Reading Popular Culture

An Anthology for Writers

SECOND EDITION

Michael Keller
South Dakota State University

With Contributions By

Kelly Bradbury
Ohio State University

Curriculum Committee

Steven Binkley

José Iglesias-Urquízar

Amber Jensen

Marina López-Casoli

Emily Olson

South Dakota State University

KENDALL/HUNT PUBLISHING COMPANY
4050 Westmark Drive   Dubuque, Iowa 52002

Contents

chapter 3 **Gender Matters: Representations of Men and Women on Television, in Film, and in Literature**

chapter 4 **Democracy in the Balance: The Fate of Intellectualism in Higher Ed and the Public Sphere**

chapter 5   *That's Entertainment: Politics and the News*

chapter 6   *Is Nothing What It Seems?: Mediation and Its Problems*

chapter 7   **How the West Was Spun: History, Hollywood, and the Narrative of Nationhood**

Thematic Contents

chapter 3   *Gender Matters: Representations of Men and Women on Television, in Film, and in Literature*

chapter 6   *Is Nothing What It Seems?: Mediation and Its Problems*

chapter 7   *How the West Was Spun: History, Hollywood, and the Narrative of Nationhood*

It's a Material World:

Tales of Consumption

The May-Pole of Merry Mount

Nathaniel Hawthorne

There is an admirable foundation for a philo-sophic romance, in the curious history of the early settlement of Mount Wollaston, or Merry Mount. In the slight sketch here attempted, the facts, recorded on the grave pages of our New England annalists, have wrought themselves, almost spontaneously, into a sort of allegory. The masques, mummeries, and festive customs, described in the text, are in accordance with the manners of the age. Authority on these points may be found in Strutt's Book of English Sports and Pastimes.

Bright were the days at Merry Mount, when the May-Pole was the banner staff of that gay colony! They who reared it, should their banner be triumphant, were to pour sunshine over New England's rugged hills, and scatter flower-seeds throughout the soil. Jollity and gloom were con-tending for an empire. Midsummer eve had come, bringing deep verdure to the forest, and roses in her lap, of a more vivid hue than the tender buds of Spring. But May, or her mirthful spirit, dwelt all the year round at Merry Mount, sporting with the Summer months, and revelling with Autumn, and basking in the glow of Winter's fireside. Through a world of toil and care, she flitted with a dreamlike smile, and came hither to find a home among the lightsome hearts of Merry Mount.

Never had the May-Pole been so gaily decked as at sunset on midsummer eve. This venerated emblem was a pine tree, which had preserved the slender grace of youth, while it equalled the lofti-est height of the old wood monarchs. From its top

Nathaniel Hawthorne (1804–1864) is one of the major figures in American literature. His novels—The Scarlet Letter (1850), The House of the Seven Gables (1851), The Blithedale Romance (1852), and The Marble Faun (1860)—and numerous short stories rank among the most celebrated and widely read works by any American writer of fiction. Descended from one of the magistrates who prosecuted women during the Salem witch trials of 1692, Hawthorne in his work typi-cally explores notions of guilt, secrecy, obsession, and desire.

From *Selected Tales and Sketches* by Nathaniel Hawthorne.

streamed a silken banner, colored like the rainbow. Down nearly to the ground, the pole was dressed with birchen boughs, and others of the liveliest green, and some with silvery leaves, fastened by ribbons that fluttered in fantastic knots of twenty different colors, but no sad ones. Garden flowers, and blossoms of the wilderness, laughed gladly forth amid the verdure, so fresh and dewy, that they must have grown by magic on that happy pine tree. Where this green and flowery splendor terminated, the shaft of the May-Pole was stained with the seven brilliant hues of the banner at its top. On the lowest green bough hung an abundant wreath of roses, some that had been gathered in the sunniest spots of the forest, and others, of still richer blush, which the colonists had reared from English seed. Oh, people of the Golden Age, the chief of your husbandry, was to raise flowers!

But what was the wild throng that stood hand in hand about the May-Pole? It could not be, that the Fauns and Nymphs, when driven from their classic groves and homes of ancient fable, had sought refuge, as all the persecuted did, in the fresh woods of the West. These were Gothic monsters, though perhaps of Grecian ancestry. On the shoulders of a comely youth, uprose the head and branching antlers of a stag; a second, human in all other points, had the grim visage of a wolf; a third, still with the trunk and limbs of a mortal man, showed the beard and horns of a venerable he-goat. There was the likeness of a bear erect, brute in all but his hind legs, which were adorned with pink silk stockings. And here again, almost as wondrous, stood a real bear of the dark forest, lending each of his fore paws to the grasp of a human hand, and as ready for the dance as any in that circle. His inferior nature rose half-way, to meet his companions as they stooped. Other faces wore the similitude of man or woman, but distorted or extravagant, with red noses pendulous before their mouths, which seemed of awful depth, and stretched from ear to ear in an eternal fit of laughter. Here might be seen the Salvage Man, well known in heraldry, hairy as a baboon, and girdled with green leaves. By his side, a nobler figure, but still a counterfeit, appeared an Indian hunter, with feathery crest and wampum belt. Many of this strange company wore fools-caps, and had little bells appended to their garments, tinkling with a silvery sound, responsive to the inaudible music of their gleesome spirits. Some youths and maidens were of soberer garb, yet well maintained their places in the irregular throng, by the expression of wild revelry upon their features. Such were the colonists of Merry Mount, as they stood in the broad smile of sunset, round their venerated May-Pole.

Had a wanderer, bewildered in the melancholy forest, heard their mirth, and stolen a half-affrighted glance, he might have fancied them the crew of Comus, some already transformed to brutes, some midway between man and beast, and the others rioting in the flow of tipsy jollity that foreran the change. But a band of Puritans, who watched the scene, invisible themselves, compared the masques to those devils and ruined souls, with whom their superstition peopled the black wilderness.

Within the ring of monsters, appeared the two airiest forms, that had ever trodden on any more solid footing than a purple and golden cloud. One was a youth, in glistening apparel, with a scarf of the rainbow pattern crosswise on his breast. His right hand held a gilded staff, the ensign of high dignity among the revellers, and his left grasped the slender fingers of a fair maiden, not less gaily decorated than himself. Bright roses glowed in contrast with the dark and glossy curls of each, and were scattered round their feet, or had sprung up spontaneously there. Behind this lightsome couple, so close to the May-Pole that its boughs shaded his jovial face, stood the figure of an English priest, canonically dressed, yet decked with flowers, in heathen fashion, and wearing a chaplet of the native vine leaves. By the riot of his rolling eye, and the pagan decorations of his holy garb, he seemed the wildest monster there, and the very Comus of the crew.

'Votaries of the May-Pole,' cried the flower-decked priest, 'merrily, all day long, have the woods echoed to your mirth. But be this your merriest hour, my hearts! Lo, here stand the Lord and Lady of the May, whom I, a clerk of Oxford, and high priest of Merry Mount, am presently to join in holy matrimony. Up with your nimble spirits, ye morrice-dancers, green-men, and glee-maidens, bears and wolves, and horned gentlemen! Come; a chorus now, rich with the old mirth of Merry England, and the wilder glee of this fresh forest; and then a dance, to show the youthful pair what life is made of, and how airily they should go through it! All ye that love the May-Pole, lend your voices to the nuptial song of the Lord and Lady of the May!'

This wedlock was more serious than most affairs of Merry Mount, where jest and delusion, trick and fantasy, kept up a continual carnival. The Lord and Lady of the May, though their titles must be laid down at sunset, were really and truly to be partners for the dance of life, beginning the measure that same bright eve. The wreath of roses, that hung from the lowest green bough of the May-Pole, had been twined for them, and would be thrown over both their heads, in symbol of their flowery union. When the priest had spoken, therefore, a riotous uproar burst from the rout of monstrous figures.

'Begin you the stave, reverend Sir,' cried they all; 'and never did the woods ring to such a merry peal, as we of the May-Pole shall send up!'

Immediately a prelude of pipe, cittern, and viol, touched with practised minstrelsy, began to play from a neighboring thicket, in such a mirthful cadence, that the boughs of the May-Pole quivered to the sound. But the May Lord, he of the gilded staff, chancing to look into his Lady's eyes, was wonderstruck at the almost pensive glance that met his own.

'Edith, sweet Lady of the May,' whispered he, reproachfully, 'is yon wreath of roses a garland to hang above our graves, that you look so sad? Oh, Edith, this is our golden time! Tarnish it not by any pensive shadow of the mind; for it may be, that nothing of futurity will be brighter than the mere remembrance of what is now passing.'

'That was the very thought that saddened me! How came it in your mind too?' said Edith, in a still lower tone than he; for it was high treason to be sad at Merry Mount. 'Therefore do I sigh amid this festive music. And besides, dear Edgar, I struggle as with a dream, and fancy that these shapes of our jovial friends are visionary, and their mirth unreal, and that we are no true Lord and Lady of the May. What is the mystery in my heart?'

Just then, as if a spell had loosened them, down came a little shower of withering rose leaves from the May-Pole. Alas, for the young lovers! No sooner had their hearts glowed with real passion, than they were sensible of something vague and unsubstantial in their former pleasures, and felt a dreary presentiment of inevitable change. From the moment that they truly loved, they had subjected themselves to earth's doom of care, and sorrow, and troubled joy, and had no more a home at Merry Mount. That was Edith's mystery. Now leave we the priest to marry them, and the masquers to sport round the May-Pole, till the last sunbeam be withdrawn from its summit, and the shadows of the forest mingle gloomily in the dance. Meanwhile, we may discover who these gay people were.

Two hundred years ago, and more, the old world and its inhabitants became mutually weary of each other. Men voyaged by thousands to the West; some to barter glass beads, and such like jewels, for the furs of the Indian hunter; some to conquer virgin empires; and one stern band to pray. But none of these motives had much weight with the colonists of Merry Mount. Their leaders were men who had sported so long with life, that when Thought and Wisdom came, even these unwelcome guests were led astray, by the crowd of vanities which they should have put to flight. Erring Thought and perverted Wisdom were made to put on masques, and play the fool. The men of whom we speak, after losing the heart's fresh gaiety, imagined a wild philosophy of pleasure, and came hither to act out their latest day-dream. They gathered followers from all that giddy tribe, whose whole life is like the festal days of soberer men. In their train were minstrels, not unknown in London streets; wandering play-ers, whose theatres had been the halls of noblemen; mummers, rope-dancers, and mounte-banks, who would long be missed at wakes, church-ales, and fairs; in a word, mirth-makers of every sort, such as abounded in that age, but now began to be discountenanced by the rapid growth of Puritanism. Light had their footsteps been on land, and as lightly they came across the sea. Many had been maddened by their previous troubles into a gay despair; oth-ers were as madly gay in the flush of youth, like the May Lord and his Lady; but whatever might be the quality of their mirth, old and young were gay at Merry Mount. The young deemed themselves happy. The elder spirits, if they knew that mirth was but the counterfeit of happiness, yet followed the false shadow wilfully, because at least her garments glittered brightest. Sworn triflers of a lifetime, they would not venture among the sober truths of life, not even to be truly blest.

All the hereditary pastimes of Old England were transplanted hither. The King of Christmas was duly crowned, and the Lord of Misrule bore potent sway. On the Eve of Saint John, they felled whole acres of the forest to make bonfires, and danced by the blaze all night, crowned with garlands, and throwing flowers into the flame. At harvest time, though their crop was of the smallest, they made an image with the sheaves of Indian corn, and wreathed it with autumnal garlands, and bore it home triumphantly. But what chiefly characterized the colonists of Merry Mount, was their veneration for the May-Pole. It has made their true history a poet's tale. Spring decked the hallowed emblem with young blossoms and fresh green boughs; Summer brought roses of the deepest blush, and the perfected foliage of the forest; Autumn enriched it with that red and yellow gorgeousness, which converts each wild-wood leaf into a painted flower; and Winter silvered it with sleet, and hung it round with icicles, till it flashed in the cold sunshine, itself a frozen sunbeam. Thus each alternate season did homage to the May-Pole, and paid it a tribute of its own richest splendor. Its votaries danced round it, once, at least, in every month; sometimes they called it their religion, or their altar; but always, it was the banner-staff of Merry Mount.

Unfortunately, there were men in the new world, of a sterner faith than these May-Pole worshippers. Not far from Merry Mount was a settlement of Puritans, most dismal wretches, who said their prayers before daylight, and then wrought in the forest or the cornfield, till evening made it prayer time again. Their weapons were always at hand, to shoot down the straggling savage. When they met in conclave, it was never to keep up the old English mirth, but to hear sermons three hours long, or to proclaim bounties on the heads of wolves and the scalps of Indians. Their festivals were fast-days, and their chief pastime the singing of psalms. Woe to the youth or maiden, who did but dream of a dance! The selectman nodded to the constable; and there sat the light-heeled reprobate in the stocks; or if he danced, it was round the whipping-post, which might be termed the Puritan May-Pole.

A party of these grim Puritans, toiling through the difficult woods, each with a horse-load of iron armor to burthen his footsteps, would sometimes draw near the sunny precincts of Merry Mount. There were the silken colonists, sporting round their May-Pole; perhaps teaching a bear to dance, or striving to communicate their mirth to the grave Indian; or masquerading in the skins of deer and wolves, which they had hunted for that especial purpose. Often, the whole colony were playing at blindman's buff, magistrates and all with their eyes bandaged, except a single scape-goat, whom the blinded sinners pursued by the tinkling of the bells at his garments. Once, it is said, they were seen following a flower-decked corpse, with merriment and festive music, to his grave. But did the dead man laugh? In their quietest times, they sang ballads and told tales, for the edification of their pious visitors; or perplexed them with juggling tricks; or grinned at them through horse-collars; and when sport itself grew wearisome, they made game of their own stupidity, and began a yawning match. At the very least of these enormities, the men of iron shook their heads and frowned so darkly, that the revellers looked up, imagining that a momentary cloud had overcast the sunshine, which was to be perpetual there. On the other hand, the Puritans affirmed, that, when a psalm was pealing from their place of worship, the echo, which the forest sent them back, seemed often like the chorus of a jolly catch, closing with a roar of laughter. Who but the fiend, and his bond-slaves, the crew of Merry Mount, had thus disturbed them! In due time, a feud arose, stern and bitter on one side, and as serious on the other as any thing could be, among such light spirits as had sworn allegiance to the May-Pole. The future complexion of New England was involved in this important quarrel. Should the grisly saints establish their jurisdiction over the gay sinners, then would their spirits darken all the clime, and make it a land of clouded visages, of hard toil, of sermon and psalm, forever. But should the banner-staff of Merry Mount be fortunate, sunshine would break upon the hills, and flowers would beautify the forest, and late posterity do homage to the May-Pole!

After these authentic passages from history, we return to the nuptials of the Lord and Lady of the May. Alas! we have delayed too long, and must darken our tale too suddenly. As we glance again at the May-Pole, a solitary sunbeam is fading from the summit, and leaves only a faint golden tinge, blended with the hues of the rainbow banner. Even that dim light is now withdrawn, relinquishing the whole domain of Merry Mount to the evening gloom, which has rushed so instantaneously from the black surrounding woods. But some of these black shadows have rushed forth in human shape.

Yes: with the setting sun, the last day of mirth had passed from Merry Mount. The ring of gay masquers was disordered and broken; the stag lowered his antlers in dismay; the wolf grew weaker than a lamb; the bells of the morrice-dancers tinkled with tremulous affright. The Puritans had played a characteristic part in the May-Pole mummeries. Their darksome figures were intermixed with the wild shapes of their foes, and made the scene a picture of the moment, when waking thoughts start up amid the scattered fantasies of a dream. The leader of the hostile party stood in the centre of the circle, while the rout of monsters cowered around him, like evil spirits in the presence of a dread magician. No fantastic foolery could look him in the face. So stern was the energy of his aspect, that the whole man, visage, frame, and soul, seemed wrought of iron, gifted with life and thought, yet all of one substance with his head-piece and breast-plate. It was the Puritan of Puritans; it was Endicott himself!

'Stand off, priest of Baal!' said he, with a grim frown, and laying no reverent hand upon the surplice. 'I know thee, Blackstone!* Thou art the man, who couldst not abide the rule even of thine own corrupted church, and hast come hither to preach iniquity, and to give example of it in thy life. But now shall it be seen that the Lord hath sanctified this wilderness for his peculiar people. Woe unto them that would defile it! And first for this flower-decked abomination, the altar of thy worship!'

And with his keen sword, Endicott assaulted the hallowed May-Pole. Nor long did it resist his arm. It groaned with a dismal sound; it showered leaves and rose-buds upon the remorseless enthusiast; and finally, with all its green boughs, and ribbons, and flowers, symbolic of departed pleasures, down fell the banner-staff of Merry Mount. As it sank, tradition says, the evening sky grew darker, and the woods threw forth a more sombre shadow.

---

* Did Governor Endicott speak less positively, we should suspect a mistake here. The Rev. Mr. Blackstone, though an eccentric, is not known to have been an immoral man. We rather doubt his identity with the priest of Merry Mount.

'There,' cried Endicott, looking triumphantly on his work, 'there lies the only May-Pole in New England! The thought is strong within me, that, by its fall, is shadowed forth the fate of light and idle mirth-makers, amongst us and our posterity. Amen, saith John Endicott.'

'Amen!' echoed his followers.

But the votaries of the May-Pole gave one groan for their idol. At the sound, the Puritan leader glanced at the crew of Comus, each a figure of broad mirth, yet, at this moment, strangely expressive of sorrow and dismay.

'Valiant captain,' quoth Peter Palfrey, the Ancient of the band, 'what order shall be taken with the prisoners?'

'I thought not to repent me of cutting down a May-Pole,' replied Endicott, 'yet now I could find in my heart to plant it again, and give each of these bestial pagans one other dance round their idol. It would have served rarely for a whipping-post!'

'But there are pine trees enow,' suggested the lieutenant.

'True, good Ancient,' said the leader. 'Wherefore, bind the heathen crew, and bestow on them a small matter of stripes apiece, as earnest of our future justice. Set some of the rogues in the stocks to rest themselves, so soon as Providence shall bring us to one of our own well-ordered settlements, where such accommodations may be found. Further penalties, such as branding and cropping of ears, shall be thought of hereafter.'

'How many stripes for the priest?' inquired Ancient Palfrey.

'None as yet,' answered Endicott, bending his iron frown upon the culprit. 'It must be for the Great and General Court to determine, whether stripes and long imprisonment, and other grievous penalty, may atone for his transgressions. Let him look to himself! For such as violate our civil order, it may be permitted us to show mercy. But woe to the wretch that troubleth our religion!'

'And this dancing bear,' resumed the officer. 'Must he share the stripes of his fellows?'

'Shoot him through the head!' said the energetic Puritan. 'I suspect witchcraft in the beast.'

'Here be a couple of shining ones,' continued Peter Palfrey, pointing his weapon at the Lord and Lady of the May. 'They seem to be of high station among these mis-doers. Methinks their dignity will not be fitted with less than a double share of stripes.'

Endicott rested on his sword, and closely surveyed the dress and aspect of the hapless pair. There they stood, pale, downcast, and apprehensive. Yet there was an air of mutual support, and of pure affection, seeking aid and giving it, that showed them to be man and wife, with the sanction of a priest upon their love. The youth, in the peril of the moment, had dropped his gilded staff, and thrown his arm about the Lady of the May, who leaned against his breast, too lightly to burthen him, but with weight enough to express that their destinies were linked together, for good or evil. They looked first at each other, and then into the grim captain's face. There they stood, in the first hour of wedlock, while the idle pleasures, of which their companions were the emblems, had given place to the sternest cares of life, personified by the dark Puritans. But never had their youthful beauty seemed so pure and high, as when its glow was chastened by adversity.

'Youth,' said Endicott, 'ye stand in an evil case, thou and thy maiden wife. Make ready presently; for I am minded that ye shall both have a token to remember your wedding-day!'

'Stern man,' cried the May Lord, 'how can I move thee? Were the means at hand, I would resist to the death. Being powerless, I entreat! Do with me as thou wilt, but let Edith go untouched!'

'Not so,' replied the immitigable zealot. 'We are not wont to show an idle courtesy to that sex, which requireth the stricter discipline. What sayest thou, maid? Shall thy silken bridegroom suffer thy share of the penalty, besides his own?'

'Be it death,' said Edith, 'and lay it all on me!'

Truly, as Endicott had said, the poor lovers stood in a woeful case. Their foes were triumphant, their friends captive and abased, their home desolate, the benighted wilderness around them, and a rigorous destiny, in the shape of the Puritan leader, their only guide. Yet the deepening twilight could not altogether conceal, that the iron man was softened; he smiled, at the fair spectacle of early love; he almost sighed, for the inevitable blight of early hopes.

'The troubles of life have come hastily on this young couple,' observed Endicott. 'We will see how they comport themselves under their present trials, ere we burthen them with greater. If, among the spoil, there be any garments of a more decent fashion, let them be put upon this May Lord and his Lady, instead of their glistening vanities. Look to it, some of you.'

'And shall not the youth's hair be cut?' asked Peter Palfrey, looking with abhorrence at the love-lock and long glossy curls of the young man.

'Crop it forthwith, and that in the true pumpkin-shell fashion,' answered the captain. 'Then bring them along with us, but more gently than their fellows. There be qualities in the youth, which may make him valiant to fight, and sober to toil, and pious to pray; and in the maiden, that may fit her to become a mother in our Israel, bringing up babes in better nurture than her own hath been. Nor think ye, young ones, that they are the happiest, even in our lifetime of a moment, who misspend it in dancing round a May-Pole!'

And Endicott, the severest Puritan of all who laid the rock foundation of New England, lifted the wreath of roses from the ruin of the May-Pole, and threw it, with his own gauntleted hand, over the heads of the Lord and Lady of the May. It was a deed of prophecy. As the moral gloom of the world overpowers all systematic gaiety, even so was their home of wild mirth made desolate amid the sad forest. They returned to it no more. But, as their flowery garland was wreathed of the brightest roses that had grown there, so, in the tie that united them, were intertwined all the purest and best of their early joys. They went heavenward, supporting each other along the difficult path which it was their lot to tread, and never wasted one regretful thought on the vanities of Merry Mount.

Understanding the Text

1. How would you characterize the inhabitants of Merry Mount and the Puritans—the two forces at odds in the story?

2. By the end of the story, what becomes of the Lady and Lord of May? Of what significance is this?

3. Hawthorne writes that "[t]he future complexion of New England was involved in this important quarrel." What was the nature of this "quarrel"? And what insight might Hawthorne's story provide us into the nature of American culture today?

Beyond Veblen: Rethinking Consumer Culture in America

Jackson Lears

A portrait of Thorstein Veblen in the faculty lounge at Yale University shows him leaning back in his chair, one leg tossed easily over the other, smoking a cigarette. He is surveying the passing scene of academic pomp with just the hint of a twinkle in his eye. Despite his mythic marginality, Veblen looks more bemused than embittered. And were he alive today, Veblen might be pardoned some bemusement. The ideas of the celebrated iconoclast have become part of the conventional wisdom about American society and conspicuous consumption. Many serious analysts of American culture have clasped Veblen to their bosoms, and more than a few would agree with Max Lerner's assertion that Veblen possessed "the most creative mind American social thought has produced."[1]

In many ways the reputation is deserved. Veblen broke new ground, much of which is still neglected. He was one of the first theorists to move away from the producer orientation of nineteenth-century economics and focus on consumption as an important category of social and economic behavior. He rejected the utilitarian psychology of orthodox economic thought, demolished through caricature the "Economic Man," and effectively focused on the irrationality and absurdity inherent in many acts of consumption. Having immersed himself in anthropological literature, Veblen could add a cultural dimension to Karl Marx's famous distinction between use-value and exchange-value. Much of what passed for exchange-value, he noted, was also a form of symbolic value. The orgies of display at Newport and the parading of ornamental wives on

Jackson Lears, one of the nation's most prominent and prolific cultural historians, is a professor of history at Rutgers University and edits the journal *Raritan*. His books include *Something for Nothing: Luck in America* (2003), *Fables of Abundance: A Cultural History of Advertising in America* (1994), and *No Place of Grace: Antimodernism and the Transformation of American Culture, 1880–1920* (1983). He also has published numerous articles and reviews in scholarly journals and in *The New Republic, The Nation, The Washington Post, The New York Times,* and other publications.

From *Consuming Visions: Accumulation and Display of Goods in America, 1880–1920* by Simon J. Bronner. Copyright © 1989 by The Henry Francis du Pont Winterthur Museum, Inc. Used by permission of W. W. Norton & Company, Inc.

Fifth Avenue corresponded to similar ceremonies among "primitive" tribes: the captain of industry, like the Kwakiutl chieftain, was eager to demonstrate his prowess by showing off his trophies. But unlike many anthropologists of his own time or ours, Veblen preserved a keen sense of hierarchical social structure and of how that structure was reinforced by patterns of consumption. By remaining sensitive to the interaction between culture and power relations, Veblen plunged forward where orthodox Marxism pulled up short. He was able to see how subordinate groups could develop allegiances to a dominant culture that may not have reflected their own best interests. He anticipated some of Antonio Gramsci's insights into the ways dominant groups exercise cultural hegemony under organized capitalism.[2]

Despite Veblen's achievements, his persistent influence has been a mixed blessing. His republican moral commitments prevented him from realizing the near universality of conspicuous consumption and conspicuous display. He himself habitually resorted to conspicuous display in the guise of antidisplay. Veblen's unkempt appearance and bizarre attire, his thick woolen stockings supported by pins clipped to his trouser legs, were aspects of costume that contributed crucially to his legendary status as a bohemian intellectual. Despite his anthropological perspective, he could not see accumulation and display as patterns interwoven by different social groups throughout the whole fabric of a culture. He insisted on attributing the dominant patterns of consumption to the pernicious influence of a parasitic "leisure class." His assumption that cultural influences flow only from the top downward is not borne out by the historical record. Lois Banner's recent and comprehensive study of American fashion, for example, demonstrates that the pacesetters in the beauty sweepstakes were courtesans and chorus girls who were often aped by their social betters.[3]

Veblen's top-down model of cultural domination melded with his desire to stress the irrationality of consumption. As a result, his psychology remained narrow. His thinking was, to be sure, a step beyond the simple-minded utilitarianism of orthodox economics, but he still reduced complex social rituals to one-dimensional examples of "pecuniary emulation." Nothing—from a funeral to a wedding to any form of "devout observance"—was allowed its true, multivalent significance. Veblen realized that all consumption enacted cultural meaning, but he was willing to assign it only one meaning: status-striving. Moreover, since nearly all cultural artifacts and practices contain elements of display, Veblen's furious assault on display amounted to an "attack on culture" itself, as Theodor Adorno recognized more than forty years ago.[4] Veblen's polemical intent led him to a sweeping dismissal of art, religion, and nearly all sensuous or material cultural forms in the name of a utopian alternative: a rational state where sturdy producer-citizens would be ruled by the discipline of the machine rather than the irrationalities of consumption.

What is amazing is how often this bleak vision has continued to inspire critics of consumer culture, particularly on the Left, and how often they have perpetuated Veblen's misconceptions.[5] Why has Veblen's influence been so durable? In part, I would suggest, because his critique resonates with a long tradition in Anglo-American Protestant culture: the Puritan's plain-speak assault on theatrical artifice and effete display. The ensuing essay furthers this argument by situating Veblen historically by tracing the tensions between authenticity and artifice in nineteenth-century American market culture and by suggesting how those tensions were reorchestrated during the period from 1880 to 1920, the period when Veblen consolidated his data base.

The origins of the plain-speech tradition lay in a fundamental project of the Protestant Reformation: the effort to create an alternative to the method of constructing meaning through the assemblage and display of objects, the method that anthropologists claim is virtually universal and timeless. The pietist tradition in Protestantism insisted that salvation lay in faith rather than works, in inner being rather than outward form. They believed that the objective surface of things concealed rather than revealed meaning. Appearances, for the early Protestant, were always deceptive.[6]

The problem of appearances was exacerbated by the emergence of a modern, placeless market, as Jean-Christophe Agnew has persuasively argued. Theatrical modes of artifice were detached from their customary ritual moorings; they became modes of self-aggrandizement in the fluid, boundless world of market relations.[7] Puritan and later evangelical Protestants aimed to create a new and tighter set of boundaries around the simple, striving self and to control the flood of meanings unleashed in market society by insisting on unadorned communication in language as well as material goods. Plain speech complemented plain living: both served the vision of social transparency; that is, a society where people said what they meant and meant what they said. That vision, of course, remained provokingly just out of reach, as market society multiplied goods and the meanings attached to them.

The tension between authenticity and artifice transferred slowly to American shores. American public culture was born in opposition to European-style luxury and display, nurtured in dreams of Spartan simplicity. But by the early and mid nineteenth century, representatives of the national and international market began to fan out from the cities into a countryside that was still dominated in many areas by household production. We are just beginning to glimpse the ways that this expanding world of goods was represented in popular culture, but preliminary evidence suggests that it may be a mistake to argue a shift from the plodding nineteenth century to the carnivalesque twentieth: the carnival may have been in town all the time.[8]

Certainly the nineteenth-century market signified entertainment and exoticism, offering new sensations as well as new goods. Exotica were the stock-in-trade of museum promoters from P. T. Barnum to his backwoods emulators; Barnum's first and most famous estate—itself a gigantic advertisement for his work—was Iranistan, a fabulous oriental villa built in 1846. From the 1830s on, many consumer goods (such as clothing, cosmetics, jewelry, patent medicines) were surrounded by an aura of sensuous mystery, even magical self-transformation. The mysterious East had long been associated with marketable goods, and mid Victorian writers kept that link before the reading public. "India is the Ophir of commerce," a *Godey's*

Lady's Book contributor announced in 1853. Fashion magazines printed engravings of bare-breasted brown ladies, such as "The Circassian Beauty" in *Peterson's* for 1851, providing a kind of sanctioned Victorian pornography. By the 1850s, fashionable clothes were often surrounded with exotic attributes: the Turkish shawl, the Castilian cloak, the Echarpe Orientale. New York department store magnate A. T. Stewart chose oriental motifs for the interior of the store he built at Broadway and Tenth Street in 1863, complete with "luxurious hassocks . . . soft Persian mats . . . [and] fairy-like frostings of lace draperies." The tie between the market and exotic oriental goods was firmly implanted in the bourgeois imagination.[9] Representatives of the market reinforced those connections. Many, to be sure, were complaisant shopkeepers; but many others were more aggressive and intrusive peddlers whose wares were sometimes just as enticing as those found in the fashionable shops.

For many Americans, particularly those outside the urban upper classes, the market was personified in the itinerant peddler. The primal scene of the emerging market culture in the mid nineteenth century was the peddler entering the isolated village or rural community, laden with glittering goods that were ornamental as well as useful: scissors, knives, tools, tinware, clocks, patent medicines, jewelry, perfumes, and fabrics. The peddler embodied a multitude of cultural associations. Certainly he was a trickster figure, a confidence man who achieved his goal through guile rather than strength, particularly through a skillful theatricality. What was perhaps most striking about the peddler was his liminality. He was constantly on the move, scurrying along the fringes of established society. He occupied the threshold not only between the village and the cosmopolitan world beyond but also between the natural and the supernatural. He was an emissary of the marvelous, promising his audience magical transformations not through religious conversion, but through the purchase of a bit of silk, a pair of earrings, or a mysterious elixir. Like the traditional conjurer multiplying rabbits, doves, or scarves, the peddler opened his pack and presented a startling vision of abundance. (In Clement Moore's famous poem "A Visit from St. Nicholas" [1822], Santa Claus himself "looked like a peddler opening his pack.") Despite his secular concerns, the peddler, particularly if he was the impresario of a patent medicine show, had much in common with the evangelical ministry: itineracy, a special appeal to women, and a rhetorical style that combined exhortation with the invocation of testimonials from the saved. From Johnson Jones Hooper's Simon Suggs to Mark Twain's Beriah Sellers, humorists presented the confidence man as preacher, and vice versa.[10]

The peddler's persona resonated with magic and religion. Those resonances varied depending on regional or ethnic circumstances. Folklore tended to label all peddlers (at least up to the Civil War) as either Yankees or Jews. Both groups were proverbially alleged to be rootless and conniving avatars of the market, aggressively penetrating the countryside, and both provoked a mingling of fear, hostility, and fascination. After the 1830s, as German Jews became a more palpable presence in peddling and its lore, popular assumptions tended increasingly to conflate the peddler's mobility and marginality with his Jewishness. "The Jews are proverbially a restless, roving class," announced Luke Shortfield, the hero of John Beauchamp Jones's *Western Merchant* (1849). "The Shylocks prefer to be on navigable streams, where it is convenient for them to take passage for 'parts unknown,' should their necessities or indications render it expedient for them to do so." Mid Victorian imagery presented the Jew as a liminal figure who was even more exotic than the Yankee. "These wonderful people bear the imprint of their Oriental origin even to this day," wrote novelist Joseph Holt Ingraham in 1860. In physical appearance and social behavior, the Jewish peddler epitomized the commercial arts of the mysterious East. Beginning with *The Monk,* written by Monk Lewis in 1796, the literary Wandering Jew was gradually transformed from an exemplar of Christian doctrine to "a black magician whose sorcery was interesting on secular grounds." The peddler was a Wandering Jew with a pack on his back, promising a brief deliverance through the magical powers of purchase.[11] Whatever his ethnic persuasion, the peddler became a lighting rod for the anxieties and aspirations of a developing market society. The encounter between the peddler and his prospective customer was exciting but also disturbing. It prefigured later, more structured rituals of purchase in department stores and other urban settings.

The common link between earlier and later cultural forms was the tendency to see selling as seduction. The peddler was not only a potential poacher on what the husband conceived to be his private sexual realm but also a participant in the mysterious power of "influence"—the Victorian belief in the capacity of one individual to form or deform another's malleable character forever. The peddler—like that other liminal confidence man, the mesmerist—seemed particularly adept at influencing women. If he sold patent medicine, he also resembled the mesmerist in his access to hidden lore: the word *nostrum* derives from *our secret.* If he sold clothes, perfume, and jewelry, he dealt in "fascination" and "glamour"; both words originally referred to magic spells.[12]

The peddler's brand of influence had powerful connotations; at its worst, it could even promote a kind of addiction. This was suggested by Ann Porter's "Banishment of the Peddlers," a *Godey's* poem published in 1848, deep enough into the era of German Jewish peddling to contain a harsh note of anti-Semitism. The poem tells the story of a small town where the ladies decide to boycott the shopkeepers until they refuse to sell any more liquor. All but one yield.

> "Ladies," said he, "you know full well,
>   That peddlers haunt this place
> And for their knick-knacks take your cash,
>   A low and vulgar race.
> But if you will refuse to trade,
>   With this same Jewish clan,
> I'll quit the sale of spirits now,
>   Nor sell a dram again."

Although "the ladies had some feeling for these men of heavy packs," they bow to the will of the "brave man": peddlers and liquor alike are banished from the village. This poem dramatizes a developing social conflict between established Protestant retailers and itinerant Jewish peddlers: it is not consumption per se that is equated with addiction to alcohol, but consumption from a particularly "influential" source. In suggesting that equation, "The Banishment of the Peddlers" identified the act of purchase as an arena of gender conflict; it also evoked the fear that, without proper boundaries, the market could undermine self-control.[13]

That fear lay at the heart of Victorian moralism. Participation in the market, given its associations with avarice and exotic sensuality, posed fundamental temptations. The moralists' nightmarish vision was that the self's moral and intellectual gyroscope would spin out of control as it entered the magnetic field of market relations, resulting in the pursuit of worldly goods that would lead to madness and death. Novelist Catherine Sedgwick, recalling the speculative fever of the 1830s, charged, "the atmosphere was poisoned, and the silly and the wise alike went mad." Popular fiction confirmed the threat, as the mad speculator became a stock figure. An 1858 *Godey's* story introduced a Mr. Brandon, who, "in the reckless spirit of the age, had entered speculation after speculation until success had made him mad; and when failure had met him he still madly persisted until inevitable ruin stared him in the face." Nor were women immune. A *Peterson's* editorial of 1866 presented an imaginary conversation between a doctor and another male observer at a fashionable ball; their decorous exchange is frequently interrupted by the screeching "mad laugh" of a lovely and elegant young matron, the most fashionably dressed and wittiest woman in the room. The doctor believes that he detects insanity in her laugh, and, sure enough, after her husband's death in a warehouse accident six months later, the woman has to be admitted to an asylum. The quest for social brilliance could be as perilous as the speculative plunge, sapping one's resources and leaving one vulnerable to psychic as well as financial collapse.[14]

The fears of self-ruination, rooted in a persistent Puritan-republican ethos, pervaded bourgeois culture throughout much of the nineteenth century. So it should come as no surprise that the proliferation of marketable goods and sensations generated protest as well as fascination. Among artisans and farmers, heirs of the plain-speech tradition mounted a powerful critique of individual accumulation at the expense of the social whole, a critique energized by the principles of labor republicanism. Among intellectuals, dreams of social transparency led to discomfort amid a new world of manufactured appearances, expressed as longings to strike through the pasteboard mask of artifice (as Melville's Ahab said), and experience unmediated life directly.[15] Longings could be expressed in the idiom of romantic transcendentalism or, later, as austere positivist scientism. Veblen participated in this latter trend; nearly all his work is pervaded by the desire to unmask the duplicities of polite society or conventional wisdom.

During the mid nineteenth century (1840–80), the arbiters of taste in fashion magazines and other popular periodicals groped for a middle ground between authenticity and artifice.

Sensing that market relations could be integrated into bourgeois society only if their centrifugal impact were controlled, these makers of mainstream culture sought an idiom that would meld aristocratic fashion and republican simplicity. They wanted to penetrate behind the veil of appearances, but not too far. They implicitly anticipated an idea articulated by Joseph Conrad, Henrik Ibsen, and Sigmund Freud at the end of the century: the notion that civilization was in some sense dependent on a delicate tissue of necessary lies.

Longings for sincerity persisted, however, and led to a bit of a muddle. Fashion was justifiable only insofar as it expressed the true self within; appearances meant everything and nothing.[16] Aesthetic moralists wanted to maintain a tightly controlled equipoise between respectability and extravagance, authenticity and artifice. As expressed by Charles J. Peterson, editor of *Peterson's* magazine, in 1873, "Wise men or women make their dress so thoroughly in accordance with their person or character, that no one notices it any more than the frame of a picture; but to be clothed shabbily in the hopes that our inner perfections will overshadow our dress, is but the extreme of vanity." Yet in the same magazine, one finds extraordinarily elaborate directions for assembling the appropriate ensemble at the appropriate time, as in these comments on the chemisette from an 1851 issue: "The undersleeves should correspond as nearly as possible, in style and pattern, with the collar and chemisette with which they are intended to be worn. This rule should be observed whether the undersleeves are open or closed at the end. We may mention that undersleeves should be reserved exclusively for evening dress, or at least confined to indoor wear." One can find similar descriptions in almost any issue of *Peterson's, Godey's,* or other fashion magazines during the middle decades of the nineteenth century, coexisting with obsessive references to simplicity and suitability. The editors recognized the need to express one's true self, but also to fit in, not to appear eccentric.[17] A sense of unified character began to erode gradually beneath the layers of appearances. What emerged was an antifashionable ideology of fashion, in which the authentic self became a constructed objet d'art, carefully framed by its material surroundings.

Fashion ideologues constantly emphasized the control and care with which clothes and other goods should be presented to the world. The meanings associated with goods, especially fashionable or luxury goods, were always shifting, unstable, and perhaps even dangerous; they embodied the decadence of the aristoi, the sybaritic delights of the demimonde, and the exotic sensuality of the "uncivilized" periphery. Madness, the literature implied, bubbled just beneath the surface of select society. So there was a constant need to organize the meanings attached to consumption—to domesticate and moralize them. This was the role played by fashion magazine editors and authors of advice literature.

The tendency to link the glittering theatricality of consumer culture with a frightening loss of control was more than puritanism; it was rooted in the insecurities of everyday life in an expanding market society. Popular fiction and the files of Dun and Bradstreet were pervaded by tales of rapid rise and overnight ruin. In searching for explanations for wild fluctuations of fortune, moralists predictably conflated the impersonal operations of the market with personal moral choice, in particular the choice of extravagance or overconsumption. They flayed men for indulging in wine, cigars, and stag outings and criticized women for improvident expenditures on clothes and household furnishings.[18]

The idiom of control was sentimental moralism, and its material embodiment was the domestic household. Home became the necessary counterweight to the centrifugal forces unleashed by the market. Few scenes were more distressing to moralists than the forced auction of household goods—the invasion of the home by the corrosive powers of cash. Used repeatedly as a symbol of doom in popular fiction, the unwise purchase of a Brussels carpet meant that the household gods would soon be toppled from their pedestals and the auctioneer's red flag would soon be hoisted over the family home. In "The New Carpets" (1881), Fannie Swift decides that she must have new carpets even though things are difficult financially for her husband, Charlie. Charlie's banker sees the carpets being delivered, considers the purchase to be a wild extravagance, given Charlie's current financial condition, and decides that Charlie is a poor credit risk. Three weeks after the banker turns down Charlie for a crucial loan, the auctioneer's flag signals the dissolution of the Swift home. It is a bitter lesson, but Fannie learns it. Through industry and economy, she and Charlie fight their way back from ruin. In this story, as in many others, not only extravagance but also the appearance of extravagance is the key to a disastrous fall. Appearances, so often dismissed as nothing, again turn out to be everything.[19]

Overall, during the period from 1840 to 1880, fashion ideologues were engaged in a continuing search for some means of organizing and controlling the chaotic potential of the proliferating meanings attached to commodities. The search was pervaded by tension between simplicity and extravagance, as well as authenticity and artifice, and by the implicit realization that obsessive preoccupation with either authenticity or artifice could lead to catastrophe. The result was the well-known Victorian compromise, respectability, rooted in tense ambivalence.

From 1880 to 1920, the period when Veblen began to survey the dominant culture, the tensions between authenticity and artifice increased for a wide variety of reasons. The most obvious reasons involved the increase of wealth, the elaboration of ornament, and the strutting social performance among elites—the tendencies that Veblen anatomized and anathematized in *The Theory of the Leisure Class* (1899). Another reason was the rise of European aestheticism, which exalted fluid theatricality and the manipulation of surfaces. The career of Oscar Wilde personified these tendencies. His delight in language as artifice, as well as his flamboyant self-fashionings, rejection of conventional gender roles, and dramaturgical conception of life, all dramatized the blurring of boundaries that Victorians attempted to control. Americans' ambivalent fascination with Wilde deserves closer scrutiny. It is worth noting that a character in an 1882 story names her rooster after him and that trade cards for goods from fertilizer to perfume satirized Wildean poseurs through the 1890s. An additional reason for increasing anxiety over issues of authenticity and artifice was the arrival of immigrants from non-Protestant traditions of ritual and carnivalesque display. Finally, within what might be called the vernacular entrepreneurial tradition, there was a continuing elaboration of exotic, sensuous display in trade card iconography and, as William Leach and John Kasson have shown, the rise of two new institutions for popularizing exoticism and commercial theatricality: department stores and amusement parks. It is not surprising that Veblen and other, more conventional plain speakers felt ill at ease in this developing cultural environment.[20]

At the same time, the fin de siècle also saw a new and more rigorous search for dark truth behind the veil of appearances. For J. G. Frazer, Freud, and others, the surface of civilization was nothing, a mere veneer covering primal irrationality. In both high and popular cultures, one can see an emergent fascination with instinctual experience unmediated by surface conventionality, a quest for what D. H. Lawrence called "blood knowledge." As Lionel Trilling suggested, the Victorian ideal of simplicity was becoming the modernist ideal of authenticity: more rigorous, demanding, and dangerous.[21]

Both the spread of exotic theatricality and the recovery of primal irrationality involved the resurfacing of instinctual energy that was submerged, although never absent, in the Victorian imagination. Both pointed toward the upsetting of equipoise, the loss of control, and the renewed need to balance tension between authenticity and artifice. Fortunately for the survival of civilization as we know it, cultural elites did develop new means of orchestrating familiar tensions—new ways of mediating the meanings attached to goods, domesticating fashion, and sanitizing exoticism. The idiom of mediation shifted from moralism to professionalism as new structures of control arose, including professional associations, national corporations, and bureaucratic organizations of all kinds. Licensing laws stopped the mobile peddler in his tracks and put him behind the counter of a department store, transforming him from a liminal figure into a complaisant shopkeeper. Advertising sought to shed its Barnumesque inheritance and achieve professional respectability. Corporations acquired unprecedented control over the visual and verbal images attached to goods. These changes helped to reorganize cultural meanings in many different arenas of consumption, of which two are particularly representative: the domestic interior and the body. There was a similar pattern in both cases: a moralized nature had become increasingly surfeited with lush and decadent imagery. Professional designers on the one hand and professional advertisers on the other sought to sanitize that imagery and to purge it of unhealthy exoticism.

The nineteenth-century interior was the woman's sphere. Women not only provided moral uplift but also gave constant attention to the messy details of biological existence often ignored or denied by the male world outside. It is therefore no surprise that the Victorian interior embodied the iconography of female experience; it domesticated and moralized natural fecundity and sexual energy with floral wallpaper, globular lamps, cavorting cupids in the bedroom, and Ceres in the dining room. The vogue of potted plants epitomized the pattern of a domesticated nature straining at the seams of its civilized constraints.[22] For men—and for some more privileged women—the interior was associated with retreat to a world of private revery and leisured aesthetic contemplation. Late Victorian architects aimed to individualize and compartmentalize interior space as much as possible. Alongside natural imagery, exoticism and theatrical display intensified during the last two decades of the nineteenth century. Curio cabinets filled with bric-a-brac from many lands, the Turkish corner, the Egyptian booth, the vogue of chinoiserie, and the riot of eclectic architectural motifs, all betokened the rise of the interior as a stage set for private fantasy. As fiction and advice literature makes clear, some parts of that domestic stage could also be set for fashionable social performance.[23]

But by the turn of the century, there was a growing sense of oppressiveness, nearly suffocation, amid the clutter of theatrical props. Male fantasies of entombment, which pervaded the work of Edgar Allan Poe, Joris-Karl Huysmans, and Gustav Klimt, became more widespread and less gender-specific. In Charlotte Perkins Gilman's "Yellow Wallpaper" (1891), for example, the narrator not only recoils from the "sprawling, flamboyant patterns" in the wallpaper but also associates its "florid arabesque" with a nightmarish vision of fecundity—a fungus: "if you could imagine a toadstool in joints, an interminable string of toadstools, budding and sprouting in endless convolutions—why, that is something like it." Here and elsewhere, domestic artifice can hardly contain the monstrous energies of nature.[24]

The more drastic aesthetic response to this oppressive anxiety was enacted by the European modernists, who preached a gospel of secular puritanism, rationality, and efficiency in the guise of liberation from the airless, closed box of the nineteenth-century interior. In a sense, European modernism was a return to plain speech in architectural style. Severe functionalists like Ludwig Mies van der Rohe and Gerrit Rietveld were animated by a blend of Dutch Calvinism and German pietism; the bedrooms designed by Marcel Breuer began to look like gymnasiums.[25] Anglo-Americans never warmed to this sterilized vision, although there was a brief flurry of scientific management in the home. Ellen Richards introduced "euthenics"—the "science of the controlled environment"—to middle-class audiences who were initially enthusiastic, but the appeal of euthenics never went beyond a few ideologues. It is also true that *House Beautiful* magazine and the arts and crafts movement attacked "the tyranny of things" and "the poor taste of the rich," warring against clutter in the name of taste, health, and sanity. They argued in the new professional/scientific language of expertise to do away with heavy drapes that sheltered microbes and "nervous, discordant" colors that bred neurasthenia. The overall result of American design reform, however, was a compromise between puritanical plain speech and riotous ornament.[26]

Frank Lloyd Wright's prairie houses expressed that compromise perfectly. He opened up and deindividualized the floor plan, providing fewer opportunities for morbid introspection and private fantasy. He brought the outdoors indoors, using the large, flat sheets of plate glass that were industrially available for the first time in the 1880s. These were moves in the direction of Bauhaus-style functionality. Wright used wood and stone rather than steel in keeping with the "organic" preoccupations of the arts and crafts movement. And he never fully rationalized the domestic ideal; he aimed to impart a sacramental aura to traditional family gathering places like the hearth and the dining room. In the pages of House Beautiful and other decorating magazines, the compromise was even more apparent. A good deal of ornament survived the assault on clutter, and by the 1910s a Morrisite commitment to "sincerity" in design—always an ambiguous goal at best—had given way to a tasteful eclecticism.[27]

The sanitizing of late Victorian imagery was even more apparent in the commercial iconography of the body. There was a dramatic movement away from exoticism and display, toward rationality and control. The vernacular entrepreneurial tradition of trade cards and patent medicine almanacs yielded to national corporate advertising planned by bureaucratic organizations—called advertising agencies—in New York City. These organizations were staffed overwhelmingly by educated, upper-class, WASP men with the same social and cultural background as the Protestant arbiters of nineteenth-century taste.[28]

Through the late nineteenth century, patent medicine advertising had preserved an exotic aura. Advertisements were steeped in herbalist lore and claims of primitive tribal origin. They fell into a common imperialist pattern: the white man penetrates the dark interior of a tropical land, extracts mysterious remedies, and puts them to the service of "civilization." A Warner's Safe Remedy pamphlet from 1882 captures the imperialist pattern; it shows a white man's head on a muscular brown body, paddling a canoe toward the heart of primitive darkness.[29]

Advertising for cosmetics also wallowed in exotic settings redolent of luxuriant sensuality during the late nineteenth century. Often advertisements toyed with overt eroticism in displaying the languorous ease of voluptuous women from the subculture of sensuality. Corsets were associated with images of explosive fecundity and even peep show-style prurience. These advertisements suggest a more complex picture of late Victorian culture than the prim and bloodless one presented by its early twentieth-century critics.[30]

After 1900 exoticism survived within the entrepreneurial tradition, inscribed on the walls of restaurants and movie theaters; however, in corporate iconography, it declined or was channeled into more productive outlets. Advertisers who promoted the tanning vogue of the early twentieth century, for example, detached dark skin from overtones of tropical sensuality and linked it with bracing outdoor vigor. The imperialist pattern was transformed from extraction of dark secrets to imposition of white values. In an Ivory soap series from 1900, for instance, an assembly of Plains Indians recalled that their blankets had been smeared with "grease and stains / from buffalo meat and settlers' veins" until "Ivory soap came like a ray / of light across our darkened way." Cleanliness had been a key emblem of refinement for at least half a century; what emerged after the turn of the century was a certain kind of cleanliness, purged of decadent hedonistic associations, oriented toward productive activism and a broader agenda of control. In corporate advertising, there was a growing emphasis on standardized, sanitized images of youthful physical perfection: the voluptuous woman and the bearded man yielded to smoother, cleaner, more activist and athletic models of beauty. The sanitation of body imagery was paralleled by an increased sensitivity to odors, culminating in the drive for "an absolute cleanliness of person, a real surgical cleanliness" announced by Zonite antiseptic in 1932. Euthenics triumphed in advertising, if not in actuality; a Lysol campaign from the early 1930s showed a cellophane-wrapped guest at a suburban front door, claiming, "If callers also arrived in sanitary packages, we wouldn't need Lysol."[31]

There are a number of explanations for this intensified emphasis on control of the biological universe. One involves the consolidation of scientific authority because of therapeutic breakthroughs and the growing preoccupation with the germ theory of disease. Another encompasses the broad process that Max Weber identified as the "disenchantment of the world": the reduction of nature, including one's own body, to a commodity, a manipulable thing. But there are more specific historical reasons as well, involving the ethnic, class, and intellectual background of the ad men themselves. They were members of a WASP elite group surrounded by swarming immigrants and troubling Darwinian theories. If one had apes for ancestors and Hottentots for cousins, the old cultural boundaries between civilization and barbarism, body and soul, no longer seemed so clear. Anglo-Saxon elites felt a strong need to distinguish themselves from primitives, exotics, and the "lower races"—the whole lot of brute creation. As Mary Douglas has suggested, a concern with bodily purification can reflect broader anxieties; pollution taboos reassert the reality of established social boundaries. The American preoccupation with sanitized, hairless bodies and sterile households was a means of redrawing familiar boundaries in a period of critical social stress. The standardized model of physical perfection offered a distinct alternative to the simian stereotypes of immigrant ethnic groups, the sort of people that Attorney Gen. A. Mitchell Palmer characterized in 1919 as "alien filth with sly and crafty eyes, lopsided faces, sloping brows, and misshapen features." Correct appearance became a mark of political normality and of civilization itself. More dramatically than in the domestic interior, in the iconography of the body one sees a farewell to exoticism, a triumph of control, and a steering away from both primitivism and decadence in favor of a moderate norm.[32]

One can only imagine what Veblen would think of this analysis. Maybe he would see the rationalizing tendencies I have described as a partial vindication of his own critique, a process by which the American ruling class refused to become a leisure class, instead creating new sanctions for self-control and disciplined achievement. And perhaps he would recognize that the reorganization of cultural meaning between 1880 and 1920 was too complex to be captured in any linear scheme of progress or decline. What is particularly suspect is the idea, derived partly from Veblen, that the emergence of new ways of assigning meaning to goods meant the rise of self-indulgent materialism and hedonism. We have always had materialism with us, in the sense that people have always used material goods to make cultural meaning; the history of hedonism has yet to be written.

Meanwhile, the tension between authenticity and artifice is still very much alive. Indeed it has acquired a global significance, as multinational corporations cry their commodities in every corner of the "developing" world. The cacophony helps to conceal older, quieter relationships of imperial coercion, at least from postmodern theorists in the West who have taken to celebrating the agreeably meaningless signifiers of mass cultural fashion. But the discourse of authenticity survives outside Anglo-Saxon traditions of plain speech, among anti-imperialist leaders in the third world who invoke national or tribal loyalties in their attempts to exorcise the demons of Western artifice. Whether their project will be any more successful than Veblen's remains to be seen.

Notes

[1] Max Lerner, ed., *The Portable Veblen* (New York: Viking Press, 1948), back cover.

[2] Thorstein Veblen, *The Theory of the Leisure Class: An Economic Study in the Evolution of Institutions* (New York: Macmillan Co., 1899); John Patrick Diggins, *The Bard of Savagery* (New York: Seabury Press, 1978); T. J. Jackson Lears, "The Concept of Cultural Hegemony: Problems and Possibilities," *American Historical Review* 90, no. 3 (June 1985): 567–93.

[3] Lois Banner, *American Beauty* (New York: Alfred A. Knopf, 1983). For an influential discussion of consumption as a way that various groups throughout a society can create cultural meaning, see Mary Douglas and Baron Isherwood, *The World of Goods: Towards an Anthropology of Consumption* (New York: W. W. Norton, 1979). For a somewhat more sophisticated version of this argument, see Mihaly Csikszentmihalyi and Eugene Rochberg-Halton, *The Meaning of Things: Domestic Symbols and the Self* (New York: Cambridge University Press, 1981).

[4] Theodor Adorno, "Veblen's Attack on Culture" (1941), reprinted in Theodor Adorno, *Prisms*, trans. Samuel and Sherry Weber (Cambridge, Mass.: MIT Press, 1981), pp. 73–94.

[5] See, for example, Stuart Chase, *The Tragedy of Waste* (New York: Macmillan, 1925); John Kenneth Galbraith, *The Affluent Society* (New York: New American Library, 1958); and John Kenneth Galbraith, *The New Industrial State* (Boston: Houghton Mifflin Co., 1967).

[6] This issue is discussed in Edmund Morgan, *Visible Saints: The History of a Puritan Idea* (New York: New York University Press, 1963); and the issue is deftly brought into the nineteenth century in Karen Halttunen, *Confidence Men and Painted Women: A Study of Middle-Class Culture in America, 1830–1870* (New Haven: Yale University Press, 1982), esp. p. 45.

[7] Jean-Christophe Agnew, *Worlds Apart: The Market and the Theater in Anglo-American Thought, 1550–1750* (New York: Cambridge University Press, 1986).

[8] Here I do not mean to abandon my own and other historians' stress on the late nineteenth century as a period of crucial transformation. But I now believe that an understanding of that transformation requires a subtler conceptual framework than simply the notion of a shift from a Protestant "producer culture" to a secular "consumer culture." For statements of that earlier view, see T. J. Jackson Lears, "From Salvation to Self-Realization: Advertising and the Therapeutic Roots of the Consumer Culture, 1880–1930," in *The Culture of Consumption: Critical Essays in American History, 1880–1980,*

ed. Richard Wightman Fox and T. J. Jackson Lears (New York: Pantheon Books, 1983) pp. 3–38; and Warren I. Susman, *Culture as History: The Transformation of American Society in the Twentieth Century* (New York: Pantheon Books, 1984), esp. Introduction.

[9] P. T. Barnum, *Struggles and Triumphs; or, Forty Years' Recollections of P. T. Barnum* (Buffalo: Warren, Johnson, 1872), p. 263; Henry P. Haynes, "The East," *Godey's Lady's Book* 47 (July 1853): 33; engraving, "The Circassian Beauty," in *Peterson's* 29, no. 3 (September 1851), frontispiece; "Work Department: The Ottoman," *Godey's Lady's Book* 56 (June 1858): 555; advertisement for "The Castiglione" in *Godey's Lady's Book* 58 (January 1858): 9; Emily May, "The Echarpe Orientale," *Peterson's* 27, no. 1 (January 1855): 89–90; "Chitchat upon Prevailing Fashions," *Godey's Lady's Book* 48 (May 1854): 479–80; Alice B. Haven, "A Morning at Stewart's," *Godey's Lady's Book* 66 (May 1863): 429–33.

[10] The standard works on peddlers are Richardson Wright, *Hawkers and Walkers in Early America: Strolling Peddlers, Preachers, Lawyers, Doctors, Players, and Others, from the Beginning to the Civil War* (Philadelphia: J. B. Lippincott Co., 1927); and J. R. Dolan, *The Yankee Peddlers of Early America* (New York: Clarkson N. Potter, 1964). Also helpful are Frazar Kirkland, *Cyclopedia of Commercial and Business Anecdotes,* 2 vols. (New York: D. Appleton, 1864); and B. A. Botkin, *A Treasury of New England Folklore* (rev. ed.; New York: Crown Publishers, 1965). The concept of liminality is associated with the work of Victor Turner, who is threatening to displace Clifford Geertz as the anthropologist most cited by historians. The most relevant writings on liminality include Victor Turner, *The Ritual Process: Structure and Anti-Structure* (Chicago: University of Chicago Press, 1969), esp. chap. 3; and Victor Turner, *Dramas, Fields, and Metaphors* (Ithaca: Cornell University Press, 1974), esp. chaps. 1, 6, 7. On the link between ancient conjuring lore and dreams of fantastic abundance, see Paul Bouissiac, *Circus and Culture: A Semiotic Approach* (Bloomington: Indiana University Press, 1975), p. 78. See also Clement Moore, "A Visit from St. Nicholas" (1822), reprinted as *The Night before Christmas* (Philadelphia: J. B. Lippincott Co., 1954); Johnson Jones Hooper, *Adventures of Capt. Simon Suggs* (Philadelphia: T. B. Peterson Co., 1846); Samuel L. Clemens and Charles Dudley Warner, *The Gilded Age: A Tale of To-Day* (1872; reprint, Indianapolis: Bobbs-Merrill, 1972).

[11] John Beauchamp Jones, *The Western Merchant* (Philadelphia: Grigg, Elliot, 1849), p. 289; Joseph Holt Ingraham, *The Sunny South; or, The Southerner at Home, Embracing Five Years' Experience of a Northern Governess in the Land of Sugar and the Cotton* (1860; reprint, New York: Negro Universities Press, 1968); Edgar Rosenberg, *From Shylock to Svengali: Jewish Stereotypes in English Fiction* (Stanford: Stanford University Press, 1960), p. 206. See also Louis Harap, *The Image of the Jew in American Literature, from the Early Republic to Mass Immigration* (Philadelphia: Jewish Publication Society, 1974); Rudolf Glanz, *The Jew in the Old American Folklore* (New York: Privately printed, 1961), esp. pp. 2–8, 187 n. 21; and Mac E. Barrick, "The Image of the Jew in South-Central Pennsylvania," *Pennsylvania Folklife* 34, no. 3 (Spring 1985): 133–38.

[12] On influence, see Halttunen, *Confidence Men,* pp. 4–5. The explicitly sexual connotations of mesmerism are discussed in John Haller, *American Medicine in Transition, 1840–1910* (Urbana: University of Illinois Press, 1974), p. 105. For the etymologies mentioned in this paragraph, see the relevant entries in *Oxford English Dictionary,* s. v. "fascination," "glamour." On fascination in particular, see Herbert Leventhal, *The Shadow of the Enlightenment* (New York: New York University Press, 1974), pp. 138–39.

[13] Ann E. Porter, "The Banishment of the Peddlers," *Godey's Lady's Book* 37 (October 1848): 227.

[14] Mrs. C. M. Sedgwick, "Wilton Harvey," *Godey's Lady's Book* 24 (March 1842): 122; "Blanche Brandon," *Godey's Lady's Book* 56 (April 1858): 306; "Editor's Table," *Peterson's* 50, no. 3 (September 1866): 210.

[15] Herman Melville, *Moby Dick; or, The White Whale* (1851; reprint, New York: New American Library, 1961), p. 167.

[16] "All is not gold that glitters" was an obsessive theme in women's magazines throughout the 1840–80 period; for example, see Harriet Beecher Stowe, "Art and Nature," *Godey's Lady's Book* 19 (September 1839); Ellen Ashton, "Keeping Up Appearances," *Peterson's* 24, no. 6 (December 1853): 283–84; and L. MacDonnell, "Grace Eversleigh's Golden Hair," *Peterson's* 62, no. 1 (July 1872): 23–24.

[17] "Editor's Table," *Peterson's* 63, no. 6 (June 1873): 442; "Fashions for September," *Peterson's* 20, no. 3 (September 1851): 134. See also "Editor's Table," *Peterson's* 28, no. 6 (December 1855): 410; "Descriptions of Fashions," *Godey's Lady's Book* 18 (January 1839); "The Art of Dress," *Godey's Lady's Book* 57 (October 1848); and "New Furniture," *Godey's Lady's Book* 40 (February 1850): 152–53.

[18] Mrs. Lambert, "Margaret Compton," *Lady's National* 4, no. 4 (October 1843): 109–18; Alice B. Neal, "Furnishing; or, Two Ways of Commencing Life," *Godey's Lady's Book* 41 (November 1850): 299–305; Mrs. Child, "Our Treasury: Hints about Furniture," *Godey's Lady's Book* 46 (June 1853): 467–68; Charles J. Peterson, "Waifs by the Wayside," *Peterson's* 32, no. 3 (September 1857): 247; Mrs. J. E. M'Conaughey, "Saving Matches," *Peterson's* 69, no. 2 (February 1876): 109–10.

[19] Mrs. J. E. M'Conaughey, "The New Carpets," *Peterson's* 80, no. 2 (August 1881): 148–49. See also Edgar Wayne, "Eleanor Hartley," *Lady's National* 11, no. 6 (June 1847): 201; and Helen B. Thornton, "The Red Flag," *Peterson's* 58, no. 2 (August 1870): 101–2.

[20] Veblen, *Theory*, pp. 33–131; Mary Hayes, "An Esthete's Heart," *Peterson's* 81, no. 5 (November 1882): 371–77; John F. Kasson, *Amusing the Millions: Coney Island at the Turn of the Century* (New York: Hill and Wang, 1978); William Leach, "Transformations in a Culture of Consumption: Women and Department Stores, 1890–1925," *Journal of American History* 71, no. 2 (September 1984): 319–42.

[21] James G. Frazer, *The Golden Bough: A Study in Comparative Religion*, 2 vols. (London and New York: Macmillan Co., 1890); Sigmund Freud, *The Interpretation of Dreams*, trans. A. A. Brill (New York: Macmillan Co., 1913); D. H. Lawrence, *Studies in Classic American Literature* (1924; reprint, London: William Heinemann, 1937), p. 86; Lionel Trilling, *Sincerity and Authenticity* (Cambridge, Mass.: Harvard University Press, 1972).

[22] Bonnie G. Smith, *Ladies of the Leisure Class: The Bourgeoises of Northern France in the Nineteenth Century* (Princeton: Princeton University Press, 1981), pp. 82–85, 87; Mario Praz, *An Illustrated History of Furnishing from the Renaissance to the Twentieth Century*, trans. William Weaver (New York: George Braziller, 1964), p. 327; Carroll Smith-Rosenberg, "The Female World of Love and Ritual," *Signs* 1, no. 1 (Autumn 1975): 1–29; Catharine E. Beecher and Harriet Beecher Stowe, *The American Woman's Home, or, Principles of Domestic Science; Being a Guide to the Formation and Maintenance of Economical, Healthful, Beautiful, and Christian Homes* (1869; reprint, Hartford, Conn.: Stowe-Day Foundation, 1975).

[23] Walter Benjamin, "Paris, Capital of the Nineteenth Century," in Walter Benjamin, *Reflections*, trans. Edmund Jephcott (New York: Harper and Row, 1978), esp. pp. 154–56; Gwendolyn Wright, *Moralism and the Model Home: Domestic Architecture and Cultural Conflict in Chicago, 1873–1913* (Chicago: University of Chicago Press, 1980), pp. 28–40.

[24] Charlotte Perkins Gilman, "The Yellow Wallpaper" (1891) in *A Charlotte Perkins Gilman Reader*, ed. Anne Lane (New York: Pantheon Books, 1980), pp. 3–20. For other examples of these developing claustrophobic sentiments, see Joris-Karl Huysmans, *Against the Grain*, trans. John Howard (New York: Modern Library, 1930); and Carl Schorske, *Fin de Siècle Vienna: Politics and Culture* (New York: Alfred A. Knopf, 1980), esp. chap. 5.

[25] Herbert Bayer, Walter Gropius, and Ise Gropius, *Bauhaus, 1919–1928* (2nd ed.; Boston: Houghton Mifflin Co., 1952), esp. p. 126; Charles Edouard Jeanneret-Gris [Le Corbusier, pseud.], *The New World of Space* (New York: Reynal and Hitchcock, 1948), p. 48; Hans Ludwig C. Jaffee, *De Stijl 1917–1931: The Dutch Contribution to Modern Art* (Amsterdam: J. M. Meulenhoff, 1956), pp. 5, 42, 59.

[26] See, for example, Helen Campbell, "Household Art and the Microbe," *House Beautiful* 6, no. 5 (October 1899): 218–20; Esther Morton, "The Tyranny of Things," *House Beautiful* 36, no. 4 (September 1914): 113; Katherine W. Hand, "Nerves and Decoration," *House Beautiful* 37, no. 6 (May 1915): 184–85; and Wright, *Moralism*, pp. 234, 291. On feminist efforts to create alternative household arrangements, see Dolores Hayden, *The Grand Domestic Revolution* (Cambridge, Mass.: MIT Press, 1981).

[27] Here I follow the stimulating suggestions of Robert Twombly, "Saving the Family: Middle Class Attraction to Wright's Prairie House, 1901–1909," *American Quarterly* 27, no. 1 (March 1975): 57–72. See, for example, Claude Bragdon, "The Architecture of the Home: Some Fundamental Principles," *House Beautiful* 16, no. 1 (June 1904): 10; and Richard Bowland Kimball, "Keeping the House Alive," *House Beautiful* 47, no. 5 (May 1920): 404.

[28] On the social background of advertising agency people, see Roland Marchand, *Advertising the American Dream: Making Way for Modernity, 1920–1940* (Berkeley: University of California Press, 1985), pp. 130–38; and Wallace Boren, "Bad Taste in Advertising," *JWT Forum*, January 7, 1936 (J. Walter Thompson Company Archives, New York).

[29] *Wright's Indian Vegetable Pills* (Philadelphia, 1844), box 33, Lyon Manufacturing Co., *Morning, Noon, and Night* (1872), box 20, *Peruvian Catarrh Cure* (New York, 1890), box 25, *Warner's "Safe" Remedies* (Rochester, N.Y., 1883), box 34, in Patent Medicines, Warshaw Collection of Business Americana, National Museum of American History, Smithsonian Institution.

[30] In addition to those illustrated, see trade cards for F. J. Taney and Co. Angostura Bitters, 1876, box 31a, Patent Medicines, and Love's Incense, 1880, and Taylor's Premium Cologne, ca. 1890, box 108, Cosmetics, Warshaw Collection. For other examples of nineteenth-century exoticism, see Banner, *American Beauty*, esp. pp. 111–17

[31] Advertisement for Mennen's Borated Talcum Powder, in *Town and Country*, June 19, 1909, in box 109, Cosmetics, Warshaw Collection; Ivory Soap Co., *What a Cake of Soap Will Do* (ca. 1900), in box "Proctor and Gamble," Soap, Warshaw Collection; advertisement for Zonite Antiseptic, *Good*

Housekeeping 92, no. 4 (April 1931): 126; advertisement for Lysol Antiseptic, *Good Housekeeping* 90, no. 4 (April 1930): 143. The upper-class counterattack on the belle ideal of voluptuous womanhood is discussed in Banner, *American Beauty,* pp. 130–31.

[32] On the consolidation of authority by the mainstream medical profession, see Paul Starr, *The Social Transformation of American Medicine* (New York Basic Books, 1982), esp. chap. 3. The best concise explication of disenchantment is Peter Berger, *The Sacred Canopy: Elements of a Sociological Theory of Religion* (Garden City, N.Y.: Doubleday, 1967). For an insightful discussion of late Victorian anxieties about the blurred boundaries between humanity and animality, see James Turner, *Reckoning with the Beast: Animals, Pain, and Humanity in the Victorian Mind* (Baltimore: Johns Hopkins University Press, 1980), esp. pp. 63–69. The classic analysis of the relationship between pollution taboos and social boundaries is Mary Douglas, *Purity and Danger: An Analysis of Concepts of Pollution and Taboo* (London: Routledge and Kegan Paul, 1966). Palmer is quoted in Michael Paul Rogin, *Ronald Reagan, the Movie, and Other Episodes in Political Demonology* (Berkeley: University of California Press, 1987), pp. 238–39.

Understanding the Text

1. Though he commends Veblen for his many insights into the nature of consumpton, Lears finds some of Veblen's thinking on the topic limited. Discuss one such instance.

2. According to Lears, peddlers in the nineteenth century exerted an especially powerful, seductive influence upon which group of consumers?

3. According to Lears, how did "the tension between authenticity and artifice" shape consumer culture in late-nineteenth/early-twentieth-century America?

Delectable Materialism: Were the Critics of Consumer Culture Wrong All Along?

Michael Schudson

On January 31, 1990, when McDonald's opened in Moscow, Soviet citizens seemed stunned by the politeness of the people behind the cash registers who smiled and said, "May I help you?" They were delighted at the efficiency of the service despite a wait of two hours; many took home their McDonald's logo-laden refuse as souvenirs. Tongue in cheek, *The New York Times* wrote of hope-starved Soviet consumers won over to "delectable materialism." *The Washington Post*, similarly jocular, painted a portrait of a factory worker standing beneath the golden arches and said of him, "He had seen the future—and it tasted good."

American journalists poke fun at the Soviet passion for American consumer goods because they cannot think of consumerism in the United States without ambivalence. It takes an immigrant, or these days a Soviet visitor, to speak of American abundance in beatific terms. Boris Yeltsin, now president of the Russian Republic, returned from a nine-day American tour in the fall of 1989 effusive about the extraordinary wealth of American life: "Their supermarkets have 30,000 food items," he told supporters in his first public appearance back home. "You can't imagine it. It makes the people feel secure." Yeltsin urged that "at least 100 million Soviets must pass through the American school of supermarkets," to understand the American system. "The leaders must be first."

Michael Schudson is a professor of communications and sociology at the University of California at San Diego. He is one of the nation's leading authorities on the history and sociology of the media, which he has explored in a number of books, including *The Sociology of News* (2003), *The Power of News* (1995), *Advertising, The Uneasy Persuasion* (1984), and *Discovering the News: A Social History of American Newspapers* (1978). He also writes about consumerism, citizenship, and public culture, and has published numerous articles and reviews in a wide range of journals and magazines.

Reprinted with permission for Michael Schudson, "Delectable Materialism: Were the Critics of Consumer Culture Wrong All Along?" *The American Prospect*, Volume 2, Number 5, March 21, 1991. The American Prospect, 2000 L Street, NW, Suite 717, Washington, DC 20036. All rights reserved.

While resembling the simple immigrant's astonishment at American abundance, Yeltsin's comments reveal something more. Abundance and choice, he is saying, provide a feeling of security, social and even spiritual comfort. This celebratory attitude toward American materialism is far from the skepticism shared by home-grown American journalists and intellectuals. The native American view of materialism draws on the anti-capitalism of the left, anti-bourgeois attitudes redolent of aristocratic values, and most of all a distaste for consumerism at the very heart of the American tradition. Jimmy Carter, in his famous 1978 "malaise" speech on America's spiritual crisis, had no trouble finding in his own evangelical Protestantism the anxiety that "too many of us now worship self-indulgence and consumption" and the affirmation that "owning things and consuming things does not satisfy our longing for meaning."

CRITICISM FROM WITHIN

Contemporary social critics may imagine their critiques of consumer culture to be deeply radical and subversive, but they are generally only versions of a critique that American culture itself has long nurtured. And confused versions, at that. Take, for example, criticism of advertising, often attacked as the most egregious emblem of materialism, even as its cause. In fact, America was materialist, consumerist, and enterprising, as Tocqueville observed, long before advertising held much visibility or importance in American cultural life. Yet advertising is today the chief symbol, if not the chief engine, of consumer culture.

As the chief symbol of consumer culture, advertising has also been a chief subject of analysis for critics looking for the hidden springs of American life. David Potter, a widely respected American historian, got it wrong forty years ago in his classic study of consumer culture, *People of Plenty* (1954), and much American thinking about advertising and culture has yet to recover from the error he expressed more directly and clearly than anyone else. Potter held that a society that moves from a producer orientation to a consumer orientation must develop a culture to correspond to it. Advertising responds to "the need to stimulate desire for the goods which an abundant economy has to offer and which a scarcity economy would never have produced."

For Potter, advertising was one of a very few institutions that can "properly be called instruments of social control." And what is an institution of social control? It is one that guides a person "by conceiving of him in a distinctive way and encouraging him to conform as far as possible to the concept." Potter used as examples the church, which conceives of a person as having an immortal soul; the schools, conceiving of the person as a reasonable creature; and the free-enterprise economy, conceiving of the person as a useful producer. Advertising, in contrast, "conceives of man as a consumer."

* * *

The trouble with Potter's argument is that advertising is not at all like church, school, and workplace, the institutions he lists as archetypal institutions of social control. (The sociologist would be more likely to list the church, school, and family.) Having recently watched my five-year-old go off to kindergarten, I have no illusion that the kind of control advertising exercises is half as determinative, controlling, influential, or potentially as destructive as that exerted by the institution of schooling. Even if children were to spend as much time watching commercial television as they do in school (and they do not—television is turned on in the average American household seven hours a day but no individual member of the family watches it for that length of time), children would be able to exercise freedoms in front of the television that they instantly lose in the classroom. Before the television, they can come and go as they like; they can choose to attend or not to attend without fear of the punishing glance, voice, or raised eyebrows of the advertiser responding immediately to their inattention; they can like or dislike, scowl or smile as they wish, without the fear that thirty others will be examining and taking cues from their behavior. In short, the television advertisement can offer no social punishment, no social reward, no social reference group.

Potter, like many others, fails to distinguish the social control exercised by schools and churches from the cultural influence exercised by the mass media. Social control always has a cultural or symbolic dimension; symbols are one of the media through which schools, churches, families, and workplaces operate. These institutions use not only threats, coercion through measures such as confinement, and even physical violence, but more ordinarily symbolic inducements and enticements. The symbolic dimensions are so important that, mistakenly, we may even identify churches with their doctrines and schools with their curricula. But religions are defined as much—if not more—by their social practices as by their doctrine. Similarly, the schools inculcate patterns of behavior in children through a "hidden curriculum" of social control, as sociologists have described it in many studies since the 1950s.

But while social control always has a cultural dimension, the reverse is not true. A cultural or symbolic medium, like advertising, does not necessarily have a social dimension. Or, to put it another way, the social aspects of consumption do not depend on advertising. For example, when we feel good and think we look smart wearing a cashmere coat, we may be reflecting some influence of advertising. But we are just as likely reflecting the practices of other people in the social set to which we belong or aspire. Big houses give a feeling of privacy, space, and security; advertising does not induce that sensation. Owning a book rather than borrowing it, or owning a washer and dryer rather than using the neighborhood laundromat, gives a pleasure of possession, convenience, and self-possession that ads for Stephen King blockbusters or laundry detergents have no part in. If the things we buy did not satisfy or seduce, the images conjured up by advertising would ordinarily fade. The consumer culture is sustained socially not by manufactured images but by the goods themselves as they are used.

* * *

Potter's analysis seems to suggest, as did other analyses of the 1950s that still guide our thought on this matter, that people need to be instructed in the emotions as well as the arts of consumption. People have to learn to desire more goods. That was the argument made by liberals like Potter and John Kenneth Galbraith and by the social critic Vance Packard. It was the point argued by Marxists Paul Baran and Paul Sweezy and taken up later by Stuart Ewen. It is also a notion pushed by the people responsible for selling propaganda to business—that is, by advertising agencies themselves.

Curiously, both the critics of advertising and its spokesmen seem to share the peculiar premise that material goods require force feeding. But is consuming so unpleasant? Is wanting more so unnatural? Is aping the neighbors or seeking to be fashionable so unheard of that a multibillion dollar enterprise is required to coax us into it? Is desire for possessions so rare? Is pleasure in goods so unusual a joy?

I do not claim that wanting more is universal. I certainly do not claim any universality for the peculiar features of the Protestant ethic that Max Weber identified as leading our culture to value hard work aimed at accumulating riches. But I do claim that in America—which in the person of Benjamin Franklin best exemplified for Weber the spirit of capitalism—no multibillion dollar industry was needed to make people want more and more or to breed in them a dissatisfaction that they could quell only in the marketplace.

In this society, as I read it, an insistent ideological campaign promoted self-discipline and self-denial. The assumption was that people would naturally want to consume more and that an elaborate ideological system had to keep desire in check. This Puritan superstructure aimed at constraining old Adam was in the nineteenth century increasingly directed at working-class and immigrant communities, as it still is in the class-skewed movement now against tobacco and alcohol use. Put this way, the underlying assumption in Potter and company seems preposterous. But, then, what is advertising for if not to turn us into desiring consumers? And why should people as smart as David Potter have tried to explain advertising as the instigator of desire for goods if this is so absurd a proposition?

WHAT DOES ADVERTISING DO?

The first question is easily answered. Large outcomes, like the rise of advertising, do not require large causes. Slight ecological advantage may cause large institutional change. Men and women share all chromosomes but one; that little one-forty-sixth of the genetic makeup makes all the difference. Advertising is a complex, wasteful, often distasteful informational system for a consumer economy of competitive businesses and competitive, otherwise unsubsidized mass media. It is an important signaling system between business and business, business and consumer, wholesaler and retailer, consumer and consumer.

But it isn't more important than that. Along with films and novels, advertising provides the iconography, but not the engine, for abundance. Its emergence was not a response to a need to educate consumers' desires and tastes but a response to specific problems and opportunities in production and marketing in certain late nineteenth-century industries—an adjustment by a range of manufacturers and retailers to a new urban life with central business districts, public transportation, and mass circulation newspapers.

* * *

The second question—why smart people should accept a notion with neither evidence nor logic to support it—has to do with the availability, almost the inescapability, of long-standing intellectual traditions of distrust of material goods. Criticism of consumer culture has deep roots in America. Indeed, criticism of what today we call consumer culture originated before anything very closely resembling consumer culture had emerged—certainly before advertising as the central institutional expression of abundance took root.

This criticism emerged not so much from a single tradition as from a set of traditions that have become intermingled in contemporary criticism of consumer culture. I see five principal traditions at work—three that lie within bourgeois culture and two that lie outside it, critical not only of advertising but of bourgeois society and capitalism in general. Teasing out these strands of thought may help us to straighten out our own very conflicted relationship to the world of goods today.

PURITANS, QUAKERS, AND REPUBLICANS

I will first take up the three bourgeois objections to consumer culture. Some critics, whom I shall call Puritans, attack popular attitudes toward material goods in pursuit of spirituality; some critics, whom I shall call Quakers, attack features of the goods themselves in pursuit of simplicity; and some, whom I shall label republicans, attack the consequences of possession, notably complacency and the inappropriate transfer of consumer values to other arenas of life, in pursuit of civic virtue.

The Puritan critique worries about whether people invest an appropriate amount of meaning in goods. By "Puritan," I refer to the conviction, symbolized by the sturdy and sober New England colonists, that pleasure should be subordinated to duty and temporal concerns to religious obligations. In this view, the meaning people invest in worldly possessions should be less than that invested in spiritual pursuits. Yet the Puritan critics do not necessarily agree about what degree of meaning-investment in material possessions would be appropriate. Some critics have argued that American attitudes toward goods are not crassly materialist enough, that people find goods insufficient without investing meaning in them. The British critic Raymond Williams, for instance, referring generally to capitalist societies, writes that modern advertising is proof that people in modern capitalist societies are not materialist—because the job of the ad is to convey added value to the product itself.

"If we were sensibly materialist," Williams writes, ". . . beer would be enough for us, without the additional promise that in drinking it we show ourselves to be manly, young in heart, or neighbourly." For Williams, the trouble with contemporary attitudes toward goods is that goods in themselves are undervalued, in their associations, overspiritualized.

In contrast, the American intellectual historian and critic Christopher Lasch suggests that people underspiritualize goods. In *The Minimal Self* (1984), Lasch complains that manufactured goods are inferior to handmade goods in that they cannot serve, in the manner of Linus's blanket, to bridge the psychological gap between an individual's inner self and the external world. For Lasch, handcrafted goods have the mark of human activity upon them, while commodities are elements in a pre-fab dream world so far removed that they cannot aid us in gaining any sense of mastery over our experience. In his latest work, *The True and Only Heaven* (1991), he again writes with admiration of manual labor and craftsmanship or, at least, with resentment of intellectuals who fail to appreciate manual labor as he does. But his larger point is that contemporary attitudes toward goods are more satanized than spiritualized, that we are possessed by our possessions, in a word, addicted. As in his earlier work, *The Culture of Narcissism,* Lasch refuses to see this as conventionally hedonistic. He describes it as addictive, compulsive, and linked intrinsically to consumer capitalism.

There are implicitly empirical claims in the notion that Americans overspiritualize or underspiritualize goods, with little proffered evidence one way or the other. Is Williams right to suppose people do not find most advertising "insanely irrelevant"? My reading of the evidence is that people ignore the vast amount of advertising they see and distrust much of the little advertising they do take in. Is Lasch correct that mass-produced goods fail as "transitional objects"? I see no evidence, certainly not from my own children, that mass-produced blankets are inferior to grandma-made afghans as "transitional objects," although adults may be more discriminating and I wish that my daughter were as attached to the quilt my wife made or the afghan my grandmother made as to the cotton blanket we got from J. C. Penney's, but she isn't. Do I overspiritualize goods in this desire? Does my daughter underspiritualize? And what is the appropriate standard?

* * *

The Quaker critique looks less at attitudes toward goods than at features of the goods themselves. It is less concerned with how people feel about goods than with objectionable features of the products themselves, usually their wastefulness or extravagance. This is part of Thorstein Veblen's attack on consumer society. Christopher Lasch, whose multifarious critiques of consumerism fit into just about all of my categories, has taken up the old complaint that modern industry is dictated by "planned obsolescence" or Sloanism, the annual model change that Alfred P. Sloan introduced at General Motors to coax people to buy a new car even when they have a serviceable old one. Here changes in products are not only useless but manipulative, aimed only at pointless product differentiation to which people will attribute unfounded meaning. The fashion industry in its various forms is a regular target of such criticism, as it was for the Quakers themselves in their adherence to plain dress.

Critics, however, have too easily generalized from a few salient examples. Does Sloanism actually guide American industry? Does it even guide the automobile industry? While General Motors was developing the annual model change, other companies were producing washing machines, radios, single-family homes, bicycles, phonographs, long-distance telephone lines, and bathroom fixtures that were designed to last, and did last, for years. Sloanism is an important aspect of the American economy, but it is a marketing strategy for a certain set of conditions rather than a strategic psychological tool or a deep cultural force.

In the case of the automobile industry, consumers were not, in fact, happily holding onto their cars for years until Sloan found a way to introduce wasteful fashion to utilitarian transport vehicles. Years before Sloan dreamt of the annual model change, the used car market was huge and by 1927 its volume outstripped new car sales. People were obviously "buying up" as they could afford to, reproducing in the automobile an objective correlative of already existing systems of class and status distinction. They were resisting the implications of Henry Ford's one model, one price policy. For reasons no more calculating, so were many of Detroit's auto makers, as historian Donald Davis has shown in a recent study. Many of Detroit's entrepreneurs were building more expensive cars, pricing themselves out of the lucrative mass market, and ultimately bankrupting themselves in a status-driven effort to manufacture cars of a sort appropriate to their own station, or desired station, in Detroit society. They went too far up-market while Ford controlled the lower end of the market and Sloan looked to the middle. As Sloan said, "Middle-income buyers created the demand for progress in their cars, for comfort, convenience, power and style. This was the actual trend of American life, and those who adapted to it prospered." The fashion-consciousness that Sloan helped institutionalize in the automobile industry may indeed be wasteful, but "planned obsolescence" as critics still call it, does not characterize most of American industry and was in its origins as much a response to the desire of consumers to be fashionable as a cause of fashion-consciousness.

But granting that some kinds of consumption are more practical, less ostentatious, and less wasteful than others, and therefore morally more defensible, what is the appropriate level of workmanship and luxury for products? This evaluative question is even more slippery than the empirical one of determining the extent of Sloanism. How should we weigh the Cadillac or BMW against the subcompact Chevy? The former may use more resources and be less fuel-efficient, but it also may be a better—and safer—car. Some practical and spartan products may not only be aesthetically unappealing but ecologically unsound. Paper plates and towels may be easier to use and dispose of than china and cloth towels that are designed for regular re-use, but they are wasteful.

Not that wastefulness is always easy to measure. "Polyester" has long been a term of abuse in some circles because it is artificial and, so go the rationalizations, it doesn't last like cotton. But the manufacturers have argued that the polyester takes less energy to produce and to maintain (never needs ironing) than the cotton shirt and, over the lifetime of the shirt, absorbs less of the earth's total energy and resources. A similar case has been made for disposable diapers. (See "Changing the Waste Makers," *The American Prospect,* Fall 1990.) This is not to mention social expenditure, exploitation, and waste—a product that never needs ironing, or a convenient diaper, saves not only electricity but human, almost invariably female, labor.

The Quaker critique, then, says goods should not be pointlessly differentiated or that goods should not be made useful, efficient, speedy, or convenient beyond some consensual standard of what level of usefulness is normative or that goods should not be multiplied if they can be made durable for sharing or personal re-use. But what is the standard of appropriate convenience and who is to set it? On what grounds is the Boeing 747 okay but the Concorde wasteful? In my house, the electric blender is acceptable but not the electric can opener, the electric toothbrush but not the electric blanket. On what grounds are such decisions made? How do we arrive at a baseline for consensus—and, if we can't (and I think that we can't), then what is the character of the moral objection to excessive consumption?

* * *

The last of the bourgeois objections to consumption, the republican perspective, is concerned not with attitudes toward goods nor with the wastefulness of goods themselves but with the corrupting influence on public life of a goods-orientation in private life. A goods-orientation or consumerist orientation seems to include two features. First, it is passive. Satisfaction with goods produces acquiescence in politics. People who transfer their passive orientation toward goods to the world of politics expect political life to be prefabricated and to participate in it simply by making a choice between predetermined alternatives. This conception of politics reduces a voting booth to a vending machine.

Second, the republican critique of consumerism objects to the priority given to goods-possession rather than to production as a defining feature of personal identity. "Lifestyle" surpasses a person's work life in a consumer society as the defining feature of existence. The republican critic sees this emphasis as not only a misunderstanding of human nature, but a politically conservative misunderstanding, since it diverts attention from the task of making our work lives more vital and democratic.

But is a consumerist orientation to goods necessarily passive? Some research suggests a much more "active" involvement by consumers in shaping the meaning of the goods they buy. In a study of automobile consumption, for example, H. F. Moorhouse examines the appropriation by young people of Detroit-made cars in the "hot rod" culture of the 1940s. Teenagers did not passively accept automobiles but decorated, redesigned, and even re-engineered them for their own purposes in racing (often illegally). The ethos of hot rod culture, in

Moorhouse's view, was not passivity but commitment "to labour, to strive, to plan, to exercise skill, to compete, to succeed, to risk." One does not have to look back to the 1940s, of course, to find that kind of active involvement.

I do not mean to protest too much here. Certainly even the most active forms of watching baseball are on some dimensions more passive than the most passive ways of playing the game (like the daydreaming elementary-school right-fielder). But it is important to note that there are degrees of activity in consumption just as there are degrees of disengagement in labor.

The role of work in human identity is scarcely self-evident. Many sociological studies of labor, whether or not Marxist in inspiration, assume that only in labor can "real" satisfaction in life be attained; all other satisfactions have to be regarded as substitutes, more or less unsatisfying and illusory. But why treat consumption, a priori, as peripheral to key matters of human fulfillment? Labor and occupation are very important, but it is some brand of meta-physics that makes labor the defining feature of human life.

Look at a standard obituary. It ends with a list of the people the dead person is "survived by," an emphasis on social relations, not occupation, as definitive of the person. It is the rare headstone that will declare "an honest merchant" or "a loyal worker" rather than "beloved husband and father" or "cherished sister and daughter."

SOCIALISTS AND ARISTOCRATS

I will discuss more quickly the non-bourgeois or anti-bourgeois objections to consumer culture since, in a variety of ways, they have been bootlegged into bourgeois self-criticism. The Marxist or socialist objection is that however beneficent the economic system may appear on the side of consumption, it rests on the exploitation of workers under the capitalist system of production. Indeed, Marxists and others have argued, this is part of the point of the con-sumer society—to distract the minds and bodies of workers, to serve as an opiate of the peo-ple, submerging dissatisfaction with life in the exploitative workplace.

"The tired worker," Christopher Lasch writes in *The Culture of Narcissism,* "instead of attempting to change the conditions of his work, seeks renewal in brightening his immediate surroundings with new goods and services." The questionable assumption here, as in other criticism, is that the satisfactions achieved through the world of goods are illusory. Ordinarily, they are quite real. The critics may see goods as distractions, but they can also be seen as authentic sources of meaning. Moreover, they may be as often motivation for political activity as a substitute for it. The recent experience of social transformation in Eastern Europe, galva-nized by economic aspirations as well as by political hope, is a case in point.

The aristocratic objection to consumer society is primarily aesthetic. Where the socialist critique of consumer culture emphasizes the exploitation of workers, the aristocratic or elitist objection to consumer society is an attack on ugliness in defense of Culture. Mass-produced goods are ugly. The trouble with this critique, clearly, is its anti-democratic bias. Mass-produced goods may be judged ugly by some, but they are often significantly cheaper than hand-crafted products. The evidence on this is not only before our eyes but available in the historical record. For instance, carpets were once available only to the wealthy; the power loom made them available to most citizens. Ready-to-wear clothing was available by the mid-nineteenth century to working-class people who could not have afforded items of such quality before. A great amount of home-made wear was shoddy and ill-fitting.

Again, the problem is one of standards and relativism. We cannot just smuggle in an assurance that we know what valid culture is: no one does. Worse, as economist Fred Hirsch argued, "positional" goods such as parks, vacation spots, and restaurants are found "beautiful" in part because of their exclusiveness, spaciousness, quiet, and seclusion—in short, because of the absence of other people. Valuing what is exclusive, we call it fine, rare, beautiful, and so incorporate social distinction into our very definition of quality. So the problem of not having aesthetic standards on which we could all agree is compounded by the problem of having too readily at hand aesthetic standards that are intrinsically anti-democratic.

THINKING THROUGH GOODS

In questioning whether the critics of consumerism have got it right, I have not suggested their views have no merit. I myself am something of a Puritan, Quaker, republican, Marxist, and aristocrat in my own everyday life—in my objections to someone else's consumption, in my debating in my own head or with my wife about a purchase, in my war with myself about the uses of money.

My opinions in these matters, however, are not absolute moral judgments. They are social and socializing, that is, both shaped by my particular set of social relations and designed at some level to identify and characterize myself within my set of social relations. I want to reserve as reasonable standards for my own consumption and for judging the consumption of others the heritage of a Puritanism that recognizes possession as an inappropriate aim of life, however valuable a means; of a Quakerism that recognizes the vanity of goods and, in a modern ecological variant, moves from objecting to the vanity of goods before God to the wastefulness of goods before a resource-scarce and unequal world; of a republicanism that scouts out dangers of private satisfaction in the face of public squalor—not that private satisfaction is in itself wrong but that insofar as it removes people from a concern for essential elements of a common life it is dangerous; of a Marxist or socialist vision that sees that for every act of consumption there is an act of production and that a calculus that would weigh the moral worth of the consumption of goods must take into account the human dignity of the work that went into their production; and of an aesthetic elitism that, without making beauty a class privilege or craftsmanship a religious cult, honors both utilitarian and aesthetic standards of grace and durability, form and function.

I want to say that these are all important standards of judgment to keep in mind. People should live by some set of moral rules for their consumption; how much and what we consume has moral consequences. Our increasing awareness of environmental deterioration and ecological interconnectedness makes this more apparent than ever before. Yet, I do not see any likelihood of establishing a calculus that will enable us to reach agreement about whether our own or anyone else's purchases and uses of products are justified.

The economic collapse of the Soviet Union and Eastern Europe has stimulated a new round of reflection about consumer culture. It would be a mistake to interpret the success of capitalism in producing goods as a justification for its failures, at least in America, to meet many citizens' basic needs of affordable shelter, health care, and economic security. But the time has come to scrutinize the repeated criticisms of consumer culture that have flourished in Western societies living in relative affluence and to recognize an ambivalence about consumption in our intellectual life as in our culture generally that extends back at least to Adam Smith, if not to Adam. It is time to face that ambivalence en route to a political and moral position beyond the snickering, joking, and invariably hypocritical posturing of most criticism of consumer culture.

* * *

Advertising at times seems to be materialism at its worst, the sizzle without the steak, the idolatry of goods divorced from the utility and enjoyment goods provide, but even this is too simple a view. It recognizes neither the aesthetic appeal of some advertising that touches us nor the plain wrapping, anti-magical character of most advertising. The most common advertising is, in a sense, Quaker itself—it points to price and so helps keep in mind economy as a chief criterion in buying. Or it is Puritan—recommending a product not because it provides moral or social or theological salvation but because it serves certain banal purposes well. It cleans your sink. It gets you to New York in time for your business meeting. It provides high-fidelity sound recording.

True, advertising is rarely republican—it does not focus on the needs of public life. And it often takes a stance toward the public life that may not be healthy. If views of the person and the society can be ranged along a continuum between those that emphasize the moral embeddedness of the individual in a community and those that emphasize the isolation of the autonomous individual, then advertising typically falls near the latter end of the continuum.

Advertising offers and is expressive of an ideology of choice. It unifies us around a belief in difference, variety, abundance, pluralism, choice, democracy. Consumer culture and advertising, along with elections, are the most important institutions that promote an ideology of choice. Yet while elections and advertising do present real choices, they also distract us from the structure of choosing, the hidden choices behind the choices. We become fascinated with the agenda and forget who sets it. And perhaps we come to believe, at bottom, that popular sovereignty governs both politics and economic life. So if the politician is corrupt, we learn to say that "we get what we deserve." And if the product fails, we learn to say that "you get what you pay for." We learn to dissent by exit rather than by voice. We are instructed in choice but not in living with or against the choices we make.

In the past generation, people have listened to one set of voices from the East and have borrowed notions of a simple life, a life of self-discipline and self-denial, from Buddhist traditions of Asia. Now we are listening to a different set of voices from a different East—the voices of Yeltsins and the unashamed emulation of economic abundance. Eastern European nations, as symbol and substance of their legitimacy on a world stage, are seeking to partake in the kind of consumer affluence the West has enjoyed for two generations.

We see this and it should stir us to question our received criticisms of consumer culture. At the same time, we have growing concerns about environmental and ecological catastrophe and the distribution of consumption not only among rich and poor within a society but among rich and poor nations within a world system. We should not learn the lessons of Eastern Europe so well as to deny ourselves the right to criticize consumerism. But it must be a new critique. Freeing ourselves from Biblical or republican or Marxist moralisms and recognizing a certain dignity and rationality in the desire for material goods, we should seek to reconstruct an understanding of our moral and political view of consumption that we and others can live with.

Understanding the Text

1. According to Schudson, what is the difference between "social control" and "cultural influence"? Which term, in his view, best describes advertising? Why?

2. Briefly describe the differences between the Puritan, Quaker, and Republican critiques of consumer culture.

3. Toward the end of his essay, Schudson writes that "[a]dvertising offers and is expressive of an ideology of choice." What does he mean by this? And what does this ideology conceal?

Two Cheers for Materialism

James B. Twitchell

Of all the strange beasts that have come slouching into the 20th century, none has been more misunderstood, more criticized, and more important than materialism. Who but fools, toadies, hacks, and occasional loopy libertarians have ever risen to its defense? Yet the fact remains that while materialism may be the most shallow of the 20th century's various -isms, it has been the one that has ultimately triumphed. The world of commodities appears so antithetical to the world of ideas that it seems almost heresy to point out the obvious: most of the world most of the time spends most of its energy producing and consuming more and more stuff. The really interesting question may be not why we are so materialistic, but why we are so unwilling to acknowledge and explore what seems the central characteristic of modern life.

When the French wished to disparage the English in the 19th century, they called them a nation of shopkeepers. When the rest of the world now wishes to disparage Americans, they call us a nation of consumers. And they are right. We are developing and rapidly exporting a new material culture, a mallcondo culture. To the rest of the world we do indeed seem not just born to shop, but alive to shop. Americans spend more time tooling around the mallcondo—three to four times as many hours as our European counterparts—and we have more stuff to show for it. According to some estimates, we have about four times as many things as Middle Europeans, and who knows how much more than people in the less developed parts of the world. The quantity and disparity are increasing daily, even

James B. Twitchell is a professor of English and advertising at the University of Florida. He has written extensively about advertising, consumerism, and popular culture in numerous books, including *Shopping for God: How Christianity Went from In Your Heart to In Your Face* (2007), *Where Men Hide* (2006), *Branded Nation: The Marketing of Megachurch, College Inc., and Museumworld* (2004), *Living It Up: America's Love Affair with Luxury* (2002), *Twenty Ads That Shook the World: The Century's Most Groundbreaking Advertising and How It Changed Us All* (2000), *Lead Us Into Temptation: The Triumph of American Materialism* (1999), and *Adcult USA: The Triumph of Advertising in American Culture* (1995). His work also has appeared in numerous journals and magazines.

though, as we see in Russia and China, the "emerging nations" are playing a frantic game of catch-up.

This burst of mallcondo commercialism has happened recently—in my lifetime—and it is spreading around the world at the speed of television. The average American consumes twice as many goods and services as in 1950; in fact, the poorest fifth of the current population buys more than the average fifth did in 1955. Little wonder that the average new home of today is twice as large as the average house built in the early years after World War II. We have to put that stuff somewhere—quick!—before it turns to junk.

Sooner or later we are going to have to acknowledge the uncomfortable fact that this amoral consumerama has proved potent because human beings love things. In fact, to a considerable degree we live for things. In all cultures we buy things, steal things, exchange things, and horde things. From time to time, some of us collect vast amounts of things, from tulip bulbs to paint drippings on canvasses to matchbook covers. Often these objects have no observable use.

We live through things. We create ourselves through things. And we change ourselves by changing our things. In the West, we have even developed the elaborate algebra of commercial law to decide how things are exchanged, divested, and recaptured. Remember, we call these things "goods," as in "goods and services." We don't—unless we are academic critics—call them "bads." This sounds simplistic, but it is crucial to understanding the powerful allure of materialism.

Our commercial culture has been blamed for the rise of eating disorders, the spread of "affluenza," the epidemic of depression, the despoliation of cultural icons, the corruption of politics, the carnivalization of holy times like Christmas, and the gnat-life attention span of our youth. All of this is true. Commercialism contributes. But it is by no means the whole truth. Commercialism is more a mirror than a lamp. In demonizing it, in seeing ourselves as helpless and innocent victims of its overpowering force, in making it the scapegoat du jour, we reveal far more about our own eagerness to be passive in the face of complexity than about the thing itself.

Anthropologists tell us that consumption habits are gender-specific. Men seem to want stuff in the latent and post-midlife years. That's when the male collecting impulse seems to be felt. Boys amass playing marbles first, Elgin marbles later. Women seem to gain potency as consumers after childbirth, almost as if getting and spending is part of a nesting impulse.

Historians, however, tell us to be careful about such stereotyping. Although women are the primary consumers of commercial objects today, they have enjoyed this status only since the Industrial Revolution. Certainly in the pre-industrial world men were the chief hunter-gatherers. If we can trust works of art to accurately portray how booty was split (and cultural historians such as John Berger and Simon Schama think we can), then males were the prime consumers of fine clothes, heavily decorated furniture, gold and silver articles, and of course, paintings in which they could be shown displaying their stuff.

Once a surplus was created, in the 19th century, women joined the fray in earnest. They were not duped. The hegemonic phallocentric patriarchy did not brainwash them into thinking goods mattered. The Industrial Revolution produced more and more things not simply because it had the machines to do so, and not because nasty producers twisted their handlebar mustaches and whispered, "We can talk women into buying anything," but because both sexes are powerfully attracted to the world of things.

Karl Marx understood the magnetism of things better than anyone else. In The Communist Manifesto (1848), he wrote:

> The bourgeoisie, by the rapid improvement of all instruments of production, by the immensely facilitated means of communication, draws all, even the most barbarian nations into civilization. The cheap prices of its commodities are the heavy artillery with which it batters down all Chinese walls. . . . It compels all nations, on pain of extinction, to adopt the bourgeois mode of production; it compels them to introduce what it calls civilization into their midst, i.e. to become bourgeois themselves. In one word, it creates a world after its own image.

Marx used this insight to motivate the heroic struggle against capitalism. But the struggle should not be to deter capitalism and its mad consumptive ways, but to appreciate how it works so its furious energy may be understood and exploited.

Don't turn to today's middle-aged academic critic for any help on that score. Driving about in his totemic Volvo (unattractive and built to stay that way), he can certainly criticize the bourgeois afflictions of others, but he is unable to provide much actual insight into their consumption practices, much less his own. Ask him to explain the difference between "Hilfiger" inscribed on an oversize shirt hanging nearly to the knees and his rear-window university decal (My child goes to Yale, sorry about yours), and you will be met with a blank stare. If you were then to suggest that what that decal and automotive nameplate represent is as overpriced as Calvin Klein's initials on a plain white T-shirt, he would pout that you can't compare apples and whatever. If you were to say next that aspiration and affiliation are at the heart of both displays, he would say that you just don't get it, just don't get it at all.

If you want to understand the potency of American consumer culture, ask any group of teenagers what democracy means to them. You will hear an extraordinary response. Democracy is the right to buy anything you want. Freedom's just another word for lots of things to buy. Appalling perhaps, but there is something to their answer. Being able to buy what you want when and where you want it was, after all, the right that made 1989 a watershed year in Eastern Europe. Recall as well that freedom to shop was another way to describe the right to be served in a restaurant that provided one focus for the early civil rights movement. Go back further. It was the right to consume freely which sparked the fires of separation of this country from England. The freedom to buy what you want (even if you can't pay for it) is what most foreigners immediately spot as what they like about our culture, even though in the next breath they will understandably criticize it.

The pressure to commercialize—to turn things into commodities and then market them as charms—has always been particularly Western. As Max Weber first argued in The Protestant Ethic and the Spirit of Capitalism (1905), much of the Protestant Reformation was geared toward denying the holiness of many things that the Catholic church had endowed with meanings. From the inviolable priesthood to the sacrificial holy water, this deconstructive movement systematically unloaded meaning. Soon the marketplace would capture this offloaded meaning and apply it to secular things. Buy this, you'll be saved. You deserve a break today. You, you're the one. We are the company that cares about you. You're worth it. You are in good hands. We care. Trust in us. We are here for you.

Materialism, it's important to note, does not crowd out spiritualism; spiritualism is more likely a substitute when objects are scarce. When we have few things we make the next world holy. When we have plenty we enchant the objects around us. The hereafter becomes the here and now.

We have not grown weaker but stronger by accepting the self-evidently ridiculous myths that sacramentalize mass-produced objects; we have not wasted away but have proved inordinately powerful; have not devolved and been rebarbarized, but seem to have marginally improved. Dreaded affluenza notwithstanding, commercialism has lessened pain. Most of us have more pleasure and less discomfort in our lives than most of the people most of the time in all of history.

As Stanley Lebergott, an economist at Wesleyan University, argues in *Pursuing Happiness* (1993), most Americans have "spent their way to happiness." Lest this sound overly Panglossian, what Lebergott means is that while consumption by the rich has remained relatively steady, the rest of us—the intractable poor (about four percent of the population) are the exception—have now had a go of it. If the rich really are different, as F. Scott Fitzgerald said, and the difference is that they have longer shopping lists and are happier for it, then we have, in the last two generations, substantially caught up.

The most interesting part of the book is the second half. Here Lebergott unloads reams of government statistics and calculations to chart the path that American consumption has taken in a wide range of products and services: food, tobacco, clothing, fuel, domestic service, and medicine—to name only a few. Two themes emerge strongly from these data. The first, not surprisingly, is that Americans were far better off by 1990 than they were in 1900. And the second is that academic critics—from Robert Heilbroner, Tibor Scitovsky, Robert and Helen Lynd, and Christopher Lasch to Juliet Schor, Robert Frank, and legions of others—who've censured the waste and tastelessness of much of American consumerism have simply missed the point. Okay, okay, money can't buy happiness, but you stand a better chance than with penury.

The cultural pessimists counter that it may be true that materialism offers a temporary palliative against the anxiety of emptiness, but we still must burst joy's grape. Consumption will turn sour because so much of it is based on the chimera of debt. Easy credit = overbuying = disappointment = increased anxiety.

This is not just patronizing, it is wrongheaded. As another economist, Lendol Calder, has argued in *Financing the American Dream* (1999), debt has been an important part of families' financial planning since the time of Washington and Jefferson. And although consumer debt has consistently risen in recent times, the default rate has remained remarkably stable. More than 95.5 percent of consumer debt gets paid, usually on time. In fact, the increased availability of credit to a growing share of the population, particularly to lower-income individuals and families, has allowed many more "have nots" to enter the economic mainstream.

There is, in fact, a special crippling quality to poverty in the modern Western world. For the penalty of intractable, transgenerational destitution is not just the absence of things; it is also the absence of meaning, the exclusion from participating in the essential socializing events of modern life. When you hear that some ghetto kid has killed one of his peers for a pair of branded sneakers or a monogrammed athletic jacket you realize that chronically unemployed poor youths are indeed living the absurdist life proclaimed by existentialists. The poor are truly the selfless ones in commercial culture.

Clearly what the poor are after is what we all want: association, affiliation, inclusion, magical purpose. While they are bombarded, as we all are, by the commercial imprecations of being cool, of experimenting with various presentations of disposable self, they lack the wherewithal to even enter the loop.

The grandfather of today's academic scolds is Thorstein Veblen (1857–1929), the eccentric Minnesotan who coined the phrase "conspicuous consumption" and has become almost a cult figure among critics of consumption. All of his books (save for his translation of the *Lexdaela Saga*) are still in print. His most famous, *The Theory of the Leisure Class,* has never been out of print since it was first published in 1899. Veblen claimed that the leisure class set the standards for conspicuous consumption. Without sumptuary laws to protect their markers of distinction, the rest of us could soon make their styles into our own—the Industrial Revolution saw to that. But since objects lose their status distinctions when consumed by the hoi polloi, the leisure class must eternally be finding newer and more wasteful markers. Waste is not just inevitable, it is always increasing as the foolish hounds chase the wily fox.

Veblen lumped conspicuous consumption with sports and games, "devout observances," and aesthetic display. They were all reducible, he insisted, to "pecuniary emulation," his characteristically inflated term for getting in with the in-crowd. Veblen fancied himself a socialist looking forward to the day when "the discipline of the machine" would be turned around to promote stringent rationality among the entire population instead of wasted dispersion. If only we had fewer choices we would be happier, there would be less waste, and we would accept each other as equals.

The key to Veblen's argumentative power is that like Hercules cleaning the Augean stables, he felt no responsibility to explain what happens next. True, if we all purchased the same toothpaste things would be more efficient and less wasteful. Logically we should all read *Consumer Reports,* find out the best brand, and then all be happy using the same product. But we aren't. Procter & Gamble markets 36 sizes and shapes of Crest. There are 41 versions of Tylenol. Is this because we are dolts afflicted with "pecuniary emulation," obsessed with making invidious distinctions, or is the answer more complex? Veblen never considered that consumers might have other reasons for exercising choice in the marketplace. He never considered, for example, that along with "keeping up with the Joneses" runs "keeping away from the Joneses."

Remember in *King Lear* when the two nasty daughters want to strip Lear of his last remaining trappings of majesty? He has moved in with them, and they don't think he needs so many expensive guards. They whittle away at his retinue until only one is left. "What needs one?" they say. Rather like governments attempting to redistribute wealth or like academics criticizing consumption, they conclude that Lear's needs are excessive. They are false needs. Lear, however, knows otherwise. Terrified and suddenly bereft of purpose, he bellows from his innermost soul, "Reason not the need."

Lear knows that possessions are definitions—superficial meanings, perhaps, but meanings nonetheless. And unlike Veblen, he knows those meanings are worth having. Without soldiers he is no king. Without a BMW there can be no yuppie, without tattoos no adolescent rebel, without big hair no Southwestern glamourpuss, without Volvos no academic intellectual, and, well, you know the rest. Meaning is what we are after, what we need, especially when we are young.

What kind of meaning? In the standard academic view, growing out of the work of the Frankfurt school theorists of the 1950s and '60s (such as Antonio Gramsci, Theodor Adorno, and Max Horkheimer) and later those of the Center for Contemporary Cultural Studies at the University of Birmingham, it is meaning supplied by capitalist manipulators. What we see in popular culture, in this view, is the result of the manipulation of the many for the profit of the few.

For an analogy, take watching television. In academic circles, we assume that youngsters are being reified (to borrow a bit of the vast lexicon of jargon that accompanies this view) by passively consuming pixels in the dark. Meaning supposedly resides in the shows and is transferred to the sponge-like viewers. So boys, for example, see flickering scenes of violence, internalize these scenes, and willy-nilly are soon out jimmying open your car. This is the famous Twinkie interpretation of human behavior—consuming too much sugar leads to violent actions. Would listening to Barry Manilow five hours a day make adolescents into loving, caring people?

Watch kids watching television and you see something quite different from what is seen by the critics. Most consumption, whether it be of entertainment or in the grocery store, is active. We are engaged. Here is how I watch television. I almost never turn the set on to see a particular show. I am near the machine and think I'll see what's happening. I know all the channels; any eight-year-old does. I am not a passive viewer. I use the remote control to pass through various programs, not searching for a final destination but making up a shopping basket, as it were, of entertainment.

But the academic critic doesn't see this. He sees a passive observer who sits quietly in front of the set letting the phosphorescent glow of mindless infotainment pour over his consciousness. In the hypodermic analogy beloved by critics, the potent dope of desire is pumped into the bleary dupe. This paradigm of passive observer and active supplier, a receptive moron and smart manipulator, is easily transported to the marketplace. One can see why such a system would appeal to the critic. After all, since the critic is not being duped, he should be empowered to protect the young, the female, the foreign, the uneducated, and the helpless from the onslaught of dreck.

In the last decade or so, however, a number of scholars in the humanities and social sciences have been challenging many of the academy's assumptions.[1] What distinguishes the newer thinking is that scholars have left the office to actually observe and question their subjects. Just one example: Mihaly Csikszentmihalyi, a psychology professor at the University of Chicago, interviewed 315 Chicagoans from 82 families, asking them what objects in the home they cherished most. The adult members of the five happiest families picked things that reminded them of other people and good times they'd had together. They mentioned a memento (such as an old toy) from their childhood 30 percent of the time. Adults in the five most dissatisfied families cited such objects only six percent of the time.

In explaining why they liked something, happy family members often described, for example, the times their family had spent on a favorite couch, rather than its style or color. Their gloomier counterparts tended to focus on the merely physical qualities of things. What was clear was that both happy and unhappy families derived great meaning from the consumption and interchange of manufactured things. The thesis, reflected in the title of his co-authored 1981 book, *The Meaning of Things: Domestic Symbols and the Self,* is that most of the "work" of consumption occurs after the act of purchase. Things do not come complete; they are forever being assembled.

Twentieth-century French sociologists have taken the argument even further. Two of the most important are Pierre Bourdieu, author of *Distinction: A Social Critique of the Judgement of Taste* (1984), and Jean Baudrillard, whose books include *The Mirror of Production* (1983) and *Simulacra and Simulation* (1994). In the spirit of reader-response theory in literary criticism, they see meaning not as a single thing that producers affix to consumer goods, but as something created by the user, who jumbles various interpretations simultaneously. Essentially, beneath the jargon, this means that the Budweiser you drink is not the same as the one I drink. The meaning tastes different. The fashion you consider stylish, I think is ugly. If we buy the package not the contents, it is because the package means more.

The process of consumption is creative and even emancipating. In an open market, we consume the real and the imaginary meanings, fusing objects, symbols, and images together to end up with "a little world made cunningly." Rather than lives, individuals since midcentury have had lifestyles. For better or worse, lifestyles are secular religions, coherent patterns of valued things. Your lifestyle is not related to what you do for a living but to what you buy. One of the chief aims of the way we live now is the enjoyment of affiliating with those who share the same clusters of objects as we do.

Mallcondo culture is so powerful in part because it frees us from the strictures of social class. The outcome of material life is no longer preordained by coat of arms, pew seat, or trust fund. Instead, it evolves from a never-ending shifting of individual choice. No one wants to be middle class, for instance. You want to be cool, hip, with it, with the "in" crowd, instead.

One of the reasons terms like Yuppie, Baby Boomer, and GenX have elbowed aside such older designations as "upper middle class" is that we no longer understand social class as well as we do lifestyle, or what marketing firms call "consumption communities." Observing stuff is the way we understand each other. Even if no one knows exactly how much money it takes to be a yuppie, or how young you have to be, or how upwardly aspiring, everybody knows where yuppies gather, how they dress, what they play, what they drive, what they eat, and why they hate to be called yuppies.

For better or worse, American culture is well on its way to becoming world culture. The Soviets have fallen. Only quixotic French intellectuals and anxious Islamic fundamentalists are trying to stand up to it. By no means am I sanguine about such a material culture. It has many problems that I have glossed over. Consumerism is wasteful, it is devoid of other-worldly concerns, it lives for today and celebrates the body, and it overindulges and spoils the young with impossible promises.

"Getting and spending" has eclipsed family, ethnicity, even religion as a defining matrix. That doesn't mean that those other defining systems have disappeared, but that an increasing number of young people around the world will give more of their loyalty to Nike than to creeds of blood, race, or belief. This is not entirely a bad thing, since a lust for upscale branding isn't likely to drive many people to war, but it is, to say the least, far from inspiring.

It would be nice to think that materialism could be heroic, self-abnegating, and redemptive. It would be nice to think that greater material comforts will release us from racism, sexism, and ethnocentrism, and that the apocalypse will come as it did at the end of romanticism in Shelley's *Prometheus Unbound,* leaving us "Scepterless, free, uncircumscribed . . . Equal, unclassed, tribeless, and nationless."

But it is more likely that the globalization of capitalism will result in the banalities of an ever-increasing worldwide consumerist culture. The French don't stand a chance. The untranscendent, repetitive, sensational, democratic, immediate, tribalizing and unifying force of what Irving Kristol calls the American Imperium need not necessarily result in a Bronze Age of culture. But it certainly will not produce what Shelley had in mind.

We have not been led into this world of material closeness against our better judgment. For many of us, especially when young, consumerism is our better judgment. We have not just asked to go this way, we have demanded. Now most of the world is lining up, pushing and shoving, eager to elbow into the mall. Getting and spending has become the most passionate, and often the most imaginative, endeavor of modern life. While this is dreary and depressing to some, as doubtless it should be, it is liberating and democratic to many more.

Note

[1] This reconsideration of consumption is an especially strong current in anthropology, where the central text is *The World of Goods: Towards an Anthropology of Consumption* (1979), by Mary Douglas and Baron Isherwood. It can also be seen in the work of scholars such as William Leiss in communication studies; Dick Hebdige in sociology; Jackson Lears in history; David Morley in cultural studies; Michael Schudson in the study of advertising; Sidney Levy in consumer research; Tyler Cowan in economics; Grant McCracken in fashion; and Simon Schama in art history. There are many other signs of change. One of the more interesting recent shows at the Museum of Modern Art, "Objects of Desire: The Modern Still Life," actually focused on the salutary influence of consumer culture on high culture.

Understanding the Text

1. In Twitchell's opinion, what does he readily acknowledge that most academics don't?

2. According to Twitchell, what is the nature of the relation between materialism and spiritualism?

3. Why, ultimately, does Twitchell think that we collect possessions—that, in most cases, we seek to have more rather than fewer of them?

Buying and Nothingness

Andrew Sullivan

Between 1967 and 1982, the number of print and broadcast advertisements in the United States increased by 103 percent. On current trends, this rate of growth will accelerate in the '90s. As media markets boom—cable, video, free newspapers, direct mail—ads are growing in number and intensity. The 15-second television ad, an innovation of the '80s, is now common. There isn't even the consolation that it's all just a blur: research shows that shorter ads with speeded-up voice-overs are better retained by the human brain than longer, slower ones. In newspapers, 65 percent of the pages are now ads, up from 40 percent half a century ago. And the saturation level is never reached: ads are now found on soda cans and coffee mugs, in cabs and check-out lines, on trash cans and executive desks, on mobile billboards and immobile restroom doors. Even plain white notepaper now has advertising printed along its edges. The average consumer is exposed to some 50 to 100 sources of advertising between getting out of bed in the morning and finishing the newspapers at work an hour or so later, assuming that the television isn't on.

Speed and ubiquity are only part of the transformation. The content of advertising has been changing, too. The banal early techniques—the conveying of information about a product—have ceded to a kinder, subtler ministration. "Mood" advertising, the sort that vaguely links class, myth, fantasy, or beauty with a product, rather than relaying a product's features or communicating any other consumer information, has become the most prevalent

Andrew Sullivan, born and raised in England, received his Ph.D. in government from Harvard University, and has lived in the United States since 1984. He has written for *Time* and *The New Republic,* which he also edited from 1991 to 1996, and currently writes for *The Atlantic* and *The Sunday Times* of London. He founded his blog, *The Daily Dish,* in 2000, and has since been one of the more popular and controversial bloggers in the nation. He is the author of three books: *The Conservative Soul: How We Lost It, How to Get It Back* (2006), *Love Undetectable: Notes on Friendship, Sex, and Survival* (1998), and *Virtually Normal: An Argument About Homosexuality* (1995).

Reprinted by permission of *The New Republic,* May 8, 1989, The New Republic, LLC.

form. In his witty, thorough tour of the contemporary advertising industry, Eric Clark cites a survey of ten years ago that posited 14 items of information about a product (price, quality of performance, and so on) that might be mentioned in a mildly informative advertisement. Over half the television ads in a single night's viewing did not contain a single item. Only one percent contained three or more. Fourteen percent of magazine ads contained no such information at all.

But the most unnerving revelation of Clark's book to those unversed in ad culture concerns the care with which the industry calibrates these images to the minds and souls of specific individuals. In the last 20 years there has been a slow but inexorable abandonment of class-based marketing, rendering much traditional criticism of advertising—that it exploits the poor—virtually irrelevant. False consciousness, if that is what it is, has long since left a crude socioeconomic base. To be sure, the class angle is still there, but it is increasingly submerged in appeals to individualist vanity, self-esteem, "values." The new marketing hones in on a consumer's "lifestyle" (marital status, education, region, sex) and "attitudes" (religion, ambition, optimism, etc). These days they're better signals than someone's income.

Clark cites the state-of-the-art technique known as VALS, short for "value and lifstyles." The categories manage to be both insipid and sinister. There are "survivors" (poor, old), and "sustainers" (struggling, young), "belongers" (traditional conformists), and "emulators" (macho yuppies), "achievers" (familial workaholics), and "I-Am-Mes" (young '80s individualists), "experientials" (menopausal new agers), and the "societally conscious" ('60s nostalgics). The most prestigious are the "integrated": mature, intelligent, sensitive, successful—and two percent of the population. The categories sell: they're used by *Time,* AT&T, Coca-Cola, Procter & Gamble, Tupperware, and the British Conservative Party, institutions not renowned for romantic delusion. And their insistent implications are clear. They assume a certain self-consciousness on the part of the consumer, an increasing awareness of personal as well as socioeconomic identity. They succeed by flattering the individual's fantasy about himself, not by expressly relating his identity to a class. They work because they play more on our fantasies about the future than on any reality about our past. In short, they are beginning to evoke a new character on the sociological stage: the bourgeois without a bourgeoisie.

All this sociology does not require, of course, that we take advertising seriously. Perhaps the sanest response to ad culture—to its ubiquity, its power, its flattery—has been the bemusement most appropriate for a 15-second message for Liquid Drano. And much of advertising journalism (the genre is growing relentlessly) has a suitably cheerful feel to it, as if the subject of trends is best seen as some sort of relief from real news. And yet the premise of ad criticism also pivots on the understanding that ad culture reveals something unanswerable about our collective psyche, and is therefore in some way, though we're not quite sure how, primordially important.

Most treatment of the subject treads, then, this ambiguous line, deeply confused, implying profundity, conveying a joke, describing a darkness whose manifestations are essentially light. Normally, thankfully, the light wins out. Clark cites a cheering survey in Britain that found that a quarter of viewers of the network news on a given night had seen none of the commercials. (Twenty-six percent simply didn't pay attention, 21 percent were fixing a drink, 20 percent left the room, 11 percent were doing something else, eight percent switched channels, six percent went to the bathroom, and five percent actually talked to someone.) More ads may lead to more cynicism, not less. And the proliferation of new media disperses and dilutes the sources of advertising's homogenizing power. Even the growth of mood advertising may mean no more than a response to the expanding market. To break through the noise of other ads, a commercial has to be visual, emotive, even silent.

And yet, as Eric Clark, Stuart Ewen, and Gilles Lipovetsky all make clear, and as the growing academic and journalistic credibility of advertising studies suggests, the argument for seeing advertising as the essential cultural influence of our time is gaining strength. It rests on two grounds. The first, the more credible, is simply that advertising is the most faithful reflection of the newly powerful market economy and the society it is generating. It is the most faithful since its very essence is to sell. For Americans, this connection has always been there, though the Reagan years underscored it. For Europeans, the 1980s saw a clear rebuttal of social democracy as a model for politics and the nervous embrace of market economics. To them, the significance of advertising is that it is a cultural premonition of a social and economic future that is fast arriving. It is telling that Clark is British and Lipovetsky is French: the cultural impact of advertising is still novel enough to shock them.

The second reason for taking advertising's claims to cultural pre-eminence seriously is less abstract. It is advertising's growing economic power over other media. Like most parasites, advertising is now devouring the organs that once sustained it. Its grip on television, journalism, and politics is profound. Clark's most interesting chapter shows systematically that the last decade witnessed the sharp decline of almost all forms of ad-free culture. Public television retreated all over Europe. The expansion of cable and VCRs dented the networks' monopoly and further extended market mechanisms in the media. Free newspapers displaced regular newspapers. Advertising replaced subscriptions as the main source of newspaper and magazine income: magazines came to exist not simply by advertising, but for advertising. Pseudo-editorial magazines with single source advertising, directed at closed markets, boomed. Advertorials deliberately blurring the distinction between ads and editorials became commonplace,

Clark shows how this transformed the market. Ad men who could not afford to waste money concentrated resources on the highest circulation newspaper in a town, and crowded out equally ad-dependent competitors. Monopolies followed: a cozy setup for advertisers and newspaper-owners, but a disaster for editorial standards. The result is that 98 percent of American cities now have a morning and an evening paper rather than two morning papers.

Newspapers are just one area, however, in which ad power is having an effect. In television, networks now unveil their fall schedules to advertisers before they show them to their affiliates, let alone to their audience. In movies, products are featured seamlessly in the editorial story line. A lot of this is not new, of course; but the magnitude of advertising's power to sustain or to destroy other media *is* new. Parasitism is perhaps no longer the right metaphor. We can speak less and less of our culture and the advertising that feeds off it as two separate entities. They are increasingly entangled. In the forseeable future, they will be indistinguishable. It is only a slight exaggeration to say that advertising will soon no longer be supporting our culture, our culture will be supporting advertising: or rather, our culture will *be* advertising.

Is this too stark? The merit of Clark's study is its commonsensical belief that this development need not be fully completed, or entirely corrupting. Mozart sponsored by IBM is still Mozart. A moviegoer who sees Steve Martin grasping a bottle of Perrier still knows which of the two is the actor. As consumers become used to such techniques, their guard is raised. And yet Clark also documents a process whose effects are subtler and profounder than common sense is fully able to counter. There *does* come a point at which our facility with advertising dims our conception of the values that might lie beyond it. We are not merely mesmerized by the sheer volume of advertising, we find it harder to remember the justification and the meaning of a culture that exists beyond the market, or in spite of it. We have also, to be more mundane about it, been transformed by the shortening of our attention span. The impact on politics is too well documented to bear repeating. But the effect elsewhere may be just as deep. We are fast generating a society whose commonest form of communication is less a debate—let alone a conversation—than a three-second shot: whose ethic, finally, is an aesthetic.

Stuart Ewen's analysis of precisely this phenomenon is focused on the object of ad culture: us. He subtitles his book "*The Politics of Style,*" since for him the ethic of constant change, the principle of "fashion," is the controlling principle of the ad age. For Ewen, advertising is merely the pusher. "Style" is the drug. We are the junkies. Ewen recounts tales of his style-obsessed students in New York, depicting an aestheticization of modern life that is depressingly convincing. He gives an account of advertising's role in this process that echoes what are by now commonplace observations. This requires, of course, that Ewen dismiss the idea that ad fantasies have any intrinsic worth. They are, for Ewen, inherently unstable and debilitating, never satisfied by the act of purchase. A Ralph Lauren scarf does not transform the New York sales rep into an English aristocrat; it may delude him with that image, but eventually it serves to remind him of the difference between his life and the life of the man in the ad. And this leads, in turn, to greater or newer fantasies, in a spiral of alienated distraction.

Ewen's unstated but clear villain is, of course, capitalism. His theme is that modern culture amounts to a variety of mass hypnosis.

Ewen's contribution lies, however, not in his somewhat tired Frankfurt School criticism of ad culture, but in his understanding of how that culture actually came to be formed. He traces the process to early Modernist designers, from Le Corbusier onward, who explicitly attempted to construct a unified "style" for modernity, and from whom advertising grafted its mission. And the aesthetic itself is telling. As our economy moved inexorably away from real goods and industrial production, its design became literally more insubstantial. Reality was replaced by image; tangible goods by design. Ewen sees no coincidence that Wall Street—the industry of invisibles—is housed in linear buildings made of glass, aimed at the sky, reflecting thin air. Nor is there any accident in the new ethic of slimness in the human body:

> The external, *social* ideal of thinness is a byproduct of modernity. It speaks for a life that claims to live beyond the consequences of nature. . . . Conforming to ideals that have informed development in architecture, design, advertising imagery, and fashion, the ideal body is one that no longer materially exists . . . regardless of the shape one's body takes, whatever flesh remains is *too much;* image must be freed from the liabilities of substance.

There is a cost to such stimulating coherence, not least in its strained attempts to squeeze all-too-deep meanings into the clutter of modern living. (Does one really have to wish to disappear into thin air to want to avoid cholesterol?) And one scours Ewen's book in vain for any trace of humor, irony, or amusement. At one point he earnestly points out that Chardon jeans need only lose one letter to become "hardon." And if Ewen has a morbid respect for the power of fantasy to distort people's minds, he belittles the complexity of the lives with which fantasy necessarily interacts. His picture of the modern consumer is one of hopelessly false consciousness. No distinctions are drawn between various levels of ad addiction. A junkie, to Ewen, is a junkie. The increasing sophistication of advertising, suggesting, as it does, an increasingly sophisticated audience, is lost on him.

The history of popular culture and style, as well as the history of market capitalism, is too varied, too interesting, for Ewen's to convince. For all his attempt to unify the direction of modern style, no single designer has been able to recast or dominate a fragmented market; no single mode of capitalism has been coterminous with the development of fashion, even in this century; no trend has failed to spur a countertrend, and these trends have competed with each other as much as sustained a mutually fulfilling cycle. Nor does Ewen's picture of individual enslavement square fully with what we know of the new research techniques: that (as VALS suggest) the new models imply at least a complicity on the part of modern consumers, whose entrapment, if entrapment it is, is clearly more linked with individual dreams than with class hypnosis and whose delusions have increased at the same time as their real economic power has expanded.

Ewen shows no sense, in short, that even within the captivity of consumerism, the consumer still has some room to maneuver: that she can choose this fantasy over another, this product over another; that she can outwit by mockery, humor—or even simply boredom—the schemes of an industry as much at war with itself as it is intent on capturing her. The modern world of advertising, in other words, cannot be simply reduced to a monochrome plane of capitalist oppression, without missing something essential. Its tyrannies are the tyrannies of seduction, not rape.

And if it is Ewen's aim to explain the human soul involved in this seduction, he doesn't do so subtly or persuasively. Mostly this is because his reductionist approach to advertising—its umbilical relationship with capitalism—refuses to see where that relationship can be broken: at the point at which human imagination makes the advertiser's fantasy its own. Thus Ewen misses the sometimes exquisite nature of the modern psyche's predicament. Take his treatment of the students in his New York class, some from traditional backgrounds, now floating listlessly in a metropolitan world of hairstyles, music, dance clubs and videos, finding in "style" a postmodern identity. Shortly after introducing them, he enters familiar territory:

> We cannot, in evaluating the patterns of individual style, disregard the fact that over the past century, an ongoing lament has been that of aloneness, isolation, invisibility, and insignificance; a desperate thirst for recognition, often expressed as a desire for fame.

The problem is not that Ewen is wrong, but that he is only half-right. Of course there is a sense of aloneness in the strangers Ewen laments in the dance clubs of New York. But that aloneness is surely accompanied, and modified, by a sense of exhilaration. The ennui of the dance-clubbing classes is oddly frenzied, if it is ennui at all. Those flickering faces gazing into a video screen are filled with freedom as well as submission; and to miss that irony is to miss the contemporary condition of "style" entirely.

The real paradox of style is that shallowness can also be a kind of liberation. By self-consciously acting on the surface, by allowing a part of our lives to be moderated by the evanescent, we may gain a genuine release from mundanity, a release that is not to be despised simply because it is not fully coherent. This freedom, which only comes with a certain level of superficiality, is the freedom of distraction: a fleeting freedom, maybe, but a freedom nonetheless. I do not mean to endorse the abolition or the abnegation of deeper experience. Still, in the vagaries of style and the seductive strategies of consumerism, there is an attempt to color, as well as to mask, the occasional alienation of modern life.

We may not, as Ewen would insist, fully escape alienation, but we may, with the help of style, modify it; and that is not a contemptible endeavor. We have long understood, in any case, that alienation is also a form of belonging, that there are communities of the alienated. If such communities are now created by style, rather than by a church or a father or a government, that does not reduce their affective power. And the mild, often playful communities of style are a good deal more benign, and sustain a good deal more individual autonomy, than some others we may think of: say, the communities of cults, ideology, or political messianism.

Gilles Lipovetsky's book, which created a stir in France when it was published, sees these intimations of liberation in the hegemony of style, grasps some of the ironies involved, and turns them into an ideology. His is an undifferentiated celebration of modern narcissistic freedom: a defense of bourgeois individualism without the constraints of bourgeois morality. For Lipovetsky, fashion is a simple sign of autonomy, beginning in the aristocratic rivalries of the 14th century and developing into the concrete freedom of the modern 1980s consumer who can pick his or her identity off the rack. In this way, "style" provides new social identities for modern individuals otherwise stripped of meaningful roles. It sustains a form of transcendence for moderns whose familiarity with genuine transcendence is increasingly faint—and it can do so more accurately than other forms of distraction because it is more finely attuned to the intricacies of demand than any other. VALS, unlike even Hollywood, can give each of us exactly what we want.

In one of his more ingenious arguments, Lipovetsky also claims that style plays a profound role in the legitimation of Western democracies. It does this by aestheticizing, and thereby defanging, the abstraction of ideological, anti-liberal politics. Lipovetsky cites the way in which the "revolution" of '68 differed from previous ones: it was led by consumers, not by the genuinely oppressed, motivated by the aesthetic of revolution rather than by its real justifications, and it was therefore deservedly impotent. He might have added, as a political counter-example, that Reaganism's production values undermined its ideology, that preference for image over argument ultimately sapped its ability to revolutionize the polity. The anti-ideological acid of style can cut both ways.

Lipovetsky also disposes of the economic arguments against style. He argues that there is nothing intrinsically unstable about an economy geared to the insubstantial, nothing dangerous about relying on advertising rather than steel, say, as a source of economic strength, if advertising is a good that a country can produce better. In America in particular, fantasy has long been an important economic product, and the emergence of a burgeoning market for it both here and around the world is, for Lipovetsky, a cause for economic hope, not pessimism. Britain's recovery has largely been premised on exactly that exploitation of economic advantage: British skills in language, presentation, irony have been central to British domination, even in the United States, of the ad industry.

Much of Lipovetsky's case, curiously like Ewen's, has the power and the exhilaration of all reductionist models, although his rhetoric is a good deal more accomplished. He is also far more engaged in the contemporary predicament. He sees the sophistication of modern advertising; he is alive to the social possibilities of our cultural transformation, while Ewen can only lament them. And because he embraces, rather than merely dismisses, the new age, he understands it better. The intimations of autonomy, the exhilaration of bourgeois fantasy, the growth of individualism, are all properly central to Lipovetsky's concerns.

And yet Lipovetsky's enthusiasm is clearly overblown. To see no threat in the enormous power of advertising is glibly to dismiss the fact that autonomy is not merely awarded to individuals; it has to be won. And there is a Whig historicism to Lipovetsky's account of "freedom through style" that is as deterministic and as unconvincing as Ewen's warmed-up version of Horkheimer and Adorno. There is also an ugly complacency to his politics, as if defanging ideology (as style may well accomplish) did not risk defanging real politics as well, sapping it of its essential conflict, blinding us to those rare moments when radicalism may be necessary.

The determinism is both suffocating and deeply out of place with its subject. It is given away in the title: we are in the "empire" of the ephemeral. For this postmodern liberal, style is not simply the central reality of our times; it rules our times. Lipovetsky's era of autonomy is remarkably heteronomous in its scope: it controls, it orders, it dispenses. Sometimes his book reads like an apologia for power. Unwilling to distinguish between mass trash and mass amusement, he is forced to defend all forms of mass culture as mass enlightenment:

> Under the complete hegemony of style, the human mind is less sure but more open to criticism, less stable but more tolerant, less certain of itself but more open to difference, to proof, to argument. . . . The unreason of style contributes to the development of individual reason. Style has its reasons of which reason knows nothing.

This is incantation. It should be possible to construct a theory of style and advertising that can admit its importance and yet distinguish between higher and lower forms of pap. Nor should a defense of advertising imply a defense of the market in all its forms. To see the possibilities in style for human autonomy, to see the benignity of much of advertising's penetration of our lives, does not necessitate a complete suspension of critical judgment. We should be able to perceive where style diverts and where it corrupts, when it sustains and stimulates other media and when it perverts them.

One of the fertile paradoxes of advertising is that this modern, shallow phenomenon need not generate a shallowly modern response. If style, after all, turns on some intimation of human autonomy, then something quite contrary to either Ewen's or Lipovetsky's determinism follows. Style can be rejected as well as chosen. It can be something we treat with the frivolity and the seriousness of genuine play, an activity whose point is not simply that it amuses, but also that it ends. This is a point about distraction that both Ewen and Lipovetsky dismiss, but that the ad age makes increasingly apparent. Modern distraction is premised on a profound consensus: that there is a place to be distracted from.

Understanding the Text

1. Sullivan claims that advertising has a parasitic relation to the "organs that once sustained it." What does he mean by this? And what examples does he provide to support his claim? (Identify three.)

2. In his discussion of style, Sullivan claims that "[t]he real paradox of style is that shallowness can also be a kind of liberation." In what sense is this possible?

3. In the three books he reviews, Sullivan finds arguments to praise and to criticize. Overall, though, what main point does he wish to make about advertising and its role in contemporary culture?

Captive Audiences: The Commercialization of Public Schools

Juliet B. Schor

At one time, television ads represented two-thirds of total expenditures targeted to children. By the mid-1990s, television had been eclipsed by direct marketing, promotions, and sponsorships, which were estimated to account for 80 percent of all marketing dollars. With this shift, children's advertising has moved beyond the confines of the living room to virtually all public spaces and institutions, with houses of worship being the one major exception. The St. Louis Zoo houses the Monsanto Insectarium and the Anheuser-Busch Hippo Harbor. In Boston's Science Museum, the exhibitions are giant structures built from Lego and K'Nex toys. The children's hospital at UCLA was renamed Mattel's Children's Hosptial, and Hasbro's got an equivalent on the East Coast. Indeed, almost anywhere one finds children, there are attempts to market to them, whether it's at doctors' offices or nature centers. The jewel in the marketers' crown of commercial infiltration has been the nation's public schools.

Corporate influence in public schools is not wholly new. Packaged goods and agricultural companies have sponsored health and nutrition education for decades. But since 1990, commercial activities in schools have expanded substantially, with an explosive rise in nearly all types of school-based marketing since 1997. Schools were an especially appealing target to marketers. They had been relatively insulated from advertising, a rare clutter-free island in the larger sea of commercial messages. Teachers and administrators enjoy tremendous trust and authority, and products that appear under their

Juliet B. Schor is a professor of sociology at Boston College and a leading authority on the subjects of work, leisure, and consumerism. Her books include *Born to Buy* (2004), *The Overspent American: Upscaling, Downshifting and the New Consumer* (1998), and *The Overworked American: The Unexpected Decline of Leisure* (1992). Her work appears in numerous academic journals.

imprimatur can benefit from their seal of approval. Finally, and most important, students are as close to a captive audience as advertisers are ever likely to get.

The Shop-Rite Gym, Exclusive Coke, and SweeTart Art: Sponsorships, Ads, Contests, and Revenue Deals

The school commercialization trend has proceeded quite far and encompasses a wide range of practices. In 2001, the Omaha, Nebraska, district hatched a plan to tear up its gymnasium floor and replace it with segments painted with corporate logos, each costing $10,000. A Pennsylvania school board announced plans to sell advertising time over the PA system. The Oscar Mayer corporation sponsors an annual elementary school contest for the best version of its familiar jingle, with the winning school receiving $10,000.

The practice that has drawn the most scrutiny is the sale of "pouring rights," in which school districts enter into exclusive contracts with soft drink companies. The first such contract was signed in 1997 in Madison, Wisconsin. Hundreds of other school districts followed suit, earning hundreds of thousands of dollars in the process, despite the association of sodas with tooth decay, obesity, and bone fractures. Vending machines began to proliferate through hallways. The Centers for Disease Control reports that soft and other sugar-added drinks are sold in 94 percent of the nation's high schools, 84 percent of middle and junior high schools, and 58 percent of elementary schools.

In some cases school officials encourage students to buy these drinks. Anticommercialization activists found and publicized a memo from a zealous Colorado administrator, who called himself "The Coke Dude," urging teachers to push Coke's products, to the point of allowing drinks inside the classroom, a typically taboo practice. Schools line up as either "Pepsi" or "Coke" and in some cases go to great lengths to prove their fealty to the corporate sponsor. In 1998, an independent-minded Georgia high school student named Mike Cameron was suspended by his principal for wearing a Pepsi shirt on "Coke Education Day." His plight attracted worldwide media attention and numerous questions about why the principal had chosen to have students devote a day to baking Coke cakes, devising marketing plans for Coke's discount cards, and using their bodies to spell out the four letters in Coke. Pressures on students to support their school's soda brand continue, as journalist Alissa Quart reported in the *New York Times,* discussing a Texas school where students are prevented from drinking any brand but the sponsoring one.

Schools are selling ad space on buses and stadium walls, and even inside school buildings and classrooms. In 2001, NetworkNext announced 500 contracts with schools to show ads in return for a mobile computer unit to use for PowerPoint and other presentations. When the teacher shows a slide, banner ads for Rock Star video games, Wal-Mart, Visa Buxx cards, and Coty products appear on the screen. This promotion also incorporates a survey feedback component in the contracts to let advertisers know how effective the technique proved to be. Product giveaways with corporate logos or ads are also common. Cover Concepts distributes millions of ad-festooned book covers a year. At the beginning of the 2003 academic year, 500,000 New York City kids received "free" annual planners with thirty pages of national advertising. In a telling example of how deeply corporate branding has infiltrated the education process, math textbook writers began to insert brand names, even without payment from the companies involved, on the grounds that kids would better relate to the word problems if they involved branded products. That practice is now illegal in California, following widespread publicity about word problems in a McGraw-Hill math textbook that included Nike, Gatorade, Topps trading cards, and Disneyland as examples. Advertising and sponsorship of athletic programs, teams, and activities are everywhere, with logos on uniforms and corporate branded scoreboards. In-school sports are reported to be one of the fastest-growing areas in all of American corporate marketing.

In what was publicized as the first deal of its kind, an elementary school in Brooklawn, New Jersey, sold naming rights for its gymnasium to the supermarket chain Shop-Rite, in return for what ended up being about $5,000 a year. Superintendent John Kellmayer noted, "We'll be the first school district to be branded with a corporate logo. You hope children can become sophisticated enough to deal with it." Naming rights discussions are cropping up at school board meetings around the country, as more and more schools mull selling off sponsorships of classrooms, libraries, and other marketable pieces of real estate.

Another major area of corporate infiltration is incentive programs, in which sponsors agree to give discounts or free products if students collect a requisite number of coupons or shop at certain stores. General Mills Box Tops for Education, supermarket loyalty programs, and Pizza Hut's Book-It program fall into this category. The Pizza Hut program, which gives free pizzas to kids who read a certain number of books, has involved tens of millions of students and has been expanded to preschools. Other fast food companies are also heavily involved in incentive and sponsorship programs. McDonald's McTeacher Nights send teachers (to work) and families (to spend) to the restaurants, with a portion of wages going to the schools. Ironically, former California governor Gray Davis, whose legislature led the way in efforts to decommercialize education, made McDonald's McTeacher Night official with a state proclamation. Corporate contests have also become common across the country There's a Dunkin' Donuts competition for the best one-minute commercial to "sell" kids on the value of homework. The grand prize is $6,000, but many of the participants get coupons for free doughnuts at the stores. Nestlé's sponsors the SweeTart contest, in which more than 5,000 schools participate, submitting entries such as a Mona Lisa made of SweeTarts and a Sweetmobile car covered with the candy. Georgia Pacific, through its Angel Soft toilet paper brand, gives money to winners of a community service program. Corporations are also trying to enlist teachers to push their products or the company's point of view. A Crayola marketer I talked to explained they use teachers as "brand ambassadors." Logging giant Weyerhauser runs a six-week summer program on science and environment that pays teachers to attend. General Mills paid Minnesota teachers $250 each to paint ads for Reese's Puffs cereal on their cars and instructed them to place the cars next to where the school buses parked. Eventually opposition forced the company to end that program.

The main impetus for commercialization is the chronic underfunding of schools. As budgets tighten, officials become more receptive to selling access to their students. Debates about exclusive soda contracts, Channel One, corporate sponsorships, and naming rights have all focused on the challenges of funding, with proponents of the deals stressing the monies they anticipate. But there's another factor operating as well. Alex Molnar, author of *Giving Kids the Business: The Commercialization of America's Schools* and the nation's leading expert on school commercialization, has shown that current trends have roots in a larger push, which began during the Reagan administration, to increase corporate influence and activity in public schools. Corporate involvement has extended to training, curriculum development, the promotion of new technologies, and partnership models. Alongside these efforts is an ongoing attempt by conservatives and their business allies to privatize public education through voucher systems, for-profit schools, private testing services, anti-union activities, and charter schools. One part of the plan is to siphon public money out of the schools and into profit-making ventures, such as testing companies and education providers, to ease the path to privatization. The public debate about testing has focused on the failures of schools and the need to improve education, but behind the rhetoric, for-profit companies with ties to the Bush administration are reaping millions of public dollars. The ongoing criticism of public education has also opened the doors to for-profit education companies that have long wanted to capture streams of public revenue. A second component is to open up schools as places to advertise, market, and sell. The career of Christopher Whittle, founder of Channel One and current president of Edison, the nation's largest for-profit education provider, combines both objectives.

Corporations Write the Curriculum

Perhaps the most egregious of the in-school commercial activities is the corporate incursion into academic content. Roberta Nusim is a pioneer in the business of corporate-sponsored curricular materials. As an English teacher in New York's South Bronx in the 1970s, Nusim became dissatisfied with the materials she had to work with. Curriculums were textbook based, and textbooks were out of date. Nusim, who had attended the same school she was teaching in, recounts that she would find herself opening textbooks only to find her own name on the inside cover. These materials lagged one and even two decades behind, and weren't chronicling either the momentous social changes that were occurring in the sixties and seventies or the differences in the ways kids were growing up. Nusim felt that her students, the "*Sesame Street* generation," needed a more visually oriented presentation and faster-paced materials. She improvised for a while, bringing in cereal boxes to teach from and assigning television programs for her children to watch and discuss. But her improvisation prompted a thought. Why not go to corporations and ask them to sponsor innovative curricular materials? Nusim ruled out approaching her own school administration or district, because she felt those bureaucracies moved too slowly and didn't have money for new initiatives. With corporations, she anticipated success, because she could sell her venture as a clear case of self-interest. "Corporate America was waking up to kids' buying power," she explained. Companies were starting to take notice of James McNeal's estimates of child spending and recognizing that their influence was expanding beyond what cereal moms would buy.

Nusim's first project was in 1978 with Columbia Pictures, producer of the film *Kramer versus Kramer*. Together, they developed a curriculum on family living and communication, thinking that the growth of divorce was a good subject for in-school conversations. Children saw the film and then spent class time discussing the issues it raised. Teachers could not require that students go to the movie, but they could strongly encourage it. Soon enough, the phones were ringing off the hook with calls from companies, and Nusim's venture became a raging success.

Since then, Nusim has branched out to a wide range of issues. In the late 1970s, in the wake of the energy crisis, she began doing curricula for utility companies. In the 1980s, as the country was becoming more health conscious, she approached food companies with the idea of doing nutrition curricula, and over the years she has worked with all the major food corporations and soft drink manufacturers, including Pepsi, Coke, and the National Soft Drink Association. Nusim gets clients by keying in on social trends and current events, especially those she feels are underrepresented among existing school materials, and then approaching those companies whose products are relevant.

Nusim's company, Youth Marketing International, has produced 1,500 curricular programs. She now has many competitors, who annually produce thousands of these sponsored educational materials, or SEMs. They start targeting virtually after birth and stick with the kids through high school. Lifetime Learning Systems, which publishes *My Weekly Reader,* is now a national leader in corporate-sponsored materials. Scholastic alone boasts a staff of forty professionals dedicated to in-school marketing, and it promises its clients that it can "harness the incredible brand building power" not of educational materials but of educationally based "marketing programs." Scholastic trades on its long-term relationships with teachers but also gets them on board by offering rewards, such as free products. The company claims that 92 percent of U.S. teachers use its programs and that its reach extends to 53 million of the nation's 69 million students. Scholastic has also turned its magazines into advertising vehicles by creating special issues that are sponsored by individual companies. Canon sponsored a special issue of *Art and Man Magazine* with three pages of company ads. Discover credit card is another Scholastic sponsor.

SEMs have made huge inroads into American classrooms in the past two decades, with little awareness by parents and the public. The cost of an SEM ranges from lows of about $25,000 to more than $1 million. These large sums of money have yielded an unprecedented ability to put out corporate messages. Revlon's curriculum taught kids about "good and bad hair days" and asked them to list their three must-have hair care products if they were stranded on a desert island. Campbell Soup Company's Science Curriculum included the "Prego Thickness Experiment" with a "slotted spoon test" to figure out whether Prego or Ragu spaghetti sauce was thicker. The Gushers Wonders of the World package included free samples and instructions to kids to bite down on the candy to create an in-mouth volcanic eruption. The Sunkist "Just One Orange" a day unit teaches children such educational facts as the theme of the first ad by the California Fruit Exchange, the number of growers that make up the Sunkist Growers corporation, and how to make a smoothie with a Sunkist orange. Other nutrition curricula are even more problematic in their selective use of information. For example, a Kellogg's breakfast curriculum presents fat content as the only thing to worry about when choosing breakfast food. There is no mention of the sugar and salt in Kellogg's cereals. A first-grade reading curriculum has the kids start out by recognizing logos from K-Mart, Pizza Hut, M&M's, Jell-O, and Target. Another first-grade program has children design a McDonald's restaurant, explains how it works, and gives them information on how to apply for a job at McDonald's. SEMs have also established a strong presence at earlier ages. In the summer of 2003, Nusim's company targeted a third of the nation's preschools with a Care Bears promotional package from American Greetings, and Scholastic placed a curriculum based on the cartoon dog Clifford in preschools all over Texas. For corporations, one of the appealing aspects of SEMs is that they can market covertly, and thereby more effectively Evan Shapiro, senior vice president of marketing for Courtroom Television, brags about the Forensics in the Classroom Curriculum, a $60,000 investment that "reaches 400,000 students and 1.2 million consumers without EVER seeming like marketing" and has had "enormous impact for Court TV on brand awareness, ratings and revenues."

Another development in sponsored curricula is the use of school trips for marketing purposes. A ten-year-old Chicago-based company, the Field Trip Factory, has organized more than 20,000 outings in forty-four states to important educational institutions such as Domino's Pizza, The Sports Authority, Petco, and Toys 'R' Us stores. The trips often include free samples, discount coupons, and exposure to advertising materials. More than 600,000 elementary school students, including kindergartners, have taken part in these exercises in early brand exposure and loyalty building.

In the mid-1990s, after sponsored materials began to flood into schools, Consumers Union undertook a study of their nature and quality surveying seventy-seven corporate-sponsored kits and packets. It found that nearly 80 percent of the materials surveyed were guilty of blatant bias, commercial pitches, significant inaccuracies, or all of these. It judged more than half to be "commercial or highly commercial." These materials are intentionally biased in their choice of information, in order to make the corporate point of view seem reasonable, objective, and educational. One California administrator whose job involved screening materials explained how difficult her task was. She kept sending back the slanted submissions, but the corporations got the message and began to circumvent her, sending materials directly to schools. In the end, it didn't matter, because she was laid off, her position cut due to budget shortfalls, the very problem that opened the door to corporate-sponsored curricula to begin with.

Some of the worst examples of bias have been found among corporate environmental materials. In the early 1990s, energy, paper, and other primary materials companies became concerned about what they considered an excessively proenvironmental attitude among the nation's youth. They worried that existing environmental education curricula were exacerbating those sentiments. So the companies began what can only be described as an expensive propaganda effort to obscure the nature of the environmental problems facing the planet. For example, Consumers Union concluded that Exxon's elaborate Energy Cube curriculum "implies that fossil fuels pose few environmental problems and that alternative energy is costly and unattainable." It minimizes the problem of oil spills and strip mining. American Coal Foundation materials dismiss the greenhouse effect, saying the "earth could benefit rather than be harmed from increased carbon dioxide." A Chevron lesson plan took a similar tack and attempted to rebut the existence of global warming. One waste curriculum defined plastics' incineration as "recycling." Materials from the Pacific Logging Congress described clear-cutting as "environmentally responsible." Procter & Gamble stopped distributing its Decision Earth, which taught that clear-cut logging is good for the environment, after attorneys general in eleven states were asked to investigate its truthfulness. Overall, Consumers Union found a "distorted picture of the problems, choices and trade-offs inherent in the issues these materials cover."

These corporations were trying to put a good face on themselves, but sometimes it seems that they prefer to hide their involvement, to make propaganda look like truth. One example is a classroom video that promoted the idea that plastics were not a threat to the environment. All but one of the "experts" who appeared in the video were full-time employees of the plastics industry. At one viewing session, arranged by a newspaper investigating corporate-sponsored materials, students thought the film was produced by an environmental group. Stewart Allen, the journalist who organized the viewing, noted that the students missed "the minuscule Mobil copyright sign that appears at the end of the video, the only indication it was created by one of the country's largest manufacturers of plastics." A similar stealth sponsorship approach has been used by the governments of Saudi Arabia and Israel, each of which collaborated (separately, of course) with U.S. firms to produce classroom materials that portrayed their countries in a positive light.

Why do teachers use these materials? In the early days, Nusim got her products into schools through an intensive grassroots effort. She began by relying on her contacts in the field. She attended industry conferences, setting up a booth to showcase the materials she was offering, free of charge, to any teachers or administrators who wanted them. She was a frequent speaker at education meetings. All of this effort paid off. Nusim developed a core of teachers who use her materials on an ongoing basis. They then recruited other teachers through word of mouth and targeting of potential new recruits to corporate curricula. Eventually she developed access to every school in the United States and Canada, and the ability to cull specialized lists from her database (for example, chairs of middle school English departments). She attributes her success in large part to money. Current estimates are that the average teacher spends more than $521 of his or her own money each year to purchase classroom materials, and that number has been climbing steadily. The corporate materials are provided free of charge and designed for easy duplication. But schools are often getting what they pay for—shoddy and biased materials that serve commercial interests. Nusim emphasized that "educational value is first and foremost for me," but her company's survival depends on serving her clients' interests. Moreover, she concedes that others in the industry lack standards.

The growth of sponsored materials, advertising within schools, and schools' deliberate marketing of junk food can ultimately be traced to the very real problem of inadequate funding. But commercialization is a troubling response and raises important questions. Businesses are willing to spend millions of dollars on crummy classroom materials, but have proven unwilling to pay taxes to support high-quality, serious curricula for the nation's children. There's a national discourse paying homage to equality of opportunity, but schools in low-income districts have far fewer resources and are more likely to turn to insidious products like Channel One. As Molnar and others have detailed, right-wing efforts to increase corporate influence in schools have succeeded, to the detriment of children's education and well-being.

In the past few years, a backlash to school commercialization has gathered momentum The soft drink companies are on the defensive, as some districts, including Madison, have rejected or failed to renew contracts, citing health impacts, parental opposition, and revenue streams that did not meet expectations. After a spate of bad publicity, Coca-Cola announced that the parent company, although not its bottling affiliates, would no longer promote (in contrast to enter into) exclusive contracts. In 2002, the Los Angeles Unified School District, where 40 percent of the children have been found to be obese, voted to enact a ban on soft drink sales to take effect in January 2004. The Oakland School District banned sales of sugared drinks and candy in schools in what is perhaps the nation's strictest regulation.

There has been opposition to other school-based commercial activities as well. After defeating Zapme! a coalition of organizations put together by the Nader-inspired group Commercial Alert was instrumental in Senate passage of the Dodd-Shelby privacy provision that requires schools to obtain parental permission before allowing marketers to elicit personal information from children. Seattle, where there is an active anticommercialization group, has enacted a new policy curtailing advertising on school property, and Channel One will be banned in 2004. Whether these victories signal a longer-term trend is unclear. Vigorous corporate lobbying by the soft drink industry, Channel One, and others defeated the Maryland legislature's attempt in 2001 to ban ads and exclusive soft drink contracts in public schools. As fast as activists can win victories, the marketers develop new schemes.

Under the Wholesome Halo

One of the keys to corporate successes in gaining access to kids has been that they glide in under the "wholesome halo." That glow is not merely reserved for cereals. Whole companies bask in it. And increasingly, those are some of the most aggressive commercializers around. Scholastic is a good example. It has a longstanding reputation as a quality educational enterprise and represents itself as the "most trusted name in publishing, education and entertainment." While it enjoys a reputation as a benign, educationally based company, Scholastic is a $2 billion giant that has been one of the leading and most aggressive forces for introducing corporate influence into schools through its sponsored curricula, licensed products at fairs, and sales of toys and other products on its book order forms. A telling example of Scholastic's transformation is the content of its well-known and loved book order forms. Once a cheap and convenient way of getting books to children, they have become a bonanza for media and toy companies. A recent order form includes four different Nickelodeon sections selling SpongeBob figurines, cards, and stickers; a *Rugrats* movie promotion; and offers of key chain giveaways with Nickelodeon characters. Disney has a number of sections, including a *Life with Lizzie* (McGuire) pack and poster next to an ad urging kids to "Watch it on Disney ABC Kids," and other products promoting Disney movies *The Hulk* and *Freaky Friday.* Other branded products represented were Hershey's, with its Hershey's Kisses math book, Hello Kitty toys and art supplies, as well as products featuring Scooby Doo, DragonBall Z, and Mary Kate and Ashley. There are guidebooks for PlayStation 2 and Lego's Bionicle action figures. There is also an array of unbranded toys.

PBS is another company that has been able to pursue commercial activities aggressively under its wholesome halo, such as its market research in schools and the introduction of *Teletubbies,* TV for one year olds, complete with fast food toy tie-ins. Lego's Bionicle action figure line benefited from the company's reputation as a maker of nonviolent toys, although its story line is violent and the figures come with extensive weaponry. Companies without the halo team up with those that have it to get access to kids and places they might not otherwise succeed with. Agencies enlist nonprofits to partner with for marketing efforts. For those who care to look, the wholesome halos are looking awfully tattered. But the companies are counting on the fact that few of us are looking.

Notes

[69] On 80 percent of marketing dollars, see Wartella (1995).

[69] On corporate sponsorship of public institutions, see Halpert (2001).

[69] On commercial infiltration of public schools, there is now a large literature. See Molnar (1996), Consumers Union (1995), GAO (2000), Manning (1999a, 1999b, 1999c), Fax (1996). Jarvis (2001), and Golding (1999). There is also a large amount of online material available. See the Web sites of the Center for the Analysis of Commercialism and Education, and Commercial Alert. Consumers Union 1995, available at www.consunion.org/other/captivekids/evaluations.htm.

[69] On the explosive rise of in-school commercialism after 1997, see Molnar (2002). The Commercialisrn in Education Research Unit of Arizona State University compiles an annual index of media reports of commercial activities in schools. The index began to rise in 1991 and nearly tripled between 1997 and 2000. See Molnar (2002) available at http://www.asu.edu/educ/epsl/CERU/CERU_Annual_Report.htm.

[70] Omaha gymnasium floor and Pennsylvania ads from Molnar (2002).

[70] Oscar Mayer contest from Mayer (2003).

[70] Centers for Disease Control figures of 94, 84, and 58 percent of schools offering soft drinks for sale are from fact sheet on Food Service, available at http://cdc.gov/nocdphp/dash/shpps/factsheets/fs01_food_service.html.

[70] For a report on the Mike Cameron incident, see Molnar (1998), available at http://www.asu.edu/educ/epsl/CERU/Annual%20reports/cace-98-0l.htm. A sampling of press coverage is available at http://www.adbusters.org/campaigns/commercialfree/toolbox/coke.html.

[70] On the Texas school with soft drink exclusivity, see Quart (2003b).

[70] On NetworkNext, see Lindeman (2001).

[71] On free planners to New York City students, see Feuer (2002).

[71] Sports as "fastest-growing areas" is from E. Fisher, writing in the *Washington Times,* March 9, 2001, cited by Molnar (2002), p. 9.

[71] John Kellmayer quote from Russakoff (2001).

[71] Tens of millions participating in Pizza Hut program and expansion to preschools from Schlosser (2001), p. 56.

[71] For more information on these promotions, see past issues of *Not for Sale!,* the newsletter of the Center for Commercial-Free Public Education.

[71] Contest examples are from Mayer (2003).

[72] Weyerhauser summer program from Molnar (2002), p. 19.

[72] On General Mills paying teachers, see Applebaum (2003), p. 24.

[72] On the roots of current trends, see Molnar (1996).

[72] On the content of corporate curricula. see Borowski (1999), who focuses on environmental curricula; Consumers Union (1995); Manning (1999c), p. 17; and materials from the Center for Commercial-Free Public Education.

[73] Scholastic's in-school marketing is described in company promotional material. Data on total school enrollment are from the Department of Education Web site. http://nces.ed.gov//lpubs2002/digest2001/tables/dt003.asp.

[73] The Scholastic magazines example is from Consumers Union (1995), p. 11.

[74] Examples of first-grade curricula are from "Information Packet on Commercialism in Schools," from the Center for Commercial-Free Public Education, March 20, 2000, provided to the author. Other examples include a Domino's pizza counting exercise and a Visa curriculum that promotes credit cards to kids by showing all the stuff kids can buy with a card.

[74] On Care Bears and Clifford in preschools, see Hays (2003).

[74] The Evan Shapiro quote on Court TV's curriculum is from the 2003 TeenPower Conference brochure.

[74] Details on the Field Trip Factory are available from its Web site, www.fleldtripfactory.com.

[74] Nearly 80 percent of materials biased from Consumers Union (1995), The report is available at www.consumersunion.org/other/captivekids/.

[75] California administrator anecdote from Allen (1992).

[75] Consumers Union quote on Exxon's energy cube, American Coal Foundation materials quote, and Chevron lesson plan are all from Consumers Union (1995), p. 5.

[75] Incineration as "recycling" is from Jacobson (1995). Responsible clear-cutting is from Molnar (2002), p. 19.

[75] Procter & Gamble's Decision Earth is from Consumers Union (1995), p. 5.

[75] Plastics video incident and quotes are from Allen (1992).

[75] Saudi Arabia and Israeli sponsorships are discussed in Molnar (1996).

[76] The $521 figure is from Goodnough (2002).

[76] Los Angeles and Oakland bans on soft drink sales are reported in Molnar (2002).

[76] On the backlash to school commercialization, see Zernike (2001) and Manning (2001) on soft drinks, and www.commercialalert.org on Zapme! and Channel One. In 1999, the California legislature passed two bills limiting school commercialism.

[76] On the Dodd-Shelby privacy provision, a coalition led by Commercial Alert, and including the right-wing groups Eagle Forum and Focus on the Family, was active in gaining this provision.

[77] On industry opposition to the Maryland law, see LeDuc (2001).

[77] The "most trusted name" quote is from Scholastic promotional materials.

Understanding the Text

1. According to Schor, what is the chief reason that schools have sought outside corporate funding?

2. Why does Schor object to corporate influence in school curricula? (Identify two reasons.) And why, in her view, do teachers use these curricula?

3. What is the "wholesome halo" effect and how, according to Schor, does it function?

Why Johnny Can't Dissent

The public be damned! I work for my stockholders.
>   —William H. Vanderbilt, 1879

Break the rules. Stand apart. Keep your head. Go with your heart.
>   —TV commercial for Vanderbilt
>   perfume, 1994

Thomas Frank

Thomas Frank received his Ph.D. in history from the University of Chicago in 1994. He is the founding editor of *The Baffler*, a journal of cultural politics, and the author of three books: *What's the Matter with Kansas?* (2004), *One Market Under God: Extreme Capitalism, Market Populism, and the End of Economic Democracy* (2000), and *The Conquest of Cool* (1997). His essays have appeared in a number of magazines.

Capitalism is changing, obviously and drastically. From the moneyed pages of the *Wall Street Journal* to TV commercials for airlines and photocopiers we hear every day about the new order's globe-spanning, cyber-accumulating ways. But our notion about what's wrong with American life and how the figures responsible are to be confronted haven't changed much in thirty years. Call it, for convenience, the "countercultural idea." It holds that the paramount ailment of our society is conformity, a malady that has variously been described as over-organization, bureaucracy, homogeneity, hierarchy, logocentrism, technocracy, the Combine, the Apollonian. We all know what it is and what it does. It transforms humanity into "organization man," into "the man in the gray flannel suit." It is "Moloch whose mind is pure machinery," the "incomprehensible prison" that consumes "brains and imagination." It is artifice, starched shirts, tailfins, carefully mowed lawns, and always, always, the consciousness of impending nuclear destruction. It is a stiff, militaristic order that seeks to suppress instinct, to forbid sex and pleasure, to deny basic human impulses and individuality, to enforce through a rigid uniformity a meaningless plastic consumerism.

From *The Baffler*, No. 6, 1995 by Thomas Frank. Copyright © 1995 by Baffler Magazine. Reprinted by permission.

As this half of the countercultural idea originated during the 1950s, it is appropriate that the evils of conformity are most conveniently summarized with images of 1950s suburban correctness. You know, that land of sedate music, sexual repression, deference to authority, Red Scares, and smiling white people standing politely in line to go to church. Constantly appearing as a symbol of arch-backwardness in advertising and movies, it is an image we find easy to evoke.

The ways in which this system are to be resisted are equally well understood and agreed-upon. The Establishment demands homogeneity; we revolt by embracing diverse, individual lifestyles. It demands self-denial and rigid adherence to convention; we revolt through immediate gratification, instinct uninhibited, and liberation of the libido and the appetites. Few have put it more bluntly than Jerry Rubin did in 1970: "Amerika says: Don't! The yippies say: Do It!" The countercultural idea is hostile to any law and every establishment. "Whenever we see a rule, we must break it," Rubin continued. "Only by breaking rules do we discover who we are." Above all rebellion consists of a sort of Nietzschean antinomianism, an automatic questioning of rules, a rejection of whatever social prescriptions we've happened to inherit. Just Do It is the whole of the law.

The patron saints of the countercultural idea are, of course, the Beats, whose frenzied style and merry alienation still maintain a powerful grip on the American imagination. Even forty years after the publication of *On the Road,* the works of Kerouac, Ginsberg, and Burroughs remain the *sine qua non* of dissidence, the model for aspiring poets, rock stars, or indeed anyone who feels vaguely artistic or alienated. That frenzied sensibility of pure experience, life on the edge, immediate gratification, and total freedom from moral restraint, which the Beats first propounded back in those heady days when suddenly everyone could have their own TV and powerful V-8, has stuck with us through all the intervening years and become something of a permanent American style. Go to any poetry reading and you can see a string of junior Kerouacs go through the routine, upsetting cultural hierarchies by pushing themselves to the limit, straining for that gorgeous moment of original vice when Allen Ginsberg first read "Howl" in 1955 and the patriarchs of our fantasies recoiled in shock. The Gap may have since claimed Ginsberg and *USA Today* may run feature stories about the brilliance of the beloved Kerouac, but the rebel race continues today regardless, with ever-heightening shit-references calculated to scare Jesse Helms, talk about sex and smack that is supposed to bring the electricity of real life, and ever-more determined defiance of the repressive rules and mores of the American 1950s—rules and mores that by now we know only from movies.

But one hardly has to go to a poetry reading to see the countercultural idea acted out. Its frenzied ecstasies have long since become an official aesthetic of consumer society, a monotheme of mass as well as adversarial culture. Turn on the TV and there it is instantly: the unending drama of consumer unbound and in search of an ever-heightened good time, the inescapable rock 'n' roll soundtrack, dreadlocks and ponytails bounding into Taco Bells, a drunken, swinging-camera epiphany of tennis shoes, outlaw soda pops, and mind-bending dandruff shampoos. Corporate America, it turns out, no longer speaks in the voice of oppressive order that it did when Ginsberg moaned in 1956 that *Time* magazine was

> always telling me about responsibility. Business-
> men are serious. Movie producers are serious.
> Everybody's serious but me.

Nobody wants you to think they're serious today, least of all Time Warner. On the contrary: the Culture Trust is now our leader in the Ginsbergian search for kicks upon kicks. Corporate America is not an oppressor but a sponsor of fun, provider of lifestyle accouterments, facilitator of carnival, our slang-speaking partner in the quest for that ever-more apocalyptic orgasm. The countercultural idea has become capitalist orthodoxy, its hunger for transgression upon transgression now perfectly suited to an economic-cultural regime that runs on ever-faster cyclings of the new; its taste for self-fulfillment and its intolerance for the confines of tradition now permitting vast latitude in consuming practices and lifestyle experimentations.

Consumerism is no longer about "conformity" but about "difference." Advertising teaches us not in the ways of puritanical self-denial (a bizarre notion on the face of it), but in orgiastic, never-ending self-fulfillment. It counsels not rigid adherence to the tastes of the herd but vigilant and constantly updated individualism. We consume not to fit in, but to prove, on the surface at least, that we are rock 'n' roll rebels, each one of us as rule-breaking and hierarchy-defying as our heroes of the 60s, who now pitch cars, shoes, and beer. This imperative of endless difference is today the genius at the heart of American capitalism, an eternal fleeing from "sameness" that satiates our thirst for the New with such achievements of civilization as the infinite brands of identical cola, the myriad colors and irrepressible variety of the cigarette rack at 7-Eleven.

As existential rebellion has become a more or less official style of Information Age capitalism, so has the countercultural notion of a static, repressive Establishment grown hopelessly obsolete. However the basic impulses of the countercultural idea may have disturbed a nation lost in Cold War darkness, they are today in fundamental agreement with the basic tenets of Information Age business theory. So close are they, in fact, that it has become difficult to understand the countercultural idea as anything more than the self-justifying ideology of the new bourgeoisie that has arisen since the 1960s, the cultural means by which this group has proven itself ever so much better skilled than its slow-moving, security-minded forebears at adapting to the accelerated, always-changing consumerism of today. The anointed cultural opponents of capitalism are now capitalism's ideologues.

The two come together in perfect synchronization in a figure like Camille Paglia, whose ravings are grounded in the absolutely noncontroversial ideas of the golden sixties. According to Paglia, American business is still exactly what it was believed to have been in that beloved decade, that is, "puritanical and desensualized." Its great opponents are, of course, liberated figures like "the beatniks," Bob Dylan, and the Beatles. Culture is, quite simply, a binary battle between the repressive Apollonian order of capitalism and the Dionysian impulses of the counterculture. Rebellion makes no sense without repression; we must remain forever convinced of capitalism's fundamental hostility to pleasure in order to consume capitalism's rebel products as avidly as we do. It comes as little surprise when, after criticizing the "Apollonian capitalist machine" (in her book, *Vamps & Tramps*), Paglia applauds American mass culture (in *Utne Reader*), the preeminent product of that "capitalist machine," as a "third great eruption" of a Dionysian "paganism." For her, as for most other designated dissidents, there is no contradiction between replaying the standard critique of capitalist conformity and repressiveness and then endorsing its rebel products—for Paglia the car culture and Madonna—as the obvious solution: the Culture Trust offers both Establishment and Resistance in one convenient package. The only question that remains is why Paglia has not yet landed an endorsement contract from a soda pop or automobile manufacturer.

Other legendary exponents of the countercultural idea have been more fortunate—William S. Burroughs, for example, who appears in a television spot for the Nike corporation. But so openly does the commercial flaunt the confluence of capital and counterculture that it has brought considerable criticism down on the head of the aging beat. Writing in the *Village Voice,* Leslie Savan marvels at the contradiction between Burroughs' writings and the faceless corporate entity for which he is now pushing product. "Now the realization that *nothing* threatens the system has freed advertising to exploit even the most marginal elements of society," Savan observes. "In fact, being hip is no longer quite enough—better the pitchman be 'underground.'" Meanwhile Burroughs' manager insists, as all future Cultural Studies treatments of the ad will no doubt also insist, that Burroughs' presence actually makes the commercial "deeply subversive"—"I hate to repeat the usual mantra, but you know, homosexual drug addict, manslaughter, accidental homicide." But Savan wonders whether, in fact, it is Burroughs who has been assimilated by corporate America. "The problem comes," she writes, "in how easily any idea, deed, or image can become part of the sponsored world."

The most startling revelation to emerge from the Burroughs/Nike partnership is not that corporate America has overwhelmed its cultural foes or that Burroughs can somehow remain "subversive" through it all, but the complete lack of dissonance between the two sides. Of course Burroughs is not "subversive," but neither has he "sold out": His ravings are no longer appreciably different from the official folklore of American capitalism. What's changed is not Burroughs, but business itself. As expertly as Burroughs once bayoneted American proprieties, as stridently as he once proclaimed himself beyond the laws of man and God, he is today a respected ideologue of the Information Age, occupying roughly the position in the pantheon of corporate-cultural thought once reserved strictly for Notre Dame football coaches and positive-thinking Methodist ministers. His inspirational writings are boardroom favorites, his dark nihilistic burpings the happy homilies of the new corporate faith.

For with the assumption of power by Drucker's and Reich's new class has come an entirely new ideology of business, a way of justifying and exercising power that has little to do with the "conformity" and the "establishment" so vilified by the countercultural idea. The management theorists and "leadership" charlatans of the Information Age don't waste their time prattling about hierarchy and regulation, but about disorder, chaos, and the meaninglessness of convention. With its reorganization around information, capitalism has developed a new mythology, a sort of corporate antinomianism according to which the breaking of rules and the elimination of rigid corporate structure have become the central article of faith for millions of aspiring executives.

Dropping *Naked Lunch* and picking up *Thriving on Chaos,* the groundbreaking 1987 management text by Tom Peters, the most popular business writer of the past decade, one finds more philosophical similarities than one would expect from two manifestos of, respectively, dissident culture and business culture. If anything, Peters' celebration of disorder is, by virtue of its hard statistics, bleaker and more nightmarish than Burroughs'. For this popular lecturer on such once-blithe topics as competitiveness and pop psychology there is nothing, absolutely nothing, that is certain. His world is one in which the corporate wisdom of the past is meaningless, established customs are ridiculous, and "rules" are some sort of curse, a remnant of the foolish fifties that exist to be defied, not obeyed. We live in what Peters calls "A World Turned Upside Down," in which whirl is king and, in order to survive, businesses must eventually embrace Peters' universal solution: "Revolution!" "To meet the demands of the fast-changing competitive scene," he counsels, "we must simply learn to love change as much as we have hated it in the past." He advises businessmen to become Robespierres of routine, to demand of their underlings, "'What have you changed lately?' 'How fast are you changing?' and 'Are you pursuing bold enough change goals?'" "Revolution," of course, means for Peters the same thing it did to Burroughs and Ginsberg, Presley and the Stones in their heyday: breaking rules, pissing off the suits, shocking the bean-counters: "Actively and publicly hail defiance of the rules, many of which you doubtless labored mightily to construct in the first place." Peters even suggests that his readers implement this hostility to logocentrism in a carnivalesque celebration, drinking beer out in "the woods" and destroying "all the forms and rules and discontinued reports" and, "if you've got real nerve," a photocopier as well.

Today corporate antinomianism is the emphatic message of nearly every new business text, continually escalating the corporate insurrection begun by Peters. Capitalism, at least as it is envisioned by the best-selling management handbooks, is no longer about enforcing Order, but destroying it. "Revolution," once the totemic catchphrase of the counterculture, has become the totemic catchphrase of boomer-as-capitalist. The Information Age businessman holds inherited ideas and traditional practices not in reverence, but in high suspicion. Even reason itself is now found to be an enemy of true competitiveness, an out-of-date faculty to be scrupulously avoided by conscientious managers. A 1990 book by Charles

Handy entitled *The Age of Unreason* agrees with Peters that we inhabit a time in which "there can be no certainty" and suggests that readers engage in full-fledged epistemological revolution: "Thinking Upside Down," using new ways of "learning which can . . . be seen as disrespectful if not downright rebellious," methods of approaching problems that have "never been popular with the upholders of continuity and of the status quo." Three years later the authors of *Reengineering the Corporation* ("A Manifesto for Business Revolution," as its subtitle declares) are ready to push this doctrine even farther. Not only should we be suspicious of traditional practices, but we should cast out virtually everything learned over the past two centuries!

> Business reengineering means putting aside much of the received wisdom of two hundred years of industrial management. It means forgetting how work was done in the age of the mass market and deciding how it can best be done now. In business reengineering, old job titles and old organizational arrangements—departments, divisions, groups, and so on—cease to matter. They are artifacts of another age.

As countercultural rebellion becomes corporate ideology, even the beloved Buddhism of the Beats wins a place on the executive bookshelf. In *The Leader as Martial Artist* (1993), Arnold Mindell advises men of commerce in the ways of the Tao, mastery of which he likens, of course, to surfing. For Mindell's Zen businessman, as for the followers of Tom Peters, the world is a wildly chaotic place of opportunity, navigable only to an enlightened "leader" who can discern the "timespirits" at work behind the scenes. In terms Peters himself might use were he a more meditative sort of inspiration professional, Mindell explains that "the wise facilitator" doesn't seek to prevent the inevitable and random clashes between "conflicting field spirits," but to anticipate such bouts of disorder and profit thereby.

Contemporary corporate fantasy imagines a world of ceaseless, turbulent change, of centers that ecstatically fail to hold, of joyous extinction for the craven gray-flannel creature of the past. Businessmen today decorate the walls of their offices not with portraits of President Eisenhower and emblems of suburban order, but with images of extreme athletic daring, with sayings about "diversity" and "empowerment" and "thinking outside the box." They theorize their world not in the bar car of the commuter train, but in weepy corporate retreats at which they beat their tom-toms and envision themselves as part of the great avant-garde tradition of edge-livers, risk-takers, and ass-kickers. Their world is a place not of sublimation and conformity, but of "leadership" and bold talk about defying the herd. And there is nothing this new enlightened species of businessman despises more than "rules" and "reason." The prominent culture-warriors of the right may believe that the counterculture was capitalism's undoing, but the antinomian businessmen know better. "One of the t-shirt slogans of the sixties read, 'Question authority,'" the authors of *Reengineering the Corporation* write. "Process owners might buy their reengineering team members the nineties version: 'Question assumptions.'"

The new businessman quite naturally gravitates to the slogans and sensibility of the rebel sixties to express his understanding of the new Information World. He is led in what one magazine calls "the business revolution" by the office-park subversives it hails as "business activists," "change agents," and "corporate radicals." He speaks to his comrades through commercials like the one for "Warp," a type of IBM computer operating system, in which an electric guitar soundtrack and psychedelic video effects surround hip executives with earrings and hairdos who are visibly stunned by the product's gnarly 'tude (It's a "totally cool way to run your computer," read the product's print ads). He understands the world through *Fast Company,* a successful new magazine whose editors take their inspiration from Hunter S. Thompson and whose stories describe such things as a "dis-organization" that inhabits an "anti-office" where "all vestiges of hierarchy have disappeared" or a computer scientist who is also "a rabble rouser, an agent provocateur, a product of the 1960s who never lost his activist fire or democratic values." He is what sociologists Paul Leinberger and Bruce Tucker have called "The New Individualist," the new and improved manager whose arty worldview and creative hip derive directly from his formative sixties days. The one thing this new executive is definitely *not* is Organization Man, the hyper-rational counter of beans, attender of church, and wearer of stiff hats.

In television commercials, through which the new American businessman presents his visions and self-understanding to the public, perpetual revolution and the gospel of rule-breaking are the orthodoxy of the day. You only need to watch for a few minutes before you see one of these slogans and understand the grip of antinomianism over the corporate mind:

Sometimes You Gotta Break the Rules	*—Burger King*
If You Don't Like the Rules, Change Them	*—WXRT-FM*
The Rules Have Changed	*—Dodge*
The Art of Changing	*—Swatch*
There's no one way to do it.	*—Levi's*
This is different. Different is good.	*—Arby's*
Just Different From the Rest	*—Special Export beer*
The Line Has Been Crossed: The Revolutionary New Supra	*—Toyota*
Resist the Usual	*—the slogan of both Clash Clear Malt and Young & Rubicam*
Innovate Don't Imitate	*—Hugo Boss*
Chart Your Own Course	*—Navigator Cologne*
It separates you from the crowd	*—Vision Cologne*

In most, the commercial message is driven home with the vanguard iconography of the rebel: screaming guitars, whirling cameras, and startled old timers who, we predict, will become an increasingly indispensable prop as consumers require ever-greater assurances that, Yes! You *are* a rebel! Just look at how offended they are!

Our businessmen imagine themselves rebels, and our rebels sound more and more like ideologists of business. Henry Rollins, for example, the maker of loutish, overbearing music and composer of high-school-grade poetry, straddles both worlds unproblematically. Rollins' writing and lyrics strike all the standard alienated literary poses: He rails against overcivilization and yearns to "disconnect." He veers back and forth between vague threats toward "weak" people who "bring me down" and blustery declarations of his weightlifting ability and physical prowess. As a result he ruled for several years as the preeminent darling of *Details* magazine, a periodical handbook for the young executive on the rise, where rebellion has achieved a perfect synthesis with corporate ideology. In 1992 *Details* named Rollins a "rock 'n' roll samurai," an "emblem . . . of a new masculinity" whose "enlightened honesty" is "a way of being that seems to flesh out many of the ideas expressed in contemporary culture and fashion." In 1994 the magazine consummated its relationship with Rollins by naming him "Man of the Year," printing a fawning story about his muscular worldview and decorating its cover with a photo in which Rollins displays his tattoos and rubs his chin in a thoughtful manner.

Details found Rollins to be such an appropriate role model for the struggling young businessman not only because of his music-product, but because of his excellent "self-styled identity," which the magazine describes in terms normally reserved for the breast-beating and soul-searching variety of motivational seminars. Although he derives it from the quality-maximizing wisdom of the East rather than the unfashionable doctrines of Calvin, Rollins' rebel posture is identical to that fabled ethic of the small capitalist whose regimen of positive thinking and hard work will one day pay off. *Details* describes one of Rollins' songs, quite seriously, as "a self-motivational superforce, an anthem of empowerment," teaching lessons that any aspiring middle-manager must internalize. Elsewhere, Iggy Pop, that great chronicler of the ambitionless life, praises Rollins as a "high achiever" who "wants to go somewhere." Rollins himself even seems to invite such an interpretation. His recent spoken-word account of touring with Black Flag, delivered in an unrelenting two-hour drill-instructor staccato, begins with the timeless bourgeois story of opportunity taken, of young Henry leaving the security of a "straight job," enlisting with a group of visionaries who were "the hardest working people I have ever seen," and learning "what hard work is all about." In the liner notes he speaks proudly of his Deming-esque dedication to quality, of how his bandmates "Delivered under pressure at incredible odds." When describing his relationship with his parents for the readers of *Details,* Rollins quickly cuts to the critical matter, the results that such dedication has brought: "Mom, Dad, I outgross both of you put together," a happy observation he repeats in his interview with the *New York Times Magazine.*

Despite the extreme hostility of punk rockers with which Rollins had to contend all through the 1980s, it is he who has been chosen by the commercial media as the godfather of rock 'n' roll revolt. It is not difficult to see why. For Rollins the punk rock decade was but a lengthy seminar on leadership skills, thriving on chaos, and total quality management. Rollins' much-celebrated anger is indistinguishable from the anger of the frustrated junior executive who finds obstacles on the way to the top. His discipline and determination are the automatic catechism of any small entrepreneur who's just finished brainwashing himself with the latest leadership and positive-thinking tracts; his poetry is the inspired verse of *21 Days to Unlimited Power* or *Let's Get Results, Not Excuses.* Henry Rollins is no more a threat to established power in America than was Dale Carnegie. And yet Rollins as king of the rebels—peerless and ultimate—is the message hammered home wherever photos of his growling visage appear. If you're unhappy with your lot, the Culture Trust tells us with each new tale of Rollins, if you feel you must rebel, take your cue from the most disgruntled guy of all: Lift weights! Work hard! Meditate in your back yard! Root out the weaknesses deep down inside yourself! But whatever you do, *don't* think about who controls power or how it is wielded.

The structure and thinking of American business have changed enormously in the years since our popular conceptions of its problems and abuses were formulated. In the meantime the mad frothings and jolly apolitical revolt of Beat, despite their vast popularity and insurgent air, have become powerless against a new regime that, one suspects, few of Beat's present-day admirers and practitioners feel any need to study or understand. Today that beautiful countercultural idea, endorsed now by everyone from the surviving Beats to shampoo manufacturers, is more the official doctrine of corporate America than it is a program of resistance. What we understand as "dissent" does not subvert, does not challenge, does not even question the cultural faiths of Western business. What David Rieff wrote of the revolutionary pretentions of multiculturalism is equally true of the countercultural idea: "The more one reads in academic multiculturalist journals and in business publications, and the more one contrasts the speeches of CEOs and the speeches of noted multiculturalist academics, the more one is struck by the similarities in the way they view the world." What's happened is not co-optation or appropriation, but a simple and direct confluence of interest.

The problem with cultural dissent in America isn't that it's been co-opted, absorbed, or ripped-off. Of course it's been all of these things. But it has proven so hopelessly susceptible to such assaults for the same reason it has become so harmless in the first place, so toothless even before Mr. Geffen's boys discover it angsting away in some bar in Lawrence, Kansas: It is no longer any different from the official culture it's supposed to be subverting. The basic impulses of the countercultural idea, as descended from the holy Beats, are about as threatening to the new breed of antinomian businessmen as Anthony Robbins, selling success & how to achieve it on a late-night infomercial.

The people who staff the Combine aren't like Nurse Ratched. They aren't Frank Burns, they aren't the Church Lady, they aren't Dean Wormer from *Animal House,* they aren't those repressed old folks in the commercials who want to ban Tropicana Fruit Twisters. They're hipper than you can ever hope to be because *hip is their official ideology,* and they're always going to be there at the poetry reading to encourage your "rebellion" with a hearty "right on, man!" before you even know they're in the auditorium. You can't outrun them, or even stay ahead of them for very long: it's their racetrack, and that's them waiting at the finish line to congratulate you on how *outrageous* your new style is, on how you *shocked* those stuffy prudes out in the heartland.

ADDITIONAL READINGS

Barber, Benjamin R. *Consumed: How Markets Corrupt Children, Infantilize Adults, and Swallow Citizens Whole.* New York: Norton, 2007.

——. *Jihad vs. McWorld: Terrorism's Challenge to Democracy.* 1995. New York: Ballantine, 2001.

Breen, T.H. *The Marketplace of Revolution: How Consumer Politics Shaped American Independence.* New York: Oxford UP, 2004.

Bronner, Simon J., ed. *Consuming Visions: Accumulation and Display of Goods in America, 1880–1920.* New York: Norton, 1989.

Cohen, Lizabeth. *A Consumers' Republic: The Politics of Mass Consumption in Postwar America.* New York: Knopf, 2003.

Ewen, Stuart. *Captains of Consciousness: Advertising and the Social Roots of the Consumer Culture.* 1976. New York: Basic Books, 2001.

Farrell, James, J. *One Nation Under Goods: Malls and the Seductions of American Shopping.* Washington: Smithsonian, 2003.

Frank, Thomas. *The Conquest of Cool: Business Culture, Counterculture, and the Rise of Hip Consumerism.* U of Chicago P, 1997.

——. *One Market Under God: Extreme Capitalism, Market Populism, and the End of Economic Democracy.* New York: Doubleday, 2000.

Frank, Thomas and Matt Weiland, eds. *Commodify Your Dissent: Salvos from the* Baffler. New York: Norton, 1997.

de Graaf, John, David Wann, and Thomas H. Naylor. *Affluenza: The All-Consuming Epidemic.* San Francisco: Berrett-Koehler, 2001.

Heath, Joseph and Andrew Potter. *Nation of Rebels: Why Counterculture Became Consumer Culture.* New York: HarperBusiness, 2004.

Hochschild, Arlie Russell. *The Commercialization of Intimate Life: Notes from Home and Work.* Berkeley: U of California P, 2003.

Lasn, Kalle. *Culture Jam: How to Reverse America's Suicidal Consumer Binge—And Why We Must.* 1999. New York: Quill-HarperCollins, 2000.

Leach, William. *Land of Desire: Merchants, Power, and the Rise of a New American Culture.* New York: Pantheon, 1993.

Mamiya, Christin J. *Pop Art and Consumer Culture: American Super Market.* American Studies Series. Austin: U Texas P, 1992.

McGovern, Charles F. *Sold American: Consumption and Citizenship, 1890–1945.* Chapel Hill: U of North Carolina P, 2006.

Ohmann, Richard. *Selling Culture: Magazines, Markets, and Class at the Turn of the Century.* The Haymarket Series. London: Verso, 1996.

Rosenblatt, Roger, ed. *Consuming Desires: Consumption, Culture, and the Pursuit of Happiness.* Washington: Shearwater Books-Island Press, *1999.*

Schor, Juliet B. *Born to Buy.* 2004. New York: Scribner, 2005

———. *The Overspent American: Upscaling, Downshifting and the New Consumer.* 1998. New York: HarperPerennial, 1999.

Sennett, Richard. *The Fall of Public Man.* 1976. New York: Norton, 1992.

Trachtenberg, Alan. *The Incorporation of America: Culture and Society in the Gilded Age.* American Century Series. New York: Hill and Wang, 1982.

Twitchell, James B. *Branded Nation: The Marketing of Megachurch, College Inc., and Museumworld.* New York: Simon & Schuster, 2004.

———. *Lead Us Into Temptation: The Triumph of American Materialism.* New York: Columbia UP, 1999.

———. *Living It Up: America's Love Affair with Luxury.* 2002. New York: Simon & Schuster, 2003.

Veblen, Thorstein. *The Theory of the Leisure Class.* 1899. New York: Viking, 1967.

Weber, Max. *The Protestant Ethic and the Spirit of Capitalism.* 1930. Trans. Talcott Parsons. London: Routledge Classics, 2001.

After These Messages:
Advertising and Its Effects

Selling to
Ms. Consumer

Carol Ascher

Consumerism and its handmaiden, advertising, developed in the late 1800s and the first decades of the twentieth century. Like many historical trends, these two grew largely outside of any direct decisions by those who were most affected by them—in this case, women. The period around the turn of the century was a time when, in fact, fewer women held professional roles than they had only two or three decades earlier. Moreover, active women of the period threw their energies into either the suffrage movement or various social welfare fights. Even Florence Kelly, executive secretary to the Consumer Union in the early 1900s, saw it as her role to generate pressure to improve the working conditions in which products were made rather than to create a movement to fight the growth of advertising or buying.

Without women's participation at higher levels in business and industry or an active women's movement concerned with these issues, the home was increasingly shaped by forces whose interests were not its own. As one woman argued in 1908, "Perhaps the real danger to the home lies in the fact that women . . . are not free to control the industrial changes which affect it, and that these changes are being determined too largely by commercial interests."[1]

Nonetheless, there was much about the condition of women that made them receptive to the changes taking place. It is this receptivity that I want to explore. For history is never completely beyond people's control, even when they are not at the helm where decisions are made.

Carol Ascher is Senior Research Scientist at the Institute for Education and Social Policy, Steinhardt School of Education, New York University. Trained as an anthropologist, she is also a novelist and essayist, and has published widely in journals. She is also the author of several books, including *Simone de Beauvoir: A Life of Freedom* (1981) and *Hard Lessons: Public Schools and Privatization* (with Norm Fruchter and Bob Berne, 1996).

Between 1890 and 1920, when America became transformed into a consumer society, women's lives continued on the almost runaway course of change begun much earlier in the nineteenth century. For those women who moved outside the home, new supports and new possibilities for selfhood became potentially available, though none were easily won or even easy to live with once attained. But for women in the home, the period had a shattering quality, much as the late sixties and early seventies have had for housewives today. And the loss of old norms and ties made these women vulnerable to solutions posed by the world of commodities.

In the early 1900s central heating, gas appliances, and running hot and cold water lightened housework for a growing number of women, particularly in the middle class. Water no longer had to be boiled for washing, nor irons heated on a stove, and coal didn't have to be brought in from a cellar and stoked throughout the day. The introduction of the fireless cooker (gas stove) was a milestone for women of this period; it meant that temperature could be controlled, and cooking done more efficiently and with greater certainty than ever before.

In the next decade, many women were able to purchase washing machines, ice boxes, and vacuum cleaners. These household appliances lightened work inside the home, but they also necessitated a reordering of women's sense of housekeeping. An example can be given with the vacuum cleaner. Here much of the early advertising consisted of retraining women to see cleaning as the rather undramatic suction process, rather than as the visually reassuring display of stirred-up dust they were used to.[2] Christine Frederick, one of the few women working with industry, expressed the disequilibrium the housewife was experiencing in the late 1920s when she said that manufacturers had to help women transform their work from the "hand-craft age" into the era of the "machine operative."[3]

The spread of the kindergarten and compulsory schooling in the first decades of the twentieth century also took some of the old childrearing responsibilities away from women. More important, these new institutions, as well as their intellectual underpinnings, began to shift the notion of who knew best how to care for children. Emerging fields of child development and education offered new methods of mothering and critiqued the old. Early standardized tests, such as the Binet, measured "objectively" how smart the child was, rendering inadequate a mother's sense of her daughter or son. Although mothers still spent years caring for their children, they increasingly did so with the specter of professional judgment hanging over them.

Women in the home were also affected by the changing order of the work world. The early home economists—domestic scientists, as they were then called—had hoped to strengthen the family and improve the woman's place in it by also insisting on the authority of the husband-father. But the new organization of industry made it difficult for men to hold on to their old controls, either at work or at home. The geographic separation of the home and work worlds made it impossible for the father to maintain the authority he had once held when he worked inside the home alongside his family. At the same time, work for most men lost its craft, and an increasing proportion of men worked for wages in large, anonymous situations where they retained little control over their work. This breakdown in the material base for male authority gave a spurt to feminism. But it also made daily life more uncertain for those women who tried to adjust old patterns to new realities.

As men's work on the outside lost its dignity, their role inside the family turned from that of patriarch to that of provider. Not only did the home have to offer solace from the workday world, but women had to bolster the wounded egos it was causing in their menfolk. It was as if by making the home a castle, women could transform their husbands back into kings.

Given the hierarchical patterns women were used to, the decreased dominion of the husband-father opened the way for women to accept a new locus of authority. This authority was being developed by science and industry. Both would have new rationales for right and wrong, and both would turn all the family, including the father, into children, to be taught, teased, and coerced. One of the most self-conscious statements of this shift in authority came toward its end, in 1931, when Edward Filene, head of the great Boston department store, wrote,

> since the head of the family is no longer in control of the economic process through which the family must get its living, he must be relieved of many ancient responsibilities and therefore of many of his prerogatives. . . . Women . . . and children are likely to discover that their economic well-being comes not from the organization of the family but from the organization of industry, and they may look more and more for individual guidance, not to their fathers, but to the truth which science is discovering.[4]

Birth control also undermined old authority patterns as well as transformed women's work in and outside the home. The shrinking of family size had started in the early nineteenth century, but it became a public "problem" in the later decades of the century when a number of social movements advocated some form of birth control and when it became a common fear that the middle class would simply cease to reproduce itself. Margaret Sanger's first clinic, which opened in 1916, was the culmination of decades of struggle for public access to birth control.[5] By the 1920s 70 to 80 percent of all middle- and upper-class women were assumed to be using some form of contraception.[6] For the first time, sex became separated from reproduction. The 1920s was a time of tremendous sexual experimentation—a time in many ways as free as today. But along with increases in sexual freedom, divorce grew rapidly. Whereas in 1890 there had been only three divorces per thousand, by 1920 the number had risen to nearly eight per thousand.[7]

Even the older feminists were caught off base by the new sexuality. Jane Addams, for example, who had grown up in the period when womanhood meant motherhood—or its more liberated variant, social housekeeping—spoke publicly of her discontent with the emphasis on sexual gratification. And Charlotte Perkins Gilman condemned the risqué clothing of the flappers. Although she felt bound to endorse sexual liberation, she believed women were displaying a "backlash of primitive femininity" that stood in the way of real sexual equality.[8]

Birth control generated the potential for women's economic independence, but it also caused a great deal of uncertainty and retrenchment. By 1920 every third worker was a woman, and 20 percent of all married women worked.[9] The proportion of single women (including those widowed and divorced) had also increased significantly in the preceding thirty years.[10] Moreover, single women were holding jobs and living outside families, rather than doing chores in return for room and board with relatives, as had been the case several decades earlier. However, Charlotte Perkins Gilman was not wrong to fear the backlash of "primitive femininity." In the first decades of the twentieth century the proportion of professional women declined. Between 1910 and 1930, for example, women doctors declined by 7 percent and women musicians and composers by 6 percent.[11] By the time the Nineteenth Amendment was passed, women posed no threat as a voting block, and few women in the 1920s ran for political office. Although many women worked, they did not aspire to the heights they once had.

Changes in work and the family had made women at home insecure; but this insecurity was exacerbated by women's increasing isolation. An important source of this isolation stemmed, in turn, from changes in the organization of the home and its relationship to the outside world.

By the turn of the century, although apartments were being built in every city, the single-family home was becoming a reality as well as an ideal for more people. Public transportation had enabled housing to spread out from city centers. Suburbanization made it possible for workers' families to live with their own separate roofs over their heads. And industrialists, home economists, and social reformers alike argued the importance of providing such dwellings for workers and their families. The *Ladies' Home Journal,* the most influential of the women's magazines, featured a model house plan for a single-family home in each of its issues.[12] Many of the industrial towns built in the late 1800s contained single-family homes in order to develop in their workers a sense of the right way to live. Some went so far as to offer courses in home economics for the wives; these courses reinforced the importance of the single-family home and the role of women in it.[13]

After World War I, the automobile furthered the sprawl of residential areas outside the cities. Thousands of men were already traveling to work over an hour each way, and neighborhoods were becoming devoid of men during working hours. While most urban women emigrees to the suburbs complained of loneliness, the idea that suburban living was important to family life, and particularly to raising children, kept the flow of families outward from the cities.

With a revolution going on in Russia and the potential for social upheaval obvious in this country, single-family dwellings became fused with a vision of preventing revolution and communism. The women's magazines supported this vision. A 1920 issue of the *Ladies' Home Journal,* for instance, "intimated that the Bolsheviks wanted most of all to destroy the single-family house and replace it with 'nationalized woman' in mass housing." The magazine also connected feminism and communism as foes of the home and motherhood, asserting that women who selfishly chose not to have children or not to raise them by themselves at home were "aiding the red cause."[14]

Along with the ideal of the single-family home came new housing styles, which lessened the housework but opened the way for commodities to enter the home. The parlor, the repository of tradition, had been the first to go, aided by a virulent campaign against it in the 1890s by the editor of the *Ladies' Home Journal,* Ed Bok. The parlor symbolized holding on to old family heirlooms and relating to guests in old, formal ways. The living room, by contrast, was to be "lived in." It could embrace new styles in commodities and human relationships.

Along with the number of rooms, room size also shrank steadily. This trend was most obvious in the kitchen, a room that had once been the center of household production. Following the industrial ideal of specialization, architects now stripped all but food preparation from the room. The ideal size for a kitchen in the early 1900s had already shrunk from its nineteenth-century expansiveness to ten by twelve feet.[15] By the end of World War I, kitchenettes began to appear.[16] The elimination of laundry space in the kitchen went along with the growth of the commercial laundry, one of the few ultimately unsuccessful campaigns to commercialize what had been women's work.[17] Small kitchens and kitchenettes also eliminated the possibility of eating inside them, and by the early 1930s one author was noting that small kitchens had forced "a good deal of eating outside the house."[18]

Small kitchens were a sign of prestige, as they both followed the ideal of efficiency and specialization and were a visual display of the fact that the husband's salary enabled the family to buy, rather than produce, most of what it used. The inverse relationship between kitchen size and workers' incomes was drawn out with exquisite detail by a Harvard social scientist. In his view, among families whose income was ten dollars a week or less, the wife spent her time "cooking, washing, caring for the children, and doing outside washing or going herself to work." The kitchen in these homes was "perforce the family living room and should be made proportionately ample." In families whose weekly income approached eighteen dollars, while the family still ate in the kitchen, it would probably want "a 'best room' in which to receive callers, actual or hoped for." Among "families of a higher income class," however, a small kitchen was most appropriate. Here, in this analyst's view, "the housewife is quite willing to carry food and dishes into the dining-room in order to escape eating the food in the place where it was cooked; also a separate dining-room is deemed more comfortable by the rest of the family."[19] Thus the middle-class housewife paid for the greater gentility of her family by preparing food alone, in a small kitchen, and carrying it to and from the dining area.

By 1920, the isolation caused by single-family homes and the specialization of rooms within them had apparently caused enough widespread distress among women at home that a book could be written entitled *The Nervous Housewife*. The book combined popular psycho-analytic notions of human needs, an ideological commitment to the single-family home with its specialized quarters, and—despite the contradiction—a detailed study of the damage it was wreaking on women. In a poignant chapter called "The Housework and the Home as Factors in the Neuroses," the author, Abraham Myerson, listed as sources of women's contemporary neuroses not only their raised expectations but also, and more important, the isolation and monotony of their work:

> All work at home has the difficulty of the segregation, the isolation of the home. Man, the social animal who needs at least some one to quarrel with, has deliberately isolated his household—on a property basis. There has grown up a definite, aesthetic need of privacy; all of modesty and the essential feeling demand it.
>
> This is good for the man, and perhaps for the children, but not for the woman. Her work is done all alone, and at the time her husband comes home and wants to stay there, she would like to get out. Work that is in the main lonely, and work that on the whole leaves the mind free, leads almost inevitably to daydreaming and introspection. These are essentials in the housework—monotony, daydreaming, and introspection.[20]

Because Myerson assumed that the need for privacy and segregation were worth nurturing in their current form, his solution to "the nervous housewife" was tentative and piecemeal. Like Charlotte Perkins Gilman, Myerson suggested that some housework would probably have to be made cooperative; but he was cautious to insist that this be done within the confines of the nuclear family and the single-family home.

Isolation inside the home began to impel women into shops and stores. Yet shopping itself provided less and less succor for isolation. For it too was becoming bereft of personal contact.

In the 1880s and 1890s department stores sprang up in all major cities. Since several hundred clerks could not be trusted to bargain in the manner of a shopkeeper, department stores began to institute the "fixed price." With the fixed price, the clerk was relegated to showing items and making change. In the same period, F. W. Woolworth began his five-and-dime stores. These further limited the contact between salesperson and customer by instituting open counters and displays. Woolworth's salespeople now only made change for purchases already chosen.

In food retailing, packaged foods around the turn of the century left the grocery store clerk without measuring functions, and shifted the focus from the actual product and the relationship between clerk and shopper to the product's appearance in its package. Brand names became the source by which the customer chose—and increasingly received her "human" contact. With packaging of food items, "self-service" came into existence. Now, instead of the storekeeper serving a woman as she filled her order, the woman was left to roam through the store while clerks stocked shelves and took inventory. Contact with the customer became limited to the checkout.

In the small shops, women had been allowed to charge and pay as their money came in. As the chain stores became the major self-service operators, the self-service stores demanded cash. The motto was "pay as you go," and nobody's personal relationship with the proprietor was good enough to warrant informal debts and charges. Instead, the larger stores began to offer installment plans, which—after some investigation of her or his personal finances—allowed the consumer to pay on time, at interest. Like self-service, installment buying aimed at stimulating purchases. But it did so without either the personal trust of the old charge account or the economic risks to the storekeepers.

Advertising developed its modern appeals during this period of upheaval and estrangement. The very technological improvements that furthered women's uncertainty and isolation also created the possibility for more effective selling. As old roles and relationships weakened, consumerism and advertising took upon themselves the burden of offering contact and promising love, trust, and security. Some of the changes in selling and advertising techniques—such as certain forms of packaging or the use of color photography—necessitated technological advances. But the dramatic alterations in the style and meaning of the messages had less to do with technology than with an increased understanding of human psychology, as it developed through psychoanalysis and its derivative movements, and with a conscious decision by businessmen to play an active role in helping to form what women and men wanted.

Before 1880, advertising messages had consisted largely of detailed instructions, diagrams and descriptions of the product by the manufacturer, or lengthy testimonials by its users. Images only indirectly connected to the product generally did not come into play. Around the 1890s, advertisers began to loosen up and experiment with new forms. Jingles and human interest trademarks appeared. Jingles told a story, often absurd, but focused on a phrase or an image that embedded the product in the customer's mind. While the emotional appeal of jingles was often their silliness, it was clear to sellers that catchy, emotionally appealing ideas, rather than long descriptions, were good selling devices. Human interest trademarks also followed the device of the simple message but began the trend of more "subjective" advertising. Human interest trademarks, such as the Wool Soap Kids or the H-O cereal baby, were characters who became known and loved for themselves.

Advertisers used images of children self-consciously in the 1890s, directing them specifically at women. *Printer's Ink,* the advertising trade journal, announced in 1896 that "the picture of a healthy, pretty child rivets the attention of most people, especially women. This fact is now generally recognized by advertisers, and the use of a multitude of child-faces as eye attractors is the result."[21] The effectiveness of children as an advertising device was heightened because motherhood had become a choice for many women. At the same time, the images served to draw women back in toward their mothering role.

From the outset, advertising theory, like much of psychoanalysis, was developed largely through experience with women. The psychology of advertising as a discipline has been dated as early as 1903, and certainly numerous insights about what motivated women were being developed around the turn of the century. However, it was with the end of World War I that an accelerated need to increase consumption and the spread of psychoanalysis in this country joined to create a new, scientific study of women as consumers. Notions about the nature of women quickly became embedded in analyses of how the consumer functioned.

Many advertising theorists took Freud's notion of the sexual drive or instinct and used it for their own purposes. Whereas Freud postulated only sexuality as an instinct that transcended history (and even this had a quite broad meaning, almost at the level of a life force), advertising theorists began to produce long lists of "instincts" that were clearly products of a specific culture and whose aim was to further embed people in that culture. For example, Christine Frederick, in her book *Selling to Mrs. Consumer,* listed eighteen "female instincts," among which were sex-love, mother-love, love of homemaking, vanity, love of mutation or change (that is, fashion), love of prestige, and love of reputation.[22] She even elevated the love of trading to an instinct in her attempt to rationalize and justify women's new consumer role. Designating all these traits as instincts removed them to a place where the society no longer had to take responsibility for their existence. Instead, those traits that would be developed, accentuated, and reinforced by advertising could be blamed on the instinctual structure.

Whatever the specific "instinct," emotionality and irrationality became the mainstay of advertising's notion of human or female nature. This was the vulgarized version of the psychoanalytic notion that the individual was driven by unconscious drives. And as emotionality and irrationality became embedded in the common sense of advertising practice, advertising language and imagery drew more and more on prestige, sexuality, isolation, and the alternative, love and contact. Carl Naether, in his classic *Advertising to Women,* argued that advertising should always "strike a personal note," because women were always involved in "the personal"; he suggested using "fanciful expressions" and "chatty tones" with women.[23] His suggestions implied an understanding that the messages of advertising would have to convey the personal contact lost to most people's lives. Like Naether, Christine Frederick also emphasized woman's emotionality. In Frederick's view, woman had a "natural" intelligence, which was "instinctive" and "practical"; but living emotionally, she often revived her spirits with "foolish purchases." Both Frederick and Naether were aware, however, of the changes women were experiencing. Whereas Naether warned industry that they must appeal to the "growing class of business women," Frederick told advertisers that "the present generation of women are not bound much by religious controls, nor by the feeling of being below men in political rights, mental ability or sex inhibition."[24]

Even in their most freedom-loving images, however, the advertisements of the 1920s never incorporated the full implications of the working woman or the possibilities of women living outside of families. Freedom was connected to leisure and romance; stability, to the family and the home. Women might hold jobs, but their main fantasies were still directed toward the family configuration. Whereas women had earlier produced the objects of their daily lives, now they were to buy them—from the objects that made them lovable (marriageable), to those that created a healthy family or a secure home life.

An analysis of the most common themes in advertising in the late 1920s is worth quoting in full, because of the clarity with which it outlines the new images of advertising. Based on a study of the *Woman's Home Companion,* the author, Otis Pease, reported two themes as paramount: "the American family at home" and "the importance of romantic love":

1. *The American family at home.* Home is never an apartment but a house, usually owned. It sanctifies leisure and recreation. It is invariably a "white collar" home. No one works or sweats; families only play at home. A housewife plays with her kitchen and her laundry, the husband plays with his boys or his radio. Homes usually have two cars and a dog. Mothers-in-law, uncles, and grandfathers live elsewhere. Single men and women do not exist. A successful man is a husband who is unfailingly cheerful, "sincere," and upwardly mobile. He may often acquire these virtues by correspondence courses and by other expenditures of money, but his failure to possess them would be a sign not of poverty, but of defective character. The worries, insecurities, and fears of modern men and women stem from failure to be liked, to adjust to one another, to find adequate sexual satisfactions, but especially from failure to live amid the accoutrements of leisure. These criteria of security are surpassingly important to all families. To possess them is to be free from tension and misery. Harmony and happiness in fact depend on the rate of consumption of gadgets. Friends are always dropping in to view the Frigidaire or dance to the Philco. No more than a good meal and a quiet deodorant are needed to keep the affection of one's husband and children. The preparation and serving of food, to be sure, is a complex function; but the housewife may trust the food industry for advice and guidance. Other large institutions perpetually bolster the family: banks, insurance companies, and utilities stand ready to protect its security and preserve its happiness. Money spent in these institutions is never an expense but an investment.

2. *The importance of romantic love.* The satisfactions of sex and the criteria of romantic love are inextricably intertwined; but whereas romantic love is indispensable to sexual satisfaction, the reverse is not the case: romantic love is desirable in and of itself and is bound up with other ends, such as prestige, social success, power and wealth. The criteria of romantic love can be acquired cheaply by purchase: youth, smoothness of skin, a prominent bust, a deodorized body, a daily ritual of body care, handsome or alluring clothes, outward manners, and a ready affirmative response to these criteria

in the other person. (Some women age so young and fade out—constipated. The wife of the Pretender to the throne of France is irresistible; she possesses the power to love; she commands attention; she uses Pond's. Look like a schoolgirl all your life; use Palmolive for your skin—it is made from natural African beauty oils.) Romantic love is available only to those who retain the appearance of youth. Men and women over forty are Mothers, Fathers, Grandmothers, Grandfathers, Business Executives, Professional People; they are no longer capable of romantic love or, therefore, of sexual interests. They seek, instead, prestige and social success; they are content merely to conform to their assigned roles as Mother, Father, etc. Romantic love is also a function of wealth and the ability to consume it. Romantic love depends on leisure time, shopping, parties, sports, vacations, cruises, night clubs, and usually on the premise that the pair are not yet married. Real satisfaction is attainable from sex only upon acquiring the criteria of romantic love.[25]

As women shopped, these images drew them in. They promised solutions to unfulfilled needs and escapes from anxieties. For isolation, there was the promise of contact and communication; for uncertainty, a world where values and ideals were clear. Adventure and freedom could be gained through romantic love; security, protection, and nourishment, through family life. The concrete solution to these desires, however, was to be mere things—commodities that had taken on the emotional overtones conveyed by the ads.

And if the anxieties and insecurities aroused naturally by contemporary life were not enough to sell products, then these feelings were provoked and drawn out by the advertisements themselves. Commodities from mouthwash to life insurance used the possibilities of marital disaster to sell their products. Women's beauty products, which became a major industry during the twenties, helped to inject into physical beauty much of the uncertainty about being a woman and maintaining a marriage. Advertisements were increasingly aimed at heightening women's insecurity so that their product might then be sold as a solution. As Stuart Ewen, who studied advertising in the 1920s, put it,

> Keen and critical glances constantly threatened her. As her home-making skills had become reconstituted into a process of accumulating possessions, her sexuo-economic capacities were reinforced on a commercial plane. An ad for Woodbury soap (1922) offered women "the possession of a beautiful skin" which might arm them to meet a hostile world "proudly—confidently—without fear." Another Woodbury ad warned women that "a man expects to find daintiness, charm, refinement in the woman he knows," and that in order to maintain his pleasure, a woman must constantly spend on her appearance.[26]

Without an alternative vision, women were easily caught in the solutions that advertising offered. If femininity was valued in a period of great instability between women and men, then the loveliness that cosmetics offered was hard to resist. If marriage seemed the only alternative in a time when so many forces made it less secure, then anything from life insurance to mouthwash might be grasped at. Commodities appeared to fill the cracks of a shattered world, and promised to make that world secure in an exciting new way.

The individual that psychoanalysis and psychology were discovering was rapidly channeled into a narrow range of possible wishes and desires. The liberating potential inherent in the loosening of family ties was transformed into a romance of sexuality and family life. Life choices would increasingly be seen in terms of choices about commodities, whose images would symbolize to the isolated, insecure consumer the satisfaction of her well-chiseled desires.

Notes

[1] Caroline Hunt, *Home Problems from a New Standpoint* (Boston: Whitcomb & Barrows, 1908), pp. 143–144.

[2] Frank G. Hoover, *Fabulous Dustpan* (Cleveland: The World, 1955).

[3] Christine Frederick, *Selling to Mrs. Consumer* (New York: The Business Course, 1929), p. 181.

[4] Edward Filene, *Successful Living in the Machine Age* (1931), p. 96; quoted in Stuart Ewen, "Advertising as a Way of Life," *Liberation,* January 1975, p. 17.

[5] Linda Gordon, *Woman's Body, Woman's Right: A Social History of Birth Control in America* (New York: Viking Press, 1976).

[6] Norman Himes, *Medical History of Contraception* (1963), p. 340; quoted in Mary P. Ryan, *Womanhood in America from Colonial Times to the Present* (New York: Franklin Watts, 1975), p. 268.

[7] Paul H. Jacobson, *American Marriage and Divorce* (New York: Holt, Rinehart, 1959), pp. 1–19.

[8] Ryan, *Womanhood in America,* p. 262.

[9] Margaret Mead and Frances Bagley Kaplan, eds., *American Woman: The Report of the President's Commission on the Status of Women, and other Publications of the Commission* (New York: Scribner, 1965), pp. 46–47.

[10] Mary Ross, "The New Status of Women in America," in *Women's Coming of Age: A Symposium,* ed. Samuel D. Schmalhausen and V. F. Calhoun (New York: Horace Liveright, 1931), p. 537.

[11] Sophonisba Breckinridge, "The Activities of Women Outside the Home" (1933), p. 723; quoted in William O'Neil, *Everyone Was Brave: A History of Feminism in America* (Chicago: Quadrangle, 1961), p. 305.

[12] An analysis of these homes, as well as other reforms proposed by the *Ladies' Home Journal* editor, Ed Bok, can be found in Helen Woodward, *The Lady Persuaders* (New York: Ivan Obolensky, 1960).

[13] G. W. W. Hanger, *Housing of the Working People in the United States,* Bulletin of the Bureau of Labor no. 54 (Washington, D.C.: GPO, 1904); quoted in Gwendolyn Wright, "A Woman's Place Is in the Home: Changes in Domestic Architecture and in American Family Life, 1880–1915" (UCLA, 1976, typescript).

[14] Quoted in Wright, "A Woman's Place."

[15] Isabel Bevier, *The House, Its Plan, Decoration and Care* (Chicago: American School of Home Economics, 1907), pp. 86–87.

[16] Stuart Ewen, *Captains of Consciousness: Advertising and the Social Roots of the Consumer Culture* (New York: McGraw-Hill, 1976), p. 28.

[17] Heidi Hartman, *Capitalism and Women's Work in the Home, 1900–1930* (Ph.D. diss., Yale University, 1974).

[18] Albert Farwell Bemes, *The Evolving House,* vol. 2: *The Economics of Shelter* (Cambridge, Mass.: MIT Press, 1934), p. 69.

[19] Winthrop Hamlin, "Low Cost Construction in America" (Cambridge, Mass.: Department of Social Ethics, Harvard University, 1917); quoted in Wright, "A Woman's Place."

[20] Abraham Myerson, *The Nervous Housewife* (Boston: Little, Brown, 1920), pp. 77–78.

[21] Frank Presbrey, *The History and Development of Advertising* (1928; New York: Greenwood, 1968), p. 387.

[22] Frederick, *Selling to Mrs. Consumer,* p. 45.

[23] Carl Naether, *Advertising to Women* (New York: Prentice-Hall, 1928).

[24] Frederick, *Selling to Mrs. Consumer,* p. 23.

[25] Otis Pease, *Responsibilities of American Advertising* (New Haven: Yale University Press, 1958), pp. 38–40.

[26] Stuart Ewen, *Captains of Consciousness,* p. 178.

Understanding the Text

1. According to Ascher, why were women around the turn of the last century especially "vulnerable to solutions posed by the world of commodities"? (Identify and discuss two reasons.)

2. During the same era, according to Ascher, what changes at home and at work were men experiencing?

3. According to Ascher, what became of the kitchen during this era? For what reasons?

"In Your Face . . . All over the Place": Advertising Is Our Environment

Jean Kilbourne

Advertisers like to tell parents that they can always turn off the TV to protect their kids from any of the negative impact of advertising. This is like telling us that we can protect our children from air pollution by making sure they never breathe. Advertising is our *environment*. We swim in it as fish swim in water. We cannot escape it. Unless, of course, we keep our children home from school and blindfold them whenever they are outside of the house. And never let them play with other children. Even then, advertising's messages are inside our intimate relationships, our homes, our hearts, our heads.

Advertising not only appears on radio and television, in our magazines and newspapers, but also surrounds us on billboards, on the sides of buildings, plastered on our public transportation. Buses now in many cities are transformed into facsimiles of products, so that one boards a bus masquerading as a box of Dunkin' Donuts (followed, no doubt, by a Slimfast bus). The creators of this atrocity proudly tell us in their ad in *Advertising Age,* "In your face . . . all over the place!" Indeed.

Trucks carry advertising along with products as part of a marketing strategy. "I want every truck we have on the road making folks thirsty for Bud Light," says an ad in *Advertising Age,* which refers to a truck as a "valuable moving billboard." Given that almost half of all automobile crashes are alcohol-related, it's frightening to think of people becoming thirsty for Bud Light while driving their cars. A Spanish company has paid the drivers of seventy-five cars in Madrid to turn their cars into

Jean Kilbourne received her Ed.D. from Boston University and has become one of the nation's leading experts on the effects of advertising, especially upon women. She is a popular lecturer on college campuses and has produced several award-winning documentaries, including *Killing Us Softly: Advertising's Image of Women, Deadly Persuasion: The Advertising of Alcohol & Tobacco,* and *Slim Hopes.* Her book *Deadly Persuasion: Why Women and Girls Must Fight the Addictive Power of Advertising* appeared in 1999.

Pall Mall cigarette packages, and hopes to expand its operation throughout Spain. Imagine cars disguised as bottles of beer zipping along our highways. If we seek to escape all this by taking a plane, we become a captive audience for in-flight promotional videos.

Ads are on the videos we rent, the shopping carts we push through stores, the apples and hot dogs we buy, the online services we use, and the navigational screens of the luxury cars we drive. A new device allows advertisers to print their messages directly onto the sand of a beach. "This is my best idea ever—5,000 imprints of Skippy Peanut Butter jars covering the beach," crowed the inventor. Added the promotion director, "I'm here looking at thousands of families with kids. If they're on the beach thinking of Skippy, that's just what we want." Their next big idea is snow imprinting at ski resorts. In England the legendary white cliffs of Dover now serve as the backdrop for a laser-projected Adidas ad. American consumers have recently joined Europeans in being offered free phone calls if they will also listen to commercials. Conversations are interrupted by brief ads, tailored to match the age and social profiles of the conversants. And beer companies have experimented with messages posted over urinals, such as "Time for more Coors" or "Put used Bud here."

The average American is exposed to at least three thousand ads every day and will spend three years of his or her life watching television commercials. Advertising makes up about 70 percent of our newspapers and 40 percent of our mail. Of course, we don't pay direct attention to very many of these ads, but we are powerfully influenced, mostly on an unconscious level, by the experience of being immersed in an advertising culture, a market-driven culture, in which all our institutions, from political to religious to educational, are increasingly for sale to the highest bidder. According to Rance Crain, editor-in-chief of *Advertising Age,* the major publication of the advertising industry, "Only eight percent of an ad's message is received by the conscious mind; the rest is worked and reworked deep within the recesses of the brain, where a product's positioning and repositioning takes shape." It is in this sense that advertising is subliminal: not in the sense of hidden messages embedded in ice cubes, but in the sense that we aren't consciously aware of what advertising is doing.

Children who used to roam their neighborhoods now often play at McDonald's. Families go to Disneyland or other theme parks instead of state and national parks—or to megamalls such as the Mall of America in Minneapolis or Grapevine Mills in Texas, which provide "shop-pertainment." One of the major tourist destinations in historic Boston is the bar used in the 1980s hit television series *Cheers.* The Olympics today are at least as much about advertising as athletics. We are not far off from the world David Foster Wallace imagined in his epic novel *Infinite Jest,* in which years are sponsored by companies and named after them, giving us the Year of the Whopper and the Year of the Tucks Medicated Pad.

Commercialism has no borders. There is barely any line left between advertising and the rest of the culture. The prestigious Museum of Fine Arts in Boston puts on a huge exhibit of Herb Ritts, fashion photographer, and draws one of the largest crowds in its history. In

1998 the museum's Monet show was the most popular exhibit in the world. Museum officials were especially pleased by results of a survey showing 74 percent of visitors recognized that the show's sponsor was Fleet Financial Group, which shelled out $1.2 million to underwrite the show.

Bob Dole plays on his defeat in the presidential election in ads for Air France and Viagra, while Ed Koch, former mayor of New York City, peddles Dunkin' Donuts' bagels. Dr. Jane Goodall, doyenne of primatology, appears with her chimpanzees in an ad for Home Box Office, and Sarah Ferguson, the former duchess of York, gets a million dollars for being the official spokeswoman for Weight Watchers (with a bonus if she keeps her weight down).

Dead celebrities, such as Marilyn Monroe and Humphrey Bogart and John Wayne, are brought to life through computer magic and given digitized immortality in ads (how awful it is to see classy Fred Astaire dancing with electric brooms and hand vacs). Even worse, advertising often exploits cultural icons of rebellion and anticommercialism. Jimi Hendrix was raised from the dead by Aiwa to sell stereos, and John Lennon's haunting song "Imagine" is used by American Express. The Beatles' "Revolution," Bob Dylan's classic anthem "The Times They Are A-Changin'," and Janis Joplin's "Oh Lord, won't you buy me a Mercedes-Benz?" have all been used as advertising jingles, appealing to baby-boomers' nostalgia while completely corrupting the meaning of the songs. And the Rolling Stones, those aging rebels, have allowed Sprint to put a straight-pin through the band's tongue logo. However, when Neil Young recorded a video for his song "This Note's for You," which states that he won't sing for Pepsi or Coke and includes the lines "I don't sing for nobody/Makes me look like a joke," MTV refused to run it.

Live celebrities line up to appear in ads and people who simply appear in ads become celebrities. Today little girls constantly rate the supermodels high on their list of heroes, and most of us know them by their first names alone . . . Cindy, Elle, Naomi, Iman. Imagine—these women are *heroes* to little girls, not because of their courage or character or good deeds, but because of their perfect features and poreless skin. Models become more famous than film and television stars and rock stars, and the stars themselves often become pitchmen (and women) for a variety of products ranging from candy to cigarettes to alcohol.

Stars such as Harrison Ford, Woody Allen, Paul Newman, Whoopi Goldberg, and Bruce Willis, who don't want to tarnish their image in the United States, gladly appear in foreign television ads and commercials. Antonio Banderas and Kevin Costner have pushed cars, Brad Pitt watches, Dennis Hopper bath salts, Michael J. Fox fishing tackle, and Jennifer Aniston shampoo. In a commercial for Nippon Ham, Sylvester Stallone munched sausages at a garden party. After the success of *Titanic,* Leonardo DiCaprio was paid $4 million to play a noodle-eating detective in a Japanese commercial for credit cards. And in a commercial for Austrian Railways, Arnold Schwarzenegger rebuffs a steward who offers him a drink with the reply, "Hasta la vista, baby." Not surprisingly, he agreed to make the commercial only on the condition that the international media not be told about it. Madonna has a similar deal with Max Factor, which is paying her $6.5 million to sell cosmetics on TV, billboards, and in magazines throughout Britain, Europe, and Asia, but is prohibited from circulating photos from the ad campaign in the United States.

We are also influenced by advertising that we do not recognize as such, like the use of brand names during televised sporting events (during one ninety-minute car race, the word "Marlboro" appeared 5,933 times). In 1983 Sylvester Stallone wrote a letter to the Brown & Williamson tobacco company in which he promised to use their tobacco products in five feature films in exchange for half a million dollars. Compare this with the old days of "Brand X," the days when Julia Child covered the brand name "Pyrex" on her measuring cup!

Increasingly, films and television shows carry these hidden commercials. Often characters use certain products, the brands are prominently displayed, but the audience remains unaware that money has changed hands. New technology allows advertisers to have products digitally added to a scene, such as a Coca-Cola can on a desk or commercial billboards in the background of baseball games. At the very least, these "commercials" should be directly acknowledged in the credits. Writer and cartoonist Mark O'Donnell suggests that someday there will be tie-ins in literature as well, such as "All's Well That Ends With Pepsi," "The Old Man, Coppertone and the Sea," and "Nausea, and Periodic Discomfort Relief."

Sometimes the tie-ins are overt. Diet Coke obtained the rights to the cast of the hit series *Friends* and built a promotion around a special episode of the show that aired after the Super Bowl. In 1997 ABC and American Airlines announced a program that grants bonus miles and vacation credits to enrolled members who can correctly answer questions about shows that recently aired on the network. In the spring of 1998 product peddling on television was brought to new heights (or a new low) when a character in the hit show *Baywatch* created a line of shoes in her fashion-design class that viewers can actually buy. Stay tuned for *Shoe-watch*.

Far more important than the tie-ins, however, is the increasing influence of advertising on the form and content of films, television shows, and music videos (which aren't so much *like* ads as they *are* ads). Among other things, advertisers prefer that their products be associated with upbeat shows and films with happy endings, shows that leave people in the mood to buy. "People have become less capable of tolerating any kind of darkness or sadness," says media scholar Mark Crispin Miller. "I think it ultimately has to do with advertising, with a vision of life as a shopping trip." Steven Stark, another media critic, holds advertising responsible for a shift in television programs from glamorizing private detectives to glamorizing the police. According to Stark, "A detective show often leaves the audience with the impression that the system, police included, is corrupt and incompetent. An audience left with that message is in less mood to buy than an audience reassured, night after night, that the system works because the police are doing their job."

The cast of *Seinfeld* were the most successful hucksters in TV history, so successful that in 1994 *Advertising Age* gave their Star Presenter of the Year award to the entire cast. As Jerry Seinfeld, star of the show, said, "It is a good combination. When you're on TV in a sitcom, there's a loose reality that lends itself to doing commercials, which are also on TV. As long as you're on TV pretending to be something you're not anyway, why not do it for a commercial?" Opening an advertising agency, one of the paths Seinfeld is reportedly now considering, wouldn't be much of a leap (not that there's anything wrong with that). No wonder Seinfeld was one of the celebrities featured in a 1999 ad placed by *Forbes* magazine in *Advertising Age* that said, "These days, kids don't want to grow up to be athletes, comedians or movie stars. They want to be highly leveraged brands." The ad continues, "The real power in America no longer belongs to the most talented celebrities. But the most marketable ones."

The 1997 James Bond film *Tomorrow Never Dies* broke new ground for global integrated film tie-ins. In an ongoing effort to raise its profile, beer marketer Heineken USA featured James Bond, portrayed by Pierce Brosnan, in point-of-purchase displays worldwide and also offered a James Bond holiday catalog of electronic devices. During one scene in the film Bond crashes a car into a Heineken truck. Other marketers with major tie-ins to the film include Heublein's Smirnoff vodka brand, Omega watches, Avis, L'Oreal, and Visa International. More recently, the 1998 hit movie *You've Got Mail* basically costarred America Online, which in turn spent millions on television and online advertising for the movie. "Warner Brothers came to us and we agreed to be as helpful as we possibly could," said an AOL spokeswoman.

And independent films are becoming as tight with Madison Avenue as are the big flicks. Although I have no evidence that it was intentional, *The Brothers McMullen* prominently featured Heineken and Budweiser beer, which was ironic given its underlying theme of the havoc wreaked by family alcoholism. According to Ted Hope, the film's producer, "We struggle with product placement all the time, and I know other producers and directors struggle with it. I actively discourage it in movies but there are times when I contradict myself."

According to Paul Speaker, director of marketing for the independent production company responsible for *Sling Blade,* the key "is not only to find opportunities to seamlessly place products, but more importantly to associate brand to the entire film relevance." In order to appear hip and cool, major clothing manufacturers, such as Dockers, Tommy Hilfiger, and Polo Ralph Lauren, are associating their products with the low-budget independent films that are usually seen as "counterculture." Hilfiger provided the wardrobe for the independent film *The Faculty* and, in exchange, the teenage actors in the film appeared in commercials for Hilfiger. Andy Hilfiger, the company's vice-president of marketing, said, "The cast is great, and they went so well with our clothing."

The music world is in the game too, as rappers launch clothing lines and designers start record labels. Maurice Malone, who designs sportswear and has a record company, says, "You can use your music videos and your artists on your label to show your clothes," and, "You can talk about your clothes in the songs and hype the name." In 1999 designer Tommy Hilfiger sponsored concert tours for the Rolling Stones, Lilith Fair, and Britney Spears. All the musicians wore Hilfiger items onstage, while ads in fashion magazines depicted staged scenes from the concerts.

Not everyone is enthusiastic about this trend. Chris Gore, publisher of the Webzine *Film Threat,* thinks that sponsorship will inevitably guide what kinds of films get made, discouraging those with less consumer-friendly content. "Think of classic movies, like *The Wizard of Oz* or *Gone With the Wind,* and the products that could have been branded with them," he said. "Not only would that date them, it would be pathetic. We're not creating classics here—this is about commerce."

In spite of the fact that we are surrounded by more advertising than ever before, most of us still ridicule the idea that we might be personally influenced by it. The ridicule is often extremely simplistic. The argument essentially is, "I'm no robot marching down to the store to do advertising's bidding and therefore advertising doesn't affect me at all." This argument was made by Jacob Sullum, a senior editor at *Reason* magazine, in an editorial in *The New York Times.* Writing about "heroin chic," the advertising fad in the mid-1990s of using models who looked like heroin addicts, Sullum says, "Like you, I've seen . . . ads featuring sallow, sullen, scrawny youths. Not once have I had an overwhelming urge to rush out and buy some heroin." He concludes from this in-depth research that all critics of advertising are portraying "people not as independent moral agents but as mindless automatons," as if there were no middle ground between rushing out to buy heroin and being completely uninfluenced by the media images that surround us—or no possibility that disaffected teens are more vulnerable than middle-aged executives. After all, Sullum is *not* the target audience for heroin chic ads.

Of course, most of us feel far superior to the kind of person who would be affected by advertising. *We* are not influenced, after all. We are skeptical, even cynical . . . but ignorant (certainly not stupid, just uninformed). Advertising is familiar, but not known. The fact that we are surrounded by it, that we can sing the jingles and identify the models and recognize the logos, doesn't mean that we are educated about it, that we understand it. As Sut Jhally says, "To not be influenced by advertising would be to live outside of culture. No human being lives outside of culture."

Advertisers want us to believe that we are not influenced by ads. As Joseph Goebbels said, "This is the secret of propaganda: Those who are to be persuaded by it should be completely immersed in the ideas of the propaganda, without ever noticing that they are being immersed in it." So the advertisers sometimes play upon our cynicism. In fact, they co-opt our cynicism and our irony just as they have co-opted our rock music, our revolutions and movements for liberation, and our concern for the environment. In a current trend that I call "anti-advertising," the advertisers flatter us by insinuating that we are far too smart to be taken in by advertising. Many of these ads spoof the whole notion of image advertising. A scotch ad tells the reader "This is a glass of Cutty Sark. If you need to see a picture of a guy in an Armani suit sitting between two fashion models drinking it before you know it's right for you, it probably isn't."

And an ad for shoes says, "If you feel the need to be smarter and more articulate, read the complete works of Shakespeare. If you like who you are, here are your shoes." Another shoe ad, this one for sneakers, says, "Shoe buying rule number one: The image wears off after the first six miles." What a concept. By buying heavily advertised products, we can demonstrate that we are not influenced by advertising. Of course, this is not entirely new. Volkswagens were introduced in the 1960s with an anti-advertising campaign, such as the ad that pictured the car and the headline "Lemon." But such ads go a lot further these days, especially the foreign ones. A British ad for Easy jeans says, "We don't use sex to sell our jeans. We don't even screw you when you buy them." And French Connection UK gets away with a double-page spread that says "fcuk advertising."

A Sprite campaign plays on this cynicism. One commercial features teenagers partying on a beach while drinking a soft drink called Jooky. As the camera pulls back, we see that this is a fictional television commercial being watched by two teens, who open their own cans of Jooky and experience absolutely nothing. "Image is nothing. Thirst is everything," says the slogan. However, there is nothing in the ad about thirst—or taste, for that matter—or anything intrinsic to Sprite. The campaign is about nothing but image. Of course, what other way is there to sell sweetened, flavored carbonated water? If thirst is really everything, our best bet is water, and not high-priced bottled water either, such as Evian, which costs more than some champagne (no wonder that Evian backward spells "naive").

When Nike wanted to reach skateboarders, it had to overcome the fact that skateboarders are "about the most cynical bunch of consumers around" and often downright hostile to the idea of Nike entering the market. By putting a humorous spin on a powerful insight about how skateboarders want to be treated, Nike created the "What if we treated all athletes the way we treat skateboarders?" campaign, which has "won over skateboarders around the country and made them believe that Nike knows them and has the guts to defend them and their sport." Who cares if this is true—what is important is that skateboarders believe that it is true.

Some advertisers use what they chillingly call "viral communications" as a way to reach teenagers alienated from traditional forms of advertising. They use posters on construction sites and lampposts, sidewalk markings, and e-mail to infiltrate youth culture and cultivate the perception that their product is hot. One marketing consultant suggests picturing the mind as a combination lock and says, "One has to know what the particular stimuli are that are the 'clicks' heard by the inner mind of the target market and then allow the target market to open the lock so it is their own 'Aha!'—their own discovery, and so their own commitment."

Some ads make fun of high-pressure tactics. "Perhaps you'd consider buying one," says an ad for Saturn, and then in brackets below, "Sorry, we didn't mean to pressure you like that." Another car ad declares, "We're not trying to sell you this car. We're just letting you know it exists." An ad for sneakers tells us that "marketing is just hype." This is a bit like a man unbuttoning a woman's blouse, all the while telling her that she is far too smart to be seduced by the likes of him.

Cynicism is one of the worst effects of advertising. Cynicism learned from years of being exposed to marketing hype and products that never deliver the promised goods often carries over to other aspects of life. This starts early: A study of children done by researchers at Columbia University in 1975 found that heavy viewing of advertising led to cynicism, not only about advertising, but about life in general. The researchers found that "in most cultures, adolescents have had to deal with social hypocrisy and even with institutionalized lying. But today, TV advertising is stimulating *preadolescent* children to think about socially accepted hypocrisy. They may be too young to cope with such thoughts without permanently distorting their views of morality, society, and business." They concluded that "7- to 10-year-olds are strained by the very existence of advertising directed to them." These jaded children become the young people whose mantra is "whatever," who admire people like David Letterman (who has made a career out of taking nothing seriously), whose response to almost every experience is "been there, done that," "duh," and "do ya think?" Cynicism is not criticism. It is a lot easier than criticism. In fact, easy cynicism is a kind of naiveté. We need to be more critical as a culture and less cynical.

Cynicism deeply affects how we define our problems and envision their solutions. Many people exposed to massive doses of advertising both distrust every possible solution *and* expect a quick fix. There are no quick fixes to the problems our society faces today, but there are solutions to many of them. The first step, as always, is breaking through denial and facing the problems squarely. I believe it was James Baldwin who said, "Not everything that is faced can be changed, but nothing can be changed until it is faced." One of the things we need to face is that we and our children are indeed influenced by advertising.

Although some people, especially advertisers, continue to argue that advertising simply reflects the society, advertising does a great deal more than simply reflect cultural attitudes and values. Even some advertisers admit to this: Rance Crain of *Advertising Age* said great advertising "plays the tune rather than just dancing to the tune." Far from being a passive mirror of society, advertising is an effective and pervasive medium of influence and persuasion, and its influence is cumulative, often subtle, and primarily unconscious. Advertising performs much the same function in industrial society as myth performed in ancient and primitive societies. It is both a creator and perpetuator of the dominant attitudes, values, and ideology of the culture, the social norms and myths by which most people govern their behavior. At the very least, advertising helps to create a climate in which certain attitudes and values flourish and others are not reflected at all.

Advertising is not only our physical environment, it is increasingly our spiritual environment as well. By definition, however, it is only interested in materialistic values. When spiritual values or religious images show up in ads, it is only to appropriate them in order to sell us something. Sometimes this is very obvious. Eternity is a perfume by Calvin Klein. Infiniti is an automobile and Hydra Zen a moisturizer. Jesus is a brand of jeans. "See the light," says an ad for wool, while a face powder ad promises "an enlightening experience" and "absolute heaven." One car is "born again" and another promises to "energize your soul." In a full-page ad in *Advertising Age,* the online service Yahoo! proclaims, "We've got 60 million followers. That's more than some religions," but goes on to assure readers, "Don't worry. We're *not* a religion." When Pope John Paul II visited Mexico City in the winter of 1999, he could have seen a smiling image of himself on bags of Sabritas, a popular brand of potato chips, or a giant street sign showing him bowing piously next to a Pepsi logo with a phrase in Spanish that reads, "Mexico Always Faithful." In the United States, he could have treated himself to pope-on-a-rope soap.

An ad for kosher hot dogs pictures the Bible beside a hot dog with the caption, "If you liked the book, you'll love the hot dog." The campaign slogan is, "We answer to a higher authority." "God bless America," says a full-page newspaper ad featuring a little boy with his hand over his heart. The copy continues, "Where else can you find one company that offers phone, cable and internet service?" And an ad for garage doors says, "The legendary architect Mies van der Rohe said, 'God is in the details.' If that's so, could these be the pearly gates?"

Sometimes the allusion to the spiritual realm is more subtle, as in the countless alcohol ads featuring the bottle surrounded by a halo of light. Indeed products are often displayed, such as jewelry shining in a store window, as if they were sacred objects. Buy this and your life will be better. Advertising co-opts our sacred symbols and sacred language in order to evoke an immediate emotional response. Neil Postman refers to this as "cultural rape" that leaves us deprived of our most meaningful images.

But advertising's co-optation of spirituality goes much deeper than this. It is commonplace these days to observe that consumerism has become the religion of our time (with advertising its holy text), but the criticism usually stops short of what is most important, what is at the heart of the comparison. Advertising and religion share a belief in transformation and transcendence, but most religions believe that this requires work and sacrifice. In the world of advertising, enlightenment is achieved instantly by purchasing material goods. As James Twitchell, author of *Adcult USA,* says, "The Jolly Green Giant, the Michelin Man, the Man from Glad, Mother Nature, Aunt Jemima, Speedy Alka-Seltzer, the White Knight, and all their otherworldly kin are descendants of the earlier gods. What separates them is that they now reside in manufactured products and that, although earlier gods were invoked by fasting, prayer, rituals, and penance, the promise of purchase calls forth their modern ilk."

Advertising constantly promotes the core belief of American culture: that we *can* re-create ourselves, transform ourselves, transcend our circumstances—but with a twist. For generations Americans believed this could be achieved if we worked hard enough, like Horatio Alger. Today the promise is that we can change our lives instantly, effortlessly—by winning the lottery, selecting the right mutual fund, having a fashion makeover, losing weight, having tighter abs, buying the right car or soft drink. It is this belief that such transformation is possible that drives us to keep dieting, to buy more stuff, to read fashion magazines that give us the same information over and over again. Cindy Crawford's makeup is carefully described as if it could transform us into her. On one level, we know it won't—after all, most of us have tried this approach many times before. But on another level, we continue to try, continue to believe that this time it will be different. This American belief that we can transform ourselves makes advertising images much more powerful than they otherwise would be.

The focus of the transformation has shifted from the soul to the body. Of course, this trivializes and cheapens authentic spirituality and transcendence. But, more important, this junk food for the soul leaves us hungry, empty, malnourished. The emphasis on instant salvation is parodied in an ad from *Adbusters* for a product called Mammon, in which a man says, "I need a belief system that serves my needs right away" The copy continues, "Dean Sachs has a mortgage, a family and an extremely demanding job. What he doesn't need is a religion that complicates his life with unreasonable ethical demands." The ad ends with the words, "Mammon: Because you deserve to enjoy life—guilt free."

As advertising becomes more and more absurd, however, it becomes increasingly difficult to parody ads. There's not much of a difference between the ad for Mammon and the real ad for cruises that says "It can take several lifetimes to reach a state of inner peace and tranquillity. Or, it can take a couple of weeks." Of course, we know that a couple of weeks on a cruise won't solve our problems, won't bring us to a state of peace and enlightenment, but it is so tempting to believe that there is some easy way to get there, some ticket we can buy.

To be one of the "elect" in today's society is to have enough money to buy luxury goods. Of course, when salvation comes via the sale, it becomes important to display these goods. Owning a Rolex would not impress anyone who didn't know how expensive it is. A Rolex ad itself says the watch was voted "most likely to be coveted." Indeed, one of advertising's purposes is to create an aura for a product, so that other people will be impressed. As one marketer said recently in *Advertising Age*, "It's no fun to spend $100 on athletic shoes to wear to high school if your friends don't know how cool your shoes are."

Thus the influence of advertising goes way beyond the target audience and includes those who could never afford the product, who will simply be envious and impressed—perhaps to the point of killing someone for his sneakers or jacket, as has sometimes happened in our poverty-stricken neighborhoods. In the early 1990s the city health commissioner in Philadelphia issued a public health warning cautioning youths against wearing expensive leather jackets and jewelry, while in Milwaukee billboards depicted a chalk outline of a body and the warning, "Dress Smart and Stay Alive." Poor children in many countries knot the laces of their Nikes around their ankles to avoid having them stolen while they sleep.

Many teens fantasize that objects will somehow transform their lives, give them social standing and respect. When they wear a certain brand of sneaker or jacket, they feel, "This is important, therefore I am important." The brand gives instant status. No wonder they are willing, even eager, to spend money for clothes that advertise the brands. A *USA Today*-CNN-Gallup Poll found that 61 percent of boys and 44 percent of girls considered brand names on clothes "very important" or "somewhat important." As ten-year-old Darion Sawyer from Baltimore said, "People will tease you and talk about you, say you got on no-name shoes or say you shop at Kmart." Leydiana Reyes, an eighth-grader in Brooklyn, said, "My father always tells me I could buy two pairs of jeans for what you pay for Calvin Klein. I know that. But I still want Calvin Klein." And Danny Shirley, a fourteen-year-old in Santa Fe decked out in Tommy Hilfiger regalia, said, "Kids who wear Levi's don't really care about what they wear, I guess."

In the beginning, these labels were somewhat discreet. Today we see sweatshirts with fifteen-inch "Polo" logos stamped across the chest, jeans with four-inch "Calvin Klein" labels stitched on them, and a jacket with "Tommy Hilfiger" in five-inch letters across the back. Some of these outfits are so close to sandwich boards that I'm surprised people aren't paid to wear them. Before too long, the logo-free product probably will be the expensive rarity.

What people who wear these clothes are really buying isn't a garment, of course, but an *image.* And increasingly, an image is all that advertising has to sell. Advertising began centuries ago with signs in medieval villages. In the nineteenth century, it became more common but was still essentially designed to give people information about manufactured goods and services. Since the 1920s, advertising has provided less information about the product and focused more on the lives, especially the emotional lives, of the prospective consumers. This shift coincided, of course, with the increasing knowledge and acceptability of psychology, as well as the success of propaganda used to convince the population to support World War I.

Industrialization gave rise to the burgeoning ability of businesses to mass produce goods. Since it was no longer certain there would be a market for the goods, it became necessary not just to mass-produce the goods but to mass-produce markets hungry for the goods. The problem became not too little candy produced but not enough candy consumed, so it became the job of the advertisers to *produce consumers.* This led to an increased use of psychological research and emotional ploys to sell products. Consumer behavior became recognized as a science in the late 1940s.

As luxury goods, prepared foods, and nonessential items have proliferated, it has become crucial to create artificial needs in order to sell unnecessary products. Was there such a thing as static cling before there were fabric softeners and sprays? An [ad] says, "I never thought of my lips as a problem area until Andrea

Most brands in a given category are essentially the same. [...] two or three manufacturers. Blindfolded smokers or beer-drink[ers...] brand they are smoking or drinking, including their own. Wh[en...] select products primarily because of the image reflected in the.. advertising. Very few ads give us any real information at all. Sometimes it is impossible to tell what is being advertised. "This is an ad for the hair dryer," says one ad, featuring a woman lounging on a sofa. If we weren't told, we would never know. A joke made the rounds a while ago about a little boy who wanted a box of tampons so that he could effortlessly ride bicycles and horses, ski, and swim.

Almost all tobacco and alcohol ads are entirely image-based. Of course, when you're selling a product that kills people, it's difficult to give honest information about it. Think of all the cigarette ads that never show cigarettes or even a wisp of smoke. One of the most striking examples of image advertising is the very successful and long-running campaign for Absolut vodka. This campaign focuses on the shape of the bottle and the word "Absolut," as in "Absolut Perfection," which features the bottle with a halo. This campaign has been so successful that a coffee-table book collection of the ads published just in time for Christmas, the perfect gift for the alcoholic in your family, sold over 150,000 copies. Collecting Absolut ads is now a common pastime for elementary-school children, who swap them like baseball cards.

Adbusters magazine often parodies the Absolut ads. One such parody, headlined "Absolut Nonsense," pictures a bottle with the following copy on the label: "This superb marketing scheme has been carefully distilled for smoothness. . . . Although no one pays attention to advertising, after one year of this campaign, sales soared from 54,000 cases to 2.4 million cases." Since all vodka is essentially the same, all the campaign can sell us is image.

Even the advertisers admit to this. Carol Nathanson-Moog, an advertising psychologist, said, "More and more it seems the liquor industry has awakened to the truth. It isn't selling bottles or glasses or even liquor. It's selling fantasies." An article in *Advertising Age* went further, stating that "product image is probably the most important element in selling liquor. The trick for marketers is to project the right message in their advertisements to motivate those often motionless consumers to march down to the liquor store or bar and exchange their money for a sip of image."

"A sip of image." Just as simple films relying on crude jokes and violence are perfect for the global marketplace, since they require little translation, so is advertising that relies entirely on image. Bare breasts and phallic symbols are understood everywhere. As are the nude female buttocks featured in the Italian and German ads for similar worthless products to remedy the imaginary problem of cellulite. Unfortunately, such powerful imagery often pollutes the cultural environment. Certainly this is so with the Olivetti ad that ran in a Russian publica-

[handwritten margin note: which makes this ad odd, since it advertises the product of milk and not the brand — likely because milk is sold locally and this is a national campaign.]

tion. In case the image is too subtle for some, the copy says "Fax me." Sexism in advertising, although increasingly recognized as a problem, remains an ongoing global issue.

How does all this affect us? It is very difficult to do objective research about advertising's influence because there are no comparison groups, almost no people who have not been exposed to massive doses of advertising. In addition, research that measures only one point in time does not adequately capture advertising's real effects. We need longitudinal studies, such as George Gerbner's twenty-five-year study of violence on television.

The advertising industry itself can't prove that advertising works. While claiming to its clients that it does, it simultaneously denies it to the Federal Trade Commission whenever the subject of alcohol and tobacco advertising comes up. As an editorial in *Advertising Age* once said, "A strange world it is, in which people spending millions on advertising must do their best to prove that advertising doesn't do very much!" According to Bob Wehling, senior vice-president of marketing at Procter & Gamble, "We don't have a lot of scientific studies to support our belief that advertising works. But we have seen that the power of advertising makes a significant difference."

What research can most easily prove is usually what is least important, such as advertising's influence on our choice of brands. This is the most obvious, but least significant, way that advertising affects us. There are countless examples of successful advertising campaigns, such as the Absolut campaign, that have sent sales soaring. A commercial for I Can't Believe It's Not Butter featuring a sculptress whose work comes alive in the form of romance-novel hunk Fabio boosted sales about 17 percent. Tamagotchis—virtual pets in an egg—were introduced in the United States with a massive advertising campaign and earned $150 million in seven months. And Gardenburger, a veggie patty, ran a thirty-second spot during the final episode of *Seinfeld* and, within a week, sold over $2 million worth, a market share jump of 50 percent and more than the entire category sold in the same week the previous year. But advertising is more of an art than a science, and campaigns often fail. In 1998 a Miller beer campaign bombed, costing the company millions of dollars and offending a large segment of their customers. The 1989 Nissan Infiniti campaign, known as the "Rocks and Trees" campaign, was the first ever to introduce a car without showing it and immediately became a target for Jay Leno's monologues. And, of course, the Edsel, a car introduced by Ford with great fanfare in 1957, remains a universal symbol of failure.

The unintended effects of advertising are far more important and far more difficult to measure than those effects that are intended. The important question is not "Does this ad sell the product?" but rather "What else does this ad sell?" An ad for Gap khakis featuring a group of acrobatic swing dancers probably sold a lot of pants, which, of course, was the intention of the advertisers. But it also contributed to a rage for swing dancing. This is an innocuous example of advertising's powerful unintended effects. Swing dancing is not binge drinking, after all.

Advertising often sells a great deal more than products. It sells values, images, and concepts of love and sexuality, romance, success, and, perhaps most important, normalcy. To a great extent, it tells us who we are and who we should be. We are increasingly using brand names to create our identities. James Twitchell argues that the label of our shirt, the make of our car, and our favorite laundry detergent are filling the vacuum once occupied by religion, education, and our family name.

Even more important, advertising corrupts our language and thus influences our ability to think clearly. Critic and novelist George Steiner once talked with an interviewer about what he called "anti-language, that which is transcendentally annihilating of truth and meaning." Novelist Jonathan Dee, applying this concept to advertising, writes that "the harm lies not in the ad itself; the harm is in the exchange, in the collision of ad language, ad imagery, with other sorts of language that contend with it in the public realm. When Apple reprints an old photo of Gandhi, or Heineken ends its ads with the words 'Seek the Truth,' or Winston suggests that we buy cigarettes by proposing (just under the surgeon general's warning) that 'You have to appreciate authenticity in all its forms,' or Kellogg's identifies itself with the message 'Simple is Good,' these occasions color our contact with those words and images in their other, possibly less promotional applications." The real violence of advertising, Dee concludes, is that "words can be made to mean anything, which is hard to distinguish from the idea that words mean nothing." We see the consequences of this in much of our culture, from "art" to politics, that has no content, no connection between language and conviction. Just as it is often difficult to tell what product an ad is selling, so is it difficult to determine what a politician's beliefs are (the "vision thing," as George Bush so aptly called it, albeit unintentionally) or what the subject is of a film or song or work of art. As Dee says, "The men and women who make ads are not hucksters; they are artists with nothing to say, and they have found their form." Unfortunately, their form deeply influences all the other forms of the culture. We end up expecting nothing more.

This has terrible consequences for our culture. As Richard Pollay says, "Without a reliance on words and a faith in truth, we lack the mortar for social cohesion. Without trustworthy communication, there is no communion, no community, only an aggregation of increasingly isolated individuals, alone in the mass."

Advertising creates a worldview that is based upon cynicism, dissatisfaction, and craving. The advertisers aren't evil. They are just doing their job, which is to sell a product, but the consequences, usually unintended, are often destructive to individuals, to cultures, and to the planet. In the history of the world, there has never been a propaganda effort to match that of advertising in the twentieth century. More thought, more effort, and more money go into advertising than has gone into any other campaign to change social consciousness. The story that advertising tells is that the way to be happy, to find satisfaction—and the path to political freedom, as well—is through the consumption of material objects. And the major motivating force for social change throughout the world today is this belief that happiness comes from the market.

So, advertising has a greater impact on all of us than we generally realize. The primary purpose of the mass media is to deliver us to advertisers. Much of the information that we need from the media in order to make informed choices in our lives is distorted or deleted on behalf of corporate sponsors. Advertising is an increasingly ubiquitous presence in our lives, and it sells much more than products. We delude ourselves when we say we are not influenced by advertising. And we trivialize and ignore its growing significance at our peril.

Notes

[113] *"advertising's messages are inside"*: Jhally, 1998.

[113] *"almost half of all automobile crashes"*: According to the U.S. Department of Transportation, over 40 percent of all fatal traffic accidents in 1996 were alcohol-related. National Highway Traffic Safety Administration, 1999.

[114] *"'This is my best idea ever'"*: Sharkey, 1998, 2.

[114] *"Their next big idea"*: Rosenberg, 1999, A3.

[114] *"In England the legendary white cliffs of Dover"*: Liu. 1999, 15A.

[114] *"American consumers have recently joined Europeans"*: Mohl, 1999, A1. Also Tagliabue, 1997, 1.

[114] *"Conversations are interrupted"*: Bidlake, 1997, I49.

[114] *"beer companies have experimented"*: Twitchell, 1996, 62.

[114] *"The average American is exposed"*: Jacobson and Mazur, 1995, 13.

[114] *"Advertising makes up about 70 percent of our newspapers"*: Twitchell, 1996, 71.

[114] *"40 percent of our mail"*: McCarthy, 1990, F3.

[114] *"According to Rance Crain"*: Crain, 1997, 25.

[114] *"advertising is subliminal"*: Twitchell, 1996, 116.

[114] *"Grapevine Mills in Texas"*: Grunwald, 1997, A1.

[114] *"the world David Foster Wallace imagined"*: Wallace, 1996.

[115] *"In 1998 the museum's Monet show"*: Monet show sets world record, 1999, E2.

[115] *"Bob Dole plays on his defeat"*: Angier, 1996, 4E.

[115] *"Sarah Ferguson"*: Lewis, 1997, 22.

[115] *"And the Rolling Stones, those aging rebels"*: Pareles, 1998, D1.

[115] *"when Neil Young recorded a video"*: Twitchell, 1996, 21–22.

[115] *"Stars such as Harrison Ford"*: Angier, 1996, 4E.

[115] *"Antonio Banderas and Kevin Costner have pushed cars"*: Ads not infinitum, 1998, 10.

[115] *"Leonardo DiCaprio was paid $4 million"*: Wentz, 1998, 12.

[116] *"In 1983 Sylvester Stallone wrote"*: What do they have in common? 1994, 4. Also Levin, 1994, 1.

[116] *"New technology allows"*: Bauder, 1999, E6.

[116] *"Writer and cartoonist Mark O'Donnell"*: O'Donnell, 1995, 64.

[116] *"Diet Coke obtained the rights"*: Gleason, 1997, S1.

[116] *"In 1997 ABC and American Airlines":* Cheers & Jeers, 1997, 10.

[116] *"a character in the hit show* Baywatch": Logan, 1998, 8.

[116] *"'People have become less capable'":* Kakutani, 1997, 32.

[116] *"Steven Stark, another media critic":* Stark, 1990, 15.

[117] *"As Jerry Seinfeld, star of the show, said":* Mandese, 1995, 1.

[117] *"The 1997 James Bond film":* Arndofer, 1997, 24

[117] *"the 1998 hit movie* You've Got Mail": Maddox and Jensen, 1998, 48.

[117] *"And independent films are becoming as tight":* Hudes, 1998, 43.

[117] *"Hilfiger provided the wardrobe":* Lee, 1998, 2 ST.

[117] *"Maurice Malone":* Ryan, 1999, F1.

[118] *"Chris Gore, publisher of the Webzine* Film Threat": Lee, 1998, 2 ST.

[118] *"This argument was made by Jacob Sullum":* Sullum, 1997, A31.

[118] *"As Sut Jhally says":* Jhally, 1998.

[118] *"As Joseph Goebbels":* Goebbels, 1933, March 28. Quoted in Jacobson and Mazur, 1995, 15.

[119] *"no wonder that Evian backwards":* My thanks to Bob McCannon for this observation.

[119] *"When Nike wanted to reach skateboarders":* Nike, 1997, 54.

[119] *"Some advertisers use what they chillingly call":* Espen, 1999, 54–59.

[119] *"One marketing consultant suggests":* Crain, 1997, 25.

[120] *"A study of children done by researchers at Columbia University":* Bever, Smith, Bengen, and Johnson, 1975, 119.

[120] *"'7- to 10-year-olds are strained'":* Bever, Smith, Bengen, and Johnson, 1975, 120.

[120] *"Rance Crain of Advertising Age":* Crain, 1999, 23.

[121] *"When Pope John Paul II":* Chacon and Ribadeneira, 1999, A8.

[121] *"Neil Postman refers":* Curtis, 1998, 49.

[121] *"'The Jolly Green Giant'":* Twitchell, 1996, 30.

[122] *"'It's no fun to spend $100 on athletic shoes'":* Peppers and Rogers, 1997, 32.

[123] *"the city health commissioner in Philadelphia":* Worthington, 1992, 15.

[123] *"A* USA Today-*CNN-Gallup Poll":* Jacobson and Mazur, 1995, 26.

[123] *"Leydiana Reyes":* Leonhardt, 1997, 65.

[123] *"Danny Shirley":* Espen, 1999, 59.

[123] *"sweatshirts with fifteen-inch 'Polo' logos":* Ryan, 1996, D1.

[123] *"Consumer behavior":* Woods, 1995.

[124] *"Most shampoos":* Twitchell, 1996, 252.

[124] *"Blindfolded smokers":* Twitchell, 1996, 125.

[124] *"This campaign has been so successful":* Enrico, 1997, 4B.

[124] *"Collecting Absolut ads":* Tye, 1997, 1, 13.

[124] *"Carol Nathanson-Moog, an advertising psychologist":* Nathanson-Moog, 1984, 18.

[124] *"product image is probably the most important element":* Nathanson-Moog, 1984, 18.

[125] *"A strange world it is'":* Bernstein, 1978, August 7.

[125] *"According to Bob Wehling":* Crain, 1998, 24.

[125] *"A commercial for I Can't Believe It's Not Butter":* Haran, 1996, 12.

[125] *"Tamagotchis":* Goldner, 1998, S43.

[125] *"And Gardenburger":* Gardenburger hits the spot, 1998, 17.

[125] *"In 1998 a Miller beer campaign":* Crain, 1998, 24.

[125] *"The 1989 Nissan Infiniti":* Horton, 1996, S28.

[125] *"the Edsel":* Horton, 1996, S30.

[125] *"An ad for Gap khakis":* Cortissoz, 1998, A10.

[126] *"James Twitchell argues":* University of Florida news release, quoted by Orlando, 1999, http://www.sciencedaily.com/releases/1999/05/990518114815.htm.

[126] *"Critic and novelist George Steiner":* Dee., 1999, 65–66.

[126] *"As Richard Pollay":* Pollay, 1986.

[126] *"there has never been a propaganda effort":* Jhally, 1998.

Works Cited

Ads not infinitum (1998, December 14). *People,* 10–11.

Angier, N. (1996, November 24). Who needs this ad most? *New York Times,* 4E.

Arndofer, J. B. (1997, July 28). 007's sponsor blitz. *Advertising Age,* 24.

Bauder, D. (1999, March 31). Ads creep into TV content. *Boston Globe,* E6.

Bernstein, S. (1978, August 7). Do ads promote spirited imbibing? *Advertising Age,* 14.

Bever, T. G., Smith, M. L., Bengen, B., and Johnson, T. G. (1975). Young viewers' troubling response to TV ads. *Harvard Business Review,* 53, 109–20.

Bidlake, S. (1997, September). Commercials support free phone calls. *Advertising Age International,* I47, I49.

Chacon, R. and Ribadeneira, D. (1999, January 22), *Boston Globe,* A1, A10.

Cheers and Jeers (1997, June 21). *TV Guide,* 10.

Cortissoz, A. (1998, July 25). For young people, swing's the thing. *Boston Globe,* A1, A10.

Crain, R. (1997, June 9). Who knows what ads lurk in the hearts of consumers? The inner mind knows. *Advertising Age,* 25.

Crain, R. (1998, November 30). Miller's horrendous mistake example of how little we know. *Advertising Age,* 24.

Crain, R. (1999, January 18). When ads don't produce sales, watch the (phony) excuses fly. *Advertising Age,* 23.

Curtis, J. (1998, May/June). Wait a minute, Mr. Postman. *Applied Arts Magazine,* 49–54.

Dee, J. (1999, January). But is it advertising? *Harper's,* 61–72.

Enrico, D. (1997, September 15). Absolut vodka's ad spots withstand the test of time. *USA Today,* 4B.

Espen, H. (1999, March 21). Levi's blues. *New York Times Magazine,* 54–59.

Gardenburger hits the spot (1998, September 14). *Advertising Age,* 17.

Gleason, M. (1997, March 17). Events & promotions. *Advertising Age,* S1.

Goldner, B. (1998, June 29). Tamagotchi. *Advertising Age,* S43.

Grunwald, M. (1997, December 9). Megamall sells stimulation. *Boston Globe,* A1, A26.

Haran, L. (1996, March 18). Madison Avenue visits dream land. *Advertising Age,* 12.

Horton, C. (1996, January 8). Admen lament: If only we could take it back. *Advertising Age,* S28, S30, S48.

Hudes, K. (1998, November 15). Independent film, but with a catch: a corporate logo. *New York Times,* 43.

Jacobson, M. F. and Mazur, L. A. (1995). *Marketing Madness: A survival guide for a consumer society.* Boulder, CO: Westview Press.

Jhally, S. (1998). Advertising and the end of the world (a video). Northampton, MA: Media Education Foundation.

Kakutani, M. (1997, November 9). Bananas for rent. *New York Times Magazine,* 32.

Lee, L. (1998, May 31). Pass the popcorn (and the khakis). *New York Times,* 2 ST.

Leonhardt, D. (1997, June 30). Hey kid, buy this! *Business Week,* 61–67.

Levin, M. (1994, May 19). Tobacco firm paid $950,000 to place cigarettes in films. *Los Angeles Times,* 1.

Lewis, M. (1997, February 9). Royal scam. *New York Times Magazine,* 22.

Liu, E. (1999, March 25). Remember when public space didn't carry brand names? *USA Today,* 15A.

Logan, M. (1998, April 18). A big step for *Baywatch. TV Guide,* 8.

Maddox, K. and Jensen, J. (1998, October 5). Online marketers race for tie-ins with *You've Got Mail. Advertising Age,* 48.

Mandese, J. (1995, September 25). Star presenter of the year. *Advertising Age,* 1, 6.

McCarthy, C. (1990, November 11). In thingdom, laying waste our powers. *Washington Post,* F3.

Mohl, B. (1999, January 13). Lend them your ear, and your call is free. *Boston Globe,* A1, A10.

Monet show sets world record (1999, February 2). *Boston Globe,* E2.

Nathanson-Moog, C. (1984, July 26). Brand personalities undergo psychoanalysis. *Advertising Age,* 18.

Nike (1997). *30 years of Effie.* New York: American Marketing Association.

O'Donnell, M. (1995, January 22). From the notebooks of a genius. *New York Times Magazine,* 64.

Orlando, S. (1999, May 19). A material world: Defining ourselves by consumer goods. *http://www.sciencedaily.com/releases/1999/05/990518114815.htm.*

Pareles, J. (1998, February 8). Edging off rock's high road. *New York Times,* D1, D30.

Peppers, D. and Rogers, M. (1997, June 2). Marketer-customer dialogue comes to fore. *Advertising Age,* 32.

Pollay, R. W. (1986, April). The distorted mirror: reflections on the unintended consequences of advertising. *Journal of Marketing,* vol. 50, 18–36.

Rosenberg, A. S. (1999, February 1). Ad ideas etched in sand. *Boston Globe,* A3.

Ryan, S. (1996, December 18). They're not afraid to be labeled. *Boston Globe,* D1, D5.

Ryan, S. C. (1999, May 26). Fusion is the fashion. *Boston Globe,* F1, F6.

Sharkey, J. (1998, July 5). Beach-blanket babel: Another reason to stay at the pool. *New York Times,* 2.

Stark, S. (1990, July 23). Cops are tops—cowboys out. *Boston Globe,* 15.

Sullum, J. (1997, May 23). Victims of everything. *New York Times,* A31.

Tagliabue, J. (1997, September 28). Europe offering free calls, but first a word from . . . *New York Times,* 1, 8.

Twitchell, J. B. (1996). *Adcult USA: The triumph of advertising in American culture.* New York: Columbia University Press.

Tye, L. (1997, January 5). For some, it's an Absolut mania. *Boston Globe,* 1, 13.

Wallace, D. F. (1996). *Infinite jest.* Boston: Little Brown.

Wentz, L. (1998, May 11). Global village. *Advertising Age International,* 12.

What do they have in common? (1994, Summer). *Tobacco-Free Youth Reporter,* 3–4.

Woods, G. B. (1995). *Advertising and marketing to the new majority.* Belmont, CA: Wadsworth.

Worthington, R. (1992, January 19). 'Cultural psychosis' defense in teen fashion killing. *Chicago Tribune,* 15.

Reading Bodies

Susan Bordo

For sometime during the last seven years, we seem to have entered an unabashed Reign of the Ram. Fashion ads today routinely feature men in underwear who are amazingly endowed ("He looks like he has *two* penises in there!" a student of mine said of one), their poses directing the viewer's attention to their crotches. Some ads show men cupping their genitals; in others, the penis seems to be fully erect. *Playgirl,* clearly doing double duty for both gay and straight readers, has become a cornucopia of humongous male organs of every race, class, and age. Rap musicians (and, aping them, Madonna) have made crotch grabbing a common cultural code for sexual power and virility. Surgical phalloplasty is big business today—and, by the way, has provided John Bobbitt with a new, happier ending to his saga. Bobbit has not only been re-membered but enhanced ("It's like a beer can," he boasted after the operation). So will someone send a thank-you card to Lorena already?

This is not the first time in history that penises have been culturally visible. Modernity has been especially squeamish, it seems, about the male body. Until the creation of trousers at the beginning of the eighteenth century, men's pants were more like what we call "tights," through which the shape of the genitals could often be clearly discerned. However, as Anne Hollander points out in *Sex and Suits,* the simulation or suggestion of male nakedness had a very different significance then than it does today. In 1998, we look at the frontal bulges of fashion models clad in clinging jersey briefs and think: "Sex." From the early Renaissance

Susan Bordo is a professor of English and women's studies at the University of Kentucky. Her books and many articles on the relation between the body and consumer culture have established her as a leading authority on issues of masculinity and femininity. Her books include *The Male Body: A New Look at Men in Public and Private* (1999), *Twilight Zones: The Hidden Life of Cultural Images from Plato to O.J.* (1997), and *Unbearable Weight: Feminism, Western Culture, and the Body* (1993).

to the eighteenth century, it was just the opposite. Revealing the basic outline of male legs and genitals while covering those parts of a woman's body with voluminous materials, drapes, hoops, and the like meant the male body was a more utilitarian, "authentic," no-nonsense, *truthful* body, while the woman's body was an object of artifice, fantasy, and illusion, her clothing designed to stimulate the sexual imagination rather than represent her anatomy accurately.

The example shows that exploring attitudes toward clothing, nakedness, and masculinity means recognizing their historical and cultural variability. It also suggests that we need to think about the body not only as a physical entity—which it assuredly is—but also as a cultural form that carries *meaning* with it. The notion that bodies are just material things, collections of instincts, mechanical processes put in place by God the watchmaker, ticking away in pretty much the same way from culture to culture, era to era, goes back to the philosopher Descartes. Darwinian science profoundly altered the Cartesian picture by showing that the body's mechanisms aren't timeless and unchanging, but have evolved dramatically over time. What's still missing from this picture, though—and what was ultimately supplied in the twentieth century—is the recognition that when we look at bodies (including our own in the mirror), we don't just see biological nature at work, but values and ideals, differences and similarities that *culture* has "written," so to speak, on those bodies.

What this means is that the body doesn't carry only DNA, it also carries human history with it. Biologically, a penis is a penis (more or less). But as Hollander's research shows, a seventeenth-century spectator would have seen something very different than we do when confronted with the sight of a man in genital-revealing tights. Another example of how history and culture affect the way we see bodies is provided by the Jockey ad on the next page. The two parts to the ad are parallel—five good-looking men (doctors, surgeons, and physical therapists) and five good-looking women (riders, ranchers, and cowgirls) with their pants around their ankles, revealing their Jockeys underneath. Some features of these ads are pretty obvious. The open expressions on the women's faces versus the mostly serious, semi-challenging male stares; the men's "feet planted firm" posture versus the women's flirtatiously bent knees—these are standard stuff in the depiction of men and women's bodies. As for what's "new"—Jockey clearly means to tweak the cultural stereotypes of doctors and cowboys with its unexpectedly muscular, macho docs and curvy, feminine ranchers. And to convey a message of equality too, by having the women and men in equal states of undress.

The thing is, they're *not* in equal states of undress—because pants-around-the-ankles convey something different on the bodies of the men than they do on the bodies of the women. The men's genitals in the Jockey ad are much more visible than the women's. Actually, the women, by contemporary standards, are hardly undressed at all. Yet somehow, they *seem* more exposed than the men. It's those pants around the ankles. Mentally remove them—or just cover them up with your hands—and you get a very different feeling from the ad. With the men, on the other hand, the "dropped trou"—the expression seems appropriate for them, but not for the girls—barely signify at all. Cover them up or leave them in, the guys' bodies project much the same confident, slightly challenging machismo either way. Their bodies are very sexy. But they do not seem stripped or exposed.

Partly, this is because we read the bodies in the Jockey ad against the backdrop of depictions of male and female bodies that we are used to, and until recently, the conventions governing the two sexes have been very different. In countless movies, we've grown used to seeing women take off their clothes for sex, or to display themselves erotically, or to be unsuspectingly spied on. The act of getting undressed is an act of uncovering, exposing; a secret sexual self is revealed. In contrast, men, until very recently, would only be shown undressing with some "utilitarian" fiction written into the scene—changing from business suits into sweats, putting on athletic uniforms, and so on. Anne Hollander would probably argue that all of this has to do with the lingering of those old ideas about the utilitarian form of the male body. And when you examine the accessories that have been included in the Jockey ads, it seems that there's something to that. The docs seem ready to get to work. They've got their stethoscopes around their necks, their surgical masks ready to tie on; all they need to do is pull up those pants, whip out that knife, and start bossing the nurses around. The cowgirls, in contrast, are ill equipped to round up anything beyond male winks. (Those hats are cute, though.)

There's a more unnerving piece to this too. With women, pants-around-the-ankles subtly recalls movie scenes of rape (think Jodie Foster on that pinball machine in *The Accused*) and the discovered bodies of female murder victims. Such images are not part of a feminist's paranoid delusion, but belong to a common lexicon of cultural motifs that we are almost all familiar with and are very difficult (if not impossible) to erase from the unconscious. The fact that the models in the Jockey ad are *not* coming on like sexual temptresses but have bright, sunny smiles only enhances the lascivious juxtaposition between their own definition of themselves (as active, happy girls) and the perspective of the viewer, in whose eyes they seem vulnerable, unknowingly exposed. You feel, in some subliminal corner of the brain, that while the men have "dropped trou" themselves someone has pulled those girls' pants down (or asked them to pull them down, or is peeping around the corner). Yes, I know the *actual* models don't feel that way at all . . . and would probably have a good hoot if they read this too. I'm not talking about how the models *feel* but about elements suggested in the representation they posed for.

You may not see the same things in this ad that I do. Representations of the body have a history, but so too do viewers, and they bring that history—both personal and cultural—to their perception and interpretation. Different viewers may see different things. In pointing to certain elements in ads, or movies, or fashion, I'm not ignoring the differences in how people may see things, but deliberately trying to direct your attention to what I see as significant. I'm making an argument, and you may or may not find it convincing. You might think—as my students sometimes do—that I'm "making too much" of certain elements. Or your own background, values, "ways of seeing" may enable you to discern things that I do not. Or it may be that even as I offer my ideas, the cultural context has already begun to shift in ways that answer my interpretation or make it obsolete. Cultural interpretation is an ongoing, always incomplete process, and no one gets the final word.

Hollander's insights, for example, while useful in interpreting some aspects of the Jockey ad, ultimately come up against the fact that we *do* live in the second half of the twentieth century, and despite the utilitarian accessorizing, the doctors' discernible genitals, no less than the girls' body parts, *are* the stuff of sex. With all the naked bodies around nowadays, this sensibility may ultimately reach its historical limit too, as we get jaded and bored with all the (mostly plastic) flesh around. But for now, as a general rule, the more a piece of clothing outlines and reveals what's underneath, the "sexier" it is to our cultural eyes.

The kind of sex the docs project is different, though, than the sex the cowgirls project. Nowadays, men—the Chippendales, for example, and men in ads as well—*do* strip for erotic display. But when they do so, they tend to present their bodies aggressively and so rarely seem truly exposed. Being undressed does not necessarily mean being naked. Most men in underwear ads today . . . Well, you wouldn't want to meet one coming round a dark corner. When, in the 1996 French film *Ridicule,* an aristocrat took his penis out of his pants and pissed in the lap of another man, he seemed more to be whipping out a weapon than a body part. And what can a viewer's eyes do but admire the bulging bundles and gleaming muscles of the Chippendales and their ilk? Their bodies are a kind of natural armor. Being "stripped," it seems—much more than merely being undressed—has been anathema to masculinity.

Work Cited

Hollander, Anne. (1994). *Sex and Suits: The Evolution of Modern Dress.* New York: Kodansha International.

Hard Bodies

Stuart Ewen

Writing in 1934, the sociologists George A. Lundberg, Mirra Komarovsky, and Mary Alice McInerny addressed the question of "leisure" in the context of an emerging consumer society. Understanding the symbiotic relationship between mass-production industries and a consumerized definition of leisure, they wrote of the need for society to achieve a compatibility between the worlds of work and daily life. "The ideal to be sought," they proposed, "is undoubtedly the gradual obliteration of the psychological barrier which today distinguishes work from leisure."[1]

That ideal has been realized in the daily routine of Raymond H——, a thirty-four-year-old middle-management employee of a large New York City investment firm. He is a living cog in what Felix Rohatyn has termed the new "money culture," one in which "making things" no longer counts; "making money," as an end in itself, is the driving force.[2] His days are spent at a computer terminal, monitoring an endless flow of numerical data.

When his workday is done, he heads toward a local health club for the relaxation of a "workout." Three times a week this means a visit to the Nautilus room, with its high, mirrored walls, and its imposing assembly line of large, specialized "machines." The workout consists of exercises for his lower body and for his upper body, twelve "stations" in all. As he moves from Nautilus machine to Nautilus machine, he works on his hips, buttocks, thighs, calves, back, shoulders, chest, upper arms, forearms, abdomen, and neck, body part by body part.

Stuart Ewen is a professor of media studies at Hunter College and of sociology and history at the City University of New York Graduate Center. He is a widely recognized authority on mass-mediated culture and is the author of a number of books on this subject, including *All Consuming Images: The Politics of Style in Contemporary Culture* (1988), *Channels of Desire: Mass Images and the Shaping of American Consciousness* (with Elizabeth Ewen, 1982), and *Captains of Consciousness: Advertising and the Social Roots of the Consumer Culture* (1976). Bill Moyers drew heavily upon Ewen's work in his PBS series, *The Public Mind*.

At the first station, Raymond lies on the "hip and back machine," making sure to align his hip joints with the large, polished, kidney shaped cams which offer resistance as he extends each leg downward over the padded roller under each knee. Twelve repetitions of this, and he moves on to the "hip abduction machine," where he spreads his legs outward against the padded restraints that hold them closed. Then leg extensions on the "compound leg machine" are followed by leg curls on the "leg curl machine." From here, Raymond H—— proceeds to the "pullover/torso arm machine," where he begins to address each piece of his upper body. After a precise series of repetitions on the "double chest machine," he completes his workout on the "four-way neck machine."

While he alternates between different sequential workouts, and different machines, each session is pursued with deliberate precision, following exact instructions.

Raymond H—— has been working on his body for the past three years, ever since he got his last promotion. He is hoping to achieve the body he always wanted. Perhaps it is fitting that this quintessential, single, young, urban professional—whose life has become a circle of work, money culture, and the cultivation of an image—has turned himself, literally, into a piece of work. If the body ideal he seeks is *lean,* devoid of fatty tissue, it is also *hard.* "Soft flesh," once a standard phrase in the American erotic lexicon, is now—within the competitive, upscale world he inhabits—a sign of failure and sloth. The hard shell is now a sign of achievement, visible proof of success in the "rat race." The goal he seeks is more about *looking* than *touching.*

To achieve his goal, he approaches his body piece by piece; with each machine he performs a discrete task. Along the way he also assumes the job of inspector, surveying the results of each task in the mirrors that surround him. The division of labor, the fragmentation of the work process, and the regulating function of continual measurement and observation—all fundamental to the principles of "scientific management"—are intrinsic to this form of recreation. Like any assembly line worker, H—— needs no overall knowledge of the process he is engaged in, only the specific tasks that comprise that process. "You don't have to understand *why* Nautilus equipment works," writes bodybuilder Mike Mentzer in the forward to one of the most widely read Nautilus manuals. "With a tape measure in hand," he promises, you will see what happens."[3]

The body ideal Raymond H—— covets is, itself, an aestheticized tribute to the broken-wn work processes of the assembly line. "I'm trying to get better definition," H—— says. into Nautilus because it lets me do the necessary touch-up work. Free weights [barbells] ood for building up mass, but Nautilus is great for definition."[4] By "definition," H—— is ying the lingo of the gym, a reference to a body surface upon which each muscle, each group, appears segmented and distinct. The perfect body is one that ratifies the frag-process of its construction, one that mimics—in flesh—the illustrative qualities of a drawing, or an anatomy chart.

Surveying his work in the mirror, H—— admires the job he has done on his broad, high pectorals, but is quick to note that his quadriceps "could use some work." This ambivalence, this mix of emotions, pursues him each time he comes for a workout, and the times in between. He is never quite satisfied with the results. The excesses of the weekend-past invariably leave their blemish. An incorrectly struck pose reveals an overmeasure of loose skin, a sign of weakness in the shell. Despite all efforts, photogenic majesty is elusive.

The power of the photographic idiom, in his mind's eye, is reinforced, again and again, by the advertisements and other media of style visible everywhere. The ideal of the perfectly posed machine—the cold, hard body in response—is paraded, perpetually, before his eyes and ours. We see him, or her, at every glance.

An advertisement for home gym equipment promises a "Body By Soloflex." Above is the silent, chiaroscuro portrait of a muscular youth, his torso bare, his elbows reaching high, pulling a thin-ribbed undershirt up over his head, which is faceless, covered by shadow. His identity is situated below the neck, an instrumentally achieved study in brawn. The powerful expanse of his chest and back is illuminated from the right side. A carefully cast shadow accentuates the paired muscle formations of his abdominal wall. The airbrush has done its work as well, effecting a smooth, standardized, molded quality, what John Berger has termed "the skin without a biography." A silent, brooding hulk of a man, he is the unified product of pure engineering. His image is a product of expensive photographic technology, and expensive technical expertise. His body—so we are informed—is also a technical achievement. He has reached this captured moment of perpetual perfection on a "machine that fits in the corner" of his home. The machine, itself, resembles a stamping machine, one used to shape standardized, industrial products. Upon this machine, he has routinely followed instructions for "twenty-four traditional iron pumping exercises, each correct in form and balance." The privileged guidance of industrial engineering, and the mindless obedience of work discipline, have become legible upon his body; yet as it is displayed, it is nothing less than a thing of beauty, a transcendent aspiration.

This machine-man is one of a generation of desolate, finely tuned loners who have cropped up as icons of American style. Their bodies, often lightly oiled to accentuate definition, reveal their inner mechanisms like costly, open-faced watches, where one can see the wheels and gears moving inside, revealing—as it were—the magic of time itself. If this is eroticism, it is one tuned more to the mysteries of technology than to those of the flesh.

In another magazine advertisement, for Evian spring water from France, six similarly anatomized figures stand across a black and white two-page spread. From the look of things, each figure (three men and three women) has just completed a grueling workout, and four of them are partaking of Evian water as part of their recovery. The six are displayed in a lineup, each one displaying a particularly well-developed anatomical region. These are the new icons of beauty, precisely defined, powerful machines. Below, on the left, is the simple caption: "Revival of the Fittest." Though part of a group, each figure is conspicuously alone.

Once again, the modern contours of power, and the structures of work discipline, are imprinted upon the body. In a world of rampant careerism, self-absorption is a rule of thumb. If the division of labor sets each worker in competition with every other, here that fragmentation is aestheticized into the narcissism of mind and body.

Within this depiction, sexual equality is presented as the meeting point between the anorectic and the "nautilized." True to gender distinctions between evanescent value and industrial work discipline, the three women are defined primarily by contour, by the thin lines that their willowy bodies etch upon the page. Although their muscles are toned, they strike poses that suggest pure, disembodied form. Each of the men, situated alternately between the women, gives testimony on behalf of a particular fraction of segmented flesh: abdomen, shoulders and upper arms, upper back. In keeping with the assembly line approach to muscle building, each man's body symbolizes a particular station within the labor process.

Another ad, for a health and fitness magazine, contains an alarmingly discordant statement: "Today's women workers are back in the sweat shop." There is a basis to this claim. In today's world, powerful, transnational corporations search the globe looking for the cheapest labor they can find. Within this global economy, more and more women—from Chinatown to Taiwan—are employed at tedious, low-paying jobs, producing everything from designer jeans to computer parts.

Yet this is not the kind of sweatshop the ad has in mind. The photographic illustration makes this clear. Above the text, across the two-page color spread, is the glistening, heavily muscled back of a woman hoisting a chrome barbell. Her sweat is self-induced, part of a "new woman" life-style being promoted in *Sport* magazine, "the magazine of the new vitality." Although this woman bears the feminine trademark of blonde, braided hair, her body is decidedly masculine, a new body aesthetic in the making. Her muscles are not the cramped, biographically induced muscles of menial labor. Hers is the brawn of the purely symbolic, the guise of the middle-class "working woman."

While the text of the advertisement seems to allude to the real conditions of female labor, the image transforms that truth into beauty, rendering it meaningless. Real conditions are copywritten into catchy and humorous phrases. The harsh physical demands of women's work are reinterpreted as regimented, leisure-time workouts at a "health club." Real sweat is reborn as photogenic body oil.

The migration of women into the social structures of industrial discipline is similarly aestheticized in an ad for Jack LaLanne Fitness Centers. A black and white close-up of a young woman wrestling with a fitness "machine" is complemented by the eroticized grimace on her face. Once again, the chiaroscuro technique accentuates the straining muscles of her arms.

The high-contrast, black and white motif may also suggest the "night and day" metamorphosis that will occur when one commits to this particular brand of physical discipline.

In large white letters, superimposed across the shadowy bottom of the photograph, are the words: "Be taut by experts." With a clever play on words the goal of education moves from the mind to the body. Muscle power is offered as an equivalent substitute for brain power. No problem. In the search for the perfectly regulated self, it is implicit that others will do the thinking. This woman, like the Soloflex man, is the product of pure engineering, of technical expertise:

> We were building bodies back when you were building blocks. . . . We know how to perfectly balance your workout between swimming, jogging, aerobics and weight training on hundreds of the most advanced machines available. . . . Sure it may hurt a little. But remember. *You only hurt the one you love* [emphasis added].

These advertisements, like Raymond H——'s regular visits to the Nautilus room, are part of the middle-class bodily rhetoric of the 1980s. Together they mark a culture in which self-absorbed careerism, conspicuous consumption, and a conception of *self* as an object of competitive display have fused to become the preponderant symbols of achievement. The regulated body is the nexus where a cynical ethos of social Darwinism, and the eroticism of raw power, meet. Yet despite the currency of this body ideal, the roots of the regulated body have been deeply implanted in the terrain of Western culture since the Enlightenment.

Within the dialectic of Enlightenment thinking, two different but interwoven conceptions of human perfectionism emerged. The first stood at the emancipatory heart of democratic movements and ideals. It held that with Reason, and through scientific, secular education ("improvement"), people could dismantle the repressive, unenlightened hierarchies of the past and become the masters of their own lives. Such thinking spurred ideas of cooperative commonwealth and individual liberty.

Yet the rise of commercial power in the Age of Reason also fueled more instrumental notions of human transformation. While likewise making reference to the touchstones of Reason and Science, these ideas suggested that the rational perfection of an individual could be engineered by another, armed with a knowledge of scientific law, and employing modern techniques of social management. Whereas the bodies within the egalitarian tradition of perfection were those of free individuals, this latter tradition gave rise to the notion of malleable bodies, trainable or teachable for whatever purpose. If the first tradition sparked ideas of liberation among the underclasses, the dark side of Enlightenment was possessed by ideas of controlling and shaping them.

From the mid-eighteenth century on, the rise of this managerial sensibility began to be imprinted on more and more bourgeois social institutions. Particularly where the social organization of power was essential, Michel Foucault has argued, "a policy of coercions that act upon the body, a calculated manipulation of its elements, its gestures, its behaviour," began to be employed.[5]

An example of this, discussed by Foucault, may be found in the military, in the body of the soldier. In the early seventeenth century, he relates, the "ideal figure of the soldier" was still conceived in reference to a great chain of being. His military bearing was understood to be inborn, inseparable from his identity as a person within the social order:

> To begin with, the soldier was someone who could be recognized from afar; he bore certain signs: the natural signs of his strength and his courage, the marks, too, of his pride; his body was the blazon of his strength and valour; and although it is true that he had to learn the profession of arms little by little—generally in actual fighting—movements like marching and attitudes like the bearing of the head belonged for the most part to a bodily rhetoric of honour; "The signs for recognizing those most suited to this profession are a lively, alert manner, an erect head, a taut stomach, broad shoulders, long arms, strong fingers, a small belly, thick thighs, slender legs and dry feet, because a man of such a figure could not fail to be agile and strong.[6]

The body of this soldier bore the marks of muscular strength, but it was also implicit that this strength was intrinsic to the man. He was motivated, from within, by natural courage and pride, not by the techniques of externally imposed discipline. His "strength and valour" were signs of his elite status among men.

By the end of the eighteenth century this had changed. With the consolidation of national sovereignty, the development of a world market, and the spread of colonialism, the military requirements of Europe escalated. The recruitment of armies from among the "masses" necessitated a technique for producing soldiers. Under the rubric of this priority, Foucault argues, the human body entered "a machinery of power that explores it, breaks it down and rearranges it." The notion of the born soldier gave way to that of *basic training:*

> By the late eighteenth century, the soldier has become something that can be made; out of a formless clay, an inapt body, the machine required can be constructed; posture is gradually corrected; a calculated constraint runs slowly through each part of the body, mastering it, making it pliable, ready at all times, turning silently into the automatism of habit; in short, one has "got rid of the peasant' and given him "the air of a soldier" (ordinance of 20 March 1764). Recruits become accustomed to "holding their heads high and erect; to standing upright, without bending the back, to sticking out the belly, throwing out the chest and throwing back the shoulders; and, to help them acquire the habit, they are given this position while standing against a wall in such a way that the heels, the thighs, the waist and the shoulders touch it, as

also do the backs of the hands, as one turns the arms outwards, without moving them away from the body. . . . Likewise, they will be taught never to fix their eyes on the ground, but to look straight at those they pass . . . to remain motionless until the order is given, without moving the head, the hands or the feet . . . lastly to march with a bold step, with knee and ham taut, on the points of the feet, which should face outwards" (ordinance of 20 March 1764).[7]

Foucault's discussion, here, focuses on the changing conception of the soldier, but the implications of this discussion shed light on changes within an ever-widening sphere of social activities from the eighteenth century onward. In the routinization of labor, in the rote teaching of schoolchildren, in the measured strides of fashion models, even in the detailed positional instructions of exercise tapes or sex manuals, Foucault's "well-trained regiments" can be heard marching in the distance.

Against this historical panorama, the monitored, regulated and segmented body ideal goes against its own claims for itself. On the aesthetic plane of the commercial culture this bodily motif suggests self-motivated, individual power. But its historic roots and its method of construction ("bodybuilding") reveal a person who is, to quote Foucault, the "object and target of power."[8] In their aestheticization, the modern structures of power are turned on their heads, posed as symbols of a *free individual.* In the world of style, where images seem to float, disconnected from the world that produces them, mastery can be confused with obedience.

Notes

[1] George A. Lundberg et al., *Leisure: A Suburban Study* (1934), p. 3.

[2] *New York Times,* 3 June 1987, p. A27.

[3] Ellington Darden, *The Nautilus Bodybuilding Book* (1986), pp. viii–ix.

[4] Style Project, interview I-13.

[5] Michel Foucault, *Discipline and Punish* (1977), p. 138.

[6] *Ibid.,* p. 135.

[7] *Ibid.,* pp. 135–36, 138.

[8] *Ibid.,* p. 136.

Understanding the Text

1. According to Ewen, in what ways does Raymond H____'s "workout" replicate "the processes of the assembly line"?

2. One ad that Ewen examines, for Jack LaLanne Fitness Centers, urges readers to "Be taut by experts." How does Ewen interpret the pun on "taut"?

3. On the surface, bodybuilding represents "self-motivated, individual power," Ewen suggests. But in light of its "historic roots," what else does he think it represents?

Getting Dirty

Mark Crispin Miller

We are outside a house, looking in the window, and this is what we see: a young man, apparently nude and half-crazed with anxiety, lunging toward the glass. "Gail!" he screams, as he throws the window open and leans outside, over a flowerbox full of geraniums: "The most important shower of my life, and you switch deodorant soap!" He is, we now see, only half-naked, wearing a towel around his waist; and he shakes a packaged bar of soap—"Shield"—in one accusing hand. Gail, wearing a blue man-tailored shirt, stands outside, below the window, clipping a hedge. She handles this reproach with an ease that suggests years of contempt. "Shield is better," she explains patiently, in a voice somewhat deeper than her husband's. "It's extra strength." (Close-up of the package in the husband's hand, Gail's efficient finger gliding along beneath the legend, THE EXTRA STRENGTH DEODORANT SOAP.) "Yeah," whimpers Mr. Gail, "but my first call on J. J. Siss [sic], the company's *toughest customer,* and now *this*!" Gail nods with broad mock-sympathy, and stands firm: "Shield fights odor better, so you'll feel *cleaner,*" she assures her husband, who darts away with a jerk of panic, as Gail rolls her eyes heavenward and gently shakes her head, as if to say, "What a half-wit!"

Cut to our hero, as he takes his important shower. No longer frantic, he now grins down at himself, apparently delighted to be caked with Shield, which, in its detergent state, has the consistency of wet cement. He then goes out of focus, as if glimpsed through a shower door. "Clinical tests prove," proclaims an eager baritone, "Shield fights

Mark Crispin Miller is a professor of media studies at New York University and has written extensively about television, advertising, propaganda, and politics. His books include *Fooled Again: How the Right Stole the 2004 Election & Why They'll Steal the Next One Too (Unless We Stop Them)* (2005), *The Bush Dyslexicon: Observations on a National Disorder* (2001), and *Boxed In: The Culture of Television* (1988). He has published widely in journals and magazines and also is a frequent guest on television and radio programs.

odor better than the *leading* deodorant soap!" A bar of Shield (green) and a bar of that other soap (yellow) zip up the screen with a festive toot, forming a sort of graph which demonstrates that Shield does, indeed, "fight odor better, so you'll feel *cleaner!*"

This particular contest having been settled, we return to the major one, which has yet to be resolved. Our hero reappears, almost transformed: calmed down, dressed up, his voice at least an octave lower. "I *do* feel cleaner!" he announces cheerily, leaning into the doorway of a room where Gail is arranging flowers. She pretends to be ecstatic at this news, and he comes toward her, setting himself up for a profound humiliation by putting on a playful air of suave command. Adjusting his tie like a real man of the world, he saunters over to his wife and her flower bowl, where he plucks a dainty purple flower and lifts it to his lapel: "And," he boasts throughout all this, trying to make his voice sound even deeper, "with old J. J.'s business and my brains—" "—you'll . . . *clean up again?*" Gail asks with suggestive irony, subverting his authoritative pose by leaning against him, draping one hand over his shoulder to dangle a big yellow daisy down his chest. Taken aback, he shoots her a distrustful look, and she titters at him.

Finally, the word SHIELD appears in extreme close-up and the camera pulls back, showing two bars of the soap, one packaged and one not, on display amidst an array of steely bubbles. "Shield fights odor better, so you'll feel *cleaner!*" the baritone reminds us, and then our hero's face appears once more, in a little square over the unpackaged bar of soap: "I feel *cleaner* than *ever before!*" he insists, sounding faintly unconvinced.

Is all this as stupid as it seems at first? Or is there, just beneath the surface of this moronic narrative, some noteworthy design, intended to appeal to (and to worsen) some of the anxieties of modern life? A serious look at this particular trifle might lead us to some strange discoveries.

We are struck, first of all, by the commercial's pseudofeminism, an advertising ploy with a long history, and one ubiquitous on television nowadays. Although the whole subject deserves more extended treatment, this commercial offers us an especially rich example of the strategy. Typically, it woos its female viewers—i.e., those who choose the soap in most households—with a fantasy of dominance; and it does so by inverting the actualities of woman's lot through a number of imperceptible details. For instance, in this marriage it is the wife, and not the husband, who gets to keep her name; and Gail's name, moreover, is a potent one, because of its brevity and its homonymic connotation. (If this housewife were more delicately named, called "Lillian" or "Cecilia," it would lessen her illusory strength.) She is also equipped in more noticeable ways: she's the one who wears the button-down shirt in this family, she's the one who's competent both outdoors and in the house, and it is she, and only she, who wields the tool.

These visual details imply that Gail is quite a powerful housewife, whereas her nameless mate is a figure of embarrassing impotence. This "man," in fact, is actually Gail's *wife:* he is utterly feminized, striking a posture and displaying attributes which men have long deplored in women. In other words, this commercial, which apparently takes the woman's side, is really the expression (and reflection) of misogyny. Gail's husband is dependent and hysterical, entirely without that self-possession which we expect from solid, manly types, like Gail. This is partly the result of his demeanor: in the opening scene, his voice sometimes cracks ludicrously, and he otherwise betrays the shrill desperation of a man who can't remember where he left his scrotum. The comic effect of this frenzy, moreover, is subtly enhanced by the mise-en-scène, which puts the man in a conventionally feminine position—in dishabille, looking down from a window. Thus we infer that he is sheltered and housebound, a modern Juliet calling for his/her Romeo; or—more appropriately—the image suggests a scene in some suburban red-light district, presenting this husband as an item on display, like the flowers just below his stomach, available for anyone's enjoyment, at a certain price. Although in one way contradictory, these implications are actually quite congruous, for they both serve to emasculate the husband, so that the wife might take his place, or play his part.

Such details, some might argue, need not have been the conscious work of this commercial's makers. The authors, that is, might have worked by instinct rather than design, and so would have been no more aware of their work's psychosocial import than we ourselves: they just wanted to make the guy look like a wimp, merely for the purposes of domestic comedy. While such an argument certainly does apply to many ads, in this case it is unlikely. Advertising agencies do plenty of research, by which we can assume that they don't select their tactics arbitrarily. They take pains to analyze the culture which they help to sicken, and then, with much wit and cynicism, use their insights in devising their small dramas. This commercial is a subtle and meticulous endorsement of castration, meant to play on certain widespread guilts and insecurities; and all we need to do to demonstrate this fact is to subject the two main scenes to the kind of visual analysis which commercials, so brief and broad, tend to resist (understandably). The ad's visual implications are too carefully achieved to have been merely accidental or unconscious.

The crucial object in the opening shot is that flower box with its bright geraniums, which is placed directly in front of the husband's groin. This clever stroke of composition has the immediate effect of equating our hero's manhood with a bunch of flowers. This is an exquisitely perverse suggestion, rather like using a cigar to represent the Eternal Feminine: flowers are frail, sweet, and largely ornamental, hardly an appropriate phallic symbol, but (of course) a venerable symbol of *maidenhood.* The geraniums stand, then, not for the husband's virility, but for its absence.

More than a clever instance of inversion, furthermore, these phallic blossoms tell us something odd about this marital relationship. As Gail, clippers in hand, turns from the hedge to calm her agitated man, she appears entirely capable of calming him quite drastically, if she hasn't done so already (which might explain his hairless chest and high-pitched voice). She has the power, that is, to take away whatever slender potency he may possess, and uses the power repeatedly, trimming her husband (we infer) as diligently as she prunes her foliage.

And, as she can snip his manhood, so too can she restore it, which is what the second scene implies. Now the flower bowl has replaced the flower box as the visual crux, dominating the bottom center of the frame with a crowd of blooms. As the husband, cleaned and dressed, comes to stand beside his wife, straining to affect a new authority, the flower bowl too appears directly at his lower center; so that Gail, briskly adding flowers to the bouquet, appears to be replenishing his vacant groin with extra stalks. He has a lot to thank her for, it seems: she is his helpmate, confidante, adviser, she keeps his house and grounds in order, and she is clearly the custodian of the family jewels.

Of course, her restoration of his potency cannot be complete, or he might shatter her mastery by growing a bit too masterful himself. He could start choosing his own soap, or take her shears away, or—worst of all—walk out for good. Therefore, she punctures his momentary confidence by taunting him with that big limp daisy, countering his lordly gesture with the boutonniere by flaunting that symbol of his floral status. He can put on whatever airs he likes, but she still has his fragile vigor firmly in her hand.

Now what, precisely, motivates this sexless battle of the sexes? That is, what really underlies this tense and hateful marriage, making the man so weak, the woman so contemptuously helpful? The script, seemingly nothing more than a series of inanities, contains the answer to these questions, conveying, as it does, a concern with cleanliness that amounts to an obsession: "Shield fights odor better, so you'll feel cleaner!" "I *do* feel cleaner!" "Shield fights odor better, so you'll feel *cleaner!*" "I feel *cleaner* than *ever before!*" Indeed, the commercial emphasizes the feeling of cleanliness even more pointedly than the name of the product, implying, by its very insistence, a feeling of dirtiness, an apprehension of deep filth.

And yet there is not a trace of dirt in the vivid world of this commercial. Unlike many ads for other soaps, this one shows no sloppy children, no sweatsoaked workingmen with blackened hands, not even a bleary housewife in need of her morning shower. We never even glimpse the ground in Gail's world, nor is her husband even faintly smudged. In fact, the filth which Shield supposedly "fights" is not physical but psychological besmirchment: Gail's husband feels soiled because of what he has to do for a living, in order to keep Gail in that nice big house, happily supplied with shirts and shears.

"My first call on J. J. Siss, the company's *toughest customer,* and now *this!*" The man's anxiety is yet another feminizing trait, for it is generally women, and not men, who are consumed by doubts about the sweetness of their bodies, which must never be offensive to the guys who run the world. (This real anxiety is itself aggravated by commercials.) Gail's husband must play the female to the mighty J. J. Siss, a name whose oxymoronic character implies perversion: "J. J." is a stereotypic nickname for the potent boss, while "Sis" is a term of endearment, short for "sister" (and perhaps implying "sissy," too, in this case). Gail's husband must do his boyish best to please the voracious J. J. Siss, just as a prostitute must satisfy a demanding trick, or "tough customer." It is therefore perfectly fitting that this employee refer to the encounter, not as a "meeting" or "appointment," but as a "call"; and his demeaning posture in the window—half dressed and bent over—conveys, we now see, a definitive implication.

Gail's job as the "understanding wife" is not to rescue her husband from these sordid obligations, but to help him meet them successfully. She may seem coolly self-sufficient, but she actually depends on her husband's attractiveness, just as a pimp relies on the charm of his whore. And, also like a pimp, she has to keep her girl in line with occasional reminders of who's boss. When her husband starts getting uppity *après la douche,* she jars him from the very self-assurance which she had helped him to discover, piercing that "shield" which was her gift.

"And, with old J. J.'s business and my brains—" "— you'll . . . *clean up again?*" He means, of course, that he'll work fiscal wonders with old J. J.'s account, but his fragmentary boast contains a deeper significance, upon which Gail plays with sadistic cleverness. "Old J. J.'s business and my brains" implies a feminine self-description, since it suggests a variation on the old commonplace of "brains vs. brawn": J. J.'s money, in the world of this commercial (as in ours), amounts to brute strength, which the flexible husband intends to complement with his mother wit. Gail's retort broadens this unconscious hint of homosexuality: "—you'll . . . *clean up again?*" Given the monetary nature of her husband's truncated remark, the retort must mean primarily, "You'll make a lot of money." If this were all it meant, however, it would not be a joke, nor would the husband find it so upsetting. Moreover, we have no evidence that Gail's husband ever "cleaned up"—i.e., made a sudden fortune—in the past. Rather, the ad's milieu and *dramatis personae* suggest upward mobility, gradual savings and a yearly raise, rather than one prior killing. What Gail is referring to, in fact, with that "again," is her husband's shower: she implies that what he'll have to do, after his "call" on J. J. Siss, is, quite literally, wash himself off. Like any other tidy hooker, this man will have to clean up after taking on a tough customer, so that he might be ready to take on someone else.

These suggestions of pederasty are intended, not as a literal characterization of the husband's job, but as a metaphor for what it takes to get ahead: Gail's husband, like most white-collar workers, must debase himself to make a good impression, toadying to his superiors, offering himself, body and soul, to the corporation. Maybe, therefore, it isn't really Gail who has neutered him; it may be his way of life that has wrought the ugly change. How, then, are women represented here? The commercial does deliberately appeal to women, offering them a sad fantasy of control; but it also, perhaps inadvertently, illuminates the unhappiness which makes that fantasy attractive.

The husband's status, it would seem, should make Gail happy, since it makes her physically comfortable, and yet Gail can't help loathing her husband for the degradations which she helps him undergo. For her part of the bargain is, ultimately, no less painful than his. She has to do more than put up with him; she has to prepare him for his world of affairs, and then must help him to conceal the shame. Of course, it's all quite hopeless. She clearly despises the man whom she would bolster; and the thing which she provides to help him "feel cleaner than ever before" is precisely what has helped him do the job that's always made him feel so dirty. "A little water cleans us of this deed" is her promise, which is false, for she is just as soiled as her doomed husband, however fresh and well-ironed she may look.

Of course, the ad not only illuminates this mess, but helps perpetuate it, by obliquely gratifying the guilts, terrors, and resentments that underlie it and arise from it. The strategy is not meant to be noticed, but works through the apparent comedy, which must therefore be studied carefully, not passively received. Thus, thirty seconds of ingenious advertising, which we can barely stand to watch, tell us something more than we might want to know about the souls of men and women under corporate capitalism.

Weasel Words

William Lutz

One problem advertisers have when they try to convince you that the product they are pushing is really different from other, similar products is that their claims are subject to some laws. Not a lot of laws, but there are some designed to prevent fraudulent or untruthful claims in advertising. Even during the happy years of nonregulation under President Ronald Reagan, the FTC did crack down on the more blatant abuses in advertising claims. Generally speaking, advertisers have to be careful in what they say in their ads, in the claims they make for the products they advertise. Parity claims are safe because they are legal and supported by a number of court decisions. But beyond parity claims there are weasel words.

Advertisers use weasel words to appear to be making a claim for a product when in fact they are making no claim at all. Weasel words get their name from the way weasels eat the eggs they find in the nests of other animals. A weasel will make a small hole in the egg, suck out the insides, then place the egg back in the nest. Only when the egg is examined closely is it found to be hollow. That's the way it is with weasel words in advertising: Examine weasel words closely and you'll find that they're as hollow as any egg sucked by a weasel. Weasel words appear to say one thing when in fact they say the opposite, or nothing at all.

"Help"—The Number One Weasel Word

The biggest weasel word used in advertising doublespeak is "help." Now "help" only means to

William Lutz is a professor of English at Rutgers University-Camden and is the former editor of the *Quarterly Review of Doublespeak*. He also holds a Doctor of Law degree and has served as an expert witness on language issues. He has written numerous books, including *Doublespeak Defined* (1999) and *The New Doublespeak: Why No One Knows What Anyone's Saying Anymore* (1996). His articles on doublespeak and on other linguistic issues have appeared in a wide range of newspapers and magazines.

aid or assist, nothing more. It does not mean to conquer, stop, eliminate, end, solve, heal, cure, or anything else. But once the ad says "help," it can say just about anything after that because "help" qualifies everything coming after it. The trick is that the claim that comes after the weasel word is usually so strong and so dramatic that you forget the word "help" and concentrate only on the dramatic claim. You read into the ad a message that the ad does not contain. More importantly, the advertiser is not responsible for the claim that you read into the ad, even though the advertiser wrote the ad so you would read that claim into it.

The next time you see an ad for a cold medicine that promises that it "helps relieve cold symptoms fast," don't rush out to buy it. Ask yourself what this claim is really saying. Remember, "helps" means only that the medicine will aid or assist. What will it aid or assist in doing? Why, "relieve" your cold "symptoms." "Relieve" only means to ease, alleviate, or mitigate, not to stop, end, or cure. Nor does the claim say how much relieving this medicine will do. Nowhere does this ad claim it will cure anything. In fact, the ad doesn't even claim it will *do* anything at all. The ad only claims that it will aid in relieving (not curing) your cold symptoms, which are probably a runny nose, watery eyes, and a headache. In other words, this medicine probably contains a standard decongestant and some aspirin. By the way, what does "fast" mean? Ten minutes, one hour, one day? What is fast to one person can be very slow to another. Fast is another weasel word.

Ad claims using "help" are among the most popular ads. One says, "Helps keep you young looking," but then a lot of things will help keep you young looking, including exercise, rest, good nutrition, and a facelift. More importantly, this ad doesn't say the product will keep you young, only "young *looking*." Someone may look young to one person and old to another.

A toothpaste ad says, "Helps prevent cavities," but it doesn't say it will actually prevent cavities. Brushing your teeth regularly, avoiding sugars in food, and flossing daily will also help prevent cavities. A liquid cleaner ad says, "Helps keep your home germ free," but it doesn't say it actually kills germs, nor does it even specify which germs it might kill.

"Help" is such a useful weasel word that it is often combined with other action-verb weasel words such as "fight" and "control." Consider the claim, "Helps control dandruff symptoms with regular use." What does it really say? It will assist in controlling (not eliminating, stopping, ending, or curing) the *symptoms* of dandruff, not the cause of dandruff nor the dandruff itself. What are the symptoms of dandruff? The ad deliberately leaves that undefined, but assume that the symptoms referred to in the ad are the flaking and itching commonly associated with dandruff. But just shampooing with *any* shampoo will temporarily eliminate these symptoms, so this shampoo isn't any different from any other. Finally, in order to benefit from this product, you must use it regularly. What is "regular use"—daily, weekly, hourly? Using another shampoo "regularly" will have the same effect. Nowhere does this advertising claim say this particular shampoo stops, eliminates, or cures dandruff. In fact, this claim says nothing at all, thanks to all the weasel words.

Look at ads in magazines and newspapers, listen to ads on radio and television, and you'll find the word "help" in ads for all kinds of products. How often do you read or hear such phrases as "helps stop . . . ," "helps overcome . . . ," "helps eliminate . . . ," "helps you feel . . . ," or "helps you look . . ."? If you start looking for this weasel word in advertising, you'll be amazed at how often it occurs. Analyze the claims in the ads using "help," and you will discover that these ads are really saying nothing.

There are plenty of other weasel words used in advertising. In fact, there are so many that to list them all would fill the rest of this book. But, in order to identify the doublespeak of advertising and understand the real meaning of an ad, you have to be aware of the most popular weasel words in advertising today.

Virtually Spotless

One of the most powerful weasel words is "virtually," a word so innocent that most people don't pay any attention to it when it is used in an advertising claim. But watch out. "Virtually" is used in advertising claims that appear to make specific, definite promises when there is no promise. After all, what does "virtually" mean? It means "in essence or effect, although not in fact." Look at that definition again. "Virtually" means *not in fact.* It does *not* mean "almost" or "just about the same as," or anything else. And before you dismiss all this concern over such a small word, remember that small words can have big consequences.

In 1971 a federal court rendered its decision on a case brought by a woman who became pregnant while taking birth control pills. She sued the manufacturer, Eli Lilly and Company, for breach of warranty. The woman lost her case. Basing its ruling on a statement in the pamphlet accompanying the pills, which stated that, "When taken as directed, the tablets offer virtually 100% protection," the court ruled that there was no warranty, expressed or implied, that the pills were absolutely effective. In its ruling, the court pointed out that, according to *Webster's Third New International Dictionary,* "virtually" means "almost entirely" and clearly does not mean "absolute" (*Whittington* v. *Eli Lilly and Company,* 333 F. Supp. 98). In other words, the Eli Lilly company was really saying that its birth control pill, even when taken as directed, *did not in fact* provide 100 percent protection against pregnancy. But Eli Lilly didn't want to put it that way because then many women might not have bought Lilly's birth control pills.

The next time you see the ad that says that this dishwasher detergent "leaves dishes virtually spotless," just remember how advertisers twist the meaning of the weasel word "virtually." You can have lots of spots on your dishes after using this detergent and the ad claim will still be true, because what this claim really means is that this detergent does not *in fact* leave your dishes spotless. Whenever you see or hear an ad claim that uses the word "virtually," just translate that claim into its real meaning.

So the television set that is "virtually trouble free" becomes the television set that is not in fact trouble free, the "virtually foolproof operation" of any appliance becomes an operation that is in fact not foolproof, and the product that "virtually never needs service" becomes the product that is not in fact service free.

New and Improved

If "new" is the most frequently used word on a product package, "improved" is the second most frequent. In fact, the two words are almost always used together. It seems just about everything sold these days is "new and improved." The next time you're in the supermarket, try counting the number of times you see these words on products. But you'd better do it while you're walking down just one aisle, otherwise you'll need a calculator to keep track of your counting.

Just what do these words mean? The use of the word "new" is restricted by regulations, so an advertiser can't just use the word on a product or in an ad without meeting certain requirements. For example, a product is considered new for about six months during a national advertising campaign. If the product is being advertised only in a limited test market area, the word can be used longer, and in some instances has been used for as long as two years.

What makes a product "new"? Some products have been around for a long time, yet every once in a while you discover that they are being advertised as "new." Well, an advertiser can call a product new if there has been "a material functional change" in the product. What is "a material functional change," you ask? Good question. In fact it's such a good question it's being asked all the time. It's up to the manufacturer to prove that the product has undergone such a change. And if the manufacturer isn't challenged on the claim, then there's no one to stop it. Moreover, the change does not have to be an improvement in the product. One manufacturer added an artificial lemon scent to a cleaning product and called it "new and improved," even though the product did not clean any better than without the lemon scent. The manufacturer defended the use of the word "new" on the grounds that the artificial scent changed the chemical formula of the product and therefore constituted "a material functional change."

Which brings up the word "improved." When used in advertising, "improved" does not mean "made better." It only means "changed" or "different from before." So, if the detergent maker puts a plastic pour spout on the box of detergent, the product has been "improved," and away we go with a whole new advertising campaign. Or, if the cereal maker adds more fruit or a different kind of fruit to the cereal, there's an improved product. Now you know why manufacturers are constantly making little changes in their products. Whole new advertising campaigns, designed to convince you that the product has been changed for the better, are based on small changes in superficial aspects of a product. The next time you see an ad for an "improved" product, ask yourself what was wrong with the old one. Ask yourself just how "improved" the product is. Finally, you might check to see whether the "improved" version costs more than the unimproved one. After all, someone has to pay for the millions of dollars spent advertising the improved product.

Of course, advertisers really like to run ads that claim a product is "new and improved." While what constitutes a "new" product may be subject to some regulation, "improved" is a subjective judgment. A manufacturer changes the shape of its stick deodorant, but the shape doesn't improve the function of the deodorant. That is, changing the shape doesn't affect the deodorizing ability of the deodorant, so the manufacturer calls it "improved." Another manufacturer adds ammonia to its liquid cleaner and calls it "new and improved." Since adding ammonia does affect the cleaning ability of the product, there has been a "material functional change" in the product, and the manufacturer can now call its cleaner "new," and "improved" as well. Now the weasel words "new and improved" are plastered all over the package and are the basis for a multimillion-dollar ad campaign. But after six months the word "new" will have to go, until someone can dream up another change in the product. Perhaps it will be adding color to the liquid, or changing the shape of the package, or maybe adding a new dripless pour spout, or perhaps a _____. The "improvements" are endless, and so are the new advertising claims and campaigns.

"New" is just too useful and powerful a word in advertising for advertisers to pass it up easily. So they use weasel words that say "new" without really saying it. One of their favorites is "introducing," as in, "Introducing improved Tide," or "Introducing the stain remover." The first is simply saying, here's our improved soap; the second, here's our new advertising campaign for our detergent. Another favorite is "now," as in, "Now there's Sinex," which simply means that Sinex is available. Then there are phrases like "Today's Chevrolet," "Presenting Dristan," and "A fresh way to start the day." The list is really endless because advertisers are always finding new ways to say "new" without really saying it. If there is a second edition of this book, I'll just call it the "new and improved" edition. Wouldn't you really rather have a "new and improved" edition of this book rather than a "second" edition?

Acts Fast

"Acts" and "works" are two popular weasel words in advertising because they bring action to the product and to the advertising claim. When you see the ad for the cough syrup that "Acts on the cough control center," ask yourself what this cough syrup is claiming to do. Well, it's just claiming to "act," to do something, to perform an action. What is it that the cough syrup does? The ad doesn't say. It only claims to perform an action or do something on your "cough control center." By the way, what and where is your "cough control center"? I don't remember learning about that part of the body in human biology class.

Ads that use such phrases as "acts fast," "acts against," "acts to prevent," and the like are saying essentially nothing, because "act" is a word empty of any specific meaning. The ads are always careful not to specify exactly what "act" the product performs. Just because a brand of aspirin claims to "act fast" for headache relief doesn't mean this aspirin is any better than any other aspirin. What is the "act" that this aspirin performs? You're never told. Maybe it just dissolves quickly. Since aspirin is a parity product, all aspirin is the same and therefore functions the same.

Works Like Anything Else

If you don't find the word "acts" in an ad, you will probably find the weasel word "works." In fact, the two words are almost interchangeable in advertising. Watch out for ads that say a product "works against," "works like," "works for," or "works longer." As with "acts," "works" is the same meaningless verb used to make you think that this product really does something, and maybe even something special or unique. But "works," like "acts," is basically a word empty of any specific meaning.

Like Magic

Whenever advertisers want you to stop thinking about the product and to start thinking about something bigger, better, or more attractive than the product, they use that very popular weasel word, "like." The word "like" is the advertiser's equivalent of a magician's use of misdirection. "Like" gets you to ignore the product and concentrate on the claim the advertiser is making about it. "For skin like peaches and cream" claims the ad for a skin cream. What is this ad really claiming? It doesn't say this cream will give you peaches-and-cream skin. There is no verb in this claim, so it doesn't even mention using the product. How is skin ever like "peaches and cream"? Remember, ads must be read literally and exactly, according to the dictionary definition of words. (Remember "virtually" in the Eli Lilly case.) The ad is making absolutely no promise or claim whatsoever for this skin cream. If you think this cream will give you soft, smooth, youthful-looking skin, you are the one who has read that meaning into the ad.

The wine that claims "It's like taking a trip to France" wants you to think about a romantic evening in Paris as you walk along the boulevard after a wonderful meal in an intimate little bistro. Of course, you don't really believe that a wine can take you to France, but the goal of the ad is to get you to think pleasant, romantic thoughts about France and not about how the wine tastes or how expensive it may be. That little word "like" has taken you away from crushed grapes into a world of your own imaginative making. Who knows, maybe the next time you buy wine, you'll think those pleasant thoughts when you see this brand of wine, and you'll buy it. Or, maybe you weren't even thinking about buying wine at all, but now you just might pick up a bottle the next time you're shopping. Ah, the power of "like" in advertising.

How about the most famous "like" claim of all, "Winston tastes good like a cigarette should"? Ignoring the grammatical error here, you might want to know what this claim is saying. Whether a cigarette tastes good or bad is a subjective judgment because what tastes good to one person may well taste horrible to another. Not everyone likes fried snails, even if they are called escargot. (*De gustibus non est disputandum,* which was probably the Roman rule for advertising as well as for defending the games in the Colosseum.) There are many people who say all cigarettes taste terrible, other people who say only some cigarettes taste all right, and still others who say all cigarettes taste good. Who's right? Everyone, because taste is a matter of personal judgment.

Moreover, note the use of the conditional, "should." The complete claim is, "Winston tastes good like a cigarette should taste." But should cigarettes taste good? Again, this is a matter of personal judgment and probably depends most on one's experiences with smoking. So, the Winston ad is simply saying that Winston cigarettes are just like any other cigarette: Some people like them and some people don't. On that statement R. J. Reynolds conducted a very successful multimillion-dollar advertising campaign that helped keep Winston the number-two-selling cigarette in the United States, close behind number one, Marlboro.

CAN IT BE UP TO THE CLAIM?

Analyzing ads for doublespeak requires that you pay attention to every word in the ad and determine what each word really means. Advertisers try to wrap their claims in language that sounds concrete, specific, and objective, when in fact the language of advertising is anything but. Your job is to read carefully and listen critically so that when the announcer says that "Crest can be of significant value . . ." you know immediately that this claim says absolutely nothing. Where is the doublespeak in this ad? Start with the second word.

Once again, you have to look at what words really mean, not what you think they mean or what the advertiser wants you to think they mean. The ad for Crest only says that using Crest "can be" of "significant value." What really throws you off in this ad is the brilliant use of "significant." It draws your attention to the word "value" and makes you forget that the ad only claims that Crest "can be." The ad doesn't say that Crest *is* of value, only that it is "able" or "possible" to be of value, because that's all that "can" means.

It's so easy to miss the importance of those little words, "can be." Almost as easy as missing the importance of the words "up to" in an ad. These words are very popular in sale ads. You know, the ones that say, "Up to 50% Off!" Now, what does that claim mean? Not much, because the store or manufacturer has to reduce the price of only a few items by 50 percent. Everything else can be reduced a lot less, or not even reduced. Moreover, don't you want to know 50 percent off of what? Is it 50 percent off the "manufacturer's suggested list price," which is the highest possible price? Was the price artificially inflated and then reduced? In other ads, "up to" expresses an ideal situation. The medicine that works "up to ten times faster," the battery that lasts "up to twice as long," and the soap that gets you "up to twice as clean" all are based on ideal situations for using those products, situations in which you can be sure you will never find yourself.

UNFINISHED WORDS

Unfinished words are a kind of "up to" claim in advertising. The claim that a battery lasts "up to twice as long" usually doesn't finish the comparison—twice as long as what? A birthday candle? A tank of gas? A cheap battery made in a country not noted for its technological achievements? The implication is that the battery lasts twice as long as batteries made by other battery makers, or twice as long as earlier model batteries made by the advertiser, but the ad doesn't really make these claims. You read these claims into the ad, aided by the visual images the advertiser so carefully provides.

Unfinished words depend on you to finish them, to provide the words the advertisers so thoughtfully left out of the ad. Pall Mall cigarettes were once advertised as "A longer finer and milder smoke." The question is, longer, finer, and milder than what? The aspirin that claims it contains "Twice as much of the pain reliever doctors recommend most" doesn't tell you what pain reliever it contains twice as much of. (By the way, it's aspirin. That's right; it just contains twice the amount of aspirin. And how much is twice the amount? Twice of what amount?) Panadol boasts that "nobody reduces fever faster," but, since Panadol is a parity product, this claim simply means that Panadol isn't any better than any other product in its parity class. "You can be sure if it's Westinghouse," you're told, but just exactly what it is you can be sure of is never mentioned. "Magnavox gives you more" doesn't tell you what you get more of. More value? More television? More than they gave you before? It sounds nice, but it means nothing, until you fill in the claim with your own words, the words the advertiser didn't use. Since each of us fills in the claim differently, the ad and the product can become all things to all people, and not promise a single thing.

Unfinished words abound in advertising because they appear to promise so much. More importantly, they can be joined with powerful visual images on television to appear to be making significant promises about a product's effectiveness without really making any promises. In a television ad, the aspirin product that claims fast relief can show a person with a headache taking the product and then, in what appears to be a matter of minutes, claiming complete relief. This visual image is far more powerful than any claim made in unfinished words. Indeed, the visual image completes the unfinished words for you, filling in with pictures what the words leave out. And you thought that ads didn't affect you. What brand of aspirin do you use?

Some years ago, Ford's advertisements proclaimed "Ford LTD—700% quieter." Now, what do you think Ford was claiming with these unfinished words? What was the Ford LTD quieter than? A Cadillac? A Mercedes Benz? A BMW? Well, when the FTC asked Ford to substantiate this unfinished claim, Ford replied that it meant that the inside of the LTD was 700% quieter than the outside. How did you finish those unfinished words when you first read them? Did you even come close to Ford's meaning?

COMBINING WEASEL WORDS

A lot of ads don't fall neatly into one category or another because they use a variety of different devices and words. Different weasel words are often combined to make an ad claim. The claim, "Coffee-Mate gives coffee more body, more flavor," uses Unfinished Words ("more" than what?) and also uses words that have no specific meaning ("body" and "flavor"). Along with "taste" (remember the Winston ad and its claim to taste good), "body" and "flavor" mean nothing because their meaning is entirely subjective. To you, "body" in coffee might mean thick, black, almost bitter coffee, while I might take it to mean a light brown, delicate coffee. Now, if you think you understood that last sentence, read it again, because it said nothing of objective value; it was filled with weasel words of no specific meaning: "thick," "black," "bitter," "light brown," and "delicate." Each of those words has no specific, objective meaning, because each of us can interpret them differently.

Try this slogan: "Looks, smells, tastes like ground-roast coffee." So, are you now going to buy Taster's Choice instant coffee because of this ad? "Looks," "smells," and "tastes" are all words with no specific meaning and depend on your interpretation of them for any meaning. Then there's that great weasel word "like," which simply suggests a comparison but does not make the actual connection between the product and the quality. Besides, do you know what "ground-roast" coffee is? I don't, but it sure sounds good. So, out of seven words in this ad, four are definite weasel words, two are quite meaningless, and only one has any clear meaning.

Remember the Anacin ad—"Twice as much of the pain reliever doctors recommend most"? There's a whole lot of weaseling going on in this ad. First, what's the pain reliever they're talking about in this ad? Aspirin, of course. In fact, any time you see or hear an ad using those words "pain reliever," you can automatically substitute the word "aspirin" for them. (Makers of acetaminophen and ibuprofen pain relievers are careful in their advertising to identify their products as nonaspirin products.) So, now we know that Anacin has aspirin in it. Moreover, we know that Anacin has twice as much aspirin in it, but we don't know twice as much as what. Does it have twice as much aspirin as an ordinary aspirin tablet? If so, what is an ordinary aspirin tablet, and how much aspirin does it contain? Twice as much as Excedrin or Bufferin? Twice as much as a chocolate chip cookie? Remember those Unfinished Words and how they lead you on without saying anything.

Finally, what about those doctors who are doing all that recommending? Who are they? How many of them are there? What kind of doctors are they? What are their qualifications? Who asked them about recommending pain relievers? What other pain relievers did they recommend? And there are a whole lot more questions about this "poll" of doctors to which I'd like to know the answers, but you get the point. Sometimes, when I call my doctor, she tells me to take two aspirin and call her office in the morning. Is that where Anacin got this ad?

ADDITIONAL READINGS

Hays, Constance L. *The Real Thing: Truth and Power at the Coca-Cola Company.* New York: Random House, 2004.

Klein, Naomi. *No Logo.* New York: Picador, 2000.

Kilbourne, Jean. *Deadly Persuasion: Why Women and Girls Must Fight the Addictive Power of Advertising.* New York: Free Press, 1999.

Laird, Pamela Walker. *Advertising Progress: American Business and the Rise of Consumer Marketing. Studies in Industry and Society.* Baltimore: Johns Hopkins UP, 1998.

Lears, Jackson. *Fables of Abundance: A Cultural History of Advertising in America.* New York: BasicBooks, 1994.

Marchand, Roland. *Advertising the American Dream: Making Way for Modernity, 1920–1940.* Berkeley: U of California P, 1985.

Quart, Alissa. *Branded: The Buying and Selling of Teenagers.* Cambridge, MA: Perseus, 2003.

Reichert, Tom. *The Erotic History of Advertising.* Amherst, NY: Prometheus, 2003.

Samuel, Lawrence R. *Brought to You Buy: Postwar Television Advertising and The American Dream.* Austin: U Texas P, 2001.

Savan, Leslie. *The Sponsored Life: Ads, TV, and American Culture.* Philadelphia: Temple UP, 1994.

Schudson, Michael. *Advertising, The Uneasy Persuasion: Its Dubious Impact on American Society.* New York: BasicBooks, 1984.

Twitchell, James B. *ADCULT USA: The Triumph of Advertising in American Culture.* New York: Columbia UP, 1996.

———. *Twenty Ads That Shook the World: The Century's Most Groundbreaking Advertising and How It Changed Us All.* New York: Three Rivers Press, 2000.

Gender Matters:
Representations of Men and Women on Television, in Film, and in Literature

Genies and Witc.

Susan Douglas

While my friends and I were upstairs blasting Beatles records and planning how many times we would go see *A Hard Day's Night,* our mothers were downstairs in the kitchen or the laundry room fuming, and fantasizing about a jailbreak of their own. They soon discovered they weren't alone. Political rumblings about women's second-class status, and their desire for more opportunities and choices, now registered on America's media seismographs. Some of our mothers, it turned out, wanted to break down some barricades themselves. The prevailing line in the print media of the early 1960s was that American women, as the *Ladies' Home Journal* put it, "never had it so good": they controlled the family's purse strings and the nation's wealth, had an array of household technologies that made housework effortless, had plenty of free time to play bridge or do volunteer work, and enjoyed unprecedented equality. The *Journal* continued, "They have rights and opportunities today the likes of which the Western world has never seen. . . . Indeed, women today are in many respects much better off than men." In its special supplement of October 1962 entitled "The American Female," *Harper's* maintained that American women were "repelled by the slogans of old-fashioned feminism."[1]

But *Harper's* also thought it saw a trend in 1962 and named it "crypto-feminism." Women were reexamining their roles as "wives, mothers, and members of the human race" because motherhood was short-lived as a full-time job, more women wanted or needed to work outside the home, yet many

Susan Douglas is a professor of communications at the University of Michigan. She is a popular lecturer on college campuses and a frequent guest on television and radio programs. Her widely read books include *The Mommy Myth: The Idealization of Motherhood and How It Undermines Women* (with Meredith Michaels, 2004), *Listening In: Radio and the American Imagination* (1999), *Where the Girls Are: Growing Up Female with the Mass Media* (1994), and *Inventing American Broadcasting, 1899–1922* (1987). Her essays appear in numerous journals and magazines.

women found that "the institutions that are supposed to serve women are not very helpful." Women, in fact, faced a "void." Articles kept appearing in the early and mid-1960s with titles like "Our Greatest Waste of Talent Is Women," "Women—Neglected Assets," and "Women—Emancipation Is Still to Come," articles at odds with the "women have it made" line. Clearly, a new turbulence was emerging.

Professional women, in particular, were fed up with their second-class salaries and their image as freaks of nature, and they lobbied the Kennedy administration to do something. In one of the more famous scenes from John Kennedy's press conferences, the indefatigable journalist May Craig stood up and asked the president what he was doing for women. Kennedy quipped that he was sure that, whatever it was, it wasn't enough, implying that women were *never* satisfied, and shared a big laugh with the predominantly male press corps. Nonetheless, in 1961, Kennedy established a Presidential Commission on the Status of Women, with Eleanor Roosevelt as its head, to ascertain how to eradicate the "prejudices and outmoded customs [that] act as barriers to the full realization of women's basic rights." The Kennedy administration also outlawed discrimination in the federal civil service and in 1963 pushed through Congress the Equal Pay Act, which prohibited paying men and women different salaries for the same jobs. The Kennedy Commission's report, *American Women,* published just six weeks before the president's death, recommended the establishment of child-care services, advocated equal opportunities for women in employment and education, urged women to seek public office, and argued that the government's mission should be to secure "equality of rights for women." The front-page story in *The New York Times* headlined the report with "U.S. Panel Urges Women to Sue for Equal Rights."[2]

The real tip-off that many of our mothers hated their assigned positions, weren't sure whether to hate themselves or the men around them, and were tired of straddling the untenable contradictions in their lives was the eagerness with which thousands of them ran out to buy Betty Friedan's *The Feminine Mystique,* which they put on the best-seller list from April through July 1963. In 1964, while teenagers were discovering the Beatles, older women made *The Feminine Mystique* the number one best-selling paperback in the country.[3] Trashing "biology as destiny," Freud, and penis envy, castigating the phony happy housewife heroine of the women's magazines, and enumerating the emptiness, resentments, and self-doubt of many housewives' lives, Friedan reminded women of the unfinished work of the women's movement and urged her sisters to stop being doormats and to fight for equality.

Portions of Friedan's book were condensed in women's magazines, and the book inspired other investigations into the status of women. In "Whatever Happened to Women's Rights?" published in the *Atlantic Monthly* in March 1964, Paul Foley stacked up a tower of statistics to emphasize women's second-class status. Only two U.S. senators and 11 of the 435 members of the House of Representatives were women. Only 3 of the 422 federal judges were female. Women were confined to low-paying, dead-end jobs, they married too young, and they were not encouraged to pursue advanced degrees. Foley's article was condensed and reprinted in Reader's Digest.[4] *U.S. News and World Report* in 1966 also itemized the various ways in which women were discriminated against and underrepresented in American business and political institutions, and it noted that sociologists "warn that the U.S. may be building up a new generation of 'unhappy women.'" The article also focused on a significant trend: women were "going to work in droves," often combining a job, marriage, and motherhood. But the article concluded that "'full equality' for women appears far off."[5] Foley, however, claimed that "for public scrutiny on the American woman, 1963 was a banner year," and he was right: this was to be a turning point.

It was within this context of prefeminist agitation, combined with the unsettling phenomenon of wild packs of girls chasing the four mop-tops across America, that there appeared on TV, and with a vengeance, a new female mutant, a hybrid of old and new, of negative and positive stereotypes. We saw the ghoulish Morticia in *The Addams Family* as a femme fatale; a genie who was not a rotund, balding man but a shapely and beautiful young woman; a witch who was not a murderous old hag but an attractive young housewife; a cute, perky nun who could fly.

All of a sudden, female characters in TV sitcoms were capable of magic. They had fantastic supernatural powers. Yet this was more than just the ultimate in kitsch or the triumph of special effects. If we put these TV shows and the impulses behind them on the shrink's couch for a minute, we see that a significant proportion of the pop culture moguls were trying to acknowledge the impending release of female sexual and political energy, while keeping it all safely in a straitjacket. Sure, it would be great if women, especially young women, were more sexually liberated. But prefeminist rumblings about economic and political liberation were another matter. You could almost see these guys holding their nuts for dear life. Sensing they were playing with fire, they tried to contain it technologically, through images of levitation, twitching noses, and poofs of fake smoke.

In these shows, the potentially monstrous and grotesque was beautified and tamed; what we saw, in other words, was the containment of the threat posed by unleashed female sexuality, especially in the wake of Beatlemania and Helen Gurley Brown. Since viewers had been socialized to regard female sexuality as monstrous, TV producers addressed the anxieties about letting it loose by domesticating the monster, by making her pretty and sometimes slavish, by shrinking her and keeping her locked up in a bottle, and by playing the situation for laughs.[6]

In shows like *Bewitched, I Dream of Jeannie*, and *The Flying Nun*, a new version of Pandora's box was acted out. Seemingly normal-looking female characters possessed magical powers, which men begged them not to use; if women did use them, their powers had to be confined to the private sphere. Whenever women used these powers outside the home, in the public sphere, the male world was turned completely upside down. Business simply could not be conducted as usual, and logic and rationality were often overthrown and rendered useless. Men were made impotent by these powers, and the husbands (or husband figures) of such women were stripped of their male authority and made to look foolish and incompetent in front of their male superiors. After all, how can you explain men turned into dogs, or co-workers sent to Antarctica? Although the men insisted (usually unsuccessfully) that their women not use these powers, there were three exceptions that the shows' narrative systems permitted: to complete domestic chores, to compete over men, and to help the men out of embarrassing situations, which usually had been created by the woman's unauthorized use of her magic powers in the first place.

The two most successful examples of this genre were *Bewitched* and *I Dream of Jeannie.* Bewitched was extremely popular; it was the biggest hit series produced by ABC up to that time, running from 1964 to 1972. For its first five seasons it was among the top twenty high-est rated shows; the year of its debut, it soared to number two, topped only by *Bonanza.*[7] It is easy to dismiss Bewitched as one of the dumbest and kitchiest shows ever produced, but it would be a mistake to do so. *Bewitched* was such a success in part because of its novelty and its skillful use of special effects, which played to some fairly basic fantasies about magic and control. But it was also successful because it was one of the few shows with an appealing female lead character who offered female viewers a respite from, as well as a critique of, male domination. In *Bewitched* we have a woman's dream and a man's nightmare. Darrin was sur-rounded by an endearing yet constantly troublesome matriarchy, a domestic situation in which his wife, mother-in-law, daughter, and other relatives were all witches, endowed with magical powers, which constantly threatened his professional status and his authority as head of the household.

A show like *Bewitched* was an updated, blander, yet trickier version of *I Love Lucy.* Lucy didn't have magical powers, and she certainly didn't need them to get into trouble. Always struggling to break out of the confines of the domestic sphere and enter Ricky's glamorous world in the public limelight, Lucy was set up by the physical slapstick of the show as a clown, as a woman constantly using her face and body to fight the strictures of femininity. Samantha, however, was not a clown: she always remained a lady. This was one of the show's many con-cessions to traditional femininity and conventional gender roles. Elizabeth Montgomery didn't have to use her face or body the way Lucy did: she had technically mastered special effects to be disruptive for her. Aside from twitching her nose, nodding her head, or raising her hands, she did not become physically grotesque when disrupting Darrin's world. Young, slim, blond, and beautiful, with practical, intelligent ideas about what needed to be done in her commu-nity, yet a witch, Samantha stood at the intersection between middle-class definitions of the ideal young wife and rebelliousness against those definitions.

Samantha embodied important contradictions, for she was a happy, respectable suburban housewife who exerted power beyond the kitchen or the living room. She was at once traditional and modern. The show often suggested that women, especially younger women, were smarter, more creative, and more versatile than men. Samantha had magical powers, but she also excelled at the more mundane female duties of ensuring that social interactions ran smoothly. Often it was up to her to come up with an explanation to Darrin's boss or other outsiders for the bizarre goings-on. Invariably, her explanation placated the irate or confused father figure, and often she succeeded in using the explanation to make Darrin or some other hapless man look good in the eyes of the older male authority figure. Samantha engineered the outcome so that Darrin got the credit for coming up with a great idea or doing a great job, but the audience knew who was the real power behind the throne. And it was key to the show that Darrin have all the sex appeal of egg albumen. Had he really been handsome, sexy, or magnetic, her magic and power would have been too threatening, both to the man and to the viewer.

The question of whether Samantha could use her powers, and under what circumstances, defined the entire series. In the first show, on their wedding night, just before they are supposed to go to bed, Samantha reveals to Darrin that she is a witch. Dressed in her peignoir, Samantha shows a skeptical Darrin just what she can do by making a broken cigarette lighter he's trying to use suddenly ejaculate a flame and by moving an ashtray around the coffee table so he can't successfully flick his ash. (And you thought all that subliminal stuff only went on in liquor ads.) When he nearly faints realizing she really is a witch, Samantha kisses him seductively and he says they'll discuss the problem tomorrow. We know what happens next. The mere suggestion that these two are going to have sex was revolutionary for television at that time. The next day, Darrin makes Samantha promise never to use her powers again. Samantha assures him, "Darling, I'll be the best wife a man ever had." He gets specific. "You're going to have to learn how to be a suburban housewife. . . . And you'll have to learn to cook and clean and keep house and go to my mother's house every Friday night." Samantha says it sounds wonderful. We don't believe her for a minute. There wasn't a woman in the audience who would have given up that kind of power.

We know she won't be able to keep her promise, and her restraint is tested right away. A former girlfriend of Darrin's, dark-haired, rich, seductive, and patronizingly sophisticated—in other words, a bitch—invites Darrin and Samantha over for dinner. During the course of the evening, she openly flirts with Darrin while making insufferably catty remarks to Samantha about her hair and clothes; she's clearly the real demon here. Under an assault like this, when another woman is challenging her for her man, Samantha can't possibly keep her promise to Darrin. Using her magical powers, she makes the rival's hair fall into her eyes, places a large hunk of spinach on one of her front teeth, has her dinner slide into her lap, her dress nearly fall off, and her wig blow off her head. The rival is humiliated and Samantha's use of witchcraft completely justified. At the end of the show, in what became a classic scene in *Bewitched,* Darrin is urging Samantha to come up to bed, and we know exactly what he's got on his mind. But the kitchen is a mess. Samantha says she'll be right up, then raises her arms and zaps the kitchen clean. She says with a self-satisfied smile, "Maybe I'll taper off," a joke rife with ambiguity. Taper off, my ass.

It is also important to note that Samantha's mother—indeed, all her relatives—is strongly opposed to Samantha not using her powers just because of Darrin. Endora constantly casts him as a mere mortal to whom Samantha is superior, and as someone who is constraining Samantha, trying to make her life too confined, boring, and predictable. For Endora, Samantha has another, more exciting destiny, a destiny that spans history and geography. And while Samantha insists that marriage to Darrin is what she wants, she gets to have it both ways, to have the reassurances of being a suburban wife and the adventures of being a more unconventional woman.

What is especially interesting about the show, premiering as it did in 1964, not long after Betty Friedan's *The Feminine Mystique* was a best-seller, is the way it offered, yet sought to diminish, a criticism of female confinement in the home. It is hard to imagine a woman watching who did not identify with the fantasy of cleaning the kitchen or preparing dinner just by twitching her nose. But there were other telling fantasies, repeated week in and week out, about having some real influence in the outside world, and how the world might be better if men just listened to women once in a while. In an episode from the first season, Samantha and Endora eat at Mario's Pizza and decide the food is so good that Mario deserves some publicity. Samantha, by twitching her nose, stops the presses at the local paper and inserts a full-page ad that reads "Eat at Mario's." When the ad comes out, Mario's competitor, the head of Perfect Pizza, is outraged and drops Darrin's ad agency for letting Mario's get the upper hand. When Samantha learns that her husband's account is in jeopardy, she works to repair the damage. She and Endora, using their magic, fill the town's billboards with ads, cover the sky with skywriting, and place "Eat Perfect Pizza" placards on all the pedestrians in town. The delight they take in orchestrating this ad campaign is clear as each tackles a new medium, giggling and saying, "It's your turn," and "Now yours." At the end of the show, with the account saved, Darrin complains, "I'd appreciate your letting me handle my accounts by myself," to which Endora responds sarcastically, "Do you think you can?" Samantha insists with a smile, "Of course he can—except under special circumstances."

In other episodes, Samantha uses her magic to get the mayor to fix the town's traffic lights, to persuade a French fashion designer to design clothes that look good on "the average American woman" and not just on fashion models, and to expose political corruption and help get a reform candidate elected to the city council. In this last episode, Darrin wrongly accuses a corrupt councilman of fraudulent dealings in a city construction contract. Samantha and Endora transport themselves to the councilman's office and use their witchcraft to open his locked file cabinet and study his records. It takes Samantha just a few seconds to confirm that all his dealings, with the sole exception of the one that pea-brained Darrin had tried to expose, had been crooked, another Darrin blunder that causes Endora great mirth. Yet Endora casts various spells to vindicate Darrin and indict the councilman. At the end of the show, we see Darrin, completely befuddled, mumbling to himself as he walks upstairs, while Samantha and Endora stand shoulder to shoulder, leaning slightly into each other with their arms crossed over their chests, smiling knowingly and patronizingly at poor, dumbo Darrin.

The repeated combination of magic, diplomacy (her forte), and good common sense made Samantha's solutions to problems the ones that were clearly the most viable and sensible. Here was a housewife with logical and creative ideas about how to make the world better, and with an ability to act on those ideas and get them a fair hearing, even if she had to do so through her bumbling surrogate, Darrin. (The character was such a zero that Dick York, Darrin number one, was easily replaced in 1969 by another Dick, last name Sargent, as Darrin number two.) Samantha's interventions in advertising, politics, and marketing were a mixed blessing, but often they expedited the solution to a particular problem. And despite his anger and frustration over the personal humiliations, Darrin always loved and admired Samantha. This was one of the first post-1950s sitcoms to show a husband and wife sharing a double bed, and we often saw Darrin looking at Sam with desire.

Samantha stood in contrast to the older women in the show, who were grotesque by comparison and conformed more closely to the age-old archetype of the witch as a wrinkled and disorderly crone.[8] Grotesque women—the battle-axes, villainesses, shrews, and over-the-hill whores of popular culture—with their aging faces and sagging, protruding bodies, were ostracized, pitied, and often destroyed in movies and TV shows because they had moved outside the norms of femininity. But such women also rebelled against and often disrupted the rigid gender codes of society, and the female grotesque par excellence of *Bewitched*—Endora—was no exception. With her overly bouffant, bright red hairdos, two-inch-long false eyelashes, and thick eyeliner that shot up at a forty-five-degree angle to her eyes, Endora made gestures to femininity that were exaggerated, like a Mardi Gras mask. But it was this defiance that gave her power, and made her such a liberatory character. Darrin hated her interventions, and often Samantha did too. She was blunt, honest, catty, and self-indulgent, and she did not waste her time trying to soothe others' feelings or placate men the way Samantha did. She was a caricature of the meddling, hard-edged mother-in-law girls were supposed to cast themselves against. But as played by Agnes Moorehead, Endora also had an arch sophistication and a biting tongue that enabled her to get away with—and enjoy—her assaults on arbitrary male authority, especially when it was imposed on her daughter. Female viewers agreed with her dismissive assessment of Darrin as an impotent doofus and took great delight in her outrageous transgressions, and in her unmovable loyalty to Samantha. Endora got to say what many women wished they could say, and her complete indifference to the approval of men was a joy and relief to watch, even as we knew we did not want to be like her.

The other grotesque female, the baggy-faced, chinless, relentlessly nosy neighbor Mrs. Kravitz, was given none of Endora's protective coloration. There was no masquerade of femininity here. Mrs. Kravitz was a warning, the darker side of female aging. She kept spying on the Stevens house, looking where she wasn't supposed to. Thus, even though she saw "the truth," her reports made her appear crazy. Ugly, unadorned, shrill, she never succeeded in getting anyone else to see what she saw. She was the parody of the old housewife with too much time on her hands and nothing to do except live through others. Old women who become voyeurs, who neglect their appearance and their husbands, are pathetic. This, girls, is who you could become if you pay too much attention to the outside world and not enough to your face, body, and home. Mrs. Kravitz embodied the costs of not adhering to traditional femininity: her husband held her in contempt, and everyone else laughed at and pitied her. Unlike Samantha, who knew how to juggle her domestic duties and her forays into the outside world, Mrs. Kravitz had lost her balance. She spent too much time looking out her window and not enough looking in her mirror, too much surveillance in the wrong direction.

The character we identified with, Samantha—most frequently referred to by her masculine nickname, Sam—was passive and active, flouted her husband's authority yet complied with the role of suburban housewife, was both conforming and rebellious: she gave expression to traditional norms and prefeminist aspirations. The show hailed young female viewers by providing, and seeking to reconcile, images of female equality—and, often, even images of female superiority—with images of female subordination. Samantha's talent and success as a wife lay in knowing when to intervene and when to hold back. She often made mistakes, but because she had the traditional female traits of empathy, tact, flattery, and the ability to craft a compromise, all coupled with her magic, she was able repeatedly to rescue her husband, herself, and her marriage.

The show acknowledged that young women wanted more than confinement in the home, that housework was drudgery, and that husbands were often inept clods. Samantha skillfully managed the contradictions of being a superior being (a witch with power) and a subordinate being (a wife with a husband). She made these contradictions work for her, and she also smoothed them over, demonstrating the juggling act young girls were meant to do when they got married. While the show reaffirmed the primacy of traditional female roles and behaviors, it also provided powerful visual representations of what many young women would like to do if they just had a little power: zap that housework and a few men as well.

I Dream of Jeannie ran from 1965 to 1970 and also featured a woman with magical powers, but this show was predicated on a more flagrant sexual display of Jeannie's body and her desires, even if the network censors made sure Barbara Eden's belly button was discreetly hidden. The premise rested on a male fantasy of a regular guy discovering a beautiful, naive, unworldly woman who will do anything for him and calls him "master," or, more formally, by his military title. (That the "regular guy" was an astronaut played into another male fantasy for good measure.) But the implied power and availability of Jeannie's sexuality were always a threat to her master, Captain (later, Major) Tony Nelson, and sometimes he was most relieved and happiest when she was "in her bottle." Jeannie was always more amorous and sexualized than her master, and this, of course, is what got them into so much trouble. Captain Nelson tried in vain to contain Jeannie both physically and sexually, and in those episodes where Jeannie's bottle was lost, there was considerable tension until it was found and Jeannie could get back inside it again.

I Dream of Jeannie differed from *Bewitched* in crucial ways that already suggested a backlash against the earlier show's discourse of empowerment. Jeannie did not intervene in community affairs the way Samantha did; in fact, she cared little for the public sphere. She was not the ideal 1960s wife who happened to have magical powers. In her pink chiffon harem pants, red bra, pom-pom-trimmed bolero jacket, and chiffon-draped headpiece, Jeannie was from another place and time, an anachronism in 1960s suburban America. She was the dumb, shapely, ditzy blonde with too much power, which she often used impetuously. Hyperfeminized, Jeannie was unreasonably jealous and possessive, giggled a lot, and was overly enthusiastic about whatever her master did: in fact, she often behaved and was treated like a child. Although she got her master into embarrassing situations, unlike Samantha she left him to explain his own way out. She was not seen as shrewder or more creative than Captain Nelson; after all, he was an astronaut, embedded in a world of science, technology, and the military-industrial complex women allegedly *couldn't* master. Jeannie's main goal was to serve Captain Nelson obsequiously, get him to pay more attention to her, and, she hoped, get him to marry her. Although Captain Nelson kept insisting he was the master of the house, Jeannie's magic constantly undermined that assertion. Yet the balance of power always tilted toward him, because Jeannie was more devoted to him and more emotionally dependent on him than he was on her.

The fact that Jeannie didn't know how to behave like a "normal" woman was the basis for a number of the plots in the show. In one telling episode, we see how this show, despite its reliance on many of the same visual gags and tricks as *Bewitched,* differed ideologically from its predecessor. In a 1965 episode, "The Americanization of Jeannie," Jeannie comes to feel that Captain Nelson devotes too much time and attention to his work and not enough to her. She reads a women's magazine and finds an article titled "The Emancipation of Modern Women." She asks, "What does emancipation mean?" and he answers, "You don't have to worry about anything like that." "Oh, yes I do," she insists. "I want to understand your way of life so I can please you." She continues reading the article. "Are you a loser in the battle between the sexes? Is the man in your life aloof, indifferent, difficult to please? Does he fail to appreciate what you have to offer as a female? Answer: Challenge his masculine arrogance. Be independent, self-reliant, unpredictable. You must learn to cope with him on his own grounds. In short, you must become a modern, American woman."

The next day, Nelson comes home to find the house a mess and no dinner on the table. Jeannie walks into the living room in a bathrobe and curlers and says, "Hiya, old boy," instead of her usual, more fawning greeting. Nelson accuses her of not doing any housework, but Jeannie responds by citing part of her magazine article, "How Not to Be a Drudge." "'Share the work with him,'" reads Jeannie as she reaches for a box of chocolates. "I'm an astronaut, not a housekeeper," explodes Nelson. "You must broaden your horizons," retorts Jeannie as she hands him a broom.

Needless to say, Nelson tells Jeannie that a real woman doesn't behave this way, and his reactions, as well as the narrative, repudiate the role reversal she proposes. At the end of the episode, their original relationship is restored, and Nelson advises her, "You need an outlet for your affection. You need a pet." Advice from a magazine about female emancipation turns out to be very bad advice because it undermines the woman's femininity, makes her appear ridiculous, and alienates the man's affections. The advice, of course, is a parody of feminism, for it urges women to be deliberately unattractive and completely self-indulgent, and to make men do the housework while the women do nothing at all.

Bewitched never took such a head-on approach to role reversal, thus it didn't draw such stark boundaries between male and female spheres. *Bewitched* blurred gender roles; *I Dream of Jeannie* accentuated them. Yet both shows anticipated feminism and hailed the prefeminist viewer. Samantha was clearly a role model, while Jeannie was an extreme version of femininity that girls ought not to model themselves after. When women like that got power, look out. Thus, *I Dream of Jeannie* was more of a warning. In *Bewitched*, Darrin's work in an advertising agency was repeatedly compromised by the inappropriate exercise of female power. In *I Dream of Jeannie*, the ante was upped: now, magic inspired by female desire, jealousy, and possessiveness threatened to disrupt one of the crowning achievements of 1960s male technocracy, the U.S. space program. Even NASA was no match for female power and sexuality run amok. In *Bewitched*, female power could be accommodated; in *Jeannie*, it could not. Because of these differences, the central mixed message remains: female power, when let loose in the public sphere, is often disruptive to male authority, but sometimes it also bolsters that authority. These colliding messages made *Bewitched* and *I Dream of Jeannie* simultaneously cautionary and liberatory. The schizophrenic female persona such shows helped constitute saw female obsequiousness amply rewarded. But she also had empowering images of physically zapping things—and men—into their proper place.

In 1964 and 1965, images of female possession were everywhere. In two sitcoms, *The Munsters* and *The Addams Family*, the mothers were black-clad female vampires with often macabre idiosyncrasies. The antithesis of Donna Reed, these moms did not bake chocolate chip cookies or take the PTA seriously. They were more likely making frog-eyeball stew or teaching the kids how to tie hangman's knots and build toy guillotines. Again, it was only through such quasimonsters—totally unrealistic yet unthreatening women from the realms of the supernatural—that females' rebellion against their traditional roles got expressed on TV. And as with *Bewitched* and *I Dream of Jeannie,* the sexual tension between regular guys and newly empowered women was a prominent subtext. A running joke on *The Addams Family* had Gomez unable to restrain himself from planting passionate kisses all along Morticia's irresistible arm. Here we saw the clearest connection between female sexuality and ghoulishness: her monstrous power turned him into a helpless, slavering fool.

Then, in the 1967–68 season, we had a fusion of *Bewitched* and *Gidget,* in the form of the poor, benighted Sally Field as Sister Bertrille. In *The Flying Nun,* perkiness took to the air. It took Sally Field ten years and the ability to portray dozens of personalities in *Sybil* to live down this role. Now we had a female character who could fly, but lest anyone do a Freudian reading, she was, by vocational choice, chaste and asexual. Her flying wasn't always in her control, but when you walk around with headgear shaped like a paper airplane on steroids, the updrafts sometimes just take you away. She often ended up in places where females, especially those from nunneries, weren't supposed to be; she was once nearly shot down as an enemy plane and, on another occasion, pursued by a lovestruck pelican.[9] Here we see the progression from Samantha to Sister Bertrille, from the woman having control of her magical powers and using them, at times, in ways that embarrassed men to the woman's magical powers having control of and embarrassing her. This was, of course, wishful thinking on the part of TV producers, for out in the viewing audience young women were feeling more, not less, empowered.

It is no surprise that, at the moment girls took to the streets in an outpouring of female resistance against the status quo, and in pursuit of new, supposedly false gods, while their mothers flocked to buy a book demanding equal rights for women, the witch and other women with supernatural powers would reappear on the cultural landscape of America. Television shows tried to suggest that if girls and women were feeling a bit restless, a tad mischievous, a mite defiant, these unruly impulses could be managed. But in an effort to co-opt this rebellion, and to translate it into Nielsen ratings, this media strategy backfired. For as we watched Darrin Stevens turned into a Yorkshire terrier, or Major Tony Nelson transported to seventh-century Persia, we saw that male authority wasn't so impregnable or impressive at all.

In real life, teenage girls blithely ignored or pushed through police barricades, with few negative consequences. What many of us experienced and saw, although we barely knew it at the time, was the beginning of a war. It was a battle between sexual rebellion and sexual containment, between the old masculinity and the new androgyny, a fight over how much more masquerading had to go on between men and women. After trying on the personas of the rebel, the sexual sophisticate, the knowing girl who was bonded to other girls in a group, the pursuer, and the witch, some girls decided they didn't want to imagine, fantasize, or pretend anymore. Girls were stepping over old boundaries, and there was no going back. We were on the verge of revolt.

Notes

[1] "The American Female," *Harper's,* October 1962, p. 117.

[2] Marjorie Hunter, "U.S. Panel Urges Women to Sue for Equal Rights," *New York Times,* October 12, 1963, p. 1.

[3] *Publisher's Weekly,* January 18, 1965, pp. 68, 72.

[4] Paul Foley, "Whatever Happened to Women's Rights," *Atlantic Monthly,* March 1964, pp. 63–65; Foley, "Women's Rights—and What They Don't Do about Them," *Reader's Digest,* May 1964, pp. 22–23.

[5] "How Women's Role in U.S. Is Changing," *U.S. News & World Report,* May 30, 1966, pp. 58–60.

[6] For a discussion of the monstrosity of female sexuality see Linda Williams, "When the Woman Looks," in Mary Ann Doane et al., eds., *Re-Vision: Essays in Feminist Film Criticism* (Frederick, MD: University Publications of America, 1984).

[7] Tim Brooks and Earle Marsh, *The Complete Directory to Prime Time Network TV Shows* (New York: Ballantine, 1979), pp. 62, 806–808.

[8] The term and concept of the female grotesque comes from Mary Russo, "Female Grotesques: Carnival and Theory," in Teresa de Lauretis, ed., *Feminist Studies/Critical Studies* (Bloomington: University of Indiana Press, 1986).

[9] Brooks and Marsh, *Complete Directory,* p. 205.

Ally McBeal's Younger Sisters

Jane Rosenzweig

I n the premiere of *Wasteland,* ABC's new prime-time soap by the creator of the WB Network's *Dawson's Creek* and the film *Scream,* 26-year-old Dawnie theorizes that her generation is experiencing a "second coming of age" in which twenty- and thirty-somethings face uncertainties of growing up that used to be the exclusive province of adolescents.

"Look at me," she says. "I've spent my entire life in school, my parents still support me, human relationships baffle me, and I am acutely self-aware—to the point where I am clueless and slightly suicidal." (She is also, in an interesting twist on television's conventional mores, a virgin.) Whether or not Dawnie's hypothesis is applicable to real people—and with any luck for ABC, this will be a subject of fervent water-cooler debate around the country—it certainly applies to the young women of prime time, who are trapped in the most protracted adolescence in television history.

It is perhaps no accident that at a time when youth sells (advertising slots for shows about teenagers, like *Dawson's Creek,* can command more money than those for the consistently top-10 rated *Touched by an Angel*), American pop culture has become preoccupied with our collective inability to grow up. People are staying single longer, and the beauty industry is constantly coaxing us to make ourselves look younger if we want to stay in romantic business.

But the proliferation of teen shows is one thing; the packaging of female adulthood as an extended adolescence is something else altogether. Indeed, what's most interesting about this infantilization of

Jane Rosenzweig writes fiction and nonfiction. She teaches writing at Harvard, where she also directs the writing center.

Reprinted with permission from *The* Prospect, Volume 11, Number 1: 1999. The American Prospect Boston, MA 02109. All righ twenty- and thirty-something women—a trend started by David Kelley's *Ally McBeal* and perpetuated by the women of *Wasteland, Providence,* and to varying degrees a number of new fall programs—is that it coincides with a flood of shows about teenage girl characters who are more assertive, more independent, and more interesting than their adult counterparts. I'd say *Ally McBeal* ought to grow up—except the real problem seems to be that she already has and is still less mature than the average television teenager.

Q: What makes your problems bigger than everyone else's?
A: They're mine.

—Ally McBeal

Most of the people here have been saved by you or helped by you at one time or another.

—A classmate speaking to Buffy Summers,
Buffy the Vampire Slayer

The preoccupations of young women are not new to television; women have always been the key audience for advertisers. A teenage girl in 1963 could flip on the TV to look for facsimiles of herself on *The Patty Duke Show* and *Gidget.* Young adult women, of course, have a long history of television "role models": think of June Cleaver, Donna Reed, and Laura Petrie—or, more recently, Mary Tyler Moore. And the history of television is rife with ambiguous portrayals of women: Are they empowered or trapped in traditional roles (think of *I Dream of Jeannie* and *Charlie's Angels*)? Can brains and femininity be reconciled in a single character, or must they always be dichotomized into either *Cagney and Lacey* or *Baywatch?* Or if they can be reconciled, must the result be *Xena: Warrior Princess?* But for all this history of mixed messages, there has never been a time when the girls were more like women and the women more like girls than right now.

True, the conventional wisdom these days is that the line between adolescence and adulthood is blurring: the young are getting older, the old younger. Though if that's the case, shouldn't our television counterparts be meeting in the middle? Why, instead, do television teenagers have more mature relationships with men than the thirty-somethings do? Why are Buffy the vampire slayer, Felicity, and the girls of *Party of Five* and *Dawson's Creek* so much more emotionally intelligent than the grown-ups on other shows? Harvard psychologist Carol Gilligan and others have observed that the confidence and self-esteem of young girls diminish when they reach adolescence, at which point girls start downplaying their intellects and compromising their personalities in order to adapt to society's expectations—and to be attractive to boys. If current television is any indication, the cultural manifestation of this trend now occurs twice (W*asteland's* Dawnie may be onto something bigger than she knows): if girls go ditzy when they reach adolescence, they seem to be going ditzier still as they pass into young adulthood.

with this phenomenon, I think, can be explained at least in part by our cultural preoccupation biological clocks, a preoccupation that has clearly constrained the imaginations of today's television writers. Can't they conceive of any other kinds of lives for women? If we succumb to the creative failure represented by the latest crop of television shows, the danger is that we, as viewers, will find ourselves accepting these same constraints in our own lives.

> I want to save the world. I just want to get married first.
>
> —Ally McBeal

It has become fashionable to loathe Ally McBeal. Her contribution to the putative death of feminism, her diminutive cuteness, her short skirts, and her perky pouts all combine to make her an insult to any actual Harvard law graduate—or any graduate of any school in any field, for that matter. While the show is still at times clever and even resonant in its focus on the lonely search for a soul mate, Ally is a hard character to sympathize with. It may be kind of funny when she says, "I'm tempted to become a street person cut off from society, but then I wouldn't get to wear my outfits," but it's also pathetic. By the end of last season, when she schemed to win back her boyfriend by hiring a gigolo to make him jealous and then propositioned the gigolo, she'd lost all credibility as an adult character. Mary Tyler Moore wouldn't be caught dead messing up her life like this.

While originally hailed as whimsical and imaginative, and even as it continues to garner accolades (most recently, in September, an Emmy for Best Comedy Series), *Ally McBeal* is well on its way to being the biggest failure of the imagination in prime time. But because of its early critical and ongoing ratings success, Ally has basically created a new category of women on television: pretty young things who, in the guise of successful career women, are actually completely defined by an inability to find a husband and have children. Ally is stalked by a holographic dancing baby meant to remind her (and us) that her biological clock is ticking. While there are women in her age group on television who do care about their careers in some workplace-centered shows—most notably Carol Hathaway on *ER*—most of the dramas and comedy-dramas that focus on personal lives feature immature women who share more with Ally McBeal than with the people we know in real life. Lindsay Dole on Kelley's *The Practice* throws tantrums in court; her unhappy housemate, played by Lara Flynn Boyle, appears more anorexic than Calista Flockhart's Ally and seems even more ill-equipped to handle her personal life. It's as though you're supposed to look at Boyle and think, If only she had a nice husband to take care of her, maybe she would eat.

Perhaps the worst example of TV's confused conception of the single woman is Dr. Sydney Hansen of NBC's *Providence,* which debuted last season. After coming home to find her boyfriend in the shower with another man, she left her lucrative job as an L.A. plastic surgeon and moved home to practice medicine at a free clinic in Providence. Sleeping once again in the room she grew up in, she regularly wakes, sweating, from dreams in which her dead mother is chastising her about her inability to find a man. Syd consistently makes dating decisions more worthy of a teenager than a smart, adult woman, which is what she is theoretically supposed to be. And her skirts are as short as Ally McBeal's; most real doctors and lawyers, it's safe to say, don't dress like that.

Unfortunately, the new fall season offers more of the same. In addition to Dawnie on *Wasteland,* there are the women of NBC's *Cold Feet,* one of whom strikes a blow to sexism by marching into her husband's business meeting to demand, for once and for all, a nanny. (And never mind that the husband appears to have no interest in either wife or child.) Another of the main characters in *Cold Feet* runs off to sulk at her mother's house when she argues with her husband. These characters are like early adolescents who relate to one another by screaming, pouting, and stamping their feet.

Funny thing is, turn the channel to the WB Network, which has made the strongest effort to stake out the youth market, and you find that the characters who actually are adolescent girls do not stamp their feet. They are calm and collected, surprisingly analytical. Television's message: only when they're not worrying about their biological clocks can women have fully developed characters. Is it really the case that only women who are still in high school have the luxury of thinking about things other than themselves without constantly being interrupted by thoughts of their own reproductive limits?

> I need to find out if I'm capable of being a whole person without you.
>
> —15-year-old Joey Potter to her boyfriend Dawson
> on the WB's *Dawson's Creek*

Don't get me wrong: teenage girls on television are not ideal role models. They all have clear skin and shiny hair and don't seem afflicted by any of the maladies of girlhood described by experts. It's not hard to see how some critics would assert that these characters are the primary contributors to body image problems of ordinary girls. (The actress who plays Buffy, Sarah Michelle Gellar, is a spokesmodel for Maybelline cosmetics, whose ads run throughout the show.) And some characters are perhaps more sexually active earlier than we would like the role models for our children to be. But I would rather have my girls watch *Dawson's Creek* or *Buffy* than *Ally McBeal.*

Say what you will about the fanciful premise of *Buffy,* in which Buffy Summers fights the evil denizens of hell in order to save her town. But Buffy is neither man obsessed nor self-absorbed, and she refuses to see her problems, like Ally McBeal does, as bigger than everyone else's. In fact, she balances her personal life quite elegantly with her responsibility to protect her community from evil vampires (okay, so that sounds ridiculous on its face; nevertheless, the lesson it conveys is a worthy one). The problems are of a different scale. She misses out on her own prom in order to make school safe for her friends; she gives up something but earns loyalty and respect in return. Also, her best friend Willow is intelligent, sensitive, principled, and the least stereotypical Jewish woman on television.

Similarly, peel away the music-video veneer from *Dawson's Creek* or *Party of Five* and you'll find some young women who clearly have their feet planted firmly on the ground, even in the context of formulaic television plots. Joey Potter, for example, in spite of having a dead mother and a jailed father, has enough self-awareness to realize that there is an asymmetry between her boyfriend Dawson's passion for filmmaking and her own passion for Dawson. After some initial sadness, she pulls herself together enough to think about what she really wants out of life—and to realize the folly of a self-definition that requires always having a man. Ally McBeal never shows this kind of independence. The tragedy is that, assuming television convention holds, if Joey graduates from college without having landed a husband, she'll be reduced to jabbering preadolescence. (The self-reliant title character of the WB Network's *Felicity* suggests that college women still have their own identities and therefore that it is sometime after college that life begins to be about having babies.)

Sometimes the divide between adolescent maturity and post-adolescent immaturity is starkly evident even within a single show. *Party of Five,* for instance, depicts both teenage girls and twenty-something women. The differences are striking. (Originally about a family of orphans trying to raise themselves, the show has turned into a fairly formulaic soap about adolescents and young adults coexisting in an adult-free San Francisco universe.) Sarah—whose character, now 19, is spinning off this season to a new show called *Time of Your Life*—was one of the first TV characters I saw with the self-awareness to realize that her coquettish attempts to win her boyfriend's heart (in a batch of episodes a few years ago) were not only a waste of her time but also a challenge to her self-esteem, and that she shouldn't have to compromise her intelligence to win love. In an episode at the end of last season, Sarah, now older, attempted to teach this lesson to 16-year-old Claudia while at the same time struggling to maintain her own interests as her life was increasingly overtaken by her boyfriend's responsibilities.

In contrast, twenty-something Kirsten, the girlfriend of the show's oldest sibling, is a unidimensional character painted almost entirely in terms of her inability to have children. The chain of events that followed her learning this fact was over the top: she plagiarized her Ph.D. thesis, had a nervous breakdown, married a man she didn't love, and spent several seasons obsessing about how she would hold onto a man if she couldn't bear children. Meanwhile, the only other twenty-something women on this show have been a stripper who doesn't love her child, an alcoholic who depends on a 19-year-old man to take care of her, and a hard-edged and independent—but, alas, unlovable and unappealing—social worker.

What is it in the logic of television that demands that self-possessed girls full of possibility must evolve into women who are defined entirely by their marriage status and act like spoiled children? To the extent that television reflects or defines many of our central preoccupations as a society, this is a question to take seriously. Mightn't television capture some more complex way of thinking about the role of women in society? Or must television continue to make women into one-issue vessels when they reach childbearing age? The women I know lead richly textured lives, and the ones who do feel the loneliness of being single do not deal with it by throwing tantrums in court or moving home to live with their parents; surely it's the same for the women you know, too. But that's not the impression your daughters would get— or your sons, for that matter—from watching TV.

Sadly, shows featuring teen girls are becoming more and more formulaic, their lead characters more and more flat and conventional. Television producers are like sheep; thus a few dramas about teenagers from the last two seasons have generated a trend that will feature as many as 10 such shows this season, not counting the returning sitcoms *Moesha* and *Sabrina the Teenage Witch,* or the *Moesha* spinoff *The Parkers*. As the new season starts, it will be worth watching to see which of these teen girls can sustain their level of maturity as they age and which will become ditzy stereotypes. We can only hope the girls don't lose character definition as these shows become the norm. One thing is certain: if Buffy Summers grows up to be Ally McBeal, there will be hell to pay. Literally.

Understanding the Text

1. How does Rosenzweig characterize Ally McBeal and other female characters in their twenties and thirties who appear on television?

2. How does Rosenzweig characterize the "younger sisters" to whom her title refers?

3. How does Rosenzweig account for the difference in the way television represents these sets of characters?

THE DOUBLE BIND OF MASCULINITY

. . . .

Gentleman or Beast: The Double Bind of Masculinity

Susan Bordo

In 1956, psychologist Gregory Bateson formulated the concept of the "double bind." A double bind is any situation in which a person is subject to mutually incompatible instructions, in which they are directed to fulfill two contradictory requirements at the same time. Bateson's emphasis was on the double messages that parents send to children—for example, demanding that they stand on their own but at the same time encouraging dependency. But the concept is socially applicable too. In a previous book, *Unbearable Weight*, I used the concept of the double bind to explore some of the contradictions that face young women today, living at a time when girls are encouraged to compete alongside men, to "be all that they can be," to "just do it," and so on—at the same time as they take care to not lose their femininity in the process. So we get superbly skilled, fearless young female athletes who speak in baby voices and bat their eyes like Ally McBeal.

Clearly, this culture places young boys in a double bind too. We fabulously reward those boys who succeed in our ritual arenas of primitive potency, and humiliate the boy whose sexual aggression quota doesn't match up to those standards. But at the same time, we want male aggression to bow to civilization when a girl says "no" and to be transformed into tender passion when she says "yes." The fact that these contradictory directives put a

Susan Bordo is a professor of English and women's studies at the University of Kentucky. Her books and many articles on the relation between the body and consumer culture have established her as a leading authority on issues of masculinity and femininity. Her books include *The Male Body: A New Look at Men in Public and Private* (1999), *Twilight Zones: The Hidden Life of Cultural Images from Plato to O.J.* (1997), and *Unbearable Weight: Feminism, Western Culture, and the Body* (1993).

real person in a difficult (if not impossible) double bind gets masked by the fact that we've created numerous *fictional* heroes who successfully embody both requirements, who have the sexual charisma of an untamed beast and are unbeatable in battle, but are intelligent, erudite, and gentle with women.

Edgar Rice Burroughs's Tarzan is an exemplar. The genetic offspring of British aristocrats, but raised by apes, he combines (as historian Gail Bederman puts it) "the ultimate in Anglo-Saxon manliness with the most primal masculinity . . . violent yet chivalrous; moral yet passionate . . . [and] with a superb body." These qualities make their appearance in every version of the Tarzan story that I've seen, including the recent *George of the Jungle* (Brendan Fraser had the most superb body yet). In a similar vein, Mel Gibson's Braveheart is a fluent linguist, educated in Latin, well-traveled, and a tender, sweet lover. None of that gets in the way, however, when he's called upon to lead an animal-house army of howling Scotsmen against their cruel (and effete) British oppressors. The heroes of *Pulp Fiction* are able to discourse at one moment on abstract intellectual conundrums of philosophy and religion (not to mention cultural variants of the "Big Mac") and in the next, without raising their pulses, blast away at a roomful of human beings.

The mixed messages about manliness get directed at girls as well as boys—and catch them at a very young age. In Disney's most recent version of *Beauty and the Beast,* the beast-hero not only looks and acts quite a bit like a man, but is the keeper of the flame of civilization. True, he must learn to control his anger and to have good table manners. But he owns a high-ceilinged library full of books, and is continually contrasted in the film with the provincial, arrogant, ferociously anti-intellectual hunter Gaston, whom Belle describes at one point as "primeval." (Gaston's room is decorated with antlers; even his furniture is made of antlers.) Gaston, who is a "normal" man, is represented as the truly uncivilized male of the story, because he has no appreciation for beauty (double meaning intended), while the beast, although full of animal rage to begin with, becomes fully tamed under the spell of his love for Belle.

But at the same time as the (tamed) Disney beast represents the virtues of masculine civility, he is also far more romanticized and sexualized *as* beast than in earlier versions of the tale. He growls impressively, rears up on his hind legs in phallic splendor, and has a wild passionate nature that seems almost the cartoon equivalent of Mel Gibson's William Wallace. His aggression is pure of heart, but, like Wallace's, it's pretty potent when it gets going. And this isn't lost on Beauty. In earlier versions of the story—the original tale and various movies based on it, as well as the popular television show—the main idea of the story is that love requires learning to see beyond externals, as the heroine learns to see past the grotesque exterior of the beast to discover the "real" person within (symbolized by the handsome prince who emerges at the end of the story). But in the Disney version, Beauty doesn't really need to see past the beast's externals, for he's pretty magnificent as he is. In fact, as Elaine Showalter writes, "it's a distinct letdown when the Beast turns into a blue-eyed prince"; I agree, the prince is rather lame compared to the commanding figure of the beast. (For Showalter, even the beast was "a bit too gentle for her tastes"; now there's a lover of the wild man!)

The Disney people recognized the erotic charge of their beast; they delayed making the film for a decade, worried about the sexual overtones of the story, until they finally hit on the solution of having constant chaperones around in the castle, in the form of all those talking teapots and dinnerware. But it was the makers of the film, of course, who endowed the beast with all that sex appeal to begin with. As such, the "learning to see past externals" theme becomes merged with, even supplanted by, a version of the "sleeping beauty" motif, whose main point is not the heroine's spiritual education but her sexual awakening. (That's the way contemporary Freudian commentators like Bruno Bettelheim have interpreted the beauty and beast tale too—as about the young girl's initiation into the power of male sexuality.) It's frightening for her at first ("strange, and a bit alarming," as the Disney heroine sings), but it ultimately allows her to unleash the beast within herself. Women, being ovens by nature, need the spark of the male blowtorch to set their instinctual fires going.

The notion that men's more forceful, hotter sexuality is required to turn on a woman's slow-heating oven—an idea which has a certain amount of charm, no doubt about it—is unfortunately also part of the mythology that teaches men not to take "no" for an answer. For in this version of sexual "complementarity," the woman *requires* for her own awakening that the man see past the veneer of civilization motivating her "no" to the *real,* albeit latent, desires within. Of course it's going to take a while . . . she's a slow cooker, remember. But don't give up; she'll come around. That's the way it happens in the movies, isn't it? There, you'll never see the woman who won't let go depicted as anything other than deranged (as in *Fatal Attraction*) or power-mad (as in *Disclosure*). But numerous romantic comedies reward the persistent male suitor for his efforts—with the girl's affections. Popular culture *admires* the man who won't take no for an answer.

When date rape workshops focus on women's learning to say "no" in a way that will be clear and unequivocal, they don't alter this mythology much either. For these (well-meaning) workshops are clearly still imagining women as the gatekeepers of male desire, tamers of the beast, domesticators, while continuing to view men as primitive animals who, if left to their own devices, would naturally plunder everything in sight. The script still has the male in hot pursuit, the woman with the "stop" and "go" signs. Here, women are getting some mixed messages too. John Gray says we should flirt, to stoke the fires of male desire. But popular college training manuals for the prevention of acquaintance rape seem to recommend otherwise. They caution that "flirting," which suggests a certain indecisiveness, a "wait and see what he does for me" attitude, is exactly what should be avoided: "An important part of assertiveness," one of these manuals reads, "includes clearly indicating what is intended with both words and actions. If a woman says 'no' with her mouth, and 'yes' with her body, she is giving a mixed and inconsistent message. She must know what she wants clearly before she can ask for it."

To slightly adapt the refrain that Maurice Chevalier sings in *Gigi:* "Oh, I'm so gla-ad that I-I'm not young . . . nowadays."

"THE MALE ANIMAL" AS IDEOLOGY

Destructive double messages aside, it might seem that science ought to have the last word here about what differences in male and female sexuality are "real" and which are the creations of culture. The findings of evolutionary science should be taken very seriously. I think it's also important to take note that scientific ideas about these matters have changed over time, and in not entirely disinterested or objective ways.

It might come as a surprise to contemporary men and women, but throughout the ancient and medieval periods of Western history, it was women, not men, whom science regarded as the hot-blooded, sexually insatiable sex. Women were believed to have a greater sexual appetite than men and to be less capable of controlling their urges. But these qualities carried meanings different from dominant contemporary notions that equate hair-trigger sexuality with virility. Both Greek and early Christian cultures valued sexual self-control highly (although for different reasons) and viewed domination by one's passions as a sign of weakness, *not* manliness. The truly virile man (or, within Christian tradition, the chaste and godly man) was the master of his own body. Being more at the mercy of our sexual urges was thus among the traits that, ancient science argued, were a sign of women's inferiority to men.

Women's lesser control over our sexual impulses was connected to what was believed to be our greater "passivity"—another feature of our natural inferiority. We've already seen, in an earlier chapter, how approval of male "activity" and revulsion with the man who puts himself in a passive, "feminine" position, affected Greek ideas about sex between men (and still inform some homosexual cultures). The same set of values (male = active = admirable; female = passive = inferior) also were embedded in ideas about reproduction, and demonstrate how profoundly gender ideology is capable of shaping even how "hard" scientists interpret their observations. According to Aristotle, the conception of a living being involves the vitalization of the purely material contribution of the female by the "effective, active" element—the male sperm:

> . . . [T]here must be that which generates and that from which it generates, even if these be one, still they must be distinct in form and their essence must be different . . . If, then, the male stands for the effective and active, and the female, considered as female, for the passive, it follows that what the female would contribute would not be semen but material for the semen to work upon. This is just what we find to be the case, for the catamenia (menstrual material) have in their nature an affinity to the primitive matter.

In other words, what the female contributes to conception is mere glop. The forces that will shape that glop into a distinctive human being are all contributed by the male. This view of things was so powerful that when Leeuwenhoek in 1677 first examined sperm under the newly invented microscope, he saw tiny "animalcules" in it—the "form" of the future being, to be stamped onto the shapeless dough of the menstrual matter. We no longer believe in this cookie-cutter version of reproduction, in which female stuff just lies there, waiting to be penetrated and molded by male form. But if you think we've gone beyond mistaken notions about males as "active" and females as "receptive" in the act of conception, consider this account from Alan Guttmacher's drugstore guide *Pregnancy, Birth and Family Planning:*

> Some of the sperm swim straight up the one-inch, mucus-filled canal with almost purposeful success, while others bog down on the way, getting hopelessly stranded in tissue bays and coves. A small proportion of the total number ejaculated eventually reach the cavity of the uterus and begin their upward two-inch excursion through its length . . . The undaunted ones, those not stranded in this veritable everglade, reach the openings of the two fallopian tubes . . . The one sperm that achieves its destiny has won against gigantic odds, several hundred million to one . . . No one knows just what selective forces are responsible for the victory. Perhaps the winner had the strongest constitution; perhaps it was the swiftest swimmer of all the contestants entered in the race . . . If ovulation occurred within several minutes to twenty-four hours before the sperm's journey ends, the ovum will be in the tube, awaiting fertilization; if ovulation took place more than twenty-four hours before insemination, the egg cell will already have begun to deteriorate and fragment, rendering it incapable of being fertilized by the time the spermatozoon reaches it. On the other hand, if ovulation has not yet occurred, but takes place within two or three days after intercourse, living spermatozoa will be cruising at the tubal site . . .

Guttmacher's drama of driven, supercharged sperm racing to be the first to penetrate a waiting egg is duplicated in the opening credits of *Look Who's Talking,* which depict the perilous journey of "the undaunted ones" to the tune of "I Get Around," and have the successful sperm (the one "who achieves his destiny") provide a running commentary on his progress. And there, at the end of his journey is the giant beach ball of an egg, languorously bobbing, killing time, awaiting the victor's arrival. But this picture is totally inaccurate as a depiction of a typical act of conception. On most occasions, when fertilization occurs it is actually the egg that travels to rendezvous with sperm that have been lolling around, for as much as three days, waiting for her to show up. What Guttmacher and *Look Who's Talking* present as their model is an act of intercourse at ovulation—by no means representative of the majority of fertilizations. Yet it has somehow become our paradigm. Could it be that it goes against the grain to imagine males (or their sperm surrogates) passively hanging around, waiting for Ms. Egg to "call"? (To be fair, Guttmacher does allow that sometimes the sperm will be waiting for the egg. But, significantly, he doesn't describe them as "waiting"; rather, they are "cruising," like guys driving their cars down the street, looking for chicks.)

During the Renaissance and Enlightenment, ideas about sexuality were focused less on men and women and more on race, as the group of people who now came to be seen by Western science as having a naturally hotter, more "primitive" sexuality were the "uncivilized" people of non-European descent: African, West Indian, and Native American Indian (both male and female). As Bryan Edward, a Jamaican planter and English politician, wrote in 1793:

> The Negroes in the West Indies, both men and women, would consider it to be the great exertion of tyranny, and the most cruel of all hardships, to be compelled to confine themselves to a single connection with the other sex. Their passion is mere animal desire, implanted by the great Author of all things for the preservation of the species. This the Negroes, without a doubt, possess in common with the rest of the animal creation, and they indulge it, as inclination prompts, in an almost promiscuous intercourse with the other sex.

The notion that the passion of the Negroes is "mere animal desire" was confirmed by pre-evolutionary (and, later, evolutionary) science, which plotted degrees of similarity and difference between the apes and various racial groups; drawings of Africans, the appropriate features exaggerated, were placed closest to those of apes, while sketches of fine-featured Europeans with noble expressions on their faces occupied the other end of the spectrum. Artists depicted "historical" matings between Africans and orangutans. These ideas that the African man (and woman) is closer to purely instinctual, animal nature still survive today, not only in overt racial stereotypes but also in more subtle ways. Actor Laurence Fishburne was recently depicted in *Vanity Fair* in a series of photographs posing him in menacing, lionlike postures, with captions like: "Laurence has natural grace, but he's not afraid to be savage" and "He's like a dangerous, magnificent beast."

How did we get from the identification of animal sexuality with non-Europeans of both sexes to the current notion that *men*—of all races—are hotter-blooded and more promiscuous in nature than women? It wasn't discoveries in evolutionary science that led the way, but changes in perceptions of what constituted the ideal man in an industrial, increasingly competitive society. By the end of the nineteenth century, Europeans began rethinking their attitudes toward the primitive "savage," not out of any sense of morality or political correctness, but because the primitive savage was beginning to be seen as having something the European gentleman lacked and needed. As we've seen in an earlier chapter, it was a time when the prestige of older notions of manliness was eroding, since those notions revolved around qualities no longer very useful to success in a market-driven economy. Being a "civilized gentleman" didn't get you very far in the competitive jungle of the marketplace. At the same time, "civilization" itself was increasingly being viewed as a source of human "discontent" (as Freud put it) responsible for numerous new nervous disorders seen as being caused by the stresses and strain of modern industrial life.

One of the most interesting expressions of this new mistrust of the suppression of instinct by civilization is found in the French nineteenth-century literature on rabies, which imagined the disease as an eruption of the beast through the suffocating veneer of civilization, turning the human sufferer into an animal, wild, uncontrollable, and dangerous, prone to biting and tearing apart everything in sight. Remarkably but consistently, rabies in dogs too was viewed as the result of hypercivilization and sexual repression! It was believed that dogs in the wild rarely developed rabies, that it was produced by the "unwholesome conditions of domesticity" where dogs are forced into "unnatural chastity by their mistresses."

In this context of growing concern and anxiety about the repressive effects of civilization and its "softening" of men (and dogs), fantasies of recovering an unspoiled, primitive masculinity began to emerge, and with them, a "flood of animal metaphors" poured forth to animate a new conception of masculinity. White men drew on the images and ideology of the savage Other to help them articulate this emerging construction of "passionate manhood" (as historian Anthony Rotundo calls it). The depiction of historical scenes of European rape and pillage—a motif that was formerly most prominent only in racist representations of the black male rapist or marauding Indian—became especially fashionable. Africans and other "primitive" peoples were also playacted in clubs and lodges. Bourgeois, white, American men began to speak of themselves in terms of "animal instincts" and "animal energy." They began to believe that "this nature was their male birthright and that it demanded expression."

In this way, arguably, the notion that men are passionate beasts by nature, who cannot and should not be expected to control themselves, gained cultural cachet—a cachet that has created a special sort of double bind for black men. Within racist mythology, being more instinctual means being a mere animal, a brute. But to the extent that being an untamed animal has become part of the definition of being a potent man, then being associated with sexual instinct and animal magnetism gives one the gender edge. It's no wonder, then, that black artists and athletes have sometimes exploited the stereotypes that endow them with greater potency and "animal" sexuality. Particularly when one has been historically deprived of most of the social privileges of masculinity, it would be hard to relinquish the one advantage one has. Unfortunately, the advantage comes at a high price, for that old racial mythology is still there, ready to be activated. When a white boy acts like a thug, he proves he's not a sissy to the other white guys in his group; when a black boy engages in the same behavior, the same white boys may view it as proof that he's a jungle brute after all.

Today, with many men feeling that women—particularly feminists—have been pushing them around for a couple of decades, the idea of a return to manhood "in the raw" has a refreshed, contemporary appeal. The "Return of the Alpha Male" literature and a good deal of the mythopoetic men's movement seem clearly to be "backlash" reclamations of manhood, which, like some of their Victorian counterparts, view women as responsible for having tamed the beast in man. Other Victorian conceptions, as we've seen, put the chief blame on civilization—and plenty of contemporary ads exploit that notion too, urging escape into the wild (in a luxury four-wheel-drive car). In neither case, however, is the ideal *really* for men to revert to the jungle (except perhaps on a weekend jaunt). For at the same time as we romanticize the wild man and scorn the wimp, we also—like the Greeks—still place great stock in masculine self-control. It's just that we expect it to have a potent, aggressive edge.

Such notions, and the ambivalence about "civilization" and "nature" that underlies them, are vividly illustrated in Mike Nichols's recent contemporary reworking of the werewolf story, in the movie *Wolf.* This film plays with the same idea which was so prominent in the Victorian era—that hypercivilization has made man soft, ineffective, and deadened and that his revitalization requires reconnection with his "animal" nature. Jack Nicholson's character, Will Randall, is a book editor at—oh, dear—"McLeash" House, where he performs his job with "taste, individuality and civility" and is given, at parties, to bemoaning the death of art and the triumph of TV talk shows. He's also a wonderfully "nice" person, as his boss Raymond Alden tells him, explaining why he's replacing him with his unscrupulous, ambitious assistant (who is also having an affair with Randall's wife). "What are you, the last civilized man?" the boss's daughter (Michelle Pfeiffer, wearing a buckskin jacket, by the way) cracks when he apologizes for finishing her drink, spelling it out for those of us who haven't gotten it yet. Randall is civilized, all right. But Nichols can't decide whether or not that's a good thing.

On the one hand, his niceness and love of art and gentleness are favorably contrasted with the ruthless crudeness of his boss and assistant, and the heroine explains that she loves him because he's a "good man" and that's "very exotic" to her. On the other hand, we are encouraged to see him as wimpy. He accepts being fired passively and uncomplainingly; his feminist wife (Kate Nelligan) nags and scolds him. At the beginning of the movie, the night he gets bitten by the wolf, he has just returned from closing a deal with an author; when asked by his wife how he got the author to sign the contract, he says he did it "the old-fashioned way; I begged." But being bitten changes all that for him. He gets in touch with his sexuality and aggression, makes love "like an animal" (as his wife tells him), begins to crave raw meat, and starts stalking game at night. And he gets even in primitive but effective ways with those who cross him. (For example, in a Bernhard Goetz white-man retribution moment, he bites off the fingers of a black gang member who tries to rob him in the park. In another scene, which must have delighted Camille Paglia, he pisses on the shoes of his assistant: "Just marking my territory and you got in the way," he says.)

All these, arguably, are in keeping with traditional werewolf stuff, albeit modernized. But becoming a wolf also makes Will more effective in the world of business—he sees and hears acutely, and uses this to his advantage—and most strikingly, his new wolfness makes him adept at the very kinds of ruthless machinations that the movie had portrayed so negatively earlier and juxtaposed against Will's civilized "niceness." He engineers a brilliant yet deceptive scheme to get his job back, and earns the respect of all around him. "You're my god," says his faithful editorial assistant (David Hyde Pierce) when he discovers that Will's scheme to get his job back is a bluff, based on a lie. And when the scheme succeeds, his boss tells him that if he'd known Will was "this ruthless, I'd never have fired you in the first place."

Here, the idea that real manliness (and sexual vitality and zest for life) is to be found outside man-made culture is merged with the idea of the workplace as the man-made jungle where a man might realize himself, if he's the right sort of animal. Will's transformation gives him the right stuff, and in the process he becomes something of an incoherency. He begins to speak like a character from a whole other movie. "The worm has turned and is packing an Uzi," he declares to his secretary. The bite of the wolf has turned Jack Nicholson into Arnold Schwarzenegger! Wolf man as terminator? Somehow I think the metaphors are getting mixed. In the end, the movie does suggest a final exit, with Michelle Pfeiffer, into the real jungle, where they will live fully as animals. But until then, the wolf man is allowed to have it all— spontaneous and playful animal sex with Michelle Pfeiffer, carnivorous romps in the woods, aggressive vengeance against his enemies— and more business smarts than Malcolm Forbes.

Works Cited

Aristotle. (1941). "On the Generation of Animals." Trans. Arthur Platt, 729a 25–30, p. 676. In Richard McKeon (ed). *The Basic Works of Aristotle.* New York: Random House.

Bederman, Gail. (1995). *Manliness and Civilization.* Chicago: University of Chicago Press.

Bettelheim, Bruno. (1977). *The Uses of Enchantment: The Meaning and Importance of Fairy Tales.* New York: Vintage Books.

Gray, John. (1997). *Mars and Venus on a Date.* New York: HarperCollins.

Gray, John. (1992). *Men Are from Mars, Women Are from Venus.* New York: HarperCollins.

Guttmacher, Alan. (1987). *Pregnancy, Birth and Family Planning.* New York: Signet Books.

Showalter, Elaine. (1997). "Beauty and the Beast: Disney Meets a Liberated Love Story for the 90's," *Premiere,* October, p. 66.

Singer, A. L. (1991). *Disney's Beauty and the Beast.* New York: Disney Press.

Rip Van Winkle

Washington Irving

The following Tale was found among the papers of the late Diedrich Knickerbocker, an old gentleman of New York, who was very curious in the Dutch history of the province, and the manners of the descendants from its primitive settlers. His historical researches, however, did not lie so much among books, as among men; for the former are lamentably scanty on his favourite topics; whereas he found the old burghers, and still more, their wives, rich in that legendary lore so invaluable to true history. Whenever, therefore, he happened upon a genuine Dutch family, snugly shut up in its low roofed farm house, under a spreading sycamore, he looked upon it as a little clasped volume of black letter, and studied it with the zeal of a bookworm.

The result of all these researches was a history of the province during the reign of the Dutch governors, which he published some years since. There have been various opinions as to the literary character of his work and, to tell the truth, it is not a whit better than it should be. Its chief merit is its scrupulous accuracy, which indeed was a little questioned on its first appearance, but has since been completely established; and it is now admitted into all historical collections as a book of unquestionable authority.

The old gentleman died shortly after the publication of his work, and now that he is dead and gone, it cannot do much harm to his memory to say that his time might have been much better employed in weightier labours. He, however, was apt to ride his hobby his own way; and though it

Washington Irving (1783–1859) had written several earlier collections of essays and tales, but it was the publication of *The Sketch Book* in 1820 that secured his fame in America and Britain, making him the first American fiction writer to achieve international celebrity. A number of his stories, "Rip Van Winkle" and "The Legend of Sleepy Hollow" among them (both appeared in *The Sketch Book*), are classics of American literature and esteemed for their artful prose, shrewd comedy, and insight into the national character.

did now and then kick up the dust a little in the eyes of his neighbours, and grieve the spirit of some friends for whom he felt the truest deference and affection; yet his errors and follies are remembered "more in sorrow than in anger," and it begins to be suspected that he never intended to injure or offend. But however his memory may be appreciated by criticks, it is still held dear by many folk whose good opinion is well worth having; particularly by certain biscuit bakers, who have gone so far as to imprint his likeness on their new year cakes, and have thus given him a chance for immortality, almost equal to being stamped on a Waterloo medal, or a Queen Anne's farthing.

Rip Van Winkle

A Posthumous Writing of Diedrich Knickerbocker

> By Woden, God of Saxons,
> From whence comes Wensday, that is Wodensday,
> Truth is a thing that ever I will keep
> Unto thylke day in which I creep into
> My sepulchre—
>
> *Cartwright*

Whoever has made a voyage up the Hudson must remember the Kaatskill mountains. They are a dismembered branch of the great Appalachian family, and are seen away to the west of the river swelling up to noble height and lording it over the surrounding country. Every change of season, every change of weather, indeed every hour of the day, produces some change in the magical hues and shapes of these mountains, and they are regarded by all the good wives far and near as perfect barometers. When the weather is fair and settled they are clothed in blue and purple, and print their bold outlines on the clear evening sky; but sometimes, when the rest of the landscape is cloudless, they will gather a hood of grey vapours about their summits, which, in the last rays of the setting sun, will glow and light up like a crown of glory.

At the foot of these fairy mountains the voyager may have descried the light smoke curling up from a village, whose shingle roofs gleam among the trees, just where the blue tints of the upland melt away into the fresh green of the nearer landscape. It is a little village of great antiquity, having been founded by some of the Dutch colonists in the early times of the province, just about the beginning of the government of the good Peter Stuyvesant, (may he rest in peace!) and there were some of the houses of the original settlers standing within a few years; built of small yellow bricks brought from Holland, having latticed windows and gable fronts, surmounted with weathercocks.

In that same village, and in one of these very houses (which to tell the precise truth was sadly time worn and weather beaten) there lived many years since, while the country was yet a province of Great Britain, a simple good natured fellow of the name of Rip Van Winkle. He was a descendant of the Van Winkles who figured so gallantly in the chivalrous days of Peter Stuyvesant, and accompanied him to the siege of Fort Christina. He inherited, however, but little of the martial character of his ancestors. I have observed that he was a simple good natured man; he was moreover a kind neighbour, and an obedient, henpecked husband. Indeed to the latter circumstance might be owing that meekness of spirit which gained him such universal popularity; for those men are most apt to be obsequious and conciliating abroad, who are under the discipline of shrews at home. Their tempers doubtless are rendered pliant and malleable in the fiery furnace of domestic tribulation, and a curtain lecture is worth all the sermons in the world for teaching the virtues of patience and long suffering. A termagant wife may therefore in some respects be considered a tolerable blessing—and if so, Rip Van Winkle was thrice blessed.

Certain it is that he was a great favourite among all the good wives of the village, who as usual with the amiable sex, took his part in all family squabbles, and never failed, whenever they talked those matters over in their evening gossippings, to lay all the blame on Dame Van Winkle. The children of the village too would shout with joy whenever he approached. He assisted at their sports, made their play things, taught them to fly kites and shoot marbles, and told them long stories of ghosts, witches and Indians. Whenever he went dodging about the village he was surrounded by a troop of them hanging on his skirts, clambering on his back and playing a thousand tricks on him with impunity; and not a dog would bark at him throughout the neighbourhood.

The great error in Rip's composition was an insuperable aversion to all kinds of profitable labour. It could not be from the want of assiduity or perseverance; for he would sit on a wet rock, with a rod as long and heavy as a Tartar's lance, and fish all day without a murmur, even though he should not be encouraged by a single nibble. He would carry a fowling piece on his shoulder for hours together, trudging through woods, and swamps and up hill and down dale, to shoot a few squirrels or wild pigeons; he would never refuse to assist a neighbour even in the roughest toil, and was a foremost man at all country frolicks for husking Indian corn, or building stone fences; the women of the village too used to employ him to run their errands and to do such little odd jobs as their less obliging husbands would not do for them—in a word Rip was ready to attend to any body's business but his own; but as to doing family duty, and keeping his farm in order, he found it impossible.

In fact he declared it was of no use to work on his farm; it was the most pestilent little piece of ground in the whole country; every thing about it went wrong and would go wrong in spite of him. His fences were continually falling to pieces; his cow would either go astray or get among the cabbages, weeds were sure to grow quicker in his fields than any where else;

the rain always made a point of setting in just as he had some outdoor work to do. So that though his patrimonial estate had dwindled away under his management, acre by acre until there was little more left than a mere patch of Indian corn and potatoes, yet it was the worst conditioned farm in the neighbourhood.

His children too were as ragged and wild as if they belonged to nobody. His son Rip, an urchin begotten in his own likeness, promised to inherit the habits with the old clothes of his father. He was generally seen trooping like a colt at his mother's heels, equipped in a pair of his father's cast off galligaskins, which he had much ado to hold up with one hand, as a fine lady does her train in bad weather.

Rip Van Winkle, however, was one of those happy mortals of foolish, well oiled dispositions, who take the world easy, eat white bread or brown, whichever can be got with least thought or trouble, and would rather starve on a penny than work for a pound. If left to himself, he would have whistled life away in perfect contentment, but his wife kept continually dinning in his ears about his idleness, his carelessness and the ruin he was bringing on his family. Morning noon and night her tongue was incessantly going, and every thing he said or did was sure to produce a torrent of household eloquence. Rip had but one way of replying to all lectures of the kind, and that by frequent use had grown into a habit. He shrugged his shoulders, shook his head, cast up his eyes, but said nothing. This, however, always provoked a fresh volley from his wife, so that he was fain to draw off his forces and take to the outside of the house—the only side which in truth belongs to a henpecked husband.

Rip's sole domestic adherent was his dog Wolf who was as much henpecked as his master, for Dame Van Winkle regarded them as companions in idleness, and even looked upon Wolf with an evil eye as the cause of his master's going so often astray. True it is, in all points of spirit befitting an honourable dog, he was as courageous an animal as ever scoured the woods—but what courage can withstand the ever during and all besetting terrors of a woman's tongue? The moment Wolf entered the house his crest fell, his tail drooped to the ground or curled between his legs, he sneaked about with a gallows air, casting many a sidelong glance at Dame Van Winkle, and at the least flourish of a broomstick or ladle he would fly to the door with yelping precipitation.

Times grew worse and worse with Rip Van Winkle as years of matrimony rolled on; a tart temper never mellows with age, and a sharp tongue is the only edged tool that grows keener with constant use. For a long while he used to console himself when driven from home, by frequenting a kind of perpetual club of the sages, philosophers and other idle personages of the village which held its sessions on a bench before a small inn, designated by a rubicund portrait of his majesty George the Third. Here they used to sit in the shade, through a long lazy summer's day, talking listlessly over village gossip, or telling endless sleepy stories about nothing. But it would have been worth any statesman's money to have heard the profound discussions that sometimes took place, when by chance an old newspaper fell into their hands from some passing traveller. How solemnly they would listen to the contents as drawled out by Derrick Van Bummel the schoolmaster, a dapper, learned little man, who was not to be daunted by the most gigantic word in the dictionary; and how sagely they would deliberate upon public events some months after they had taken place.

The opinions of this junto were completely controlled by Nicholaus Vedder, a patriarch of the village, and landlord of the inn, at the door of which he took his seat from morning till night, just moving sufficiently to avoid the sun and keep in the shade of a large tree; so that the neighbours could tell the hour by his movements as accurately as by a sun dial. It is true he was rarely heard to speak, but smoked his pipe incessantly. His adherents, however (for every great man has his adherents), perfectly understood him and knew how to gather his opinions. When any thing that was read or related displeased him, he was observed to smoke his pipe vehemently and to send forth short, frequent and angry puffs; but when pleased he would inhale the smoke slowly and tranquilly and emit it in light and placid clouds, and sometimes taking the pipe from his mouth and letting the fragrant vapour curl about his nose, would gravely nod his head in token of perfect approbation.

From even this strong hold the unlucky Rip was at length routed by his termagant wife who would suddenly break in upon the tranquility of the assemblage and call the members all to naught; nor was that august personage Nicholaus Vedder himself sacred from the daring tongue of this terrible virago, who charged him outright with encouraging her husband in habits of idleness.

Poor Rip was at last reduced almost to despair; and his only alternative to escape from the labour of the farm and the clamour of his wife, was to take gun in hand and stroll away into the woods. Here he would sometimes seat himself at the foot of a tree and share the contents of his wallet with Wolf, with whom he sympathised as a fellow sufferer in persecution. "Poor Wolf," he would say, "thy mistress leads thee a dog's life of it, but never mind my lad, whilst I live thou shalt never want a friend to stand by thee!" Wolf would wag his tail, look wistfully in his master's face, and if dogs can feel pity I verily believe he reciprocated the sentiment with all his heart.

In a long ramble of the kind on a fine autumnal day, Rip had unconsciously scrambled to one of the highest parts of the Kaatskill mountains. He was after his favourite sport of squirrel shooting and the still solitudes had echoed and re-echoed with the reports of his gun. Panting and fatigued he threw himself, late in the afternoon, on a green knoll, covered with mountain herbage, that crowned the brow of a precipice. From an opening between the trees he could overlook all the lower country for many a mile of rich woodland. He saw at a distance the lordly Hudson, far, far below him, moving on its silent but majestic course, with the reflection of a purple cloud, or the sail of a lagging bark here and there sleeping on its glassy bosom, and at last losing itself in the blue highlands.

On the other side he looked down into a deep mountain glen, wild, lonely and shagged, the bottom filled with fragments from the impending cliffs and scarcely lighted by the reflected rays of the setting sun. For some time Rip lay musing on this scene, evening was gradually advancing, the mountains began to throw their long blue shadows over the valleys, he saw that it would be dark, long before he could reach the village, and he heaved a heavy sigh when he thought of encountering the terrors of Dame Van Winkle.

As he was about to descend he heard a voice from a distance hallooing "Rip Van Winkle! Rip Van Winkle!" He looked around, but could see nothing but a crow winging its solitary flight across the mountain. He thought his fancy must have deceived him and turned again to descend, when he heard the same cry ring through the still evening air: "Rip Van Winkle! Rip Van Winkle!"—at the same time Wolf bristled up his back and giving a low growl, skulked to his master's side, looking fearfully down into the glen. Rip now felt a vague apprehension stealing over him; he looked anxiously in the same direction and perceived a strange figure slowly toiling up the rocks and bending under the weight of something he carried on his back. He was surprised to see any human being in this lonely and unfrequented place, but supposing it to be some one of the neighbourhood in need of his assistance he hastened down to yield it.

On nearer approach he was still more surprised at the singularity of the stranger's appearance. He was a short, square built old fellow, with thick bushy hair and a grizzled beard. His dress was of the antique Dutch fashion, a cloth jerkin strapped round the waist, several pair of breeches, the outer one of ample volume decorated with rows of buttons down the sides and bunches at the knees. He bore on his shoulder a stout keg that seemed full of liquor, and made signs for Rip to approach and assist him with the load. Though rather shy and distrustful of this new acquaintance Rip complied with his usual alacrity, and mutually relieving each other they clambered up a narrow gully apparently the dry bed of a mountain torrent. As they ascended Rip every now and then heard long rolling peals like distant thunder, that seemed to issue out of a deep ravine or rather cleft between lofty rocks, toward which their rugged path conducted. He paused for an instant, but supposing it to be the muttering of one of those transient thunder showers which often take place in mountain heights, he proceeded. Passing through the ravine they came to a hollow like a small amphitheatre, surrounded by perpendicular precipices, over the brinks of which impending trees shot their branches, so that you only caught glimpses of the azure sky and the bright evening cloud. During the whole time Rip and his companion had laboured on in silence, for though the former marvelled greatly what could be the object of carrying a keg of liquor up this wild mountain, yet there was something strange and incomprehensible about the unknown, that inspired awe and checked familiarity.

On entering the amphitheatre new objects of wonder presented themselves. On a level spot in the centre was a company of odd looking personages playing at ninepins. They were dressed in a quaint outlandish fashion—some wore short doublets, others jerkins with long knives in their belts and most of them had enormous breeches of similar style with that of the guide's. Their visages too were peculiar. One had a large head, broad face and small piggish eyes. The face of another seemed to consist entirely of nose, and was surmounted by a white sugarloaf hat, set off with a little red cock's tail. They all had beards of various shapes and colours. There was one who seemed to be the Commander. He was a stout old gentleman, with a weatherbeaten countenance. He wore a laced doublet, broad belt and hanger, high crowned hat and feather, red stockings and high heel'd shoes with roses in them. The whole group reminded Rip of the figures in an old Flemish painting, in the parlour of Dominie Van Schaick the village parson, and which had been brought over from Holland at the time of the settlement.

What seemed particularly odd to Rip was, that though these folks were evidently amusing themselves, yet they maintained the gravest faces, the most mysterious silence, and were, withal, the most melancholy party of pleasure he had ever witnessed. Nothing interrupted the stillness of the scene, but the noise of the balls, which, whenever they were rolled, echoed along the mountains like rumbling peals of thunder.

As Rip and his companion approached them they suddenly desisted from their play and stared at him with such fixed statue like gaze, and such strange uncouth, lack lustre countenances, that his heart turned within him, and his knees smote together. His companion now emptied the contents of the keg into large flagons and made signs to him to wait upon the company. He obeyed with fear and trembling; they quaffed the liquor in profound silence and then returned to their game.

By degrees Rip's awe and apprehension subsided. He even ventured, when no eye was fixed upon him, to taste the beverage, which he found had much of the flavour of excellent hollands. He was naturally a thirsty soul and was soon tempted to repeat the draught. One taste provoked another, and he reiterated his visits to the flagon so often that at length his senses were overpowered, his eyes swam in his head—his head gradually declined and he fell into a deep sleep.

On awaking he found himself on the green knoll from whence he had first seen the old man of the glen. He rubbed his eyes—it was a bright, sunny morning. The birds were hopping and twittering among the bushes, and the eagle was wheeling aloft and breasting the pure mountain breeze. "Surly," thought Rip, "I have not slept here all night." He recalled the occurrences before he fell asleep. The strange man with a keg of liquor—the mountain ravine—the wild retreat among the rocks—the woe begone party at ninepins—the flagon—"ah! that flagon! that wicked flagon!" thought Rip—"what excuse shall I make to Dame Van Winkle?"

He looked round for his gun, but in place of the clean well oiled fowling piece he found an old firelock lying by him, the barrel encrusted with rust; the lock falling off and the stock worm eaten. He now suspected that the grave roysters of the mountain had put a trick upon him, and having dosed him with liquor, had robbed him of his gun. Wolf too had disappeared, but he might have strayed away after a squirrel or partridge. He whistled after him and shouted his name—but all in vain; the echoes repeated his whistle and shout, but no dog was to be seen.

He determined to revisit the scene of the last evening's gambol, and if he met with any of the party, to demand his dog and gun. As he arose to walk he found himself stiff in the joints and wanting in his usual activity. "These mountain beds do not agree with me," thought Rip, "and if this frolick should lay me up with a fit of the rheumatism, I shall have a blessed time with Dame Van Winkle." With some difficulty he got down into the glen; he found the gully up which he and his companion had ascended the preceding evening, but to his astonishment a mountain stream was now foaming down it; leaping from rock to rock, and filling the glen with babbling murmurs. He, however, made shift to scramble up its sides working his toilsome way through thickets of birch, sassafras and witch hazel, and sometimes tripped up or entangled by the wild grape vines that twisted their coils and tendrils from tree to tree, and spread a kind of net work in his path.

At length he reached to where the ravine had opened through the cliffs, to the amphitheatre—but no traces of such opening remained. The rocks presented a high impenetrable wall over which the torrent came tumbling in a sheet of feathery foam, and fell into a broad deep basin black from the shadows of the surrounding forest. Here then poor Rip was brought to a stand. He again called and whistled after his dog—he was only answered by the cawing of a flock of idle crows, sporting high in air about a dry tree that overhung a sunny precipice; and who, secure in their elevation seemed to look down and scoff at the poor man's perplexities.

What was to be done? The morning was passing away and Rip felt famished for want of his breakfast. He grieved to give up his dog and gun; he dreaded to meet his wife; but it would not do to starve among the mountains. He shook his head, shouldered the rusty fire lock and with a heart full of trouble and anxiety, turned his steps homeward.

As he approached the village he met a number of people, but none whom he knew, which somewhat surprised him for he had thought himself acquainted with every one in the country round. Their dress too was of a different fashion from that to which he was accustomed. They all stared at him with equal marks of surprise, and whenever they cast their eyes upon him, invariably stroked their chins. The constant recurrence of this gesture induced Rip involuntarily to do the same, when to his astonishment he found his beard had grown a foot long!

He had now entered the skirts of the village. A troop of strange children ran at his heels, hooting after him and pointing at his grey beard. The dogs too, not one of which he recognized for an old acquaintance, barked at him as he passed. The very village was altered—it was larger and more populous. There were rows of houses which he had never seen before, and those which had been his familiar haunts had disappeared. Strange names were over the doors—strange faces at the windows—every thing was strange. His mind now misgave him; he began to doubt whether both he and the world around him were not bewitched. Surely this was his native village which he had left but the day before. There stood the Kaatskill mountains—there ran the silver Hudson at a distance—there was every hill and dale precisely as it had always been—Rip was sorely perplexed—"That flagon last night," thought he, "has addled my poor head sadly!"

It was with some difficulty that he found the way to his own house, which he approached with silent awe, expecting every moment to hear the shrill voice of Dame Van Winkle. He found the house gone to decay—the roof fallen in, the windows shattered and the doors off the hinges. A half starved dog that looked like Wolf was skulking about it. Rip called him by name but the cur snarled, shewed his teeth and passed on. This was an unkind cut indeed— "My very dog," sighed poor Rip, "has forgotten me!"

He entered the house, which, to tell the truth, Dame Van Winkle had always kept in neat order. It was empty, forlorn and apparently abandoned. This desolateness overcame all his connubial fears—he called loudly for his wife and children— the lonely chambers rung for a moment with his voice, and then all again was silence.

He now hurried forth and hastened to his old resort, the village inn—but it too was gone. A large, ricketty wooden building stood in its place, with great gaping windows, some of them broken, and mended with old hats and petticoats, and over the door was printed "The Union Hotel, by Jonathan Doolittle." Instead of the great tree, that used to shelter the quiet little Dutch inn of yore, there now was reared a tall naked pole with something on top that looked like a red night cap, and from it was fluttering a flag on which was a singular assemblage of stars and stripes—all this was strange and incomprehensible. He recognized on the sign, however, the ruby face of King George under which he had smoked so many a peaceful pipe, but even this was singularly metamorphosed. The red coat was changed for one of blue and buff; a sword was held in the hand instead of a sceptre; the head was decorated with a cocked hat, and underneath was printed in large characters GENERAL WASHINGTON.

There was as usual a crowd of folk about the door; but none that Rip recollected. The very character of the people seemed changed. There was a busy, bustling disputatious tone about it, instead of the accustomed phlegm and drowsy tranquility. He looked in vain for the sage Nicholaus Vedder with his broad face, double chin and fair long pipe, uttering clouds of tobacco smoke instead of idle speeches. Or Van Bummel the schoolmaster doling forth the contents of an ancient newspaper. In place of these a lean bilious looking fellow with his pockets full of hand bills, was haranguing vehemently about rights of citizens—elections— members of Congress—liberty—Bunker's hill—heroes of seventy six—and other words which were a perfect babylonish jargon to the bewildered Van Winkle.

The appearance of Rip with his long grizzled beard, his rusty fowling piece his uncouth dress and an army of women and children at his heels soon attracted the attention of the tavern politicians. They crowded around him eying him from head to foot, with great curiosity. The orator bustled up to him, and drawing him partly aside, enquired "on which side he voted?"—Rip stared in vacant stupidity. Another short but busy little fellow, pulled him by the arm and rising on tiptoe, enquired in his ear " whether he was Federal or Democrat?"—Rip was equally at a loss to comprehend the question—when a knowing, self important old gentleman, in a sharp cocked hat, made his way through the crowd, putting them to the right and left with his elbows as he passed, and planting himself before Van Winkle, with one arm akimbo, the other resting on his cane, his keen eyes and sharp hat penetrating as it were into his very soul, demanded in an austere tone—"what brought him to the election with a gun on his shoulder and a mob at his heels, and whether he meant to breed a riot in the village?"— "Alas gentlemen," cried Rip, somewhat dismayed, "I am a poor quiet man, a native of the place, and a loyal subject of the King—God bless him!"

Here a general shout burst from the byestanders—"A tory! a tory! a spy! a Refugee! hustle him! away with him!"—It was with great difficulty that the self important man in the cocked hat restored order; and having assumed a ten fold austerity of brow demanded again of the unknown culprit, what he came there for and whom he was seeking. The poor man humbly assured him that he meant no harm; but merely came there in search of some of his neighbours, who used to keep about the tavern.

"—Well—who are they?—name them."

Rip bethought himself a moment and enquired, "Where's Nicholaus Vedder?"

There was a silence for a little while, when an old man replied, in a thin, piping voice, "Nicholaus Vedder? why he is dead and gone these eighteen years! There was a wooden tombstone in the church yard that used to tell all about him, but that's rotted and gone too."

"Where's Brom Dutcher?"

"Oh he went off to the army in the beginning of the war; some say he was killed at the storming of Stoney Point—others say he was drowned in a squall at the foot of Antony's Nose—I don't know—he never came back again."

"Where's Van Bummel the schoolmaster?"

"He went off to the wars too—was a great militia general, and is now in Congress."

Rip's heart died away at hearing of these sad changes in his home and friends, and finding himself thus alone in the world—every answer puzzled him too by treating of such enormous lapses of time and of matters which he could not understand—war—Congress, Stoney Point—he had no courage to ask after any more friends, but cried out in despair, "Does nobody here know Rip Van Winkle?"

"Oh. Rip Van Winkle?" exclaimed two or three—"oh to be sure!—that's Rip Van Winkle— yonder—leaning against the tree."

Rip looked and beheld a precise counterpart of himself, as he went up the mountain: apparently as lazy and certainly as ragged! The poor fellow was now completely confounded.

He doubted his own identity, and whether he was himself or another man. In the midst of his bewilderment the man in the cocked hat demanded who he was,—what was his name?

"God knows," exclaimed he, at his wit's end, "I'm not myself.—I'm somebody else—that's me yonder—no—that's somebody else got into my shoes—I was myself last night; but I fell asleep on the mountain—and they've changed my gun—and every thing's changed—and I'm changed—and I can't tell what's my name, or who I am!"

The byestanders began now to look at each other, nod, wink significantly and tap their fingers against their foreheads. There was a whisper also about securing the gun, and keeping the old fellow from doing mischief—at the very suggestion of which, the self important man in the cocked hat retired with some precipitation. At this critical moment a fresh likely looking woman pressed through the throng to get a peep at the greybearded man. She had a chubby child in her arms, which frightened at his looks began to cry. "Hush Rip," cried she, "hush you little fool, the old man won't hurt you." The name of the child, the air of the mother, the tone of her voice all awakened a train of recollections in his mind. "What is your name my good woman?" asked he.

"Judith Gardenier."

"And your father's name?"

"Ah, poor man, Rip Van Winkle was his name, but it's twenty years since he went away from home with his gun and never has been heard of since—his dog came home without him—but whether he shot himself, or was carried away by the Indians no body can tell. I was then but a little girl."

Rip had but one question more to ask, but he put it with a faltering voice—

"Where's your mother?"—

Oh she too had died but a short time since—she broke a blood vessel in a fit of passion at a New England pedlar.—

There was a drop of comfort at least in this intelligence. The honest man could contain himself no longer—he caught his daughter and her child in his arms.—"I am your father!" cried he—"Young Rip Van Winkle once—old Rip Van Winkle now!—does nobody know poor Rip Van Winkle!"

All stood amazed, until an old woman tottering out from among the crowd put her hand to her brow and peering under it in his face for a moment exclaimed—"Sure enough!— it is Rip Van Winkle—it is himself—welcome home again old neighbour—why, where have you been these twenty long years?"

Rip's story was soon told, for the whole twenty years had been to him but as one night. The neighbours stared when they heard it; some were seen to wink at each other and put their tongues in their cheeks, and the self important man in the cocked hat, who when the alarm was over had returned to the field, screwed down the corners of his mouth and shook his head—upon which there was a general shaking of the head throughout the assemblage.

It was determined, however, to take the opinion of old Peter Vanderdonk, who was seen slowly advancing up the road. He was a descendant of the historian of that name, who wrote one of the earliest accounts of the province. Peter was the most ancient inhabitant of the village and well versed in all the wonderful events and traditions of the neighbourhood. He recollected Rip at once, and corroborated his story in the most satisfactory manner. He assured the company that it was a fact handed down from his ancestor the historian, that the Kaatskill mountains had always been haunted by strange beings. That it was affirmed that the great Hendrick Hudson, the first discoverer of the river and country, kept a kind of vigil there every twenty years, with his crew of the Half Moon—being permitted in this way to revisit the scenes of his enterprize and keep a guardian eye upon the river and the great city called by his name. That his father had once seen them in their old Dutch dresses playing at nine pins in a hollow of the mountain; and that he himself had heard one summer afternoon the sound of their balls, like distant peals of thunder.

To make a long story short—the company broke up, and returned to the more important concerns of the election. Rip's daughter took him home to live with her; she had a snug well furnished house, and a stout cheery farmer for a husband whom Rip recollected for one of the urchins that used to climb upon his back. As to Rip's son and heir, who was the ditto of himself seen leaning against the tree; he was employed to work on the farm; but evinced an hereditary disposition to attend to any thing else but his business.

Rip now resumed his old walks and habits; he soon found many of his former cronies, though all rather the worse for the wear and tear of time; and preferred making friends among the rising generation, with whom he soon grew into great favour. Having nothing to do at home, and being arrived at that happy age when a man can be idle, with impunity, he took his place once more on the bench at the inn door and was reverenced as one of the patriarchs of the village and a chronicle of the old times "before the war." It was some time before he could get into the regular track of gossip, or could be made to comprehend the strange events that had taken place during his torpor. How that there had been a revolutionary war—that the country had thrown off the yoke of Old England and that instead of being a subject of his majesty George the Third, he was now a free citizen of the United States. Rip in fact was no politician; the changes of states and empires made but little impression on him; but there was one species of despotism under which he had long groaned and that was petticoat government. Happily that was at an end—he had got his neck out of the yoke of matrimony, and could go in and out whenever he pleased without dreading the tyranny of Dame Van Winkle. Whenever her name was mentioned, however, he shook his head, shrugged his shoulders and cast up his eyes; which might pass either for an expression of resignation to his fate or joy at his deliverance.

He used to tell his story to every stranger that arrived at Mr. Doolittle's Hotel. He was observed at first to vary on some points, every time he told it, which was doubtless owing to his having so recently awaked. It at last settled down precisely to the tale I have related and not a man woman or child in the neighbourhood but knew it by heart. Some always pretended to doubt the reality of it, and insisted that Rip had been out of his head, and that this was one point on which he always remained flighty. The old Dutch inhabitants, however, almost universally gave it full credit—Even to this day they never hear a thunder storm of a summer afternoon about the Kaatskill, but they say Hendrick Hudson and his crew are at their game of nine pins; and it is a common wish of all henpecked husbands in the neighbourhood, when life hangs heavy on their hands, that they might have a quieting draught out of Rip Van Winkle's flagon.

NOTE

. . . .

The foregoing tale one would suspect had been suggested to Mr. Knickerbocker by a little German superstition about the emperor Frederick *der Rothbart* and the Kypphauser Mountain; the subjoined note, however, which he had appended to the tale, shews that it is an absolute fact, narrated with his usual fidelity.—

"The story of Rip Van Winkle may seem incredible to many, but nevertheless I give it my full belief, for I know the vicinity of our old Dutch settlements to have been very subject to marvellous events and appearances. Indeed I have heard many stranger stories than this, in the villages along the Hudson; all of which were too well authenticated to admit of a doubt. I have even talked with Rip Van Winkle myself, who when last I saw him was a very venerable old man and so perfectly rational and consistent on every other point, that I think no conscientious person could refuse to take this into the bargain—nay I have seen a certificate on the subject taken before a country justice and signed with a cross in the justice's own hand writing. The story therefore is beyond the possibility of doubt.

D.K."

POSTSCRIPT

. . . .

The following are travelling notes from a memorandum book of Mr. Knickerbocker.

The Kaatsberg or Catskill mountains have always been a region full of fable. The Indians considered them the abode of spirits who influenced the weather, spreading sunshine or clouds over the landscape and sending good or bad hunting seasons. They were ruled by an old squaw spirit, said to be their mother. She dwelt on the highest peak of the Catskills and had charge of the doors of day and night to open and shut them at the proper hour. She hung up the new moons in the skies and cut up the old ones into stars. In times of drought, if properly propitiated, she would spin light summer clouds out of cobwebs and morning dew, and send them off, from the crest of the mountain, flake after flake, like flakes of carded cotton to float in the air: until, dissolved by the heat of the sun, they would fall in gentle showers, causing the grass to spring, the fruits to ripen and the corn to grow an inch an hour. If displeased, however, she would brew up clouds black as ink, sitting in the midst of them like a bottle bellied spider in the midst of its web; and when these clouds broke—woe betide the valleys!

In old times say the Indian traditions, there was a kind of Manitou or Spirit, who kept about the wildest recesses of the Catskill mountains, and took a mischievous pleasure in wreaking all kinds of evils and vexations upon the red men. Sometimes he would assume the form of a bear a panther or a deer, lead the bewildered hunter a weary chace through tangled forests and among rugged rocks; and then spring off with a loud ho! ho! leaving him aghast on the brink of a beetling precipice or raging torrent.

The favorite abode of this Manitou is still shewn. It is a great rock or cliff in the loneliest part of the mountains, and, from the flowering vines which clamber about it, and the wild flowers which abound in its neighborhood, is known by the name of the Garden Rock. Near the foot of it is a small lake the haunt of the solitary bittern, with water snakes basking in the sun on the leaves of the pond lillies which lie on the surface. This place was held in great awe by the Indians, insomuch that the boldest hunter would not pursue his game within its precincts. Once upon a time, however, a hunter who had lost his way, penetrated to the garden rock where he beheld a number of gourds placed in the crotches of trees. One of these he seized and made off with it, but in the hurry of his retreat he let it fall among the rocks, when a great stream gushed forth which washed him away and swept him down precipices where he was dashed to pieces, and the stream made its way to the Hudson and continues to flow to the present day; being the identical stream known by the name of the Kaaters-kill.

Understanding the Text

1. Characterize Rip Van Winkle and his wife in detail. What is Rip's attitude toward work? What is his wife's response to this attitude?

2. Why does Rip go to the mountains, and what happens to him there? What happens to his wife back in the village?

3. When he returns home, what does Rip discover has happened in the country and in his village? How many other Rips does he encounter? Who are they?

Superstars, Superheroes and the Male Body Image: The Visual Implications of Football Uniforms

Charlotte A. Jirousek

Charlotte A. Jirousek is an associate professor of textiles and apparel at Cornell University. She writes on the historical and social contexts of textile and clothing design.

INTRODUCTION

Anne Hollander has argued most successfully that there is a relationship between the cut of clothes and concepts of the ideal body, and that the body ideal changes as fashions change (84–87). Although football uniforms are not daily dress, they have been the costume of heroes idolized by young boys and grown men alike as the embodiment of American manhood in the middle of the twentieth century. It can be argued that the evolution of the high tech protective armor worn under the uniform created an exaggerated image of male musculature, particularly in the years from World War II through the 1980s. This silhouette has exerted a relentless pressure on the ideal form of the unadorned male body. This pressure can also be discerned in recent fashion trends.

To be sure, not all men are sports fans. Martin and Koda make a persuasive case for a set of options from which men can choose to define their personal style (7–9). The preeminent choice they offer is between the look of the "Jock" and the "Nerd." They present the recent rehabilitation of the fashion image of the Nerd as a backlash against the ultra-macho Jock notion of manhood. Even with this alternative, the relentless images of muscular bodies presented by the media must be difficult for any man to ignore completely.

Football has been described as the ultimate expression of manly skill and aggressiveness, a metaphor for male roles and social relationships.

From *Journal of American Culture*, Vol. 19, No. 2, Summer 1996 by Charlotte A. Jirousek. Copyright © 1996 by Journal of American & Comparative Cultures. Reprinted by permission.

In the introduction to a history of the National Football League, football is described as a "symbolic war":

> Professional football is basically a physical assault by one team upon another in a desperate fight for land. Most people see themselves as the sum of their possessions—I am what I own. The most basic possession, land, is the issue in football and the most basic weapon, the body, is the means of acquiring it. It is a game of physical dominance; the weak are punished unmercifully and the unskilled are run off the field. So much of a man's personality is at stake that the game becomes a fanatical crusade." (*The First Fifty Years*)

There are several possible reasons why football rose in importance by the midpoint of this century. Social scientists have made a case for territoriality as a basic human trait. As our population has grown, becoming more urban and crowded, the appeal of this turf-oriented sport increased. This has also been a period of unparalleled technical development, social upheaval, alienation and anger. Football reflects an increasingly high tech, fast-moving culture, generating metaphors of violence, high tech strategy, corporate style team-work, and high tech-augmented physical power. These images resonate with the temper of society in a way that the slow-paced, graceful virtuosity of that other great American pastime, baseball, can no longer do as effectively. As football gained in popularity, it was discovered that television and football were remarkably well suited to each other. The continuous action and visual impact of football came across dramatically on television. The enormous success of televised football has firmly planted the football hero in the pantheon of male icons.

THE EVOLUTION OF THE FOOTBALL UNIFORM

Football began as a college sport, and although in recent years professional football has gained preeminence, college football has retained a passionate following. Since its beginnings, football has been followed fervently at the University of Alabama, and with great success. This was particularly true during the tenure of coach Paul "Bear" Bryant from 1958 to 1982. The opening of the Paul W. Bryant Museum in 1988 celebrated this history. The museum houses an extensive archive of visual and written material on football. In addition, there is a collection of football uniforms, equipment, and related materials that document the history of football from its beginnings in the 19th century to the present. As seen in these collections, the Alabama experience of football encapsulates the national experience. This material can be used to illustrate some interesting parallels between the evolution of the football uniform and the evolution of ideals for male body image.

The first intercollegiate football game in the United States took place in 1869 between Princeton and Rutgers. Within the next two years, Yale, Columbia, and Harvard established teams, and the "Ivy League" was born. Alabama came to the sport as a relative latecomer in 1892, and the Southern Intercollegiate Athletic Conference was formed in 1894 (Edson 23).

Early football players had no protective gear to exaggerate the body silhouette. The body image of the Victorian and Edwardian football hero was that of the natural athletic body. In the nineteenth and early twentieth century, the ideal for the fit male body was slender, with smooth muscular definition, corresponding to Classical sculpture (Mrozek 21–22). On the first Alabama team, the average weight of the players was 148 pounds (Bolton 62). The uniform of Alabama's early teams consisted of ordinary knickers and a wool sweater.

At this early period in its development, the game of football was virtually without rules, a violent free-for-all that was little more than a planned brawl. Gradually, because of the serious injuries that occurred, protective features were added to football wear, although many players resisted these innovations. Initially these precautions were rather minimal. In 1894, Alabama players were photographed wearing thicker (probably canvas) pants. A sleeveless canvas vest and a jersey were also worn under or instead of the sweater. These specialized garments may have saved wear and tear on the player's personal wardrobe, but they provided little protection for his body. In 1896, some padding was added to the elbows, and by the turn of the century jerseys had replaced sweaters (Shores). Not until 1900 did the first helmet (a rather inadequate leather article) appear at Alabama. However, helmets would remain optional until the late 1920s. Also introduced at the University of Alabama in 1900 was a type of canvas pants with attached vest. This garment included quilted patches filled with cotton, which also might be stiffened with lead inserts. In addition, patches were sewn to the pants and/or vest, into which rows of small reeds were inserted.

By 1901, separate leather shoulder pads began to come into use. A photograph of the 1901 University of Michigan team includes a player with his sweater off and pads visible over his jersey. In 1903, the first shoulder pads appeared at Alabama. During the next 25 years, the size of shoulder pads would gradually increase, as would the bulk and padding of the canvas knee pants. However, protective shoulder padding continued to be relatively unobtrusive before World War I. Such gear was a personal choice, often added only to protect an injury that would otherwise prevent the player from playing. Routine use of excessive protective gear was generally considered unmanly, and the wide-shouldered look of pads was de-emphasized as a result.

After World War I, as a generation of American young men set off to college, America was in a youthful, freewheeling mood. The college boy and his sport of football surged in popularity. In 1919, professional football made its appearance with the founding of the National Football League. The NFL introduced football to non-college audiences in towns throughout the midwest, and eventually, the whole country. The 1920s has been described as "the decade in which sport assumed its modern position as a cornerstone of American culture" (McChesney 55). This was also the first era in which radio and especially film could bring sports and its stars to the broader public (Treat).

By the 1920s, the shoulder padding was sufficient to be noticeable, but still seemed not to exaggerate the shoulder musculature in the way later uniforms would do. The bulky pants in use by this time often made the legs and hips appear wider than the upper body. This was also a characteristic of men's suits in the late twenties. The suit jacket became somewhat wider in the shoulders, but although the waist was indicated, the jacket was essentially straight and loosely fitted, giving width to the whole body. Pants were also cut wide. In the extreme form, the youthful fad for a style of wide-legged pants known as "Oxford bags" decidedly counterbalanced any appearance of width in the shoulders.

By the 1930s, some players, particularly linemen, began to wear shoulder pads that did add substantial width to the shoulders as compared to the lower body. At the same time, the uniform pants became more closely fitted, following the narrower contour of leg and hips, but augmented by the protective thigh padding. The more noticeable pads began to take on the look of exaggerated muscle development in the shoulders and thighs. Men's suits also began to take the form of an inverted triangle; wide at the shoulders, tapering to a clearly demarcated waist, and descending to narrower hips and pants.

Over the years the game became somewhat more regulated and less overtly dangerous. From the 1940s to the 1970s the protective padding developed into a form of virtual armor that increasingly exaggerated the athletic male form, and therefore exaggerated the superhero image of the football player. Thus, football became a less directly brutal spectacle, with the illusion of protection for its players, who at the same time evoked an image of superhuman size and strength. As the violence became more sublimated, the image of strength became more fantastic.

There is some evidence that the power of the football image is beginning to wane, however. Particularly among younger people, basketball has been on the rise as the sport of choice,[1] and basketball stars have gained prominence in television sports and advertising imagery (Weismann 810). This may signal a paradigm shift in the image offered by the sports hero. The basketball hero still offers a larger than life body image, but the uniform exposes the real body, significantly different in proportions from the artificially exaggerated football silhouette. Yet football continues to be the leading American sport in terms of attendance and earnings, and clearly continues to be a pervasive media presence.[2]

THE MEDIA AND THE DEVELOPMENT OF THE SUPERHERO BODY IMAGE

Football was first seen on television as a demonstration at the RCA pavilion during the New York World's Fair of 1939. Even in that first fuzzy broadcast football was seen as the perfect television sport:

Science has scored a touchdown at the kickoff of football by television. So sharp are the pictures, that the televiewer sits in his parlor wondering why he should leave the comforts of home to watch a gridiron battle in a sea of mud on a chilly autumnal afternoon. . . . When the players gallop directly in front of the camera, the televiewer feels that he is plunging right through the line or sliding out of bounds with the ball runner. . . . There is plenty of action on the gridiron and that is why football is classed as a "natural" for the camera (Patton 15).

Commercial television had to wait until after World War II to become a reality. Football games were broadcast from time to time throughout the 1950s. However, it was not until after the spectacular sudden death National Championship game televised in 1958 that the networks took up football in earnest. In 1962, the first contract with the NFL was signed by CBS.

As televised football grew in popularity, the images of football increased in importance. Television created many individual stars, whose image and lifestyle had substantial influence. As a result, this period saw an increasing use of football and other sports stars for advertising, which further augmented their image power. Johnny Unitas, Frank Gifford, and Alex Karras were among the first beneficiaries of this attention (Patton 38–42). Joe Namath, whose career began at the University of Alabama, became one of the great celebrities of the sixties when he led the New York Jets to their first Superbowl victory. He was as well known for his playboy lifestyle and pantyhose ads as he was for his prowess on the field (Jenkins 42).

Although changes in male body image and fashions are certainly caused by a number of factors, the parallels between the functional evolution of the football player's protective gear and the aesthetic evolution of the male silhouette are striking. The steady rise in the popularity of football was concurrent with the increasing augmentation of the player's body. The protective gear under his uniform ultimately created an irresistible image of male power which has in turn affected standards of male strength and beauty. The power of this image has contributed to a national obsession with physical fitness and sport in general, in the pursuit of the ideal body (Ames 91–94). This trend has been particularly discernible in the last thirty years, the era in which football became the preeminent sport, its image and mythology promoted by the ubiquitous force of television.

It is interesting to compare the evolution of the football uniform with other media images of male strength and attractiveness in comparable periods. In the late 1930s and 1940s, comic books were a popular form of literature for children, particularly for boys. Superman first appeared in 1938, followed quickly by Batman in 1939 (*Superman at Fifty;* Vaz 31–32). These superheroes were idolized for their incredible bravery, moral superiority, and (for the time) fantastic physical strength and proportions. Since Superman and Batman were supposed to be more powerful than ordinary men, they were drawn with physiques that exceeded the currently accepted standards of strength and fitness. In every comic book there was also an ad for Charles Atlas's body building program, holding out the promise that even a "97-pound weakling" could hope to look like Superman. Of course, the image of Charles Atlas in the ads looked suspiciously like that of the superhero shown in the adventure stories. Clearly this advertiser thought that the muscular appearance of the comic heroes was fascinating to the young reader.

For the most part, real muscle men of the day could not match this super image. The accepted ideals of strength and fitness for men idealized the classical Greek prototype, with smooth sleek lines and limited muscle definition (Ames 91). In actual fact, few if any men then encountered in real life could be compared to Superman's original physique, with the possible exception of a few obscure body builders—and a uniformed football player. Apart from the cape, the uniform of Superman or Batman actually looked rather like the football uniform of the day, but with super shoulders instead of pads.

As football uniforms and padding grew more exaggerated in the years that followed World War II, these fictional superheroes seemed to grow more powerful in appearance as well. In their comic book versions, the physiques of Superman and Batman have decidedly improved with age. Between the late thirties and the post sixties era, the bulk and articulation of muscles increased markedly.

Even more dramatic is the contrast between Adam West's 1960s portrayal of Batman and Michael Keaton's 1989 movie version. Adam West was filming his campy television series at the beginning of the televised football era, before the subsequent fitness craze set in (Eisner 14). West's body looks quite unremarkable to our eyes today. On the other hand, Keaton's body had to be augmented with supermuscular armor to accomplish a satisfactory superhero effect. Clearly the standards for super bodies had been revised in the interim.

The most dramatic changes in the ideal body silhouette occurred after the introduction of regularly televised football in the 1960s. By the end of 1961, there were numerous assertions by the elder statesmen of both football and baseball that football had replaced baseball as the national pastime (Marshall 10; "National Game" 15). Although this was an opinion subject to debate, there was no question that football was now center stage.

Television enormously increased the impact of the football body image. It can be no coincidence that the rise of televised football also corresponded to an explosion of interest in physical fitness in general and the amateur sport of body building in particular. As football became more popular, football players were getting bigger, both in fact as well as in silhouette ("Hefty Pros" 43). Certainly factors such as improved nutrition had contributed to larger, stronger athletes, particularly in the first half of the century. Yet improved nutrition alone cannot account for the growing fascination with well developed muscles.

Although body building had a long history as a minor sport, it had not previously captured mainstream attention. As the new physical fitness craze began in the late 1950s, California led the way with the success of Vic Tanny's sanitized gyms that offered fitness regimes and weight training for the amateur, male or female (Bunzel 45). Throughout the

1960s, interest in body building grew. By the early 1970s, *Sports Illustrated,* for the first time, began to cover major body building events, such as the Mr. Olympia competition, on a regular basis (Kram 128–48; McDermott 92). This interest in body building began to produce real life superheroes whose bodies looked as though football pads had been installed underneath their skin. These images of exaggerated muscles, looked upon as freakish in earlier periods, were now admired. The standard for jock manliness-of-form had escalated right out of normal reality.

It might be a temptation to dismiss the extreme results of body building as an aberration, followed by a rather obsessive subculture, and not relevant to mainstream tastes. Yet even if one does not choose to participate in the pursuit of this physical ideal, the pressure of this superheroic image can modify tastes and attitudes. Definitions of physical attractiveness are to a large extent cultural. Therefore, self concept, and our response to the appearance of others, is colored by such norms. There is no denying that standards of male attractiveness, as represented by public taste in popular entertainment stars, have shifted toward the more muscular. It should be pointed out that these images are sometimes intended to appeal to a female public rather than a male one, and, therefore, may not always inspire male emulation. At least in some cases, the media hero's silhouette may be more of a reflection of changing standards of male attractiveness than a source of these standards. However, this does not change the fact that both female and male audiences gradually accepted a more exaggerated aesthetic for the ideal male body.

The earliest male heart-throbs were, if anything, on the skinny side, and exaggerated muscularity was absent even among the square-shouldered and square-jawed. In fact, the nude upper body was rarely seen except in rather exotic settings until the 1930s and after. Douglas Fairbanks was a rather small and slender hero of 1920s swashbuckler epics. He could be best described as wiry rather than muscular, although he was generally held to be a model of fitness and athleticism for his time (Mrozek 26). Like football stars, movie stars seemed to become more broad shouldered as time passed. In the thirties, Olympic swimming stars such as Johnny Weismuller and Buster Crabbe played superheroes Tarzan and Flash Gordon, while Clark Gable and Cary Grant were playing more conventional romantic leads. These stars offered an increasingly broad shouldered and solid silhouette, but not one with pronounced muscles. This was also the first period in which football uniforms presented a noticeably broad shouldered silhouette. In the forties and fifties, Kirk Douglas and Burt Lancaster played many romantic and adventure roles. They offered somewhat more muscular shoulders, but not a look that could qualify as superheroic by today's standards. Charlton Heston seemed to be the actor of choice for superheroic roles in the 1960s, and in this first decade of televised football, he provided an image which was both large of frame and decidedly muscular. However, as televised football grew, and the subsequent sports and fitness boom developed, the standard for the heroic body became Sylvester Stallone or Arnold Schwarzenegger. By the time Schwarzenegger appeared in *Conan the Barbarian* in 1982, movie stars had become truly larger than life (Kroll 100). The overdeveloped muscles of these stars would have seemed unnatural—even repugnant, to many—a few years earlier. Is it not possible that this silhouette had become acceptable, and in fact, necessary as a bodily image of superpower after years of continuous televised exposure to the supermen of the gridiron?

Certainly athletics has enormously influenced the marketing of clothing for both men and women in this century. Athletic wear such as turtle neck sweaters, T shirts, sweat shirts and jogging suits have all entered the wardrobes of even the most determined couch potato. Athletic images have also become stock-in-trade for marketing clothing and anything else that can be vaguely associated with sexual attractiveness. It can be said that the mark of fashion in the 1980s was the shoulder pad, which did with clothing what Arnold Schwarzenegger has done with the body. Although shoulder pads are certainly not a new idea, there has been no period in which they were more exaggerated.

Also, as in the movies, the individuals chosen to wear the clothing and underwear in magazine ads have decidedly more athletic-looking bodies than was the case in earlier decades. In fact, a perusal of male fashion layouts could create the impression that if a man wants a career in modeling today, he will need to include weight training in his plans.

In recent years, however, the more extreme body builder images have begun to decline somewhat in fashion spreads. Though it is still manifestly clear that male models weight train to maintain their athletic looks, the more exaggerated muscle men are being replaced by men with more balanced proportions. This may be a result of the sports trends which are leading away from the predominance of the football hero toward the more proportional athleticism of the basketball star, as described above. Yet, we still have super male models such as Fabio, and the muscle man has by no means disappeared from the media, any more than football has disappeared as a national sport (Linden 73). However, Fabio's image as a romance novel cover boy and fashion model is clearly aimed at women more than men. His image cannot be seen primarily as an icon of male aspirations. In any case, the media continue to offer professionally developed athletic bodies as the standard of attractiveness.

IMPLICATIONS

For men, athletics and fitness have been the source of standards of body image and appearance more than fashion images (Ames 91–92). The pursuit of beauty is therefore translated into the pursuit of a healthy athletic body. Indeed, until relatively recently, articles offering men advice on their appearance were invariably offered under the guise of health and fitness. The rare discussion of male concerns with appearance seemed to be confined to women's fashion magazines.[3] Even in these articles, male concerns are presented primarily as health issues. However, health is not the only concern. In a study by Larry Tucker conducted at Auburn University, self concepts of male students were examined (McCarthy 12). Tucker compared students in a health class with members of a weight training course. Although both groups displayed similar profiles on a pretest, there was a significant difference between the groups at the end of the course. The weight training students experienced an improvement in self-confidence and general satisfaction levels with their bodies which corresponded to the visible changes in their physique. In another study by Adam Drenowski and Doris Yee, it was determined that although men and women are equally likely to be unhappy with their weight, women want to lose weight, while men want to gain (626–634). Therefore, women diet, and men exercise.

Much has been said about the unrealistic standards of beauty that have been foisted upon women by movies and fashion marketing. Since the 1960s, fashion magazines have portrayed a feminine ideal body which is wholly unattainable for most. The medical community has decried the resulting epidemic of bulimia and anorexia as desperate young women tried to achieve the impossible.

It seems that the athletic heroes sold through the media as a standard for manhood have placed an unrealistic pressure on young men not unlike that presented by the fashion model to young women. Images of sports surround a boy from earliest childhood. Many adolescents and young men have been motivated to actively pursue the kind of superbody silhouette embodied in the uniformed football player. The result has been a boom in weight training. Certainly the desire to compete and succeed in a variety of athletic endeavors is an important stimulus for this trend; yet it is undeniable that muscle building is done for the sake of image and attractiveness. For some, the desire to achieve supermuscles has become so great that they turn to artificial aids. In the 1980s, use of anabolic steroids to achieve this goal became an epidemic among high school-aged as well as older athletes (Fackelmann 391).

Fitness is a laudable goal, and to the extent that health is improved, disciplines mastered, and excellence achieved, society is well served. However, the exaggerations of body form encouraged by media images are perhaps not so healthy. It would seem that the super body as envisioned in the image of the uniformed football hero has provided an unrealistic standard of male strength and beauty. In turn, this image became the measure for other male icons of physical beauty, such as movie stars and fashion models.

In an era of overwhelming change, constant crisis, and deep disillusionment with old values, the metaphor of football in particular and sports in general has fulfilled the immensely important role of a cultural myth. It is clear that the images of men reflected in the game and its players speak powerfully to many people, both men and women. Our institutions may help to select and shape these myths, but once they are in place, they shape us all.

Notes

[1] J. Fierman, "Advertisers Show Signs of Football Fatigue," *Fortune* 110 (15 Oct. 1984), 141. Fierman reports that for the first time ratings for ABC's Monday night football have dropped 12%, and other football broadcasts show similar declines. Meanwhile, basketball revenues and viewership were rising (B. Welling, "Basketball: Business is Booming," *Business Week* [28 Oct. 1985], 72–5; and M. Landler, "It's Not Just the Fans on the Edge of Their Seats: Advertisers on CBS are Reaping a Bonanza from NCAA Basketball Fever," *Business Week* [13 Apr. 1992], 40).

[2] J. Lieber, "Fat and Unhealthy," *Sports Illustrated* 76 (27 Apr. 1992), 32–4. Lieber reports that although football revenues appeared to have peaked in 1990–93, and basketball earnings have been rising steadily for a decade, projections for 1994 show that football revenues will still be almost triple those of basketball for the same period.

[3] Men In Vogue: Charlton Heston Stays in Shape and Tells How," *Vogue* 151 (1 Jan. 1968), 67; "Men and Their Looks," *Vogue* 146 (15 Nov. 1965), 181; and "Male Body Beautiful," *Harper's Bazaar* 105 (June 1972), 106.

Works Cited

Ames, W. "Does He or Doesn't He? Use of Anabolic Steroids." *Sports Illustrated* 5 Dec. 1977: 91–92.

Bolton, Carl. *The Crimson Tide: A Story of Alabama Football.* Birmingham: The Strode Publishers, 1972.

Bunzel, Peter. "Health Kick's High Priest." *Life* 29 Sept. 1958: 71–80.

Drenowski, Adam and Doris Yee. "Men and Body Image: Are Males Satisfied With Their Body Weight?" *Psychosomatic Medicine* 49 (1987): 626–34.

Edson, James S. *Alabama's Crimson Tide.* Montgomery: Paragon P, 1946.

Eisner, Joel. *The Official Batman Batbook.* Chicago: Contemporary Books, 1986.

Fackelmann, K. A. "Male Teenagers and Steroid Abuse." *Science News* 17 Dec. 1988: 391.

Fierman, J. "Advertisers Show Signs of Football Fatigue." *Fortune* 16 Oct. 1984: 141.

The First Fifty Years: A Celebration of the National Football League in its Fiftieth Season. Ed. B. Oates. New York: Simon & Schuster, 1970.

"Hefty Pros Get Even Heftier." *Life* 18 Nov. 1957: 68–70.

Hollander, Anne. *Seeing through Clothes.* New York: Penguin Books, 1988.

Jenkins, Dan. "Sweet Life of Swinging Joe." *Sports Illustrated* 17 Oct. 1966: 42–44.

Kram, Mark. "Looking for a Lift." *Sports Illustrated* 12 Sept. 1966: 128–48.

Kroll, J. "Conan the Barbarian." *Newsweek* 17 May 1982: 100.

Landler, M. "It's Not Just the Fans on the Edge of their Seats." *Business Week* 13 Apr. 1992: 40.

Lieber, J. "Fat and Unhealthy." *Sports Illustrated* 27 April 1992: 32–4.

Linden, D. W. and M. Rees. "Pinup Boy." *Forbes* 6 July 1992: 73.

"Male Body Beautiful." *Harpers Bazaar* 105 (1972): 106.

Marshall, George P. "Speaking Out: Baseball Isn't Our National Sport." *Saturday Evening Post* 9 Dec. 1961: 10–14.

Martin, Richard and Harold Koda. *Jocks and Nerds: Men's Style in the Twentieth Century.* New York: Rizzoli, 1989.

McCarthy, Paul. "Body Beautiful." *Psychology Today* July/Aug. 1988: 12.

McChesney, Robert W. "Media Made Sport: A History of Sports Coverage in the United States." *Media, Sports and Society.* Ed. L. A. Wenner. Newberry Park, CA: SAGE Publications, 1989.

McDermott, Barry. "Trying to Muscle In." *Sports Illustrated* 21 Oct. 1974: 92.

"Men and Their Looks." *Vogue* 15 Nov. 1965: 181–221.

"Men in Vogue: Charlton Heston Stays in Great Shape and Tells How." *Vogue* 1 Jan. 1968: 67.

Mrozek, Donald J. "Sport in American Life: From National Health to Personal Fulfillment, 1890–1940." *Fitness in American Culture.* Ed. K. Grover. Amherst, MA: U of Massachusetts P, 1989.

"National Game." *Sports Illustrated* 18 Dec. 1961: 7.

Patton, Phil. *Razzle Dazzle: The Curious Marriage of Television and Football.* New York: Doubleday and Co., 1984.

Shores, Gary. History of Football Uniforms at Alabama. Unpublished summary. Archives, Paul W. Bryant Museum, Tuscaloosa, AL: University of Alabama.

Superman at Fifty: The Persistence of a Legend. Eds. Dennis Dooley and Gary Engle. Cleveland: Octavia Press, 1987.

Treat, Roger. *The Encyclopedia of Football.* New York: A.S. Barnes & Co., 1979.

Vaz, Mark. *Tales of the Dark Knight: Batman's First Fifty Years, 1939–1989.* New York: Ballantine Books, 1989.

Weisman, J. "Acolytes in the Temple of Nike." *The Nation* 17 June 1991: 810.

Welling, B. "Basketball: Business is Booming." *Business Week* 28 Oct. 1985: 72–5.

Les Très Riches Heures de Martha Stewart

Margaret Talbot

Margaret Talbot is a staff writer for *The New Yorker* and has also published articles in *The New Republic, The New York Times Magazine,* and *The Atlantic.*

Every age gets the household goddess it deserves. The '60s had Julia Child, the sophisticated French chef who proved as permissive as Dr. Spock. She may have proselytized for a refined foreign cuisine from her perch at a Boston PBS station, but she was always an anti-snob, vowing to "take a lot of the la dee dah out of French cooking." With her madras shirts and her penumbra of curls, her 6'2 frame and her whinny of a voice, she exuded an air of Cambridge eccentricity—faintly bohemian and a little tatty, like a yellowing travel poster. She was messy and forgiving. When Julia dropped and thing or collapsed a soufflé, she shrugged and laughed. "You are alone in the kitchen, nobody can see you, and cooking is meant to be fun," she reminded her viewers. She wielded lethal-looking kitchen knives with campy abandon, dipped her fingers in crème anglaise and wiped her chocolate-smeared hands on an apron tied carelessly at her waist. For Child was also something of a sensualist, a celebrant of appetite as much as a pedant of cooking.

In the '90s, and probably well into the next century, we have Martha Stewart, corporate overachiever turned domestic overachiever, Mildred Pierce in earth-toned Armani. Martha is the anti-Julia. Consider the extent of their respective powers. At the height of her success, Child could boast a clutch of bestselling cookbooks and a *gemütlich* TV show shot on a single set. And that may or may not be the height of her success, here's what Stewart can claim: a 5-year-old magazine, *Martha Stewart Living,* with a circulation has leapt to

1.5 million; a popular cable TV show, also called *Martha Stewart Living* and filmed at her luscious Connecticut and East Hampton estates; a dozen wildly successful gardening, cooking and lifestyle books; a mail-order business, Martha-by-Mail; a nationally syndicated newspaper column, "Ask Martha"; a regular Wednesday slot on the *Today* show; a line of $110-a-gallon paints in colors inspired by the eggs her Araucana hens lay; plans to invade cyberspace—in short, an empire.

Julia limited herself to cooking lessons, with the quiet implication that cooking was a kind of synecdoche for the rest of bourgeois existence; but Martha's parish is vaster, her field is all of life. Her expertise, as she recently explained to *Mediaweek* magazine, covers, quite simply, "Beautiful soups and how to make them, beautiful houses and how to build them, beautiful children and how to raise them." (From soups to little nuts.) She presides, in fact, over a phenomenon that, in other realms, is quite familiar in American society and culture: a cult, devoted to her name and image.

In the distance between these two cynosures of domestic life lies a question: What does the cult of Martha mean? Or, to put it another way, what have we done, exactly, to deserve her?

If you have read the paper or turned on the television in the last year or so, you have probably caught a glimpse of the WASPY good looks, the affectless demeanor, the nacreous perfection of her world. You may even know the outlines of her story. Middle-class girl from a Polish-American family in Nutley, New Jersey, works her way through Barnard in the early '60s, modeling on the side. She becomes a stockbroker, a self-described workaholic and insomniac who by the '70s is making six figures on Wall Street, and who then boldly trades it all in . . . for life as a workaholic, insomniac evangelist for domesticity whose business now generates some $200 million in profits a year. (She herself, according to the *Wall Street Journal,* makes a salary of $400,000 a year from Time Inc., which generously supplements this figure with a $40,000 a year clothing allowance and other candies.) You may even have admired her magazine, with its art-book production values and spare design, every kitchen utensil photographed like an Imogen Cunningham nude, every plum or pepper rendered with the loving detail of an eighteenth-century botanical drawing, every page a gentle exhalation of High Class.

What you may not quite realize, if you have not delved deeper into Stewart's oeuvre, is the ambition of her design for living—the absurd, self-parodic dream of it. To read Martha Stewart is to know that there is no corner of your domestic life that cannot be beautified or improved under careful tutelage, none that should not be colonized by the rhetoric and the discipline of quality control. Work full time though you may, care for your family though you must, convenience should never be your watchword in what Stewart likes to call, in her own twee coinage, "homekeeping." Convenience is the enemy of excellence. "We do not pretend that these are 'convenience' foods," she writes loftily of the bread and preserves recipes in a 1991 issue of the magazine. "Some take days to make. But they are recipes that will produce the very best results, and we know that is what you want." Martha is a kitchen-sink idealist. She scorns utility in the name of beauty. But her idealism, of course, extends no further than surface appearances, which makes it a very particular form of idealism indeed.

To spend any length of time in Martha-land is to realize that it is not enough to serve your guests homemade pumpkin soup as a first course. You must present it in hollowed-out, hand-gilded pumpkins as well. It will not do to serve an Easter ham unless you have baked it in a roasting pan lined with, of all things, "tender, young, organically-grown grass that has not yet been cut." And, when serving a "casual" lobster and corn dinner al fresco, you really ought to fashion dozens of cunning little bamboo brushes tied with raffia and adorned with a chive so that each of your guests may butter their corn with something pretty.

To be a Martha fan (or more precisely, a Martha adept) is to understand that a terracotta pot is just a terracotta pot until you have "aged" it, painstakingly rubbing yogurt into its damp-ened sides, then smearing it with plant food or "something you found in the woods" and patiently standing by while the mold sprouts. It is to think that maybe you could do this *kind* of thing, anyway—start a garden, say, in your scruffy backyard—and then to be brought up short by Martha's enumeration, in *Martha Stewart's Gardening,* of forty-nine "essential" gar-dening tools. These range from a "polesaw" to a "corn fiber broom" to three different kinds of pruning shears, one of which—the "loppers"—Martha says she has in three different sizes. You have, perhaps, a trowel. But then Martha's garden is a daunting thing to contemplate, what with its topiary mazes and state-of-the-art chicken coop; its "antique" flowers and geometric herb garden. It's half USDA station, half Sissinghurst. And you cannot imagine making any-thing remotely like it at your own house, not without legions of artisans and laborers and graduate students in landscape design, and a pot of money that perhaps you'll unearth when you dig up the yard.

In *The Culture of Narcissism,* Christopher Lasch describes the ways in which pleasure, in our age, has taken on "the qualities of work," allowing our leisure-time activities to be meas-ured by the same standards of accomplishment that rule the workplace. It is a phenomenon that he memorably characterizes as "the invasion of play by the rhetoric of achievement." For Lasch, writing in the early '70s, the proliferation of sex-advice manuals offered a particularly poignant example. Today, though, you might just as easily point to the hundreds of products and texts, from unctuous home-furnishings catalogs to upscale "shelter" magazines to self-help books like *Meditations for Women Who Do Too Much,* that tell us exactly how to "nest" and "cocoon" and "nurture," how to "center" and "retreat," and how to measure our success at these eminently private pursuits. Just as late-nineteenth-century marketers and experts prom-ised to bring Americans back in touch with the nature from which modern industrial life had alienated them, so today's "shelter" experts—the word is revealingly primal— promise to reconnect us with a similarly mystified home. The bourgeois home as lost paradise, retriev-able through careful instruction.

Martha Stewart is the apotheosis of this particular cult of expertise, and its most resourceful entrepreneur. She imagines projects of which we would never have thought—gathering dewy grass for our Easter ham, say—and makes us feel the pressing need for training in them. And she exploits, brilliantly, a certain estrangement from home that many working women feel these days. For women who are working longer and longer hours at more and more demanding jobs, it's easy to think of home as the place where chaos reigns and their own competence is called into doubt: easy to regard the office, by comparison, as the bulwark of order. It is a reversal, of course, of the hoary concept of home as a refuge from the tempests of the marketplace. But these days, as the female executives in a recent study attested, the priority they most often let slide is housekeeping: they'll abide disorder at home that they wouldn't or couldn't abide at the office. No working couple's home is the oasis of tranquility and Italian marble countertops that Marthaism seems to promise. But could it be? Should it be? Stewart plucks expertly at that chord of doubt.

In an era when it is not at all uncommon to be cut off from the traditional sources of motherwit and household lore—when many of us live far from the families into which we were born and have started our own families too late to benefit from the guidance of living parents or grandparents— domestic pedants like Martha Stewart rightly sense a big vacuum to fill. Stewart's books are saturated with nostalgia for lost tradition and old moldings, for her childhood in Nutley and for her mother's homemade preserves. In the magazine, her "Remembering" column pines moralistically for a simpler era, when beach vacations meant no television or video games, just digging for clams and napping in hammocks. Yet Stewart's message is that such simplicity can only be achieved now through strenuous effort and a flood of advice. We might be able to put on a picnic or a dinner party without her help, she seems to tell us, but we wouldn't do it properly, beautifully, in the spirit of excellence that we expect of ourselves at work.

It may be that Stewart's special appeal is to women who wouldn't want to take their mother's word anyway, to baby-boomer daughters who figure that their sensibilities are just too different from their stay-at-home moms', who can't throw themselves into housekeeping without thinking of their kitchen as a catering business and their backyards as a garden show. In fact, relatively few of Martha's fans are housewives—72 percent of the subscribers to *Martha Stewart Living* are employed outside the home as managers or professionals—and many of them profess to admire her precisely because she isn't one, either. As one such Martha acolyte, an account executive at a Christian radio station, effused on the Internet: "[Stewart] is my favorite independent woman and what an entrepreneur! She's got her own television show, magazine, books and even her own brand of latex paint. . . . Martha is a feisty woman who settles for nothing less than perfection."

For women such as these, the didactic faux-maternalism of Martha Stewart seems the perfect answer. She may dispense the kind of homekeeping advice that a mother would, but she does so in tones too chill and exacting to sound "maternal," singling out, for example, those "who will always be too lazy" to do her projects. She makes housekeeping safe for the professional woman by professionalizing housekeeping. And you never forget that Stewart is herself a mogul, even when she's baking rhubarb crisp and telling you, in her Shakeresque mantra, that "It's a Good Thing."

It is tempting to see the Martha cult purely as a symptom of anti-feminist backlash. Though she may not directly admonish women to abandon careers for hearth and home, Stewart certainly exalts a way of life that puts hearth and home at its center, one that would be virtually impossible to achieve without *somebody's* full-time devotion. (Camille Paglia has praised her as "someone who has done a tremendous service for ordinary women—women who identify with the roles of wife, mother, and homemaker.") Besides, in those alarming moments when Stewart slips into the social critic's mode, she can sound a wee bit like Phyllis Schlafly—less punitive and more patrician, maybe, but just as smug about the moral uplift of a well-ordered home. Her philosophy of cultivating your own walled garden while the world outside is condemned to squalor bears the hallmarks of Reagan's America—it would not be overreading to call it a variety conservatism. "Amid the horrors of genocidal war in Bosnia and Rwanda, the AIDS epidemic and increasing crime in many cities," Stewart writes in a recent column, "there are those of us who desire positive reinforcement of some very basic tenets of good living." And those would be? "Good food, gardening, crafts, entertaining and home improvement." (Hollow out the pumpkins, they're starving in Rwanda.)

Yet it would, in the end, be too simplistic to regard her as a tool of the feminine mystique, or as some sort of spokesmodel for full-time mommies. For one thing, there is nothing especially June Cleaverish, or even motherly, about Stewart. She has taken a drubbing, in fact, for looking more convincing as a businesswoman than a dispenser of milk and cookies. (Remember the apocryphal tale that had Martha flattening a crate of baby chicks while backing out of a driveway in her Mercedes?) Her habitual prickliness and Scotchguard perfectionism are more like the badges of the striving good girl, still cut to the quick by her classmates' razzing when she asked for extra homework.

Despite the ritual obeisance that Martha pays to Family, moreover, she is not remotely interested in the messy contingencies of family life. In the enchanted world of Turkey Hill, there are no husbands (Stewart was divorced from hers in 1990), only loyal craftsmen, who clip hedges and force dogwood with self-effacing dedication. Children she makes use of as accessories, much like Parisian women deploy little dogs. The books and especially the magazine are often graced with photographic spreads of parties and teas where children pale as waxen angels somberly disport themselves, their fair hair shaped into tasteful blunt cuts, their slight figures clad in storybook velvet or lace. "If I had to choose one essential element for the success of an Easter brunch," she writes rather menacingly in her 1994 *Menus for Entertaining,* "it would be children." The homemade Halloween costumes modeled by wee lads and lasses in an October 1991 issue of *Martha Stewart Living* do look gorgeous—the Caravaggio colors, the themes drawn from nature. But it's kind of hard to imagine a 5-year-old boy happily agreeing to go as an acorn this year, instead of say, Batman. And why should he? In Marthaland, his boyhood would almost certainly be overridden in the name of taste.

If Stewart is a throwback, it's not so much to the 1950s as to the 1850s, when the doctrine of separate spheres did allow married or widowed women of the upper classes a kind of power—unchallenged dominion over the day-to-day functioning of the home and its servants, in exchange for ceding the public realm to men. At Turkey Hill, Stewart is the undisputed chatelaine, micromanaging her estate in splendid isolation. (This hermetic pastoral is slightly marred, of course, by the presence of cameras.) Here the domestic arts have become ends in themselves, unmoored from family values and indeed from family.

Stewart's peculiar brand of didacticism has another nineteenth-century precedent—in the domestic science or home economics movement. The domestic scientists' favorite recipes—"wholesome" concoctions of condensed milk and canned fruit, rivers of white sauce—would never have passed Martha's muster; but their commitment to painstakingly elegant presentation, their concern with the look of food even more than its taste, sound a lot like Stewart's. And, more importantly, so does their underlying philosophy. They emerged out of a tradition: the American preference for food writing of the prescriptive, not the descriptive, kind, for food books that told you, in M. F. Fisher's formulation, not about eating but about what to eat. But they took this spirit much further. Like Stewart, these brisk professional women of the 1880s and '90s believed that true culinary literacy could not be handed down or casually absorbed; it had to be carefully taught. (One of the movement's accomplishments, if it can be called that, was the home ec curriculum.)

Like Stewart, the domestic scientists were not bent on liberating intelligent women from housework. Their objective was to raise housework to a level worthy of intelligent women. They wished to apply rational method to the chaos and the drudgery of housework and, in so doing, to earn it the respect accorded men's stuff like science and business. Neither instinct, nor intuition, nor mother's rough-hewn words of advice would have a place in the scientifically managed home of the future. As Laura Shapiro observes in *Perfection Salad,* her lively and perceptive history of domestic science, the ideal new housewife was supposed to project, above all, "self-sufficiency, self-control, and a perfectly bland façade." Sound familiar?

It is in their understanding of gender roles, however, that the doyennes of home ec most closely prefigure Marthaism. Like Stewart, they cannot be classified either as feminists or traditionalists. Their model housewife was a pseudo-professional with little time for sublimating her ego to her husband's or tenderly ministering to his needs. She was more like a factory supervisor than either the Victorian angel of the home or what Shapiro calls the courtesan type, the postwar housewife who was supposed to zip through her chores so she could gussy herself up for her husband. In Martha's world, too, the managerial and aesthetic challenges of "homekeeping" always take priority, and their intricacy and ambition command a respect that mere wifely duties never could. Her husbandless hauteur is rich with the self-satisfaction of financial and emotional independence.

In the end, Stewart's fantasies have as much to do with class as with gender. The professional women who read her books might find themselves longing for a breadwinner, but a lifestyle this beautiful is easier to come by if you've never needed a breadwinner in the first place. Stewart's books are a dreamy advertisement for independent wealth—or, more accurately, for its facsimile. You may not have a posh pedigree, but with a little effort (okay, a lot) you can adopt its trappings. After all, Martha wasn't born to wealth either, but now she attends the weddings of people with names like Charles Booth-Clibborn (she went to his in London, the magazine tells us) and caters them for couples named Sissy and Kelsey (see her *Wedding Planner,* in which their yacht is decorated with a "Just Married" sign).

She is not an American aristocrat, but she plays one on TV. And you can play one, too, at least in your own home. Insist on cultivating only those particular yellow plums you tasted in the Dordogne, buy your copper cleaner only at Delherin in Paris, host lawn parties where guests come "attired in the garden dress of the Victorian era," and you begin to simulate the luster of lineage. Some of Stewart's status-augmenting suggestions must strike even her most faithful fans as ridiculous. For showers held after the baby is born, Martha "likes presenting the infant with engraved calling cards that the child can then slip into thank you notes and such for years to come." What a great idea. Maybe your baby can gum them for a while first, thoughtfully imprinting them with his signature drool.

The book that best exemplifies her class-consciousness is *Martha Stewart's New Old House,* a step-by-step account of refurbishing a Federal-style farmhouse in Westport, Connecticut. Like all her books, it contains many, many pictures of Martha; here she's frequently shown supervising the work of plasterers, carpenters and other "seemingly taciturn men." *New Old House* establishes Stewart's ideal audience: a demographic niche occupied bv the kind of people who, like her, can afford to do their kitchen countertops in "mottled, gray-green, hand-honed slate from New York state, especially cut" for them. The cost of all this (and believe me, countertops are only the beginning) goes unmentioned. If you have to ask, maybe you're not a Martha kind of person after all.

In fact, Stewart never seems all that concerned with reassuring her readers of their ability to afford such luxuries or their right to enjoy them. She's more concerned with establishing her own claims. Her reasoning seems to go something like this: the houses that she buys and renovates belong to wealthy families who passed them down through generations. But these families did not properly care for their patrimony. The widowed Bulkeley sisters, erstwhile owners of Turkey Hill, had let the estate fall "into great disrepair. All the farms and outbuildings were gone. . . . The fields around had been sold off by the sisters in 2-acre building lots;

suburbia encroached." The owner of the eponymous New Old House was a retired librarian named Miss Adams who "had little interest in the house other than as a roof over her head. Clearly a frugal spirit, she had no plans to restore the house, and she lived there until she could no longer cope with the maintenance and upkeep of the place. The house was in dire need of attention, and since no other family member wanted to assume responsibility, Miss Adams reluctantly decided to sell her family home. I wanted very much to save the Adams house, to put it to rights, to return its history to it, to make it livable once again."

It's a saga with overtones of Jamesian comedy: a family with bloodlines but no money is simultaneously rescued and eclipsed by an energetic upstart with money but no bloodlines. The important difference—besides the fact that Martha is marrying the house, not the son—is that she also has taste. And it's taste, far more than money, she implies, that gives her the right to these splendid, neglected piles of brick. Unlike the "frugal" Misses Bulkeley, she will keep suburbia at bay; unlike the careless Miss Adams, she would never resort to "hideous rugs" in (yuck) shades of brown. They don't understand their own houses; she does, and so she *deserves* to own their houses. But leave it to Martha to get all snippy about these people's aesthetic oversights while quietly celebrating their reversion to type. They're useful to her, and not only because their indifference to decor bolsters her claim to their property. Like the pumpkin pine floors and original fixtures, these quaintly cheeseparing New Englanders denote the property's authenticity.

The fantasy of vaulting into the upper crust that Martha Stewart fulfilled, and now piques in her readers, is about more than just money, of course. Among other things, it's about time, and the luxurious plenitude of it. Living the Martha way would mean enjoying a surfeit of that scarce commodity, cooking and crafting at the artisanal pace her projects require. Trouble is, none of us overworked Americans has time to spare these days—and least of all the upscale professional women whom Stewart targets. Martha herself seemed to acknowledge this when she told *Inside Media* that she attracts at least two classes of true believers: the "Be-Marthas," who have enough money and manic devotion to follow many of her lifestyle techniques, and the "Do-Marthas, " who "are a little bit envious" and "don't have as much money as the Be-Marthas."

To those fulsome categories, you could surely add the "watch Marthas" or the "read Marthas," people who might consider, say, making their own rabbit-shaped wire topiary forms, but only consider it, who mostly just indulge in the fantasy of doing so, if only they had the time. There is something undeniably soothing about watching Martha at her absurdly time-consuming labors. A female "media executive" explained the appeal to Barbara Lippert in *New York* magazine: "I never liked Martha Stewart until I started watching her on Sunday mornings. I turn on the TV, and I'm in my pajamas, still in this place between sleep and reality. And she's showing you how to roll your tablecloths in parchment paper. She's like a character when she does her crafts. It reminds me of watching Mr. Green Jeans on Captain Kangaroo. I remember he had a shoebox he took out that was filled with craft things. There would be a close-up on his hands with his buffed nails. And then he would show you how to cut an oaktag with a scissor, or when he folded paper, he'd say: 'There you go, boys and girls,' and it was very quiet. It's like she brings out this great meditative focus and calm."

The show does seem strikingly unfrenetic. Unlike just about everything else on TV, including the *Our Home* show, which follows it on Lifetime, it eschews Kathy Lee-type banter, perky music, swooping studio shots and jittery handheld cameras. Instead there's just Martha, alone in her garden or kitchen, her teacherly tones blending with birdsong, her recipes cued to the seasons. Whimsical recorder music pipes along over the credits. Martha's crisply ironed denim shirts, pearl earrings, and honey-toned highlights bespeak the fabulousness of Connecticut. Her hands move slowly, deliberately over her yellow roses or her Depression glasses. Martha is a Puritan who prepares "sinful" foods—few of her recipes are low-fat or especially health-conscious—that are redeemed by the prodigious labors, the molasses afternoons, involved in serving them. (She preys upon our guilt about overindulgence, then hints at how to assuage it.) Here at Turkey Hill, time is as logy as a honey-sated bumblebee. Here on Lifetime, the cable channel aimed at baby-boom women, Martha's stately show floats along in a sea of stalker movies, Thighmaster commercials and "Weddings of a Lifetime" segments, and by comparison, I have to say, she looks rather dignified. Would that we all had these *très riches heures*.

But if we had the hours, if we had the circumstances, wouldn't we want to fill them with something of our own, with a domestic grace of our own devising? Well, maybe not anymore. For taste is no longer an expression of individuality. It is, more often, an instrument of conformism, a way to assure ourselves that we're living by the right codes, dictated or sanctioned by experts. Martha Stewart's "expertise" is really nothing but another name for the perplexity of her cowed consumers. A lifestyle cult as all-encompassing as hers could thrive only at a time when large numbers of Americans have lost confidence in their own judgment about the most ordinary things. For this reason, *Martha Stewart Living* isn't really living at all.

Understanding the Text

1. Based on your reading of Talbot's essay, describe the phenomenon of Martha Stewart.

2. "Every age gets the household goddess it deserves," Talbot proclaims in the first sentence of her essay. Why, in her view, do we deserve Martha Stewart? (Identify and discuss two reasons.)

3. According to Talbot, what was the main "objective" of the domestic science movement?

ADDITIONAL READINGS

Bly, Robert. *Iron John: A Book About Men*. 1990. New York: Vintage-Random House, 1992.

Bordo, Susan. *The Male Body: A New Look at Men in Public and Private*. New York: Farrar, Straus and Giroux, 1999.

———. *Unbearable Weight: Feminism, Western Culture, and the Body*. Berkeley: U of California P, 1993.

Brownmiller, Susan. *Femininity*. 1984. New York: Fawcett-Ballantine, 1985.

Brumberg, Joan Jacobs. *The Body Project: An Intimate History of American Girls*. New York: Random House, 1997.

Byron, Christopher M. *Martha Inc.: The Incredible Story of Martha Stewart Living Omnimedia*. New York: John Wiley, 2002.

Coward, Rosalind. *Female Desires: How They Are Sought, Bought and Packaged*. 1984. New York: Grove Weidenfeld, 1985.

Douglas, Ann. *The Feminization of American Culture*. New York: Knopf, 1977.

Douglas, Susan. *Where the Girls Are: Growing Up Female with the Mass Media*. New York: Times Books, 1994.

Ehrenreich, Barbara. *The Hearts of Men: American Dreams and the Flight from Commitment*. New York: Anchor-Doubleday, 1983.

Faludi, Susan. *Backlash: The Undeclared War Against American Women*. New York: Crown, 1991.

———. *Stiffed: The Betrayal of the American Man*. New York: William Morrow, 1999.

Garvey, Ellen Gruber. *The Adman in the Parlor: Magazines and the Gendering of Consumer Culture, 1880s to 1910s*. New York: Oxford UP, 1996.

Hollander, Anne. *Sex and Suits: The Evolution of Modern Dress*. New York: Knopf, 1994.

Horowitz, Helen Lefkowitz. *Rereading Sex: Battles over Sexual Knowledge and Suppression in Nineteenth-Century America*. New York: Knopf, 2002.

Kitch, Carolyn. *The Girl of the Magazine Cover: The Origins of Visual Stereotypes in American Mass Media*. Chapel Hill: U of North Carolina P, 2001.

McCabe, Janet and Kim Akass, eds. *Reading Desperate Housewives: Beyond the White Picket Fence*. Reading Contemporary Television Series. London: I.B. Tauris, 2006.

Levy, Ariel. *Female Chauvinist Pigs: Women and the Rise of Raunch Culture*. New York: Free Press, 2005.

Luciano, Lynne. *Looking Good: Male Body Image in Modern America*. New York: Hill and Wang, 2001.

Macdonald, Myra. *Representing Women: Myths of Femininity in the Popular Media*. London: Arnold, 1995.

Peiss, Kathy. *Hope in a Jar: The Making of America's Beauty Culture*. New York: Metropolitan-Henry Holt, 1998.

Shapiro, Laura. *Perfection Salad*. New York: Farrar, Straus and Giroux, 1986.

Shields, Vickie Rutledge and Dawn Heinecken. *Measuring Up: How Advertising Affects Self-Image*. Philadelphia: U of Pennsylvania P, 2002.

Strasser, Susan. *Never Done: A History of American Housework*. 1982. New York: Owl-Henry Holt, 2000.

Stratton, Jon. *The Desirable Body: Cultural Fetishism and the Erotics of Consumption.* Urbana: U of Illinois P, 1996.

Tiger, Lionel. *The Decline of Males: The First Look at an Unexpected New World for Men and Women.* New York: St. Martin's, 2000.

Twitchell, James B. *Where Men Hide.* New York: Columbia UP, 2006.

Wolf, Naomi. *The Beauty Myth: How Images of Beauty Are Used Against Women.* New York: William Morrow, 1991.

Democracy in the Balance:

The Fate of

Intellectualism in Higher

Ed and the Public Sphere

INTELLECTUALISM AND DEMOCRACY

Democracy and Anti-Intellectualism in America

Richard Hofstadter

American education today is in the midst of a great crisis, the general outlines of which I believe we can all recognize. About the first part of this crisis, its financial aspect, I shall have nothing to say. A second part of it comes from outside education, in the shape of tremendous pressures to conform, for we live in a society in which the most dynamic force is provided by a small group of politicians who seek to base careers upon the policing of opinion. About the problems of freedom and conformity, I will speak briefly. The third part of this crisis, which concerns me most, is internal; it is less dramatic and perceptible than the others and it has been going on for a longer time. It stems from an inner failure of nerve, for it is nothing less than the growing loss of confidence among educators in the importance and value of the life of the mind, a capitulation within the educational world—indeed, in many quarters an eager capitulation—to the non-intellectual or anti-intellectual criteria that many forces in our society wish to impose upon education and which we might well consider it the bounden duty of educators to resist. It is about this that I wish primarily to speak; and I hope to suggest some relations between this species of educational failure and our popular democracy.

Since I am speaking about education and intellectualism, I want to make it entirely clear that I do

Richard Hofstadter (1916–70) was one of the most revered, prolific, and widely read American historians of the twentieth century. He balanced an academic career, teaching at Columbia University for over two decades, with that of a public intellectual—engaging in the political debates of his day and generally preferring to publish his essays in magazines that appealed to a wide audience such as *Harper's* and *American Heritage* rather than in academic journals that served a more exclusive readership. Among his many books are *Social Darwinism in American Thought, 1860–1915* (1944), *The American Political Tradition and the Men Who Made It* (1948), *The Age of Reform: from Bryan to F.D.R* (1955), and *Anti-intellectualism in American Life* (1963). The last two each received the Pulitzer Prize in nonfiction.

From *The Michigan Alumnus Quarterly Review*, Vol. LIX, Nu. 21, August 8, 1953 by Richard Hofstadter. Copyright © 1953 by Alumni Association of the University of Michigan. Reprinted by permission.

not make the mistake of identifying higher education in general with intellectualism. Quite the contrary; I propose to emphasize the extent to which anti-intellectualism is rampant within the educational community. But it is also probably true that in America the greater part of the leadership of those who can be called intellectuals lives and works in academic communities. And if higher education can be said to be under fire today, it can be said with greater certainty that the distinctively intellectual part of the educational community is the part that stands to lose most.

The crisis in higher education is also a crisis in the history of the intelligentsia. Today, everywhere in America, intellectuals are on the defensive. They have been identified with the now-defeated inheritance of the New Deal and the Fair Deal. That this identification should have been made is ironical, because the New Deal itself, for all its Brain Trusters, had its own streak of anti-intellectualism. But it has also been unfair: the intellectuals are never given credit for the successes of the New Deal, but they have had to take the blame for everything that has been charged up to the Democratic administrations of the past twenty years—with so-called creeping socialism, with the war, with the alleged failure at Yalta, even with treason. In the late presidential campaign a political leader who embodied the kind of traits that the intellectual would most like to see in our national leadership found the support of the intellectuals of slight value in overcoming the disadvantages of his party and his hour. During that campaign the nation also found the epithet for the intellectuals that it has so long wanted—"egg-heads."

Do not imagine, however, that the intellectual is going into permanent eclipse. He always has his day posthumously, for the very men who are most forward in proclaiming their dislike of living intellectuals are the most abject followers of the dead ones. They may not like contemporary intellectuals but they are often quite hypnotized by the intellectual leavings of Adam Smith or Herbert Spencer, or Edmund Burke, or Thomas Aquinas, or similar gods of the past. They have restored an old slogan of the frontiersman with a new meaning and a new object: "The only good intellectual is a dead intellectual."

But what is an intellectual, really? This is a problem of definition that I found, when I came to it, far more elusive than I had anticipated. A great deal of what might be called the journeyman's work of our culture—the work of engineers, physicians, newspapermen, and indeed of most professors—does not strike me as distinctively intellectual, although it is certainly work based in an important sense on ideas. The distinction that we must recognize, then, is one originally made by Max Weber between living *for* ideas and living *off* ideas. The intellectual lives for ideas; the journeyman lives off them. The engineer or the physician—I don't mean here to be invidious—needs to have a pretty considerable capital stock in frozen ideas to do his work; but they serve for him a purely instrumental purpose: he lives off them, not for them. Of course he may also be, in his private role and his personal ways of thought, an intellectual, but it is not necessary for him to be one in order to work at his profession. There is in fact no profession which demands that one be an intellectual. There do seem to be vocations, however, which almost demand that one be an anti-intellectual, in which those who live off ideas seem to have an implacable hatred for those who live for them. The marginal intellectual workers and the unfrocked intellectuals who work in journalism, advertising, and mass communication are the bitterest and most powerful among those who work at such vocations.

It will help, too, to make the further distinction between living for ideas and living for *an idea.* History is full of cases of great men with good minds, a capacity to deal with abstractions, and a desire to make systems of them—all qualities we associate with the intellectual. But when, as it has in many of them, this concern with ideas, no matter how dedicated and sincere, reduces in the end to the ingenious use of them for a central preconception, however grand, then I think we have very little intellectualism and a great deal of something else. A good historical illustration is that of Lenin, who, as his more theoretical works show, had in him a powerful element of intellectuality; but this intellectuality was rendered thin by his all-absorbing concern with certain very limiting political values. His book on philosophy, *Materialism and Empirio-Criticism,* a shrill work and an extremely depressing one to read, makes it altogether clear that the politician in him swallowed up the intellectual. I choose the illustration of Lenin because it helps me to make another point that seems unfortunately necessary because of the present tendency to identify intellectuals with subversives. That point is that the idea of a party line and political messianism is inherently inconsistent with intellectualism, and those few intellectuals who have in some way survived that tension are few, pitiable, and on the whole sterile.

The journeyman of ideas, and the janizary who makes a somewhat complicated but highly instrumental use of ideas, provide us with two illustrations of people who work with ideas but are not precisely intellectuals, as I understand the term. What, then, are the differences between the men who work with ideas but are *not* intellectuals and the men who work with ideas and *are* intellectuals?

Two things, that seem in fact to be mutually at odds, mark off the intellectual from the journeyman of ideas; one is playfulness, the other is piety.

Certainly the intellectual, if he is nothing else, is one who relishes *the play of the mind* for its own sake, for whom it is one of the major ends of life. The intellectual has a full quotient of what Veblen called "idle curiosity." His mind, instead of falling to rest when it has provided him with his girl and his automobile and his dinner, becomes even more active. Indeed if we had to define him in physiological terms, we might define him as the creature whose mind is *most* likely to be active after dinner.

I speak of playfulness too because of the peculiar nature of the relationship, in the intellectual's mind, between ideas and practicality. To the journeyman of ideas the be-all and end-all of ideas lies in their practical efficacy. Now the intellectual, by contrast, is not necessarily impractical; I can think of some intellectuals like Thomas Jefferson and Robert Owen and John Maynard Keynes who have been eminently practical, and I consider the notion that the intellectual is inherently impractical to be one of the most contemptible of the delusions with which the anti-intellectual quiets his envy—the intellectual is not impractical but primarily concerned with a quality of ideas that does not depend upon their practicality. He neither reveres nor disdains practical consequences; for him they are either marginal or irrelevant. And when he does talk about the practicality or the "relevance" of ideas, the kind of practicality that he is concerned with is itself somewhat different from the practicality of building a bridge, curing a disease, or making a profit—it is practical relevance to spiritual values themselves.

The best illustration of the intellectual's view of the purely practical that has recently come to my attention is the reaction of Clerk Maxwell, the great nineteenth-century mathematician and theoretical physicist, to the invention of the telephone. Maxwell was asked to give a lecture on the workings of this wonderful new instrument, which he began by saying how difficult it was to believe, when the word first came from America, that such a thing had actually been devised. But then, he said, "when at last this little instrument appeared, consisting, as it does, of parts, every one of which is familiar to us, and capable of being put together by an amateur, the disappointment arising from its humble appearance was only partially relieved on finding that it was really able to talk." Perhaps, then, this regrettable appearance of simplicity might be redeemed by the presence somewhere of "recondite physical principles, the study of which might worthily occupy an hour's time of an academic audience." But no; Maxwell had not met a single person who could not understand the physical processes involved, and even the science reporters for the daily press had almost got it right! The thing was a disappointing bore; it was not recondite, it was not profound, it was not complex, it was not *intellectually* new.

To be sure, what this illustration suggests is not merely that the telephone disappointed Maxwell as a pure scientist and an intellectual, but that the strain of intellectuality in him was not as broadly developed as it might have been. The telephone might well excite not merely the commercial imagination but the historical imagination. But my point is, after all, not that Maxwell was a universal intellectual, but that he was displaying the attitude of the intellectual in his particular sphere of interest.

The second element in intellectualism is its religious strain, the note of piety. What I mean by this is simply that for the intellectual the whole world of moral values becomes attached to ideas and to the life dedicated to ideas. The life given over to the search for truth takes on for him a primary moral significance. Intellectualism, although hardly confined to doubters, is often the sole piety of the skeptic. A few years ago a distinguished sociologist asked me to read a brief manuscript which he had written primarily for students planning to go on to advanced work in his field, the purpose of which was to illustrate various ways in which the life of the mind might be cultivated. The essay had about it a little too much of the how-to-do books, and my friend abandoned it. But the nub of the matter from the standpoint of our present problem was that I found myself to be reading a piece of devotional literature, comparable perhaps to Cotton Mather's *Essays to do Good* or Richard Steele's *The Tradesman's Calling*. My friend was trying to communicate his sense of dedication to the life of ideas, which he conceived much in the fashion of the old Protestant writers as a *calling*. To work is to pray. Yes, and for this kind of man, to think—really to think—is to pray. What he knows best, when he is at his best, is the pursuit of truth; but *easy* truths bore him. What he is certain of becomes unsatisfactory always; the meaning of his intellectual life lies in the quest for new uncertainties.

In a bygone day when men lived even more by dogma than they do now, there were two kinds of men whose special office it was to seek for and utter the truth; and they symbolize these two sides of the intellectual's nature. One was the angelic doctor, the learned schoolman, the conserver of old orthodoxies but also the maker of the new, and the prodder at the outer limits of received truths. The other was the jester, the professional fool, who had license to say on occasion for the purposes of amusement and release those things that bordered on lèse majesté and could not be uttered by others who were accounted serious men.

The fool and the schoolman are very far apart. No doubt you will ask whether there is not a contradiction between these two qualities of the intellectual, piety and playfulness. Certainly there is great tension between them; human beings are tissues of contradictions, and the life even of the intellectual is not logic, to borrow from Holmes, but experience. If you will think of the intellectuals you know, some will occur to you in whom the note of playfulness seems stronger, others who are predominantly pious. But I believe that in all intellectuals who have any stability as intellectuals—and that includes the angelic doctors of the middle ages—each of these characteristics is at some point qualified by the other. Perhaps the tensile strength of the intellectual can be gauged by his ability to maintain a fair equipoise between these aspects of himself. At one end of the scale, an excess of playfulness leads to triviality, to dilettantism, to cynicism, to the failure of all sustained creative effort. At the other, an excess of piety leads to fanaticism, to messianism, to ways of life that may be morally magnificent or morally mean, but in either case are not quite the ways of intellectualism. It is of the essence of the intellectual that he strikes a balance.

The widespread distrust of intellectuals in America reflects a tendency to depreciate their playfulness and distrust their piety. Ours is a society in which every form of play seems to be accepted by the majority except the play of the mind. It does not need to be explained to most people in America why sports, sex, liquor, gambling, motoring, and gourmandizing are all more or less legitimate forms of amusement for those who happen to find them amusing. The only forms of *mental* play that are similarly accepted and understood are those that do not involve the particular kinds of critical intelligence that are called into play by intellectualism; I refer, of course, to such highly cerebral amusements as bridge, chess, and the various forms of the crossword puzzle. I suppose that those who are inclined to find economic explanations will point out that the play of the mind, being the only kind that has not been susceptible to commercialization, has not been able to rally the support of a vested interest. I believe, however, that a large part of our common neglect of the humanities is attributable to the absence of a traditional and accepted leisure class which looks upon this kind of personal cultivation as a natural goal of life. The idea of leisured intellectual exercise, not put to the service of some external end, has been offensive to mass democracy. One of the best signs of this is the rhetoric adopted by college presidents and others who appeal to the public for support for education. Always these appeals tell how much education does for citizenship, science, technology, morals, or religion. Rarely do they point to the glories or pleasures of the human mind as an end in itself.

Just as the truly religious man is always a misfit in a secular society, so it is the piety of the intellectual that makes the greatest difficulties for him. Playfulness may be disdained or misunderstood, but it is not usually thought to be dangerous. Piety is another matter, for it is almost certain in the end to challenge something. It is the piety of the intellectual that puts iron into his nonconformism, if he happens to be a nonconformist. It is his piety that will make him, if anything does, a serious moral force in society. In our day the pressures operating against boldness in thought, as well as the sheer bureaucratization of intellectual life, bear hardest against the elements of piety in the intellectual. The temptation is very strong for some intellectuals to suppress the note of piety in themselves, to turn increasingly to the playful and generally more esoteric aspects of their work, to give up the office of spiritual leadership. Such self-suppression is psychologically and morally dangerous, and cannot be indulged in without paying a serious price. It does not become the intellectual, it is much too false to an important part of him, to give in altogether to playfulness and play the fool to the powerful. The jester had his prerogatives, to be sure, but we should also remember that he was usually a slave.

I have attempted thus far to define and elucidate intellectualism. Let me now explain what I mean by democracy when I say that in an important sense higher education and democracy have often been at odds. I do not mean by democracy simply the indispensable formal essentials of our society—constitutionalism, government by discussion, guarantees for the civil liberties of political minorities. These I neither challenge nor criticize; and I am sure that free higher education cannot in our time stand without them. But I do mean to criticize something that relates to the spirit of our politics, something that for lack of a better term I will call populistic democracy. Populistic democracy is neither progressive nor conservative, although it is in a perverse way equalitarian. Populistic democracy is the meeting ground, in fact, of the extreme left and the extreme right. It is government by or through the mass man, disguised behind the mask of an easy sentimentalization of the folk. It is the idea that anything done in the name of the people is *ipso facto* legitimate, even if the same act done in the name of a vested interest would be considered outrageous. It is the idea that a dozen postcards to a congressman from the wildest cranks should be given the same weight as a dozen reasoned letters from sober citizens. Transferred to the field of education, which is our concern, it is the idea that a university ought to cater to the needs of anybody who comes out of or pretends to represent the folk, whether or not he has any real need for or interest in the use of ideas. Put in terms of the state university, it is the idea that any graduate of the public high school should be accepted as a freshman no matter how dismal his prospects are as a student. Put in broader terms, it is the idea that any of the wants, real or fancied, of a mass society, should be absolute imperatives to its system of higher education.

We Americans are noted for our faith in both democracy and education. It has been our assumption that democracy and education, both being good, must be closely related and mutually reinforcing. We should have, it is argued, as much education and as much democracy as possible. It is also assumed that education serves democracy, and one of the most common shibboleths in our educational literature is the slogan "education for democracy." It is characteristically American that very few of us trouble to inquire whether democracy serves education. Whether it does indeed do so as fully and unambiguously as we might consider desirable is the question I insist we must face.

That there is any necessary relation between a vital system of higher education and a democratic society, one may readily deny on the basis of historical evidence. Two of the greatest periods in university history, that of the thirteenth and fourteenth centuries and that of the German universities in the nineteenth century, occurred in societies that were not notably democratic. In our own experience, I do not believe it incorrect to say that the great age of American university development from 1870 to 1910 was for the most part an age of political and economic oligarchy; and also that our finest universities and small colleges, by and large, have been those started and endowed by rich men and patronized chiefly by the upper classes.

All this does not mean, of course, that there is any necessary antagonism between democracy and higher education. Presumably there is no inherent or universally necessary opposition between a political democracy and a vital, respected, intellectually rich and alert university system. But I do wish to point out that there has been a historically persistent tension between our popular democracy and intellectualism that has been very sadly felt in the sphere of university and college life. The problem of how democracy and education can best serve and complement each other—as we would all, no doubt, like them to do—has not been nearly as constructively attacked as it might be for the simple reason that it has not often enough been candidly faced.

Long ago Tocqueville saw that the democratic culture that had emerged in the United States had brought with it pressures that were seriously hostile to the free use of the mind. He found that the democratic and equalitarian impulse had weakened the ability of the individual to resist the pressure of the opinion of the mass:

> The fact that the political laws of the Americans are such that the majority rules the community with sovereign sway, materially increases the power which that majority naturally exercises over the mind. For nothing is more customary in man than to recognise superior wisdom in the person of his oppressor. . . . The intellectual dominion of the greater number would probably be less absolute among a democratic people governed by a king than in the sphere of a pure democracy, but it will always be extremely absolute; and by whatever political laws men are governed in the ages of equality, it may be foreseen that faith in public opinion may become a species of religion there, and the majority its ministering prophet.
>
> Thus intellectual authority will be different, but it will not be diminished; and far from thinking that it will disappear, I augur that it may readily acquire too much preponderance and confine the action of private judgment within narrower limits than are suited either to the greatness or the happiness of the human race. In the principle of equality I very clearly discern two tendencies; the one leading the mind of every man to untried thoughts, the other inclined to prohibit him from thinking at all. And I perceive how, under the dominion of certain laws, democracy would extinguish that liberty of mind to which a democratic social condition is favourable; so that, after having broken all the bondage once imposed on it by ranks or by men, the human mind would be closely fettered to the general will of the greatest number.

Tocqueville found that in his time the most absolute monarchs in Europe were unable to prevent certain heretical notions from circulating through their dominions and even in their courts:

> Such is not the case in America; as long as the majority is still undecided, discussion is carried on; but as soon as its decision is irrevocably pronounced, a submissive silence is observed, and the friends, as well as the opponents of the measure unite in assenting to its propriety. The reason of this is perfectly clear: no monarch is so absolute as to combine all the powers of society in his own hands, and to conquer all opposition with the energy of a majority which is invested with the right of making and of executing the laws. . . .
>
> I know no country in which there is so little true independence of mind and freedom of discussion as in America. In any constitutional state in Europe every sort of religious and political theory may be advocated and propagated abroad; for there is no country in Europe so subdued by any single authority as not to contain citizens who are ready to protect the man who raises his voice in the cause of truth from the consequences of his hardihood. If he is unfortunate enough to live under an absolute government, the people is upon his side; if he inhabits a free country, he may find a shelter behind the authority of the throne, if he require one. The aristocratic part of society supports him in some countries and the democracy in others. But in a nation where democratic institutions exist, organized like those of the United States, there is but one sole authority, one single element of strength and of success, with nothing beyond it.

While I do believe that Tocqueville was exaggerating the case of the United States in 1835, he pointed to the heart of the problem of majority tyranny over the soul. It is a problem that has grown still more acute in our own age, an age of mass communications and the mass man; for now the tyranny of the majority can be spread uniformly over the surface of a great nation otherwise well suited by size and diversity to a multiplicity of opinions, and it can be to some degree forged and manipulated from a few centers. If there were any horrors in that spontaneous, grass-roots variety of popular tyranny, as Tocqueville saw it, they must be greatly compounded by the artificial and centralized means of manipulation that the communications technology of our time has made possible.

But has there been substantial historical evidence in the development of American higher education for the validity of Tocqueville's fear of mass tyranny? I believe there is certainly enough evidence to warrant a reconsideration of our views of the relation between democracy and university culture. I propose to argue that while populistic democracy has been on the side of many educational improvements and reforms, it has often been aligned as sharply with forces tending to constrain freedom in higher education and to lower its devotion to intellectual goals.

DEMOCRACY AND HIGHER EDUCATION

There may have been some popular upsurges in our history that have been auspicious for intellectualism in general, and for higher education in particular; but the popular movements that have been notable for their failure to understand the place of learning in our culture, or even on occasion for their hostility to it, are quite numerous. One of the first, the Great Awakening of the mid-eighteenth century, was notable for its hostility to a free and liberal-minded theological education such as was emerging in the older colleges; and while the Awakening must be in the end credited for enlarging the number of colleges, the goal sought at first in these enterprises was not an enhancement of the sphere of free learning but simply the creation of schools that would teach the right brand of theology. Jeffersonian democracy was not, on the whole, what I call populistic—at least not in its leadership. Its most constructive work in education, the founding of a liberal university in Virginia, was the work of aristocratic leadership. Jacksonian democracy, whatever its benefits in other areas, was identified with a widespread deterioration in the standards of professional education, masquerading under the ideology that easier access to these privileged areas of life must be made available to the people.

The founding of early state universities was badly hampered by popular hostility to advanced education that was held to be of use chiefly to the aristocrats, who, in fact, usually provided the basic impetus to the cultivation of the higher learning, whether in state-founded or private institutions. The movement that destroyed the old classical curriculum and made American universities, especially our state universities, the nurseries of all kinds of subintellectual practical skills of less than university grade was in its impetus very largely a popular movement; and while many of the consequences of that movement must be set to its credit as compensations, the undercurrent of vocationalism and anti-intellectualism was undeniable. Our history books tell us—to come toward our own time—that during the Populist-Bryan period the university professors who failed to accept the gold-standard economics of the well-to-do classes were often victims of outrageous interference; they do not usually trouble to tell us that when the Populists captured Kansas they raised hob with the University of Kansas in much the same way that they complained of so bitterly when the shoe was on the other foot. One of the most genuinely popular, and I believe democratic, political leaders in our history was William Jennings Bryan; and the sort of respect he showed for science and academic freedom is familiar to you all. His concept of the rights of the dissenting teacher reduces to his famous comment: "A man cannot demand a salary for saying what his employers do not want said."

My aim in stressing these facts is not to cast discredit upon popular democracy, whose merit in our whole scheme of things must be weighed by taking into account all its achievements as well as its deficiencies; I am simply trying to suggest that many of us have in the past made a mystique of the masses and have tended too much to attribute all the villainy in our world to the machinations of vested interests. I find it rather suggestive that the sole ruling group in our history that could be called a vested intellectual interest of any considerable power—I refer, of course, to the early Puritan clergy—has suffered the fate of being scandalously libelled by our "liberal" historians who have written in the tradition of V. L. Parrington.

Why this persistent tension between popular democracy and free higher learning? Obviously it is to some degree an aspect of social striving: a college education is a privilege that has not been open to all. While it can open up otherwise unavailable opportunities to the children of the less favored classes, it can also confirm the privileges of the upper classes by adding to those social, political, and economic advantages which are theirs by birth and family, the advantages of a superior education. Much of the early opposition to state universities was based precisely upon this argument. Why tax the poor, it was repeatedly asked, to educate the sons of the rich? No doubt there is such an element of resentment on the part of the lower classes for the privileges and attainments of the upper classes. But this, to my mind, will not get us very far in explaining why the United States in particular has been a happy hunting ground for anti-intellectualism. Class divisions exist in all western societies. Moreover, of all western nations, the United States has given by far the greatest proportion of its total population an opportunity to have a college education. In our more than 1700 colleges, for instance, we offer higher education, or a reasonable facsimile thereof, to about ten times as large a portion of our population as is done in the British Isles. Moreover, while we have always had our class stratification, class lines have been less sharp in the United States, and mobility between classes somewhat easier, than in European countries. By the showing of these facts, the United States should, in accordance with the class envy theory, have much less resentment of higher education as a source of privilege than any other country on the globe.

The evidence is all to the contrary, and this is enough to give us pause. It remains to be explained why, in a culture that seems to value education very highly, that has provided an enormous apparatus for the collegiate education of its youth, the genuine intellectual content of higher education is so little esteemed, why the teacher in general and the college professor in particular has so much less social status than he does almost anywhere else. I believe that the problem of status is, indeed, quite crucial, but that the situation cannot be explained in terms of broad assertions about the envy of manual for intellectual labor, the poor for the well-to-do, or the middle classes for the leisure classes. We must look to some of the unique factors of American historical development for our answers.

From the beginning the American people were confronted with rich resources, an immense task of continental settlement, and a shortage of labor. Their culture thus came to set a premium on practical achievement, the manipulation of material reality, and quick decision. It did not encourage reflection or a respect for the ultimate and irreducible disagreements of life. On the contrary, it suggested that it was to everyone's interest to arrive at a quick consensus, general enough to get the work done, that any disagreement on details was, in the light of the rich potentialities of organized work, unimportant. The American still sets a very high premium on such a consensus; he implicitly approaches broad intellectual and philosophical problems with that model of prompt decision in mind. "What can we agree on?" he wants to know. The wonderful persistence of irreducible differences of opinion, of the plurality of human dreams and perspectives, the exchange or contemplation of differences as an exercise in mutual understanding—all these are likely to be dark mysteries to him. He makes an ideology of normality; he asks not "What am I?" but "What is it customary and proper to be around here?" He *thinks* he is an individualist because he does truly and genuinely resent any rude coercive efforts to make him conform, but he cannot realize that he spends half his time trying to figure out how he can conform "spontaneously." One of the most appalling things in American life is the failure of those who prate most about individualism to develop any understanding of individuality. The loudest hosannas to individualism are sung by grim, regimented choruses.

The effects of our chronic shortage of labor have also struck quite directly at the teaching profession from grammar schools to graduate schools. Our historic abundance of land and other resources has continually beckoned to the inadequate resources of our labor power. The consequences of this for other areas of life than education have often been noted. Our agriculture, for instance, was dedicated from the outset to extensive and wasteful cultivation and rapid mechanization rather than to intensive and careful cultivation and farming as a settled way of life. Too little has been said about a similar trend in our educational history. I think we have cultivated man wastefully and mechanically too. The teaching of our young, for instance, has been all too regularly left over to those whose imaginations and energies were not absorbed—or not yet absorbed—in the more exciting and lucrative life of physical and economic conquest, or to those who for one reason or another were altogether incapable of entering upon it. Ichabod Crane was, I suppose, the archetype of the American schoolmaster—the timid misfit, the amiable failure, the man who was scared out of town; and when Brom Bones chased him that terrible night through Sleepy Hollow and frightened him almost to death with a pumpkin, he was passing upon him the characteristic comment of the American philistine upon the American teacher. If the teacher was not Ichabod Crane, then it was the lonely spinster, driven by desperation to take up teaching when all else failed. If not the spinster, it was the young man who was merely marking time, supporting himself before launching upon a more permanent career in business or some really serious profession. "The men teachers," wrote an observer of early Massachusetts schools—mind you, even Massachusetts schools—

> may be divided into three classes: (1) Those who think teaching is easier and possibly a little more remunerative than common labor. (2) Those who are acquiring, or have acquired, a good education, and who take up teaching as a temporary employment, either to earn money for pressing necessities or to give themselves time to choose deliberately a regular profession. (3) Those who, conscious of weakness, despair of distinction or even the means of subsistence by other means. . . . They are often very young, they are constantly changing their employment, and consequently can have but little experience; and what is worse than all, they have never had any direct preparation for their profession. . . . No standard of attainments is fixed . . . so that any one *keeps school,* which is a very different thing from *teaching school,* who wishes to do it, and can persuade by herself or her friends, a small district to employ her. And this is not a very difficult matter, especially when the remuneration for the employment is so very trifling. . . . If a young man be moral enough to keep out of State prison, he will find no difficulty in getting approbation for a schoolmaster.

An exaggeration? Possibly. But in 1930–31, even after much had been done to improve standards of teacher training in the United States, the National Survey of the Education of Teachers showed that American teacher education, although only slightly inferior to that of England, was drastically inferior to that of France, Germany, and the Scandinavian countries. The teacher of a high school in the continental countries was found to be a much superior person, attracted by the relatively high social position, higher salaries, and advanced professional morale. And while I have been speaking here of the teaching profession below the university grade, most of what I have said will apply almost as well to American colleges down at least to the last three decades of the nineteenth century.

Let us look for a moment at those old colleges and the situation of their faculties. One of the first things that any observer of American higher education is struck by is the fact that the American professoriat is the only profession in the United States that is governed by laymen. Outside the continent of North America university faculties are nowhere governed, as they are here, by lay boards of trustees. Of course it is not easy to say whether the American professor lacks status because he is not self-governing or whether he has failed to get self-government in part because he lacks status. Genetically, however, it is not too difficult to explain how the curse of absentee government came to afflict American education. American colleges were called into existence before the community had the full means to support them amply, and indeed before there was a body of learned men professionally given to teaching. The great independent, self-governing universities of the middle ages, which established the pattern for early modern university government, came into existence only where there were well-established bodies of students and masters; they took their political form from the guild model of corporate self-control and the church's model of independence from the power of the state. The American colleges were founded in a Protestant milieu, which, no longer accepting the principles of hierarchy and corporate independence, had introduced lay government of churches. From this to lay government of colleges was a natural step, made the more natural by the fact that the greater part of the teaching personnel in early American colleges, for over a century and a half, consisted of young tutors, recent graduates, who were merely waiting and studying preparatory to entering the ministry. These men usually had no permanent interest in teaching as a profession, no permanent stake in its welfare. And they were considered by the philanthropic non-teachers who founded the colleges to be too young and too transient to be entrusted with the task of governing the colleges and managing their resources. Hence governmental powers were kept in the hands of trustees. The only working member of the college who held the full stature of a master of university learning was the president who, in the absence of the trustees, took over a larger and larger share of the task of determining college policy. Hence to this day the only person in the American community who enjoys a measure of prestige and respect comparable to that enjoyed by the university professor in most countries of Europe is our college or university president. Needless to say, with the development of the modern university, a great deal of the power to govern academic affairs has informally passed into the hands of faculties. But in almost all cases, such powers are delegated and may be legally retaken on any issue at any time by trustees. While few American university professors would argue for full self-government at this date, the legal inability of the American academic community to govern itself in matters bearing on academic freedom and tenure is a major disability in its struggle against the external forces of anti-intellectualism.

It may also be said in passing that the historic lack of prestige within the American academic community has tended to feed on itself. I am sure that no man anywhere whose primary desire is for a large share of the material goods of life enters the teaching profession with the idea that it will supply them with any abundance. He enters it because of other inducements: because he wants to pursue knowledge, because he values leisure (he will be lucky if he gets it), because he likes the idea of living in an academic community, or because of the prestige of the office. But American academic life, having so little prestige to offer, has failed to recruit a very large percentage of its professorial personnel from the upper classes, as does the professoriat in England or on the continent. The American college professor is characteristically drawn from the lower middle classes. I hope you will not imagine that I am being snobbish when I argue that this has been a signal disadvantage both to the freedom and the intellectualism of the academic community. Logan Wilson, in his study of *The Academic Man* in the United States, has pointed out that the recruit from the lower middle classes often comes from a background of cultural poverty in which, of necessity, the view taken of most things has to be profoundly affected by their material efficacy. I should also add that a man who comes from a well-established family with secure connections, and has perhaps in addition some personal resources to draw on, can confront the problems of free expression with far greater boldness than the man who feels that he must cling to his academic job at all costs. I have been impressed, in studying the development of a certain measure of liberalism in the American colleges of the eighteenth century, by the important role played by men who came to academic life from secure positions of social prestige, either in great commercial families or the ministry. One of the boldest men in early academic life was Professor John Winthrop, the great Harvard astronomer, and no little part of his boldness rested upon the security derived from the fact that he was, after all, a Winthrop in Massachusetts.

The low prestige of the professor in America was matched by the low prestige of the college itself. At the end of the eighteenth century and the beginning of the nineteenth, as the American population broke through the Allegheny mountains and began to spread across the continent, a process of educational fragmentation began which still profoundly afflicts our educational system. Every sect of Protestants wanted to have a little college to service every part of a great country. Localities thought that a community college would be good for local development. Parents welcomed the opportunity to educate their sons near at home in small schools whose annual tuition was often not much larger than the cost of transportation to a distant and perhaps more formidable seat of learning. They were advised, too, that the country college was socially democratic and that it protected their offspring from the corrupting atmosphere of great cities. This passion for breaking up the educational system into small units destroyed much of the potential strength and prestige of the old college. Where English colleges had clustered at a few university centers, American colleges were strewn across three thousand miles of continent. Innumerable colleges failed because they were so flimsily launched. Many that survived were much too tiny to maintain decent teaching staffs and adequate educational standards. It became a commonplace among serious educators before the Civil War that the American college was not, in the terms of international educational standards, a college at all, but a closer equivalent to the German gymnasium, the French lycée, the English public school.

After a time the old college became the butt of a great deal of criticism. It was, of course, devoted chiefly to the inherited classical curriculum, featuring Latin, Greek, and mathematics. This kind of schooling was increasingly held to be unadapted to the needs of American business, technology, and agriculture. It was held, and quite correctly, to be too limited and rigid to be adequate to the growing fund of human knowledge. Between the educational reformers, who were dissatisfied with the low level of work that the existing colleges were unable to transcend, and the practical reformers, who wanted to make American higher education work for the community in a clearer and more easily definable way, a curiously mixed transformation was finally effected in the last half of the nineteenth century. Universities, both state and private, were at last reared on adequate foundations; graduate and professional schools were created; schools of agriculture and engineering were founded; the curriculum was broadened; and the elective system was introduced.

Within only a few decades a curriculum system that had been too tight and too rigid was made too loose and too sprawling. All kinds of practical skills that had neither professional nor intellectual stature—no matter how necessary they might be to the community—were taught, or presumed to be taught, at universities. The president of a great state university was proud to say: "The state universities hold that there is no intellectual service too undignified for them to perform." Vast numbers of students without notable intellectual interests or skills flocked to the colleges and universities, availed themselves freely of the multitude of elective courses with little or no intellectual content, and passed out into the world with padded degrees. Much of the information thus inculcated may be thought to have no place in any system of formal education. A still larger part belongs to purely technical and mechanical education of the sort that can be properly taught in formal education but is not elsewhere considered proper to a university—the sort of thing that on the continent of Europe is to be found among the offerings of the German *technische Hochschule* and its many counterparts in other countries.

Now all this has taken place at serious cost to intellectualism. It is possible, of course, to argue that the professor of some field of pure learning is not interfered with in the pursuit of his work simply because his colleague in the school of agriculture is busy teaching farmers how to raise healthy pigs. Theoretically, no; but those who are familiar with the problems of university administration and finance know that these things have a way of pulling against or tripping over each other; and that when all kinds of skills of various levels are jumbled together and taught in one institution, the hierarchy of values that places intellectual accomplishment at the top, as one would expect to do in a university, is somehow broken and destroyed. Thus the universities, that we might have expected to stand as solid barriers against the undercurrents of American anti-intellectualism, have actually intensified the push of the stream. How they could have resisted it, I do not honestly know. For one thing, our system of higher education is, unlike all the other systems in the world, a system of mass education, that today enrolls about 3,000,000 people. In a way, that is a preposterous figure, and I suppose it is altogether unreasonable to expect that students in such numbers will all get anything that could be called a common liberal education. All kinds of things pass for a college education in this country and will no doubt continue to do so for a long time to come. The difficulty is that we now have an educational system which rarely produces educators who will themselves dare to defend an education wholeheartedly directed to the goal of increasing intellectual power. The famous report of the President's Commission on Higher Education published in 1948—a report prepared by a representative group of American educators and laymen interested in education—had this to say on the subject:

> We shall be denying educational opportunity to many young people as long as we maintain the present orientation of higher education toward verbal skills and intellectual interest. Many young people have abilities of a different kind, and they cannot receive "education commensurate with their native capacities" in colleges and universities that recognize only one kind of educable intelligence.
>
> Traditionally the colleges have sifted out as their special clientele persons possessing verbal aptitudes and a capacity for grasping abstractions. But many other aptitudes—such as social sensitivity and versatility, artistic ability, motor skill and dexterity, and mechanical aptitude and ingenuity—also should be cultivated in a society depending, as ours does, on the minute division of labor and at the same time upon the orchestration of an enormous variety of talents.

I can think of no more shameful capitulation than this to the canons of anti-intellectualism: a group of educators urging that our de-intellectualized colleges become still more de-intellectualized by giving up their alleged preoccupation with "verbal aptitudes" and "a capacity for grasping abstractions"—that is, the power to think and to express thought—for a motley batch of skills which, however valuable, one does not have to go to college to learn; for "social sensitivity" that no doubt includes ballroom dancing and parlor games; for "motor skill and dexterity" that must clearly mean athletics if it does not mean the ability to wash dishes without dropping them; and for "mechanical aptitude and ingenuity" that may very well mean the ability to drive and repair an automobile. Worthy skills every single one of them, and no doubt a necessary part of our life; but why they have to be acquired in something that calls itself a college or university the Commission, whose business was supposed to be with *higher* education, did not take the trouble to explain. No doubt its members did not feel themselves to be on the defensive, for they were expressing the dominant point of view in American society.

At the top of our educational system this attitude threatens to weaken whatever intellectualism we have. At lower levels, in our grammar and high schools, it threatens to wipe out literacy altogether in the name of "progressive education" or education for "life adjustment." If you think I exaggerate, listen to the principal of a junior high school in Urbana, Illinois, speaking to a meeting of the National Association of Secondary-School Principals:

> Through the years we've built a sort of halo around reading, writing, and arithmetic. We've said they were for everybody . . . rich and poor, brilliant and not-so-mentally endowed, ones who liked them and those who failed to go for them. Teacher has said that these were something "everyone should learn." The principal has remarked, "All educated people know how to write, spell, and read." When some child declared a dislike for a sacred subject, he was warned that, if he failed to master it, he would grow up to be a so-and-so.
>
> The Three R's for All Children and All Children for the Three R's! That was it.
>
> We've made some progress in getting rid of that slogan. But every now and then some mother with a Phi Beta Kappa award or some employer who has hired a girl who can't spell stirs up a fuss about the schools . . . and ground is lost. . . .
>
> . When we come to the realization that not every child has to read, figure, write, and spell . . . that many of them either cannot or will not master these chores . . . then we shall be on the road to improving the junior high curriculum.
>
> Between this day and that a lot of selling must take place. But it's coming. We shall some day accept the thought that it is just as illogical to assume that every boy must be able to read as it is that each one must be able to perform on a violin, that it is no more reasonable to require that each girl shall spell well than it is that each one shall bake a good cherry pie. . . .
>
> When adults finally realize that fact, everyone will be happier . . . and schools will be nicer places in which to live. . . .

Of course this speaker, unlike the President's Commission, does not seem to be entirely in harmony with the prevailing sentiments of the country—at least, not yet; for it is clear that he thinks himself to be a visionary whose notions are considerably in advance of the times but whose high ideals for the future of illiteracy will some fine day be realized. I must ask you, however, to try to envisage the minds of a generation of young Americans who receive their lower education under men of this stamp and their higher education under a regime fully conforming to the President's Commission's disdain for verbal aptitudes and abstractions.

What is it, I think we may properly ask, that brings our nation's educators to such depressing disavowals of the fundamentally intellectual purposes of education? Much the same thing, I believe, that has them cringing before the onslaughts of politicians who are beyond the pale of moral decency—and that is the lack of a self-confident dedication to the life of the mind. What the root of that failure of self-confidence is, no one really knows; but I venture to suggest that it has a great deal to do with our false piety for populistic democracy, our sense of guilt at daring to suggest that there is anything wrong with the mob, even when a large part of it has obviously been whipped up by demagogues to a state of frantic suspicion of everything it does not care to understand. I think it would help us all morally, even if it would do nothing else, to face the fact that the very idea of intellectualism implies an elite of some kind—not, to be sure, a ruthless elite with special privileges or powers, but simply a group of people who have interests not shared by everyone in the community and whose very special interest is in freedom. Not everyone really wants to belong to that elite. But the primary fact is that this elite must maintain a certain spiritual autonomy in defining its own standards. I am not optimistic enough to believe that in any calculable future the rest of society can be brought to recognize that intellectuals have their own rights and interests, not special rights or privileged interests, but of the same sort that any other group has. What the intellectual community can do is what any group of sensible people will do whose values are under attack—and that is not to try to find some plausible reason for abandoning those values because they are not shared by the majority; and not to try to convince themselves that they really agree with the majority after all—but to show cohesion and firmness under fire, until the point has been reached when it is no longer profitable to encroach upon them.

This world will never be governed by intellectuals—it may rest assured. But *we* must be assured, too, that intellectuals will not be altogether governed by this world, that they maintain their piety, their long-standing allegiance to the world of spiritual values to which they should belong. Otherwise there will be no intellectuals, at least not above ground. And societies in which the intellectuals have been driven underground, as we have had occasion to see in our own time, are societies in which even the anti-intellectuals are unhappy.

Understanding the Text

1. According to Hofstadter, what is an intellectual?

2. What role does Hofstadter feel that democracy has played in education and anti-intellectualism in America?

3. Is Hofstadter hopeful about the fate of intellectualism in this country? Why or why not?

The Renaissance of Anti-Intellectualism

Todd Gitlin

The presidential campaign ended, effectively, in a tie, but it did speak clearly about the value accorded intellectuals and intellectuality in American culture. What it declared is, to say the least, inauspicious.

However the next four years play out in the White House, George W. Bush deserves a certain credit for resurrecting— though probably not intentionally—the subject of anti-intellectualism. Like Dan Quayle before him, but even more conspicuously (Bush's gaffes provided horror-comic relief during a campaign marked by its narrowed themes and horse-race obsessions), the governor of Texas proved an inadvertent shill for the comedy routines that have become an increasingly visible showcase for the spectacle of national politics.

Gov. Malaprop accomplished that dubious objective by various means: semantic spatter, most memorably "subliminable" for "subliminal," but also "subscribe" for "ascribe," "retort" for "resort," "hostile" for "hostage," and so on; inversions and juxtapositions of singular verbs and plural nouns, as in "Our priorities is our faith" and "Families is where our nation finds hope, where wings take dream"; and an ineptitude so guileless ("Social Security is not a federal program") as to embarrass the literal-minded who affect intellectual seriousness, for after a certain point it seems rude to call attention to the obvious, or "elitist" to notice something that viewers haven't noticed.

Early in the campaign, Bush had famously dubbed the inhabitants of Greece "Grecians" and flubbed a talk-show host's quiz about names of

Todd Gitlin is a professor of journalism and sociology at Columbia University. He is the author of twelve books, including *The Intellectuals and the Flag* (2006), *Media Unlimited: How the Torrent of Images and Sounds Overwhelms Our Lives* (2002), *The Twilight of Common Dreams: Why America Is Wracked by Culture Wars* (1995), and *The Whole World Is Watching: Mass Media in the Making and Unmaking of the Left*. His essays appear in numerous newspapers and magazines, and he is a frequent guest on television and radio programs.

foreign leaders. There was so much ignorance on display as to raise the suspicion, on one hand, that Bush was dyslexic or, on the other, that this lazy-minded graduate of Andover, Yale, and Harvard Business School was a chip off his father's pork rinds, appealing self-consciously to his audience's resentment of brains. Thanks to videotape and a media maw hungry for simple charges and sound bites, Duh-bya seemed to have stridden right out of central casting, a veritable personification of the politician as clown.

Yet none of the easy charges against Bush touched upon his more substantial incapacities: his lack of curiosity about the world (he has scarcely traveled outside the United States and Mexico City) and the ample evidence that he does not reason. During the debates, he was unresponsive to questions the answers to which he had not memorized. In public appearances, he spoke in sloganistic lists, not arcs. It would seem that, precisely because his thinking was disordered, the governor lost track of his points, so that items came out nonsensical, as in: "Drug therapies are replacing a lot of medicines as we used to know it."

There has been much talk since the election to the effect that "two nations" were evenly matched in the contest: roughly speaking, the rural, inland, heavily male, and white Bushland versus the urban, coastal, heavily female, black, and immigrant Goreland. To be sure, suspicion of intellectuals and intellectuality was visible in both camps, but most plainly so in Bush's. So it came to pass that half of the voting population was appalled that the other half judged this man of little discernible achievement, little knowledge of the world or curiosity about it, to be an acceptable president of the United States. His defenders were in the position of claiming that it didn't matter whether the governor was smart or not, he could hire a smart staff, thereby certifying that intelligence was something for underlings.

In the minds of many of Bush's supporters, the absence of thoughtfulness, the narrowness of scope, the presence of diminished capacity were all reduced to a question of "management style." Gore, meanwhile, suffered bad reviews for his dismissive and overbearing style of intellectual combat. In the eyes of half the population, the vice president fell prey to a suspicion that he was not only preachy but also a sharpie. In the media's campaign story line, the standard charge against Gore, shared by the Bush campaign and the comedians, was that, like the traditional confidence man, Gore—too smart for his own good—lied, while Bush was the amiable common man.

Thirty-seven years have passed since the appearance of the last substantial book to take seriously, in the words of its title, *Anti-Intellectualism in American Life*. Richard Hofstadter's tour de force, appearing in 1963, is actually a product of the 1950's. Like many intellectuals, Hofstadter was disturbed by the general disdain for "eggheads," haunted by Joseph McCarthy's thuggish assault on Dean Acheson and his Anglophilic ways, and dismayed by Eisenhower's taste for Western novels and his tangled syntax (which was not yet understood to be, at least sometimes, not simply incompetent but deliberately evasive). Had not Eisenhower himself in

1954 (no doubt in words written for him by another hand) cited a definition of an intellectual as "a man who takes more words than are necessary to tell more than he knows"? (How much more congenial was Stevenson, who once cracked: "Eggheads of the world, unite! You have nothing to lose but your yolks!")

Probing for historical roots of a mood that was sweeping (if somewhat exaggerated by intellectuals), Hofstadter found that "our anti-intellectualism is, in fact, older than our national identity." He cited, among others, the Puritan John Cotton, who wrote in 1642, "The more learned and witty you bee, the more fit to act for Satan will you bee"; and Baynard R. Hall, who wrote in 1843 of frontier Indiana: "We always preferred an ignorant bad man to a talented one, and hence attempts were usually made to ruin the moral character of a smart candidate; since unhappily smartness and wickedness were supposed to be generally coupled, and incompetence and goodness."

Yet, according to the historian Lawrence W. Levine, the illiterate Rocky Mountain scout Jim Bridger could recite long passages from Shakespeare, which he learned by hiring someone to read the plays to him. "There is hardly a pioneer's hut that does not contain a few odd volumes of Shakespeare," Alexis de Tocqueville found on his trip through America in 1831–32. Here lay a supremely American paradox: The same Americans who valued the literacy of commoners were suspicious of experts and tricksters.

In his unsurpassed survey, Hofstadter described three pillars of anti-intellectualism—evangelical religion, practical-minded business, and the populist political style. Religion was suspicious of modern relativism, business of regulatory expertise, populism of claims that specialized knowledge had its privileges. Those pillars stand. But, as Hofstadter recognized, something was changing in American life, and that was the uneasy apotheosis of technical intellect.

The rise of big science during World War II, and its normalization during the cold war, along with the Sputnik panic of 1957, made "brains" more reputable among respectable citizens who had their own ideas about the force of common sense but had to acknowledge that expertise delivered material goods Then as now, the "brains" that became admirable were brains kept in their place. To the extent that brains were admirable, it was because they were instrumental—they prevented polio, invented computers, launched satellites.

By the 1990s, the geek was an acceptable good guy, the nerd an entrepreneurial hero. That sense of the supreme position of useful intellect is preserved in the current phrase, "It's not rocket science"—implying that real rocket science is the grandest field of intellectual dreams.

Hofstadter did most of his research before Kennedy came to the White House, and he understood that Kennedy's brief ascendancy did not change the fundamentals. Kennedy was not especially serious about the life of the mind, but he was elegant, witty, and, by all accounts, enjoyed the occasional presence of intellectuals. John Kenneth Galbraith and Arthur Schlesinger

Jr. were adornments. Never mind that Kennedy's reading tilted heavily toward Ian Fleming, who in the James Bond books supplied the president with a man of action's idea of the debonair, the sort of fellow whose European accent can be mistaken for mental accomplishment.

Even into the Johnson administration, the White House ceremonially invited intellectuals and high artists to visit, culminating in the public-relations disaster of a White House festival of the arts, in 1965, that was boycotted by some writers and artists while others circulated an antiwar petition at the event.

The force of Hofstadter's insight into persistent anti-intellectualism despite the rising legitimacy of technical experts would be clear five years after he published his book. George Wallace ran well in several Democratic Party primaries, and eventually, too, as a third-party candidate, while campaigning against "pointy-headed bureaucrats"—precisely the classic identification of intellect with arbitrary power that Hofstadter had identified as the populist hallmark.

There was a left-wing version of this presupposition, too. A populist strain in the 60s student movement, identifying with the oppressed sharecroppers of the Mississippi Delta and the dispossessed miners of Appalachia, bent the principle "Let the people decide" into a suspicion of all those who were ostensibly knowledgeable. Under pressure of the Vietnam War, the steel-rimmed technocrat Robert S. McNamara came to personify the steel-trap mind untethered by insight, and countercultural currents came to disdain reason as a mask for imperial arrogance.

In his first gubernatorial campaign in 1966, Ronald Reagan deployed a classic anti-intellectual theme—portraying students as riotous decadents. Real education was essentially a matter of training, and breaches of discipline resulted in nihilism and softness on communism. The Nixon-Agnew team proceeded to mobilize resentment against "nattering nabobs of negativism," successfully mobilizing a "silent majority" against a verbose minority. That was to flower into a major neoconservative theme thereafter.

As candidate and president, the smooth-spoken if intellectually challenged Reagan succeeded in availing himself of an indulgent press and an adoring constituency that, at the least, did not mind his incapacity. He did not suffer from his evident contempt for professorial types, his half-educated ignorance of history and reliance on crackpot sources, his embrace of the notion that trees cause pollution. That he was opposed by sophisticated types only inflated his aura.

By the 1990s, "elitism" had become an all-purpose epithet, used by neoconservatives against the "new class" (consisting of all political intellectuals with the exception of themselves), but also by hard multiculturalists against "the neo-Enlightenment project," by relativists in general against objectivists in general. Populist resentment flourished even as (and, perhaps in part, because) populist egalitarianism of an economic stripe was dwindling.

The counterculture had introduced suspicion of professionalized rationality—swelling the reputation of "alternative" medicine and elevating herbs and homeopathic, chiropractic, and osteopathic treatments to alternatives to plodding old Western therapies. Hofstadter had made much of the distinction between critical intellectuals (suspected, sometimes justifiably, of being ideologues) and expert intellectuals ("on tap, not on top," in the terms of the early atomic scientists), but thanks to the postmodern mood of the intervening decades, many experts had come to be tarred with the same brush as ideologues. College students were heard to complain that certain professors were excessive in their vocabularies. Even in the classroom, "boring" became an epithet of choice.

A central force boosting anti-intellectualism since Hofstadter published his book has been the bulking up of popular culture and, in particular, the rise of a new form of faux cerebration: punditry. Everyday life, supersaturated with images and jingles, makes intellectual life look hopelessly sluggish, burdensome, difficult. In a video-game world, the play of intellect—the search for validity, the willingness to entertain many hypotheses, the respect for difficulty, the resistance to hasty conclusions—has the look of retardation.

Again, there is a continuity to the earlier nation. Long before Hollywood or MTV, Tocqueville observed that Americans were drawn to novelty, turnover, and sensation. How much more so in a world of cascading, all-pervasive images, where two-thirds of children grow up with 24/7 access to television in their bedrooms, where video and computer games flourish, where mobile phones guarantee access when and where one chooses, where the right to be instantly entertained and in-touch seems to preoccupy more of the citizenry than the right to vote and to have their votes properly counted.

There is a seeming paradox that Hofstadter did not anticipate, but would have appreciated. In the torrent of popular culture, there emerges more talk about public affairs than ever before—virtually nonstop talk about political concerns, debate on burning questions available at all hours of the day and night. But the talk that fills the channels amounts mainly to signals, gestures, and stances—not reasoning.

Television reporting and punditry are the tributes that entertainment pays to the democratic ideal of discourse. The political talk does not, in the main, evaluate or research: It "covers." When CNN's Washington bureau chief can say casually, "The Texas governor hammered home some of his major themes, including Social Security," this is shorthand, but not only shorthand—it is a surrogate for reasoning. Positions are signaled—candidates "position themselves"—rather than defended; no defending is demanded of them. A topic is a "theme" is a "position" is an "issue" is news.

All the more so does punditry diffuse a debased version of intellectual life, cornering intellect in the name of chat, operating by a sort of Gresham's law of discourse. Punditry is concerned with reviewing performances, rating "presidentiality," itemizing themes, relaying and interpreting spin, not thoughtfully assessing politicians' claims, evaluating their evidence, judging their reasoning. To assess the quality of what politicians say would require intellectual work for which the pundits do not demonstrate competency. Pundits are hired, rather, for the facility and pungency of their presentations and the ferocity and acceptability of their opinions.

The most bookish of pundits, George Will, was hired for the Anglophilic elegance of his sneers, not for logical mastery or historical depth. The punditocracy, as Eric Alterman calls it, does not assess either reason or reasons. Its job is simply to declare which issues are discussable, which positions presentable. It makes up for its intellectual deficits by supplying pre-cooked opinion. The point is not to clarify: It is never to be at a loss for words. Surely the English infusion into American journalism—the premium on corrosive wit, the fusion of intellectual name-dropping with tabloid meanness—belongs to this trend: the show of intellect without the demanding work.

When Hofstadter wrote, the dominant intellectuals were either experts or ideologues. The most influential pundit was Walter Lippmann. But the crucial public development since Hofstadter's time is the rise of the pseudo-intellectual, thanks to the premium on smirking and glibness, which, in much of the popular mind, passes for intellect. The pundit is a smart person in both senses—intelligent and a smarty-pants— and his knowingness about how the game is played is a substitute for knowledge about what would improve society. Punditry is to intellectual life as fast food is to fine cuisine.

After Gore, self-cast as wonk-expert and therefore prey to precisely the anti-intellectualism that Hofstadter identified, challenged Bush to state his position on the Dingell-Norwood patients-rights' bill during the third debate, and Bush avoided the question, the pseudo-brains of ABC's *This Week,* Cokie Roberts and Sam Donaldson, made much mirth by mocking the names. They did not think it their obligation to clarify what Gore was talking about. Deadly, that would have been. Chock full of attitude, deploying the cheap gags and knowingness that mark them as qualified for their jobs, those maestros of the Beltway paraded their superiority to knowledge while (as Michael Kinsley pointed out) refraining from showing that they knew more than the public.

Surely television is a boon to anti-intellectualism, with its encouragement of emotional chords and comfort, but the degradations of public life that afflict us are not primarily visual achievements. It is language and sound, most of all, that warp the public discourse. That is true not only in the presentation of politics but of science, education, and many another subject. The sound-bite discourse cultivated by television pumps up the imperative "Cut to the chase," reinforcing the fetish of "the bottom line."

It is not that the sound-bite culture was imposed upon what was previously unrelievedly brilliant politics. From "Tippecanoe and Tyler too" to "I like Ike," American history is soaked in sound-bite prefigurations. Warren G. Harding may not have been much better than George W. Bush. But the more striking transformation in American commentary takes us in 50 years from Walter Lippmann, a man of tremendous historical and philosophical sophistication, to

Tim Russert, an intelligent man who specializes in "Gotcha!" questions and gives Rush Limbaugh respectful interviews, defending that choice on the ground that, after all, Limbaugh "speaks to 20-million people." Thus does knowingness make its peace with populism.

In the Bushes, *père et fils,* we see another turn in the history of the American aversion to intellect. Hofstadter rightly noted the 19th-century aristocratic disdain for practical intellectuals, the business types and experts whose rising power displaced their own. The Roosevelt cousins, different in many respects, both honored the life of the mind: Theodore as writer, Franklin as a collector of advisers. Old money respected brains.

But the Bushes are men of social credentials who went to the right schools and passed through them without any detectable mark. They represent aristocracy with a populist gloss, borrowing what they can from the evangelical revival, siding with business and its distaste for time-wasting mind work, holding intellectual talent in contempt from both above and below. Pleasant enough for the pundits, they have been able to count on a surplus of populist ressentiment. That Bush *fils,* country-club Republican, could gain stature (and keep a straight face) in his presidential campaign for proposing an "education presidency" and denouncing an "education recession" tells us something about the closing of the American mind that Allan Bloom did not dream of.

Understanding the Text

1. How does Gitlin characterize Bush and Gore's performance during the 2000 campaign for president?

2. What former presidents does Gitlin discuss, and how does he assess their performance in regard to intellectualism?

3. What is "punditry"? According to Gitlin, how does it contribute to the rise of anti-intellectualism in American political discourse?

On the Uses of a Liberal Education: As Lite Entertainment for Bored College Students

Mark Edmundson

Today is evaluation day in my Freud class, and everything has changed. The class meets twice a week, late in the afternoon, and the clientele, about fifty undergraduates, tends to drag in and slump, looking disconsolate and a little lost, waiting for a jump start. To get the discussion moving, they usually require a joke, an anecdote, an off-the-wall question—When you were a kid, were your Halloween getups ego costumes, id costumes, or superego costumes? That sort of thing. But today, as soon as I flourish the forms, a buzz rises in the room. Today they write their assessments of the course, their assessments of *me,* and they are without a doubt wide-awake. "What is your evaluation of the instructor?" asks question number eight, entreating them to circle a number between five (excellent) and one (poor, poor). Whatever interpretive subtlety they've acquired during the term is now out the window. Edmundson: one to five, stand and shoot.

And they do. As I retreat through the door—I never stay around for this phase of the ritual—I look over my shoulder and see them toiling away like the devil's auditors. They're pitched into high writing gear, even the ones who struggle to squeeze out their journal entries word by word, stoked on a procedure they have by now supremely mastered. They're playing the informed consumer, letting the provider know where he's come through and where he's not quite up to snuff.

But why am I so distressed, bolting like a refugee out of my own classroom, where I usually hold easy sway? Chances are the evaluations will

Mark Edmundson is a professor of English at the University of Virginia. He lectures frequently on college campuses and has published numerous essays on literature and teaching in journals and magazines. He has published five books, the most recent of which are *Why Read?* (2004) and *Teacher: The One Who Made the Difference* (2002).

287

be much like what they've been in the past—they'll be just fine. It's likely that I'll be commended for being "interesting" (and I am commended, many times over), that I'll be cited for my relaxed and tolerant ways (that happens, too), that my sense of humor and capacity to connect the arcana of the subject matter with current culture will come in for some praise (yup). I've been hassled this term, finishing a manuscript, and so haven't given their journals the attention I should have, and for that I'm called—quite civilly, though—to account. Overall, I get off pretty well.

Yet I have to admit that I do not much like the image of myself that emerges from these forms, the image of knowledgeable, humorous detachment and bland tolerance. I do not like the forms themselves, with their number ratings, reminiscent of the sheets circulated after the TV pilot has just played to its sample audience in Burbank. Most of all I dislike the attitude of calm consumer expertise that pervades the responses. I'm disturbed by the serene belief that my function—and, more important, Freud's, or Shakespeare's, or Blake's—is to divert, entertain, and interest. Observes one respondent, not at all unrepresentative: "Edmundson has done a fantastic job of presenting this difficult, important & controversial material in an enjoyable and approachable way."

Thanks but no thanks. I don't teach to amuse, to divert, or even, for that matter, to be merely interesting. When someone says she "enjoyed" the course—and that word crops up again and again in my evaluations—somewhere at the edge of my immediate complacency I feel encroaching self-dislike. That is not at all what I had in mind. The off-the-wall questions and the sidebar jokes are meant as lead-ins to stronger stuff—in the case of the Freud course, to a complexly tragic view of life. But the affability and the one-liners often seem to be all that land with the students; their journals and evaluations leave me little doubt.

I want some of them to say that they've been changed by the course. I want them to measure themselves against what they've read. It's said that some time ago a Columbia University instructor used to issue a harsh two-part question. One: What book did you most dislike in the course? Two: What intellectual or characterological flaws in you does that dislike point to? The hand that framed that question was surely heavy. But at least it compels one to see intellectual work as a confrontation between two people, student and author, where the stakes matter. Those Columbia students were being asked to relate the quality of an *encounter,* not rate the action as though it had unfolded on the big screen.

Why are my students describing the Oedipus complex and the death drive as being interesting and enjoyable to contemplate? And why am I coming across as an urbane, mildly ironic, endlessly affable guide to this intellectual territory, operating without intensity, generous, funny, and loose?

Because that's what works. On evaluation day, I reap the rewards of my partial compliance with the culture of my students and, too, with the culture of the university as it now operates. It's a culture that's gotten little exploration. Current critics tend to think that liberal-arts education is in crisis because universities have been invaded by professors with peculiar ideas: deconstruction, Lacanianism, feminism, queer theory. They believe that genius and tradition are out and that P.C., multiculturalism, and identity politics are in because of an invasion by tribes of tenured radicals, the late millennial equivalents of the Visigoth hordes that cracked Rome's walls.

But mulling over my evaluations and then trying to take a hard, extended look at campus life both here at the University of Virginia and around the country eventually led me to some different conclusions. To me, liberal-arts education is as ineffective as it is now not chiefly because there are a lot of strange theories in the air. (Used well, those theories *can* be illuminating.) Rather, it's that university culture, like American culture writ large, is, to put it crudely, ever more devoted to consumption and entertainment, to the using and using up of goods and images. For someone growing up in America now, there are few available alternatives to the cool consumer worldview. My students didn't ask for that view, much less create it, but they bring a consumer weltanschauung to school, where it exerts a powerful, and largely unacknowledged, influence. If we want to understand current universities, with their multiple woes, we might try leaving the realms of expert debate and fine ideas and turning to the classrooms and campuses, where a new kind of weather is gathering.

From time to time I bump into a colleague in the corridor and we have what I've come to think of as a Joon Lee fest. Joon Lee is one of the best students I've taught. He's endlessly curious, has read a small library's worth, seen every movie, and knows all about showbiz and entertainment. For a class of mine he wrote an essay using Nietzsche's Apollo and Dionysus to analyze the pop group The Supremes. A trite, cultural-studies bonbon? Not at all. He said striking things about conceptions of race in America and about how they shape our ideas of beauty. When I talk with one of his other teachers, we run on about the general splendors of his work and presence. But what inevitably follows a JL fest is a mournful reprise about the divide that separates him and a few other remarkable students from their contemporaries. It's not that some aren't nearly as bright—in terms of intellectual ability, my students are all that I could ask for. Instead, it's that Joon Lee has decided to follow his interests and let them make him into a singular and rather eccentric man; in his charming way, he doesn't mind being at odds with most anyone.

It's his capacity for enthusiasm that sets Joon apart from what I've come to think of as the reigning generational style. Whether the students are sorority/fraternity types, grunge aficionados, piercer/tattooers, black or white, rich or middle class (alas, I teach almost no students from truly poor backgrounds), they are, nearly across the board, very, very self-contained. On good days they display a light, appealing glow; on bad days, shuffling disgruntlement. But there's little fire, little passion to be found.

This point came home to me a few weeks ago when I was wandering across the university grounds. There, beneath a classically cast portico, were two students, male and female, having a rip-roaring argument. They were incensed, bellowing at each other, headstrong, confident, and wild. It struck me how rarely I see this kind of full-out feeling in students anymore. Strong emotional display is forbidden. When conflicts arise, it's generally understood that one of the parties will say something sarcastically propitiating ("whatever" often does it) and slouch away.

How did my students reach this peculiar state in which all passion seems to be spent? I think that many of them have imbibed their sense of self from consumer culture in general and from the tube in particular. They're the progeny of 100 cable channels and omni-present Blockbuster outlets. TV, Marshall McLuhan famously said, is a cool medium. Those who play best on it are low-key and nonassertive; they blend in. Enthusiasm, à la Joon Lee, quickly looks absurd. The form of character that's most appealing on TV is calmly self-interested though never greedy, attuned to the conventions, and ironic. Judicious timing is preferred to sudden self-assertion. The TV medium is inhospitable to inspiration, improvisation, failures, slipups. All must run perfectly.

Naturally, a cool youth culture is a marketing bonanza for producers of the right products, who do all they can to enlarge that culture and keep it grinding. The Internet, TV, and magazines now teem with what I call persona ads, ads for Nikes and Reeboks and Jeeps and Blazers that don't so much endorse the capacities of the product per se as show you what sort of person you will be once you've acquired it. The Jeep ad that features hip, outdoorsy kids whipping a Frisbee from mountaintop to mountaintop isn't so much about what Jeeps can do as it is about the kind of people who own them. Buy a Jeep and be one with them. The ad is of little consequence in itself, but expand its message exponentially and you have the central thrust of current consumer culture—buy in order to be.

Most of my students seem desperate to blend in, to look right, not to make a spectacle of themselves. (Do I have to tell you that those two students having the argument under the portico turned out to be acting in a role-playing game?) The specter of the uncool creates a subtle tyranny. It's apparently an easy standard to subscribe to, this Letterman-like, Tarantino-like cool, but once committed to it, you discover that matters are rather different. You're inhibited, except on ordained occasions, from showing emotion, stifled from trying to achieve anything original. You're made to feel that even the slightest departure from the reigning code will get you genially ostracized. This is a culture tensely committed to a laid-back norm.

Am I coming off like something of a crank here? Maybe. Oscar Wilde, who is almost never wrong, suggested that it is perilous to promiscuously contradict people who are much younger than yourself. Point taken. But one of the lessons that consumer hype tries to insinuate is that we must never rebel against the new, never even question it. If it's new—a new need, a new product, a new show, a new style, a new generation—it must be good. So maybe, even at the risk of winning the withered, brown laurels of crankdom, it pays to resist newness-worship and cast a colder eye.

Praise for my students? I have some of that too. What my students are, at their best, is decent. They are potent believers in equality. They help out at the soup kitchen and volunteer to tutor poor kids to get a stripe on their résumés, sure. But they also want other people to have a fair shot. And in their commitment to fairness they are discerning; there you see them at their intellectual best. If I were on trial and innocent, I'd want them on the jury.

What they will not generally do, though, is indict the current system. They won't talk about how the exigencies of capitalism lead to a reserve army of the unemployed and nearly inevitable misery. That would be getting too loud, too brash. For the pervading view is the cool consumer perspective, where passion and strong admiration are forbidden. "To stand in awe of nothing, Numicus, is perhaps the one and only thing that can make a man happy and keep him so," says Horace in the *Epistles,* and I fear that his lines ought to hang as a motto over the university in this era of high consumer capitalism.

It's easy to mount one's high horse and blame the students for this state of affairs. But they didn't create the present culture of consumption. (It was largely my own generation, that of the Sixties, that let the counterculture search for pleasure devolve into a quest for commodities.) And they weren't the ones responsible, when they were six and seven and eight years old, for unplugging the TV set from time to time or for hauling off and kicking a hole through it. It's my generation of parents who sheltered these students, kept them away from the hard knocks of everyday life, making them cautious and overfragile, who demanded that their teachers, from grade school on, flatter them endlessly so that the kids are shocked if their college profs don't reflexively suck up to them.

Of course, the current generational style isn't simply derived from culture and environment. It's also about dollars. Students worry that taking too many chances with their educations will sabotage their future prospects. They're aware of the fact that a drop that looks more and more like one wall of the Grand Canyon separates the top economic tenth from the rest of the population. There's a sentiment currently abroad that if you step aside for a moment, to write, to travel, to fall too hard in love, you might lose position permanently. We may be on a conveyor belt, but it's worse down there on the filth-strewn floor. So don't sound off, don't blow your chance.

But wait. I teach at the famously conservative University of Virginia. Can I extend my view from Charlottesville to encompass the whole country, a whole generation of college students? I can only say that I hear comparable stories about classroom life from colleagues everywhere in America. When I visit other schools to lecture, I see a similar scene unfolding. There are, of course, terrific students everywhere. And they're all the better for the way they've had to strive against the existing conformity. At some of the small liberal-arts colleges, the tradition of strong engagement persists. But overall, the students strike me as being sweet and sad, hovering in a nearly suspended animation.

Too often now the pedagogical challenge is to make a lot from a little. Teaching Wordsworth's "Tintern Abbey," you ask for comments. No one responds. So you call on Stephen. Stephen: "The sound, this poem really flows." You: "Stephen seems interested in the music of the poem. We might extend his comment to ask if the poem's music coheres with its argument. Are they consistent? Or is there an emotional pain submerged here that's contrary to the poem's appealing melody?" All right, it's not usually that bad. But close. One friend describes it as rebound teaching: they proffer a weightless comment, you hit it back for all you're worth, then it comes dribbling out again. Occasionally a professor will try to explain away this intellectual timidity by describing the students as perpetrators of postmodern irony, a highly sophisticated mode. Everything's a slick counterfeit, a simulacrum, so by no means should any phenomenon be taken seriously. But the students don't have the urbane, Oscar Wilde-type demeanor that should go with this view. Oscar was cheerful, funny, confident, strange. (Wilde, mortally ill, living in a Paris flophouse: "My wallpaper and I are fighting a duel to the death. One or the other of us has to go.") This generation's style is considerate, easy to please, and a touch depressed.

Granted, you might say, the kids come to school immersed in a consumer mentality—they're good Americans, after all—but then the university and the professors do everything in their power to fight that dreary mind-set in the interest of higher ideals, right? So it should be. But let us look at what is actually coming to pass.

Over the past few years, the physical layout of my university has been changing. To put it a little indecorously, the place is looking more and more like a retirement spread for the young. Our funds go to construction, into new dorms, into renovating the student union. We have a new aquatics center and ever-improving gyms, stocked with StairMasters and Nautilus machines. Engraved on the wall in the gleaming aquatics building is a line by our founder, Thomas Jefferson, declaring that everyone ought to get about two hours' exercise a day. Clearly even the author of the Declaration of Independence endorses the turning of his university into a sports-and-fitness emporium.

But such improvements shouldn't be surprising. Universities need to attract the best (that is, the smartest *and* the richest) students in order to survive in an ever more competitive market. Schools want kids whose parents can pay the full freight, not the ones who need scholarships or want to bargain down the tuition costs. If the marketing surveys say that the kids require sports centers, then, trustees willing, they shall have them. In fact, as I began looking around, I came to see that more and more of what's going on in the university is customer driven. The consumer pressures that beset me on evaluation day are only a part of an overall trend.

From the start, the contemporary university's relationship with students has a solicitous, nearly servile tone. As soon as someone enters his junior year in high school, and especially if he's living in a prosperous zip code, the informational material—the advertising—comes flooding in. Pictures, testimonials, videocassettes, and CD ROMs (some bidden, some not) arrive at the door from colleges across the country, all trying to capture the student and his tuition cash. The freshman-to-be sees photos of well-appointed dorm rooms; of elaborate phys-ed facilities; of fine dining rooms; of expertly kept sports fields; of orchestras and drama troupes; of students working alone (no overbearing grown-ups in range), peering with high seriousness into computers and microscopes; or of students arrayed outdoors in attractive conversational garlands.

Occasionally—but only occasionally, for we usually photograph rather badly; in appearance we tend at best to be styleless—there's a professor teaching a class. (The college catalogues I received, by my request only, in the late Sixties were austere affairs full of professors' credentials and course descriptions; it was clear on whose terms the enterprise was going to unfold.) A college financial officer recently put matters to me in concise, if slightly melodramatic, terms: "Colleges don't have admissions offices anymore, they have marketing departments." Is it surprising that someone who has been approached with photos and tapes, bells and whistles, might come in thinking that the Freud and Shakespeare she had signed up to study were also going to be agreeable treats?

How did we reach this point? In part the answer is a matter of demographics and (surprise) of money. Aided by the G.I. bill, the college-going population in America dramatically increased after the Second World War. Then came the baby boomers, and to accommodate them, schools continued to grow. Universities expand easily enough, but with tenure locking faculty in for lifetime jobs, and with the general reluctance of administrators to eliminate their own slots, it's not easy for a university to contract. So after the baby boomers had passed through—like a fat meal digested by a boa constrictor—the colleges turned to energetic promotional strategies to fill the empty chairs. And suddenly college became a buyer's market. What students and their parents wanted had to be taken more and more into account. That usually meant creating more comfortable, less challenging environments, places where almost no one failed, everything was enjoyable, and everyone was nice.

Just as universities must compete with one another for students, so must the individual departments. At a time of rank economic anxiety, the English and history majors have to contend for students against the more success-insuring branches, such as the sciences and the commerce school. In 1968, more than 21 percent of all the bachelor's degrees conferred in America were in the humanities; by 1993, that number had fallen to about 13 percent. The humanities now must struggle to attract students, many of whose parents devoutly wish they would study something else.

One of the ways we've tried to stay attractive is by loosening up. We grade much more softly than our colleagues in science. In English, we don't give many Ds, or Cs for that matter. (The rigors of Chem 101 create almost as many English majors per year as do the splendors of Shakespeare.) A professor at Stanford recently explained grade inflation in the humanities by observing that the undergraduates were getting smarter every year; the higher grades simply recorded how much better they were than their predecessors. Sure.

Along with softening the grades, many humanities departments have relaxed major requirements. There are some good reasons for introducing more choice into curricula and requiring fewer standard courses. But the move, like many others in the university now, jibes with a tendency to serve—and not challenge—the students. Students can also float in and out of classes during the first two weeks of each term without making any commitment. The common name for this time span—shopping period—speaks volumes about the consumer mentality that's now in play. Usually, too, the kids can drop courses up until the last month with only an innocuous "W" on their transcripts. Does a course look too challenging? No problem. Take it pass-fail. A happy consumer is, by definition, one with multiple options, one who can always have what he wants. And since a course is something the students and their parents have bought and paid for, why can't they do with it pretty much as they please?

A sure result of the university's widening elective leeway is to give students more power over their teachers. Those who don't like you can simply avoid you. If the clientele dislikes you en masse, you can be left without students, period. My first term teaching I walked into my introduction to poetry course and found it inhabited by one student, the gloriously named Bambi Lynn Dean. Bambi and I chatted amiably awhile, but for all that she and the pleasure of her name could offer, I was fast on the way to meltdown. It was all a mistake, luckily, a problem with the scheduling book. Everyone was waiting for me next door. But in a dozen years of teaching I haven't forgotten that feeling of being ignominiously marooned. For it happens to others, and not always because of scheduling glitches. I've seen older colleagues go through hot embarrassment at not having enough students sign up for their courses: they graded too hard, demanded too much, had beliefs too far out of keeping with the existing disposition. It takes only a few such instances to draw other members of the professoriat further into line.

And if what's called tenure reform—which generally just means the abolition of tenure—is broadly enacted, professors will be yet more vulnerable to the whims of their customer-students. Teach what pulls the kids in, or walk. What about entire departments that don't deliver? If the kids say no to Latin and Greek, is it time to dissolve classics? Such questions are being entertained more and more seriously by university administrators.

How does one prosper with the present clientele? Many of the most successful professors now are the ones who have "decentered" their classrooms. There's a new emphasis on group projects and on computer-generated exchanges among the students. What they seem to want most is to talk to one another. A classroom now is frequently an "environment," a place highly conducive to the exchange of existing ideas, the students' ideas. Listening to one another, students sometimes change their opinions. But what they generally can't do is acquire a new vocabulary, a new perspective, that will cast issues in a fresh light.

The Socratic method—the animated, sometimes impolite give-and-take between student and teacher—seems too jagged for current sensibilities. Students frequently come to my office to tell me how intimidated they feel in class; the thought of being embarrassed in front of the group fills them with dread. I remember a student telling me how humiliating it was to be corrected by the teacher, by me. So I asked the logical question: "Should I let a major factual error go by so as to save discomfort?" The student—a good student, smart and earnest—said that was a tough question. He'd need to think about it.

Disturbing? Sure. But I wonder, are we really getting students ready for Socratic exchange with professors when we push them off into vast lecture rooms, two and three hundred to a class, sometimes face them with only grad students until their third year, and signal in our myriad professorial ways that we often have much better things to do than sit in our offices and talk with them? How bad will the student-faculty ratios have to become, how teeming the lecture courses, before we hear students righteously complaining, as they did thirty years ago, about the impersonality of their schools, about their decline into knowledge factories? "This is a firm," said Mario Savio at Berkeley during the Free Speech protests of the Sixties, "and if the Board of Regents are the board of directors, . . . then . . . the faculty are a bunch of employees and we're the raw material. But we're a bunch of raw material that don't mean . . . to be made into any product."

Teachers who really do confront students, who provide significant challenges to what they believe, *can* be very successful, granted. But sometimes such professors generate more than a little trouble for themselves. A controversial teacher can send students hurrying to the deans and the counselors, claiming to have been offended. ("Offensive" is the preferred term of repugnance today, just as "enjoyable" is the summit of praise.) Colleges have brought in hordes of counselors and deans to make sure that everything is smooth, serene, unflustered, that everyone has a good time. To the counselor, to the dean, and to the university legal squad, that which is normal, healthy, and prudent is best.

An air of caution and deference is everywhere. When my students come to talk with me in my office, they often exhibit a Franciscan humility. "Do you have a moment?" "I know you're busy. I won't take up much of your time." Their presences tend to be very light; they almost never change the temperature of the room. The dress is nondescript: clothes are in earth tones; shoes are practical—cross-trainers, hiking boots, work shoes, Dr. Martens, with now and then a stylish pair of raised-sole boots on one of the young women. Many, male and female both, peep from beneath the bills of monogrammed baseball caps. Quite a few wear sports, or even corporate, logos, sometimes on one piece of clothing but occasionally (and disconcertingly) on more. The walk is slow; speech is careful, sweet, a bit weary, and without strong inflection. (After the first lively week of the term, most seem far in debt to sleep.) They are almost unfailingly polite. They don't want to offend me; I could hurt them, savage their grades.

Naturally, there are exceptions, kids I chat animatedly with, who offer a joke, or go on about this or that new CD (almost never a book, no). But most of the traffic is genially sleepwalking. I have to admit that I'm a touch wary, too. I tend to hold back. An unguarded remark, a joke that's taken to be off-color, or simply an uncomprehended comment can lead to difficulties.

I keep it literal. They scare me a little, these kind and melancholy students, who themselves seem rather frightened of their own lives.

Before they arrive, we ply the students with luscious ads, guaranteeing them a cross between summer camp and lotusland. When they get here, flattery and nonstop entertainment are available, if that's what they want. And when they leave? How do we send our students out into the world? More and more, our administrators call the booking agents and line up one or another celebrity to usher the graduates into the millennium. This past spring, Kermit the Frog won himself an honorary degree at Southampton College on Long Island; Bruce Willis and Yogi Berra took credentials away at Montclair State; Arnold Schwarzenegger scored at the University of Wisconsin-Superior. At Wellesley, Oprah Winfrey gave the commencement address. (*Wellesley*—one of the most rigorous academic colleges in the nation.) At the University of Vermont, Whoopi Goldberg laid down the word. But why should a worthy administrator contract the likes of Susan Sontag, Christopher Hitchens, or Robert Hughes—someone who might actually say something, something disturbing, something "offensive"—when he can get what the parents and kids apparently want and what the newspapers will softly commend—more lite entertainment, more TV?

Is it a surprise, then, that this generation of students—steeped in consumer culture before going off to school, treated as potent customers by the university well before their date of arrival, then pandered to from day one until the morning of the final kiss off from Kermit or one of his kin—are inclined to see the books they read as a string of entertainments to be placidly enjoyed or languidly cast down? Given the way universities are now administered (which is more and more to say, given the way that they are currently marketed), is it a shock that the kids don't come to school hot to learn, unable to bear their own ignorance? For some measure of self-dislike, or self-discontent—which is much different than simple depression—seems to me to be a prerequisite for getting an education that matters. My students, alas, usually lack the confidence to acknowledge what would be their most precious asset for learning: their ignorance.

Not long ago, I asked my Freud class a question that, however hoary, never fails to solicit intriguing responses: Who are your heroes? Whom do you admire? After one remarkable answer, featuring T. S. Eliot as hero, a series of generic replies rolled in, one gray wave after the next: my father, my best friend, a doctor who lives in our town, my high school history teacher. Virtually all the heroes were people my students had known personally, people who had done something local, specific, and practical, and had done it for them. They were good people, unselfish people, these heroes, but most of all they were people who had delivered the goods.

My students' answers didn't exhibit any philosophical resistance to the idea of greatness. It's not that they had been primed by their professors with complex arguments to combat genius. For the truth is that these students don't need debunking theories. Long before college, skepticism became their habitual mode. They are the progeny of Bart Simpson and David Letterman, and the hyper-cool ethos of the box. It's inane to say that theorizing professors have created them, as many conservative critics like to do. Rather, they have substantially created a university environment in which facile skepticism can thrive without being substantially contested.

Skeptical approaches have *potential* value. If you have no all-encompassing religious faith, no faith in historical destiny, the future of the West, or anything comparably grand, you need to acquire your vision of the world somewhere. If it's from literature, then the various visions literature offers have to be inquired into skeptically. Surely it matters that women are denigrated in Milton and in Pope, that some novelistic voices assume an overbearing godlike authority, that the poor are, in this or that writer, inevitably cast as clowns. You can't buy all of literature wholesale if it's going to help draw your patterns of belief.

But demystifying theories are now overused, applied mechanically. It's all logocentrism, patriarchy, ideology. And in this the student environment—laid-back, skeptical, knowing—is, I believe, central. Full-out debunking is what plays with this clientele. Some have been doing it nearly as long as, if more crudely than, their deconstructionist teachers. In the context of the contemporary university, and cool consumer culture, a useful intellectual skepticism has become exaggerated into a fundamentalist caricature of itself. The teachers have buckled to their students' views.

At its best, multiculturalism can be attractive as well-deployed theory. What could be more valuable than encountering the best work of far-flung cultures and becoming a citizen of the world? But in the current consumer environment, where flattery plays so well, the urge to encounter the other can devolve into the urge to find others who embody and celebrate the right ethnic origins. So we put aside the African novelist Chinua Achebe's abrasive, troubling *Things Fall Apart* and gravitate toward hymns on Africa, cradle of all civilizations.

What about the phenomenon called political correctness? Raising the standard of civility and tolerance in the university has been—who can deny it?—a very good thing. Yet this admirable impulse has expanded to the point where one is enjoined to speak well—and only well—of women, blacks, gays, the disabled, in fact of virtually everyone. And we can owe this expansion in many ways to the student culture. Students now do not wish to be criticized, not in any form. (The culture of consumption never criticizes them, at least not *overtly*.) In the current university, the movement for urbane tolerance has devolved into an imperative against critical reaction, turning much of the intellectual life into a dreary Sargasso Sea. At a certain point, professors stopped being usefully sensitive and became more like careful retailers who have it as a cardinal point of doctrine never to piss the customers off.

To some professors, the solution lies in the movement called cultural studies. What students need, they believe, is to form a critical perspective on pop culture. It's a fine idea, no doubt. Students should be able to run a critical commentary against the stream of consumer stimulations in which they're immersed. But cultural-studies programs rarely work, because no matter what you propose by way of analysis, things tend to bolt downhill toward an uncritical discussion of students' tastes, into what they like and don't like. If you want to do a Frankfurt School-style analysis of *Braveheart,* you can be pretty sure that by mid-class Adorno and Horkheimer will be consigned to the junk heap of history and you'll be collectively weighing the charms of Mel Gibson. One sometimes wonders if cultural studies hasn't prospered because, under the guise of serious intellectual analysis, it gives the customers what they most want—easy pleasure, more TV. Cultural studies becomes nothing better than what its detractors claim it is—Madonna studies—when students kick loose from the critical perspective and groove to the product, and that, in my experience teaching film and pop culture, happens plenty.

On the issue of genius, as on multiculturalism and political correctness, we professors of the humanities have, I think, also failed to press back against our students' consumer tastes. Here we tend to nurse a pair of—to put it charitably—disparate views. In one mode, we're inclined to a programmatic debunking criticism. We call the concept of genius into question. But in our professional lives per se, we aren't usually disposed against the idea of distinguished achievement. We argue animatedly about the caliber of potential colleagues. We support a star system, in which some professors are far better paid, teach less, and under better conditions than the rest. In our own profession, we are creating a system that is the mirror image of the one we're dismantling in the curriculum. Ask a professor what she thinks of the work of Stephen Greenblatt, a leading critic of Shakespeare, and you'll hear it for an hour. Ask her what her views are on Shakespeare's genius and she's likely to begin questioning the term along with the whole "discourse of evaluation." This dual sensibility may be intellectually incoherent. But in its awareness of what plays with students, it's conducive to good classroom evaluations and, in its awareness of where and how the professional bread is buttered, to self-advancement as well.

My overall point is this: It's not that a left-wing professorial coup has taken over the university. It's that at American universities, left-liberal politics have collided with the ethos of consumerism. The consumer ethos is winning.

Then how do those who at least occasionally promote genius and high literary ideals look to current students? How do we appear, those of us who take teaching to be something of a performance art and who imagine that if you give yourself over completely to your subject you'll be rewarded with insight beyond what you individually command?

I'm reminded of an old piece of newsreel footage I saw once. The speaker (perhaps it was Lenin, maybe Trotsky) was haranguing a large crowd. He was expostulating, arm waving, carrying on. Whether it was flawed technology or the man himself, I'm not sure, but the orator looked like an intricate mechanical device that had sprung into fast-forward. To my students, who mistrust enthusiasm in every form, that's me when I start riffing about Freud or Blake. But more and more, as my evaluations showed, I've been replacing enthusiasm and intellectual animation with stand-up routines, keeping it all at arm's length, praising under the cover of irony.

It's too bad that the idea of genius has been denigrated so far, because it actually offers a live alternative to the demoralizing culture of hip in which most of my students are mired. By embracing the works and lives of extraordinary people, you can adapt new ideals to revise those that came courtesy of your parents, your neighborhood, your clan—or the tube. The aim of a good liberal-arts education was once, to adapt an observation by the scholar Walter Jackson Bate, to see that "we need not be the passive victims of what we deterministically call 'circumstances' (social, cultural, or reductively psychological-personal), but that by linking ourselves through what Keats calls an 'immortal free-masonry' with the great we can become freer—freer to be ourselves, to be what we most want and value."

But genius isn't just a personal standard; genius can also have political effect. To me, one of the best things about democratic thinking is the conviction that genius can spring up anywhere. Walt Whitman is born into the working class and thirty-six years later we have a poetic image of America that gives a passionate dimension to the legalistic brilliance of the Constitution. A democracy needs to constantly develop, and to do so it requires the most powerful visionary minds to interpret the present and to propose possible shapes for the future. By continuing to notice and praise genius, we create a culture in which the kind of poetic gamble that Whitman made—a gamble in which failure would have entailed rank humiliation, depression, maybe suicide—still takes place. By rebelling against established ways of seeing and saying things, genius helps us to apprehend how malleable the present is and how promising and fraught with danger is the future. If we teachers do not endorse genius and self-overcoming, can we be surprised when our students find their ideal images in TV's latest persona ads?

A world uninterested in genius is a despondent place, whose sad denizens drift from coffee bar to Prozac dispensary, unfired by ideals, by the glowing image of the self that one might become. As Northrop Frye says in a beautiful and now dramatically unfashionable sentence, "The artist who uses the same energy and genius that Homer and Isaiah had will find that he not only lives in the same palace of art as Homer and Isaiah, but lives in it at the same time." We ought not to deny the existence of such a place simply because we, or those we care for, find the demands it makes intimidating, the rent too high.

What happens if we keep trudging along this bleak course? What happens if our most intelligent students never learn to strive to overcome what they are? What if genius, and the imitation of genius, become silly, outmoded ideas? What you're likely to get are more and more one-dimensional men and women. These will be people who live for easy pleasures, for comfort and prosperity, who think of money first, then second, and third, who hug the status quo; people who believe in God as a sort of insurance policy (cover your bets); people who are never surprised. They will be people so pleased with themselves (when they're not in despair at the general pointlessness of their lives) that they cannot imagine humanity could do better. They'll think it their highest duty to clone themselves as frequently as possible. They'll claim to be happy, and they'll live a long time.

It is probably time now to offer a spate of inspiring solutions. Here ought to come a list of reforms, with due notations about a core curriculum and various requirements. What the traditionalists who offer such solutions miss is that no matter what our current students are given to read, many of them will simply translate it into melodrama, with flat characters and predictable morals. (The unabated capitalist culture that conservative critics so often endorse has put students in a position to do little else.) One can't simply wave a curricular wand and reverse acculturation.

Perhaps it would be a good idea to try firing the counselors and sending half the deans back into their classrooms, dismantling the football team and making the stadium into a playground for local kids, emptying the fraternities, and boarding up the student-activities office. Such measures would convey the message that American colleges are not northern outposts of Club Med. A willingness on the part of the faculty to defy student conviction and affront them occasionally—to be usefully offensive— also might not be a bad thing. We professors talk a lot about subversion, which generally means subverting the views of people who never hear us talk or read our work. But to subvert the views of our students, our customers, that would be something else again.

Ultimately, though, it is up to individuals—and individual students in particular—to make their own way against the current sludgy tide. There's still the library, still the museum, there's still the occasional teacher who lives to find things greater than herself to admire. There are still fellow students who have not been cowed. Universities are inefficient, cluttered, archaic places, with many unguarded corners where one can open a book or gaze out onto the larger world and construe it freely. Those who do as much, trusting themselves against the weight of current opinion, will have contributed something to bringing this sad dispensation to an end. As for myself, I'm canning my low-key one-liners; when the kids' TV-based tastes come to the fore, I'll aim and shoot. And when it's time to praise genius, I'll try to do it in the right style, full-out, with faith that finer artistic spirits (maybe not Homer and Isaiah quite, but close, close), still alive somewhere in the ether, will help me out when my invention flags, the students doze, or the dean mutters into the phone. I'm getting back to a more exuberant style; I'll be expostulating and arm waving straight into the millennium, yes I will.

Understanding the Text

1. How does Edmundson characterize today's typical college students—physically, intellectually, emotionally?

2. How does Edmundson characterize the university, the faculty, and the quality of education they offer?

3. How does Edmundson propose to conduct himself in the future?

On the Uses of a Liberal Education: As a Weapon in the Hands of the Restless Poor

Earl Shorris

Next month I will publish a book about poverty in America, but not the book I intended. The world took me by surprise—not once, but again and again. The poor themselves led me in directions I could not have imagined, especially the one that came out of a conversation in a maximum-security prison for women that is set, incongruously, in a lush Westchester suburb fifty miles north of New York City.

I had been working on the book for about three years when I went to the Bedford Hills Correctional Facility for the first time. The staff and inmates had developed a program to deal with family violence, and I wanted to see how their ideas fit with what I had learned about poverty.

Numerous forces—hunger, isolation, illness, landlords, police, abuse, neighbors, drugs, criminals, and racism, among many others—exert themselves on the poor at all times and enclose them, making up a "surround of force" from which, it seems, they cannot escape. I had come to understand that this was what kept the poor from being political and that the absence of politics in their lives was what kept them poor. I don't mean "political" in the sense of voting in an election but in the way Thucydides used the word: to mean activity with other people at every level, from the family to the neighborhood to the broader community to the city-state.

By the time I got to Bedford Hills, I had listened to more than six hundred people, some of them over the course of two or three years. Although my method is that of the *bricoleur*, the

Earl Shorris has worked as a journalist, novelist, and lecturer. He also founded the Clemente Course in the Humanities, which provides the poor with a college-level education. His books include *The Politics of Heaven: America in Fearful Times* (2007), *Riches for the Poor: The Clemente Course in the Humanities* (2000), and *New American Blues: A Journey Through Poverty to Democracy* (1997). He also has published numerous articles in a range of magazines, including *Harper's*, *The Atlantic*, and *The Nation*.

tinkerer who assembles a thesis of the bric-a-brac he finds in the world, I did not think there would be any more surprises. But I had not counted on what Viniece Walker was to say.

It is considered bad form in prison to speak of a person's crime, and I will follow that precise etiquette here. I can tell you that Viniece Walker came to Bedford Hills when she was twenty years old, a high school dropout who read at the level of a college sophomore, a graduate of crackhouses, the streets of Harlem, and a long alliance with a brutal man. On the surface Viniece has remained as tough as she was on the street. She speaks bluntly, and even though she is HIV positive and the virus has progressed during her time in prison, she still swaggers as she walks down the long prison corridors. While in prison, Niecie, as she is known to her friends, completed her high school requirements and began to pursue a college degree (psychology is the only major offered at Bedford Hills, but Niecie also took a special interest in philosophy). She became a counselor to women with a history of family violence and a comforter to those with AIDS.

Only the deaths of other women cause her to stumble in the midst of her swaggering step, to spend days alone with the remorse that drives her to seek redemption. She goes through life as if she had been imagined by Dostoevsky, but even more complex than his fictions, alive, a person, a fair-skinned and freckled African-American woman, and in prison. It was she who responded to my sudden question, "Why do you think people are poor?"

We had never met before. The conversation around us focused on the abuse of women. Niecie's eyes were perfectly opaque—hostile, prison eyes. Her mouth was set in the beginning of a sneer.

"You got to begin with the children," she said, speaking rapidly, clipping out the street sounds as they came into her speech.

She paused long enough to let the change of direction take effect, then resumed the rapid, rhythmless speech. "You've got to teach the moral life of downtown to the children. And the way you do that, Earl, is by taking them downtown to plays, museums, concerts, lectures, where they can learn the moral life of downtown."

I smiled at her, misunderstanding, thinking I was indulging her. "And then they won't be poor anymore?"

She read every nuance of my response, and answered angrily, "And they won't be poor *no more.*

"What you mean is —"

"What I mean is what I said—a moral alternative to the street."

She didn't speak of jobs or money. In that, she was like the others I had listened to. No one had spoken of jobs or money. But how could the "moral life of downtown" lead anyone out from the surround of force? How could a museum push poverty away? Who can dress in statues or eat the past? And what of the political life? Had Niecie skipped a step or failed to take a step? The way out of poverty was politics, not the "moral life of downtown." But to enter the public world, to practice the political life, the poor had first to learn to reflect. That was what Niecie meant by the "moral life of downtown." She did not make the error of divorcing ethics from politics. Niecie had simply said, in a kind of shorthand, that no one could step out of the panicking circumstance of poverty directly into the public world.

Although she did not say so, I was sure that when she spoke of the "moral life of downtown" she meant something that had happened to her. With no job and no money, a prisoner, she had undergone a radical transformation. She had followed the same path that led to the invention of politics in ancient Greece. She had learned to reflect. In further conversation it became clear that when she spoke of "the moral life of downtown" she meant the humanities, the study of human constructs and concerns, which has been the source of reflection for the secular world since the Greeks first stepped back from nature to experience wonder at what they beheld. If the political life was the way out of poverty, the humanities provided an entrance to reflection and the political life. The poor did not need anyone to release them; an escape route existed. But to open this avenue to reflection and politics a major distinction between the preparation for the life of the rich and the life of the poor had to be eliminated.

Once Niecie had challenged me with her theory, the comforts of tinkering came to an end; I could no longer make an homage to the happenstance world and rest. To test Niecie's theory, students, faculty, and facilities were required. Quantitative measures would have to be developed; anecdotal information would also be useful. And the ethics of the experiment had to be considered: I resolved to do no harm. There was no need for the course to have a "sink or swim" character; it could aim to keep as many afloat as possible.

When the idea for an experimental course became clear in my mind, I discussed it with Dr. Jaime Inclán, director of the Roberto Clemente Family Guidance Center in lower Manhattan, a facility that provides counseling to poor people, mainly Latinos, in their own language and in their own community. Dr. Inclán offered the center's conference room for a classroom. We would put three metal tables end to end to approximate the boat-shaped tables used in discussion sections at the University of Chicago of the Hutchins era,[1] which I used as a model for the course. A card table in the back of the room would hold a coffeemaker and a few cookies. The setting was not elegant, but it would do. And the front wall was covered by a floor-to-ceiling blackboard.

Now the course lacked only students and teachers. With no funds and a budget that grew every time a new idea for the course crossed my mind, I would have to ask the faculty to donate its time and effort. Moreover, when Hutchins said, "The best education for the best is the best education for us all," he meant it: he insisted that full professors teach discussion sections in the college. If the Clemente Course in the Humanities was to follow the same pattern, it would require a faculty with the knowledge and prestige that students might encounter in their first year at Harvard, Yale, Princeton, or Chicago.

I turned first to the novelist Charles Simmons. He had been assistant editor of *The New York Times Book Review* and had taught at Columbia University. He volunteered to teach poetry, beginning with simple poems, Housman, and ending with Latin poetry. Grace Glueck, who writes art news and criticism for the *New York Times,* planned a course that began with cave paintings and ended in the late twentieth century. Timothy Koranda, who did his graduate work at MIT, had published journal articles on mathematical logic, but he had been away from his field for some years and looked forward to getting back to it. I planned to teach the American history course through documents, beginning with the Magna Carta, moving on to the second of Locke's *Two Treatises of Government,* the Declaration of Independence, and so on through the documents of the Civil War. I would also teach the political philosophy class.

Since I was a naif in this endeavor, it did not immediately occur to me that recruiting students would present a problem. I didn't know how many I needed. All I had were criteria for selection:

Age: 18–35.

Household income: Less than 150 percent of the Census Bureau's Official Poverty Threshold (though this was to change slightly).

Educational level: Ability to read a tabloid newspaper.

Educational goals: An expression of intent to complete the course.

Dr. Inclán arranged a meeting of community activists who could help recruit students. Lynette Lauretig of The Door, a program that provides medical and educational services to adolescents, and Angel Roman of the Grand Street Settlement, which offers work and training and GED programs, were both willing to give us access to prospective students. They also pointed out some practical considerations. The course had to provide bus and subway tokens, because fares ranged between three and six dollars per class per student, and the students could not afford sixty or even thirty dollars a month for transportation. We also had to offer dinner or a snack, because the classes were to be held from 6:00 to 7:30 P.M.

The first recruiting session came only a few days later. Nancy Mamis-King, associate executive director of the Neighborhood Youth & Family Services program in the South Bronx, had identified some Clemente Course candidates and had assembled about twenty of her clients and their supervisors in a circle of chairs in a conference room. Everyone in the room was black or Latino, with the exception of one social worker and me.

After I explained the idea of the course, the white social worker was the first to ask a question: "Are you going to teach African history?"

"No. We'll be teaching a section on American history, based on documents, as I said. We want to teach the ideas of history so that —"

"You have to teach African history."

"This is America, so we'll teach American history. If we were in Africa, I would teach African history, and if we were in China, I would teach Chinese history."

"You're indoctrinating people in Western culture."

I tried to get beyond her. "We'll study African art," I said, "as it affects art in America. We'll study American history and literature; you can't do that without studying African-American culture, because culturally all Americans are black as well as white, Native American, Asian, and so on." It was no use; not one of them applied for admission to the course.

A few days later Lynette Lauretig arranged a meeting with some of her staff at The Door. We disagreed about the course. They thought it should be taught at a much lower level. Although I could not change their views, they agreed to assemble a group of Door members who might be interested in the humanities.

On an early evening that same week, about twenty prospective students were scheduled to meet in a classroom at The Door. Most of them came late. Those who arrived first slumped in their chairs, staring at the floor or greeting me with sullen glances. A few ate candy or what appeared to be the remnants of a meal. The students were mostly black and Latino, one was Asian, and five were white; two of the whites were immigrants who had severe problems with English. When I introduced myself, several of the students would not shake my hand, two or three refused even to look at me, one girl giggled, and the last person to volunteer his name, a young man dressed in a Tommy Hilfiger sweatshirt and wearing a cap turned sideways, drawled, "Henry Jones, but they call me Sleepy, because I got these sleepy eyes —"

"In our class, we'll call you Mr. Jones."

He smiled and slid down in his chair so that his back was parallel to the floor.

Before I finished attempting to shake hands with the prospective students, a waiflike Asian girl with her mouth half-full of cake said, "Can we get on with it? I'm bored."

I liked the group immediately.

Having failed in the South Bronx, I resolved to approach these prospective students differently. "You've been cheated," I said. "Rich people learn the humanities; you didn't. The humanities are a foundation for getting along in the world, for thinking, for learning to reflect on the world instead of just reacting to whatever force is turned against you. I think the humanities are one of the ways to become political, and I don't mean political in the sense of voting in an election but in the broad sense." I told them Thucydides' definition of politics.

"Rich people know politics in that sense. They know how to negotiate instead of using force. They know how to use politics to get along, to get power. It doesn't mean that rich people are good and poor people are bad. It simply means that rich people know a more effective method for living in this society.

"Do all rich people, or people who are in the middle, know the humanities? Not a chance. But some do. And it helps. It helps to live better and enjoy life more. Will the humanities make you rich? Yes. Absolutely. But not in terms of money. In terms of life."

"Rich people learn the humanities in private schools and expensive universities. And that's one of the ways in which they learn the political life. I think that is the real difference between the haves and have-nots in this country. If you want real power, legitimate power, the kind that comes from the people and belongs to the people, you must understand politics. The humanities will help.

"Here's how it works: We'll pay your subway fare; take care of your children, if you have them; give you a snack or a sandwich; provide you with books and any other materials you need. But we'll make you think harder, use your mind more fully, than you ever have before. You'll have to read and think about the same kinds of ideas you would encounter in a first-year course at Harvard or Yale or Oxford.

"You'll have to come to class in the snow and the rain and the cold and the dark. No one will coddle you, no one will slow down for you. There will be tests to take, papers to write. And I can't promise you anything but a certificate of completion at the end of the course. I'll be talking to colleges about giving credit for the course, but I can't promise anything. If you come to the Clemente Course, you must do it because you want to study the humanities, because you want a certain kind of life, a richness of mind and spirit. That's all I offer you: philosophy, poetry, art history, logic, rhetoric, and American history.

"Your teachers will all be people of accomplishment in their fields," I said, and I spoke a little about each teacher. "That's the course. October through May, with a two-week break at Christmas. It is generally accepted in America that the liberal arts and the humanities in particular belong to the elites. I think you're the elites."

The young Asian woman said, "What are you getting out of this?"

"This is a demonstration project. I'm writing a book. This will be proof, I hope, of my idea about the humanities. Whether it succeeds or fails will be up to the teachers and you."

All but one of the prospective students applied for admission to the course.

I repeated the new presentation at the Grand Street Settlement and at other places around the city. There were about fifty candidates for the thirty positions in the course. Personal interviews began in early September.

Meanwhile, almost all of my attempts to raise money had failed. Only the novelist Starling Lawrence, who is also editor in chief of W. W. Norton, which had contracted to publish the book; the publishing house itself; and a small, private family foundation supported the experiment. We were far short of our budgeted expenses, but my wife, Sylvia, and I agreed that the cost was still very low, and we decided to go ahead.

Of the fifty prospective students who showed up at the Clemente Center for personal interviews, a few were too rich (a postal supervisor's son, a fellow who claimed his father owned a factory in Nigeria that employed sixty people) and more than a few could not read. Two home-care workers from Local 1199 could not arrange their hours to enable them to take the course. Some of the applicants were too young: a thirteen-year-old and two who had just turned sixteen.

Lucia Medina, a woman with five children who told me that she often answered the door at the single-room occupancy hotel where she lived with a butcher knife in her hand, was the oldest person accepted into the course. Carmen Quiñones, a recovering addict who had spent time in prison, was the next eldest. Both were in their early thirties. The interviews went on for days.

Abel Lomas[2] shared an apartment and worked part-time wrapping packages at Macy's. His father had abandoned the family when Abel was born. His mother was murdered by his stepfather when Abel was thirteen. With no one to turn to and no place to stay, he lived on the streets, first in Florida, then back in New York City. He used the tiny stipend from his mother's Social Security to keep himself alive.

After the recruiting session at The Door, I drove up Sixth Avenue from Canal Street with Abel, and we talked about ethics. He had a street tough's delivery, spitting out his ideas in crudely formed sentences of four, five, eight words, strings of blunt declarations, with never a dependent clause to qualify his thoughts. He did not clear his throat with badinage, as timidity teaches us to do, nor did he waste his breath with tact.

"What do you think about drugs?" he asked, the strangely breathless delivery further coarsened by his Dominican accent. "My cousin is a dealer."

"I've seen a lot of people hurt by drugs."

"Your family has nothing to eat. You sell drugs. What's worse? Let your family starve or sell drugs?"

"Starvation and drug addiction are both bad, aren't they?"

"Yes," he said, not "yeah" or "uh-huh" but a precise, almost formal "yes."

"So it's a question of the worse of two evils? How shall we decide?"

The question came up near Thirty-fourth Street, where Sixth Avenue remains hellishly traffic-jammed well into the night. Horns honked, people flooded into the street against the light. Buses and trucks and taxicabs threatened their way from one lane to the next where the overcrowded avenue crosses the equally crowded Broadway. As we passed Herald Square and made our way north again, I said, "There are a couple of ways to look at it. One comes from Immanuel Kant, who said that you should not do anything unless you want it to become a universal law; that is, unless you think it's what everybody should do. So Kant wouldn't agree to selling drugs or letting your family starve."

Again he answered with a formal "Yes."

"There's another way to look at it, which is to ask what is the greatest good for the greatest number: in this case, keeping your family from starvation or keeping tens, perhaps hundreds of people from losing their lives to drugs. So which is the greatest good for the greatest number?"

"That's what I think," he said.

"What?"

"You shouldn't sell drugs. You can always get food to eat. Welfare. Something."

"You're a Kantian."

"Yes."

"You know who Kant is?"

"I think so."

We had arrived at Seventy-seventh Street, where he got out of the car to catch the subway before I turned east. As he opened the car door and the light came on, the almost military neatness of him struck me. He had the newly cropped hair of a cadet. His clothes were clean, without a wrinkle. He was an orphan, a street kid, an immaculate urchin. Within a few weeks he would be nineteen years old, the Social Security payments would end, and he would have to move into a shelter.

Some of those who came for interviews were too poor. I did not think that was possible when we began, and I would like not to believe it now, but it was true. There is a point at which the level of forces that surround the poor can become insurmountable, when there is no time or energy left to be anything but poor. Most often I could not recruit such people for the course; when I did, they soon dropped out.

Over the days of interviewing, a class slowly assembled. I could not then imagine who would last the year and who would not. One young woman submitted a neatly typed essay that said, "I was homeless once, then I lived for some time in a shelter. Right now, I have got my own space granted by the Partnership for the Homeless. Right now, I am living alone, with very limited means. Financially I am overwhelmed by debts. I cannot afford all the food I need . . ."

A brother and sister, refugees from Tashkent, lived with their parents in the farthest reaches of Queens, far beyond the end of the subway line. They had no money, and they had been refused admission by every school to which they had applied. I had not intended to accept immigrants or people who had difficulty with the English language, but I took them into the class.

I also took four who had been in prison, three who were homeless, three who were pregnant, one who lived in a drugged dream-state in which she was abused, and one whom I had known for a long time and who was dying of AIDS. As I listened to them, I wondered how the course would affect them. They had no public life, no place; they lived within the surround of force, moving as fast as they could, driven by necessity, without a moment to reflect. Why should they care about fourteenth-century Italian painting or truth tables or the death of Socrates?

Between the end of recruiting and the orientation session that would open the course, I made a visit to Bedford Hills to talk with Niecie Walker. It was hot, and the drive up from the city had been unpleasant. I didn't yet know Niecie very well. She didn't trust me, and I didn't know what to make of her. While we talked, she held a huge white pill in her hand. "For AIDS," she said.

"Are you sick?"

"My T-cell count is down. But that's neither here nor there. Tell me about the course, Earl. What are you going to teach?"

"Moral philosophy."

"And what does that include?"

She had turned the visit into an interrogation. I didn't mind. At the end of the conversation I would be going out into "the free world"; if she wanted our meeting to be an interrogation, I was not about to argue. I said, "We'll begin with Plato: the *Apology,* a little of the *Crito,* a few pages of the *Phaedo* so that they'll know what happened to Socrates. Then we'll read Aristotle's *Nicomachean Ethics.* I also want them to read Thucydides, particularly Pericles' Funeral Oration in order to make the connection between ethics and politics, to lead them in the direction I hope the course will take them. Then we'll end with *Antigone,* but read as moral and political philosophy as well as drama."

There's something missing," she said, leaning back in her chair, taking on an air of superiority.

The drive had been long, the day was hot, the air in the room was dead and damp. "Oh, yeah," I said, "and what's that?"

"Plato's Allegory of the Cave. How can you teach philosophy to poor people without the Allegory of the Cave? The ghetto is the cave. Education is the light. Poor people can understand that."

At the beginning of the orientation at the Clemente Center a week later, each teacher spoke for a minute or two. Dr. Inclán and his research assistant, Patricia Vargas, administered the questionnaire he had devised to measure, as best he could, the role of force and the amount of reflection in the lives of the students. I explained that each class was going to be videotaped as another way of documenting the project. Then I gave out the first assignment: "In preparation for our next meeting, I would like you to read a brief selection from Plato's *Republic:* the Allegory of the Cave."

I tried to guess how many students would return for the first class. I hoped for twenty, expected fifteen, and feared ten. Sylvia, who had agreed to share the administrative tasks of the course, and I prepared coffee and cookies for twenty-five. We had a plastic container filled with subway tokens. Thanks to Starling Lawrence, we had thirty copies of Bernard Knox's *Norton Book of Classical Literature,* which contained all of the texts for the philosophy section except the *Republic* and the *Nicomachean Ethics.*

At six o'clock there were only ten students seated around the long table, but by six-fifteen the number had doubled, and a few minutes later two more straggled in out of the dusk. I had written a time line on the blackboard, showing them the temporal progress of thinking—from the role of myth in Neolithic societies to *The Gilgamesh Epic* and forward to the Old Testament, Confucius, the Greeks, the New Testament, the Koran, the *Epic of Son-Jara,* and ending with Nahuatl and Maya poems, which took us up to the contact between Europe and America, where the history course began. The time line served as context and geography as well as history: no race, no major culture was ignored. "Let's agree," I told them, "that we are all human, whatever our origins. And now let's go into Plato's cave."

I told them that there would be no lectures in the philosophy section of the course; we would use the Socratic method, which is called maieutic dialogue. "'Maieutic' comes from the Greek word for midwifery. I'll take the role of midwife in our dialogue. Now, what do I mean by that? What does a midwife do?"

It was the beginning of a love affair, the first moment of their infatuation with Socrates. Later, Abel Lomas would characterize that moment in his no-nonsense fashion, saying that it was the first time anyone had ever paid attention to their opinions.

Grace Glueck began the art history class in a darkened room lit with slides of the Lascaux caves and next turned the students' attention to Egypt, arranging for them to visit the Metropolitan Museum of Art to see the Temple of Dendur and the Egyptian Galleries. They arrived at the museum on a Friday evening. Darlene Codd brought her two-year-old son. Pearl Lau was late, as usual. One of the students, who had told me how much he was looking forward to the museum visit, didn't show up, which surprised me. Later I learned that he had been arrested for jumping a turnstile in a subway station on his way to the museum and was being held in a prison cell under the Brooklyn criminal courthouse. In the Temple of Dendur, Samantha Smoot asked questions of Felicia Blum, a museum lecturer. Samantha was the student who had burst out with the news, in one of the first sessions of the course, that people in her neighborhood believed it "wasn't no use goin' to school, because the white man wouldn't let you up no matter what." But in a hall where the statuary was of half-human, half-animal female figures, it was Samantha who asked what the glyphs meant, encouraging Felicia Blum to read them aloud, to translate them into English. Toward the end of the evening, Grace led the students out of the halls of antiquities into the Rockefeller Wing, where she told them of the connections of culture and art in Mali, Benin, and the Pacific Islands. When the students had collected their coats and stood together near the entrance to the museum, preparing to leave, Samantha stood apart, a tall, slim young woman, dressed in a deerstalker cap and a dark blue peacoat. She made an exaggerated farewell wave at us and returned to Egypt—her ancient mirror.

Charles Simmons began the poetry class with poems as puzzles and laughs. His plan was to surprise the class, and he did. At first he read the poems aloud to them, interrupting himself with footnotes to bring them along. He showed them poems of love and of seduction, and satiric commentaries on those poems by later poets. "Let us read," the students demanded, but Charles refused. He tantalized them with the opportunity to read poems aloud. A tug-of-war began between him and the students, and the standoff was ended not by Charles directly but by Hector Anderson. When Charles asked if anyone in the class wrote poetry, Hector raised his hand.

"Can you recite one of your poems for us?" Charles said.

Until that moment, Hector had never volunteered a comment, though he had spoken well and intelligently when asked. He preferred to slouch in his chair, dressed in full camouflage gear, wearing a nylon stocking over his hair and eating slices of fresh cantaloupe or honeydew melon.

In response to Charles's question, Hector slid up to a sitting position. "If you turn that camera off," he said. "I don't want anybody using my lyrics." When he was sure the red light of the video camera was off, Hector stood and recited verse after verse of a poem that belonged somewhere in the triangle formed by Ginsberg's *Howl,* the Book of Lamentations, and hip-hop. When Charles and the students finished applauding, they asked Hector to say the poem again, and he did. Later Charles told me, "That kid is the real thing." Hector's discomfort with Sylvia and me turned to ease. He came to our house for a small Christmas party and at other times. We talked on the telephone about a scholarship program and about what steps he should take next in his education. I came to know his parents. As a student, he began quietly, almost secretly, to surpass many of his classmates.

Timothy Koranda was the most professorial of the professors. He arrived precisely on time, wearing a hat of many styles—part fedora, part Borsalino, part Stetson, and at least one-half World War I campaign hat. He taught logic during class hours, filling the blackboard from floor to ceiling, wall to wall, drawing the intersections of sets here and truth tables there and a great square of oppositions in the middle of it all. After class, he walked with students to the subway, chatting about Zen or logic or Heisenberg.

On one of the coldest nights of the winter, he introduced the students to logic problems stated in ordinary language that they could solve by reducing the phrases to symbols. He passed out copies of a problem, two pages long, then wrote out some of the key phrases on the blackboard. "Take this home with you," he said, "and at our next meeting we shall see who has solved it. I shall also attempt to find the answer."

By the time he finished writing out the key phrases, however, David Iskhakov raised his hand. Although they listened attentively, neither David nor his sister Susana spoke often in class. She was shy, and he was embarrassed at his inability to speak perfect English.

"May I go to blackboard?" David said. "And will see if I have found correct answer to zis problem."

Together Tim and David erased the blackboard, then David began covering it with signs and symbols. "If first man is earning this money, and second man is closer to this town . . . ," he said, carefully laying out the conditions. After five minutes or so, he said, "And the answer is: B will get first to Cleveland!"

Samantha Smoot shouted, "That's not the answer. The mistake you made is in the first part there, where it says who earns more money."

Tim folded his arms across his chest, happy. "I shall let you all take the problem home," he said.

When Sylvia and I left the Clemente Center that night, a knot of students was gathered outside, huddled against the wind. Snow had begun to fall, a slippery powder on the gray ice that covered all but a narrow space down the center of the sidewalk. Samantha and David stood in the middle of the group, still arguing over the answer to the problem. I leaned in for a moment to catch the character of the argument. It was even more polite than it had been in the classroom, because now they governed themselves.

One Saturday morning in January, David Howell telephoned me at home. "Mr. Shores," he said, Anglicizing my name, as many of the students did.

"Mr. Howell," I responded, recognizing his voice.

"How you doin', Mr. Shores?"

"I'm fine. How are you?"

"I had a little problem at work."

Uh-oh, I thought, bad news was coming. David is a big man, generally good-humored but with a quick temper. According to his mother, he had a history of violent behavior. In the classroom he had been one of the best students, a steady man, twenty-four years old, who always did the reading assignments and who often made interesting connections between the humanities and daily life. "What happened?"

"Mr. Shores, there's a woman at my job, she said some things to me and I said some things to her. And she told my supervisor I had said things to her, and he called me in about it. She's forty years old and she don't have no social life, and I have a good social life, and she's jealous of me."

"And then what happened?" The tone of his voice and the timing of the call did not portend good news.

"Mr. Shores, she made me so mad, I wanted to smack her up against the wall. I tried to talk to some friends to calm myself down a little, but nobody was around."

"And what did you do?" I asked, fearing this was his one telephone call from the city jail.

"Mr. Shores, I asked myself, 'What would Socrates do?'"

David Howell had reasoned that his co-worker's envy was not his problem after all, and he had dropped his rage.

One evening, in the American history section, I was telling the students about Gordon Wood's ideas in *The Radicalism of the American Revolution.* We were talking about the revolt by some intellectuals against classical learning at the turn of the eighteenth century, including Benjamin Franklin's late-life change of heart, when Henry Jones raised his hand.

"If the Founders loved the humanities so much, how come they treated the natives so badly?"

I didn't know how to answer this question. There were confounding explanations to offer about changing attitudes toward Native Americans, vaguely useful references to views of Rousseau and James Fenimore Cooper. For a moment I wondered if I should tell them about Heidegger's Nazi past. Then I saw Abel Lomas's raised hand at the far end of the table. "Mr. Lomas," I said.

Abel said, "That's what Aristotle means by incontinence, when you know what's morally right but you don't do it, because you're overcome by your passions."

The other students nodded. They were all inheritors of wounds caused by the incontinence of educated men; now they had an ally in Aristotle, who had given them a way to analyze the actions of their antagonists.

Those who appreciate ancient history understand the radical character of the humanities. They know that politics did not begin in a perfect world but in a society even more flawed than ours: one that embraced slavery, denied the rights of women, practiced a form of homosexuality that verged on pedophilia, and endured the intrigues and corruption of its leaders. The genius of that society originated in man's re-creation of himself through the recognition of his humanness as expressed in art, literature, rhetoric, philosophy, and the unique notion of freedom. At that moment, the isolation of the private life ended and politics began.

The winners in the game of modern society, and even those whose fortune falls in the middle, have other means to power: they are included at birth. They know this. And they know exactly what to do to protect their place in the economic and social hierarchy. As Allan Bloom, author of the nationally best-selling tract in defense of elitism, *The Closing of the American Mind,* put it, they direct the study of the humanities exclusively at those young people who "have been raised in comfort and with the expectation of ever increasing comfort."

In the last meeting before graduation, the Clemente students answered the same set of questions they'd answered at orientation. Between October and May, students had fallen to AIDS, pregnancy, job opportunities, pernicious anemia, clinical depression, a schizophrenic child, and other forces, but of the thirty students admitted to the course, sixteen had completed it, and fourteen had earned credit from Bard College. Dr. Inclán found that the students' self-esteem and their abilities to divine and solve problems had significantly increased; their use of verbal aggression as a tactic for resolving conflicts had significantly decreased. And they all had notably more appreciation for the concepts of benevolence, spirituality, universalism, and collectivism.

It cost about $2,000 for a student to attend the Clemente Course. Compared with unemployment, welfare, or prison, the humanities are a bargain. But coming into possession of the faculty of reflection and the skills of politics leads to a choice for the poor—and whatever they choose, they will be dangerous: they may use politics to get along in a society based on the game, to escape from the surround of force into a gentler life, to behave as citizens, and nothing more; or they may choose to oppose the game itself. No one can predict the effect of politics, although we all would like to think that wisdom goes our way. That is why the poor are so often mobilized and so rarely politicized. The possibility that they will adopt a moral view other than that of their mentors can never be discounted. And who wants to run that risk?

On the night of the first Clemente Course graduation, the students and their families filled the eighty-five chairs we crammed into the conference room where classes had been held. Robert Martin, associate dean of Bard College, read the graduates' names. David Dinkins, the former mayor of New York City, handed out the diplomas. There were speeches and presentations. The students gave me a plaque on which they had misspelled my name. I offered a few words about each student, congratulated them, and said finally, "This is what I wish for you: May you never be more active than when you are doing nothing . . ." I saw their smiles of recognition at the words of Cato, which I had written on the blackboard early in the course. They could recall again too the moment when we had come to the denouement of Aristotle's brilliantly constructed thriller, the *Nicomachean Ethics*—the idea that in the contemplative life man was most like God. One or two, perhaps more of the students, closed their eyes. In the momentary stillness of the room it was possible to think.

The Clemente Course in the Humanities ended a second year in June 1997. Twenty-eight new students had enrolled; fourteen graduated. Another version of the course will begin this fall in Yucatán, Mexico, using classical Maya literature in Maya.

On May 14, 1997, Viniece Walker came up for parole for the second time. She had served more than ten years of her sentence, and she had been the best of prisoners. In a version of the Clemente Course held at the prison, she had been my teaching assistant. After a brief hearing, her request for parole was denied. She will serve two more years before the parole board will reconsider her case.

A year after graduation, ten of the first sixteen Clemente Course graduates were attending four-year colleges or going to nursing school; four of them had received full scholarships to Bard College. The other graduates were attending community college or working full-time. Except for one: she had been fired from her job in a fast-food restaurant for trying to start a union.

Notes

[1] Under the guidance of Robert Maynard Hutchins (1929–1951), the University of Chicago required year-long courses in the humanities, social sciences, and natural sciences for the Bachelor of Arts degree. Hutchins developed the curriculum with the help of Mortimer Adler, among others; the Hutchins courses later influenced Adler's Great Books program.

[2] Not his real name.

Understanding the Text

1. According to Shorris, what does Viniece Walker mean by the phrase "the moral life of downtown"? And how does one acquire this "moral life"?

2. Why does Viniece Walker insist that Shorris teach Plato's "Allegory of the Cave" in his moral philosophy class?

3. Toward the end of his essay, Shorris claims that as a result of finishing the Clemente course, his students, all of them poor, "will be dangerous." In what ways?

Stealth TV

Russ Baker

At Clifton High School, a mostly white, working-class institution in suburban New Jersey, it's time for second period—and for Channel One, a public-affairs TV broadcast available exclusively for school viewing. Mounted high in a corner of every classroom—as omnipresent an icon as the American flag—is a large-screen television set, provided by Channel One. The face on the screen is that of school principal William Cannici. Speaking into a microphone, he tries a few jokes, then announces student vocational-award winners. In Mrs. Rossi's Spanish class, restless students begin talking among themselves. Suddenly, the teacher shushes her charges: It's show time.

The hip-hop music starts. Heads bounce to the beat. Cut to two young, fashionably dressed anchorwomen, one white and one black. First up in the news is a tough sell to almost any viewership: the census. Point: Without an accurate count, schools can't get their rightful aid. The census form flashes on the screen. "Hey, I got that!" remarks a student. Channel One's reporter interviews a census spokesperson, a sexually ambiguous-looking woman with her hair pulled back in a ponytail. "What the heck is that?" a student in the back of the room asks with a chortle.

Time for a commercial break. Teens snowboard and dirt-bike their way through the Mountain Dew life (170 calories, 46 grams of sugar per can): "Do the Dew!" Then a Twinkies spot (150 calories, 14 grams of sugar per two-pack).

Russ Baker is an investigative journalist and has published hundreds of articles in the nation's leading magazines and newspapers. He also has taught journalism as an adjunct instructor at Columbia University.

Reprinted with permission from *The American Prospect*, Volume 12, Number 3: February 12, 2001. The American Prospect, 5 Broad Street, Boston, MA 02109. All rights reserved.

Back to the news. As a story airs about the pope's groundbreaking mea culpa over the Catholic Church's transgressions toward the Jews, much of the class is deep in chitchat; the teacher tries, without success, to silence the talk. Other students appear to be doing their homework. Two young women are checking their makeup, and four are resting their heads on their desks. Not one person has a comment about the story, described by *The New York Times* as "the most sweeping papal apology ever."

Another commercial break. As the first frames roll, a student shrieks, "Pokémon!" Declares another: "I need to get that." Next ad: Join the Marines. One viewer chimes along with the script: "The Few. The Proud. . . ."

For 10 years now, the folks behind Channel One have been able to offer advertisers a dream demographic: a captive audience composed of nearly half of all American teenagers. (And they truly are captive, as Carlotta and D.J. Maurer, two students at Perrysburg Junior High School in Ohio, can attest. Their refusal to watch Channel One in school bought them a day in the Wood County Juvenile Detention Center.) On the condition that all teachers will air and all students will watch its daily satellite-broadcast programs, Channel One lends television sets and other equipment to schools. The company, which claims to reach a teen market 50 times larger than MTV's, profits by selling two of every 12 program minutes for commercials coupled with call-in contests and cool banter.

As noxious as these school-sanctioned ads are, Channel One's success is part of a larger trend toward in-school marketing: Textbook manufacturers insert proprietary brand names into math equations, corporations provide book covers emblazoned with their logos, soda companies entice school officials into signing deals for on-campus product exclusivity, and companies donate computers that have the ability, in some cases, to track the online behavior of individual students. A whole new industry of consultants has sprung up to help corporate clients position their products in schools.

Even in today's thoroughly commercialized environment, there is something especially insidious about school-endorsed product pushing. For one thing, schools are supposed to offer a haven from the worst the world has to offer. We authorize metal detectors and locker sweeps to prevent deadly violence on campus. But there are other dangers to impressionable minds. Channel One's hyperkinetic blend of "current-affairs broadcasting" and carefully targeted commercials blurs the line between fact and fiction, between reporting that at least tries to be objective and the self-serving rhetoric of the advertising business. Unquestionably, young people lack the media "literacy" skills necessary to understand fully what they are dealing with: A recent study cited in *Education Week* shows that ninth-graders who watched ads in which professional athletes endorsed products thought the athletes had themselves paid for the ads.

CHANNEL WHAT?

• • • • • • • • • • • • • • • •

Few American adults have ever heard of Channel One—a remarkable fact, considering that one in four middle and high schools now broadcasts it and an estimated 40 percent of all high school students are compelled to watch its programming every single school day. Perhaps parents do not know about Channel One because their kids (some eight million of them, in 12,000 schools) do not tell them about it. As for the key American institutions—governmental, educational—that might be expected to raise an alarm, they have mostly been looking the other way.

Last fall the first-ever government study of commercialization in the schools was published. The General Accounting Office (GAO) report, requested by two Democrats—Representative George Miller of California and Senator Christopher Dodd of Connecticut—notes that in-school marketing is dramatically on the rise and that deals between schools and companies are being made on a district-by-district basis. Local educators are not equipped to negotiate with crafty marketers bearing freebies, much less to address the larger educational issues. While the GAO study was being circulated, the Federal Trade Commission released a report specifically condemning the marketing of violent content to underage children.

In some ways, the "new" political interest in protecting our children from the onslaught of the marketers harks back to 1989, when Channel One was launched by entrepreneur Chris Whittle (later, in 1994, he sold the company to K-III Communications, now called Primedia). Initially, the service faced heavy criticism from liberal groups and from educational power-houses such as the national Parent-Teacher Association, the American Federation of Teachers (AFT), the National Education Association (NEA), and various principals' associations; even the American Academy of Pediatrics frowned upon for-profit classroom television. But the well-financed company won over school system after school system, and effective opposition dried up.

Of late, none of the major teachers' or school administrators' organizations has seemed willing to mount a serious challenge to Channel One. Two years ago, NEA officials told Channel One critics that while the association remains opposed to the service, removing it from America's classrooms was not a priority. The AFT offered a similar line. And the National Association of School Principals rebuffed Channel One opponents several times when they requested a meeting. As a result, the battle against Channel One is being waged by several tiny public-interest groups and through scattered, small-scale parent uprisings. The educational establishment apparently believes that the issue lacks urgency.

Governmental bodies tend to accept the claim that the free equipment and the "news value" of Channel One more than make up for any downside; besides, the argument goes, local governments can address the matter if they so choose. Even the GAO report declares that it is impossible to differentiate the effects of bombardment by Channel One from those of the commercial messages directed at young people outside school hours. Although the GAO researchers were undoubtedly well-meaning, such a claim is a cop-out: Many in-school marketers specially design ads, promotions, contests, and the like to track the impact of their sales pitches.

Can anyone doubt that the ads on Channel One are grossly out of place in an academic environment? Mark Crispin Miller, a professor of media and culture at New York University who studied Channel One's content in 1997, concluded that its commercial messages reinforced bad body image, emphasized the importance of buying things, and glamorized boorish and loutish behavior. To ensure "stickiness," the ad campaigns often feature interactive components. One that I saw urged students to watch a film called *Never Been Kissed,* then to call in and answer questions about the movie's content in order to qualify for a chance to win a $500 shopping spree and a watch.

Rather than defend the indefensible, Channel One insists that the ads are not what matters. At the company's Madison Avenue headquarters, sleek, gunmetal-silver placards fit for the starship *Enterprise* proclaim "Education" and "Our Missions: To Inform and Empower Young People." These displays imply that the ads are a necessary evil that makes possible a bounty of fresh educational content and free equipment. Indeed, in a meeting with me last year, Channel One officials sought repeatedly to focus attention on the educational merits of their product. The company has been able to orchestrate favorable publicity ranging from a laudatory *New York Times* op-ed by a Catholic priest who is also a principal in a Channel One school to supportive statements from the ordinarily populist Senator Paul Wellstone of Minnesota.

Company executives claim that the broadcasts hold students' interest because they deliver important information in an appealing manner. (The students appear to identify with the youthful newscasters as stars; indeed, one of them, Lisa Ling, has moved on to anchoring a commercial-network morning show.) The solution to disaffection among youths, say executives, is to deliver a product that shows them how world affairs are relevant to them and their families. "We go to Kosovo and talk to kids who are their age," said Susan Tick, an outside PR representative for Channel One. "You don't connect with them otherwise."

Even by these standards, the compilation tape Channel One gave me was not impressive: It included a segment summarizing the Bill Clinton impeachment situation, delivered at a rapid-fire pace that seemed harder for an average teen to follow than a conventional news broadcast. The commentary is often self-promotional, with Channel One correspondents and anchors gushing about how they've gotten to travel to exotic places, and with interviewed students identified as attendees of "a Channel One school."

If we are to accept Channel One's request that it be judged on its news content, we have to face the fact that there just isn't much there. Of the 10 minutes of "news," only two to three minutes is breaking news, according to William Hoynes, a Vassar College sociologist who studies the intersection of media and education. The remainder is a hodgepodge of contests, self-promotion, light features and profiles, music intros, and pop quizzes. And Hoynes concludes that even those paltry hard-news minutes frame the issues in rigid terms that do not promote original thought or critical thinking.

Not surprisingly, Channel One doesn't offer any statistics to prove that its programs benefit students. "We have attitudinal studies showing that teachers believe it to be productive," said Jeffrey Ballabon, a Channel One executive vice president. "They know kids don't read newspapers. They also don't watch the evening news." Perhaps the citation of "attitudinal" evidence is necessitated by the findings of one study the company did commission: A 1994 University of Michigan analysis found that students performed just 5 percent better in high schools that aired the programs and 8 percent better in participating middle schools—and then only in an "exemplary" (read: highly atypical) environment in which the teacher actively sought to incorporate the broadcast content into the class and made sure the students were paying attention. There was no measurable increase in discussion of news outside the school or in efforts to seek out additional information from outside news sources.

Nevertheless, most administrators and teachers seem to love their Channel One. With good reason: The company provides TV sets and a broadcast system that the schools use for their own purposes, including the principal's morning addresses. "Our district is not a real wealthy district," explains Lawrence Westerfield, principal of Mt. Healthy South Middle School in Cincinnati, Ohio, which airs Channel One. If you want the technology, says Westerfield, "you have to count on advertisers to pay."

Yet there is evidence that the schools aren't getting a very good deal. A 1998 study co-authored by Alex Molnar, an education professor at the University of Wisconsin-Milwaukee, concluded that broadcasting Channel One takes up six or seven days of instruction over the school year and costs American taxpayers $1.8 billion annually. Molnar, who heads the Center for Education Research, Analysis, and Innovation, compared the average cost of 12 daily minutes of a secondary school's time, or about $158,000 a year, with the total value of Channel One's equipment ($17,000) and the annual rental value of the equipment ($4,000). Even the value of the time spent watching the two minutes of commercials ($26,000) exceeded the value of the equipment. And those Channel One minutes add up. A child who views the shows from sixth grade to graduation will lose seven weeks of school time.

AD NAUSEAM

Despite Channel One's self-proclaimed educational mission, the company offers a different story to advertisers. As Channel One's then-president bragged to a youth marketing conference in 1994, "The biggest selling point to advertisers [is that] . . . we are forcing kids to watch two minutes of commercials. . . . The advertiser gets a group of kids who cannot go to the bathroom, who cannot change the station, who cannot listen to their mother yell in the background, who cannot be playing Nintendo, who cannot have their headsets on." Channel One continually conducts surveys about the spending patterns of teens; and its Web site, heavily touted on the shows themselves, provides an ideal means of obtaining direct feedback from the students.

Channel One also makes much of its public-service announcements, including those warning students to resist peer pressure to take drugs. Meanwhile, it airs ads stressing ways to be cool and brags to advertisers that controlled viewing in the classroom is the ideal way to play on teens' insecurity and desire to fit in.

Channel One makes a lot of money—$346 million in 1999 ad revenues—for its financially troubled parent company, Primedia, which reported a net loss of $120 million that year. With an estimated $200,000 price per 30-second ad (a rate comparable to the major networks'), Channel One is a crucial element in the company's future strategy. In its 1999 stockholder report, Primedia declared: "Our products serve highly specialized niches and capitalize on the growing trend toward targeted rather than mass information distribution. Many of the company's products, such as . . . CHANNEL ONE NEWS, . . . afford advertisers with an opportunity to directly reach niche market audiences. CHANNEL ONE NEWS *has no direct competition in the schools* [my emphasis] but does compete for advertising dollars with other media aimed at teenagers."

With so vast a market at stake, Channel One has not been reluctant to spend in order to protect its franchise. When Republican Senator Richard Shelby of Alabama, an ally of the ragtag band of Channel One opponents, initiated Senate hearings in 1999, Channel One dumped almost $1 million into a lobbying effort led by former Christian Coalition Director Ralph Reed and the powerful law firm of Preston, Gates, and Ellis—and effectively kept a lid on further action or hearings. Last spring a Shelby-sponsored sense-of-the-Senate resolution opposing commercialization of the schools was blocked by Republican Senator Sam Brownback of Kansas and heavy lobbying by Reed and former New York Senator Alfonse D'Amato. The company has other means of winning support: Channel One's Ballabon insisted on faxing me a mound of positive letters; several from students mentioned free trips to Channel One's Los Angeles production studios.

Lined up against Channel One's PR juggernaut is a spirited and diverse coalition that includes Professor Molnar's group; Ralph Nader's D.C.-based Commercial Alert; the Center for Commercial-Free Public Education, located in Oakland, California; and Obligation, Inc., a group from Birmingham, Alabama, headed by Republican businessman Jim Metrock. When Metrock found out that his children were watching Channel One, he did his own study; he's been a committed opponent ever since. He has helped recruit a number of socially conservative groups—like Phyllis Schlafly's Eagle Forum and James Dobson's Focus on the Family—some of which are more concerned with what they perceive as risqué content than with commercialism per se. In addition, Channel One's critics convinced the 15.8-millionmember Southern Baptist Convention to pass a resolution in 1999 opposing the enterprise.

That's about it on a national scale. Channel One likes to keep the battleground local, where school officials often lack the training and policy sophistication to ask tough questions about content control and educational philosophy. Thus far, only one state, New York, has banned Channel One from the public schools.

Still, a few small districts have voted to bar Channel One, and Metrock says that some teachers in schools contractually obligated to show the programs are nevertheless switching them off. The company has apparently responded by warning errant schools that it will yank its equipment. And Channel One has now retained Nielsen Media Research to measure student viewing in 1,500 schools.

Sooner or later, it seems, educational advocates are going to have to make Channel One and its ilk a priority. If we are really on the brink of a top-to-bottom reconstitution of American education, then surely the intrusion of corporate products must be addressed. And enthusiasm for these new methods of "improving" the educational experience bears scrutiny if the letters of support from teachers and principals that Channel One's Ballabon forwarded to me are any evidence. Many contained the sorts of appalling errors—in spelling, grammar, syntax, and exposition—that these educators are supposed to be helping students avoid.

Were the topic ever to reach the national agenda, many vexing questions about education itself would be raised. For example, Channel One advocates contend that the broadcasts make it easier to teach young people about the news because the young hosts know how to speak kids' language. This, of course, suggests that adult educators (and parents, for that matter) are incapable of discussing the ways of the world in a compelling manner—a sentiment not everyone shares. And anyway, in an America awash in exhortations to buy and consume, shouldn't institutions of learning and discussion be free from the constant pressures toward superficiality and conformity?

Meanwhile, Primedia has announced a merger with the Internet company About.com, which has intricate business partnerships with pornography purveyors. Conservatives are upset by that, as they are with Senator Brownback, who is a leader in denouncing violence in the media yet enthusiastically backs Channel One, with its advertising for violent movies.

This year opponents are likely to concentrate on challenging the federal government's role as a major Channel One benefactor through its paid advertising for the armed services and the Office of National Drug Control Policy. But if there's strong, broad, untapped sentiment against the juggernaut, it probably needs to coalesce fairly soon: Channel One officials told me the company looks forward to rolling out the programs in thousands of additional schools.

Understanding the Text

1. According to Baker, what kind of material typically airs on Channel One? In how many states does Channel One provide programming?

2. What arguments do Channel One supporters offer in its favor?

3. What do its critics say against it?

Athletes, Outcasts, and Partyers

Dianne Williams Hayes

Dianne Williams Hayes writes for *Black Issues in Higher Education.*

Films about African Americans in higher education are a relatively new phenomenon but they, like other films about Blacks, still frequently resort to stereotypes.

In Spike Lee's *School Daze,* John Singleton's *Higher Learning,* and other less-known movies such as *Blue Chips* and *The Program,* African-American students tend to be shown as athletes, outcasts or partyers with little interest or engagement in the academic life of colleges and universities.

"There has been a very narrow portrayal," said Henry Hampton, producer of the award-winning *Eyes on the Prize* civil rights documentary. "For the last five to seven years, more Black films are in production, but the stereotypes persist and characters are one-dimensional. The problem is that we need to get more thoughtful portrayals," Hampton said.

"I am particularly concerned about the lack of portrayals of people who succeed academically. At the same time, we allow them without protest. Young people have got to have academic excellence as an attainable goal that is represented in film. There's a missed opportunity to show variety."

Reality for many minority students in higher education is that they often have to overcome the notion that they are getting a "free ride" or are in some way less qualified than other students. One of the reasons to be concerned about one-sided portrayals of the college experience for minorities is that the images may extend beyond the dark movie theaters into the minds of professors and fellow students.

Spike Lee's film *School Daze* was one of the first films produced by an African-American director that addressed life on a predominantly Black campus during the 1980s. While some report that many of the portrayals were accurate, it fell short of exploring the academic dimension of college life. Its premise was to take a hard and honest look at the social side of college life dealing with fraternities and sororities, classism and prejudice among African Americans.

Monty Ross, who co-produced the movie with Spike Lee, described it as an exercise in dealing with many of the issues that carry over into the classroom. "Overall, the weekend of homecoming was used to deal with issues affecting the school and inner activities of the student body as it relates to skin color, hair and African-American support of the school, as well as hazing," Ross said. "It explored the issues of sororities and fraternities, but the classroom was part of it."

SUBTLE ISSUES OVERWHELMED

More recently, John Singleton attempted to address issues of race relations and campus polarization on a majority campus in his film *Higher Learning*. However, the day-to-day subtle issues that are a fact of life on many American campuses were overshadowed by stereotypical images outside the norm. Its main white character was recruited by neo-Nazis because of bad experiences with an insensitive Black roommate, and its main Black character spent his time demanding his athletic scholarship money and dodging bullets and violence on campus.

Singleton did offer some new elements, such as an older perpetual student played by rapper Ice Cube. Ice Cube began by benignly guiding newcomers, but his advice quickly became one of advocating violence as a solution to problems. The Black characters who weren't athletes were from the "hood." And none of the main Black characters were presented in a way to endear the audience. Before the athlete was hunted down by his former roommate-turned-neo-Nazi, we saw him expect special favors from the only Black faculty member we see, demand scholarship money, and show up late for track practice because he feels superior to everyone else on the team.

Frequently, African-American students on campus are portrayed as athletes with serious deficiencies in reading and basic skills and the classroom is merely a backdrop to the football field, basketball court or track. Movies such as *Blue Chips, The Program* and the highly-acclaimed documentary *Hoop Dreams* all deal with the experience of talented athletes whose primary goal is to transcend their struggling economic backgrounds with sports. College is simply a vehicle to their dreams.

While the movies address an overwhelming sentiment among many young students that sports can lead to riches and fame as coaches help them through college, there is little balance or representation of the majority of students who do not enter college on athletic scholarships. Nor do they tend to represent the middle- and upper-class students who go to class every day, graduate in four years and have aspirations of becoming doctors, lawyers and engineers.

"Blacks are portrayed as being generally deficient," said Dr. Jesse A. Rhines, assistant professor of African-American studies with a concentration in film at Rutgers University, Newark campus. "There is . . . a preference for sports and entertainment over education in these films."

Hoop Dreams is credited with being more ambitious in its complex depiction of the dream that many poor, urban youth carry of becoming the next Shaquille O'Neal. In the film, two boys are followed as they grow, from the playground to the Catholic high school that produced Isiah Thomas. Their lives are shown in detail as one is forced back to his neighborhood school while the other continues the struggle to lift his family out of poverty. College is only a way to continue to play basketball and be noticed by scouts. In this true story, few teachers or coaches talk to him about other career choices besides shooting a basketball.

"The current crop of jock films are primarily the fish out of water stories," said Butch Robinson, cowriter and producer of the film *Drop Squad,* which was released in 1994. The film, which Spike Lee executive produced, is about an African-American advertising executive who teaches his firm how to push unwanted products on his community in order to rise to the top. "The presentation of Blacks in higher education is extremely stereotypical in breadth, with no complexity to the characters." Robinson said.

"I think whites in general like their Negroes docile and concerned about things other than politics, education and their rights. The idea even with *Hoop Dreams* and the majority of films that receive the green light [is that they] provide a certain comfort for the majority viewers who do not see African Americans expressing the same desires as them. It makes more sense to perpetuate the idea of life in the ghetto and triumph if a jump shot is hit. The wonderful back story in *Hoop Dreams* was that it didn't work," said Robinson.

Robinson adds that stereotypes persist when it comes to higher education. African-American characters in these films are always characters where their "Blackness" is the prevalent issue in their role, he said. A 1970s comedy, *Soul Man,* depicted Black actress Rae Dawn Chung at Harvard University but, unlike her counterparts, she was a single mother working in the university's cafeteria to make ends meet.

THE MEN OF MOREHOUSE

● ● ● ● ● ● ● ● ● ● ● ● ● ● ●

Short films, which are not always seen by mass audiences, are credited with doing a better job at telling a broader range of stories that are rarely seen. For example, *The Men of Morehouse,* made by California Newsreel, examines the making of the Morehouse College student, and aired last year on public television.

California Newsreel, based in San Francisco, has released several movies that address aspects of Black life including documentaries such as *Frosh,* which looks at the first-year college experience through the eyes of an array of students, some African American. Another film, *Skin Deep,* features roundtable discussions between students of different ethnic backgrounds on the subject of race. A new film, *W.E.B. DuBois: A Biography in Four Voices,* features perspectives on the educator's life from author Toni Cade Bambara and others. Many of these documentaries are being used to fill the void through PBS and find their way into the classroom.

But with all of the criticism about the shortcomings of films that address the African-American experience, particularly on the college campus, many filmmakers and those in the industry point the finger back at viewing audiences who continue to support stereotypical films. For African Americans, Robinson describes it as simply a matter of limited opportunities for Black filmmakers.

"I have yet to see a film by a Black filmmaker that was not ambitious," Robinson said. "The prevailing thought is that they may not get another shot at it. But we are asked to solve all of the problems. The (Black) audience is starving to see themselves, see their story. We don't have the luxury to tell all the stories. If you go to see a Black film, nine times out of 10 it will be a ghetto film. We are allowed to make films about survival."

In the African-American community, the mission of telling the story of the community has frequently fallen in the hands of someone else. It wasn't until the beginning of this decade that doors have begun to open to more African-American directors, who have begun to control images (under the direction of funding studios).

Sensitivity about images in the African-American community is based on a long legacy of negative portrayals of Blacks in film. Some of the earliest films depicting African Americans produced by the American Mutoscope company included such fares as *Trilby,* an excerpted moment from the popular play *Trilby,* and *Little Billee,* vignettes of African Americans in "characteristic poses." *A Hard Wash,* shows a Black woman scrubbing her child. Spectators were to consider the scene humorous since no matter how hard the mother scrubbed, she would never get him "truly clean." *Watermelon Feast* and *Dancing Darkies* were filled with stereotypes and conformed to degrading, white-imposed stereotypes. That trend continued through *Birth of a Nation,* which played on white fears of newly-freed slaves and portrayed the Ku Klux Klan in a heroic role.

Even in the hands of African Americans, films sometimes perpetuate stereotypical images. In *House Party II* the main characters, Kid and Play, spend most of their time on the college campus partying, with little representation of the average student who can't sing or dance their way through the rigors of college life.

"It is a really complicated issue," said Cornelius Moore, co-director of California Newsreel. "The reality is that there have been few movies about education. We are only talking about a handful of movies during the past few years. The debate is much more charged, because there aren't that many Black films and we want to be portrayed in the right way, whatever that is. For us, it is more than just entertainment."

Understanding the Text

1. Hayes and those she interviews are quite critical of the mainstream films they discuss. Why? And why do they believe this is such a critical issue?

2. According to Hayes and those she interviews, what are the sources of these films' failings? (Identify two.)

3. According to Hayes, what kinds of films seem to represent the situation more accurately?

Lisa and American Anti-Intellectualism

Aeon J. Skoble

American society has generally had a love-hate relationship with the notion of the intellectual. On the one hand, there is a sense of respect for the professor or the scientist, but at the same time there is great resentment of the "ivory tower" or the "bookish"; a defensiveness about intelligent or learned people. The republican ideals of the Founders presuppose an enlightened citizenry, yet today, the introduction of even remotely sophisticated analysis of political topics is decried as "elitism." Everyone respects a historian, yet a historian's opinion may be disregarded on the grounds that it is "no more valid" than that of the "working man." Populist commentators and politicians frequently exploit this resentment of expertise while relying on it as it suits them, for example when a candidate attacks his opponent for being an "Ivy League elitist" while in fact being a product of (or relying on advisers from) a similar educational background.

Similarly, a hospital may consult a bioethicist, or it may reject the counsel of bioethicists, on the grounds that they are too abstract and unconnected to the realities of medicine. Indeed, it seems as though most people like being able to support their positions by citing experts, but then invoke populist sentiment when the experts don't support their view. For instance, I may lend support to my argument by citing an expert who agrees with me, but if an expert disagrees, I may respond "what does he know?" or "I'm entitled to my opinion too." Oddly, we see anti-intellectualism even among intellectuals. For example, at many universities today, both among the student body and the faculty, the role of

Aeon J. Skoble is an associate professor of philosophy at Bridgewater State College (Massachusetts). He has published numerous articles on philosophy and popular culture and is co-editor of three collections of essays that explore the connections between them: *The Philosophy of TV Noir* (2007), *Woody Allen and Philosophy* (2004), and *The Simpsons and Philosophy* (2000).

the classics, and humanities generally, has been greatly diminished. The trend has clearly been to develop pre-professional programs and emphasize "relevance"; whereas traditional humanities classes are regarded as a luxury or an enhancement, but not truly necessary features of a college education. At best they are seen as vehicles for developing "transferable skills" such as composition or critical thinking.

There seem to be periodic pendulum swings: in the 1950s and early 1960s, there was tremendous respect for scientists, as the nation found itself competing against the Soviets in such areas as space exploration. Today, it seems the pendulum has reversed swing, as the current *Zeitgeist* holds all opinions to be equally valid. But at the same time, people still seem interested in what alleged experts have to say. A cursory review of TV talk shows or newspaper letters-to-the-editor reveals this ambivalence. The talk show will book an expert because, presumably, people will be interested in that person's analysis or opinion. But the panelists or audience members who disagree with the expert will argue that their opinions, their perspectives, are just as worthwhile. A newspaper will run an opinion column by a specialist, whose analysis on a situation may be better informed than the average person's, but the letters from people who disagree will often be based on the underlying (if unstated) premise that "No one really knows anything" or "It's all a matter of opinion, and mine counts too." This last rationale is particularly insidious: in fact, if it were true that everything were merely a matter of opinion, then it actually would follow that mine is as relevant as the expert's; indeed there would be no such thing as expertise.

So, it is fair to say that American society is conflicted about intellectuals. Respect for them seems virtually to go hand in hand with resentment. This is a puzzling social problem, and also one of great importance, for we seem to be on the verge of a new "dark ages," where not only the notion of expertise, but all standards of rationality are being challenged. This clearly has significant social consequences. As a vehicle for exploring this issue, it may be surprising to choose a TV show which, at first glance, seems devoted to the idea that dumber is better; but actually, of the many things that *The Simpsons* skillfully illustrates about society, the American ambivalence about expertise and rationality is clearly one of them.[1]

On *The Simpsons,* Homer is a classic example of an anti-intellectual dolt, as are most of his acquaintances, and his son. But his daughter, Lisa, is not only pro-intellectual, she is smart beyond her years. She is extremely intelligent and sophisticated, and is often seen out-thinking those around her. Naturally, for this she is mocked by the other children at school and generally ignored by the adults. On the other hand, her favorite TV show is the same one as her brother's: a mindlessly violent cartoon. Her treatment on the show, I argue, captures the love-hate relationship American society has with intellectuals.[2] Before turning to the ways in which it does this, let's have a closer look at the problem.

FALLACIOUS AUTHORITY AND REAL EXPERTISE

It is a staple of introductory logic courses that it is a fallacy to "appeal to authority," yet people typically make more out of this than is appropriate. Strictly in terms of logic, it's always a mistake to argue that a proposition is true because so-and-so says it is, but appeals to authority are more commonly used to show that we have good reason to believe the proposition, as opposed to being proof of its truth. Like all fallacies involving relevance, the problem with most appeals to authority is that they are invoking the authority in an irrelevant way. For example, in matters which really are subjective, such as which pizza or soft drink I should buy, invoking anyone else is irrelevant, since I may not have the same tastes.[3] In other cases, the error is in assuming that because a person is an authority about one thing, that person's expertise should carry the day in all areas. We see this in celebrity endorsements for products unrelated to that person's field. For example, Troy McClure endorsing Duff Beer would not constitute a valid appeal to authority, since being an actor doesn't make one an expert on beer. (And experience is not the same as expertise: Barney is not an expert on beer either.) In other cases, the appeal is fallacious on the grounds that some matters cannot be settled by appeal to experts, not because they are subjective, but because they are unknowable, for instance the future of scientific progress. The classic example here is Einstein's claim in 1932 that "there is not the slightest indication that [nuclear] energy will ever be obtainable."[4]

But after building up all this skepticism about appeals to authority, it's worth remembering that some people actually do know more about some things than other people, and in many cases, the fact that an authority on a subject tells us something really is a good reason to believe it. For example, since I have no first-hand knowledge of the Battle of Marathon, I am going to have to rely on what other people tell me, and a classical historian is precisely the sort of person I should go to, whereas a physician probably is not.[5]

Often what people resent is the application of wisdom, especially to moral or social ideals. People may argue that yes, there is such a thing as being an expert on the Greco-Persian Wars, but that doesn't mean that person can inform our discussion about world politics today.[6] You may be an expert on Aristotle's moral theory, but that doesn't mean you can tell me how I should live. This sort of resistance to expertise stems partly from the nature of a democratic regime, and the problem is not new, but was identified by philosophers as early as Plato. Since, in a democracy, all voices get heard, this can lead people to conclude that all voices have equal value. Democracies tend to justify themselves by contrast to the aristocracies or oligarchies they replace or resist. In those elitist societies, some presume to know more, or actually to be better people; whereas we democrats know better: all are equal. But of course, political equality doesn't imply that no one can possess knowledge that others lack, and indeed few people think this about most skills, for example plumbing or auto repair. No one, though (they say), can know more than anyone else about how to live, how to be just. Hence a kind of relativism develops: from the rejection of ruling elites, who in fact may not have had any better idea than anyone else about justice, to a rejection of the notion of objective standards of right and wrong entirely. What is right is what I feel is right, what is right-for-me. Today, there is a trend even in the academy to dispute notions of objectivity and expertise. There are said to be no true histories, only different interpretations of history.[7] There are no correct interpretations of literary works, only different interpretations.[8] Even physical science is said to be value-laden and non-objective.[9]

So we have all these factors contributing to a climate in which the notion of expertise is eroded, yet at the same time we see countervailing trends. If there's no such thing as expertise, and all opinions are equally valid, why are the talk shows and bestseller lists populated by experts on love and angels? Why watch those shows or read books in the first place? Why send the kids to school? Clearly, people do still put some stock in the notion of expertise, and in many cases, yearn for its guidance. People actually seem to have some tendencies towards wanting to be told what to do. Some critics of religion ascribe its influence to this psychological need, but we need look no further than the political realm to see evidence of it. People look to political figures for their "leadership": we're having a problem with unemployment—doesn't anyone know how to do something about that? This person would make a better president than that one because he knows how to reduce crime, end poverty, make our children better, and so on. But the ambivalence shows itself very clearly in these contexts. If candidate Smith bases his appeal on his expertise and ability to "get the job done," candidate Jones will likely charge Smith with being an elite, a "pointy-head." We also see the paradoxical situation wherein celebrities' pronouncements on political matters taken seriously, as if being a talented musician or actor gave greater weight to one's political views, while at the same time the notion of being an expert on government is derided. With whose views are most Americans more familiar, Alec Baldwin and Charlton Heston, or John Rawls and Robert Nozick?

In addition to political expertise, people also yearn for, and seem least ambivalent about, technological expertise. Most people are quick to acknowledge their own incompetence at plumbing, auto repair, and surgery, and happily turn those tasks over to the experts. In the case of the surgeon, we do see another manifestation of the ambivalence I have in mind, namely when people defend alternative medicine or spiritual healing—what do doctors know? This is a trickle-down from the currently-fashionable trend in academia which maintains that all science is value-laden and non-objective. But we don't have any advocates of "alternative plumbing" or "spiritual auto repair," so these people's expertise is more generally accepted; and do-it-your-selfers are not a counter-example, since that's more a matter of regarding oneself as that sort of craftsman, rather than denying that anyone else is. Also, since plumbers and mechanics less frequently position themselves as experts in fields beyond their own, as surgeons might position themselves as ethicists, they are less susceptible to being regarded skeptically.[10]

DO WE ADMIRE OR LAUGH AT LISA?

American anti-intellectualism, then, is pervasive but not all-encompassing. As it does with many other aspects of modern society, *The Simpsons* often uses this theme as fodder for its satire. In the Simpson family, only Lisa could really be described as an intellectual. But her portrayal as such is not unequivocally flattering. In contrast to her relentlessly ignorant father, she is often shown having the right answer to a problem or a more perceptive analysis of a situation, for example when she exposes political corruption[11] or when she gives up her dream of owning a pony so that Homer won't have to work three jobs.[12] When Lisa discovers the truth behind the myth of Jebediah Springfield, many people are unconvinced, but Homer says, "you're always right about this sort of thing."[13] In "Homer's Triple Bypass," Lisa actually talks Dr. Nick through a heart operation and saves her father's life. But other times, her intellectualism is itself used as the butt of the joke, as if she were "too" smart, or merely preachy. For instance, her principled vegetarianism is revealed as dogmatic and inconsistent,[14] and she uses Bart in a science experiment without his knowledge,[15] evoking examples of the worst sort of arrogance, such as the infamous Tuskegee study.[16] She agitates to join the football team, but it turns out she is more interested in making a point than in playing.[17] So although her wisdom is sometimes presented as valuable, other times it is presented as a case of being sanctimonious or condescending.

One common populist criticism of the intellectual is that "you're no better than the rest of us." The point of this attack seems to be that if I can show that the alleged sage is "really" a regular person, then maybe I don't have to be as impressed with his opinion. Thus the expression "Hey, he puts his pants on one leg at a time just like the rest of us." The implication of this non-sequitur is clearly "he is just a regular person like you and me, so why should we be awed by his alleged expertise?" In Lisa's case, we are shown that she has many of the same foibles as many kids: she joins her non-intellectual brother in revelry as they watch the mindlessly violent *Itchy and Scratchy* cartoon, she worships the teen idol Corey, she plays with Springfield's analogue to the Barbie Doll, Malibu Stacy. So we are given ample opportunity to see Lisa as "no better" in many respects, thus giving us another window for not taking her smarts seriously. Of course, it is true that she is a young girl, and one might argue that this is merely typical young girl behavior, but since in so many other cases she is presented not simply as a prodigy but as preternaturally wise, the fondness for *Itchy and Scratchy* and Corey seem to be highlighted, taking on greater significance. Lisa is portrayed as the avatar of logic and wisdom, but then she also worships Corey, so she's "no better." In "Lisa the Skeptic," Lisa is the sole voice of reason when the town becomes convinced that "the skeleton of an angel" has been found (it's a hoax), but when it seems to speak, Lisa is as afraid as everyone else.

Lisa's relationship with the Malibu Stacy doll actually takes center stage in one episode,[18] and even this highlights an ambivalence in society about rationalism. It gradually occurs to Lisa that the Malibu Stacy doll does not offer a positive role model for young girls, and she presses for (and actually contributes to) the development of a different doll which encourages girls to achieve and learn. But the makers of Malibu Stacy counter with a new version of their doll, which triumphs on the toy market. The fact that the "less intellectual" doll is vastly preferred over Lisa's doll, even though all of Lisa's objections are reasonable, demonstrates the ways in which reasonable ideas can be made to take a back seat to "having fun" and "going with the flow." This debate is often played out in the real world, of course: Barbie is the subject of perennial criticism along the lines of Lisa's critique of Malibu Stacy, yet remains immensely popular, and in general, we often see intellectual critiques of toys dismissed as "out of touch" or elitist.[19]

PHILOSOPHER KINGS? D'OH!

A more specific instance of the way *The Simpsons* reflects American ambivalence towards the intellectual is found in the episode "They Saved Lisa's Brain."[20] In this episode, Lisa joins the local chapter of Mensa, which already includes Professor Frink, Dr. Hibbert, and the Comic Book Guy. Together they end up in charge of Springfield. Lisa rhapsodizes about the rule of the intellectuals, a true rationalist utopia, but too many of their programs alienate the regular citizens of the town (including, of course, Homer, who leads the charge of the idiot brigade). It would be easy enough to see this sequence of events as a satire on the way the average person is too stupid to recognize the rule of the wise, but more than that is being satirized here. Also under attack is the very notion of rule of the wise—the Mensans have some legitimately good ideas (more rational traffic patterns), but also some ridiculous ones (censorship, mating rituals inspired by *Star Trek*), and they squabble amongst themselves. The Mensans offer something of value, especially in contrast to the corrupt regime of Mayor Quimby or the reign of idiocy that Homer represents, and Lisa's intentions are good, but it is impossible to see this episode as unequivocally pro-intellectual, since one theme is clearly that utopian schemes by elites are unstable, inevitably unpopular, and sometimes foolish. As Paul Cantor argues, "the utopia episode embodies the strange mixture of intellectualism and anti-intellectualism characteristic of *The Simpsons*. In Lisa's challenge to Springfield, the show calls attention to the cultural limitations of small-town America, but it also reminds us that intellectual disdain for the common man can be carried too far and that theory can all too easily lose touch with common sense."[21]

It is actually true, however, that utopian schemes by elites tend to be ill-conceived, or are power-grabbing schemes masquerading as the common good. But is the only alternative Homer's mob or Quimby's oligarchy? The framers of the United States Constitution hoped to combine democratic principles (a Congress) with some of the benefits of an undemocratic elite rule (a Senate, a Supreme Court, a Bill of Rights). This has had mixed results, but in contrast to other alternatives seems to have fared well. Is all of our society's ambivalence about intellectuals due to this constitutional tension? Surely not. That is part of it, but, more likely than not, this ambivalence is a manifestation of deeper psychological conflicts. We want to have authoritative guidance, but we also want autonomy. We don't like feeling stupid, yet when we are honest we realize we need to learn some things. We respect the accomplishments of others, but sometimes feel threatened and resentful. We have a respect for authorities when it suits us, and embrace relativism in other cases. The "we" here is, of course, a generalization: some people manifest this conflict less than others (or in a few cases not at all), but it seems an apt description of a general social outlook. Unsurprisingly, *The Simpsons,* our most profoundly satirical TV show, both illustrates and instantiates it.

The ambivalence in American society towards the intellectual, if it is indeed a deep-rooted psychological phenomenon, is not likely to go away any time soon. But no one is better off for encouraging or promoting anti-intellectualism. Those who wish to save the republic from the tyranny of Professor Frink and The Comic Book Guy need to find ways to argue against it that do not entail a wholesale attack on the ideal of intellectual development. Those who champion the common man ought not do so in ways that belittle the achievements of the learned. That approach is tantamount to defending Homer's right to live as a stupid person by criticizing Lisa for being smart.[22] That's not a sound idea for the development of the nation or of any individual.[23]

Notes

[1] Is it anti-intellectual for a Ph.D. in philosophy to write an essay about a TV show? As we argued in the Introduction, not necessarily: it depends on whether or not the show can illuminate some philosophical problem, or serve as an accessible example when explaining a point. If we wanted to adopt an anti-intellectual approach, we could argue that all one needs to know about life can be learned from watching TV, but that's clearly not what we are saying; indeed, we're trying to use people's interest in the show as a way to get them to read more philosophy.

[2] Intellectuals and experts are not the same thing, of course: many intellectuals are not experts in anything. But I suspect that the antipathy towards both is similarly rooted, and that the distinction is lost on those who would be inclined to reject or scorn both.

[3] This is not to address the arguments concerning whether or not there can be objective criteria for judging food, but simply to distinguish between the way in which Smith's preference for chocolate over vanilla is really different from Jones's preference for murder over counseling.

[4] Quoted in Christopher Cerf and Victor Navasky, *The Experts Speak* (New York: Pantheon Books, 1984), p. 215.

[5] Of course, there are the odd cases where the physician in question is, say, as a hobby, also an expert on the Battle of Marathon, but I am speaking here of the physician qua physician.

[6] In case you're wondering, see Peter Green's *The Greco-Persian Wars* (Berkeley: University of California Press, 1996).

[7] See for example, Mary Lefkowitz's book *Not Out of Africa* (New York: Basic Books, 1996), in which she recounts her experiences as a classicist trying to maintain standards of rational inquiry in the heated area of race-based archeology.

[8] For a rare objective account of artistic interpretation, see William Irwin's *Intentionalist Interpretation: A Philosophical Explanation and Defense* (Westport, CT: Greenwood Press, 1999). Ironically, at the same time the notion of truth and expertise is being challenged within the academy—there are no such things as experts on morality—the talk shows and bestseller lists are populated with experts on such things as relationships, horoscopes, and angels. But these experts are heeded, I think, only to the extent that they confirm a person's predispositions, and rejected on grounds I have outlined when they do not. To be sure, the rejection of knowledge claims in the realm of values is different from the rejection of knowledge claims in physical matters, but what is interesting is that we do see both, and at the same time we also see bogus claims of expertise on a host of inappropriate matters.

[9] See, for example, Alan Sokal and Jean Bricmont, *Fashionable Nonsense: Postmodern Intellectuals' Abuse of Science* (New York: Picador, 1998). The springboard for this book was Sokal's now-famous hoax, in which he submitted a bogus essay based on this theme, which was readily accepted by scientifically challenged journal editors as a fine work. That essay was "Transgressing the Boundaries: Toward a Transformative Hermeneutics of Quantum Gravity," originally published in *Social Text* 46–47, (1996), pp. 217–252.

[10] This also highlights ways in which popular attitudes towards "authorities" and "intellectuals" are not exactly the same. People are less resistant to an authority or expert when the area seems not to be an intellectual one, as for example we all recognize the plumber's expertise; but of course being an expert in anything requires a degree of intellectualism, so the distinction is a fallacious one, and is more a reflection of people's attitudes than a statement about the intellectual level of expert craftsmen. Expert craftsmen obviously do possess wisdom, but are often seen as less threatening to those who don't possess the wisdom. This might be due to the fact that when we speak of "intellectuals" or "smart people," we are describing a general characteristic which sets the person apart, whereas when we speak of an "expert," we are only describing an attribute which we may regard as isolated, and thus feel less threatened. Lisa is an intellectual (valuing the pursuit of wisdom) and very smart, while not specifically an "expert" on anything.

[11] "Mr. Lisa Goes to Washington."

[12] "Lisa's Pony."

[13] "Lisa the Iconoclast."

[14] "Lisa the Vegetarian."

[15] "Duffless."

[16] This was a case in which the doctors experimented without consent, and with little regard for the well-being of the "participants," who were infected with syphilis.

[17] "Bart Star."

[18] "Lisa vs. Malibu Stacy."

[19] GI Joe, for example, is criticized for promoting militarism and violence, as do all "gun" toys, yet parents overwhelmingly reject the calls of some intellectuals that kids should be guided towards different play.

[20] For futher discussion of this episode, see Chapter 11 of this volume.

[21] Ibid., p. 178.

[22] Some argue that, indeed, Homer does not have the right to live as a stupid person. There may be something to this, but it's neither here nor there with respect to the narrower argument I am making here.

[23] I am grateful to Mark Conard and William Irwin for helping me clarify several of my points and reminding me of several useful examples.

Understanding the Text

1. According to Skoble, how do Americans typically view expertise? Why?

2. Skoble entitles one section of his article, "Do We Admire or Laugh at Lisa?" What is his answer?

3. According to Skoble, how does the episode "They Saved Lisa's Brain" represent intellectualism?

Watching TV Makes You Smarter

Steven Johnson

The Sleeper Curve

> SCIENTIST A: *Has he asked for anything special?*
> SCIENTIST B: *Yes, this morning for breakfast . . . he requested something called "wheat germ, organic honey and tiger's milk."*
> SCIENTIST A: *Oh, yes. Those were the charmed substances that some years ago were felt to contain life-preserving properties.*
> SCIENTIST B: *You mean there was no deep fat? No steak or cream pies or . . . hot fudge?*
> SCIENTIST A: *Those were thought to be unhealthy.*
>
> —From Woody Allen's "Sleeper"

On Jan. 24, the Fox network showed an episode of its hit drama "24," the real-time thriller known for its cliffhanger tension and often- gruesome violence. Over the preceding weeks, a number of public controversies had erupted around "24," mostly focused on its portrait of Muslim terrorists and its penchant for torture scenes. The episode that was shown on the 24th only fanned the flames higher: in one scene, a terrorist enlists a hit man to kill his child for not fully supporting the jihadist cause; in another scene, the secretary of defense authorizes the torture of his son to uncover evidence of a terrorist plot.

But the explicit violence and the post-9/11 terrorist anxiety are not the only elements of "24" that would have been unthinkable on prime-time network television 20 years ago. Alongside the notable change in content lies an equally notable change in form. During its 44 minutes—a real-time hour, minus 16 minutes for commercials—the episode

Steven Johnson writes about science and technology for a number of magazines, including *Discover Magazine, Slate, Wired,* and *The New York Times Magazine.* He is the author of five books: *The Ghost Map: The Story of London's Most Terrifying Epidemic and How It Changed Science, Cities, and the Modern World* (2006), *Everything Bad Is Good for You: How Today's Popular Culture Is Actually Making Us Smarter* (2005), *Mind Wide Open: Your Brain and the Neuroscience of Everyday Life* (2004), *Emergence: The Connected Lives of Ants, Brains, Cities, and Software* (2001), and *Interface Culture: How New Technology Transforms the Way We Create and Communicate* (1997). He lectures widely and is a frequent guest on television and radio programs.

347

connects the lives of 21 distinct characters, each with a clearly defined "story arc," as the Hollywood jargon has it: a defined personality with motivations and obstacles and specific relationships with other characters. Nine primary narrative threads wind their way through those 44 minutes, each drawing extensively upon events and information revealed in earlier episodes. Draw a map of all those intersecting plots and personalities, and you get structure that—where formal complexity is concerned—more closely resembles "Middlemarch" than a hit TV drama of years past like "Bonanza."

For decades, we've worked under the assumption that mass culture follows a path declining steadily toward lowest-common-denominator standards, presumably because the "masses" want dumb, simple pleasures and big media companies try to give the masses what they want. But as that "24" episode suggests, the exact opposite is happening: the culture is getting more cognitively demanding, not less. To make sense of an episode of "24," you have to integrate far more information than you would have a few decades ago watching a comparable show. Beneath the violence and the ethnic stereotypes, another trend appears: to keep up with entertainment like "24," you have to pay attention, make inferences, track shifting social relationships. This is what I call the Sleeper Curve: the most debased forms of mass diversion—video games and violent television dramas and juvenile sitcoms—turn out to be nutritional after all.

I believe that the Sleeper Curve is the single most important new force altering the mental development of young people today, and I believe it is largely a force for good: enhancing our cognitive faculties, not dumbing them down. And yet you almost never hear this story in popular accounts of today's media. Instead, you hear dire tales of addiction, violence, mindless escapism. It's assumed that shows that promote smoking or gratuitous violence are bad for us, while those that thunder against teen pregnancy or intolerance have a positive role in society. Judged by that morality-play standard, the story of popular culture over the past 50 years—if not 500—is a story of decline: the morals of the stories have grown darker and more ambiguous, and the antiheroes have multiplied.

The usual counterargument here is that what media have lost in moral clarity, they have gained in realism. The real world doesn't come in nicely packaged public-service announcements, and we're better off with entertainment like "The Sopranos" that reflects our fallen state with all its ethical ambiguity. I happen to be sympathetic to that argument, but it's not the one I want to make here. I think there is another way to assess the social virtue of pop culture, one that looks at media as a kind of cognitive workout, not as a series of life lessons. There may indeed be more "negative messages" in the mediasphere today. But that's not the only way to evaluate whether our television shows or video games are having a positive impact. Just as important—if not more important—is the kind of thinking you have to do to make sense of a cultural experience. That is where the Sleeper Curve becomes visible.

TELEVISED INTELLIGENCE

Consider the cognitive demands that televised narratives place on their viewers. With many shows that we associate with "quality" entertainment—"The Mary Tyler Moore Show," "Murphy Brown," "Frasier"—the intelligence arrives fully formed in the words and actions of the characters on-screen. They say witty things to one another and avoid lapsing into tired sitcom clichés, and we smile along in our living rooms, enjoying the company of these smart people. But assuming we're bright enough to understand the sentences they're saying, there's no intellectual labor involved in enjoying the show as a viewer. You no more challenge your mind by watching these intelligent shows than you challenge your body watching "Monday Night Football." The intellectual work is happening on-screen, not off.

But another kind of televised intelligence is on the rise. Think of the cognitive benefits conventionally ascribed to reading: attention, patience, retention, the parsing of narrative threads. Over the last half-century, programming on TV has increased the demands it places on precisely these mental faculties. This growing complexity involves three primary elements: multiple threading, flashing arrows and social networks.

According to television lore, the age of multiple threads began with the arrival in 1981 of "Hill Street Blues," the Steven Bochco police drama invariably praised for its "gritty realism." Watch an episode of "Hill Street Blues" side by side with any major drama from the preceding decades—"Starsky and Hutch," for instance, or "Dragnet"—and the structural transformation will jump out at you. The earlier shows follow one or two lead characters, adhere to a single dominant plot and reach a decisive conclusion at the end of the episode. Draw an outline of the narrative threads in almost every "Dragnet" episode, and it will be a single line: from the initial crime scene, through the investigation, to the eventual cracking of the case. A typical "Starsky and Hutch" episode offers only the slightest variation on this linear formula: the introduction of a comic subplot that usually appears only at the tail ends of the episode, creating a structure that looks like the graph below. The vertical axis represents the number of individual threads, and the horizontal axis is time.

"STARSKY AND HUTCH" (ANY EPISODE)

A "Hill Street Blues" episode complicates the picture in a number of profound ways. The narrative weaves together a collection of distinct strands—sometimes as many as 10, though at least half of the threads involve only a few quick scenes scattered through the episode. The number of primary characters—and not just bit parts—swells significantly. And the episode has fuzzy borders: picking up one or two threads from previous episodes at the outset and leaving one or two threads open at the end. Charted graphically, an average episode looks like this:

Critics generally cite "Hill Street Blues" as the beginning of "serious drama" native to the television medium—differentiating the series from the single-episode dramatic programs from the 50's, which were Broadway plays performed in front of a camera. But the "Hill Street" innovations weren't all that original; they'd long played a defining role in popular television, just not during the evening hours. The structure of a "Hill Street" episode—and indeed of all the critically acclaimed dramas that followed, from "thirtysomething" to "Six Feet Under"—is the structure of a soap opera. "Hill Street Blues" might have sparked a new golden age of television drama during its seven-year run, but it did so by using a few crucial tricks that "Guiding Light" and "General Hospital" mastered long before.

Bochco's genius with "Hill Street" was to marry complex narrative structure with complex subject matter. 'Dallas" had already shown that the extended, interwoven threads of the soap-opera genre could survive the weeklong interruptions of a prime-time show, but the actual content of "Dallas" was fluff. (The most probing issue it addressed was the question, now folkloric, of who shot J.R.) "All in the Family" and "Rhoda" showed that you could tackle complex social issues, but they did their tackling in the comfort of the sitcom living room. "Hill Street" had richly drawn characters confronting difficult social issues and a narrative structure to match.

Since "Hill Street" appeared, the multi-threaded drama has become the most widespread fictional genre on prime time: "St. Elsewhere," "L.A. Law," "thirtysomething," "Twin Peaks," "N.Y.P.D. Blue," "E.R.," "The West Wing," "Alias," "Lost." (The only prominent holdouts in drama are shows like "Law and Order" that have essentially updated the venerable "Dragnet" format and thus remained anchored to a single narrative line.) Since the early 80's, however, there has been a noticeable increase in narrative complexity in these dramas. The most ambitious show on TV to date, "The Sopranos," routinely follows up to a dozen distinct threads over the course of an episode, with more than 20 recurring characters. An episode from late in the first season looks like this:

THE SOPRANOS (EPISODE 8)

The total number of active threads equals the multiple plots of "Hill Street," but here each thread is more substantial. The show doesn't offer a clear distinction between dominant and minor plots; each story line carries its weight in the mix. The episode also displays a chordal mode of storytelling entirely absent from "Hill Street": a single scene in "The Sopranos" will often connect to three different threads at the same time, layering one plot atop another. And every single thread in this "Sopranos" episode builds on events from previous episodes and continues on through the rest of the season and beyond.

Put those charts together, and you have a portrait of the Sleeper Curve rising over the past 30 years of popular television. In a sense, this is as much a map of cognitive changes in the popular mind as it is a map of on-screen developments, as if the media titans decided to condition our brains to follow ever-larger numbers of simultaneous threads. Before "Hill Street," the conventional wisdom among television execs was that audiences wouldn't be comfortable following more than three plots in a single episode, and indeed, the "Hill Street" pilot, which was shown in January 1981, brought complaints from viewers that the show was too complicated. Fast-forward two decades, and shows like "The Sopranos" engage their audiences with narratives that make "Hill Street" look like "Three's Company." Audiences happily embrace that complexity because they've been trained by two decades of multi-threaded dramas.

Multi-threading is the most celebrated structural feature of the modern television drama, and it certainly deserves some of the honor that has been doled out to it. And yet multi-threading is only part of the story.

THE CASE FOR CONFUSION

Shortly after the arrival of the first-generation slasher movies—"Halloween," "Friday the 13th"—Paramount released a mock-slasher flick called "Student Bodies," parodying the genre just as the "Scream" series would do 15 years later. In one scene, the obligatory nubile teenage baby sitter hears a noise outside a suburban house; she opens the door to investigate, finds nothing and then goes back inside. As the door shuts behind her, the camera swoops in on the doorknob, and we see that she has left the door unlocked. The camera pulls back and then swoops down again for emphasis. And then a flashing arrow appears on the screen, with text that helpfully explains: "Unlocked!"

That flashing arrow is parody, of course, but it's merely an exaggerated version of a device popular stories use all the time. When a sci-fi script inserts into some advanced lab a nonscientist who keeps asking the science geeks to explain what they're doing with that particle accelerator, that's a flashing arrow that gives the audience precisely the information it needs in order to make sense of the ensuing plot. ("Whatever you do, don't spill water on it, or you'll set off a massive explosion!") These hints serve as a kind of narrative hand-holding. Implicitly, they say to the audience, "We realize you have no idea what a particle accelerator is, but here's the deal: all you need to know is that it's a big fancy thing that explodes when wet." They focus the mind on relevant details: "Don't worry about whether the baby sitter is going to break up with her boyfriend. Worry about that guy lurking in the bushes." They reduce the amount of analytic work you need to do to make sense of a story. All you have to do is follow the arrows.

By this standard, popular television has never been harder to follow. If narrative threads have experienced a population explosion over the past 20 years, flashing arrows have grown correspondingly scarce. Watching our pinnacle of early 80's TV drama, "Hill Street Blues," we find there's an informational wholeness to each scene that differs markedly from what you see on shows like "The West Wing" or "The Sopranos" or "Alias" or "E.R."

"Hill Street" has ambiguities about future events: will a convicted killer be executed? Will Furillo marry Joyce Davenport? Will Renko find it in himself to bust a favorite singer for cocaine possession? But the present-tense of each scene explains itself to the viewer with little ambiguity. There's an open question or a mystery driving each of these stories—how will it all turn out?—but there's no mystery about the immediate activity on the screen. A contemporary drama like "The West Wing," on the other hand, constantly embeds mysteries into the present-tense events: you see characters performing actions or discussing events about which crucial information has been deliberately withheld. Anyone who has watched more than a handful of "The West Wing" episodes closely will know the feeling: scene after scene refers to some clearly crucial but unexplained piece of information, and after the sixth reference, you'll find yourself wishing you could rewind the tape to figure out what they're talking about, assuming you've missed something. And then you realize that you're supposed to be confused. The open question posed by these sequences is not "How will this turn out in the end?" The question is "What's happening right now?"

The deliberate lack of hand-holding extends down to the microlevel of dialogue as well. Popular entertainment that addresses technical issues—whether they are the intricacies of passing legislation, or of performing a heart bypass, or of operating a particle accelerator—conventionally switches between two modes of information in dialogue: texture and substance. Texture is all the arcane verbiage provided to convince the viewer that they're watching Actual Doctors at Work; substance is the material planted amid the background texture that the viewer needs to make sense of the plot.

Conventionally, narratives demarcate the line between texture and substance by inserting cues that flag or translate the important data. There's an unintentionally comical moment in the 2004 blockbuster "The Day After Tomorrow" in which the beleaguered climatologist (played by Dennis Quaid) announces his theory about the imminent arrival of a new ice age to a gathering of government officials. In his speech, he warns that "we have hit a critical desalinization point!" At this moment, the writer-director Roland Emmerich—a master of brazen arrow-flashing—has an official follow with the obliging remark: "It would explain what's driving this extreme weather." They might as well have had a flashing "Unlocked!" arrow on the screen.

The dialogue on shows like "The West Wing" and "E.R.," on the other hand, doesn't talk down to its audiences. It rushes by, the words accelerating in sync with the high-speed tracking shots that glide through the corridors and operating rooms. The characters talk faster in these shows, but the truly remarkable thing about the dialogue is not purely a matter of speed; it's the willingness to immerse the audience in information that most viewers won't understand. Here's a typical scene from "E.R.":

[WEAVER *and* WRIGHT *push a gurney containing a 16-year-old girl. Her parents,* JANNA *and* FRANK MIKAMI, *follow close behind.* CARTER *and* LUCY *fall in.*]

WEAVER: 16-year-old, unconscious, history of biliary atresia.
CARTER: Hepatic coma?
WEAVER: Looks like it.
MR. MIKAMI: She was doing fine until six months ago.
CARTER: What medication is she on?
MRS. MIKAMI: Ampicillin, tobramycin, vitamins A, D and K.
LUCY: Skin's jaundiced.
WEAVER: Same with the sclera. Breath smells sweet.
CARTER: Fetor hepaticus?
WEAVER: Yep.
LUCY: What's that?
WEAVER: Her liver's shut down. Let's dip a urine. [*To* CARTER] Guys, it's getting a little crowded in here, why don't you deal with the parents? Start lactulose, 30 cc's per NG.
CARTER: We're giving medicine to clean her blood.
WEAVER: Blood in the urine, two-plus.
CARTER: The liver failure is causing her blood not to clot.

MRS. MIKAMI: Oh, God. . . .

CARTER: Is she on the transplant list?

MR. MIKAMI: She's been Status 2a for six months, but they haven't been able to find her a match.

CARTER: Why? What's her blood type?

MR. MIKAMI: AB.

[*This hits* CARTER *like a lightning bolt.* LUCY *gets it, too. They share a look.*]

There are flashing arrows here, of course—"The liver failure is causing her blood not to clot"—but the ratio of medical jargon to layperson translation is remarkably high. From a purely narrative point of view, the decisive line arrives at the very end: "AB." The 16-year-old's blood type connects her to an earlier plot line, involving a cerebral-hemorrhage victim who—after being dramatically revived in one of the opening scenes—ends up brain-dead. Far earlier, before the liver-failure scene above, Carter briefly discusses harvesting the hemorrhage victim's organs for transplants, and another doctor makes a passing reference to his blood type being the rare AB (thus making him an unlikely donor). The twist here revolves around a statistically unlikely event happening at the E.R.—an otherwise perfect liver donor showing up just in time to donate his liver to a recipient with the same rare blood type. But the show reveals this twist with remarkable subtlety. To make sense of that last "AB" line—and the look of disbelief on Carter's and Lucy's faces—you have to recall a passing remark uttered earlier regarding a character who belongs to a completely different thread. Shows like "E.R." may have more blood and guts than popular TV had a generation ago, but when it comes to storytelling, they possess a quality that can only be described as subtlety and discretion.

EVEN BAD TV IS BETTER

Skeptics might argue that I have stacked the deck here by focusing on relatively highbrow titles like "The Sopranos" or "The West Wing," when in fact the most significant change in the last five years of narrative entertainment involves reality TV. Does the contemporary pop cultural landscape look quite as promising if the representative show is "Joe Millionaire" instead of "The West Wing"?

I think it does, but to answer that question properly, you have to avoid the tendency to sentimentalize the past. When people talk about the golden age of television in the early 70's—invoking shows like "The Mary Tyler Moore Show" and "All in the Family"—they forget to mention how awful most television programming was during much of that decade. If you're going to look at pop-culture trends, you have to compare apples to apples, or in this case, lemons to lemons. The relevant comparison is not between "Joe Millionaire" and

"MASH"; it's between "Joe Millionaire" and "The Newlywed Game," or between "Survivor" and "The Love Boat."

What you see when you make these head-to-head comparisons is that a rising tide of complexity has been lifting programming at the bottom of the quality spectrum and at the top. "The Sopranos" is several times more demanding of its audiences than "Hill Street" was, and "Joe Millionaire" has made comparable advances over "Battle of the Network Stars." This is the ultimate test of the Sleeper Curve theory: even the junk has improved.

If early television took its cues from the stage, today's reality programming is reliably structured like a video game: a series of competitive tests, growing more challenging over time. Many reality shows borrow a subtler device from gaming culture as well: the rules aren't fully established at the outset. You learn as you play.

On a show like "Survivor" or "The Apprentice," the participants—and the audience—know the general objective of the series, but each episode involves new challenges that haven't been ordained in advance. The final round of the first season of "The Apprentice," for instance, threw a monkey wrench into the strategy that governed the play up to that point, when Trump announced that the two remaining apprentices would have to assemble and manage a team of subordinates who had already been fired in earlier episodes of the show. All of a sudden the overarching objective of the game—do anything to avoid being fired—presented a potential conflict to the remaining two contenders: the structure of the final round favored the survivor who had maintained the best relationships with his comrades. Suddenly, it wasn't enough just to have clawed your way to the top; you had to have made friends while clawing. The original "Joe Millionaire" went so far as to undermine the most fundamental convention of all— that the show's creators don't openly lie to the contestants about the prizes—by inducing a construction worker to pose as man of means while 20 women competed for his attention.

Reality programming borrowed another key ingredient from games: the intellectual labor of probing the system's rules for weak spots and opportunities. As each show discloses its conventions, and each participant reveals his or her personality traits and background, the intrigue in watching comes from figuring out how the participants should best navigate the environment that has been created for them. The pleasure in these shows comes not from watching other people being humiliated on national television; it comes from depositing other people in a complex, high-pressure environment where no established strategies exist and watching them find their bearings. That's why the water-cooler conversation about these shows invariably tracks in on the strategy displayed on the previous night's episode: why did Kwame pick Omarosa in that final round? What devious strategy is Richard Hatch concocting now?

When we watch these shows, the part of our brain that monitors the emotional lives of the people around us—the part that tracks subtle shifts in intonation and gesture and facial expression—scrutinizes the action on the screen, looking for clues. We trust certain characters implicitly and vote others off the island in a heartbeat. Traditional narrative shows also trigger emotional connections to the characters, but those connections don't have the same participatory effect, because traditional narratives aren't explicitly about strategy. The phrase "Monday-morning quarterbacking" describes the engaged feeling that spectators have in relation to games as opposed to stories. We absorb stories, but we second-guess games. Reality programming has brought that second-guessing to prime time, only the game in question revolves around social dexterity rather than the physical kind.

THE REWARDS OF SMART CULTURE

The quickest way to appreciate the Sleeper Curve's cognitive training is to sit down and watch a few hours of hit programming from the late 70's on Nick at Nite or the SOAPnet channel or on DVD. The modern viewer who watches a show like "Dallas" today will be bored by the content—not just because the show is less salacious than today's soap operas (which it is by a small margin) but also because the show contains far less information in each scene, despite the fact that its soap-opera structure made it one of the most complicated narratives on television in its prime. With "Dallas," the modern viewer doesn't have to think to make sense of what's going on, and not having to think is boring. Many recent hit shows— "24," "Survivor," "The Sopranos," "Alias," "Lost," "The Simpsons," "E.R."—take the opposite approach, layering each scene with a thick network of affiliations. You have to focus to follow the plot, and in focusing you're exercising the parts of your brain that map social networks, that fill in missing information, that connect multiple narrative threads.

Of course, the entertainment industry isn't increasing the cognitive complexity of its products for charitable reasons. The Sleeper Curve exists because there's money to be made by making culture smarter. The economics of television syndication and DVD sales mean that there's a tremendous financial pressure to make programs that can be watched multiple times, revealing new nuances and shadings on the third viewing. Meanwhile, the Web has created a forum for annotation and commentary that allows more complicated shows to prosper, thanks to the fan sites where each episode of shows like "Lost" or "Alias" is dissected with an intensity usually reserved for Talmud scholars. Finally, interactive games have trained a new generation of media consumers to probe complex environments and to think on their feet, and that gamer audience has now come to expect the same challenges from their television shows. In the end, the Sleeper Curve tells us something about the human mind. It may be drawn toward the sensational where content is concerned—sex does sell, after all. But the mind also likes to be challenged; there's real pleasure to be found in solving puzzles, detecting patterns or unpacking a complex narrative system.

In pointing out some of the ways that popular culture has improved our minds, I am not arguing that parents should stop paying attention to the way their children amuse themselves. What I am arguing for is a change in the criteria we use to determine what really is cognitive junk food and what is genuinely nourishing. Instead of a show's violent or tawdry content, instead of wardrobe malfunctions or the F-word, the true test should be whether a given show engages or sedates the mind. Is it a single thread strung together with predictable punch lines every 30 seconds? Or does it map a complex social network? Is your on-screen character running around shooting everything in sight, or is she trying to solve problems and manage resources? If your kids want to watch reality TV, encourage them to watch "Survivor" over "Fear Factor." If they want to watch a mystery show, encourage "24" over "Law and Order." If they want to play a violent game, encourage Grand Theft Auto over Quake. Indeed, it might be just as helpful to have a rating system that used mental labor and not obscenity and violence as its classification scheme for the world of mass culture.

Kids and grown-ups each can learn from their increasingly shared obsessions. Too often we imagine the blurring of kid and grown-up cultures as a series of violations: the 9-year-olds who have to have nipple broaches explained to them thanks to Janet Jackson; the middle-aged guy who can't wait to get home to his Xbox. But this demographic blur has a commendable side that we don't acknowledge enough. The kids are forced to think like grown-ups: analyzing complex social networks, managing resources, tracking subtle narrative intertwinings, recognizing long-term patterns. The grown-ups, in turn, get to learn from the kids: decoding each new technological wave, parsing the interfaces and discovering the intellectual rewards of play. Parents should see this as an opportunity, not a crisis. Smart culture is no longer something you force your kids to ingest, like green vegetables. It's something you share.

Understanding the Text

1. What does Johnson mean by the "Sleeper Curve"?

2. According to Johnson, what do the activities of reading and of watching contemporary television drama have in common?

3. What is Johnson's assessment of so-called "reality" programming such as *Survivor* and *The Apprentice*? For what reasons? (Identify two.)

Game Theory

Russell Jacoby

Wander down the abandoned alleys of Trotskyism and there is no telling where you might turn up: on Main Street with contemporary neoconservatives, on campuses with respected literary critics or on the margins of the margins, where political savants probe the zeitgeist. In one of those quarters lived Josef Weber, a forgotten essayist who pondered, among other things, popular culture, which did not please him. To establish its impact, Weber in a 1957 essay posited a law of the dwindling force of cognition in bourgeois society.

Weber's law suggested that despite vast growth in scientific and technological information, knowledge of society declines. People increasingly know about things and decreasingly about social reality. Later reformulated as the law of the falling rate of intelligence, it posits that intelligence sinks in society as the production, selling and advertising of commodities rises. We face a crisis of the overproduction of idiocy. These notions represent a classic stance about the dumbing-down of popular culture. Cases in point: The most popular sporting event in the United States is the Indianapolis 500, in which nearly half a million people pay good money to watch grown men drive fast automobiles in a circle. Viewers by the millions follow contestants on reality television as they compete to eat bugs and worms.

Steven Johnson, a savvy writer on technology and its pleasures, offers a thorough-going challenge to this bleak outlook on popular culture. To be sure, Johnson's contrariness may be a pose, inasmuch as it depends on opposition that has all but melted

Russell Jacoby is a professor of history at UCLA. He is the author of many books, including *Picture Imperfect: Utopian Thought for an Anti-Utopian Age* (2005), *The End of Utopia: Politics and Culture in the Age of Apathy* (1999), *Dogmatic Wisdom: How the Culture Wars Divert Education and Distract America* (1994), and *The Last Intellectuals: American Culture in the Age of Academe* (1987). He also has published numerous articles and reviews in *American Historical Review,* the *Los Angeles Times, Harper's,* and elsewhere.

Reprinted with permission from the June 27, 2006 issue of *The Nation.* For subscription information call 1-800-333-8536. Portions of each week's Nation magazine can be accessed at http://www.thenation.com.

away. Apart from a few depressed followers of Josef Weber and his ilk, who today believes in falling cognition? Champions of popular culture can be found throughout this broad land. One need not venture very far to discover courses on soap operas, situation comedies or *Star Trek* offered by cultural studies professors, who wax about the profundity of television. To be sure, doubt about the legitimacy of their subject matter haunts even the most avid boosters of popular culture. I sometimes ask my students a variant of an Internet dating question: Whom would you rather date, someone who indicates their favorite pastime is to stay home to play video games or to step out to a ballet or museum? Even the most avid enthusiasts of television balk at dating their soul mates.

In *Everything Bad Is Good for You,* Johnson tells a "progressive story," in which popular culture, far from dumbing us down, becomes ever more complex, intellectually stimulating and sophisticated each year. He recalls that his father partook of an intricate game of simulated professional baseball in which one mastered endless data in order to field teams. While this game required dice, cards and graphs, Johnson Jr. grew up on video games, which serve as the touchstone for his argument. For Johnson these games and kindred television programs require an ability to command mountains of information and characters. They are not easy to play or enjoy; they call for patience and intelligence. Aficionados study guidebooks and cheat sheets. The most debased forms of mass diversion—video games and violent television dramas and juvenile sitcoms—turn out to be nutritional after all. Neither the masses nor the mass media are getting dumber. "The exact opposite is happening: the culture is getting more intellectually demanding, not less."

Johnson worships the god of complexity, but it may prove a false idol. He makes much of the new complexity, not simply of video games—the transition from a simplistic Pac-Man to an intricate Grand Theft Auto—but of television programs and films. Old shows like *Dragnet* consisted of a single narrative structure with two or three lead characters and ended decisively. New shows like *The Sopranos* juggle numerous characters and maintain an ongoing story. Johnson even offers a spatial graph of the Fox series *24* to demonstrate that it's at least three times as complex as the old *Dallas.* These shows presumably demand increasing attention from the viewer, who must recall previous episodes and follow multiple story lines. Although the trend is not so evident, films too have become increasingly complicated. Johnson compares *Star Wars,* with ten characters, to *Lord of the Rings,* with almost thirty. He suggests that new children's films such as *Toy Story* and *Shrek* present much more intricate paths than earlier ones like *Mary Poppins* and *Bambi.*

Johnson's argument is not quite as contrived as it appears. He limits his thesis to narrow cognitive and mental skills that may increase due to gaming, television and Internet surfing. He makes a halfhearted stab at giving a scientific confirmation of his belief that popular culture and its customers are becoming smarter, but he often writes in the comfortably vague style of "studies have shown." He appeals to evidence of rising IQs over the decades, based on the work of an American philosopher named James Flynn, which supposedly rebuts any notion of dwindling cognition in society.

Yet the idea that IQ scores are rising remains contested; and even if it were true, it is not clear what its causes are or—more important—what its consequences are. Hence when Johnson tells us that "moderately intelligent people today are much smarter" than "moderately intelligent people were a hundred years ago," we moderately intelligent might wonder what this means. True, many of us today can simultaneously drive a car, talk on a cell phone, shuffle music CDs and sip coffee, which a denizen of a century ago would find bewildering. But is this a measure of intelligence? Does it have any bearing on knowledge of self and society? Not in the least.

This is the rub about the complexity argument: how complex is complexity? Or, more precisely, does an ability to master complex narratives and intricate games reflect an expansion of general intelligence? It's odd that Johnson's paean to the impact of mass media nowhere mentions "attention-deficit disorder," which has only been recognized as a syndrome by the American Psychiatric Association since 1980. Whatever its medical basis, the syndrome would seem a revealing counterpoint to media complexity: Many people today cannot focus on one thing for long. "Complex" television programs with ten characters and six plots may respond to this phenomenon; something is always happening, unlike a simple narrative, which might require a willingness or ability to stick to one story. Johnson half knows this, and late in his book he qualifies his thesis: The new complex intelligence does not foster a capacity to follow the "sustained" argument of a typical book. Johnson must make this concession—after all, he offers us an argumentative book, not a blog or a video game.

However, the concession hardly salvages his thesis. Today's media may require skills that stand in no relationship to an aptitude to think about the world. It's hardly news that many Americans command vast amounts of information about automobiles and sports, and just a few hazy facts about society. My own basketball pals can talk with ardor and knowledge about an army of ball players, coaches, high school prospects, old games and new, salaries and draft choices, but few of them address politics with any comparable expertise. Media complexity may express the dwindling force of cognition in the era of attention-deficit disorder.

If Johnson trumpets the new media, Thomas de Zengotita questions it. De Zengotita believes that the media have "mediated" life to the point that we no longer know, or care about, the difference between reality and its representation. "We have been consigned to a new plane of being engendered by mediating representations of fabulous quality and inescapable ubiquity." If this sounds portentous, de Zengotita generally is not: "Ask yourself this: is there anything you do that remains essentially unmediated, anything you don't experience reflexively through some commodified representation of it? Birth? Marriage? Illness?"

For de Zengotita we live in a period where reality and representation, or things and their sheen, blur. Everything seems to flow and merge, a world of endless choices, crystallized in the expression "whatever." We watch fake reality TV and live real fake lives.

De Zengotita, who teaches at a progressive private school in New York City, has a good eye for life's foibles in an age of surfeit. At a school event in which political clubs made presentations, seventy-five adults showed but only a few students. An indignant woman arose, a 1960s veteran, to lambaste the lack of "opportunities" at a "school like this" for "our students to bring their concerns to the community." Wrong, as de Zengotita realized. There were not too few but too many opportunities.

We have entered the period of "niche commitments" and politics, he writes. "It was that evening that I first grasped the dialectic of 'whatever.'" At another panel, a speaker let drop that he had attended an "Advocacy Institute." De Zengotita wondered, "Advocacy of what?" The speaker replied, "Anything."

De Zengotita breezes through subjects such as television, movies, adolescence and parenting, and he sometimes sounds like Johnson with a caveat. The transition from *Leave It to Beaver* or *Father Knows Best* to *The Simpsons,* he writes breathlessly, says "so much" about the "new millennium." In *The Simpsons,* anarchy reigns. We are no longer "charmed" by children as they "slowly learn to make sense of a world that does, in fact, make sense. Because it doesn't. The world of *The Simpsons* is chaos."

Unfortunately, de Zengotita has an eye for media excess and excess media, but not much more. *Mediated* consists of loosely connected vignettes and observations punctuated by epiphanies de Zengotita experienced during panels or watching television. To the extent he has an argument, his best chapter, on "The Cult of the Child," bears little relationship to it, which de Zengotita coolly admits. The sanctification of children seems "to sit strangely" amid a society of mediation, where everything is about choices and representation. "But mediation is nothing if not a fount of paradox. No need to make the factual case" about the cult of the child. With this approach one could also take up Bush's foreign policy or the health insurance crisis as instances of media mediation, which de Zengotita almost does. He rants about Bush but does not get beyond telling us that the President belongs to the "age of mediation" while pretending he doesn't.

De Zengotita's best and worst case for his argument may be his own book. It's not clear whether *Mediated* is a real book or a knockoff; whether it is written in English or a facsimile. It reads like a magazine piece on uppers, and parts of it did appear in *Harper's Magazine.* "Ah those iPods," runs a typical passage. "Plato would have flipped out. Which brings us to attitude." So it goes for several hundred pages. "But enough politics. Let's have fun instead. Here's one of my favorite examples. . . . I'll never forget—it was during the Christmas season of 1999, during those heady dot-com days, and Jeff Bezos was sharing his vision with the masses in a TV interview. . . . Bezos saith. . . ." Or this: "I hate to be a drag, but, have you noticed? Movie endings are getting lamer and lamer lately, especially in the action/sci-fi/scary area." Ironically it's Johnson, the champion of the mass media, who has written an old-fashioned book; the putative detractor, de Zengotita, offers us the literary equivalent of Post-its.

The critic Dwight Macdonald befriended the German refugee Josef Weber, perhaps because of a shared suspicion of the culture industry. "Those who consume Masscult," Macdonald wrote more than forty years ago, "might as well be eating ice cream sodas, while those who fabricate it are no more expressing themselves than are the stylists, who design the latest atrocity from Detroit." The day for sweeping denunciations of popular culture like these is obviously over, probably for the better. The vision of media complexity and profundity, however, that pervades Johnson's and de Zengotita's books may represent not simply an advance—a new sophistication—but an old conformism.

Understanding the Text

1. In his 1957 essay, what did Josef Weber argue about the relation between consumerism and intelligence?

2. What does Steven Johnson argue in *Everything Bad is Good for You?* And what are Jacoby's chief objections to this argument?

3. As he compares the books by Johnson and de Zengotita, why does Jacoby find their relation ironic?

ADDITIONAL READINGS

Birkerts, Sven: *The Gutenberg Elegies: The Fate of Reading in an Electronic Age.* 1994. New York: Fawcett-Ballantine, 1995.

Bledstein, Burton J. *The Culture of Professionalism: The Middle Class and the Development of Higher Education in America.* New York: Norton, 1976.

Bloom, Alan. *The Closing of the American Mind.* New York: Simon and Schuster, 1987.

Bok, Derek. *Our Underachieving Colleges: A Candid Look at How Much Students Learn and Why They Should Be Learning More.* Princeton: Princeton UP, 2006.

———. *Universities in the Marketplace: The Commercialization of Higher Education.* Princeton: Princeton UP, 2003.

Callahan, Raymond C. *Education and the Cult of Efficiency: A Study of the Social Forces That Have Shaped the Administration of the Public Schools.* Chicago: U of Chicago P, 1962.

Claussen, Dane S. *Anti-Intellectualism in American Media: Magazines and Higher Education.* Questions about the Purpose(s) of Colleges & Universities 11. New York: Peter Lang, 2004.

Denby, David. *Great Books: My Adventures with Homer, Rousseau, Woolf, and Other Indestructible Writers of the Western World.* New York: Simon & Schuster, 1996.

Frank, Marcie. *How to Be an Intellectual in the Age of TV: The Lessons of Gore Vidal.* Public Planet Series. Durham: Duke UP, 2005.

Graff, Gerald. *Clueless in Academe: How Schooling Obscures the Life of the Mind.* New Haven: Yale UP, 2003.

Hersh, Richard H. and John Merrow, eds. *Declining by Degrees: Higher Education at Risk.* New York: Palgrave Macmillan, 2005.

Hirsch, E.D. *Cultural Literacy: What Every American Needs to Know.* Boston: Houghton Mifflin, 1987.

Hofstadter, Richard. *Anti-Intellectualism in American Life.* New York: Random House, 1963.

Jacoby, Russell. *The Last Intellectuals: American Culture in the Age of Academe.* New York: Basic Books, 1987.

Johnson, Steven. *Everything Bad Is Good for You: How Today's Popular Culture Is Actually Making Us Smarter.* New York: Riverhead Books, 2005.

Kirp, David L. *Shakespeare, Einstein, and the Bottom Line: The Marketing of Higher Education.* Cambridge: Harvard UP, 2003.

Marc, David. *Bonfire of the Humanities: Television, Subliteracy, and Long-Term Memory Loss.* The Television Series. Syracuse: Syracuse UP, 1995.

Miller, Mark Crispin. *The Bush Dyslexicon: Observations on a National Disorder.* New York: Norton, 2001.

Nathan, Rebekah. *My Freshman Year: What a Professor Learned by Becoming a Student.* Ithaca: Cornell UP, 2005.

Newman, John Henry. *The Idea of a University.* 1852. Notre Dame: U of Notre Dame P, 1982.

Oppenheimer, Todd. *The False Promise of Technology in the Classroom and How Learning Can Be Saved.* New York: Random House, 2003.

Ross, Andrew. *No Respect: Intellectuals & Popular Culture.* New York: Routledge, 1989.

Sanders, Barry. *A Is for Ox: Violence, Electronic Media, and the Silencing of the Written Word.* New York: Pantheon, 1994.

Shor, Ira. *Culture Wars: School and Society in the Conservative Restoration, 1969–1984.* Critical Social Thought. Boston: Routledge & Kegan Paul, 1986.

Sperber, Murray. *Beer and Circus: How Big-time College Sports Is Crippling Undergraduate Education.* New York: Henry Holt, 2000.

———. *College Sports Inc.: The Athletic Department vs. the University.* New York: Henry Holt, 1990.

Washburn, Katharine and John Thornton. *Dumbing Down: Essays on the Strip-Mining of American Culture.* New York: Norton, 1996.

White, Curtis. *The Middle Mind: Why Americans Don't Think for Themselves.* New York: HarperSanFrancisco, 2003.

Wolfe, Tom. *I am Charlotte Simmons.* New York: Farrar, Straus, and Girioux, 2004.

That's Entertainment:
Politics and the News

The Age of Show Business

Neil Postman

A dedicated graduate student I know returned to his small apartment the night before a major examination only to discover that his solitary lamp was broken beyond repair. After a whiff of panic, he was able to restore both his equanimity and his chances for a satisfactory grade by turning on the television set, turning off the sound, and with his back to the set, using its light to read important passages on which he was to be tested. This is one use of television—as a source of illuminating the printed page.

But the television screen is more than a light source. It is also a smooth, nearly flat surface on which the printed word may be displayed. We have all stayed at hotels in which the TV set has had a special channel for describing the day's events in letters rolled endlessly across the screen. This is another use of television—as an electronic bulletin board.

Many television sets are also large and sturdy enough to bear the weight of a small library. The top of an old-fashioned RCA console can handle as many as thirty books, and I know one woman who has securely placed her entire collection of Dickens, Flaubert, and Turgenev on the top of a 21-inch Westinghouse. Here is still another use of television—as bookcase.

I bring forward these quixotic uses of television to ridicule the hope harbored by some that television can be used to support the literate tradition. Such a hope represents exactly what Marshall McLuhan used to call "rear-view mirror" thinking: the assumption that a new medium is merely an

Neil Postman (1931–2003) was a professor and chair of the Department of Culture and Communication at New York University, where he taught for over four decades. In his seventeen books, Postman wrote about education, the media, and the influence of technology. His books continue to reach a wide audience and include *Building a Bridge to the Eighteenth Century: Ideas from the Past that Can Improve Our Future* (1999), *The End of Education: Redefining the Value of School* (1995), *Technopoly: The Surrender of Culture to Technology* (1993), and *Amusing Ourselves to Death: Public Discourse in the Age of Show Business* (1985).

extension or amplification of an older one; that an automobile, for example, is only a fast horse, or an electric light a powerful candle. To make such a mistake in the matter at hand is to misconstrue entirely how television redefines the meaning of public discourse. Television does not extend or amplify literate culture. It attacks it. If television is a continuation of anything, it is of a tradition begun by the telegraph and photograph in the mid-nineteenth century, not by the printing press in the fifteenth.

What is television? What kinds of conversations does it permit? What are the intellectual tendencies it encourages? What sort of culture does it produce?

These are the questions to be addressed in the rest of this [essay], and to approach them with a minimum of confusion, I must begin by making a distinction between a technology and a medium. We might say that a technology is to a medium as the brain is to the mind. Like the brain, a technology is a physical apparatus. Like the mind, a medium is a use to which a physical apparatus is put. A technology becomes a medium as it employs a particular symbolic code, as it finds its place in a particular social setting, as it insinuates itself into economic and political contexts. A technology, in other words, is merely a machine. A medium is the social and intellectual environment a machine creates.

Of course, like the brain itself, every technology has an inherent bias. It has within its physical form a predisposition toward being used in certain ways and not others. Only those who know nothing of the history of technology believe that a technology is entirely neutral. There is an old joke that mocks that naive belief. Thomas Edison, it goes, would have revealed his discovery of the electric light much sooner than he did except for the fact that every time he turned it on, he held it to his mouth and said, "Hello? Hello?"

Not very likely. Each technology has an agenda of its own. It is, as I have suggested, a metaphor waiting to unfold. The printing press, for example, had a clear bias toward being used as a linguistic medium. It is *conceivable* to use it exclusively for the reproduction of pictures. And, one imagines, the Roman Catholic Church would not have objected to its being so used in the sixteenth century. Had that been the case, the Protestant Reformation might not have occurred, for as Luther contended, with the word of God on every family's kitchen table, Christians do not require the Papacy to interpret it for them. But in fact there never was much chance that the press would be used solely, or even very much, for the duplication of icons. From its beginning in the fifteenth century, the press was perceived as an extraordinary opportunity for the display and mass distribution of written language. Everything about its technical possibilities led in that direction. One might even say it was invented for that purpose.

The technology of television has a bias, as well. It is conceivable to use television as a lamp, a surface for texts, a bookcase, even as radio. But it has not been so used and will not be so used, at least in America. Thus, in answering the question, What is television?, we must understand as a first point that we are not talking about television as a technology but television as a medium. There are many places in the world where television, though the same technology as it is in America, is an entirely different medium from that which we know. I refer to places where the majority of people do not have television sets, and those who do have only one; where only one station is available; where television does not operate around the clock; where most programs have as their purpose the direct furtherance of government ideology and policy; where commercials are unknown, and "talking heads" are the principal image; where television is mostly used as if it were radio. For these reasons and more television will not have the same meaning or power as it does in America, which is to say, it is possible for a technology to be so used that its potentialities are prevented from developing and its social consequences kept to a minimum.

But in America, this has not been the case. Television has found in liberal democracy and a relatively free market economy a nurturing climate in which its full potentialities as a technology of images could be exploited. One result of this has been that American television programs are in demand all over the world. The total estimate of U.S. television program exports is approximately 100,000 to 200,000 hours, equally divided among Latin America, Asia and Europe.[1] Over the years, programs like *Gunsmoke, Bonanza, Mission: Impossible, Star Trek, Kojak,* and more recently, *Dallas* and *Dynasty* have been as popular in England, Japan, Israel and Norway as in Omaha, Nebraska. I have heard (but not verified) that some years ago the Lapps postponed for several days their annual and, one supposes, essential migratory journey so that they could find out who shot J.R. All of this has occurred simultaneously with the decline of America's moral and political prestige, worldwide. American television programs are in demand not because America is loved but because American television is loved.

We need not be detained too long in figuring out why. In watching American television, one is reminded of George Bernard Shaw's remark on his first seeing the glittering neon signs of Broadway and 42nd Street at night. It must be beautiful, he said, if you cannot read. American television is, indeed, a beautiful spectacle, a visual delight, pouring forth thousands of images on any given day. The average length of a shot on network television is only 3.5 seconds, so that the eye never rests, always has something new to see. Moreover, television offers viewers a variety of subject matter, requires minimal skills to comprehend it, and is largely aimed at emotional gratification. Even commercials, which some regard as an annoyance, are exquisitely crafted, always pleasing to the eye and accompanied by exciting music. There is no question but that the best photography in the world is presently seen on television commercials. American television, in other words, is devoted entirely to supplying its audience with entertainment.

Of course, to say that television is entertaining is merely banal. Such a fact is hardly threatening to a culture, not even worth writing a book about. It may even be a reason for rejoicing. Life, as we like to say, is not a highway strewn with flowers. The sight of a few blossoms here and there may make our journey a trifle more endurable. The Lapps undoubtedly thought so. We may surmise that the ninety million Americans who watch television every night also think so. But what I am claiming here is not that television is entertaining but that it has made entertainment itself the natural format for the representation of all experience. Our television set keeps us in constant communion with the world, but it does so with a face whose smiling countenance is unalterable. The problem is not that television presents us with entertaining subject matter but that all subject matter is presented as entertaining, which is another issue altogether.

To say it still another way: Entertainment is the supra-ideology of all discourse on television. No matter what is depicted or from what point of view, the overarching presumption is that it is there for our amusement and pleasure. That is why even on news shows which provide us daily with fragments of tragedy and barbarism, we are urged by the newscasters to "join them tomorrow." What for? One would think that several minutes of murder and mayhem would suffice as material for a month of sleepless nights. We accept the newscasters' invitation because we know that the "news" is not to be taken seriously, that it is all in fun, so to say. Everything about a news show tells us this—the good looks and amiability of the cast, their pleasant banter, the exciting music that opens and closes the show, the vivid film footage, the attractive commercials—all these and more suggest that what we have just seen is no cause for weeping. A news show, to put it plainly, is a format for entertainment, not for education, reflection or catharsis. And we must not judge too harshly those who have framed it in this way. They are not assembling the news to be read, or broadcasting it to be heard. They are televising the news to be seen. They must follow where their medium leads. There is no conspiracy here, no lack of intelligence, only a straightforward recognition that "good television" has little to do with what is "good" about exposition or other forms of verbal communication but everything to do with what the pictorial images look like.

I should like to illustrate this point by offering the case of the eighty-minute discussion provided by the ABC network on November 20, 1983, following its controversial movie *The Day After.* Though the memory of this telecast has receded for most, I choose this case because, clearly, here was television taking its most "serious" and "responsible" stance. Everything that made up this broadcast recommended it as a critical test of television's capacity to depart from an entertainment mode and rise to the level of public instruction. In the first place, the subject was the possibility of a nuclear holocaust. Second, the film itself had been attacked by several influential bodies politic, including the Reverend Jerry Falwell's Moral Majority. Thus, it was important that the network display television's value and serious intentions as a medium of information and coherent discourse. Third, on the program itself no musical theme was used as background—a significant point since almost all television programs are embedded in music, which helps to tell the audience what emotions are to be called forth. This is a standard theatrical device, and its absence on television is always ominous. Fourth, there were no commercials during the discussion, thus elevating the tone of the event to the state of reverence usually reserved for the funerals of assassinated Presidents.

And finally, the participants included Henry Kissinger, Robert McNamara, and Elie Wiesel, each of whom is a symbol of sorts of serious discourse. Although Kissinger, somewhat later, made an appearance on the hit show *Dynasty,* he was then and still is a paradigm of intellectual sobriety; and Wiesel, practically a walking metaphor of social conscience. Indeed, the other members of the cast—Carl Sagan, William Buckley and General Brent Scowcroft—are, each in his way, men of intellectual bearing who are not expected to participate in trivial public matters.

The program began with Ted Koppel, master of ceremonies, so to speak, indicating that what followed was not intended to be a debate but a *discussion.* And so those who are interested in philosophies of discourse had an excellent opportunity to observe what serious television means by the word "discussion." Here is what it means: Each of six men was given approximately five minutes to say something about the subject. There was, however, no agreement on exactly what the subject was, and no one felt obliged to respond to anything anyone else said. In fact, it would have been difficult to do so, since the participants were called upon seriatim, as if they were finalists in a beauty contest, each being given his share of minutes in front of the camera. Thus, if Mr. Wiesel, who was called upon last, had a response to Mr. Buckley, who was called upon first, there would have been four commentaries in between, occupying about twenty minutes, so that the audience (if not Mr. Wiesel himself) would have had difficulty remembering the argument which prompted his response. In fact, the participants—most of whom were no strangers to television—largely avoided addressing each other's points. They used their initial minutes and then their subsequent ones to intimate their position or give an impression. Dr. Kissinger, for example, seemed intent on making viewers feel sorry that he was no longer their Secretary of State by reminding everyone of books he had once written, proposals he had once made, and negotiations he had once conducted. Mr. McNamara informed the audience that he had eaten lunch in Germany that very afternoon, and went on to say that he had at least fifteen proposals to reduce nuclear arms. One would have thought that the discussion would turn on this issue, but the others seemed about as interested in it as they were in what he had for lunch in Germany. (Later, he took the initiative to mention three of his proposals but they were not discussed.) Elie Wiesel, in a series of quasi-parables and paradoxes, stressed the tragic nature of the human condition, but because he did not have the time to provide a context for his remarks, he seemed quixotic and confused, conveying an impression of an itinerant rabbi who has wandered into a coven of Gentiles.

In other words, this was no discussion as we normally use the word. Even when the "discussion" period began, there were no arguments or counterarguments, no scrutiny of assumptions, no explanations, no elaborations, no definitions. Carl Sagan made, in my opinion, the most coherent statement—a four-minute rationale for a nuclear freeze—but it contained at least two questionable assumptions and was not carefully examined. Apparently, no one wanted to take time from his own few minutes to call attention to someone else's. Mr. Koppel, for his part, felt obliged to keep the "show" moving, and though he occasionally pursued what he discerned as a line of thought, he was more concerned to give each man his fair allotment of time.

But it is not time constraints alone that produce such fragmented and discontinuous language. When a television show is in process, it is very nearly impermissible to say, "Let me think about that" or "I don't know" or "What do you mean when you say . . . ?" or "From what sources does your information come?" This type of discourse not only slows down the tempo of the show but creates the impression of uncertainty or lack of finish. It tends to reveal people in the *act of thinking,* which is as disconcerting and boring on television as it is on a Las Vegas stage. Thinking does not play well on television, a fact that television directors discovered long ago. There is not much to *see* in it. It is, in a phrase, not a performing art. But television demands a performing art, and so what the ABC network gave us was a picture of men of sophisticated verbal skills and political understanding being brought to heel by a medium that requires them to fashion performances, rather than ideas. Which accounts for why the eighty minutes were very entertaining, in the way of a Samuel Beckett play: The intimations of gravity hung heavy, the meaning passeth all understanding. The performances, of course, were highly professional. Sagan abjured the turtle-neck sweater in which he starred when he did *Cosmos.* He even had his hair cut for the event. His part was that of the logical scientist speaking in behalf of the planet. It is to be doubted that Paul Newman could have done better in the role, although Leonard Nimoy might have. Scowcroft was suitably military in his bearing—terse and distant, the unbreakable defender of national security. Kissinger, as always, was superb in the part of the knowing world statesman, weary of the sheer responsibility of keeping disaster at bay. Koppel played to perfection the part of a moderator, pretending, as it were, that he was sorting out ideas while, in fact, he was merely directing the performances. At the end, one could only applaud those performances, which is what a good television program always aims to achieve; that is to say, applause, not reflection.

I do not say categorically that it is impossible to use television as a carrier of coherent language or thought in process. William Buckley's own program, *Firing Line,* occasionally shows people in the act of thinking but who also happen to have television cameras pointed at them. There are other programs, such as *Meet the Press* or *The Open Mind,* which clearly strive to maintain a sense of intellectual decorum and typographic tradition, but they are scheduled so that they do not compete with programs of great visual interest, since otherwise, they will not be watched. After all, it is not unheard of that a format will occasionally go against the bias of its medium. For example, the most popular radio program of the early 1940's featured a ventriloquist, and in those days, I heard more than once the feet of a tap dancer on the *Major Bowes' Amateur Hour.* (Indeed, if I am not mistaken, he even once featured a pantomimist.) But ventriloquism, dancing and mime do not play well on radio, just as sustained, complex talk does not play well on television. It can be made to play tolerably well if only one camera is used and the visual image is kept constant—as when the President gives a speech. But this is not television at its best, and it is not television that most people will choose to watch. The single most important fact about television is that people *watch* it, which is why it is called "tele*vision*." And what they watch, and like to watch, are moving pictures—millions of them, of short duration and dynamic variety. It is in the nature of the medium that it must suppress the content of ideas in order to accommodate the requirements of visual interest; that is to say, to accommodate the values of show business.

Film, records and radio (now that it is an adjunct of the music industry) are, of course, equally devoted to entertaining the culture, and their effects in altering the style of American discourse are not insignificant. But television is different because it encompasses all forms of discourse. No one goes to a movie to find out about government policy or the latest scientific advances. No one buys a record to find out the baseball scores or the weather or the latest murder. No one turns on radio anymore for soap operas or a presidential address (if a television set is at hand). But everyone goes to television for all these things and more, which is why television resonates so powerfully throughout the culture. Television is our culture's principal mode of knowing about itself. Therefore—and this is the critical point— how television stages the world becomes the model for how the world is properly to be staged. It is not merely that on the television screen entertainment is the metaphor for all discourse. It is that off the screen the same metaphor prevails. As typography once dictated the style of conducting politics, religion, business, education, law and other important social matters, television now takes command. In courtrooms, classrooms, operating rooms, board rooms, churches and even airplanes, Americans no longer talk to each other, they entertain each other. They do not exchange ideas; they exchange images. They do not argue with propositions; they argue with good looks, celebrities and commercials. For the message of television as metaphor is not only that all the world is a stage but that the stage is located in Las Vegas, Nevada.

In Chicago, for example, the Reverend Greg Sakowicz, a Roman Catholic priest, mixes his religious teaching with rock 'n' roll music. According to the Associated Press, the Reverend Sakowicz is both an associate pastor at the Church of the Holy Spirit in Schaumburg (a suburb of Chicago) and a disc jockey at WKQX. On his show, *The Journey Inward,* Father Sakowicz chats in soft tones about such topics as family relationships or commitment, and interposes his sermons with "the sound of *Billboard's* Top 10." He says that his preaching is not done "in a churchy way," and adds, "You don't have to be boring in order to be holy."

Meanwhile in New York City at St. Patrick's Cathedral, Father John J. O'Connor put on a New York Yankee baseball cap as he mugged his way through his installation as Archbishop of the New York Archdiocese. He got off some excellent gags, at least one of which was specifically directed at Mayor Edward Koch, who was a member of his audience; that is to say, he was a congregant. At his next public performance, the new archbishop donned a New York

Mets baseball cap. These events were, of course, televised, and were vastly entertaining, largely because Archbishop (now Cardinal) O'Connor has gone Father Sakowicz one better: Whereas the latter believes that you don't have to be boring to be holy, the former apparently believes you don't have to be holy at all.

In Phoenix, Arizona, Dr. Edward Dietrich performed triple bypass surgery on Bernard Schuler. The operation was successful, which was nice for Mr. Schuler. It was also on television, which was nice for America. The operation was carried by at least fifty television stations in the United States, and also by the British Broadcasting Corporation. A two-man panel of narrators (a play-by-play and color man, so to speak) kept viewers informed about what they were seeing. It was not clear as to why this event was televised, but it resulted in transforming both Dr. Dietrich and Mr. Schuler's chest into celebrities. Perhaps because he has seen too many doctor shows on television, Mr. Schuler was uncommonly confident about the outcome of his surgery. "There is no way in hell they are going to lose me on live TV," he said.[2]

As reported with great enthusiasm by both WCBS-TV and WNBC-TV in 1984, the Philadelphia public schools have embarked on an experiment in which children will have their curriculum sung to them. Wearing Walkman equipment, students were shown listening to rock music whose lyrics were about the eight parts of speech. Mr. Jocko Henderson, who thought of this idea, is planning to delight students further by subjecting mathematics and history, as well as English, to the rigors of a rock music format. In fact, this is not Mr. Henderson's idea at all. It was pioneered by the Children's Television Workshop, whose television show *Sesame Street* is an expensive illustration of the idea that education is indistinguishable from entertainment. Nonetheless, Mr. Henderson has a point in his favor. Whereas *Sesame Street* merely attempts to make learning to read a form of light entertainment, the Philadelphia experiment aims to make the classroom itself into a rock concert.

In New Bedford, Massachusetts, a rape trial was televised, to the delight of audiences who could barely tell the difference between the trial and their favorite mid-day soap opera. In Florida, trials of varying degrees of seriousness, including murder, are regularly televised and are considered to be more entertaining than most fictional courtroom dramas. All of this is done in the interests of "public education." For the same high purpose, plans are afoot, it is rumored, to televise confessionals. To be called *Secrets of the Confessional Box,* the program will, of course, carry the warning that some of its material may be offensive to children and therefore parental guidance is suggested.

On a United Airlines flight from Chicago to Vancouver, a stewardess announces that its passengers will play a game. The passenger with the most credit cards will win a bottle of champagne. A man from Boston with twelve credit cards wins. A second game requires the passengers to guess the collective age of the cabin crew. A man from Chicago guesses 128, and wins another bottle of wine. During the second game, the air turns choppy and the Fasten Seat Belt sign goes on. Very few people notice, least of all the cabin crew, who keep up a steady flow of gags on the intercom. When the plane reaches its destination, everyone seems to agree that it's fun to fly from Chicago to Vancouver.

On February 7, 1985, *The New York Times* reported that Professor Charles Pine of Rutgers University (Newark campus) was named Professor of the Year by the Council for the Support and Advancement of Education. In explaining why he has such a great impact on his students, Professor Pine said: "I have some gimmicks I use all the time. If you reach the end of the blackboard, I keep writing on the wall. It always gets a laugh. The way I show what a glass molecule does is to run over to one wall and bounce off it, and run over to the other wall." His students are, perhaps, too young to recall that James Cagney used this "molecule move" to great effect in *Yankee Doodle Dandy.* If I am not mistaken, Donald O'Connor duplicated it in *Singin' in the Rain.* So far as I know, it has been used only once before in a classroom: Hegel tried it several times in demonstrating how the dialectical method works.

The Pennsylvania Amish try to live in isolation from mainstream American culture. Among other things, their religion opposes the veneration of graven images, which means that the Amish are forbidden to see movies or to be photographed. But apparently their religion has not got around to disallowing seeing movies *when* they are being photographed. In the summer of 1984, for example, a Paramount Pictures crew descended upon Lancaster County to film the movie *Witness,* which is about a detective, played by Harrison Ford, who falls in love with an Amish woman. Although the Amish were warned by their church not to interfere with the film makers, it turned out that some Amish welders ran to see the action as soon as their work was done. Other devouts lay in the grass some distance away, and looked down on the set with binoculars. "We read about the movie in the paper," said an Amish woman. "The kids even cut out Harrison Ford's picture." She added: "But it doesn't really matter that much to them. Somebody told us he was in *Star Wars* but that doesn't mean anything to us."[3] The last time a similar conclusion was drawn was when the executive director of the American Association of Blacksmiths remarked that he had read about the automobile but that he was convinced it would have no consequences for the future of his organization.

In the Winter, 1984, issue of the *Official Video Journal* there appears a full-page advertisement for "The Genesis Project." The project aims to convert the Bible into a series of movies. The end-product, to be called *The New Media Bible,* will consist of 225 hours of film and will cost a quarter of a billion dollars. Producer John Heyman, whose credits include *Saturday Night Fever* and *Grease,* is one of the film makers most committed to the project. "Simply stated," he is quoted as saying, "I got hooked on the Bible." The famous Israeli actor Topol, best known for his role as Tevye in *Fiddler on the Roof,* will play the role of Abraham. The advertisement does not say who will star as God but, given the producer's background, there is some concern that it might be John Travolta.

At the commencement exercises at Yale University in 1983, several honorary degrees were awarded, including one to Mother Teresa. As she and other humanitarians and scholars each in turn, received their awards, the audience applauded appropriately but with a slight hint of reserve and impatience, for it wished to give its heart to the final recipient who waited shyly in the wings. As the details of her achievements were being recounted, many people left their seats and surged toward the stage to be closer to the great woman. And when the name Meryl Streep was announced, the audience unleashed a sonic boom of affection to wake the New Haven dead. One man who was present when Bob Hope received his honorary doctorate at another institution said that Dr. Streep's applause surpassed Dr. Hope's. Knowing how to please a crowd as well as anyone, the intellectual leaders at Yale invited Dick Cavett, the talk-show host, to deliver the commencement address the following year. It is rumored that this year, Don Rickles will receive a Doctorate of Humane Letters and Lola Falana will give the commencement address.

Prior to the 1984 presidential elections, the two candidates confronted each other on television in what were called "debates." These events were not in the least like the Lincoln-Douglas debates or anything else that goes by the name. Each candidate was given five minutes to address such questions as, What is (or would be) your policy in Central America? His opposite number was then given one minute for a rebuttal. In such circumstances, complexity, documentation and logic can play no role, and, indeed, on several occasions syntax itself was abandoned entirely. It is no matter. The men were less concerned with giving arguments than with "giving off" impressions, which is what television does best. Post-debate commentary largely avoided any evaluation of the candidates' ideas, since there were none to evaluate. Instead, the debates were conceived as boxing matches, the relevant question being, Who KO'd whom? The answer was determined by the "style" of the men—how they looked, fixed their gaze, smiled, and delivered one-liners. In the second debate, President Reagan got off a swell one-liner when asked a question about his age. The following day, several newspapers indicated that Ron had KO'd Fritz with his joke. Thus, the leader of the free world is chosen by the people in the Age of Television.

What all of this means is that our culture has moved toward a new way of conducting its business, especially its important business. The nature of its discourse is changing as the demarcation line between what is show business and what is not becomes harder to see with each passing day. Our priests and presidents, our surgeons and lawyers, our educators and newscasters need worry less about satisfying the demands of their discipline than the demands of good showmanship. Had Irving Berlin changed one word in the title of his celebrated song, he would have been as prophetic, albeit more terse, as Aldous Huxley. He need only have written, There's No Business But Show Business.

Notes

[1] On July 20, 1984, *The New York Times* reported that the Chinese National Television network had contracted with CBS to broadcast sixty-four hours of CBS programming in China. Contracts with NBC and ABC are sure to follow. One hopes that the Chinese understand that such transactions are of great political consequence. The Gang of Four is as nothing compared with the Gang of Three.

[2] This story was carried by several newspapers, including the *Wisconsin State Journal,* February 24, 1983, Section 4, p. 2.

[3] As quoted in *The New York Times,* June 7, 1984, Section A, p. 20.

Understanding the Text

1. "A news show," Postman asserts, "is a format for entertainment, not for education, reflection or catharsis." Why does he think so? (Identify four reasons.)

2. Why is Postman critical of the "discussion" that followed ABC's airing of *The Day After* in 1983? (Identify two reasons.)

3. The "critical point," Postman says, is that "how television stages the world becomes the model for how the world is properly to be staged." What, exactly, does he mean by this, and why is it a problem?

The Yuckster: Bob Dole, After Politics

John J. Miller

When the people behind *Bartlett's Familiar Quotations* consider whether to put any of Bob Dole's utterances in their next edition—he has none in the current one—they'll have plenty of choices. There's the bitter line from the 1988 GOP primaries, spoken to then-Vice President George Bush: "Stop lying about my record." There's one of the great blunders of recent political history, from the 1976 debate with Walter Mondale: "I figured it up the other day: If we added up the killed and wounded in Democrat wars in this century, it would be about 1.6 million Americans—enough to fill the city of Detroit." A later, self-deprecating quip on this unfortunate statement may itself deserve status as a minor classic: "They told me to go for the jugular, so I did: mine."

Now there's a very late entry: "Easy, boy."

On March 25, during ABC's broadcast of the Oscars, Pepsi unveiled an ad in which belly-baring 19-year-old pop star Britney Spears vamps about shaking her hips, flaunting her cleavage, and singing her tune. Flash to Bob Dole, sitting in an armchair and watching the same commercial. He appears transfixed at the sight of Spears and her come-hither looks. His dog barks. Dole doesn't budge, except to nod and speak two words: "Easy, boy."

It's the sort of double entendre more suited to a cheap sitcom than to a former presidential candidate, and it's hard to imagine, say, Michael Dukakis pulling it off. Dole can, simply because he's universally known not just as a former politician, but as a septuagenarian pitchman for an erection drug.

John J. Miller is a political reporter for the *National Review* and also writes for the *Wall Street Journal,* the *New York Times,* and the *New Criterion.*

What a long way we've come since Dole ran for the White House. Back in 1995, he traveled to Hollywood and delivered a bold speech attacking the entertainment industry for its "mindless violence and loveless sex." It was a fight Dole didn't especially need to pick, and it voiced the belief of millions of Americans that contemporary movies and music pander far too much to people's worst urges. Dole's rhetoric soared, in what remains one of the finest speeches of his career: "The mainstreaming of deviancy must come to an end, but it will only stop when the leaders of the entertainment industry recognize and shoulder their responsibility." "The mainstreaming of deviancy"—that's a nice phrase, and a useful one. So it's too bad that Bob Dole, by portraying a dirty old man in a Pepsi commercial, now embodies a trend he once condemned with such eloquence.

Conservatives never were entirely comfortable with Dole as the Republican nominee—Newt Gingrich once described him as "the tax collector for the welfare state"—but the stoic Kansan nevertheless earned respect on the right for his rugged Midwestern dignity. He was a plainspoken war hero, a gruff member of the Greatest Generation who seemed attractively out of place in the age of Slick Willie. During one of the debates in 1996, Dole even criticized Clinton's manners: "I'm addressing [Clinton] all evening as 'Mr. President,'" he said. "He didn't extend that courtesy to President Bush." Here was a man who probably would have refused to answer the most memorably indecent question of the 1992 presidential campaign: boxers or briefs? Conservatives also admired his loyalty: Dole was capable of resilient partisanship when necessary, and remained faithful to the first President Bush even after they fought through that rough primary in 1988.

Despite this appeal, Dole was not a good presidential candidate. It would have taken a truly exceptional campaign to beat Bill Clinton in 1996, but Dole's effort was worse than lackluster. The one thing most people remember is not that he proposed a tax cut or that he promised to restore character to the Oval Office, but that time he tumbled off the stage in Chico, California

It's hard to believe, then, that Dole has been even worse as an ex-presidential candidate—but it's true. Dole started out playing the good loser, and his shtick worked. He went on David Letterman's show within days of his defeat. "Bob, what have you been doing lately?" asked Letterman. "Apparently not enough," Dole deadpanned. He also showed up on *Saturday Night Live* for a skit with Norm MacDonald, the man who had been impersonating him. They commiserated about their dim futures. Dole said that at least he had a job answering phones at the Red Cross. "My wife pulled some strings," he explained, referring to the fact that Elizabeth Dole was president of the organization. Then he satirized his own penchant for talking about himself in the third person by demonstrating his telephone skills: "Hello, Red Cross. How might Bob Dole direct your call?"

These appearances were funny. They also communicated the fundamentally conservative message that politics isn't everything. As Dole wrote in his recent book, *Great Political Wit* (an amusing collection of one-liners and anecdotes), "I wanted to show that there is indeed life after politics. And that losing an election does not mean losing your sense of humor."

But some of his behavior following the election was a bit unsettling. Dole immediately reneged on what seemed a simple promise, made during his surprise speech announcing he would retire from the Senate: "I will seek the presidency with nothing to fall back on but the judgment of the people, and nowhere to go but the White House or home." By "home," most listeners assumed he meant Kansas, which he had represented in Congress for decades. But it turned out that home really meant the Watergate complex, where he owned a one-bedroom apartment; Kansas was no more Bob Dole's home than Tennessee was Al Gore's.

Next came a slew of commercials. Other losing candidates—Dan Quayle, Geraldine Ferraro, Mario Cuomo—had made commercials, but for Dole it amounted to a new career. First was an ad for Air France, featuring Dole's picture under the caption, "Not doing anything?" Then there was one for Visa, which set Dole in what seemed to be a "homecoming" parade in Russell, Kansas. (It was actually shot in a couple of Texas towns.) Dole winds up in a local store, tries to make a purchase, and is asked for ID. "I just can't win!" he cracks. Dole also appeared in ads for Dunkin' Donuts and Target. He gave much of his personal proceeds to charity, yet there was still something unseemly about it all. Losing with a smile is one thing; repeatedly poking fun at your loss—in a campaign to which thousands of people anonymously devoted themselves because they seriously believed in a man and his ideas—is another. Nowadays Dole is more likely to be seen on Comedy Central's *Daily Show* than on *Meet the Press*. He's not an elder statesman so much as an aging comic.

He is best known, of course, as a poster boy for Viagra. Impotence is surely a difficult condition, and one of the primary hurdles facing men who might benefit from the drug is the awkwardness of asking for a prescription. The whole object of Viagra's ongoing ad campaign is to destigmatize the product. As Dole himself said in his commercial, "You know, it's a little embarrassing to talk about E.D. [erectile dysfunction], but it's so important to millions of men and their partners that I decided to talk about it publicly." It's a little embarrassing to listen to Bob Dole talk about it publicly. Frankly, I'd rather know whether he wears boxers or briefs. And what's this business about men and their "partners"? Would it be too judgmental and exclusionary simply to say "wives"? Some things apparently could benefit from restigmatizing.

Bob Dole once knew the value of a good stigma. "Those who cultivate moral confusion for profit should understand this," he warned in his Hollywood speech, before turning positively Churchillian. "We will name their names and shame them as they deserve to be shamed. We will contest them for the heart and soul of every child, in every neighborhood. If we refuse to condemn evil, it is not tolerance but surrender. And we will never surrender."

At least not until we can appear in a Pepsi commercial with Britney Spears.

Understanding the Text

1. Miller praises several passages from Bob Dole's 1995 campaign speech. What was the subject of that speech?

2. Why do you think Miller quotes those passages in his essay?

3. Since he lost the 1996 presidential election, what has Bob Dole become best known for? What is Miller's response to this?

Power of Ads to Shape News

Kathleen Hall Jamieson

In October 1980 Citizens' Party candidate Barry Commoner, who would garner a quarter of a million votes in the general election, bought air time for a radio commercial that opened with the word "Bullshit!" As the ad itself admitted, it had used that word to secure news coverage for a campaign that had been ignored by the press. ABC complied (October 15, 1980). CBS and NBC ignored the ad. By getting access to ABC network news time, Commoner's ad producer Bill Zimmerman parlayed a $5000 radio buy into free television attention previously denied that campaign. But the coverage ABC gave the ad was hardly a producer's dream. Throughout, Susan King, the network reporter, uses every available moment to convey her personal distaste and that of the network for the ad.

> *King:* "Political commercials you hear on the radio are broadcast from network studios like this one at ABC in New York. Later this month ABC will be forced to carry the Citizens' Party presidential ad which ran across the country yesterday at CBS and NBC radio and which begins with the unprecedented use of vulgarity."
>
> *Ad:* "Bullshit. What? Reagan and Anderson— it's all bullshit."
>
> *King:* "Shocked? Many listeners were when they heard the ad and complained to their local radio station, but when it comes to political advertising, the candidate controls. By law the studio, or in this case the network, is bound to air the politician's message if he is involved in the ad, no matter what the message says."

Kathleen Hall Jamieson is a professor of communication and former dean of the Annenberg School of Communication at the University of Pennsylvania. She is one of the nation's leading authorities on political campaigning and advertising and the author of numerous scholarly articles on these subjects. She also is the author of fifteen books, including *unSpun: Finding Facts in a World of Disinformation* (2007), *The Press Effect: Politicians, Journalists and the Stories that Shape the Political World* (2003), *Dirty Politics: Deception, Distraction and Democracy* (1992), and *Presidential Debates: The Challenge of Creating an Informed Electorate* (1988). She also is a frequent guest on television and radio programs.

From *Dirty Politics: Deception, Distraction, and Democracy* by Kathleen Hall Jamieson, copyright © 1993 by Kathleen Hall Jamieson. Used by permission of Oxford University Press, Inc.

An expert then agrees that the law requires airing bona fide candidate ads if the candidate's picture appears or his voice is heard. [The "expert" should have added that this requirement goes into effect only when the station has aired an ad for any candidate for that office.]

> *King:* "Section 315 of the Federal Communications Act dealing with political commercials says, 'The licensee shall have no power of censorship over the material broadcast.'"
> *Commoner:* "I think the American public is mature enough to be able to withstand certain messages and register their reaction to that at the polls."

A spokesperson for Commoner decries a situation that dictates that "the only way we can attract attention is to remind people that this campaign is a hollow sham." King closes by noting that the few stations that refused the ad were being sued by the Citizens' Party. The piece ends with King saying, "No matter how uncomfortable the listener is, the candidate has the last word."

News reporting can provide a frame through which viewers understand ads. Conventional campaign wisdom holds that news sets the context for ads. If the news accounts are inconsistent with the ad, the power of the ad is diminished. When the two are consistent, the power of both is magnified. But news can only reframe ads if reporters question the legitimacy of their claims, point out the false inferences that they invite, and so on. Without such reframing by reporters, campaign ads have the potential to shape the visual and verbal language of news, and in recent campaigns they have been increasingly successful.

Eleven years after the Commoner ad aired, network norms for coverage had changed. On September 4, 1991, CBS, NBC, ABC, and CNN news stories all carried an excerpt from a Conservative Victory Committee ad urging Senate confirmation of Supreme Court nominee Clarence Thomas and attacking the integrity of his likely opponents including one who was not even on the Senate Judiciary Committee.

As a result, viewers saw and heard content they would not otherwise have been exposed to on these news programs. "Who will judge the judge?" asked a segment of the ad. "How many of these liberal Democrats could themselves pass ethical scrutiny?" [Pictures of Alan Cranston, Joseph Biden, and Edward Kennedy are shown.] As the charges unfold, they are repeated in print on the screen. "Ted Kennedy, suspended from Harvard for cheating, left the scene of the accident at Chappaquiddick where Mary Jo Kopechne died" [a headline from the *Washington Star* appears] "and this year Palm Beach [on screen, a photo of the front page of the *New York Post* showing a picture of Kennedy in casual wear and the headline "Teddy's Sexy Romp."] "Joseph Biden, found guilty of plagiarism during his presidential campaign. Alan Cranston, implicated in the Keating Five S&L scandal. Whose values should be on the Supreme Court? Clarence Thomas's or Ted Kennedy's" [The headline "Teddy's Sexy Romp" with the attached photo is juxtaposed with a photo of Thomas].

With the exception of CNN's *Crossfire,* the news broadcasts did not focus on the accuracy or fairness of the attacks but rather on the potential impact of the campaign on the Thomas hearings. A small Conservative group with a membership of 80,000 had managed to garner over a million dollars' worth of network time with an ad that cost $20,000 to produce and just under $40,000 to air on Fox and CNN in the Washington, D.C., area.

In the process of relaying the controversial segments of the ad to their viewers, the networks legitimized the unsupported inference that Kennedy had either engaged in questionable sexual behavior or, worse, was an accomplice in the alleged rape of a young woman by his nephew at the Kennedy Palm Beach home. The headline in the *New York Post* referred to a later discredited report that Kennedy, wearing only an undershirt, had chased a young woman around the Palm Beach residence. As corrected, the report revealed that the Senator had simply appeared in a living room in which a young woman was talking with Kennedy's son. The senator was at the time wearing a nightshirt that went down to his knees.

As the controversy about the ad raged, the *New York Times* ran a still from the ad on its front page. Where in 1980 two of the three networks ignored the Commoner ad, in 1991 all four networks centered coverage on the Conservative ad. Where the frame created by ABC for the Commoner ad distanced the network from it and treated it negatively, coverage of the anti-Biden, -Cranston, -Kennedy ad focused on its strategy and likely outcome.

But what the ABC coverage of 1980 and the 1991 coverage of the Thomas ad have in common is also important. Neither ABC in 1980 nor any of the networks in 1991 examined the legitimacy of the ads' claims. The Commoner ad alleged that there were no substantive differences among the major party candidates; the Conservative Victory Fund ad posited that the morality of those who would determine the qualifications of a Supreme Court nominee was a legitimate subject of inquiry. Until a subsequent charge of sexual harassment surfaced, no questions about Thomas's morality had been publicly raised by anyone.

News can provide a frame through which viewers are invited to see an ad. But 1988 was the year in which ads began routinely to contextualize news. As many have argued, in 1988 the Republicans defined the campaign terrain for Dukakis, for the press, and for voters. Ads played an important role in the Republicans' ability to set this agenda. To the extent that the spots succeeded and their images were used as visual illustration of the power of the Bush appeals, ads were contextualizing news.

Ads also contextualized news in a second sense. After a viewer has seen the same ad many times, exposure to a small segment of it can evoke the whole ad. My work with focus groups across a twenty-year period suggests that unless the verbal message is highly salient (e.g., the mention of your profession in the ad), reinforced by print on the screen, or repeatedly uttered in the ad, it is not until the third exposure to a typical production ad that the typical viewer is able to recall a substantial amount of the ad's spoken content.

But weeks after exposure to a single ad image, viewers can accurately recall whether or not they have seen it before. The discussion of whether pictures dominate words or words pictures is confused by its assumptions that one invariably dominates the other, that music plays no role in cueing recall, and that the impact of each remains the same with repeated exposure.[1]

Ads have an additional recall advantage over news. Most ads are "bedded" in a sound track that invites emotions consistent with the ad's message. So, for example, the musical backtrack for an ad about the candidate's accomplishments is upbeat and often patriotic. When a segment of the ad airs in news, its soundtrack is usually preserved. Lee Greenwood's "I'm Proud to Be an American" hitchhiked into network news in 1984 when the Reagan ads incorporating it were clipped into broadcast news stories. Although network news opens and closes with theme music, the news segments themselves aren't musically scored.

Moreover, the announcer's voice on the ad is usually more resonant than the reporter's. These factors increase the power of the embedded ad segment and dampen the corrective words spoken by the reporter.

Repeated exposure increases the likelihood that the words and pictures will be remembered. When a segment from a remembered ad is then shown on news, two things happen. First, if the segment is able to function synecdochically for the whole ad, the viewer will recall a larger part of the ad than that shown. Second, the audio that is likely to be remembered is not the reporter's words about the ad but rather some form of the audio from the ad itself.

ADS CAN SHAPE THE VISUAL AND VERBAL LANGUAGE OF NEWS

Critics from Coleridge to Kenneth Burke have recognized the power of naming. For Coleridge, a word doesn't "convey merely what a certain thing is, but the very passion and all the circumstances which were conceived as *constituting* the perception of the thing by the person who used the word."[2] One might paraphrase Burke to say that language does our thinking for us.[3] Along these lines, if the language of a candidate's ads infuses the vocabulary of reporters, the candidate has obtained a significant advantage.

In the 1988 general election the Republicans' ads, reinforced by news coverage of speeches and debates, created a pro-Bush vocabulary for reporters. Others had done so, although with less impact, before. In 1976 the Ford campaign succeeded in getting reporters to adopt the language of its most powerful attack ads. Repeatedly, Carter was faced by press queries about being or being perceived to be "wishy-washy on the issues."

In 1980 Carter achieved the same effect when the press accepted the question raised in Democratic ads and speeches, "Is Reagan too reckless to be president?" "Aides acknowledge that Reagan is having trouble shaking the perception that he might be militarily reckless," noted Barry Serafin (ABC, October 20, 1980). "Critics say his proposals border on recklessness," noted John McWethy (ABC, October 28, 1980). So, for example, after the Carter-Reagan debate, Barry Serafin (ABC, October 31, 1980) commented that Reagan's "advisers think that in his debate with Mr. Carter, he went a long way toward assuring a big audience that he would not be reckless." In their only debate, Reagan was able to dispatch the reckless image more by manner than matter. "There you go again" just aren't the words Hollywood usually scripts for Dr. Strangelove.

But where in these earlier campaigns, one side or the other occasionally enticed the press into embracing one of its words or phrases, in 1988 the Bush campaign managed to insinuate an entire vocabulary about the campaign into press coverage. Reporting on the Dukakis record on crime is illustrative. Here the Republicans secured the complicity of the press in renaming convicted murderer William Horton, in redefining the relationship between Horton's Maryland victims, in adopting such words as "torture" and "terrorize" to describe his actions while on furlough, in defining the furlough program's purpose as dispensing "weekend passes," and in talking of the policy as a "revolving door." Each of these acts of naming biased the discussion against Dukakis. Each was inaccurate. To the extent that the Republicans were able to put this language in place, however, they demonstrated the power of ads, reinforced by candidate speeches and campaign hype, to contextualize news.

Although his given name is William, he calls himself William, court records cite him as William, a July 1988 *Reader's Digest* article identifies him as William J. Horton, Jr.,[4] and press reports before the Republican ad and speech blitz name him "William," the Bush campaign and its supporting PACs identified the furloughed convict as "Willie" Horton. Even the crusading anti-Dukakis newspaper that won a Pulitzer Prize for its exposé on the furlough program consistently identifies Horton as William Horton or William Horton, Jr. When the Maryland man stabbed by the furloughed convict contacted the Lawrence *Eagle-Tribune* reporter, he too referred to Horton as William Horton.[5] In his account of the attack in the PAC ad, however, that man, Clifford Barnes, instead identifies the convict as "Willie" Horton.

One might trace the familiar "Willie" to the naming practices of slavemasters, to our patterns of talk about gangsters, or to the sort of benign paternalism that afflicts adults around small children. But whatever its origin, when discussing murder, kidnapping, and rape "Willie" summons more sinister images of criminality than does William. After all, it wasn't J. Eddie Hoover who hunted down Albert (or was it Alfred?) Capone. And during his trial, the person to that point known as Willie Smith was identified by family and attorney as either William or

Will. After his acquittal on charges of rape, the family reverted to the name by which he had been known before.

The PAC ad titled "Weekend Prison Passes" as well as the PAC ads featuring Horton's victims all refer to him as "*Willie* Horton." When his mug shot appears on the screen of "Weekend Prison Passes," print under it reads "Willie Horton." Reporters reduced Dukakis on crime to the Republican sculpted image of "Willie Horton." In news reports, "*Willie*" Horton's name was mentioned more often by reporters than by George Bush or any of his representatives. Use of dramatic, coherent narrative increases the likelihood of recall.[6] Once the Horton narrative was embedded in public consciousness, mention of his name should have been sufficient to evoke the entire story.

By the campaign's end, even the Democratic candidates had accepted the Republican identification of Horton. (Bentsen in Rather interview, CBS, October 26, 1988; Dukakis interview with Rather, October 27, 1988; Dukakis in interview with Jennings, November 9, 1988). The most prominent exception occurred before Horton became a stock feature in the Bush stump speech and the subject of PAC ads. On July 8, 1988, in the *Washington Post* Richard Cohen wrote about "*William* Horton's Furlough."

The schizophrenic labeling by the *New York Times* seemed to invite a Woody Allen to shout that the czar and the tsar were the same person. An editorial on June 30, 1988, labels Horton "Willie Horton" as do articles on October 3 and 21. Yet pieces by Robin Toner on July 5 and Martin Tolchin on October 12 refer to him as "William R. Horton." In Tolchin's article, it is Clifford Barnes who refers to Horton as "Willie Horton."[7] The difference between the two sets of articles appears to be that "Willie Horton" is written about by anonymous reporters tasked with inside reporting and given filler space. By contrast, "issue" pieces carrying bylines write of "William Horton." The contrast raises the unconfirmed possibility that the more contact a reporter had with Bush campaign insiders, the more likely the use of "Willie." The hypothesis falters on the editorial presumably written by someone safely anchored to a desk in New York.

In an October 10, 1988, *New York Times* piece, Horton is initially tagged "Willie" and then accorded "Mr. Horton," the *Times'* usual mode of address. "Clifford Barnes is making a radio commercial—to the delight of George Bush and the concern of Michael Dukakis," says the report. "More than a year ago, Mr. Barnes and his wife [*note:* she wasn't his wife at the time; they were engaged and living together], Angela, were *viciously* attacked in their suburban Maryland home by *Willie* Horton, who had fled Massachusetts while out of prison under that state's furlough program. Mr. Horton broke into their home, *slashed* Mr. Barnes with a knife, and raped Angela Barnes. *Mr. Horton* is now serving two life sentences plus 85 years in prison for the attack. Vice President Bush repeatedly cites the attack and Mr. Dukakis's support for the furlough program to charge that his rival is soft on crime. Mr. Barnes will recount his grim experience in a radio ad for a pro-George Bush group in California, the Committee for the Presidency." About the *Times'* naming of Horton, one *New York Times* reporter observed, "Once when an editor changed his name to William, I argued that no one would know who I was talking about [if he weren't called 'Willie']."

The Republicans also controlled the language that characterized the furlough program itself. The Bush furlough ad describes Dukakis's policy as giving "*weekend furloughs to first-degree murderers.*" The PAC ad titled "Weekend Passes" shows pictures of Bush, Dukakis, and Horton as it claims that Dukakis "allowed first-degree murderers to have *weekend passes* from prison. . . . Horton received ten *weekend passes* [a statement reprinted on the screen]. . . ." The ad is tagged "*Weekend prison passes:* Dukakis on crime" (emphasis added).

The press adopted the phrases "weekend furloughs" and "weekend passes" from the Republican speeches and ads that in turn located them in the Lawrence *Eagle-Tribune.* The phrases are inaccurate. Furloughs in Massachusetts ranged from one to seventy-four hours in 1987 and from one to 170 hours in 1986[8] and furloughs could be granted for any day or days of the week. In 1987, the median number of hours of leave per furlough was 19, five less than a full day and 29 less than a weekend. Horton's approved 48-hour furlough began on Friday, June 6, 1986, which means he should have returned to prison while most of us were still enjoying what we usually define as a weekend.

Bush reinforced the notion that these were weekend events by averring that he says to criminals "Make my day!" while Dukakis says "Have a nice weekend." "Weekend" suggests that the furloughs occur frequently when in fact in 1988 as in 1986 a prisoner is permitted no furloughs for the first half of his or her sentence and in 1988 may be furloughed only in the final three years before eligibility for parole or release.[9] In April 1988, Dukakis signed a bill ending furloughs for those who once were first-degree murderers not eligible for parole.

Weekend is a time for recreation. This association suggests that the assault and rapes were leisure activities for the prisoners. Bush implied as much when he asked those in his audience to question Dukakis why he had let "murderers out on vacation" (June speech to Illinois Republican Convention in Springfield).

The Bush furlough ad is titled "Revolving Door" and speaks of Dukakis's "revolving door prison policy." Although the visual in the ad itself shows not a revolving door but a turnstile, reporters also adopted the Republican announcer's characterization of the program as a "revolving door" policy. So, for example, Dan Rather asked the Democratic vice presidential nominee "[C]an't a person, or can a person, be deeply concerned about *revolving-door justice* and laxity toward criminals, even when the criminal happens to be someone who is black and still not be a racist?" (CBS, October 26, 1988).

In describing the ad, reporters adopted the Bush language as well. In an article examining inaccuracies in the ads of both campaigns, the *Washington Post's* Lloyd Grove describes "[A]nother Bush campaign commercial featuring hard-eyed men in prison garb streaming through a *revolving door*" (*Washington Post,* October 31, 1988, p. A8).

So clear was the identification that reporters quote viewers using it. In Texas Bill Cockerill described the ad to a *New York Times* reporter as "the revolving door commercial, implying that they come out as fast as they go in" (*New York Times,* October 22, 1988).[10] Despite the use of the words "turnstile or gate" in all questions to our Texas focus groups, 36 percent of respondents referred to the "furlough ad" as the "revolving door ad."

Here is an instance of the complexity of the visual-verbal relationship. The repeated use of the phrase "revolving door" couples with repeated viewing of the image of the circling actors as convicts to situate the visual-verbal link in memory. "Revolving door" too suggests a frequency and casualness in the administration of the furlough program that did not characterize the Massachusetts system.

From PAC ads made by Horton's victims, reporters adopted the words "slashed," "brutally," "terrorized," and "tortured." "For twelve hours I was beaten, slashed, and terrorized," says Clifford Barnes, "and my wife Angie was brutally raped." "Horton went on to rape and torture others," says the sister of the man killed by Horton. Bush helped set the language in place. On June 24, he stated, "In no other state would a cold-blooded murderer like *Willie* Horton have been set free to *terrorize* innocent people" (emphasis added).

"Slashed," "terrorized," and "tortured" are not the words usually used by reporters to characterize crime. Nor was it the language first used by the national press to describe Horton's actions. Before the furloughs became a campaign issue, on December 2, 1987, CBS aired a segment that "took a hard look today at a standard procedure for many of the nation's prisons. Forty-five states," says Rather, "offer furlough programs which release inmates from prison for limited times to see how they handle freedom." The language of the correspondent is the factual, calm, descriptive language characteristic of crime reporting in network news. "William Horton did strike again in this Maryland house where Cliff and Angela Barnes lived. He held them hostage for 12 hours. Horton raped her twice, tied her husband up in the basement and stabbed him 22 times." But by June 26 (Adams) and July 20 (Stahl), CBS reporters were calling Horton "Willie" and adopting the tabloid-like language of torture and terror.

Once the Republican language was in place, it became the optic through which the print media saw and invited us to see Horton's actions as well. The *Washington Post* favored the word "terrorized" (October 22, 1988; October 25, 1988; June 23, 1988, "terror"), as did columnist Tom Wicker (*New York Times,* June 24, 1988). *Newsweek* preferred to label "*Willie* Horton" "the Massachusetts murderer who *tortured* a Maryland couple" (October 31, 1988, p. 16). The *New York Times,* which on July 5 described "William Horton" as "a convicted murderer" who "broke into the couple's home, bound and stabbed Mr. Barnes and raped his wife" by mid-October had "*Willie* Horton" "viciously" attacking and also adopted Barnes's word "*slashed* with a knife" (*New York Times,* October 10, 1988, "Convict's Victim Makes an Ad" [emphasis added]).

Academics also embraced the Republican language. "The furlough program was empha-sized," writes journalism professor David Myers, "because *Willie* Horton, a black man who had been convicted of first-degree murder, had escaped to Maryland on a *weekend pass,* where he *brutalized* a white man and raped his fiancée."[11]

As interesting is the fact that when offered two different constructions of the relationship of the couple assaulted by Horton, press reports adopt the more incendiary of the two until late in the campaign. At the time of the Horton attack, Clifford Barnes and his fiancée were living together. The first PAC ad to air on the topic says accurately that Horton "kidnapped a young couple, stabbing the man and repeatedly [twice] raping his *girlfriend.*"[12] That ad began airing September 9. On October 20 a second PAC ad is aired in California. This spot features Clifford Barnes, who is now married to the woman who was his fiancée at the time of the attack by Horton. "My wife Angie was brutally raped," says Barnes.

The sources that identify "Angie" as Barnes's "wife" at the time of the attack include CBS (December 1987), Cohen in the *Washington Post,* Holman of *MacNeil/Lehrer,* and Toner in the *New York Times.* Although in an October 23 ABC report, Joe Bergantino identifies Barnes as her "boyfriend," two days later ABC's Britt Hume identifies Barnes as her husband (October 25, 1988). On NBC (October 28, 1988), this identification was reinforced in what I define as a "newsad," a segment of news that might as well have been paid candidate advertising:

> *Ken Bode:* "George Bush was here [California] again today. Again talking about crime."
> *Bush:* "I believe in safe neighborhoods, and I say I believe it is time for America to take back our streets."
> *Bode:* "Like everywhere else the Democrats have been on the defensive about crime. Willie Horton's victims made a campaign commercial."
> *Cliff Barnes in ad clip:* "For twelve hours I was beaten, slashed, and terrorized, and my wife Angie was brutally raped."
> *Bode:* "But mostly, Bush's tough talk on crime works, because it fits with what Californians see on their news each day."
> *Man:* "When you have gang murders in the headlines, day after day, I think the voters understand that there is only one candidate in this race who is truly tough on crime. Only one candidate for President who really supports the death penalty."

My final claim is that the Republican use of Horton shaped the visual portrayal of crime in network news in ways that reinforced the mistaken assumption that violent crime is dispro-portionately committed by blacks, disproportionately committed by black perpetrators against white victims, and disproportionately the activity of black males against white females. In other words, Republican use of Horton shaped the visuals in 1988 network crime coverage in a way that underscored the Bush message.

James Devitt and I have systematically examined the way in which alleged criminals are portrayed in network news from 1985 to 1989. In 911 scenes of alleged criminals in 530 network news stories, blacks are proportionately more likely than whites to be shown restrained and in actual mug shots—the two visuals shown in the Horton PAC ads. Robert Entman has found the same pattern in local news.[13]

I suspect that this disproportionate exposure to black males in mug shots increases the telegraphic power of the use of the Horton mug shot in the PAC ads. This tendency is then magnified at a statistically significant level in coverage of crime as a 1988 campaign issue ($p = .0011$). This finding raises the question: What subtle chain of inferences or visceral responses might be invited by Senator Jesse Helms's showing of a closeup still photo of his opponent Harvey Gantt?

Our data also provide a baseline telling us how often blacks are likely to appear as "alleged criminals" in news and what visual forms this representation will take. By comparing the appearance of blacks as alleged criminals in crime stories from 1985 to 1989 with appearance in stories about the issue of crime in the 1988 general election, we can determine whether the crime stories of 1988 differed significantly from earlier norms. They do. The increase in the proportion of blacks identified or shown as criminals in 1988 general election stories about crime is statistically significant ($p =.0139$). Moreover, the number of female victims per news story doubled in 1988 stories about crime.

Just as the Bush campaign verbally primed reporters' discussion of crime, so too the issue of Horton subtly primed producers and editors to include more blacks in their covering shots showing presumed criminals. The most egregious example of this occurred October 31, 1988 on ABC. The reporter was Ken Kashiwahara. All of the presumed criminals but one are black or Hispanic. All of those who say that they are afraid are white. Most are women.

To portray a black male who "killed" one white male, stabbed a second, and raped a white woman as a typical criminal is inaccurate. Blacks run a greater risk of forcible rape, robbery, and aggravated assault than whites. Low-income individuals are the most likely victims of violent crime. Men are more likely than women to be the victims of violence, blacks more often than whites.[14] FBI statistics confirm that, unlike robbery, rape and murder in the United States are primarily intraracial not interracial phenomena. In 1988, for example, 11.3 percent of reported rapes involved a black rapist and a white victim.[15]

I do not intend to minimize Thomas and Mary Edsall's claims that a higher percent of the crime committed by blacks is interracial and that in the categories of assault and robbery more than half of the robberies committed by blacks have white victims.[16] Rather, my point is that raising the fear of whites that they are likely to be murdered or raped by blacks is unjustified. It is racist to identify William Horton's actions as somehow typical, as George Bush did when he said that the Horton case had "come to symbolize, and represent . . . the misguided outlook of my opponent."

Moreover, disproportionate portrayal of blacks as criminals plays on racial fears. When discussion of crime in network news occurs in segments in which blacks are visually cast in disproportion as criminals, the news stories themselves are priming both a pro-Bush and a racist response.

In 1988 the power of the Republican campaign to export the visual and verbal language of its ads to news was indicative of a change in the relationship between news and political advertising. Where news once contextualized ads, visually evocative and easily edited oppositional ads backed by reinforcing candidate speeches and pseudo-events now have the capacity to shape the language and pictures of news.

Notes

[1] This conclusion is consistent with that of scholarship about recall of advertising and of television. Cf. D. S. Hayes and S. Pingree, "Television's Influence on Social Reality," in D. Pearl and J. Lazar, *Television and Behavior* (Washington, D.C.: U.S. Government Printing Office, 1982), 224–47; D. S. Hayes and D. W. Birnbaum, "Preschoolers' Retention of Televised Events: Is a Picture Worth a Thousand Words?" *Developmental Psychology* 16 (1980), 410–16; D. S. Hayes, B. E. Chemelaki, and D. W. Birnbaum, "Young Children's Incidental Retention of Televised Events," *Developmental Psychology* 17 (1981), 230–32; K. Pezdek and E. F. Hartman, "Children's Television Viewing: Attention and Comprehension of Auditory Versus Visual Information," *Child Development* 54 (1983), 1015–23.

The evidence does not suggest that the visual interferes with comprehension of the audio, however. Cf. D. R. Rolandelli, "Children and Television: The Visual Superiority Effect Reconsidered," *Journal of Broadcasting and Electronic Media* 33 (1989), 69–81; C. Hoffner, J. Cantor, and E. Thorson, "Children's Responses to Conflicting Auditory and Visual Features of a Televised Narrative," *Human Communication Research* 16:2, (1989), 256–78. There is evidence that the visual imagery of television changes the processing of audio. Cf. J. Beagles-Roos and I. Gat, "Specific Impact of Radio and Television on Children's Story Comprehension," *Journal of Educational Psychology* 75 (1983), 128–35.

Some have argued that Iyengar and Kinder's research calls the impact of vivid communication into question. Their summary of the existing scholarly literature states that "When vividness is defined as the contrast between personalized, case history information and abstract statistical information, the vividness hypothesis is supported every time" (p. 35). The structure of their chapter seems to suggest that they then take issue with this consensus. Yet they conclude that "Our results do not argue against vividness effects in general; they indicate only that dramatic vignettes of personal suffering do not enhance agenda setting" (p. 46). See S. Iyengar and D. Kinder, *News that Matters* (Chicago: University of Chicago Press, 1987).

Additional information on verbal/visual processing can be found in Laura M. Buchholz and Robert E. Smith, "The Role of Consumer Involvement in Determining Cognitive Response to Broadcast Advertising," *Journal of Advertising* 20:1 (1991), 4–17, and Julie Edell and Kevin Lane Keller, "The Information Processing of Coordinated Media Campaigns," *Journal of Marketing Research* 26 (May 1989), 149–63.

[2] Samuel Taylor Coleridge, *Shakespeare Criticism,* Middleton Raysor, ed. (London: Dutton, 1907).

[3] Cf. *The Philosophy of Literary Form,* 3rd ed. (Berkeley: University of California Press, 1973), 3 ff.

[4] Robert James Bidinotto, "Getting Away With Murder," *Reader's Digest* 133 (July 1988), 57–63.

[5] Susan Forrest, "How 12 Hours Shattered Two Lives," *Lawrence Eagle-Tribune,* August 16, 1987.

[6] See N. S. Johnson and J. M. Mandler, "A Tale of Two Structures: Underlying and Surface Forms in Stories," *Poetics* 9 (1980), 51–86.

[7] "Furloughs From Common Sense," *New York Times,* June 30, 1988, A22; Robin Toner, "Prison Furloughs in Massachusetts Threaten Dukakis Record on Crime," *New York Times,* July 5, 1988, B5.

[8] "1987 Annual Statistical Report of the Furlough Program," Massachusetts Department of Correction, December 1988, 6.

[9] 103CMR-157. February 2, 1990, 3.

[10] Cf. Gerald Boyd, "Bush's Attack on Crime Appeals to the Emotions," *New York Times,* October 11, 1988, 12: "In addition, Mr. Bush's campaign has aired television commercials that portray the prison system in Massachusetts, where Mr. Dukakis is the Governor, as a revolving door that releases inmates on weekend passes." Gerald Boyd "Despite Vow to be 'Gentler,' Bush Stays on Attack," *New York Times,* October 29, 1988, 8: "Mr. Fuller said that although Mr. Bush hoped to end the campaign on a 'positive note,' there were no plans to remove television commercials like the one that accuses Mr. Dukakis of operating the Massachusetts prison program as a 'revolving door.'"

[11] *The Media in the 1984 and 1988 Presidential Campaigns,* Guido H. Stempel III and John W. Windhauser, eds. (New York: Greenwood Press, 1991), 169. Note the tacit assumption that because the man is white, his fiancée must be white as well.

[12] "Weekend Prison Passes," produced by Larry McCarthy for Americans for Bush.

[13] Entman, 30.

[14] *Sourcebook,* 1988, 298. Table 3.17.

[15] U.S. Dept. of Justice *"Criminal Victimization in the United States, 1988."* December 1990. NCJ-122024. Table 43.

[16] Edsall and Edsall, *Chain Reaction,* 236.

Understanding the Text

1. According to Jamieson, when television news programs "analyze" a political ad on the air, what do they typically focus upon, and what do they ignore?

2. According to Jamieson, in what ways do ads "shape news"? (Identify and discuss two.)

3. What, according to Jamieson, were some of the inaccuracies of the Willie Horton ad? (Identify and discuss two.)

Trout or Hamburger: Politics and Telemythology

Michael Schudson

Has television taken over the practice of American politics? Have cynically manipulated images and sound bites mesmerized the American public? Have politicians bypassed the citizen's rational decision-making process with a shortcut to some image center in the brain that values appearance over substance, flash over philosophy? In American politics today, do the eyes have it?

Anyone listening to political commentary in any recent election would surely answer yes. The airwaves teem with political commercials. The newspapers overflow with commentary about the broadcast spots. And then new TV spots incorporate the print commentary about the old spots. At times, candidates and voters seem to be on the sidelines, passively observing the media consultants and ad agencies on the playing field.

As soon as the election is over, however, talk about the brilliance or mendacity of 30-second demagoguery fades. On the day before the election, every politician is a candidate, and takes a candidate's obsessive interest in every little bit of good or harm that might come from advertising. On the day after there are only winning candidates, glad to be in office, and losers, seeking some kind of solace in a bad time. The losers seem to change quickly from activists to philosophers, from political strategists to political scientists. Thus in 1990 Dianne Feinstein's campaign manager, Duane Garrett, was suddenly reminding people that for twenty-five years (with the exception of 1974, the Watergate year) California voted Republican for president and governor—so what else could one

Michael Schudson is a professor of communications and sociology at the University of California at San Diego. He is one of the nation's leading authorities on the history and sociology of the media, which he has explored in a number of books, including *The Sociology of News* (2003), *The Power of News* (1995), *Advertising, The Uneasy Persuasion* (1984), and *Discovering the News: A Social History of American Newspapers* (1978). He also writes about consumerism, citizenship, and public culture, and has published numerous articles and reviews in a wide range of journals and magazines.

From *Tikkun Magazine*, Vol. 6, No. 1, March/April 1991 by Michael Schudson. Copyright © 1995 by Tikkun Magazine. Reprinted by permission.

expect in 1990? In his post-election assessment, the story was not that Feinstein lost but that she came as close as she did.

Did Feinstein's TV spots make a difference? Did Paul Wellstone's in Minnesota? Or Jesse Helms's in North Carolina? The question is still important, but it is notoriously elusive. Despite all the attention that the press has lavished on political commercials, it is no simple task to evaluate their potency, as opposed to observing their ubiquity and decrying their negativity. Even newspaper "truth box" commentaries, which began in 1990 to monitor the accuracy of political ads on television, have been criticized for focusing on the commercials' explicit claims rather than their visual imagery—for reading television as if it were radio and failing to understand the overwhelming power of the image.

But is the image overpowering? Does the image conquer all in political television? Even that apparently safe assumption can be questioned.

Take, for instance, the story told by the media critic Michael Arlen in *Thirty Seconds* about the making of an AT&T "Reach Out and Touch Someone" commercial.[1] In one version of the commercial, a group of men have gone off to a rural retreat for a weekend of fishing. The weekend is a disaster; it is pouring rain the whole time. We see the men huddled in their cabin in the woods, cooking hamburgers, while one of them talks to friends back home, singing the praises of their manly adventure. The man on the phone is staring into a frying pan full of hamburgers while he says into the receiver, "Boy, you should see the great trout we've got cooking here." When test audiences were asked what the men were cooking for dinner, they replied overwhelmingly—trout. One of the advertising executives in charge of the project comments:

> I have to tell you we were very discouraged. Some of our guys were even talking of junking the commercial, which was a good one, with a nice humorous flow to it. Well, we ended up making it, but what we had to do was, when we came to that segment, we put the camera almost inside the frying pan, and in the frying pan we put huge, crude chunks of hamburger that were almost red. I mean, just about all you could see was raw meat. This time, when we took it to the audience, it tested OK. That is, most of the test audience—though, in fact, still not everybody— finally said "hamburger."

The trout/hamburger story has not made its way into the common culture of media consulting, political journalism, or academic criticism. The ability of verbal cues to trump the visual is forgotten, while the contrary lesson, that a picture overrides ten thousand words, is regularly retold.

A current favorite is the story of the Lesley Stahl four-and-a-half-minute piece that CBS ran during the 1984 presidential campaign. Its subject was how the White House staged events for Ronald Reagan and manipulated the press, especially television. Stahl later said that a White House official called her soon after the piece aired and said he'd loved it. "How could you?" she responded. He said, "Haven't you figured it out yet? The public doesn't pay any attention to what you say. They just look at the pictures." Stahl, on reflection—but not, I think, on very much reflection—came to believe that the White House was probably right: all she had done was to assemble, free of charge, a Republican campaign film, a wonderful montage of Reagan appearing in upbeat scenes.

In the world of media criticism and political consulting, the Stahl story is presented as powerful evidence of the triumph of pictures over words and emotion over rationality in American politics. It is a major piece of evidence for *New York Times* reporter Hedrick Smith's conclusion that the eye is more powerful than the ear in American politics; it opens journalist Martin Schram's account of television in the 1984 election; it is cited to similar account by *Washington Post* columnist David Broder and communications scholar Kathleen Jamieson.[2] But the story's punch depends on our believing that the White House official knew what he was talking about. Did he?

In this case, no one really knows. But in another case we have information that indicates that the Reagan White House did *not* understand the power of pictures on television. In 1982 the country was in the midst of a recession and the Reagan administration was faring badly in the polls. The networks were making efforts to dramatize the country's economic plight not only by reporting the national unemployment figures, but also by focusing on a particular person or family hurt by hard times. The White House was outraged and criticized the networks for presenting the sad tale of the man in South Succotash and missing the general economic trends that, according to the White House, were more positive. Obviously, the White House assumed that the emotionally compelling, visually powerful vignette had much more impact on the American public than dry statistics. But when Donald Kinder and Shanto Iyengar conducted a series of careful experiments on television viewing, they found that the captivating vignette on economic affairs did no more than the bare statistics to lead viewers to believe that economic affairs were a major problem facing the nation. In fact, the evidence in Kinder and Iyengar's *News That Matters* ran modestly in the other direction—viewers were more impressed by statistics than by down-home stories about the gravity of the economic crisis.[3] This result runs counter to common sense. Isn't it true that a picture is worth more than all those words? Are the social scientists in this case (and not for the first time) just plain wrong?

I don't think so. There is a way to understand their results that is consistent with other well-established research. People do not automatically extrapolate from individual experience, even their own, to the nation as a whole. When American citizens go to the polls, for instance, they distinguish between their own personal economic situation and their sense of how the nation as a whole is doing—and typically they vote according to their sense of how the nation as a whole is doing. They do not cast reflex-like "pocketbook" votes.[4] When people see a television story on the plight of an individual family, they do not automatically generalize to the state of the nation. Indeed, the form of the vignette encourages them to discount the story as unrepresentative. If, say, the vignette pictures a black family, a significant number of whites may routinely discount the story as a special case, not a representative one, because they do not identify with blacks. If the news pictures a farm family, an urban family may not identify with them. In a sense, these viewers are not "visually literate"; they do not follow the visual logic by which one instance of poverty or unemployment is meant to represent the general phenomenon. Viewers find more general significance, then, in Department of Labor statistics than in artfully composed and emotionally compelling photographic essays on the economy.

The Lesley Stahl episode has become part of our telemythology, a set of widely circulated stories about the dangerous powers of television. With respect to politics, three key episodes contribute to the general mythology:

- Kennedy defeated Nixon in 1960 because he presented a more attractive image in the first television debate.
- Television's graphic portrayal of the war in Vietnam sickened and horrified American viewers, who were led by harsh photographic reality to oppose the war.
- The unprecedented popularity of President Reagan has no rational explanation but can be accounted for only by the power of an actor skilled at manipulating a visual medium.

But look again at each of the episodes. Kennedy just barely defeated Nixon in November 1960, and perhaps did not actually defeat him at all—we will never know just how many ballot boxes were stuffed in Cook County on election day. Many observers of the election, including Kennedy himself, attributed his success to his fine showing in the television debates. The most discussed part of the debates concerns the failure of Nixon's makeup artists to prepare him properly for the hot lights of the television studio. Where Kennedy seemed cool, Nixon appeared to be sweating; where Kennedy was self-assured, Nixon seemed to strain. Kennedy's appearance on national television galvanized his campaign; crowds instantly seemed larger and more enthusiastic in his campaign appearances. For Nixon, who added to Kennedy's stature simply by accepting the challenge to debate in the first place, the first debate was deeply unsettling.

Social scientists cite the finding that citizens who listened to the Kennedy-Nixon debate on the radio judged Nixon the winner; those who watched television found Kennedy the winner. As with the Stahl story, this is presented as conclusive evidence of the distorting lens of television. On radio, it is assumed, one listens to pure argument; on television, one is distracted by the appearance of things, the superficial look of people rather than the cogency of their arguments.

The basis for all this is a study undertaken by a Philadelphia market research firm that found that radio listeners judged Nixon the winner by 43 percent to 20 percent, while a majority (53 percent) of television viewers judged the debate a draw or refused to name a winner. Of those willing to name a winner, 28 percent chose Kennedy and 19 percent Nixon.[5]

Even if we accept this study as valid (and it was never reported in a form to make serious analysis possible), there are two problems with the way it has been used. The first problem concerns the presumption that radio is a distortion-free medium. Is the human voice itself not a medium? Is radio not a medium, too? Are words conveyed through radio a pure rendering of logical relations? Or does the voice—specifically, the radio-transmitted voice—give special weight to sonority and to the verbal tics and tricks of an experienced and skilled debater that have no necessary relation to the validity of the arguments themselves? Might radio have exaggerated Kennedy's Boston accent as part of his nature and therefore put people off? The human voice, from the cry of a baby onward, can stir passions. It can as easily be an enemy of reason as its epitome. A medium like radio that separates the human voice from the body is not necessarily a guardian of rationality.

Second, is television imagery so obviously superficial? Was it not important, and truthful, to see that Kennedy, despite his relative youth, was able to handle the most public moment of his life with assurance? Was it not important, and truthful, to see Nixon, despite his vast experience, looking awkward and insecure? Isn't it possible to argue that the insecurity he showed betrayed his manner and motive in public life?

Let me turn briefly to Vietnam. Here we have been told repeatedly about the power that television had to turn the American public against the war. The general argument has been that the horror of war, graphically shown to the viewing public, sickened Americans. Anything that the narration might have said about the legitimacy of the military effort, the pictures stunningly undermined. What is the evidence for this belief? There is, it turns out, almost no evidence at all. The public did, over time, become more and more disenchanted with the war in Vietnam—but at just about the same rate and to just about the same degree as the public became disaffected with the untelevised Korean war. Moreover, contrary to some popular reconstructions of television coverage, the TV coverage of the Vietnam war provided very little combat footage in the years during which opposition to the war mounted. It is possible, of course, that isolated instances of combat coverage had great impact; but, as Peter Braestrup points out in his book *Battle Lines,* the television archives provide no basis for the view that a day-in, day-out television portrait of bloodshed was ever presented to the American public.[6]

The general understanding behind the "TV-turned-us-against-the-war" argument is that TV photography comes to us unmediated—it forces itself upon the viewer, who then recoils from war. In fact, Daniel Hallin argues in *The Uncensored War* that "television's visual images are extremely ambiguous." We don't know very much about how audiences construct the meaning of TV images, but "it seems a reasonable hypothesis that most of the time the audience sees what it is told it is seeing."[7] Trout, in short, not ground beef.

The final piece of telemythology I want to examine is the view that Ronald Reagan's mastery of television led to his mastery of the American public. This is another curious story. Reagan's extraordinary popularity was heralded by the news media months before he took office. The sense in Washington of his popularity was so powerful that on March 18, 1981, not yet two months into Reagan's first term, James Reston reported that Congress was very reluctant to vote against the budget of so popular a chief executive. Reston's column appeared prominently on the *New York Times* op-ed page on the same day that, in a three-inch story at the bottom of page 22, a report on the latest Gallup poll coolly stated that Reagan's public approval ratings were the lowest in polling history for a newly elected president.

As it turned out, Reagan's average approval rating for his first year in office was, according to the Gallup survey, 57 percent compared with Carter's 62 percent, Nixon's 62 percent, Kennedy's 76 percent. His second-year average was 43 percent compared with Carter's 46 percent, Nixon's 56 percent, Kennedy's 72 percent.[8] Polls that tried to separate Reagan's personal appeal from the appeal of his policies found the President to be notably more popular than his program; however, this has been the case with every president, and the margin of difference was smaller for Reagan than for other presidents.[9] Later in his first term and in much of his second term, Reagan had unusually high public approval ratings. Still, the public impression and the media consensus about his general popularity were firmly established before there was any national polling evidence to corroborate it. How did this happen?

There are a number of explanations. The most important, I think, is that the Washington establishment *liked* Reagan. That establishment, Republican and Democrat, politician and journalist, had had enough of Jimmy Carter's puritanical style of socializing and humorless style of leadership. "For the first time in years, Washington has a President that it really likes," *Washington Post* political analyst Haynes Johnson concluded by the fall of 1981.[10] Reagan was very likable, yes. He brought with him the allure and glamour of Hollywood. More than this, he turned out to be a first-rate politician in the most old-fashioned sense: he could count votes, he knew whom to invite to breakfast or dinner and when, and he employed expert staff to deal with the Congress. When his aides asked him to make a phone call here or a public appearance there, he obliged. And if this direct courtship from the White House were not enough, Reagan succeeded in mobilizing a small but highly vocal right-wing constituency that, with just a whisper from the White House staff, would deluge congressional offices with telegrams and letters.

That is probably the heart of it, but I think there is something more—the strong belief of Washington elites that the general public can be mesmerized by television images. Many journalists shared a kind of "gee whiz" awe at the media skills of the White House, according to Laurence Barrett, senior White House correspondent for *Time.* Their sense of White House media omnipotence was particularly strong because of the contrast between Reagan's smooth administrative machinery and the ineffective Carter White House.[11] Consider the view of Barrett's colleague at *Time,* Thomas Griffith, who wrote that the "people in Peoria" are more receptive to Reagan's message than people who follow public affairs closely. The Reagan administration, he felt, aimed its message at the television audience, not the close readers of print. Reagan's was a "TV presidency."[12]

What is a TV presidency? Reagan's was scarcely the first to be declared one. There was Kennedy's, of course. Even Nixon gets a vote: "Nixon is a television creation, a sort of gesturing phantom, uncomfortable in the old-fashioned world of printer's type, where assertions can be checked and verified." That unlikely judgment comes from novelist and critic Mary McCarthy.[13] Carter was regularly declared a master of symbolism and images in his first year in office. In 1976, Carter flew into office hailed as a genius at media manipulation. His own media adviser, perhaps not surprisingly, called him "the biggest television star of all time. He is the first television president." The comic strip *Doonesbury* added a new cabinet officer, the secretary of symbolism, early in the Carter administration. The *New York Times* television critic reported in 1977 that Carter is "a master of controlled images." David Halberstam wrote in 1976 that Carter "more than any other candidate this year has sensed and adapted to modern communications and national mood . . . Watching him again and again on television I was impressed by his sense of pacing, his sense of control, very low-key, soft, a low decibel count, all this in sharp contrast to the other candidates."[14] Note, however, that as is so often the case with discussions of Reagan, Halberstam attributes Carter's television power to sound, not look. A case could be made that Reagan's presence on television has to do most of all with his voice. People thought of Carter in his first years as a master of images—the President walking, rather than riding, in his inaugural procession; the informal, down-home Jimmy wearing a cardigan sweater. Reagan riding his horse on the ranch never gained the same kind of power. I suspect that we will one day recall Reagan as one of the least visual but most auditory of our presidents. What is memorable is the Reagan with the slight choke in his voice when he told a melodramatic story about a G.I. or read a letter from a little girl, his quick intelligence with a joke or a quip, the comfort, calm, and sincerity in his voice. It was not even his look. It was not his words, as such, but his way with them. Reagan knew, if his critics did not, that it was his voice, his long-lived radio asset, that made his television appearance so effective.

The power of television is perhaps more firmly an article of faith in Washington than anywhere else in the country. There is an odd sense inside the beltway that the rest of the nation is not so much concerned with freeway traffic, paying bills at the end of the month, waiting for the plumber, getting the kids off to school, and finding a nursing home for Grandma as it is with watching Washington, especially in an election year. Otherwise it seems inexplicable that George Will, for instance, should have judged Robert Dole's relatively high poll ratings among Democrats early in the 1988 Republican primary season as "an effect of the televised Senate—he's had a chance to be seen in what is manifestly his home turf, where he is very comfortable."[15] Who is watching the televised Senate? C-SPAN is just not much competition for *Wheel of Fortune, General Hospital, Roseanne,* or, I'm afraid, even *Sesame Street.* How could anyone be so hopelessly out of touch? But so as not to pick on a Republican unfairly, I call to mind Walter Mondale's mournful plaint after his landslide loss to Reagan that television never warmed up to him nor did he warm up to television.[16] Did Hoover lose to Roosevelt because he didn't warm up to radio? Could a Depression have had something to do with it? And might Mondale have lost because 1984 was a time of peace, apparent prosperity, and a likable incumbent Republican?

The phenomenon of people believing that only *others* are influenced by the mass media is what W. Phillips Davison calls the "third-person effect" in communication.[17] The assumption that gullible others, but not one's own canny self, are slaves to the media is so widespread that the actions based on it may be one of the mass media's most powerful creations. The power of the media resides in the perception of experts and decision makers that the general public is influenced by the mass media, not in the direct influence of the mass media on the general public. That is to say, the media's political appeal lies less in its ability to bend minds than in its ability to convince elites that the popular mind can be bent.

If experts overestimate the direct power of the visual, they underrate their own power to reinterpret the visual. In 1976, Gerald Ford said in his debate with Carter that "there is no Soviet domination of Eastern Europe." Although recent events suggest that his misstatement was truer than he knew, that gaffe was reputed to be a major break for Carter and the beginning of the Ford campaign's unraveling. Again, it appears, television demonstrated its enormous power in American politics.

But few television viewers noticed or cared about Ford's remark. A poll conducted by a market research organization employed by the President Ford Committee found that people judged Ford to have done a better job than Carter by 44 percent to 35 percent in the two hours immediately after the debate on the evening of October 6. By noon on October 7, Carter was judged the winner by 44 percent to 31 percent, and by that evening he was judged the winner by 61 percent to 19 percent. On the evening of October 6, not a single person interviewed mentioned the Eastern Europe statement as one of the "main things" the candidate had done "well" or "not well" during the debate. But the next morning 12 percent of the respondents mentioned it, and the next evening 20 percent mentioned it. By that time it was the most frequently mentioned criticism of Ford's performance.[18]

What happened in the interim, of course, is that the news media intervened. Journalists, print and broadcast, told viewers what they had seen and heard. Viewers did not take their hint from the cathode ray tube but from the lessons the journalists taught them after the fact. Trout or hamburger? People did not know until they were told.

In 1984, in Mondale's first debate with Reagan, there was widespread agreement that Mondale was impressive and Reagan surprisingly ill at ease and defensive. Polls conducted during the debate, however, showed that people felt, by a slight margin, that Reagan was winning. An hour after the debate, Mondale had a 1 percent edge in a poll on who won. A day later his advantage was 37 percent, and two days later 49 percent. Again, the evidence compellingly shows that even when people "see for themselves," they take as cues for their own thinking suggestions from experts that come after the fact.[19]

In this respect, Reagan's administration did understand television very well. Reagan's aides did not expect television by itself to implant in Americans a love of Reagan or his policies, and they did not treat a television appearance as simply a matter of finding an appropriate stage set and working on the president's makeup. They did all they could to assure the success of a television appearance by preparing the audience for it in rather old-fashioned ways. Before a presidential TV address, the administration's public liaison office arranged for Reagan to meet personally with groups of allies, several hundred at a time, and brief them on what he would say on television so that they could alert their comrades at home. According to political analyst Stephen Wayne, these briefings helped unleash the flood of responses the White House and Congress received on the budget and tax proposals during Reagan's first year in office.[20] This is not to say that the television appearance was without effect on the public—although recent analysis by political scientists indicates that the influence of staged television appearances was very slight in the Reagan years.[21] It is to suggest that even here Reagan was more successful at manipulating congressional opinion than public opinion—but the manipulation came through encouraging the Congress to believe that the public at large was aroused by television. Since this so readily coincided with a view that Washington elites already held as gospel, it was a relatively easy trick to manage.

If the belief in television power is a large part of what makes television powerful, it may be not television but our beliefs about it that help undo a vital politics. The fascination of critics with television as devil, in any event, takes political discourse off track. We—American citizens, cultural critics, social scientists—seek some kind of reckoning with television, the culture it presents and the culture it represents. But despite the growing abundance of media critics, I don't think we have found the language for that reckoning yet. The object of our attention keeps shifting, for one thing; we've gone from an era of the sponsor to an era of the network to the present (still undefined) era of the proliferation of cable and the declining network-share of the television audience. The kinds of television experience also seem too varied to be easily encapsulated—from the live coverage of the Kennedy funeral, the Olympics, a presidential debate, or a natural disaster to the evening news, daytime soap operas, old movies, or reruns of old sitcoms. The judgment we make of one of these genres is not likely to stick when applied to the next.

Beyond the difficulties in keeping the object of our attention steadily in view, there is the complicated problem of the mixed motives of our own curiosity. There are professional career-making ambitions, an inevitable product of the proliferation of the study of communication in the universities; there is the *ressentiment* of intellectuals who feel unfairly overlooked in an era of celebrity; there is the anger, seeking an object, that arises in the general population from a sense of impotence in dealing with the wider world that both print and television news bring to our homes daily. There is also a sense, one I certainly share, that television executives live in time-and-space capsules closely linked to research reports on market trends but very far from deeper currents of experience in the contemporary world. And since they do not yet know this, may never know this, may not want to know this, they may never tell us the stories about ourselves from which we could genuinely learn.

Notes

[1] Michael Arlen, *Thirty Seconds* (New York: Penguin, 1980).

[2] Hedrick Smith, *The Power Game* (New York: Ballantine Books, 1988) p. 409; David Broder, *Behind the Front Page* (New York: Simon & Schuster 1987), p. 182; Martin Schram, *The Great American Video Game: Presidential Politics in the Television Age* (New York: William Morrow, 1987), pp. 23–27; and Kathleen Hall Jamieson, *Eloquence in an Electronic Age* (New York: Oxford University Press, 1988), pp. 60–61.

[3] Shanto Iyengar and Donald Kinder, *News That Matters* (Chicago: University of Chicago Press, 1984), pp. 36–42.

[4] See D. Roderick Kiewiet, *Macroeconomics and Micro-politics: The Electoral Effects of Economic Issues* (Chicago: University of Chicago Press, 1983).

[5] *Broadcasting* 59 (November 7, 1960): 27–29. When I originally published this chapter, I was unaware of a very good paper criticizing the conventional wisdom on the Kennedy-Nixon debate by David L. Vancil and Sue D. Pendell, "The Myth of Viewer-Listener Disagreement in the First Kennedy-Nixon Debate," *Central States Speech Journal* 38 (1987): 16–27. Vancil and Pendell nicely demonstrate both how pervasive the myth about the Kennedy-Nixon debate is and how meager is the evidence to substantiate it.

[6] Peter Braestrup, *Battle Lines* (New York: Priority Press, 1985), pp. 68–69.

[7] Daniel C. Hallin, *"The Uncensored War": The Media and Vietnam* (New York: Oxford University Press, 1986), p. 131.

[8] Calculated from Gallup polls reported in "Reagan and His Predecessors," *Public Opinion* (September/October 1987): 40.

[9] *The Gallup Poll* 1982 (Wilmington, Del.: Scholarly Resources, 1983), pp. 107, 243.

[10] *Washington Post,* November 22, 1981.

[11] Laurence I. Barrett, *Gambling with History: Ronald Reagan in the White House* (Harmondsworth, England: Penguin Books, 1984), p. 443.

[12] *Time,* August 16, 1982.

[13] Mary McCarthy, *The Mask of State: Watergate Portraits* (New York: Harcourt Brace Jovanovich, 1974), p. 5.

[14] Barry Jogoda, quoted in William Lunch, *The Nationalization of American Politics* (Berkeley: University of California Press, 1987), p. 79; John J. O'Connor, *New York Times,* April 14, 1977, quoted in Joshua Meyrowitz, *No Sense of Place* (New York: Oxford University Press, 1985), p. 273; David Halberstam cited in Meyrowitz, *No Sense of Place,* p. 297.

[15] *San Diego Union,* January 31, 1988, p. C-8.

[16] *Los Angeles Times,* November 8, 1984, p. 1.

[17] W. Phillips Davison, "The Third-Person Effect in Communication," *Public Opinion Quarterly* 47 (1983): 1–15.

[18] Frederick T. Steeper, "Public Response to Gerald Ford's Statements on Eastern Europe in the Second Debate," in George F. Bishop, Robert G. Meadow, and Marilyn Jackson-Beeck, *The Presidential Debates: Media, Electoral, and Policy Perspectives* (New York: Praeger, 1978), pp. 81–101.

[19] Michael Robinson, "Where's the Beef? Media and Media Elites in 1984," in *The American Elections of 1984,* ed. Austin Ranney (Durham, N.C.: Duke University Press, 1985), pp. 198–199.

[20] Stephen J. Wayne, "Congressional Liaison in the Reagan White House: A Preliminary Assessment of the First Year," in *President and Congress: Assessing Reagan's First Year,* ed. Norman J. Ornstein (Washington, D.C.: American Enterprise Institute, 1982), p. 55.

[21] Charles W. Ostrom, Jr., and Dennis M. Simon, "The Man in the Teflon Suit: The Environmental Connection, Political Drama, and Popular Support in the Reagan Presidency," *Public Opinion Quarterly* 53 (1989): 353–387.

Understanding the Text

1. What assumption about the relative power of images vs. words does Schudson challenge in his essay?

2. What three historical events does Schudson examine to support his challenge? Choose one, and summarize his argument about it.

3. To what does the "Trout or Hamburger" of Schudson's title refer? What is the lesson he extracts from this reference, and how does this relate to his understanding of the influence of television upon viewers?

———

The Incredible Shrinking Sound Bite

Kiku Adatto

Standing before a campaign rally in Pennsylvania, the 1968 Democratic vice presidential candidate, Edmund Muskie, tried to speak, but a group of anti-war protesters drowned him out. Muskie offered the hecklers a deal. He would give the platform to one of their representatives if he could then speak without interruption. Rick Brody, the students' choice, rose to the microphone where, to cheers from the crowd, he denounced the candidates that the 1968 presidential campaign had to offer. "Wallace is no answer. Nixon's no answer. And Humphrey's no answer. Sit out this election!" When Brody finished, Muskie made his case for the Democratic ticket. That night Muskie's confrontation with the demonstrators played prominently on the network news. NBC showed fifty-seven seconds of Brody's speech, and more than a minute of Muskie's.

Twenty years later, things had changed. Throughout the entire 1988 campaign, no network allowed either presidential candidate to speak uninterrupted on the evening news for as long as Rick Brody spoke. By 1988 television's tolerance for the languid pace of political discourse, never great, had all but vanished. An analysis of all weekday evening network newscasts (over 280) from Labor Day to Election Day in 1968 and 1988 reveals that the average "sound bite" fell from 42.3 seconds in 1968 to only 9.8 seconds in 1988. Meanwhile the time the networks devoted to visuals of the candidates, unaccompanied by their words, increased by more than 300 percent.

Kiku Adatto is a lecturer in Social Studies at Harvard University and also has taught at the Kennedy School of Government and the Department of Sociology. She is the author of *Picture Perfect: The Art and Artifice of Public Image Making* (1993) as well as numerous articles on politics and the media.

Since the Kennedy-Nixon debates of 1960, television has played a pivotal role in presidential politics. The Nixon campaign of 1968 was the first to be managed and orchestrated to play on the evening news. With the decline of political parties and the direct appeal to voters in the primaries, presidential campaigns became more adept at conveying their messages through visual images, not only in political commercials but also in elaborately staged media events. By the time of Ronald Reagan, the actor turned president, Michael Deaver had perfected the techniques of the video presidency.

For television news, the politicians' mastery of television imagery posed a temptation and a challenge. The temptation was to show the pictures. What network producer could resist the footage of Reagan at Normandy Beach, or of Bush in Boston Harbor? The challenge was to avoid being entangled in the artifice and imagery that the campaigns dispensed. In 1988 the networks tried to have it both ways—to meet the challenge even as they succumbed to the temptation. They showed the images that the campaigns produced—their commercials as well as their media events. But they also sought to retain their objectivity by exposing the artifice of the images, by calling constant attention to their self-conscious design.

The language of political reporting was filled with accounts of staging and backdrops, camera angles and scripts, sound bites and spin control, photo opportunities and media gurus. So attentive was television news to the way the campaigns constructed images for television that political reporters began to sound like theater critics, reporting more on the stagecraft than the substance of politics.

When Bush kicked off his campaign with a Labor Day appearance at Disneyland, the networks covered the event as a performance for television. "In the war of the Labor Day visuals," CBS's Bob Schieffer reported, "George Bush pulled out the heavy artillery. A Disneyland backdrop and lots of pictures with the Disney gang." When Bruce Morton covered Dukakis riding in a tank, the story was the image. "In the trade of politics, it's called a visual," said Morton. "The idea is pictures are symbols that tell the voter important things about the candidate. If your candidate is seen in the polls as weak on defense, put him in a tank."

And when Bush showed up at a military base to observe the destruction of a missile under an arms control treaty, ABC's Brit Hume began his report by telling his viewers that they were watching a media event. "Now, here was a photo opportunity, the vice president watching a Pershing missile burn off its fuel." He went on to describe how the event was staged for television. Standing in front of an open field, Hume reported, "The Army had even gone so far as to bulldoze acres of trees to make sure the vice president and the news media had a clear view."

So familiar is the turn to theater criticism that it is difficult to recall the transformation it represents. Even as they conveyed the first presidential campaign "made for television," TV reporters in 1968 continued to reflect the print journalist tradition from which they had descended. In the marriage of theater and politics, politics remained the focus of reporting.

The media events of the day—mostly rallies and press conferences—were covered as political events, not as exercises in impression management.

By 1988 television displaced politics as the focus of coverage. Like a gestalt shift, the images that once formed the background to political events—the setting and the stagecraft—now occupied the foreground. (Only 6 percent of reports in 1968 were devoted to theater criticism, compared with 52 percent in 1988.) And yet, for all their image-conscious coverage in 1988, reporters did not escape their entanglement. They showed the potent visuals even as they attempted to avoid the manipulation by "deconstructing" the imagery and revealing its artifice.

To be sure, theater criticism was not the only kind of political reporting on network newscasts in 1988. Some notable "fact correction" pieces offered admirable exceptions. For example, after each presidential debate, ABC's Jim Wooten compared the candidates' claims with the facts. Not content with the canned images of the politicians, Wooten used television images to document discrepancies between the candidates' rhetoric and their records.

Most coverage simply exposed the contrivances of image-making. But alerting the viewer to the construction of television images proved no substitute for fact correction. A superficial "balance" replaced objectivity as the measure of fairness, a balance consisting of equal time for media events, equal time for commercials. But this created a false symmetry, leaving both the press and the public hostage to the play of perceptions the campaigns dispensed.

Even the most critical versions of image-conscious coverage could fail to puncture the pictures they showed. When Bush visited a flag factory in hopes of making patriotism a campaign issue, ABC's Hume reported that Bush was wrapping himself in the flag. "This campaign strives to match its pictures with its points. Today and for much of the past week, the pictures have been of George Bush with the American flag. If the point wasn't to make an issue of patriotism, then the question arises, what was it?" Yet only three days later, in an ABC report on independent voters in New Jersey, the media event that Hume reported with derision was transformed into an innocent visual of Bush. The criticism forgotten, the image played on.

Another striking contrast between the coverage of the 1968 and 1988 campaigns is the increased coverage of political commercials. Although political ads played a prominent role in the 1968 campaign, the networks rarely showed excerpts on the news. During the entire 1968 general election campaign, the evening news programs broadcast only two excerpts from candidates' commercials. By 1988 the number had jumped to 125. In 1968 the only time a negative ad was mentioned on the evening news was when CBS's Walter Cronkite and NBC's Chet Huntley reported that a Nixon campaign ad—showing a smiling Hubert Humphrey superimposed on scenes of war and riot—was withdrawn after the Democrats cried foul. Neither network showed the ad itself.

The networks might argue that in 1988 political ads loomed larger in the campaign, and so required more coverage. But as with their focus on media events, reporters ran the risk of becoming conduits of the television images the campaigns dispensed. Even with a critical narrative, showing commercials on the news gives free time to paid media. And most of the time the narrative was not critical. The networks rarely bothered to correct the distortions or misstatements that the ads contained. Of the 125 excerpts shown on the evening news in 1988, the reporter addressed the veracity of the commercials' claims less than 8 percent of the time. The networks became, in effect, electronic billboards for the candidates, showing political commercials not only as breaking news but as stand-ins for the candidates, and file footage aired interchangeably with news footage of the candidates.

The few cases where reporters corrected the facts illustrate how the networks might have covered political commercials. ABC's Richard Threlkeld ran excerpts from a Bush ad attacking Dukakis's defense stand by freezing the frame and correcting each mistaken or distorted claim. He also pointed out the exaggeration in a Dukakis ad attacking Bush's record on Social Security. CBS's Leslie Stahl corrected a deceptive statistic in Bush's revolving-door furlough ad, noting: "Part of the ad is false. . . . Two hundred sixty-eight murderers did not escape. . . . [T]he truth is only four first-degree murderers escaped while on parole."

Stahl concluded her report by observing, "Dukakis left the Bush attack ads unanswered for six weeks. Today campaign aides are engaged in a round of finger-pointing at who is to blame." But the networks also let the Bush furlough commercial run without challenge or correction. Before and even after her report, CBS ran excerpts of the ad without correction. In all, network newscasts ran excerpts from the revolving-door furlough ad ten times throughout the campaign, only once correcting the deceptive statistic.

It might be argued that it is up to the candidate to reply to his opponent's charges, not the press. But the networks' frequent use of political ads on the evening news created a strong disincentive for a candidate to challenge his opponent's ads. As Dukakis found, to attack a television ad as unfair or untrue is to invite the networks to run it again. In the final weeks before the election, the Dukakis campaign accused the Republicans of lying about his record on defense, and of using racist tactics in ads featuring Willie Horton, a black convict who raped and killed while on furlough from a Massachusetts prison. (See "The Making of Willie Horton" by Martin Schram.) In reporting Dukakis's complaint, all three networks ran excerpts of the ads in question, including the highly charged pictures of Horton and the revolving door of convicts. Dukakis's response thus gave Bush's potent visuals another free run on the evening news.

The networks might reply that the ads are news and thus need to be shown, as long as they generate controversy in the campaign. But this rationale leaves them open to manipulation. Oddly enough, the networks were alive to this danger when confronted with the question of whether to air the videos the campaigns produced for their conventions. "I am not into tone poems," Lane Venardos, the executive producer in charge of convention coverage at

CBS, told *The New York Times.* "We are not in the business of being propaganda arms of the political parties." But they seemed blind to the same danger during the campaign itself.

So successful was the Bush campaign at getting free time for its ads on the evening news that, after the campaign, commercial advertisers adopted a similar strategy. In 1989 a pharmaceutical company used unauthorized footage of Presidents Bush and Gorbachev to advertise a cold medication. "In the new year," the slogan ran, "may the only cold war in the world be the one being fought by us." Although two of the three networks refused to carry the commercial, dozens of network and local television news programs showed excerpts of the ad, generating millions of dollars of free airtime.

"I realized I started a trend," said Bush media consultant Roger Ailes in *The New York Times.* "Now guys are out there trying to produce commercials for the evening news." When Humphrey and Nixon hired Madison Avenue experts to help in their campaigns, some worried that, in the television age, presidents would be sold like products. Little did they imagine that, twenty years later, products would be sold like presidents.

Along with the attention to commercials and stagecraft in 1988 came an unprecedented focus on the stage managers themselves, the "media gurus," "handlers," and "spin-control artists." Only three reports featured media advisers in 1968, compared with twenty-six in 1988. And the numbers tell only part of the story.

The stance reporters have taken toward media advisers has changed dramatically over the past twenty years. In *The Selling of the President* (1969), Joe McGinniss exposed the growing role of media advisers with a sense of disillusion and outrage. By 1988 television reporters covered image-makers with deference, even admiration. In place of independent fact correction, reporters sought out media advisers as authorities in their own right to analyze the effectiveness and even defend the truthfulness of campaign commercials. They became "media gurus" not only for the candidates but for the networks as well.

For example, in an exchange with CBS anchor Dan Rather on Bush's debate performance, Stahl lavished admiration on the techniques of Bush's media advisers:

> STAHL: "They told him not to look into the camera. [She gestures toward the camera as she speaks.] You know when you look directly into a camera you are cold, apparently they have determined."
>
> RATHER [laughing]:"Bad news for anchormen I'd say."
>
> STAHL: "We have a lot to learn from this. Michael Dukakis kept talking right into the camera. [Stahl talks directly into her own camera to demonstrate.] And according to the Bush people that makes you look programmed, Dan [Stahl laughs]. And they're very adept at these television symbols and television imagery. And according to our poll it worked."
>
> RATHER: "Do you believe it?"
>
> STAHL: "Yes, I think I do, actually."

So hypersensitive were the networks to television image-making in 1988 that minor mishaps—gaffes, slips of the tongue, even faulty microphones—became big news. Politicians were hardly without mishaps in 1968, but these did not count as news. Only once in 1968 did a network even take note of a minor incident unrelated to the content of the campaign. In 1988 some twenty-nine reports highlighted trivial slips.

The emphasis on "failed images" reflected a kind of guerrilla warfare between the networks and the campaigns. The more the campaigns sought to control the images that appeared on the nightly news, the more the reporters tried to beat them at their own game, magnifying a minor mishap into a central feature of the media event.

Early in the 1988 campaign, for example, George Bush delivered a speech to a sympathetic audience of the American Legion, attacking his opponent's defense policies. In a slip, he declared that September 7, rather than December 7, was the anniversary of Pearl Harbor. Murmurs and chuckles from the audience alerted him to his error, and he quickly corrected himself.

The audience was forgiving, but the networks were not. All three network anchors highlighted the slip on the evening news. Dan Rather introduced CBS's report on Bush by declaring solemnly, "Bush's talk to audiences in Louisville was overshadowed by a strange happening." On NBC Tom Brokaw reported, "He departed from his prepared script and left his listeners mystified." Peter Jennings introduced ABC's report by mentioning Bush's attack on Dukakis, adding, "What's more likely to be remembered about today's speech is a slip of the tongue."

Some of the slips the networks highlighted in 1988 were not even verbal gaffes or misstatements, but simply failures on the part of candidates to cater to the cameras. In a report on the travails of the Dukakis campaign, Sam Donaldson seized on Dukakis's failure to play to ABC's television camera as evidence of his campaign's ineffectiveness. Showing Dukakis playing a trumpet with a local marching band, Donaldson chided, "He played the trumpet with his back to the camera." As Dukakis played "Happy Days Are Here Again," Donaldson's voice was heard from off-camera calling, "We're over here, governor."

One way of understanding the turn to image-conscious coverage in 1988 is to see how television news came to partake of the postwar modernist sensibility, particularly the pop art movement of the 1960s. Characteristic of this outlook is a self-conscious attention to art as performance, a focus on the process of image-making rather than on the ideas the images represent.

During the 1960s, when photography and television became potent forces for documentation and entertainment, they also became powerful influences on the work of artists. Photographers began to photograph the television set as part of the social landscape. Newspapers, photographs, and commercial products became part of the collage work of painters such as Robert Rauschenberg. Artists began to explore self-consciously their role in the image-making process.

For example, Lee Friedlander published a book of photography, *Self Portrait,* in which the artist's shadow or reflection was included in every frame. As critic Rod Slemmons notes, "By indicating the photographer is also a performer whose hand is impossible to hide, Friedlander set a precedent for disrupting the normal rules of photography." These "post-modernist" movements in art and photography foreshadowed the form television news would take by the late 1980s.

Andy Warhol once remarked, "The artificial fascinates me." In 1988 network reporters and producers, beguiled by the artifice of the modern presidential campaign, might well have said the same. Reporters alternated between reporting campaign images as if they were facts and exposing their contrived nature. Like Warhol, whose personality was always a presence in his work, reporters became part of the campaign theater they covered—as producers, as performers, and as critics. Like Warhol's reproductions of Campbell's soup cans, the networks' use of candidates' commercials directed our attention away from the content and toward the packaging.

The assumption that the creation of appearances is the essence of political reality pervaded not only the reporting but the candidates' self-understanding and conduct with the press. When Dan Quayle sought to escape his image as a highly managed candidate, he resolved publicly to become his own handler, his own "spin doctor." "The so-called handlers story, part of it's true," he confessed to network reporters. "But there will be no more handlers stories, because I'm the handler and I'll do the spinning." Surrounded by a group of reporters on his campaign plane, Quayle announced. "I'm Doctor Spin, and I want you all to report that."

It may seem a strange way for a politician to talk, but not so strange in a media-conscious environment in which authenticity means being master of your own artificiality. Dukakis too sought to reverse his political fortunes by seeking to be master of his own image. This attempt was best captured in a commercial shown on network news in which Dukakis stood beside a television set and snapped off a Bush commercial attacking his stand on defense. "I'm fed up with it," Dukakis declared. "Never seen anything like it in twenty-five years of public life. George Bush's negative television ads, distorting my record, full of lies, and he knows it." The commercial itself shows an image of an image—a Bush television commercial showing (and ridiculing) the media event where Dukakis rode in a tank. In his commercial, Dukakis complains that Bush's commercial showing the tank ride misstates Dukakis's position on defense.

As it appeared in excerpts on the evening news, Dukakis's commercial displayed a quintessentially modernist image of artifice upon artifice upon artifice: television news covering a Dukakis commercial containing a Bush commercial containing a Dukakis media event. In a political world governed by images of images, it seemed almost natural that the authority of the candidate be depicted by his ability to turn off the television set.

In the 1950s Edward R. Murrow noted that broadcast news was "an incompatible combination of show business, advertising, and news." Still, in its first decades television news continued to reflect a sharp distinction between the news and entertainment divisions of the networks. But by the 1980s network news operations came to be seen as profit centers for the large corporations that owned them, run by people drawn less from journalism than from advertising and entertainment backgrounds. Commercialization led to further emphasis on entertainment values, which heightened the need for dramatic visuals, fast pacing, quick cutting, and short sound bites. Given new technological means to achieve these effects—portable video cameras, satellite hookups, and sophisticated video-editing equipment—the networks were not only disposed but equipped to capture the staged media events of the campaigns.

The search for dramatic visuals and the premium placed on showmanship in the 1980s led to a new complicity between the White House image-makers and the networks. As Susan Zirinsky, a top CBS producer, acknowledged in Martin Schram's *The Great American Video Game,* "In a funny way, the [Reagan White House] advance men and I have the same thing at heart—we want the piece to look as good as [it] possibly can." In 1968 such complicity in stagecraft was scorned. Sanford Socolow, senior producer of the *CBS Evening News with Walter Cronkite,* recently observed, "If someone caught you doing that in 1968 you would have been fired."

In a moment of reflection in 1988, CBS's political correspondents expressed their frustration with image-driven campaigns "It may seem frivolous, even silly at times," said Schieffer. "But setting up pictures that drive home a message has become the No. 1 priority of the modern-day campaign. The problem, of course, is while it is often entertaining, it is seldom enlightening."

Rather shared his colleague's discomfort. But what troubled him about modern campaigns is equally troubling about television's campaign coverage. "With all this emphasis on the image," he asked, "what happens to the issues? What happens to the substance?"

Understanding the Text

1. According to Adatto, how did the focus of presidential campaign coverage change from 1968 to 1988?

2. Why is Adatto critical of the television news programs in 1988 excerpting 125 candidate ads during their broadcasts? (Identify two reasons.)

3. Adatto reports that even in the early days of television news, Edward R. Murrow, a prominent journalist, observed that it was "an incompatible combination of show business, advertising, and news." According to Adatto, what has become of this "combination" since? What evidence does she cite to support her view?

Lightning, Camera, Action

J. Hoberman

Can photographs, motion pictures, and television create social change? Or would it be more accurate to say that these camera-based forms construct a social reality? Michael Moore notwithstanding, the ultimate test case appeared 90 years ago: D.W. Griffith's *The Birth of a Nation,* released throughout America in the spring of 1915, remains the single most important movie ever made in this country, as well as the most inflammatory one.

A culmination of the hundreds of short, two-reel narratives, more or less codifying the language of narrative cinema, that Griffith ground out at the Biograph studio between 1908 and 1913, *The Birth of a Nation* was the longest, costliest, and most ambitious American movie of its day. Imagine an unholy cross between *The Passion of the Christ* and *Fahrenheit 9/11,* combined and rendered mega-*Titanic* (most movies in 1915 were still only 20 minutes long), drenched in the patriotic pathos of *Saving Private Ryan,* and tricked out with the historical shenanigans of *Forrest Gump.* It still wouldn't approximate the magnitude of Griffith's fervent, tendentious, wildly entertaining achievement.

Viewers were inundated with a cascade of images—1,500 separate shots when other features had fewer than 100. Like the Henry Ford of cine narrative, Griffith created an assembly line for cinema meaning; he broke dramatic scenes into component parts and reassembled them for maximum emotional impact. *The Birth of a Nation* hurtled through time and space, making unprecedented use of close-ups, cutaways, and parallel action. The miracle of moving pictures, less than 20 years old,

J. Hoberman writes film criticism for *The Village Voice* as well as other publications, and also teaches at Cooper Union. He is the author of a number of books of film criticism, including *On Jack Smith's Flaming Creatures* (2001), *Vulgar Modernism* (1991), and *Midnight Movies* (with Jonathan Rosenbaum, 1983).

Reprinted with permission from J. Hoberman, "Lighting, Camera, Action," *The American Prospect,* Volume 16, No. 6, June 6, 2005. The American Prospect, 2000 L Street, NW, Suite 77, Washington, DC 20036.

was projected into the past. Griffith gave motion to Matthew Brady's photographs and staged Lincoln's assassination as a "historical facsimile," complete with footnotes. Masses of extras were deployed to recreate the Battle of Petersburg and Sherman's march to the sea. Audiences were swept away; in some cities, the action was pumped with a 40-piece symphony orchestra.

In short, Griffith had produced the wonder of the age: a technological marvel, a masterpiece of promotion, a brilliantly constructed emotional roller coaster, a box-office gold mine —and an utterly unambiguous and ruthlessly demagogic attack on African Americans. *The Birth of a Nation* is not simply the precursor of every Hollywood historical epic, stalker film, and thriller ever made; adapted from a best-selling novel by the Reverend Thomas Dixon that offered a militantly white-supremacist perspective on the Civil War and Reconstruction, Griffith's movie is an ideological horror show, filled with outrageous factual distortions and vile racial stereotypes. In the Gospel according to Griffith, the American nation is born when, as one of the film's climactic intertitles has it, the Ku Klux Klan enables North and South to unite in defense of their common "Aryan birthright."

The Birth of a Nation was released for the 50th anniversary of the end of the Civil War— just as America's ultimate trauma was poised to pass from living memory into national mythology. The son of a Kentucky colonel, Griffith took it upon himself to rewrite, and re-right, a historical wrong—an act for which he sought, and received, official sanction. Two days before submitting the movie to the National Board of Review, he previewed it for President Woodrow Wilson and his cabinet. Wilson responded with the ultimate pull quote: "It is like writing history with lightning." The following night the president had it screened for the justices of the Supreme Court and members of Congress.

The film was immediately attacked by many organizations—notably the NAACP, which issued a statement declaring that "every resource of a magnificent new art has been employed with an undeniable attempt to picture Negroes in the worst possible light." But it helped revive the KKK. Some 25,000 Klansmen marched down Peachtree Street in full regalia to celebrate the Atlanta premiere. Contested virtually everywhere it opened outside the old Confederacy, *The Birth of a Nation* was banned outright in Chicago, Cleveland, St. Louis, San Antonio, and Topeka, Kansas. Boston saw the most protracted struggle: Weeks of mass meetings, demonstrations, and even legislative action reached their climax in June 1915 and came to naught when Mayor James Michael Curley simply refused to close the movie.

The Birth of Nation grossed more than $60 million—well over a billion contemporary dollars—during its first run. In New York, where it ran for 48 weeks, tickets were $2, at least 20 times as much as an ordinary picture show. Anticipating the special screenings to which secondary-school teachers escorted their classes, William Randolph Hearst's *New York Evening Journal* advised that, above all: "Children must be sent to see this masterpiece. Any parent who neglects this advice is committing an educational offense, for no film has ever produced more educational points than Griffith's latest achievement." Throughout the rural

South and Midwest, exhibitors chartered trains to bring audiences to large cities to see what Griffith had wrought.

Marshaling the resources of its medium, *The Birth of a Nation* made history. More crucially, it changed history—that is, it changed the ways by which the past might be represented. In Griffith's hands, the American past became a melodrama, at once cosmic and intimate. The Civil War is all in the family. The cataclysmic battle is punctuated by sudden close-ups of familiar characters; a distraught fictional mother meets the real Abraham Lincoln, who spares her Confederate son; in one of several metaphoric rape scenes, the Union army invades a specific southern home as the fearful family retreats from room to room.

No one has ever been more expressive than Griffith in subsuming 10,000 casualties in a single battlefield reunion or folding historical calamity in the pathos of an individual soldier's homecoming. But that, of course, is what war has become—and not just on the screen. As the most heavily televised military operation in history, the Iraq War was necessarily an exercise in image making. Although immediately exposed as a staged pseudo-event, the toppling of Saddam Hussein's statue lives on as television, broadcast when necessary to represent Iraq's liberation; the battle for Fallujah was the iconic *Los Angeles Times* photograph of a 20-year-old Marine dubbed the "Marlboro Man" for his battle-stained face and dangling cigarette.

The Iraq War's great human-interest item, the story of Private Jessica Lynch, is precisely the sort of captivity-and-rescue saga Griffith remade a dozen times as a Biograph two-reeler. Human interest is, for Griffith, history's driving force. He locates the impetus for Reconstruction in a sexual liaison between Senator Austin Stoneman, his stand-in for Senator Thaddeus Stevens, and Stoneman's mulatto housekeeper—"the great leader's weakness that is to blight a nation." History is its own allegory. (This sort of filmmaking is hardly restricted to Americans. The fervor with which German audiences embraced the recent *Downfall,* a re-enactment of Hitler's last days in the bunker, is less a testament to Bruno Ganz's performance as a "humanized" führer than the filmmakers' skill in surrounding the devil and his familiars with real yet airbrushed "ordinary" Germans to establish Germany as the first Nazi victim.)

Griffith taught the movies to take history personally, and politicians have been following his lead ever since. No one until Steven Spielberg has been better at pressing America's buttons—unless it was Ronald Reagan, whose uncanny ability to recast American life into a movie starring a wisecracking action hero like himself reached its apotheosis a year ago in the media narratives occasioned by his death. Reagan was resurrected in a particularly awful way when Arnold Schwarzenegger created his own movie within the hyper-designed triumphalist pseudo-event of the 2004 Republican national convention. (What's remarkable is how long it took right-wing Republicans to admit how much they love Hollywood's animated action figures. Would that the misdirected satire *Team America* had taken that for its subject.)

But the melodrama of American politics is not only manifested in choreographed pep rallies, prepackaged "good news" segments, or even the robotic blitz of applied movie-dialogue sound bites that Schwarzenegger offered as a panacea for California's problems. As demonstrated by *The Birth of a Nation,* the scenario rules (and so does demonization). The 2004 election was more or less decided last July with the Republicans' redefinition of John Kerry's heroism and preemptive destruction of his Viet-vet narrative. George W. Bush's premature declaration of victory in Iraq may have been a joke, but it established him as a leader at home in a pilot's costume. For all of Kerry's Hollywood support, he was outacted.

The made-for-TV *DC 9/11: Time of Crisis,* the most significant political movie of the 2004 campaign, went Griffith one better by staging a recent event with a professional cast impersonating the current president and his administration. (There's no precedent: The Kennedys contrived a Hollywood *PT-109* as a run-up to 1964; imagine if it had been a dramatization of the Cuban missile crisis!) Why not construct a narrative improvement on events as they unfold? "We're an empire now, and when we act, we create our own reality," a Bush spokesman famously told reporter Ron Suskind on the eve of the election.

As was made apparent last summer when the Silent Movie Theatre in Los Angeles was forced to cancel a well-publicized screening, *The Birth of a Nation* is all but unshowable today. It is also humiliating to watch. Every year when I teach cinema history, I must convince myself that students need to see and discuss it if they are to understand the country in which they live.

We are all citizens of the state that Griffith prophesied—the empire of total docudrama where actual figures mingle with fictional ones, real events are imbued with storybook logic, and everything is reflected in relentless hype. *The Birth of a Nation* is an object lesson in the manufacture of an image-based spectacle. Creaky as it is, the mechanism still works. The appeal is not to reason.

What's most chastening about *The Birth of a Nation* is its demonstration of what it can do, and, by extension, what all forms of camera-constructed reality can do. Griffith reminds us that movies are an authoritarian medium, that a successful film narrative is largely a function of gross emotional manipulation, and that history may not only be written but rewritten with lightning.

Understanding the Text

1. According to Hoberman, what is the content of *Birth of a Nation* and how did audiences respond to it when it appeared in 1915?

2. According to Hoberman, what made this film so powerful?

3. For what reasons does Hoberman think that *Birth of a Nation* can help us to understand contemporary political spectacle?

Politics and the English Language

George Orwell

Most people who bother with the matter at all would admit that the English language is in a bad way, but it is generally assumed that we cannot by conscious action do anything about it. Our civilization is decadent and our language—so the argument runs—must inevitably share in the general collapse. It follows that any struggle against the abuse of language is a sentimental archaism, like preferring candles to electric light or hansom cabs to aeroplanes. Underneath this lies the half-conscious belief that language is a natural growth and not an instrument which we shape for our own purposes.

Now, it is clear that the decline of a language must ultimately have political and economic causes: it is not due simply to the bad influence of this or that individual writer. But an effect can become a cause, reinforcing the original cause and producing the same effect in an intensified form, and so on indefinitely. A man may take a drink because he feels himself to be a failure, and then fail all the more completely because he drinks. It is rather the same thing that is happening to the English language. It becomes ugly and inaccurate because our thoughts are foolish, but the slovenliness of our language makes it easier for us to have foolish thoughts. The point is that the process is reversible. Modern English, especially written English, is full of bad habits which spread by imitation and which can be avoided if one is willing to take the necessary trouble. If one gets rid of these habits one can think more clearly, and to think clearly is a necessary first step towards political regeneration: so that

George Orwell is the pseudonym of Eric Blair (1903–50), one of the most widely read, respected, and influential political essayists and novelists of the twentieth century. His many books include works of nonfiction—*Down and Out in Paris and London* (1933) and *The Road to Wigan Pier* (1937), both of which address the dire circumstances of the working class, and *Homage to Catalonia* (1939), which records his experiences fighting in the Spanish Civil War in the 1930s—and collections of essays, including *Inside the Whale* (1940), *Critical Essays* (1946), and *Shooting an Elephant* (1950). But he is, perhaps, best known for his novels, especially *Animal Farm* (1945) and *1984* (1949), both of which register his intense opposition to political tyranny. Ever critical of obfuscation and deceit in political language, Orwell himself practiced a prose style that remains a model of clarity and concision.

the fight against bad English is not frivolous and is not the exclusive concern of professional writers. I will come back to this presently, and I hope that by that time the meaning of what I have said here will have become clearer. Meanwhile, here are five specimens of the English language as it is now habitually written.

These five passages have not been picked out because they are especially bad—I could have quoted far worse if I had chosen—but because they illustrate various of the mental vices from which we now suffer. They are a little below the average, but are fairly representative samples. I number them so that I can refer back to them when necessary:

(1) I am not indeed sure whether it is not true to say that the Milton who once seemed not unlike a seventeenth-century Shelley had not become out of an experience ever more bitter in each year, more alien *[sic]* to the founder of that Jesuit sect which nothing could induce him to tolerate.

—Professor Harold Laski, Essay in *Freedom of Expression*

(2) Above all, we cannot play ducks and drakes with a native battery of idioms which prescribes such egregious collocations of vocables as the Basic *put up with* for *tolerate* or *put at a loss* for *bewilder.*

—Professor Lancelot Hogben, *Interglossa*

(3) On the one side we have the free personality: by definition it is not neurotic, for it has neither conflict nor dream. Its desires, such as they are, are transparent, for they are just what institutional approval keeps in the forefront of consciousness; another institutional pattern would alter their number and intensity; there is little in them that is natural, irreducible, or culturally dangerous. But *on the other side,* the social bond itself is nothing but the mutual reflection of these self-secure integrities. Recall the definition of love. Is not this the very picture of a small academic? Where is there a place in this hall of mirrors for either personality or fraternity?

—Essay on psychology in *Politics* (New York)

(4) All the "best people" from the gentlemen's clubs, and all the frantic fascist captains, united in common hatred of Socialism and bestial horror of the rising tide of the mass revolutionary movement, have turned to acts of provocation, to foul incendiarism, to medieval legends of poisoned wells, to legalize their own destruction of proletarian organizations, and rouse the agitated petty-bourgeoisie to chauvinistic fervour on behalf of the fight against the revolutionary way out of the crisis.

—Communist pamphlet

(5) If a new spirit is to be infused into this old country, there is one thorny and contentious reform which must be tackled, and that is the humanization and galvanization of the

B.B.C. Timidity here will bespeak cancer and atrophy of the soul. The heart of Britain may be sound and of strong beat, for instance, but the British lion's roar at present is like that of Bottom in Shakespeare's *Midsummer Night's Dream*—as gentle as any sucking dove. A virile new Britain cannot continue indefinitely to be traduced in the eyes or rather ears, of the world by the effete languors of Langham Place, brazenly masquerading as "standard English." When the Voice of Britain is heard at nine o'clock, better far and infinitely less ludicrous to hear aitches honestly dropped than the present priggish, inflated, inhibited, school-ma'amish arch braying of blameless bashful mewing maidens!

—Letter in *Tribune*

Each of these passages has faults of its own, but, quite apart from avoidable ugliness, two qualities are common to all of them. The first is staleness of imagery; the other is lack of precision. The writer either has a meaning and cannot express it, or he inadvertently says something else, or he is almost indifferent as to whether his words mean anything or not. This mixture of vagueness and sheer incompetence is the most marked characteristic of modern English prose, and especially of any kind of political writing. As soon as certain topics are raised, the concrete melts into the abstract and no one seems able to think of turns of speech that are not hackneyed: prose consists less and less of *words* chosen for the sake of their meaning, and more and more of *phrases* tacked together like the sections of a prefabricated hen-house. I list below, with notes and examples, various of the tricks by means of which the work of prose-construction is habitually dodged:

DYING METAPHORS

A newly invented metaphor assists thought by evoking a visual image, while on the other hand a metaphor which is technically "dead" (e.g. *iron resolution*) has in effect reverted to being an ordinary word and can generally be used without loss of vividness. But in between these two classes there is a huge dump of worn-out metaphors which have lost all evocative power and are merely used because they save people the trouble of inventing phrases for themselves. Examples are: *Ring the changes on, take up the cudgels for, toe the line, ride roughshod over, stand shoulder to shoulder with, play into the hands of, no axe to grind, grist to the mill, fishing in troubled waters, on the order of the day, Achilles' heel, swan song, hotbed.* Many of these are used without knowledge of their meaning (what is a "rift," for instance?), and incompatible metaphors are frequently mixed, a sure sign that the writer is not interested in what he is saying. Some metaphors now current have been twisted out of their original meaning without those who use them even being aware of the fact. For example, *toe the line* is sometimes written *tow the line.* Another example is *the hammer and the anvil,* now always used with the implication that the anvil gets the worst of it. In real life it is always the anvil that breaks the hammer, never the other way about: a writer who stopped to think what he was saying would be aware of this, and would avoid perverting the original phrase.

OPERATORS OR VERBAL FALSE LIMBS

These save the trouble of picking out appropriate verbs and nouns, and at the same time pad each sentence with extra syllables which give it an appearance of symmetry. Characteristic phrases are: *render inoperative, militate against, make contact with, be subjected to, give rise to, give grounds for, have the effect of, play a leading part (role) in, make itself felt, take effect, exhibit a tendency to, serve the purpose of, etc., etc.* The keynote is the elimination of simple verbs. Instead of being a single word, such as *break, stop, spoil, mend, kill,* a verb becomes a *phrase*, made up of a noun or adjective tacked on to some general-purposes verb such as *prove, serve, form, play, render.* In addition, the passive voice is wherever possible used in preference to the active, and noun constructions are used instead of gerunds (*by examination of* instead of *by examining*). The range of verbs is further cut down by means of the *-ize* and *de-* formations, and the banal statements are given an appearance of profundity by means of the *not un-*formation. Simple conjunctions and prepositions are replaced by such phrases as *with respect to, having regard to, the fact that, by dint of, in view of, in the interests of, on the hypothesis that;* and the ends of sentences are saved from anticlimax by such resounding commonplaces as *greatly to be desired, cannot be left out of account, a development to be expected in the near future, deserving of serious consideration, brought to a satisfactory conclusion,* and so on and so forth.

PRETENTIOUS DICTION

Words like *phenomenon, element, individual* (as noun), *objective, categorical, effective, virtual, basic, primary, promote, constitute, exhibit, exploit, utilize, eliminate, liquidate,* are used to dress up simple statements and give an air of scientific impartiality to biased judgments. Adjectives like *epoch-making, epic, historic, unforgettable, triumphant, age-old, inevitable, inexorable, veritable,* are used to dignify the sordid processes of international politics, while writing that aims at glorifying war usually takes on an archaic colour, its characteristic words being: *realm, throne, chariot, mailed fist, trident, sword, shield, buckler, banner, jackboot, clarion.* Foreign words and expressions such as *cul de sac, ancien regime, deus ex machina, mutatis mutandis, status quo, gleichshaltung, weltanschauung,* are used to give an air of culture and elegance. Except for the useful abbreviations *i.e., e.g.,* and *etc.,* there is no real need for any of the hundreds of foreign phrases now current in English. Bad writers, and especially scientific, political and sociological writers, are nearly always haunted by the notion that Latin or Greek words are grander than Saxon ones, and unnecessary words like *expedite, ameliorate, predict, extraneous, deracinated, clandestine, subaqueous* and hundreds of others constantly gain ground from their Anglo-Saxon opposite numbers.[1] The jargon peculiar to Marxist writing (*hyena, hangman, cannibal, petty bourgeois, these gentry, lacquey, flunkey, mad dog, White Guard,* etc.) consists largely of words and phrases translated from Russian, German or French; but the normal way of coining a new word is to use a Latin or Greek root with the appropriate affix and, where necessary, the -ize formation. It is often easier to make up words of this kind (*deregionalize, impermissible, extramarital, nonfragmentatary* and so forth) than to think up the English words that will cover one's meaning. The result, in general, is an increase in slovenliness and vagueness.

MEANINGLESS WORDS

In certain kinds of writing, particularly in art criticism and literary criticism, it is normal to come across long passages which are almost completely lacking in meaning.[2] Words like *romantic, plastic, values, human, dead, sentimental, natural, vitality,* as used in art criticism, are strictly meaningless in the sense that they not only do not point to any discoverable object, but are hardly ever expected to do so by the reader. When one critic writes, "The outstanding feature of Mr. X's work is its living quality," while another writes, "The immediately striking thing about Mr. X's work is its peculiar deadness," the reader accepts this as a simple difference of opinion. If words like *black* and *white* were involved, instead of the jargon words *dead* and *living,* he would see at once that language was being used in an improper way. Many political words are similarly abused. The word *Fascism* has now no meaning except in so far as it signifies "something not desirable." The words *democracy, socialism, freedom, patriotic, realistic, justice,* have each of them several different meanings which cannot be reconciled with one another. In the case of a word like *democracy,* not only is there no agreed definition, but the attempt to make one is resisted from all sides. It is almost universally felt that when we call a country democratic we are praising it: consequently the defenders of every kind of regime claim that it is a democracy, and fear that they might have to stop using the word if it were tied down to any one meaning. Words of this kind are often used in a consciously dishonest way. That is, the person who uses them has his own private definition, but allows his hearer to think he means something quite different. Statements like *Marshal Pétain was a true patriot, The Soviet Press is the freest in the world, The Catholic Church is opposed to persecution,* are almost always made with intent to deceive. Other words used in variable meanings, in most cases more or less dishonestly, are: *class, totalitarian, science, progressive, reactionary, bourgeois, equality.*

Now that I have made this catalogue of swindles and perversions, let me give another example of the kind of writing that they lead to. This time it must of its nature be an imaginary one. I am going to translate a passage of good English into modern English of the worst sort. Here is a well-known verse from *Ecclesiastes:*

> I returned and saw under the sun, that the race is not to the swift, nor the battle to the strong, neither yet bread to the wise, nor yet riches to men of understanding, nor yet favour to men of skill; but time and chance happeneth to them all.

Here it is in modern English:

> Objective consideration of contemporary phenomena compels the conclusion that success or failure in competitive activities exhibits no tendency to be commensurate with innate capacity, but that a considerable element of the unpredictable must invariably be taken into account.

This is a parody, but not a very gross one. Exhibit (3), above, for instance, contains several patches of the same kind of English. It will be seen that I have not made a full translation. The beginning and ending of the sentence follow the original meaning fairly closely, but in the middle the concrete illustrations—race, battle, bread—dissolve into the vague phrase "success or failure in competitive activities." This had to be so, because no modern writer of the kind I am discussing—no one capable of using phrases like "objective consideration of contemporary phenomena"—would ever tabulate his thoughts in that precise and detailed way. The whole tendency of modern prose is away from concreteness. Now analyse these two sentences a little more closely. The first contains forty-nine words but only sixty syllables, and all its words are those of everyday life. The second contains thirty-eight words of ninety syllables: eighteen of its words are from Latin roots, and one from Greek. The first sentence contains six vivid images, and only one phrase ("time and chance") that could be called vague. The second contains not a single fresh, arresting phrase, and in spite of its ninety syllables it gives only a shortened version of the meaning contained in the first. Yet without a doubt it is the second kind of sentence that is gaining ground in modern English. I do not want to exaggerate. This kind of writing is not yet universal, and outcrops of simplicity will occur here and there in the worst-written page. Still, if you or I were told to write a few lines on the uncertainty of human fortunes, we should probably come much nearer to my imaginary sentence than to the one from *Ecclesiastes.*

As I have tried to show, modern writing at its worst does not consist in picking out words for the sake of their meaning and inventing images in order to make the meaning clearer. It consists in gumming together long strips of words which have already been set in order by someone else, and making the results presentable by sheer humbug. The attraction of this way of writing is that it is easy. It is easier—even quicker, once you have the habit—to say *In my opinion it is a not unjustifiable assumption that* than to say *I think.* If you use ready-made phrases, you not only don't have to hunt about for words; you also don't have to bother with the rhythms of your sentences, since these phrases are generally so arranged as to be more or less euphonious. When you are composing in a hurry—when you are dictating to a stenographer, for instance, or making a public speech—it is natural to fall into a pretentious, Latinized style. Tags like *a consideration which we should do well to bear in mind* or *a conclusion to which all of us would readily assent* will save many a sentence from coming down with a bump. By using stale metaphors, similes and idioms, you save much mental effort, at the cost of leaving your meaning vague, not only for your reader but for yourself. This is the significance of mixed metaphors. The sole aim of a metaphor is to call up a visual image. When these images clash—as in *The Fascist octopus has sung its swan song, the jackboot is thrown into the melting pot*—it can be taken as certain that the writer is not seeing a mental image of the objects he is naming; in other words he is not really thinking. Look again at the examples I gave at the beginning of this essay. Professor Laski (1) uses five negatives in fifty-three words. One of these is superfluous, making nonsense of the whole passage, and in addition there is the slip *alien* for akin, making further nonsense, and several avoidable pieces of clumsiness which increase the general vagueness. Professor Hogben (2) plays ducks and drakes with a battery which is able to write prescriptions, and, while disapproving of the everyday phrase *put up with,* is unwilling to look *egregious* up in the dictionary and see what it means. (3), if one takes an uncharitable attitude towards it, is simply meaningless: probably one could work out its intended meaning by reading the whole of the article in which it occurs. In (4), the writer knows more or less what he wants to say, but an accumulation of stale phrases chokes him like tea leaves blocking a sink. In (5), words and meaning have almost parted company. People who write in this manner usually have a general emotional meaning—they dislike one thing and want to express solidarity with another—but they are not interested in the detail of what they are saying. A scrupulous writer, in every sentence that he writes, will ask himself at least four questions, thus: What am I trying to say? What words will express it? What image or idiom will make it clearer? Is this image fresh enough to have an effect? And he will probably ask himself two more: Could I put it more shortly? Have I said anything that is avoidably ugly? But you are not obliged to go to all this trouble. You can shirk it by simply throwing your mind open and letting the ready-made phrases come crowding in. They will construct your sentences for you—even think your thoughts for you, to a certain extent—and at need they will perform the important service of partially concealing your meaning even from yourself. It is at this point that the special connection between politics and the debasement of language becomes clear.

In our time it is broadly true that political writing is bad writing. Where it is not true, it will generally be found that the writer is some kind of rebel, expressing his private opinions and not a "party line." Orthodoxy, of whatever colour, seems to demand a lifeless, imitative style. The political dialects to be found in pamphlets, leading articles, manifestos, White

Papers and the speeches of under-secretaries do, of course, vary from party to party, but they are all alike in that one almost never finds in them a fresh, vivid, homemade turn of speech. When one watches some tired hack on the platform mechanically repeating the familiar phrases—*bestial atrocities, iron heel, bloodstained tyranny, free peoples of the world, stand shoulder to shoulder*—one often has a curious feeling that one is not watching a live human being but some kind of dummy: a feeling which suddenly becomes stronger at moments when the light catches the speaker's spectacles and turns them into blank discs which seem to have no eyes behind them. And this is not altogether fanciful. A speaker who uses that kind of phraseology has gone some distance towards turning himself into a machine. The appropriate noises are coming out of his larynx, but his brain is not involved as it would be if he were choosing his words for himself. If the speech he is making is one that he is accustomed to make over and over again, he may be almost unconscious of what he is saying, as one is when one utters the responses in church. And this reduced state of consciousness, if not indispensable, is at any rate favourable to political conformity.

In our time, political speech and writing are largely the defence of the indefensible. Things like the continuance of British rule in India, the Russian purges and deportations, the dropping of the atom bombs on Japan, can indeed be defended, but only by arguments which are too brutal for most people to face, and which do not square with the professed aims of political parties. Thus political language has to consist largely of euphemism, question-begging and sheer cloudy vagueness. Defenceless villages are bombarded from the air, the inhabitants driven out into the countryside, the cattle machine-gunned, the huts set on fire with incendiary bullets: this is called *pacification*. Millions of peasants are robbed of their farms and sent trudging along the roads with no more than they can carry: this is called *transfer of population* or *rectification of frontiers*. People are imprisoned for years without trial, or shot in the back of the neck or sent to die of scurvy in Arctic lumber camps: this is called *elimination of unreliable elements*. Such phraseology is needed if one wants to name things without calling up mental pictures of them. Consider for instance some comfortable English professor defending Russian totalitarianism. He cannot say outright, "I believe in killing off your opponents when you can get good results by doing so." Probably, therefore, he will say something like this:

> While freely conceding that the Soviet regime exhibits certain features which the humanitarian may be inclined to deplore, we must, I think, agree that a certain curtailment of the right to political opposition is an unavoidable concomitant of transitional periods, and that the rigours which the Russian people have been called upon to undergo have been amply justified in the sphere of concrete achievement.

The inflated style is itself a kind of euphemism. A mass of Latin words fall upon the facts like soft snow, blurring the outlines and covering up all the details. The great enemy of clear language is insincerity. When there is a gap between one's real and one's declared aims, one turns as it were instinctively to long words and exhausted idioms, like a cuttlefish squirting out ink. In our age there is no such thing as "keeping out of politics." All issues are political issues, and politics itself is a mass of lies, evasions, folly, hatred and schizophrenia. When the general atmosphere is bad, language must suffer. I should expect to find— this is a guess which I have not sufficient knowledge to verify—that the German, Russian and Italian languages have all deteriorated in the last ten or fifteen years, as a result of dictatorship.

But if thought corrupts language, language can also corrupt thought. A bad usage can spread by tradition and imitation, even among people who should and do know better. The debased language that I have been discussing is in some ways very convenient. Phrases like *a not unjustifiable assumption, leaves much to be desired, would serve no good purpose, a consideration which we should do well to bear in mind,* are a continuous temptation, a packet of aspirins always at one's elbow. Look back through this essay, and for certain you will find that I have again and again committed the very faults I am protesting against. By this morning's post I have received a pamphlet dealing with conditions in Germany. The author tells me that he "felt impelled" to write it. I open it at random, and here is almost the first sentence that I see: "[The Allies] have an opportunity not only of achieving a radical transformation of Germany's social and political structure in such a way as to avoid a nationalistic reaction in Germany itself, but at the same time of laying the foundations of a cooperative and unified Europe." You see, he "feels impelled" to write—feels, presumably, that he has something new to say— and yet his words, like cavalry horses answering the bugle, group themselves automatically into the familiar dreary pattern. This invasion of one's mind by ready-made phrases (*lay the foundations, achieve a radical transformation*) can only be prevented if one is constantly on guard against them, and every such phrase anaesthetizes a portion of one's brain.

I said earlier that the decadence of our language is probably curable. Those who deny this would argue, if they produced an argument at all, that language merely reflects existing social conditions, and that we cannot influence its development by any direct tinkering with words and constructions. So far as the general tone or spirit of a language goes, this may be true, but it is not true in detail. Silly words and expressions have often disappeared, not through any evolutionary process but owing to the conscious action of a minority. Two recent examples were *explore every avenue* and *leave no stone unturned,* which were killed by the jeers of a few journalists. There is a long list of flyblown metaphors which could similarly be got rid of if enough people would interest themselves in the job; and it should also be possible to laugh the *not un-* formation out of existence,[3] to reduce the amount of Latin and Greek in the average sentence, to drive out foreign phrases and strayed scientific words, and, in general, to make pretentiousness unfashionable. But all these are minor points. The defense of the English language implies more than this, and perhaps it is best to start by saying what it does *not* imply.

To begin with it has nothing to do with archaism, with the salvaging of obsolete words and turns of speech, or with the setting up of a "standard English" which must never be departed from. On the contrary, it is especially concerned with the scrapping of every word or idiom which has outworn its usefulness. It has nothing to do with correct grammar and syntax, which are of no importance so long as one makes one's meaning clear, or with the avoidance of Americanisms, or with having what is called a "good prose style." On the other hand it is not concerned with fake simplicity and the attempt to make written English colloquial. Nor does it even imply in every case preferring the Saxon word to the Latin one, though it does imply using the fewest and shortest words that will cover one's meaning. What is above all needed is to let the meaning choose the word, and not the other way about. In prose, the worst thing one can do with words is to surrender to them. When you think of a concrete object, you think wordlessly, and then, if you want to describe the thing you have been visualizing you probably hunt about till you find the exact words that seem to fit. When you think of something abstract you are more inclined to use words from the start, and unless you make a conscious effort to prevent it, the existing dialect will come rushing in and do the job for you, at the expense of blurring or even changing your meaning. Probably it is better to put off using words as long as possible and get one's meaning as clear as one can through pictures or sensations. Afterwards one can choose—not simply *accept*—the phrases that will best cover the meaning, and then switch round and decide what impression one's words are likely to make on another person. This last effort of the mind cuts out all stale or mixed images, all prefabricated phrases, needless repetitions, and humbug and vagueness generally. But one can often be in doubt about the effect of a word or a phrase, and one needs rules that one can rely on when instinct fails. I think the following rules will cover most cases:

1. Never use a metaphor, simile or other figure of speech which you are used to seeing in print.
2. Never use a long word where a short one will do.
3. If it is possible to cut a word out, always cut it out.
4. Never use the passive where you can use the active.
5. Never use a foreign phrase, a scientific word or a jargon word if you can think of an everyday English equivalent.
6. Break any of these rules sooner than say anything outright barbarous.

These rules sound elementary, and so they are, but they demand a deep change of attitude in anyone who has grown used to writing in the style now fashionable. One could keep all of them and still write bad English, but one could not write the kind of stuff that I quoted in those five specimens at the beginning of this article.

I have not here been considering the literary use of language, but merely language as an instrument for expressing and not for concealing or preventing thought. Stuart Chase and others have come near to claiming that all abstract words are meaningless, and have used this as a pretext for advocating a kind of political quietism. Since you don't know what Fascism is, how can you struggle against Fascism? One need not swallow such absurdities as this, but one ought to recognize that the present political chaos is connected with the decay of language, and that one can probably bring about some improvement by starting at the verbal end. If you simplify your English, you are freed from the worst follies of orthodoxy. You cannot speak any of the necessary dialects, and when you make a stupid remark its stupidity will be obvious, even to yourself. Political language—and with variations this is true of all political parties, from Conservatives to Anarchists—is designed to make lies sound truthful and murder respectable, and to give an appearance of solidity to pure wind. One cannot change this all in a moment, but one can at least change one's own habits, and from time to time one can even, if one jeers loudly enough, send some worn-out and useless phrase—some *jackboot, Achilles' heel, hotbed, melting pot, acid test, veritable inferno* or other lump of verbal refuse—into the dustbin where it belongs.

Notes

[1] An interesting illustration of this is the way in which the English flower names which were in use till very recently are being ousted by Greek ones, *snapdragon* becoming *antirrkinum, forget-me-not* becoming *myosotis,* etc. It is hard to see any practical reason for this change of fashion: it is probably due to an instinctive turning-away from the more homely word and a vague feeling that the Greek word is scientific.

[2] Example: "Comfort's catholicity of perception and image, strangely Whitmanesque in range, almost the exact opposite in aesthetic compulsion, continues to evoke that trembling atmospheric accumulative hinting at a cruel, an inexorably serene timelessness. . . . Wrey Gardiner scores by aiming at simple bull's-eyes with precision. Only they are not so simple, and through this contented sadness runs more than the surface bitter-sweet of resignation." (*Poetry Quarterly.*)

[3] One can cure oneself of the *not un-* formation by memorizing this sentence: *A not unblack dog was chasing a not unsmall rabbit across a not ungreen field.*

Understanding the Text

1. In Orwell's view, what is the nature of the relation between language and thought?

2. What typifies writing that Orwell considers "easy"?

3. What social improvement does Orwell think would follow if writers improved their use of the English language? Why?

Additional Readings

Adatto, Kiku. *Picture Perfect: The Art and Artifice of Public Image Making.* New York: Basic Books, 1993.

Alterman, Eric. *Sound and Fury: The Washington Punditocracy and the Collapse of American Politics.* New York: HarperCollins, 1992.

Bagdikian, Ben. *The Media Monopoly.* 1983. Boston: Beacon Press, 2000.

Didion, Joan. *Political Fictions.* New York: Knopf, 2001.

Fallows, James. *Breaking the News: How the Media Undermine American Democracy.* New York: Pantheon 1996.

Hertsgaard, Mark. *On Bended Knee: The Press and the Reagan Presidency.* 1988. New York: Schocken, 1989.

Jamieson, Kathleen Hall. *Dirty Politics: Deception, Distraction, and Democracy.* New York: Oxford UP, 1992.

———. *Packaging the Presidency: A History and Criticism of Presidential Campaign Advertising.* 1984. New York: Oxford UP, 1996.

Kalb, Marvin. *One Scandalous Story: Clinton, Lewinski, & 13 Days That Tarnished American Journalism.* New York: Free Press, 2001.

Kellner, Douglas. *Media Spectacle and the Crisis of Democracy: Terrorism, War, and Election Battles.* Boulder: Paradigm, 2005.

Lapham, Lewis. *Lights, Camera, Democracy!: Selected Essays.* New York: AtRandom.com, 2001.

McChesney, Robert W. *Rich Media, Poor Democracy: Communication Politics in Dubious Times.* New York: New Press, 2000.

Mindich, David T.Z. *Tuned Out: Why Americans Under 40 Don't Follow the News.* New York: Oxford UP, 2005.

Postman, Neil. *Amusing Ourselves to Death: Public Discourse in the Age of Show Business.* New York: Viking, 1985.

Scheuer, Jeffrey. *The Sound Bite Society: How Television Helps the Right and Hurts the Left.* New York: Routledge, 2001.

Schroeder, Alan. *Celebrity-in-Chief: How Business Took Over the White House.* Boulder: Westview, 2004.

———. *Presidential Debates: Forty Years of High-Risk TV.* New York: Columbia UP, 2000.

Schudson, Michael. *The Power of News.* Cambridge: Harvard UP, 1995.

Stahl, Lesley. *Reporting Live.* 1999. New York: Touchstone-Simon & Schuster, 2000.

Starr, Paul. *The Creation of the Media: Political Origins of Modern Communications.* New York: Basic Books, 2004.

Thelen, David. *Becoming Citizens in the Age of Television: How Americans Challenged the Media and Seized Political Control During the Iran-Contra Debate.* Chicago: U of Chicago P, 1996.

Thomas, Helen. *Front Row at the White House: My Life and Times.* 1999. New York: Touchstone-Simon & Schuster, 2000.

Is Nothing What It Seems?:

Mediation and Its Problems

Allegory of the Cave

Plato

FROM BOOK VII

Next, said I, compare our nature in respect of education and its lack to such an experience as this. Picture men dwelling in a sort of subterranean cavern with a long entrance open to the light on its entire width. Conceive them as having their legs and necks fettered from childhood, so that they remain in the same spot, able to look forward only, and prevented by the fetters from turning their heads. Picture further the light from a fire burning higher up and at a distance behind them, and between the fire and the prisoners and above them a road along which a low wall has been built, as the exhibitors of puppet shows have partitions before the men themselves, above which they show the puppets.

All that I see, he said.

See also, then, men carrying past the wall implements of all kinds that rise above the wall, and human images and shapes of animals as well, wrought in stone and wood and every material, some of these bearers presumably speaking and others silent.

A strange image you speak of, he said, and strange prisoners.

Like to us, I said. For, to begin with, tell me do you think that these men would have seen anything of themselves or of one another except the shadows cast from the fire on the wall of the cave that fronted them?

Plato (428–348 B.C.), admirer of Socrates (470–399 B.C.) and teacher of Aristotle (384–322 B.C.), is perhaps the best known and most influential of all the ancient Greek philosophers. The majority of his writings take the form of dialogues in which the protagonist Socrates questions other characters, entrapping them in their own contradictions and thus exposing the inconsistencies in their arguments. Chief among Plato's lasting contributions to western thought are the Theory of Forms, in which Plato posits the existence of a perfect, immutable idea (or form) from which each sensate object derives, his model for the education of young rulers-to-be as a means of establishing a just and ordered state, and his idealized form of love that encouraged the lover and beloved to seek a spiritual union that rose above the level of mere sexual desire.

How could they, he said, if they were compelled to hold their heads unmoved through life?

And again, would not the same be true of the objects carried past them?

Surely.

If then they were able to talk to one another, do you not think that they would suppose that in naming the things that they saw they were naming the passing objects?

Necessarily.

And if their prison had an echo from the wall opposite them, when one of the passers-by uttered a sound, do you think that they would suppose anything else than the passing shadow to be the speaker?

By Zeus, I do not, said he.

Then in every way such prisoners would deem reality to be nothing else than the shadows of the artificial objects.

Quite inevitably, he said.

Consider, then, what would be the manner of the release and healing from these bonds and this folly if in the course of nature something of this sort should happen to them. When one was freed from his fetters and compelled to stand up suddenly and turn his head around and walk and to lift up his eyes to the light, and in doing all this felt pain and, because of the dazzle and glitter of the light, was unable to discern the objects whose shadows he formerly saw, what do you suppose would be his answer if someone told him that what he had seen before was all a cheat and an illusion, but that now, being nearer to reality and turned toward more real things, he saw more truly? And if also one should point out to him each of the passing objects and constrain him by questions to say what it is, do you not think that he would be at a loss and that he would regard what he formerly saw as more real than the things now pointed out to him?

Far more real, he said.

And if he were compelled to look at the light itself, would not that pain his eyes, and would he not turn away and flee to those things which he is able to discern and regard them as in very deed more clear and exact than the objects pointed out?

It is so, he said.

And if, said I, someone should drag him thence by force up the ascent which is rough and steep, and not let him go before he had drawn him out into the light of the sun, do you not think that he would find it painful to be so haled along, and would chafe at it, and when he came out into the light, that his eyes would be filled with its beams so that he would not be able to see even one of the things that we call real?

Why, no, not immediately, he said.

Then there would be need of habituation, I take it, to enable him to see the things higher up. And at first he would most easily discern the shadows and, after that, the likenesses or reflections in water of men and other things, and later, the things themselves, and from these he would go on to contemplate the appearances in the heavens and heaven itself, more easily by night, looking at the light of the stars and the moon, than by day the sun and the sun's light.

Of course.

And so, finally, I suppose, he would be able to look upon the sun itself and see its true nature, not by reflections in water or phantasms of it in an alien setting, but in and by itself in its own place.

Necessarily, he said.

And at this point he would infer and conclude that this it is that provides the seasons and the courses of the year and presides over all things in the visible region, and is in some sort the cause of all these things that they had seen.

Obviously, he said, that would be the next step.

Well then, if he recalled to mind his first habitation and what passed for wisdom there, and his fellow bondsmen, do you not think that he would count himself happy in the change and pity them?

He would indeed.

And if there had been honors and commendations among them which they bestowed on one another and prizes for the man who is quickest to make out the shadows as they pass and best able to remember their customary precedences, sequences, and coexistences, and so most successful in guessing at what was to come, do you think he would be very keen about such rewards, and that he would envy and emulate those who were honored by these prisoners and lorded it among them, or that he would feel with Homer and greatly prefer while living on earth to be serf of another, a landless man, and endure anything rather than opine with them and live that life?

Yes, he said, I think that he would choose to endure anything rather than such a life.

And consider this also, said I. If such a one should go down again and take his old place would he not get his eyes full of darkness, thus suddenly coming out of the sunlight?

He would indeed.

Now if he should be required to contend with these perpetual prisoners in 'evaluating' these shadows while his vision was still dim and before his eyes were accustomed to the dark—and this time required for habituation would not be very short—would he not provoke laughter, and would it not be said of him that he had returned from his journey aloft with his eyes ruined and that it was not worth while even to attempt the ascent? And if it were possible to lay hands on and to kill the man who tried to release them and lead them up, would they not kill him?

They certainly would, he said.

This image then, dear Glaucon, we must apply as a whole to all that has been said, likening the region revealed through sight to the habitation of the prison, and the light of the fire in it to the power of the sun. And if you assume that the ascent and the contemplation of the things above is the soul's ascension to the intelligible region, you will not miss my surmise, since that is what you desire to hear. But God knows whether it is true. But, at any rate, my dream as it appears to me is that in the region of the known the last thing to be seen and hardly seen is the idea of good, and that when seen it must needs point us to the conclusion that this is indeed the cause for all things of all that is right and beautiful, giving birth in the visible world to light, and the author of light and itself in the intelligible world being the authentic source of truth and reason, and that anyone who is to act wisely in private or public must have caught sight of this.

I concur, he said, so far as I am able.

Come then, I said, and join me in this further thought, and do not be surprised that those who have attained to this height are not willing to occupy themselves with the affairs of men, but their souls ever feel the upward urge and the yearning for that sojourn above. For this, I take it, is likely if in this point too the likeness of our image holds.

Yes, it is likely.

And again, do you think it at all strange, said I, if a man returning from divine contemplations to the petty miseries of men cuts a sorry figure and appears most ridiculous, if, while still blinking through the gloom, and before he has become sufficiently accustomed to the environing darkness, he is compelled in courtrooms or elsewhere to contend about the shadows of justice or the images that cast the shadows and to wrangle in debate about the notions of these things in the minds of those who have never seen justice itself?

It would be by no means strange, he said.

But a sensible man, I said, would remember that there are two distinct disturbances of the eyes arising from two causes, according as the shift is from light to darkness or from darkness to light, and, believing that the same thing happens to the soul too, whenever he saw a soul perturbed and unable to discern something, he would not laugh unthinkingly, but would observe whether coming from a brighter life its vision was obscured by the unfamiliar darkness, or whether the passage from the deeper dark of ignorance into a more luminous world and the greater brightness had dazzled its vision. And so he would deem the one happy in its experience and way of life and pity the other, and if it pleased him to laugh at it, his laughter would be less laughable than that at the expense of the soul that had come down from the light above.

That is a very fair statement, he said.

Then, if this is true, our view of these matters must be this, that education is not in reality what some people proclaim it to be in their professions. What they aver is that they can put true knowledge into a soul that does not possess it, as if they were inserting vision into blind eyes.

They do indeed, he said.

But our present argument indicates, said I, that the true analogy for this indwelling power in the soul and the instrument whereby each of us apprehends is that of an eye that could not be converted to the light from the darkness except by turning the whole body. Even so this organ of knowledge must be turned around from the world of becoming together with the entire soul, like the scene-shifting periactus in the theater, until the soul is able to endure the contemplation of essence and the brightest region of being. And this, we say, is the good, do we not?

Yes.

Of this very thing, then, I said, there might be an art, an art of the speediest and most effective shifting or conversion of the soul, not an art of producing vision in it, but on the assumption that it possesses vision but does not rightly direct it and does not look where it should, an art of bringing this about.

Yes, that seems likely, he said.

Then the other so-called virtues of the soul do seem akin to those of the body. For it is true that where they do not pre-exist, they are afterward created by habit and practice. But the excellence of thought, it seems, is certainly of a more divine quality, a thing that never loses its potency, but, according to the direction of its conversion, becomes useful and beneficent, or, again, useless and harmful. Have you never observed in those who are popularly spoken of as bad, but smart men how keen is the vision of the little soul, how quick it is to discern the things that interest it, a proof that it is not a poor vision which it has, but one forcibly enlisted in the service of evil, so that the sharper its sight the more mischief it accomplishes?

I certainly have, he said.

Observe then, said I, that this part of such a soul, if it had been hammered from childhood, and had thus been struck free of the leaden weights, so to speak, of our birth and becoming, which attaching themselves to it by food and similar pleasures and gluttonies turn downward the vision of the soul—if, I say, freed from these, it had suffered a conversion toward the things that are real and true, that same faculty of the same men would have been most keen in its vision of the higher things, just as it is for the things toward which it is now turned.

It is likely, he said.

Well, then, said I, is not this also likely and a necessary consequence of what has been said, that neither could men who are uneducated and inexperienced in truth ever adequately preside over a state, nor could those who had been permitted to linger on to the end in the pursuit of culture—the one because they have no single aim and purpose in life to which all their actions, public and private, must be directed, and the others, because they will not voluntarily engage in action, believing that while still living they have been transported to the Islands of the Blessed?

True, he said.

It is the duty of us, the founders, then, said I, to compel the best natures to attain the knowledge which we pronounced the greatest, and to win to the vision of the good, to scale that ascent, and when they have reached the heights and taken an adequate view, we must not allow what is now permitted.

What is that?

That they should linger there, I said, and refuse to go down again among those bondsmen and share their labors and honors, whether they are of less or of greater worth.

Do you mean to say that we must do them this wrong, and compel them to live an inferior life when the better is in their power?

You have again forgotten, my friend, said I, that the law is not concerned with the special happiness of any class in the state, but is trying to produce this condition in the city as a whole, harmonizing and adapting the citizens to one another by persuasion and compulsion, and requiring them to impart to one another any benefit which they are severally able to bestow upon the community, and that it itself creates such men in the state, not that it may allow each to take what course pleases him, but with a view to using them for the binding together of the commonwealth.

True, he said, I did forget it.

Observe, then, Glaucon, said I, that we shall not be wronging, either, the philosophers who arise among us, but that we can justify our action when we constrain them to take charge of the other citizens and be their guardians. For we will say to them that it is natural that men of similar quality who spring up in other cities should not share in the labors there. For they grow up spontaneously from no volition of the government in the several states, and it is justice that the self-grown, indebted to none for its breeding, should not be zealous either to pay to anyone the price of its nurture. But you we have engendered for yourselves and the rest of the city to be, as it were, king bees and leaders in the hive. You have received a better and more complete education than the others, and you are more capable of sharing both ways of life. Down you must go then, each in his turn, to the habitation of the others and accustom yourselves to the observation of the obscure things there. For once habituated you will discern them infinitely better than the dwellers there, and you will know what each of the 'idols' is and whereof it is a semblance, because you have seen the reality of the beautiful, the just and the good. So our city will be governed by us and you with waking minds, and not, as most cities now which are inhabited and ruled darkly as in a dream by men who fight one another for shadows and wrangle for office as if that were a great good, when the truth is that the city in which those who are to rule are least eager to hold office must needs be best administered and most free from dissension, and the state that gets the contrary type of ruler will be the opposite of this.

By all means, he said.

Will our alumni, then, disobey us when we tell them this, and will they refuse to share in the labors of state each in his turn while permitted to dwell most of the time with one another in that purer world?

Impossible, he said, for we shall be imposing just commands on men who are just. Yet they will assuredly approach office as an unavoidable necessity, and in the opposite temper from that of the present rulers in our cities.

For the fact is, dear friend, said I, if you can discover a better way of life than office holding for your future rulers, a well-governed city becomes a possibility. For only in such a state will those rule who are really rich, not in gold, but in the wealth that makes happiness—a good and wise life. But if, being beggars and starvelings from lack of goods of their own, they turn to affairs of state thinking that it is thence that they should grasp their own good, then it is impossible. For when office and rule become the prizes of contention, such a civil and internecine strife destroys the office seekers themselves and the city as well.

Molding Our Lives in the Image of Movies

Neal Gabler

Nearly 160 years ago, Alexis De Tocqueville observed that Americans lacked an appreciation for what he called the "pleasures of mind." Instead, he wrote, they "prefer books which may be easily procured, quickly read, and which require no learned researches to be understood. They ask for beauties self-proffered and easily enjoyed. . . . They require strong and rapid emotions, startling passages, truths or errors brilliant enough to rouse them up and to plunge them at once, as if by violence, into the midst of the subject."

Those words remain, in fact, a pretty good description of the impulses that drive American popular culture, what one might call a constant quest for ever greater sensationalism. But the characteristics Tocqueville ascribed to our books, poetry and theater are now no longer confined to amusements; they have leached into almost every aspect of American life. Any putative Tocqueville looking at America today would see a whole Republic of Entertainment in which strong and rapid emotions, startling passages and rousing truths pervade journalism, politics, education, religion, art and even crime. Indeed, ours seems to be a world molded in the image of the movies and intended for our viewing pleasure.

To most of us, this has been obvious for some time in the country's public life. However serious their subtext may be, news events like the O. J. Simpson trials and Lewinskygate are vastly entertaining spectacles that are promoted, packaged and

Neal Gabler is a prominent commentator upon American media and celebrity culture. He has taught at the University of Michigan and Pennsylvania State University and has written four books: *Walt Disney: The Triumph of the American Imagination* (2006), *Life the Movie: How Entertainment Conquered Reali'* (1998), *Winchell: Gossip, Power and the C* . *of Celebrity* (1994), and *An Empire of Th wn: How the Jews Invented Hollywood* (19̸ ie also has published numerous artic̸ ı *The New York Times, Esquire, American .age, The New Republic, Us,* and others, an̸ a frequent guest on television and radio ɾ ɟrams.

presented very much like the latest Hollywood blockbusters, only these stories happen to be written in the medium of life.

What has been less evident than the transformation of public events into entertainment, however, is something arguably much more important: the extent to which entertainment has gradually infested our own personal lives, converting them into "movies" too. It is not just that audiences may find daily life as entertaining as fictionalized stories, as *The Truman Show* and the director Ron Howard's forthcoming *EdTV* have it. It is that over the years our movie-going and television watching has been impregnating the American consciousness with the conventions and esthetics of entertainment, until we have become performers ourselves, performing our own lives out of the shards of movies. One might even think of American life, including quotidian American life, as a vast production in which virtually every object is a prop, every space is a set, every person is an actor and every experience is a scene in a continuing narrative.

It has been a long process that has brought us to this point—a process that may have been set in motion by the country's very active sense of democracy. In Europe, where the class hierarchy was rigid and class distinctions obvious, any sort of personal theatricality, aside from that of self-conscious, rebellious Bohemians, was limited to the upperclasses, which could afford flamboyant display. But in America, where class boundaries were more porous and distinctions less apparent, citizens quickly learned that how one looked and behaved largely determined how one was perceived, prompting Walt Whitman to lament the "terrible doubt of appearances."

This emphasis on class by style infused 19th century American life with a kind of subtle theatricality as the middle class and later the working class imitated the affectations of the gentry in hopes of being regarded as gentry themselves. By the early 20th century, though, these old models of gentility had yielded to new models in the mass media, especially the movies, and the change ushered in a marked difference in aspiration. What had begun in the 19th century as a way of appropriating class became in the 20th a way of making one's life more closely approximate the glamorous visions one read about in novels and picture magazines or saw on the screen.

Today, with the burgeoning of mass culture, this everyday performance art may be America's most ubiquitous art. Though obviously not everyone is willing to concede that he or she is becoming a performer, there are telltale signs everywhere that ordinary life is cinematic. Take fashion. There was a time when fashion was, as Tom Wolfe once put it, the "code language of status," a way to express where one stood in the social order. Nowadays, when nearly everyone has access to designer clothes, even if it is only a pair of jeans, fashion is less expressive than imaginative. What one wears doesn't necessarily convey who one is: it projects who one wants to be—which makes clothing into costume.

It is certainly no coincidence that America's most popular and influential designer, Ralph Lauren, has demonstrated the greatest appreciation for the costume functions of fashion. What Mr. Lauren, born Ralph Lifshitz, understood from his own love of the movies as a boy growing up in the Bronx was that people would pay to transform their lives into their cinematic fantasies: safari outfits to make one a colonialist from *Out of Africa;* denim jackets and jeans to make one a cowboy from a Hollywood western; finely tailored English suits to make one an aristocrat from any number of crisp drawing room melodramas.

At the same time, he realized that these transformations were more than a matter of costuming. With his home furnishings and accessories as well as his ad campaigns, Mr. Lauren sells an image of life, a kind of collage of movie fantasies that, in his own words, "represent living, not fashion" and that, more specifically, provide the "whole atmosphere of the good life" that movies had always purveyed. One writer called him the first image manager, which is exactly what he is. He *gave* the middle class what the upper classes and celebrities had always had: a conscious esthetic.

What Ralph Lauren is to the materials of image, Martha Stewart is to their deployment. Like Mr. Lauren's, Ms. Stewart's origins were humble, but like Mr. Lauren, she has an instinct for transporting her followers from their daily grind. Identifying with the bedraggled, unfulfilled, unappreciated middle-class housewife, Ms. Stewart, as a life style consultant, offers a vision of domestic perfection that owes more to movies and television sitcoms than to reality. "We have come to realize that the creation of a fine family, a lovely life style and a comfortable home is kind of a national art form in itself," she told her readers of her syndicated column with a nod to the theatricality of it. So devout an esthete is Ms. Stewart that she has even issued instructions on how to shovel the snow from your sidewalk: "Always leave an inch of snow so it looks nice and white. Esthetics are very important in snow removal."

While designers like Mr. Lauren and life style counselors like Ms. Stewart are in the business of image management, more and more architects are in the business of creating the sets on which the life movie could unfold. Stores like Niketown and malls like the Mall of America outside Minneapolis or Horton Plaza in San Diego, theme restaurants like the Hard Rock Cafe, Planet Hollywood or Jekyll and Hyde, and hotels, museums, churches and schools were now furnishing stages for the performance of shopping, eating, sleeping, watching, worshiping or learning. As Andy Warhol once said of New York restaurants, "They caught on that what people really care about is changing their atmosphere for a couple of hours"—that is, escaping into their own life movies.

Nor was the set restricted to individual spaces. Whole areas had become back lots, to use the Hollywood term for the studios' old tracts where outdoor scenes were shot—areas like West 57th Street and the South Street Seaport in New York or Peachtree Center in Atlanta or

Navy Pier in Chicago. The intellectual historian Thomas Bender, looking at the way America's inner cities were being colonized and commercialized by chain stores, theme restaurants and other tourist attractions, summoned a new urban vision in which the city was an "entertainment zone—a place to visit, a place to shop; it is no more than a live-in theme park," which he believed was designed to hide a grittier, dirtier, more problematic city from us.

Even so, if many of us now live on stages, dress in costumes and follow esthetic guidance, these things are only symptomatic of a larger reconceptualization of life itself. Nearly 50 years ago, the sociologist David Riesman identified the emergence of a new type of social character in America that he called "other-directed," by which he meant, essentially, that one's goals were directed toward satisfying the expectations of others—an audience. By definition, other-directed Americans were conscious of performance and of the effects of affect, a self-consciousness that led another sociologist, Erving Goffman, to conclude that in the 20th century "life itself is a dramatically enacted thing."

In Goffman's analysis, every American was engaged in a series of plays and a series of roles, an "exchange of dramatically inflated actions, counteractions, and terminating replies"— in short, an enactment of the scenes of daily life. What Goffman didn't seem to foresee when he was writing in the late 1950's was how much more complex the performance would become, how many more scenes and roles there would be to play on a daily basis and how much farther the front stage would extend into the backstage until the show never seemed to end.

In effect, the demands of daily performance at work, at school, at social engagements, even at home, would become so onerous that one could no longer be compared to a classical actor digging into his kit bag to find a character the way a Laurence Olivier had. Rather, Americans were on stage so often that they were forced to become Method actors mastering the art of playing themselves by, as Elizabeth Taylor once described the technique, "making their fiction reality." Daily life had become a show. "A whole day of life is like a whole day of television," Andy Warhol observed, anticipating *The Truman Show*. "TV never goes off the air once it starts for the day, and I don't either. At the end of the day the whole day will be a movie."

But if one lived a movie, as Warhol said, it wasn't just the day that qualified as a performance; it was the entire life. It was *life* now that had a beginning, a middle and an end like conventional movies. It was *life* now that was increasingly being plotted to let the "actor" live out his or her fantasies, albeit within the restraints of physical appearance, financial resources, talent, cooperation and a myriad of other impediments. One now chose a genre to which one aspired and then eased into the role. If you wanted to be a young professional or a Bohemian artist or a man of leisure or an outdoorsman, you conformed your life to the conventions of each. You dressed the way they dressed, acted the way they acted, associated with the kinds of people with whom they associated.

Though in practice this was all somewhat amorphous, what really seemed to illustrate how rapidly personal life was advancing toward theater was the advent of a new profession:

self-styled "life coaches," reportedly 1,300 of them, as of last year, who advise clients on how to reorient their lives to reach what one coach calls fulfillment but what someone else might call a happy ending. What the coaches do, along with routine ego boosting, is replot the client's life. They tell him how he should organize his time, how he should deal with business matters, whether or not he should host a party or take a trip. "It's like painting a canvas for a 'life assignment,'" said one coach.

Few people are as overtly self-conscious about their life movies as these clients, but a good many Americans are still embarked on a campaign to live out their life vision as it has been shaped by mass culture. "At one point in cultural history we asked whether movies furnished an adequate likeness of real life," the psychologist Kenneth Gergen once observed. "The good movies were the more realistic. Now we ask of reality that it accommodate itself to film. The good person, like the good party, should be more 'movieistic.'" Or to put it another way, where we had once measured the movies by life, we are learning to measure life itself by how well it satisfies the narrative expectations created by the movies.

In doing so, we have been changing not only the contours of our lives but the very justification for our existence. Traditionally, realizing one's dreams was only one part of the life experience. It was understood that a full life necessarily entailed both our failures and our triumphs, our agonies and our ecstasies. This was why Aldous Huxley's brave new world seemed so terrifying even though its inhabitants were in a perpetual state of bliss. In Huxley's view, they had sacrificed their humanness to their happiness.

Clearly we have not yet arrived at the point where we can shape our lives to our specifications as writers shape movies, but we are probably closer to living in *Pleasantville,* to cite the title of the new film about a 1950s television universe of unruffled joy, than any previous generation. In the movie, the town of Pleasantville is disturbed by the arrival of "real" humans who bring with them a pungent taste of "real" life. In our own Pleasantville, though, the issue is not how much more exciting reality is than our movie and television glosses; it is how little reality seems to count when life itself is a gloss. After all, when life is a movie, who needs reality?

Huxley notwithstanding, that may just turn out to be the central question of the next millennium.

Understanding the Text

1. In Gabler's view, what insights did Alexis de Tocqueville provide into the American character?

2. According to Gabler, in what ways has entertainment "infested" our lives? Why is he concerned about this?

3. Gabler suggests that America's "very active sense of democracy" might account for why elements of performance have come to so thoroughly pervade our lives. Why does he think so?

The Reality Effect

Joel Black

FROM CINEMA VERITÉ TO REALITY TV

> The networks not only remain enthusiastic about the reality genre, but the next iterations are all about one-upping the others.
>
> —Ben Silverman, the William Morris Agency

Joel Black is a professor of comparative literature at the University of Georgia and has published numerous scholarly articles on literature, film, and cultural studies. He also is the author of two books: *The Reality Effect: Film Culture and the Graphic Imperative* (2002) and *The Aesthetics of Murder: A Study in Romantic Literature and Contemporary Culture* (1991).

The media's growing influence in the digital age would seem to support the claims of critics such as Jean Baudrillard and Paul Virilio about the "crisis in the reality principle," and has led a number of commentators to lament the gradual disappearance and ultimate loss of "reality" itself.[1] For some, the problem goes back six thousand years to the earliest media technology, writing, which heralded the separation of signs and things that caused reality to become increasingly symbolic and virtual.[2] Others, such as James Carey, call attention to the fact that reality is increasingly being coopted, "preempted," "defined," and "restricted" by ever more powerful global media conglomerates that debase news and history into mindless diversions.[3] Such critiques of the media and information technology are valid as far as they go, but they overlook several key matters. By calling attention to the media's distortions of reality, they give the impression that there is some independent state of affairs "out there" that can be objectively verified. Yet as philosophers from Vico onward have insisted, human reality is always a construct and has been so since the earliest poets came up with supernatural explanations for natural phenomena. If anything, the recording revolution of the nineteenth and twentieth centuries has worked to stabilize meaning and limit interpretation rather than promote rampant invention and distortion. (Of course, this could all change with the digital revolution now under way, in which fabricated images are capable of simulating indexical records.)

Then there are claims such as Neal Gabler's that entertainment now plays such an overwhelming role in people's lives that reality hardly "seems to count . . . After all, when life is a movie, who needs reality?"[4] On the contrary, reality is never more in demand than it is in our global mass-mediated film culture, where it has become, in Carey's words, "a scarce resource." And while reality has never been more in demand, it has also never been more at issue. Reality in liberal, democratic, mass-mediated societies no longer is self-evident, but is constantly contested and up for grabs. It isn't merely that movies compete with reality; rather, movies compete with other movies (and studios with other studios) in rendering an authentic—that is, graphic—view of reality. Thus in 1998, for example, the movies *Deep Impact* and *Armageddon* both took up the hot new post–Cold War scare of an asteroid hitting the earth, while *Saving Private Ryan* and *The Thin Red Line* presented directors Steven Spielberg's and Terrence Malick's strikingly different accounts of American soldiers' experiences of World War II, and *Antz* and *A Bug's Life* offered the DreamWorks and Disney/Pixar studios' competing computer-animated visions of the anthropomorphized world of insects.

Besides the rival views of reality presented by different movies is the competition in our "mixed media culture" between movies and other media, such as TV, video, and the Internet.[5] An entire subgenre of movies has emerged, from *Network* to *Quiz Show,* critiquing the impact of television on daily life. While the protagonist of the 1998 movie *The Truman Show* is the unwitting star of a real-life TV serial and the two 1990s teenagers in *Pleasantville* become the unwilling captives of a 1950s black-and-white television drama, Ed of *EdTV* is only too eager (at least at first) to allow himself to become the star of a real-life soap opera. In each case, the medium of television is presented in all its contrived artificiality—especially in its pretense as reality TV to give viewers a direct glimpse of life. Yet movies critical of television do precisely what they fault television for doing: they present themselves as a transparent lens through which we watch the absurd interaction unfold between the artificial medium of TV and "real life." Film's own status as an artificial (and artificing) medium goes unexamined in these intramedial movies that critique TV as a mediating agency standing between viewers and (one particular view of) reality. Watching these movies about TV, we are led to forget that we are watching a movie, and more precisely a movie fiction. When the protagonists Truman and Ed renounce their fake TV world for real life, no acknowledgment is made that "real life" in these movies is nothing but another media fiction—that of *The Truman Show* and *EdTV* themselves.

Even as these end-of-the-century films critique television as an artificial medium, a case can be made that movies themselves have historically been a fantasy medium and that it is in fact TV that has led the way in presenting the real in all its gritty, graphic immediacy.[6] Whereas cinema verité uses the pretense of documentary to dramatize events or fabricate a story in order to present a thesis or to convey some deeper truth, reality TV documents "actual" events that are intrinsically dramatic, sensational, and voyeuristic (car chases and crashes, man-made and natural disasters, feuding spouses, even surgical operations).[7] The fact that the phrase "reality TV" has largely displaced "cinema verité" is itself revealing: in contrast to the immediacy of television, movies only offer a staged (after)image of reality, reality as an effect. Yet as media researcher Sandra J. Ball-Rokeach asks of infotainment TV, "in what sense is it reality programming? . . . These shows desensitize the audience to the fear and the emotions [of actual chases and shoot-outs]. The fictional police dramas are sometimes more 'real' because they give you that context. You get a much more subtle understanding of character instead of just the action."[8] Arguing along similar lines, Lincoln Kaplan points out that fictional police and courtroom dramas on television "are more effective in framing important legal choices than most of what [the real-life cable channel] Court TV broadcasts. In an era when 'reality' TV blurs the line between nonfiction and fiction by recreating events, what people see on [fictional television dramas] gets closer to the truth—especially since the events they stage are often taken from the news."[9] Once again, what is graphic and documentary is not necessarily real or true. The so-called "caught-on-video" footage of reality TV is marked by its own artificial

> verité aesthetic (shaky camerawork, static and technical glitches, time codes, and other aesthetic techniques that suggest that the footage was not studio-produced) . . . [Reality TV's] claim of realism is not achieved by stripping the imagery of all mediation to somehow reveal an unadulterated "reality"—an impossible feat. In fact, it tends to require more mediation to assert that these images are real.[10]

Narrative filmmakers might think twice before emulating the dubious realism of reality TV. Still, the fact that a number of filmmakers are striving for television's nonfictional edginess suggests that "reality" still counts for a great deal in the movies, and that film has a deeper commitment to, and connection with, the "real world" than formalist critics suspect.

Nowhere is television's vaunted realism more dubious than in the new genre of "reality shows" flourishing at the turn of the century. Many of these popular American products are not even original, but recycled European imports. The number one U.S. TV program *Who Wants to Be a Millionaire* was a British quiz show that ABC first acquired as a summer series. After its success (and the fiasco of Fox's prime-time, publicity-driven special *Who Wants to Marry a Multi-Millionaire*), three networks vied for the rights to the Dutch program *Big Brother* (another losing proposition, it turned out), in which a group of young people is confined to a house loaded with cameras and microphones that record their every move. The CBS summer-of-2000 blockbuster *Survivor,* in which sixteen contestants were stranded on (and gradually eliminated from) a jungle island near Borneo, was originally a Swedish hit. In that version, one cast member committed suicide after receiving a negative vote. If *Los Angeles Times* television columnist Brian Lowry is right, more deaths can be expected as these ratings-driven shows continue "to push the envelope farther and farther in order to make them interesting"[11]—and, we might add, in order to pursue an elusive reality which must appear ever more violent and graphic.

Not only did reality shows have the potential to be immensely popular with audiences, but they were far cheaper to produce, and therefore far more profitable, than sitcoms and crime dramas. As a partner at one talent agency remarked, "Game shows and reality shows will occupy real estate previously rented to fictional entertainment programs."[12] As of this writing, plans are already in place for a televised worldwide scavenger hunt; an American version of the European show *Jailbreak,* in which a group of contestants compete to be the first to break out of a high-technology prison; and a show in which a group of people live in an environment approximating conditions on Mars. There's even a new all-out space race for the new century: NBC's deal with Russia to broadcast a contest in which the winner is sent into space aboard a Russian rocket was followed up by negotiations between the other major networks and NASA for a show in which twenty contestants train with the space agency for the chance to spend a week aboard the new International Space Station.[13]

While the hegemony of the Hollywood movie industry is threatened by far cheaper independent films and video games, the reign of costly fictional programming on TV has been put in jeopardy by the groundswell of inexpensive "reality shows." Clearly the term is an egregious misnomer. The fact that such shows are unscripted hardly makes them real. The ubiquitous presence of television cameras and film crews, and above all the actors' awareness that they are being filmed, undercuts the pretense of reality that informs the film *The Truman Show* or, for that matter, a TV program such as *Candid Camera*—"shows" in which the subject is genuinely ignorant that he or she is on film and is being seen by millions of knowing viewers. But while shows such as MTV's *The Real World* continued to cling to the pretense of presenting people as they are, the new breed of hyperreality shows has dropped this conceit once and for all. The over-the-top, soap-opera stories contrived by the World Wrestling Federation's Vince McMahon have given up any "pretense that wrestling was real." Far from making the sport seem more legitimate and lifelike, McMahon introduced "a second layer of unreality" by alternating the rounds with a lurid, behind-the-scenes glimpse into his own dysfunctional family. In John Leland's words, "here was something to believe in: the candidly, honestly fake."[14] But McMahon seriously misgauged matters when, instead of the honestly fake, he attempted to bring a new level of realism to the hallowed institution of professional football. The XFL, or Extreme Football League, was expressly created in 2000 for a new generation of viewers who appeared to be steadily losing interest in the increasingly artificial spectacle of NFL games. By placing cameras and microphones everywhere—on the field and off the field, in the players' helmets, and in the locker rooms—the XFL promised a glimpse into the behind-the-scenes reality of the game. Such realism couldn't compete with the over-hyped spectacle of the NFL, and the XFL folded after only one season.

If viewers of the common run of reality shows willfully suspend their disbelief to the point that they can believe the "candidly, honestly fake," what's to stop them from doubting the documented truth? Indeed, while a surprising number of people are disposed to believe photographic "evidence" of UFOs and other fantastic phenomena, others reject filmed evidence of the moon landing or the liberation of the death camps at the end of World War II. Straightforward, undoctored amateur recordings of sensational events, such as the Zapruder film of JFK's assassination or the Holliday video of the Rodney King beating, not only fail to show "what really happened," but actually provoke more controversy than if they hadn't been made and hadn't become part of the public record.[15] Such seemingly accurate but ultimately ambiguous and inconclusive recordings have contributed to the skeptical attitude that many feel toward the documentary media today. Others, meanwhile, are disposed to accept whatever they are shown in the movies, regardless of its veracity or even its authenticity, as long as the special effects are sufficiently spectacular and graphic.

More than ever, film audiences are in need, if not of a new hermeneutics of suspicion, then of a code of cinematic literacy that will allow them to maintain a healthy skepticism in the face of ever more spectacular special effects. An innovative media criticism is called for that can expose the ways that film distorts the world in the process—and under the pretense—of documenting it. Of particular interest in this regard are a line of narrative films from the second half of the century—from Hitchcock's 1958 *Vertigo* to Antonioni's 1966 *Blow-Up* and Neil Jordan's 1992 *The Crying Game*—that thematize the pitfalls of credulity and stress the need to doubt visible evidence in the primarily visual medium of film. "You can't believe everything you see" ran the advertising tag for Brian De Palma's 1984 film *Body Double,* while the ads for his 1998 *Snake Eyes* warned, "Believe everything, except your eyes."[16] It's as if filmmakers increasingly find themselves in the role of sorcerer's apprentices, wielding a medium whose seductive power has become so great, thanks to ever more realistic special effects, that they actually need to remind their supposedly media-savvy audiences to suspend not their disbelief but their belief. Yet it may be too much to expect such warnings to be taken seriously by most viewers growing up in the society of the spectacle of contemporary film culture. From their earliest years they have learned that the visible is the only reality that matters and that the truth is out there—namely, on the airwaves, on whatever channel the most vivid and awesome spectacle can be found.

Notes

[1] John Johnston, "Machinic Vision," *Critical Inquiry* 26 (1999): 31.

[2] Albert Borgmann, *Holding on to Reality: The Nature of Information at the Turn of the Millennium* (Chicago: University of Chicago Press, 1999).

[3] Quoted by Eric Alterman, "A Euro without a Europe," *The Nation,* Oct. 11, 1999, 10.

[4] Neal Gabler, "Molding Our Lives in the Image of Movies," *New York Times,* Oct. 25, 1998.

[5] See Bill Kovach and Tom Rosenstiel, *Warp Speed: America in the Age of Mixed Media* (New York: The Century Foundation Press, 1999).

[6] Thus Sterngold observes that "real life, as portrayed on television, has grown so graphic that the people who write teleplays and screenplays have been forced into greater luridness just to keep up" ("For Artistic Freedom, It's Not the Worst of Times"). Don DeLillo has contrasted "choreographed movie violence" with the surveillance videos of bank robberies and shoot-outs that are shown and reshown on television news programs, commenting that while such television images are "produced in a mass-market kind of fashion," they're "also real, it's real life. It's as though this were our last experience of nature: seeing a guy with a gun totally separate from choreographed movie violence. It's all that we've got left of nature, in a strange way. But it's all happening on our TV set" (quoted in David Remnick, "Exile on Main Street," *The New Yorker,* Sept. 15, 1997, 48).

[7] Examples of medical reality shows are the Discovery Health Channel's *Operation,* the Health Network's *O.R.: Behind the Mask,* and the Learning Channel's *Trauma: Life in the E.R.* See Craig Tomashoff, "When the Reality Is Inside the Body," *New York Times,* June 11, 2000.

[8] Quoted in James Sterngold, "Bruce Nash: Seeking to Go Beyond the 'Shockumentary,'" *New York Times,* Jan. 25, 1999.

[9] Lincoln Caplan, "The Failure (and Promise) of Legal Journalism," in J. Abramson, ed., *Postmortem: The O.J. Simpson Case: Justice Confronts Race, Domestic Violence, Lawyers, Money, and the Media* (New York: Basic Books, 1996), 199–207.

[10] Tarleton Gillespie, "Narrative Control and Visual Polysemy: Fox Surveillance Specials and the Limits of Legitimation," *The Velvet Light Trap* 45 (Spring 2000): 40.

[11] Interview with Mandalit Delbarco on NPR's "Morning Edition" (Feb. 9, 2001).

[12] Peter Benedek, quoted in Bernard Weinraub, "Sudden Explosion of Game Shows Threatens the Old TV Staples," *New York Times,* Feb. 9, 2000.

[13] Bill Carter, "Space: Network TV's Commercial Frontier," *New York Times,* Sept. 21, 2000.

[14] John Leland, "Why America's Hooked on Wrestling," *Newsweek,* Feb. 7, 2000, 48.

[15] The unreliability of video evidence in the courtroom became especially apparent in the 1999 antitrust case against Microsoft; a videotape demonstration that the corporation had prepared in its defense backfired when troubling inconsistencies on the tape prompted the judge to reject it as evidence.

[16] In a marketing ploy devised by producers of the film *The X-Files,* ads for the video version advised viewers who had already seen the movie in theaters that "if you've seen it once, you haven't seen it all; now you can look closer, dig deeper." While this promotion ostensibly referred to the fact that the video—like many DVD releases—included additional scenes that weren't shown in theaters, it also hinted that *The X-Files* was a kind of hermetic text with hidden clues that required endless study, and that the video was a medium more conducive to in-depth research than the movie's theatrical presentation.

UNREAL ESTATE: FAKE TOWNS, REAL PEOPLE

Nowadays when a person lives somewhere, in a neighborhood, the place is not certified from him. More than likely he will live there sadly and the emptiness which is inside him will expand until it evacuates the entire neighborhood. But if he sees a movie which shows his very neighborhood, it becomes possible for him to live, for a time at least, as a person who is Somewhere and not Anywhere.

—Walker Percy, *The Moviegoer*

Besides *Wag the Dog,* two other noteworthy movies about the media appeared in 1998. In Gary Ross's *Pleasantville,* two contemporary siblings are transported back into a 1950s-era TV show, experiencing and exposing the blandness of that artificial world. And Peter Weir's *The Truman Show* presents the ultimate paranoid scenario: Jim Carrey's character, Truman Burbank, is a man whose entire life is a staged, ongoing soap opera, filmed by five thousand tiny hidden cameras and watched by millions on TV. Reality triumphs over artifice at the end of both movies: the TV characters in the *Pleasantville* series wake up to the unpredictability of real life, and Truman discovers the elaborate deception in which he has been both dupe and star, whereupon he abandons his closed sound-stage world in order to live an authentic life beyond the cameras' myriad probing eyes.

The Truman Show and *Pleasantville* are movies whose stories play on the unprecedented power of the visual media of television and, by extension, film at the end of the twentieth century. They especially call attention to Americans' obsessive fascination with "the surreal ordinariness" of life as embodied in the character of Truman or in the town of Pleasantville, and they self-reflexively examine the willingness of viewers "to find the most nondescript . . . experiences" of a character such as Truman "more poignant and meaningful than one's own."[1] But why do viewers find the ordinary so fascinating? Perhaps because it's become so rare in a society of the spectacle where more and more of life is mediated by the mass media. Or perhaps because in such a society the "ordinary" is anything but natural, but is itself the most surreal and extraordinary effect of all.

It's worth noting in this regard that both *The Truman Show* and *Pleasantville* are situated in towns that look like sets staged for movies or television. Oddly, the fake town of Seahaven portrayed in *The Truman Show* was *not* a set, but the actual planned community of Seaside on Florida's panhandle. The film's producers had simply reversed the customary practice of building an artificial set that looks real; instead they used a real town that looked like a set to evoke "a setting that becomes a character in its own right."[2] Viewers unaware of the fact that Seahaven is not just a set but the real town of Seaside miss the irony in the film's premise that enormous effort, incalculable expense, and ingenious special effects have been used to provide Truman with the illusion of reality—that he is living a normal life in an ordinary town—when the film was in fact shot in an actual (although thoroughly movie-mediated) town. If, as J. G. Ballard said, "the fiction is already there" for the writer whose only "task is to invent the reality," the setting for Peter Weir's film already existed as the town of Seaside. Rather than create a fake town as an "effect," Weir merely had to give this ready-made town a slightly altered name.

It's not often that the real thing suits Hollywood's artificial purposes. When an existing historical monument figures prominently in a movie, it's usually necessary to construct a fake alternative. Thus when a film about the Alamo was being made in Texas, moviemakers considered the real landmark "small and unprepossessing." As a result, they arranged for "a bigger and better Alamo" to be built in a nearby town, and today it is as much a tourist attraction as the genuine Alamo.[3] (One is reminded of the exact copy of Goethe's Garden House built a hundred yards from the original in Weimar to celebrate the writer's 250th birthday.)

Similarly, in seeking set locations, Hollywood production designers routinely settle on small, historic American towns to create a feeling of authenticity—for example the Rhode Island towns of Wickford in *Meet Joe Black* (1998) and Jamestown in *Me, Myself, and Irene* (2000). Yet although these traditional towns would seem to be utterly unlike the artificial fantasy worlds of Hollywood or the synthetic sprawl of Los Angeles, they increasingly seem quaint and unreal, as if they were constructed as movie sets. In fact, a growing number of residential communities have so assiduously simulated the pristine towns portrayed in the movies that they themselves take on the appearance of movie sets. And so the producers of *The Truman Show*—a movie satirizing the media's idealized depictions of post-World War II American life—were able to use a real-life town as a set precisely because it looked so artificial. The logical next step was for the movie companies themselves to construct new "real" communities that replicate the appearance of the few remaining towns of yesteryear, and then to use these new-old, fake-real hybrid towns as movie sets.[4]

The fact that real and fake towns can no longer be distinguished in the movies is another sign that the traditional distinction between narrative films and documentaries has been thoroughly blurred. After Michael Moore's *Roger & Me* documented the ravaged economy of Flint, Michigan, in the aftermath of General Motors plant closings and layoffs, it was only a matter of time before a virtual documentary such as Russ Hexter's 1997 movie *Dadetown* would portray the economic woes of a fake town.

> The film unrolled like an as-it-happened documentary of a small town where the factory economy was dying and giving way to the software business. Not until the credits rolled was it revealed that the town, the citizens and the upheaval were entirely fictional.
>
> Any critic who raced out at the close of the final scene reviewed a documentary they only thought they saw.[5]

While *Roger & Me* depicts the decline of an actual industrial city, a finde-siècle documentary such as James Marsh's *Wisconsin Death Trip* insidiously suggests that the apparent prosperity of the rural farming community of Black River Falls is deceptive, and that the pleasant rituals of small-town life—parades, beauty contests, high-school football games—mask occasional eruptions of criminal violence that are painfully reminiscent of the town's harrowing gothic past.

These documentaries about decaying cities and troubled towns are giving way to a new phenomenon: real towns whose survival depends on their becoming an artificial film set, a theme park, or even an advertisement. Take the small Cascade Mountain town of Cashmere, Washington, which recently faced economic ruin when its principal business, a candy company that had been based there since 1918, threatened to move to a nearby "Bavarian theme town." The company, Liberty Orchards, would agree to stay in Cashmere only if a list of demands were met that would effectively turn the town into an advertisement for its business—changing road signs and renaming streets to refer to Liberty Orchards' products, and even letting the company buy the town hall.

"It is not surprising," writes architecture critic Ada Louise Huxtable, "that much of the most popular and profitable development of the [theme park] genre is spearheaded and bankrolled by the masters of illusion; the movie and entertainment businesses have become the major innovators and investors in theme parks and related enterprises."[6] But it should also come as no surprise to learn that the media company most adept in constructing amusement parks and entertainment complexes as well as movie sets simulating small-town life in America would enter the real estate business and build actual residential communities. This is what the Walt Disney Company did when it created the town of Celebration in Florida on land acquired in the 1960s for Walt Disney World. Disney himself had wanted to create "a real town with real citizens" in central Florida to be called Epcot, the Experimental Prototype Community of Tomorrow.[7] But the Epcot that eventually opened in the early '80s as part of Disney World was a futuristic theme park that hardly conformed to the original project. Disney's dream had to wait until the company came under the management of Michael Eisner, who agreed to develop a five-thousand-acre tract of land that wasn't needed for the park's expansion into a town that he hoped "would be a model for development in the next millennium."[8] But far from being a futuristic town, Celebration—which was designed by the same architects who planned Seaside, that other artificial-looking Florida site where *The Truman Show* was filmed—is an example of "New Urbanism," a style modeled on Savannah, Georgia, and other pre-1940s southern towns. The exterior appearance of the homes are carefully regulated, from the landscaping to the pastel shades of paint to the white and off-white color of the window curtains.[9] It's fitting that the town's central feature is its movie house, designed by Cesar Pelli in the style of 1930s theaters.

For critics such as Neal Gabler, Celebration's nostalgic creation of a movie-mediated past is a sign of its unreality. Celebration is *The Truman Show* come true—a town in which all the inhabitants "were cast members on the set of their own life movies."[10] But the New Urbanist invocation of an earlier period in American culture can also be seen as a move toward a new reality. In contrast to Disney's futuristic Epcot, Celebration may be, as Kurt Andersen suggests, "the real EPCOT—the quasi-democratic, postmodern fulfillment of Walt's totalitarian, late-modern vision." To those critics who would sneer at Celebration's "picturesque fakery," Andersen responds,

> Isn't the obligatory American lawn a form of fakery? Isn't air-conditioning a fake? Aren't the crazy architectural mongrels built every day in every city in America—all the tarty Mediterranean-Colonial-Norman-Palladian raised ranches—thoroughly (and wretchedly) fake? . . . Celebration's "fakery"—its small scale, its density, its hidden garages, its pre-mall commercial core—is in the service of a coherent vision, as opposed to the accumulation of developers' cost-efficient short cuts and aesthetic bad habits that produce the random, sprawling, ghastly "real" suburbs of the late twentieth century.[11]

For end-of-the-century advocates of New Urbanism, planned fakery has become preferable to a ruthlessly unregulated reality. And Celebration's particular brand of fakery is also preferable to all the other forms of artificiality that characterize modern American life, not so much because it is more picturesque or more up-front about its pretense, but because its coherent vision of small-town life (which is really a cinematic vision à la Capra and Disney) comes closest to creating the ultimate reality effect—the illusion of "a real town with real citizens." According to this logic, the only place in late-twentieth-century America to find real people who can be spontaneously and genuinely themselves is in fake towns, communities deliberately designed to recapture the supposed simplicity of a bygone era before the advent of the very technology that transformed reality into—or revealed it as—an effect.

Ants Wars

While families were moving into Celebration's movie-set community in an attempt to re-experience real life at the close of the twentieth century, another building project of a different kind was under way on the other side of the country that was intended to challenge Disney's media hegemony. (Under Eisner's leadership, the Disney corporation had acquired the film company Miramax, allied itself with the software company Pixar, and was once again producing cutting-edge feature animation as in the days of its founder.) On a 1,087-acre stretch of marshland on the California coast, the first new Hollywood studio in sixty years was being planned by DreamWorks SKG. The complex was to be a state-of-the-art technological marvel, constructed on the very site where former film mogul Howard Hughes had built his "Spruce Goose" seaplane. Headed by director Steven Spielberg, former Disney movie chief Jeffrey Katzenberg, and record mogul David Geffen, the company was valued at $2.7 billion before it even produced its first product.[12] A project of this size had to be more than just a complex of sound stages; DreamWorks was to be the anchor tenant of the projected Playa

Vista development, which, with thirteen thousand new condos and commercial space including a new marina, and at least $75 million in city and state tax incentives, was intended to be a self-sufficient residential community with an estimated worth of $6 billion to $8 billion.

From the start, however, the ambitious project was headed for trouble. Environmentalists charged that Playa Vista threatened the Ballona wetlands, the last undeveloped tract in Los Angeles County. Ultimately, financing difficulties led DreamWorks to pull out of the project in 1999. There are limits, it seems, to the joint business ventures envisioned by dream movies and "real" estate.[13]

Nevertheless, DreamWorks was—and still is—clearly positioning itself to give Disney, one of the world's largest media companies, a run for its money. Specifically, it has sought to challenge Disney in the domain where it reigns supreme—animation—and especially in the new generation of computer-generated animation that Disney had inaugurated with its partner Pixar (the software company that Apple Computer cofounder Steve Jobs bought from George Lucas in 1986). Since the huge success of the first computer-animated feature, *Toy Story,* Pixar's staff focused exclusively on making movies, entering into a five-picture partnership with Disney and building its own base of operations on sixteen and a half acres in Emeryville, California.

Competition between DreamWorks and Disney/Pixar came to a head in the fall of 1998 with each studio's release of a blockbuster computer-generated animation feature dealing with the unlikely subject of ants. Although DreamWorks started work on *Antz* in 1995, a full year after Pixar began developing *A Bug's Life,* the film was rushed into production so that it could be released more than a month ahead of its competitor. Pixar protested that its idea for an ant movie had been stolen by Katzenberg when he quit his post as chairman of Disney Studios to join DreamWorks in August 1994—two days before the idea was pitched to Disney by Pixar director John Lasseter. (Katzenberg has denied knowing about the project.) But while DreamWorks scooped Disney in the ants animation war, *A Bug's Life* held its own and was widely hailed as a superior achievement. Besides, the technical innovations of *Antz* did not go without criticism. Film critic Anthony Lane complained about the movie's "decorative uniformity," its shiny surfaces that show no trace of

> the random ways on which physical surfaces are rubbed and scarred. This was no problem with "Toy Story," where the natural sheen of the animation coincided happily with the fact that the heroes were molded from plastic; it is more of a letdown in "Antz," which is, by definition, set in a universe of trash and crap.[14]

The movie's key scene in a garbage dump dubbed "Insectopia" fails to come off "because the garbage cannot help but suffer from the same spooky, enhanced cleanness in which computer design has wrapped the entire movie." The contradiction Lane finds between computerized cleanliness and a sort of sanitized filth that appeals to humans and vermin alike would seem to be an inevitable result of the new technology which is incapable of simulating old-ness and waste.

And why two ant films anyway? The life of insects, typically the subject of nature docu-mentaries, became the ideal subject for filmmakers eager to demonstrate the new capabilities of the most artificial of cinematic forms—animation—to reproduce the natural world. What better subject, as Edward Rothstein observes, to display "texture, character, individuality, nuance and other un-antlike characteristics" created by the new technology? "Computer ani-mation was once the sign of artificiality; now it is humanized, naturalized, and we are meant to see it at work bringing a human touch to the inhuman realm of the ant. Nature is trans-formed by artifice into seeming more natural."[15] Computer animation, the latest breakthrough in cinematic special effects, was used to produce the illusion not of the supernatural but of nature at its most ordinary, familiar, and homely. The greatest technical feat in *Toy Story 2* wasn't the lifelike animation of the toy characters but the digitized portrayal of the dachshund Buster; the four million hairs on his body are visual effects made possible by fur software developed during the movie's production. It's as if nature presents the computer-animation wizards not only with the greatest challenge, but also with an unprecedented opportunity to re-create it into something altogether new, artificial, and supremely graphic—to make reality over once and for all as an effect.

Back to the Future: Movies, the Ride

At the end of the twentieth century, Neal Gabler's claim that life has become "the biggest, most entertaining, most realistic movie of all, one that played twenty-four hours a day, 365 days a year, and featured a cast of billions" itself became the subject of movies.[16] In *The Truman Show* one man's life is nothing more than a cinematic illusion; the following year *The Matrix* revealed *all* life to be an illusion. The latter film is based on the Kabbalistic premise that the world as we know it is no longer real but a "computer-generated dream" that only a few select individuals can penetrate to the reality beyond. The irony here, of course, is that the movie *The Matrix* is itself a computer-generated dream that envelops its viewers, sealing them off in its own substitute reality. It doesn't take much imagination to see *The Matrix* as an allegory of the pervasive power of movies—especially movies loaded with special effects—to create an alternate, substitute, but ultimately false reality. A key problem with such movies is that they are utterly incapable of critically looking at or reflecting upon new developments in digital media and virtual-reality technology because for the most part they are themselves a product of that technology. A better title for the movie might have been *The Möbius Strip* since the mediated reality it depicts loops back into its own production. The use of all the advanced special effects— especially the well-hyped "Flo-Mo" sequences—give the movie the look not of real life, but of a spectacular sci-fi comic book.

The explicit thematization of virtual reality machines in movies such as *The Matrix* calls attention to the fact—already anticipated by early-twentieth-century writers such as Pirandello and Schwartz—that the ultimate machine of this kind, the ideal dream machine, is the cinematic apparatus itself and its more recent televisual derivatives. Most of today's commercial films do not encourage such reflection, however, but rather employ a powerfully synchronized combination of digital audio and visual effects to plunge the viewer into an all-encompassing, somnambulent state that all but screens out the real world. Caught up in the overwhelming imagery of Tony Scott's 1998 thriller *Enemy of the State, Newsweek's* Jack Kroll describes the

> scary fun of the movie . . . embodied in a brilliantly filmed and edited chase sequence in which [Will] Smith tries to escape the ubiquitous cyber-eyes that see every inch of his flight. In such passages Scott . . . creates a new cinematic landscape out of hurtling satellite images and flashing computer screens, turning the whole earth into a claustrophobic space that affords no escape.[17]

Scott's creation of a "new cinematic landscape" is an instance of the Kuleshov effect taken to the extreme: now not merely does the swift sequencing of scenes shot at different locations serve to create an artificial space for the viewer, who remains outside the action, but the film surrounds the viewer with a total surveillance space in which there is no escape from remote cameras, bugging devices, and concealed monitoring systems. The wording of Kroll's description leaves it unclear whether it is the actor Smith or the viewer who is unable to escape the "claustrophobic space" of the "cinematic landscape" into which "the whole earth" has been transformed—the world made film. Whether viewers want it or not, they are along for the ride.

Many of Hollywood's blockbuster films are really no longer movies, but are better described (and evaluated) as rides or games. Some movies, such as *Raiders of the Lost Ark* or *Back to the Future,* become actual rides in theme parks such as Walt Disney World and Universal City, where visitors are no longer passive spectators but have the sense of being interactive participants in cinematic events. Yet there is also a sense in which some of the most entertaining special-effects movies are more than mere rides, providing graphic, documentary evidence or even proof of a reality that has never been, and can never be, recorded on film. One thinks of the prehistoric dinosaurs reconstructed in Steven Spielberg's *Jurassic Park*: although this movie itself became a ride, and is itself *about* a ride in a futuristic theme park, it also presents a vivid picture of a "lost world" that no human being has ever witnessed, let alone documented. In contrast to Disney's talking-dinosaur movie a few years later, Spielberg endeavored to use special effects to reconstruct the most realistic visual simulation possible of these prehistoric creatures. Like all those cinematic reconstructions of JFK's assassination that tried to fill in the gaps left by the spotty film record, Spielberg was making up for the absolute absence of cameras, recording technology, or eyewitnesses during the Jurassic period. Beyond providing a graphic "record" of that lost world, he may have been giving it a kind of reality. For as the real is increasingly identified with recorded audiovisual "evidence" that dates back only to the twentieth—or the first filmed—century, there is a chance that history may appear to future generations as *beginning* with the twentieth century, or at least with what was graphically recorded at that time. (This was, after all, the logic behind the Kansas Board of Education's 1999 decision to drop evolution and the big bang theory from the state's science curriculum since such unobserved and unrecorded events are open to doubt.) The corollary of the literalist belief that the whole world is on film is the view that there's every reason to doubt the reality of whatever *isn't* on film. Given such a view, events in earlier times will have to be photographically reconstructed through dramatization and special effects if they are to appear real. A popular commercial filmmaker such as Spielberg may find himself as a documentarian not only preserving history (as in his project to record the recollections of Holocaust survivors), but also creating history as he and others face the daunting task of having to fill in the yawning gap of all of unrecorded history with realistic, graphic reconstructions.

The longest running back-to-the-future ride is George Lucas's *Star Wars* series. In a curious temporal twist, *Episode 1: The Phantom Menace*—the 1999 sequel to the trilogy of movies that appeared in the 1970s—purported to be a *prequel* that depicted events a generation before those shown in the earlier films. The first three movies dealt with the aftermath of a great debacle that reduced the former Galactic Empire (derived from Isaac Asimov's *Foundation* stories) to a primitive condition of nomadic warriors working with salvaged weaponry; the new film introduced viewers to the period preceding the debacle, when the Empire was at the height of its technological glory.[18]

In fact, this was all an ingenious strategy on Lucas's part to showcase the special-effects wizardry of his company Industrial Light and Magic, effects that were necessary to bring the pre-debacle Empire to the screen in the first place. Twenty years earlier, when the original *Star Wars* movies appeared dealing with the Empire's aftermath, a movie about the Empire could not be made because the special effects needed to represent—and, indeed, create—it did not yet exist. And so Lucas found it necessary to put the series on hold. The depiction of a lost world of marvelous but dangerous technology had to be postponed until end-of-the-century computer technology could catch up with his own imaginative scenarios. (The contradiction between the antitechnological thrust of Lucas's films and his love of special-effects technology has not gone unnoticed.)[19] As late as 1990, Lucas still didn't consider computers sufficiently cost-effective to create the effects he wanted. But with the release of his friend Spielberg's *Jurassic Park* he realized that "we can create a photo-realistic, digital character that can look as real as any actor. . . . I was just so desperate to have an alien character that I can turn into a real character who interacts with other humans." Here was a case in which a certain spectacle—in this case, the world of the Empire—could not be "recorded" on film until the special effects needed to represent that spectacle became available.

But the epic saga doesn't end here. The images of the Galactic Empire with their vast scale that Lucas's FX-driven movies made so popular have gone on to generate our very conception of the actual cosmos. It's now common to hear the three-dimensional universe described cine-matically, as a thin membrane in which we are trapped like "characters playing out their lives within the confines of a movie screen. Unknown to these shallow, two-dimensional players, a larger universe spreads into numerous extra dimensions, like theaters in a multiplex."[20] Or, as Dick Teresi puts it more dramatically, "With its fiery explosions, wormholes, white dwarfs, red giants and black holes, the big bang universe satisfies our Lucasfilm sensibilities. . . . It is the biggest-budget universe ever, with mind-boggling numbers to dazzle us. . . . Who wants to live in a smallish, low-budget universe?"[21]

Notes

[1] Janet Maslin, "'The Truman Show': So, What's Wrong with This Picture?" *New York Times,* June 5, 1998.

[2] Ibid.

[3] Ada Louise Huxtable, *The Unreal America: Architecture and Illusion* (New York: New Press, 1997). See also the scene in Walker Percy's *Lancelot* where a film company shooting a movie near New Orleans needs "to use the hurricane machine even though a real hurricane is coming, not just because the real hurricane is not yet here, but because even if it were it wouldn't be as suitable for film purposes as an artificial hurricane" (1977; New York: Picador, 1999), 191.

[4] A similar retrolook was adopted by automakers for the new millennium—e.g., Volkswagen's new Beetle and Chrysler's PT Cruiser.

[5] "Photos that Lie—and Tell the Truth," *New York Times,* Mar. 16, 1997.

[6] Timothy Egan, "Candymaker Wants to Use Town as Advertisement," *New York Times,* Oct. 6, 1997.

[7] Kurt Andersen, "Pleasantville," *The New Yorker,* Sept. 6, 1999, 74.

[8] Douglas Frantz, "Living in a Disney Town, with Big Brother at Bay," *New York Times,* Oct. 4, 1998.

[9] Ibid.

[10] Neal Gabler, *Life the Movie: How Entertainment Conquered Reality* (New York: Knopf, 1998), 213 n.

[11] Andersen, "Pleasantville," 79.

[12] Allan Sloan, "Pennies from Heaven," *Newsweek,* Apr. 3, 1995, 44–45. DreamWorks should not be confused with Dreamtime Holdings, Inc., the multimedia company based in Moffett Field, California. The company has been involved in many media projects with NASA and is currently trying to broker a new reality show with one of the major networks in which the winner of a group of contestants training at the Johnson Space Center in Houston would spend a week aboard the International Space Station.

[13] Thus, in order to expedite the creation of Disney World, the Walt Disney Company had founded an independent governmental jurisdiction called the Reedy Creek Improvement District; two decades later, when the company developed Celebration, it removed its name from the title, turned matters of

land use over to Osceola County, and turned the business of buying and selling the town's houses over to out-of-state companies.

[14] Anthony Lane, "No Picnic," *The New Yorker,* Oct. 19, 1998, 94.

[15] Edward Rothstein, "Heed the Arthropods; They May Have the Answers," *New York Times,* Nov. 23, 1998.

[16] Gabler, *Life the Movie,* 58.

[17] Jack Kroll, "Cyberspies," *Newsweek,* Nov. 23, 1998, 83.

[18] See Oliver Morton, "In Pursuit of Infinity," *The New Yorker,* May 17, 1999, 84–89. Morton argues, however, that the antitechnological thrust of Lucas's *Star Wars* films "is the antithesis of what Asimov believed. Asimov had an Enlightenment love of reason above all things; and he wanted a better future, not a stirring past" (88).

[19] See Morton: "'Star Wars' treats technology as essentially malign, inhuman, and untrustworthy (except when producing special effects)" (ibid., 88).

[20] K. C. Cole, "Unseen Dimensions Hold Theory Aloft," *Los Angeles Times,* Nov. 18, 1999, B2.

[21] Dick Teresi, "The First Squillion Years," *New York Times Book Review,* Aug. 8, 1999, 6.

Understanding the Text

1. Why is Black critical of *The Truman Show, Pleasantville,* and *EdTV*—films that are critical of television?

2. What town provided the set for *The Truman Show?* How does Black characterize this town, and why does he find it significant that *The Truman Show* was filmed there?

3. While Disney's Celebration has many critics, such as Neal Gabler, it has its supporters, too. On what basis does Kurt Andersen defend Disney's "ideal" town?

The Numbing of the American Mind: Culture as Anesthetic

Thomas de Zengotita

... the massive influx of impressions is so great; surprising, barbaric, and violent things press so overpoweringly—"balled up into hideous clumps"— in the youthful soul; that it can save itself only by taking recourse in premeditated stupidity.

—Friedrich Nietzsche

It was to have been the end of irony, remember? Superficial celebrity culture was over; a new age of seriousness was upon us. Of course, the way media celebrities focused on their own mood as the consequence of September 11 was in itself an irony so marvelous you knew immediately how wrong they were. And sure enough, the spotlight never wavered. It went on shining as it always had, on those it was meant for—on them. A guarantee of continuing superficiality right there, quite apart from unintended irony.

So we shared Dan Rather's pain, marveled at intrepid Ashleigh Banfield, scrutinizing those ferocious tribal fighters through her designer specs, and Tom Brokaw, arbiter of greatness among generations, took us on a tour of the real West Wing. But these iconic moments swam into focus only momentarily, soon to be swept away in a deluge of references, references so numerous, so relentlessly repeated, that they came at last to constitute a solid field, a new backdrop for all our public performances. How often did you hear, how often did you say, "Since the events of 9/11"? A new idiom had been deposited in the language, approaching the same plane of habituality as "by the way" or "on

Thomas de Zengotita teaches at the Draper Graduate Program at New York University and is a contributing editor at *Harper's Magazine*. His most recent book is *Mediated: How the Media Shapes Your World and the Way You Live In It* (2005).

491

the other hand." And in the process we got past it after all. Six months or so was all it took. The holidays came and went, and—if you were not personally stricken by the terror of September—chances are you got over it. You moved on.

How is that possible?

Nietzsche was not thinking I.Q. or ignorance when he used the word "stupidity." He meant stupidity as in clogged, anesthetized. Numb. He thought people at the end of the *nineteenth* century were suffocating in a vast goo of meaningless stimulation. Ever notice how, when your hand is numb, everything feels thin? Even a solid block of wood lacks depth and texture. You can't feel the wood; your limb just encounters the interrupting surface. Well, numb is to the soul as thin is to a mediated world. Our guiding metaphor. And it isn't just youthful souls either.

Here's the basic situation. On the one hand: the Web, satellite cable TV, PalmPilot, DVD, Ethernet—Virtual Environments everywhere. On the other hand: cloning, genetic engineering, artificial intelligence, robotics—Virtual Beings everywhere. Someday, when people (or whatever they are) look back on our time, all this will appear as a single development, called something like "The Information Revolution," and the lesson of that revolution will have been this: what counts is the code. Silicon- or carbon-based. Artifact or animate. The difference between them is disappearing. This is not science fiction. This is really happening. Right now, in an Atlanta hospital, there is a quadriplegic with his brain directly wired to a computer. He can move the cursor with his thoughts.

The moving cursor doesn't really need explaining—it comes down to digital bytes and neurochemical spikes. What needs explaining is our equanimity in the face of staggering developments. How can we go about our business when things like this are happening? How can we just read the article, shake our heads, turn the page? If creatures from outer space sent a diplomatic mission to the U.N., how long would it be before we were taking that in stride? Before Comedy Central send-ups were more entertaining than the actual creatures? About six months?

Soap-opera politics. The therapy industry. Online communities. Digital effects. Workshops for every workplace. Viagra, Prozac, Ritalin. Reality TV. Complete makeovers. Someday, it will be obvious that all the content on our information platforms converges on this theme: there is no important difference between fabrication and reality, between a chemical a pill introduces and one your body produces, between role-playing in marital therapy and playing your role as a spouse, between selling and making, campaigning and governing, expressing and existing. And that is why we moved on after September 11, after an event that seemed so enormous, so horrific, so stark, that even the great blob of virtuality that is our public culture would be unable to absorb it. But it could. It has. Here's how.

FABRICATION

Some people refuse to believe that reality has become indistinguishable from fabrication. But beliefs are crude reflections of the psychological processes that actually determine how we function. Fat people believe they are on the stocky side. Abject drunks believe they are poetical free spirits. Malicious prudes believe they are selfless do-gooders. And a lot of people still believe that, with some obvious exceptions involving hoaxes and errors, we know what's real and what's not. We can tell the difference between the *Kursk* and the *Titanic* (meaning the movie, of course), for example.

And maybe we can—when specifically focused on the issue. It might take a while, of course, because there *are* so many gradations when you stop to think about it. For example:

- Real real: You fall down the stairs. Stuff in your life that's so familiar you've forgotten the statement it makes.
- Observed real: You drive by a car wreck. Stuff in your life in which the image-statement is as salient as the function.
- Between real real and observed real: Stuff that oscillates between the first two categories. Like you're wearing something you usually take for granted but then you meet someone attractive.
- Edited real real: Shtick you have down so pat you don't know it's shtick anymore, but you definitely only use it in certain situations. Documentaries and videos in which people are unaware of the camera, though that's not easy to detect, actually. Candid photographs.
- Edited observed real: Other people's down-pat shtick. Shtick you are still working on. Documentaries in which people are accommodating the camera, which is actually a lot of the time, probably.
- Staged real: Formal events like weddings. Retail-clerk patter.
- Edited staged real: Pictures of the above. Homemade porn.
- Staged observed real unique: Al kisses Tipper. *Survivor.*
- Staged observed real repeated: Al kisses Tipper again and again. Anchor-desk and talk-show intros and segues. Weather Channel behavior.

(In the interests of time, we can skip the subtler middle range of distinctions and go to the other end of the spectrum:)

- Staged realistic: *The English Patient* and *NYPD Blue.*
- Staged hyperreal: Oliver Stone movies and *Malcolm in the Middle.*

- Overtly unreal realistic: S.U.V.'s climbing buildings. Digitized special effects in general, except when they are more or less undetectable.
- Covertly unreal realistic: Hair in shampoo ads. More or less undetectable digital effects, of which there are more every day.
- Between overtly and covertly unreal realistic: John Wayne in a beer ad (you have to know he's dead to know he isn't "really" in the ad).
- Real unreal: Robo-pets.
- Unreal real: Strawberries that won't freeze because they have fish genes in them.

See? No problem. The differences are perfectly clear.

But the issue isn't *can* we do it; it's *do* we do it—and the answer is, of course not. Our minds are the product of total immersion in a daily experience saturated with fabrications to a degree unprecedented in human history. People have never had to cope with so much stuff, so many choices. In kind and number.

FLOOD

● ● ● ● ● ● ● ● ● ● ● ● ● ● ●

And sheer quantity really matters, because here we collide with a real limit, one of the few that remain—namely, how much a person can register at a given instant. No innovation in techno-access or sensationalism can overcome this bottleneck. It determines the fundamental dynamic, the battle to secure attention, in every domain of our lives.

Compare, say, the cereal and juice sections of a supermarket today with those of years ago. For you youngsters out there, take it from Dad: it used to be Wheaties, Corn Flakes, Cheerios (oats), Rice Krispies—and that was about it. One for each grain, see? Same for fruit juice. But now? Pineapple/Banana/Grape or Strawberry/Orange/Kiwi anyone? And that's just a sample from Tropicana—check out Nantucket Nectars. Makes of cars? Types of sunglasses? Sneaker species? Pasta possibilities? On and on. It's all about options, as they say.

Umbrella brands toss off diverse and evolving lines of market-researched products for niches of self-inventing customers with continual access to every representational fabrication ever produced in the whole of human history. That's "the environment." You like Vedic ankle tattoos? 1930s cockney caps? Safari jackets? Inca ponchos? Victorian lace-up high-heel booties? Whatever.

No wonder that word caught on.

The moreness of everything ascends inevitably to a threshold in psychic life. A change of state takes place. The discrete display melts into a pudding, and the mind is forced to certain adaptations if it is to cohere at all.

When you find out about the moving cursor, or hear statistics about AIDS in Africa, or see your 947th picture of a weeping fireman, you can't help but become fundamentally indifferent because you are exposed to things like this all the time, just as you are to the rest of your options. Over breakfast. In the waiting room. Driving to work. At the checkout counter. *All the time.* I know you know this already. I'm just reminding you.

Which is not to say you aren't moved. On the contrary, you are moved, often deeply, very frequently—never more so, perhaps, than when you saw the footage of the towers coming down on 9/11. But you are so used to being moved by footage, by stories, by representations of all kinds—that's the point. It's not your fault that you are so used to being moved, you just are.

So it's not surprising that you have learned to move on so readily to the next, sometimes moving, moment. It's sink or surf. Spiritual numbness guarantees that your relations with the moving will pass. And the stuffed screen accommodates you with moving surfaces that assume you are numb enough to accommodate them. And so on, back and forth. The dialectic of postmodern life.

One might say, "Well, people didn't respond deeply to every development in the world 200 years ago either." And that's true, but it isn't an objection, it's a confirmation. Until the new media came along, people didn't even *know* about such developments, or not as quickly, and above all not as dramatically or frequently. Also, there weren't as many developments, period. This is crucial, another aspect of sheer moreness that gets overlooked. *Less was happening.*

The contrast is stark with, say, the Middle Ages. By the industrial era, a lot more was happening, and numbness became an issue then. Think of Baudelaire, adrift in the crowd, celebrating the artist for resisting numbness, for maintaining vulnerability—thus setting the standard for the genius of modernism. But a qualitative threshold has since been breached. Cities no longer belong to the soulful *flâneur* but to the wired-up voyeur in his soundproofed Lexus. Behind his tinted windows, with his cell phone and CD player, he gets more input, with less static, from more and different channels, than Baudelaire ever dreamed of. But it's all insulational—as if the deities at Dreamworks were invisibly at work around us, touching up the canvas of reality with existential airbrushes. Everything has that edgeless quality, like the lobby of a high-end Marriott/Ramada/Sheraton. Whole neighborhoods feel like that now. And you can be sure that whatever they do at "the site" will feel like that, too. Even if they specifically set out to avoid having it feel like that—it will still feel like that. They can't control themselves. They can't stop.

Take the new Times Square, everybody's icon for this process. All the usual observations apply—and each contributes its iota to muffling what it meant to expose. But the point here is the way everything in that place is *aimed.* Everything is firing message modules, straight for your gonads, your taste buds, your vanities, your fears. These modules seek to penetrate, but in a passing way. A second of your attention is all they ask. Nothing is firing that rends or cuts. It's a massage, really, if you just go with it. And why not? Some of the most talented people on the planet have devoted their lives to creating this psychic sauna, just for you.

And it's not just the screens and billboards, the literal signs; it's absolutely everything you encounter. Except for the eyes of the people, shuffling along, and the poignant imperfections of their bodies; they are so manifestly unequal to the solicitations lavished upon them. No wonder they stuff themselves with junk—or, trying to live up to it all, enslave themselves to regimes of improvement.

Yes, there were ersatz environments and glitzy ads back in the fifties, but this is a new order of quality and saturation. Saying that it's just more of what we had before is like saying a hurricane is just more breeze. For here, too, there is a psychological threshold. Today, your brain is, as a matter of brute fact, full of stuff that was *designed* to affect you. As opposed to the scattered furniture of nature and history that people once registered just because it happened to be there. September 11 had to accommodate the fact that our inner lives are now largely constituted by effects.

To get relief, you have to stumble into the Greyhound bus station in Albany, or some old side-street barbershop that time forgot, into someplace not yet subjected to the renovating ministrations of the International Red Brick and Iron Filigree Restoration Corporation. And "stumble" is the key concept here. Accidental places are the only real places left.

That's why a couple of weeks out in Nature doesn't make it anymore. Even if you eschew the resonant clutter of The Tour and The Gear, you will virtualize everything you encounter anyway, all by yourself. You won't see wolves, you'll see "wolves." You'll be murmuring to yourself, at some level, "Wow, look, a real wolf, not in a cage, not on TV, I can't believe it."

That's right, you can't. Natural things have become their own icons.

And you will get restless really fast if that "wolf" doesn't do anything. The kids will start squirming in, like, five minutes; you'll probably need to pretend you're not getting bored for a while longer. But if that little smudge of canine out there in the distance continues to just loll around in the tall grass, and you don't have a really powerful tripod-supported telelens gizmo to play with, you will get bored. You will begin to appreciate how much technology and editing goes into making those nature shows. The truth is that if some no-account chipmunk just happens to come around your campsite every morning for crumbs from your picnic table, it will have meant more to you than any "wolf."

Precious accidents.

Back to the new Times Square—do you parse out the real from the fabricated in that mélange? Not *can* you, but *do* you. The Fox screen is showing Elián in his Cuban school uniform on the side of a building—real or not? Some glorious babe in her underwear is sprawled across 35 percent of your visual field. She's looking you right in the eye. You feel that old feeling—real or not? A fabulous man, sculpted to perfection by more time in the health club than most parents have for their kids, is gliding by on Day-Glo Rollerblades eight inches high. He's wearing Tex-tex gear so tight it looks like it's under his skin, and the logos festooning his figure emit meaning-beeps from every angle—real or not? What about the pumped-up biceps? If he uses steroids? But, once again, the issue isn't what you *can* do when I call your attention to it. The real issue is *do* you do it as a matter of routine processing? Or do you rely instead on a general immunity that only numbness can provide, an immunity that puts the whole flood in brackets and transforms it all into a play of surfaces—over which you hover and glide like a little god, dipping in here and there for the moving experience of your choice, with the ultimate reaches of your soul on permanent remote?

FINITUDE

What about that feeling that it's all been done? Not in the techie department, of course; there, the possibility of novelty seems to be unlimited. But in those areas occupied by what platform proprietors call "content providers." What a phrase! Could anything register devastation of the spirit more completely than that little generic? Could meaning suffer more complete evacuation? Not since we landed on the moon and found nothing has our cultural unconscious encountered so traumatic a void.

Maybe the postmodern taste for recycling and pastiche is more than a phase? Maybe it's necessity. Maybe more or less everything that can be done in the plastic arts, say, has been done? How many different ways can a finite set of shapes and colors be arranged in a finite space? We aren't talking infinitely divisible Platonic geometry here. Maybe there just isn't any really new way to put x shapes and y colors into z permutations. Maybe some day it will be obvious that the characteristic gestures of twentieth-century art were flailing against this fact. Cézanne's planes, Magritte's pipe, Pollock's swirls, Warhol's soup can, Christo's draperies, Serrano's piss, the "installations"—so many desperate efforts to elude the end of originality?

Likewise with music? How many distinguishable sounds can be put in how many patterns? There has to be some limit. After you've integrated techno and Brazilian-Afro and Tibetan monko and Hump-backed Whalo, at some point, surely, there's going to be nothing left but play it again, Sam. Maybe that's why it's the age of the mix. And characters and plots, in stories and shows? What's the raw material? Sex, outlaws, illness, death, master villains, guilt, the fall of giants, fate, just deserts, the dark side, redemption by the little things, a few other themes—we all know the repertoire. Maybe it's just impossible to think of anything that couldn't be described, after the fashion of all contemporary pitches, as "It's *To the Lighthouse* meets *Married with Children*" or "It's Hannibal Lecter meets Peter Pan."

The prospect of finitude helps to account for the turn to sensation, as if intensity of presentation could make up for repetition. Of course, sensation is also a response to sheer clutter on the screen, a way to grab the most possible attention in the least amount of time. But that clutter also accounts for why everything's already been done, and so it cycles on relentlessly—fill the pages, fill the time slots, fill the channels, the websites, the roadsides, the building facades, the fronts and backs of shirts and caps, everything, everything must be saying something, every minute. But what? What's left to say? It doesn't matter. Cut to the response.

Zap. Whimper. Flinch. Cringe. Melt. Assert! Exult! Weep. Subside. Ahhh . . .

Eventually we can just wire our glands directly to a console of sensation buttons, platform to platform, and be done with this tiresome content altogether. Call it P2P communication. Talk about interactive. Thus will the human soul be compensated for the despair of finitude.

FAST

● ● ● ● ● ● ● ● ● ● ● ● ● ● ● ● ●

Remember that T-shirt from the eighties that said "High on Stress"? It was sort of true and sort of a way to bluff it out and sort of a protest—it had that "any number of meanings" quality we now prefer to depth. That's because the any-number-of-meanings quality keeps you in motion, but depth asks you to stop. Depth is to your life what dead air is to a talk show.

Being numb isn't antithetical to being totally stressed, 24-7—and asking for more. Over-scheduled busyness might seem like the opposite of numbness, but it is just the active aspect of living in a flood of fabricated surfaces. Consider the guiding metaphor again. The (absence of) sensation that is physical numbness is constituted by a multitude of thrills and tingles at a frequency beyond which you feel nothing. The numbness of busyness works on the same principle, but it relies upon its agents to abide by an agreement they must keep secret, even from themselves. The agreement is this: we will so conduct ourselves that everything becomes an emergency.

Under that agreement, stress is how reality feels. People addicted to busyness, people who don't just use their cell phones in public but display in every nuance of cell-phone deportment their sense of throbbing connectedness to Something Important—these people would suffocate like fish on a dock if they were cut off from the Flow of Events they have conspired with their fellows to create. To these plugged-in players, the rest of us look like zombies, coasting on fumes. For them, the feeling of being busy *is* the feeling of being alive.

Partly, it's a function of speed, like in those stress dramas that television provides to keep us virtually busy, even in our downtime. The bloody body wheeled into the ER, every person-jack on the team yelling numbers from monitors, screaming for meds and equipment, especially for those heart-shocker pads—that's the paradigm scene. All the others derive from it: hostage-negotiator scenes, staffers pulling all-nighters in the West Wing, detectives sweeping out of the precinct, donning jackets, adjusting holsters, snapping wisecracks. Sheer speed and Lives on the Line. That's the recipe for feeling real.

The irony is that *after* we have worked really hard on something urgent for a long time, we do escape numbness for a while—stepping out of the building, noticing the breeze, the cracks in the sidewalk, the stillness of things in the shop window. During those accidental and transitional moments, we actually get the feeling of the real we were so frantically pursuing when we were busy. But we soon get restless. We can't take the input reduction. Our psychic metabolism craves more.

Actually, stress dramas are about the lives of the media people who make them. They purport to be about hospitals or law firms, but they are actually about what it is like to make TV shows, about high-stakes teamwork in the land of celebrity, where, by definition, everything matters more than it does anywhere else, a land that welcomes diversity and foibles as long as The Job Gets Done, a land where everything personal, unconditional, intimate— everything unbounded by the task—takes place on the side. That's why, in these shows through which the celebrated teach the rest of us how to be like them, the moments of heartfelt encounter that make it all worthwhile are stolen in the corridors of power, while the verdict is awaited. If we get that real-folks-rushing-to-get-out-of-the-house-in-the-morning scene, it's just to underscore the priority of the Flow of Events that protects the busy from being left alone in the stillness with what makes it all worthwhile. Lest direction be lost, motion must be maintained.

MOVING ON

So life in a flood of surfaces means a life of perpetual motion, and TV provides the model in other modes as well. Take the transitions from story to story in newscasts, that finishing-with-a-topic moment. "Whether these supplies, still piling up after weeks of intense effort by these humanitarian workers, will actually reach the victims (pause) remains to be seen." A hint of a sigh, a slight shake of the head, eyes down-turning; the note of seasoned resignation. Profound respect is conveyed for the abandoned topic even as a note of anticipation rises to greet the (also interesting, but less burdensome) next topic—and the new camera angle at the anchor desk makes it clear that stern and external necessity, rather than any human agency, governs the shift from two minutes on mass starvation to the next episode of The Fall of the House of Enron.

Judy Woodruff is especially good at this, her particular little head nod, or shake, as the case may be, and the way her lips tighten up a tad. "If it were up to me as a human being I would *never* leave this coverage of thousands of dying innocents, but, as a newscaster, of course, I have to." And her speaking voice says, "All right, Jim, we have to go to a break now, but we will be following this story as it develops—and thanks again." "Thank you, Judy," says

Jim, echoing her gesture, and we understand that he, too, as a human being, would never allow us to move on from so ghastly and demanding a reality, but it isn't up to him as a human being either. It isn't up to anybody, actually. That's the one real reality. Moving on.

It would be irrelevant to object by asking, "Well, how else are we supposed to do it?" There isn't any other way to do it. That's the point. This isn't a consultant's memo. This is a serious diagnosis of a serious condition. Would we rather not know about it because it happens to be incurable? This goes much deeper than subject matter, or political bias, the usual fodder. It determines the way we frame everything. Like all that is most profound in human custom, this agreement is almost physical, an attunement, more music than semantics. It instills and expresses, moment by moment, the *attitude* we bring to living in this world of surfaces.

So, for example, you don't have to wait for the anchorperson to change the topic. You can change it yourself, and you don't have to sigh or tighten your lips as you make the transition. But you do. Monitor yourself next time you zap away from some disturbing something on *Lehrer* to catch the action on the *Law & Order* reruns. You mime those little gestures as you punch the buttons. These are the constituting habit structures of our culture.

And we've touched already on what awaits you when you join the gang on *Law & Order*. The stress drama re-creating, more elaborately, the basic gesture of the news show, the one you just performed when you slid away from those refugee visuals. Everything's in motion, elliptical, glancing, fungible. You see the sides of faces, the slope of shoulders, the beginnings of expressions but not the ends, the ends of expressions but not the beginnings. No matter the horror, no matter the injustice, no matter how passionate McCoy may feel, no matter how angry Bratt gets at Briscoe (actors or characters?), no matter how obnoxious the defense attorney or impatient the judge (especially in chambers), they all keep moving. And the camera keeps moving, too, gliding, peeking, glimpsing. Frightened witnesses, incoming lawyers, outgoing suspects, they're all moving—as is the traffic, the doors, hands, phones, everything. Meaningful personal encounters are bound to be interrupted, and the performers, like would-be fighters in a bar relying on friends to keep them apart, anticipate the interruption. Ferociously or tenderly, they emote in transitional interlude, awaiting inevitable rescue by events, and, gratefully regretting the passing of the moment of communion, they watch the D.A. step into the elevator and deliver the homily as the door slides shut across his grizzled visage, a homily that is never merely upbeat or despairing, never final or conclusive in any way. Because the one thing people in a TV series know is that tomorrow is another show, and they will be ready to roll. For they are pros, and pros know how to deal. It's not that they're indifferent or cynical. They care. Sometimes they win, sometimes they lose—but, either way, they move on. That's the lesson, the ultimate homily of all shows. The way we live now.

So, if we were spared a gaping wound in the flesh and blood of personal life, we inevitably moved on after September 11. We were carried off by endlessly proliferating representations of the event, and by an ever expanding horizon of associated stories and characters, and all of them, in their turn, represented endlessly, and the whole sweep of it driven by the rhythms of The Show—anthrax, postal workers, the Bronx lady, the Saddam connection, Osama tapes, Al Jazeera's commentary on Osama tapes, Christiane Amanpour's commentary on Al Jazeera's commentary on Osama tapes, a magazine story about Christiane Amanpour . . .

And that's just one thread in this tapestry of virtuality. The whole is so densely woven and finely stranded that no mind could possibly comprehend it, escape it, govern it. It's the dreamwork of culture. It just proceeds and we with it, each of us exposed to thousands, probably millions of 9/11-related representations—everything from the layout of the daily paper to rippling-flag logos to NYPD caps on tourists to ads for *Collateral Damage.* Conditioned thus relentlessly to move from representation to representation, we got past the thing itself as well; or rather, the thing itself was transformed into a sea of signs and upon it we were borne away from every shore, moving on, moving on.

What else could we do?

Understanding the Text

1. de Zengotita writes: Someday, it will be obvious that all the content on our information platforms converge on this theme: there is no important difference between fabrication and reality. . . .” What evidence does he offer to support this notion that no such “important difference” exists? (Identify two instances.)

2. de Zengotita claims that “[a]ccidental places are the only real places left.” What does he mean by this, and why does he think it is true?

3. "Flood," "Finitude," "Fast," "Moving On": de Zengotita uses each of these headings to describe a condition of contemporary life that shapes our consciousness. To what, specifically, does each refer? Together, how does he think these conditions affect our response to the events of 9/11?

Remembering Norma Rae

Robert Nathan and Jo-Ann Mort

Here are some words you are unlikely to hear in any of the movie clips shown during the Academy Awards this year:

> Ladies and gentlemen, the textile industry, in which you are spending your lives and your substance . . . is the only industry in the whole length and breadth of these United States of America that is not unionized. Therefore, they are free to exploit you, to lie to you, to cheat you and to take away from you what is rightfully yours—your health, a decent wage, a fit place to work.

"Unionized" isn't a word you hear in many American movies. "A decent wage," now there's a phrase that doesn't crop up too often. As for the evocative "your lives and your substance," poetic descriptions of the human condition aren't generally found in contemporary entertainment.

This speech is from Martin Ritt's classic 1979 film *Norma Rae*, delivered in an impassioned sermon by Ron Leibman in the role of an organizer for the Textile Workers Union of America, a real union at the time and a predecessor to the current trade union UNITE HERE. *Norma Rae* is an aberration in recent Hollywood history. The movie portrays a realistic union-organizing campaign and the fierce corporate response at the fictional O.P. Henley textile mill in the fictional town of Henleyville. As everyone knew at the time, the mill and the town were unambiguous stand-ins for J.P. Stevens and its sixteen-year war against union organizers in

Robert Nathan is co-executive producer of the television drama *Law & Order*. Jo-Ann Mort was director of communications for the labor unions ACTWU and UNITE.

Reprinted with permission from the March 12, 2007 issue of *The Nation*. For subscription information, call 1-800-333-8536. Portions of each week's Nation magazine can be accessed at http://www.thenation.com

Roanoke Rapids, North Carolina, and the movie accurately depicted the state of American labor in 1979.

The situation has not improved much since. The only remaining Stevens factory in the United States (owned by its successor company, Westpoint Home) is a unionized blanket mill in Maine. In other industries, union organizers are battling adversaries as unyielding as any in the days of *Norma Rae.* According to the labor advocacy group American Rights at Work, last year more than 23,000 Americans were fired or penalized for legal union activity.

On a human level, *Norma Rae* is the story of one woman, played by Sally Field, who finds redemption risking her life for economic justice, and of factory workers demanding to be treated as more than slaves. In the realm of the political, it is virtually the only American movie of the modern era to deal substantially with any of these subjects. Even today it remains iconic—a major studio movie about the lives of working people with a profound and, for its time, disturbing political message: The little guy may have a prayer of getting social justice, but he'll have to fight desperately to get it. Try to think of a contemporary American film with a similar message or a political statement anywhere near that blunt. The closest thing to a message in this year's crop of Oscar nominees for Best Picture can be found in *Babel,* which poses the rather mild question, Why can't we all just get along?

European filmmakers, like England's Ken Loach and Mike Leigh, don't shy from the subject of class. Loach's *Bread and Roses* dramatized the 1990 Service Employees International Union's Justice for Janitors campaign in Los Angeles, and Leigh's entire career is virtually a paean to the working class. This is not to say that American studios don't make topical mainstream films. A kind of renaissance seemed to be blossoming in 2005, with material as varied as *Good Night, and Good Luck* and *The Constant Gardener.* But *Blood Diamond*—about the 1990s civil war in Sierra Leone partly sparked by international diamond speculators—was perhaps this season's only major studio picture that could be called politically daring, and it was a box-office disappointment. In the end, of course, financially successful or not, such movies don't fundamentally threaten the established order. They're well-crafted stories delivering conventional wisdom with considerable artistic skill.

Norma Rae was different. Its subject matter, never mind its politics, was enough to make a studio executive cringe: a movie about a union. On top of that, it was a story of platonic love between a Jewish intellectual and a factory worker; in Hollywood love stories, the audience wants the heroes to end up in bed. Even with a trio of creative giants—Ritt and his writers, Irving Ravetch and Harriet Frank Jr.—this was no easy sell. Casting could have helped; stars get movies made. But several leading actresses, among them Jane Fonda and Jill Clayburgh, turned down the title role. Creative issues aside, there was the problem of location. Where would you shoot the movie? Because of J.P. Stevens's influence, taking the production to most Southern towns would be impossible, and building your own textile mill, prohibitively costly.

(With help from the union, Ritt found a unionized mill in Opelika, Alabama, where management agreed to let him shoot, with mill workers as extras playing themselves.) Finally, after overcoming all the odds, when released the movie was anything but an instant hit, and only after Sally Field won Best Actress at Cannes did it gradually go from dud to box-office success.

Since then, the entertainment community has kept its distance from the film. One indication of Hollywood's indifference came six years later, at the 1985 Academy Awards, when Field accepted her Oscar as Best Actress for *Places in the Heart.* "You like me," she said effusively, "right now, you like me." The audience response was nervous laughter, as if Sally Field were so needy as to consider an Academy Award a sign that she was "liked." This was, of course, not the case. Field had assumed, incorrectly, that most of her colleagues had seen her astonishing performance in *Norma Rae.* But in fact, many in the audience had no idea that she was referencing one of the picture's most memorable pieces of dialogue—her character's realization that her union organizer not merely respected her but liked her as a human being.

In the ensuing twenty years, the movie essentially disappeared. Otherwise movie-literate folks only vaguely remember Norma's quest. Alas, they don't know what they're missing. With Leibman and Field, the movie has two of the toughest and most generous performances in the history of American film. The film's language is simultaneously elegant and gritty. Of powerful moments, there is no end. When Norma commits herself to the organizing campaign, she asks the local minister to lend his church for a union meeting. "That's blacks and whites sitting together," Norma says. The minister, horrified, tells her, "We're going to miss your voice in the choir, Norma." She replies, "You're going to hear it raised up somewhere else."

In an unusual twist, the movie's story played itself out in reality the year following its release. Sixteen years after a successful union election at the Roanoke Rapids mill, union members finally forced J.P. Stevens to the bargaining table. The film was a key factor in a nationwide boycott against Stevens—a campaign that became a model for coalitions of union supporters and union members. The Rev. David Dyson, who helped spearhead the Stevens boycott when he was on the union's staff, recalls: "The movie came along at the two-year point in the boycott, which hadn't picked up any steam. We found Crystal Lee Jordan [now Crystal Lee Sutton, the worker who inspired the Norma Rae character]. . . . We put on a tour, including a great event in Los Angeles with Sally Field and Crystal Lee. The lights would come up and there would be the real Norma Rae and people would leap to their feet."

It's nearly impossible to imagine a similar movie that would bring them to their feet today. Television, a broader medium, is different, with an audience more fractionated and therefore, theoretically, more open to content that some might label controversial. Not so long ago there was *Roseanne,* which addressed head-on the darkness of power and social class and the tribulations of working life. Last year's Emmy winner *The Office* included a story line mocking a nasty anti-union campaign; the hugely popular *Grey's Anatomy* followed a nurses' strike with obvious sympathy for the nurses—even management, in the person of doctor George O'Malley, joined the picket line as the story revealed his upbringing in a pro-union home. One could argue that the brilliantly corrosive *Rescue Me,* about Denis Leary as a New York City firefighter and the personal lives of his colleagues, is a bold step into the interior world of the working class; but firefighters are unmistakably post-9/11 heroes. What's ultimately most telling about these examples is how unusual they are, far from television's norm, at a time when most Americans are losing economic ground. One new show this season, the polished and artful *Brothers & Sisters,* is about a wealthy family in Pasadena who own a business in which workers are nearly invisible; the primary stories involve the characters' tortured love lives. Ironically, the family matriarch—albeit a liberal ACLU-ish matriarch—is played by none other than Sally Field.

It would be easy to blame the entertainment industry for the invisibility of working people fighting to better their lives. Ask writers in show business and they'll say, "Nobody cares about seeing those people on a screen" and "If audiences wanted to see that, the studios would make it" and, finally, the answer to nearly every question about the current condition of American filmmaking, "The studios have a mega-hit mentality; they don't want to make small pictures." But maybe there's another reason. Making *Norma Rae* in 1979 was hard enough; now it would probably be impossible. The country has changed. It's more difficult to build a mass movement for social and economic change, to find large numbers of Americans who care about social solidarity. If popular entertainment is, by definition, mass entertainment, what happens when no mass exists, when an insufficient number of people occupy cultural common ground? In that case, for whom would you make *Norma Rae?*

"You live there, and you become one of them," Sally Field said in a documentary issued with the DVD of *Norma Rae,* "and you try to stand at their machine and thread it and run it, and . . . you learn to appreciate how difficult their lives are, and chances are you're never getting out." Which, for the most part, is how things remain. The American labor movement is arguably in more trouble now than it was then. Where is the next movie that might hope to change the course of history?

Of movies about ideas and social justice, Sam Goldwyn famously said, "If you want to send a message, call Western Union." In other words, moviemakers are in the movie business, not the social change business. And so tomorrow we won't go to the tenplex and find movies about Wal-Mart workers fighting for health and pension benefits, or turn on the television and find a working-class hero struggling to pay the electric bill. (Isn't it odd that people on TV hardly ever seem to worry about gas prices?) If we are to find a *Roseanne* or a *Norma Rae* again in popular entertainment, if we are to make movies that can affect the course of history, we need to find something else first, something difficult to see on the horizon. We need to find a belief in an ideal disappearing not only from our movies but also from our lives—the notion that we do, in fact, share common ground, and that if we ignore the lives of the least fortunate in our society we may well be ignoring the future of our society itself.

Understanding the Text

1. What is the chief reason that Nathan and Mort praise *Norma Rae?*

2. Why do the authors think that the film is not better known and more frequently discussed today?

3. The authors claim that *Norma Rae* influenced events in the real world. What were they?

Look at Me!
Leave Me Alone!

Joshua Gamson

I't's a beautiful fantasy, really, and a potent one right about now: you are sailing through stormy weather to the edge of this bright, false, pretty world, and ramming suddenly into what all of your life you had mistaken for the sky but turns out to be a wall, you climb out of your boat onto a staircase and up to a door, behind which things may be less pretty but certainly more real. Stepping through that door into a private darkness, you start a life that is unwatched, unproduced, unrecorded, unmarketed, unsold. This fantasy—the end of the popular dystopia *The Truman Show*—is powerful exactly because of the world we seem to live in on this side of the backdrop sky, in which privacy is a scarce commodity, in which prying eyes are everywhere, and in which everything and everyone you see is for sale, operators standing by. In this world, it's tough to know just who and what is for real.

If you've seen the film, you know that Truman Burbank was the first baby to be legally adopted by a corporation, OmniCam. Directed by the God-artiste-mogul Christof ("the big guy," or, as he puts it, "the Creator [pause] of a television show"), Truman is the unknowing star of his own enormously popular television show; his entire life is recorded by 5,000 hidden cameras and is broadcast, with constant product placement, worldwide. The manicured and predictable little island town he lives in, Seahaven, is in fact the world's biggest studio, populated entirely by actors, including those playing his wife, his mother, his best friend. Everything in it, literally, is available by mail order. Truman is the only "real" thing on the set, kept

Joshua Gamson is a professor of sociology at the University of San Francisco and publishes widely on celebrity culture in America. He is the author of three books: *The Fabulous Sylvester: The Legend, The Music, The Seventies in San Francisco* (2005), *Freaks Talk Back: Tabloid Talk Shows and Sexual Nonconformity* (1998), and *Claims to Fame: Celebrity in Contemporary America* (1994). His essays and reviews appear in numerous journals and magazines.

there by a fear of water facilitated by the staged drowning of his father, TV shows proclaiming the joys of never leaving home, and travel agency posters featuring crashing jets. Gradually, through a series of glitches such as falling studio lights, the reappearance of his dead father, and a car radio playing control room instructions, Truman begins to suspect that things are not as they appear, a perspective aided by memories of an old girlfriend, now a leader of a "Free Truman" resistance movement, who before being dragged away by a thug posing as her father had shouted "Everybody's pretending! It's a set! It's a studio!"

And so Truman begins a ratings-grabbing escape, violently opposed and exploited by Christof and OmniCam, who put in his way forest fires, a nuclear plant leak from which he is chased and subdued by men in silver protective suits, betrayals by his wife and best friend, and a search by actors and hunting dogs lined up like a lynch mob, lit by a moon-turned-searchlight and a prematurely risen sun. Eventually he is found where he's not supposed to be, on the sea. Over the objections of network executives ("We can't let him die in front of a live audience!"), he is subjected to biblical punishments by Christof ("He was born in front of a live audience!"), who, using a weather program, sends storms and giant waves in an attempt to drown his boy rather than see the show end. "There's no more truth out there than in the world I created," Christof warns Truman from his perch in the studio sky. Truman isn't buying it, and to the viewers' delight, still directed by Christof ("That's our hero shot," he says as Truman sails off defiantly), he plays the hero. "You're going to have to kill me," he screams, and he survives to hit the wall, and the staircase, and the doorway. Live free-camera-free, that is—or die.

WATCHING ME WATCHING YOU

● ● ● ● ● ● ● ● ● ● ● ● ● ● ● ●

The Truman Show is interesting not because of its originality; it borrows from and nicely updates quite a number of earlier stories of paranoid heroes starring unknowingly in films about themselves, of horrific Big Brother surveillance and pacified publics and superpowerful media, from Samuel Beckett and Aldous Huxley and George Orwell to Philip K. Dick and Robert A. Heinlein, from *Blade Runner* to *Network* to *The Twilight Zone*. It is, however, a timely satire, and one that has spurred waves of commentary about how it summarizes our current state of affairs in a big, entertaining metaphor, how we are all Truman Burbanks, trapped by the ever shrinking private life created by constant surveillance. "The movie's most frightening question comes down to this: Is the fictional specter of an all-knowing, all-seeing eye really so far removed from fact?" asked a typical *Chicago Tribune* report recently, going on to suggest it is not. Writing about information access more generally, novelist Richard Powers argued in the *New York Times* that "private life" might soon enough become a "term that had some shared meaning once but vaporized under the press of material progress." We have conceded the right to be recorded, Powers claims, having "long forsaken any hope of preserving the private—that part of life that goes unregistered."

We are trapped, another version of the argument goes, not so much by the constant registering of private life as by our insatiable appetite for the televised life. We may be victims of surveillance, but we are also its advocates, sad-sack Truman fans thrilled by the prying eyes of the cameras. The most provocative aspect of *The Truman Show,* Paul Brownfield wrote in the *Los Angeles Times,* for instance, "is not how thoroughly Big Brother can watch us but how the home viewers in the film blithely peer in at Truman's life, never stopping to consider their own complicity in the grand manipulation." If we are trapped, it is only because, as Christof asserts about Truman, we love our cell. "The captive of TV isn't Truman, it's the audience," Stanley Kauffmann suggested in the *New Republic.* "Us." And greedy media corporations are only too willing to shove cameras anywhere they can get them, feeding us the private until there's nothing left to eat.

What traps us, then, the constant watching by hidden others or our own constant watching? Which are we, the poor souls chased by camera crews or the chop-licking connoisseurs of other people's secrets? Which is the fantasy of freedom, the one in which we can see everything or the one in which we are safe from being seen? The weird thing, of course, is that both seem to be the case. Many of us are not, like Truman, running away from the cameras but running toward them, arms wide open, carrying our own spotlights—while complaining that we can't seem to get away from the lens. The fantasy of entering a camera-free realm coexists quite comfortably with the dream of a life in which all eyes are on you; the pronounced anxiety about eroded privacy (don't watch me! leave people alone!) lives happily with the avid worship of publicity (look at me! let me see!). What is new here is neither voyeurism nor exhibitionism—it is their strange relationship, in which watching and turning away, being on camera and hiding from it, are married impulses.

It's hard to know exactly where and when this all began, but the two impulses are now relentlessly chasing each other's tails. The key to understanding the chase, where anxiety about diminution of privacy begets more craving for televised moments of privacy and vice versa, is that it is not the erosion of privacy alone that really seems to be bothersome, but the erosion of moments that can be *trusted.* It is not just crass voyeurism that drives growing popular interest in the nooks and crannies of everyday life, but a sense that those nooks and crannies look more and more like stage sets. The growth of surveillance, industrialized voyeurism, and increased self-display add up to a situation in which "realness" seems harder to find; all the heightened recording of private and personal life, the invited kind and the uninvited, sets in motion a hunt for the authentic. Television, along with technological advances in surveillance technique and demographic-information capturing, has made the places where one is unwatched and unsurveyed, where one need make no adjustments for an audience, seem fewer and farther between (be careful what books you buy, your sales receipt might get subpoenaed; be careful what you do in the aisle of a drugstore, because hidden cameras are recording you). The look-at-me culture only makes the search for these moments even more untenable: the more people offer themselves for the watching, the more like performers they become. And so the search for trustable moments, really private ones, intensifies.

Television, a prime purveyor of the look-at-me principle, has stepped in to satisfy the craving for the real, unobserved life that it has helped to undermine. Media conglomerates happily and effortlessly market the pursuit of realness, exploiting it for the old-fashioned goal of getting people to watch television. Television now commonly provides fare that promises a door at the edge of the studio—showing off private moments meant to reassure us that spontaneous behaviors, actions taken without regard to cameras and publicity, still exist. It can do this very easily by drawing on the heady dream of publicity that television culture has long since codified: the fantasy of being the star of your very own show (think of programs as disparate as *Oprah* or *America's Funniest Home Videos*), if only for a few minutes, with all its attendant rewards. Yet when all kinds of people take up these invitations to celebrity, as they have more and more, the sense of private life as a performance for the cameras, as somehow not quite real, gets even stronger. These rolling cameras to which we have by now grown so accustomed bring with them the giant suspicion that everyone might be partly acting, every candid moment part of the ongoing infomercial. And the TV solution to the worry that we are too watched to be real, our lives too public to be trusted, is more watching in the hope of glimpsing the real. We are invited to see the unobserved (a snoring Truman, the unsuspecting criminals on *Cops*), the glitches in the observation system (the falling lights on Truman's stage set, goofy out-takes on *TV Censored Bloopers*), anything that takes us behind the door. But the TV offer comes with a funny sort of guarantee: the door gets farther away the faster you run toward it.

SOMEBODY'S WATCHING ME

● ● ● ● ● ● ● ● ● ● ● ● ● ●

It's an intriguing, reassuring, almost nostalgic kick to witness the innocence of the unwatched. Indeed, perhaps what makes the marketing of "private" reality an especially easy sell for television is the more and more common awareness that watchers could be pretty much anywhere. I myself, for instance, am careful not to do anything indelicate on elevators, at automatic teller machines, and in convenience stores these days, since it's hard to know if there's a camera in the corner watching me pick basil or poppy seeds out of my teeth. And I might also be well advised to compose my emails more carefully at work: along with many other such jarring examples in his new book *The Transparent Society,* David Brin cites a 1997 survey of 906 employers, 35 percent of whom were found to be conducting one or more types of "close electronic surveillance" on their employees. I should probably also be more careful about what I do on the streets of New York City, where, as in Baltimore, my behavior in some areas is recorded by hidden cameras 24 hours a day. I'll be avoiding Roslyn Heights, New York, too, where, according to the *Boston Globe,* 35 hidden surveillance cameras feed live pictures onto the Internet of anyone moving on the streets.

It seems pretty clear that new technology has made hidden surveillance much more sophisticated, easier to do, and harder to detect. There's no question that everyone needs to be vigilant as ever about sleazy, ill-intentioned intrusions and restrictions on civil liberties, but it's also worth noting that, in order to be truly effective as social control tools—and these spying techniques have indeed proved to be remarkable crime reducers—people need to know the cameras are there. This kind of surveillance, unlike Truman's, operates on the knowledge that, at least potentially, someone is watching; the cameras must be both obscured and acknowledged. This is the effect of the Panopticon famously noted by Michel Foucault: people police themselves. Who's going to light up a joint in Washington Square Park when the cameras might be rolling? Who's going to have raunchy conversations online if their boss might be reading along? The awareness of being observed, not just the observing, is what Big Brother techniques promote.

Of course, the greatest recent increase in hidden watching is less Big Brother than big business. Driving records, Social Security numbers, credit ratings, marital status, purchasing habits, membership in organizations, taxes—pretty much anyone with a little skill and a computer can find those out with just your name and address. But who really wants to know? The increased recording of information most of us thought was ours alone is not so much a matter of getting you to adjust your behavior as to generate information from which to sell you more things. America Online and others, for instance, compile names and addresses of their subscribers to sell to other companies; every magazine subscription begets unmerciful junk mail. An Internet site visit is tracked by a "cookie," a piece of software that makes note of what you look at, and the next thing you know you're getting messages from manufacturers of baldness cures or vacation resorts or people willing to take their clothes off for a small fee. A supermarket discount "club" card tracks what's in your shopping cart. It's not in fact paranoid to think that, at least when it comes to any activity that might remotely involve you in buying something, almost everything you do is on record. These surveillance activities, open or not, start to add up after a while, and you start to feel less certain that much information about yourself is yours to control, and more certain that in order to sell you things, companies of all kinds are keeping awfully close tabs.

While computerized recording of buying habits and convenience store cameras and nosy neighbors with video cameras are not bothersome in the same ways or to the same degree, together they do create the impression that not much is left unrecorded. It's this suspicion that is firmed up, popularized, and capitalized upon by the now ubiquitous phenomenon of "reality" television, in which people are filmed going about their everyday lives and those images converted into entertainment. Sometimes they know about the cameras ahead of time, sometimes they grant permission after the fact (or, more rarely, refuse to grant it) for some moment of their lives to be broadcast; sometimes the real life is loosely scripted, sometimes it's just edited for dramatic effect. A minor tradition precedes the 1990s explosion of reality TV—*Candid Camera* set people up to be the unknowing butts of televised jokes in the 1960s, the Loud family aired their laundry for PBS's *American Family* in the 1970s, David Letterman has had this cam and that cam roaming the streets and the studio since the 1980s, and daytime talk shows, for their part, have always made their money by the revelation of the everyday lives and emotions of their guests. But by now reality entertainment is a full-fledged genre, as cheap-to-produce programming meets up with an audience intrigued by dramas of "real life." MTV's *Real World* (and its spinoff *Road Rules*) brings together a combustible mix of good-looking young men and women and films them playing themselves as they might be if they had actually chosen to live together. Fox's *Cops* films police pursuing and arresting criminals, and the syndicated *Real TV* buys footage of car chases and dramatic rescue scenes. HBO's *Taxicab Confessions* places "lipstick cameras" in cabs and offers drivers, who are equipped with earphones through which they can hear producers, suggestions for questions to ask the fares. Local television news looks increasingly like some loony combination of *Cops* and *America's Funniest Home Videos.*

Watching these shows, it makes sense to wonder once again what there is left to live unobserved, whether there's a cam-less spot left. Truman may not have died on live television, but the airing of the Los Angeles freeway suicide earlier this year—and years before that, the O. J. car chase scene, which was riveting because he had a gun and was threatening suicide—has made it clear that it is indeed possible, if controversial, to watch someone die on live television. Or give birth on the Internet, as a woman named "Elizabeth" did this past summer before an audience estimated at two million. What seems especially striking in recent years is the enthusiasm with which so many people invite strangers to watch and listen to activities that are typically considered private, and the enthusiasm with which, despite the fear of lost privacy, strangers are willing to participate in the process. Apple software engineer John Kullmann has a webcam in his office that has fed his image so far to 76,000 strangers. "If I happen to be picking my nose, they catch me," he told a San Francisco reporter. Apple co-founder Steve Wozniak has four webcams in his office. "If I pick my nose," Wozniak told a Houston reporter, perhaps confirming the rumors of widespread computer industry nose-picking, "they see me." Jennifer Ringley allows you to witness her life on JenniCam for $15 a year, and Ana Voog's anacam.com allows you to watch the performance artist take baths, eat lunch, and paint herself blue in front of four webcams. According to one keeper of a list of webcam sites, between 20 and 30 people submit new sites every day

And there's still the old-fashioned route. *The Jerry Springer Show* claims to get thousands of calls every week from people volunteering to fight with their two-timing/slut-dressing/thought-he-was-a-she wife/boyfriend/mother/cousin. According to the *Los Angeles Times,* about 14,000 people volunteered to be subjects for the most recent *Real World* and *Road Rules* casts. Clearly, not everybody is all that bothered by the idea of being watched. Picking noses, telling each other's secrets, eating a peanut butter sandwich, having a baby: there are more than enough people willing to invade their own "privacy." And more than enough people willing to watch, all the while complaining that "the media" are too intrusive, sticking their microphones in the midst of private grief and joy and intrigue.

THE CURRENCY OF PUBLICITY

Although people do routinely and vehemently object to the erosion of privacy, it's puzzling that they also seem to be unbothered by quite a bit of it. For instance, while everyone pretty much agrees that the relentless, hidden information grabbing by companies is incredibly annoying, and that the companies should at least tell you when they're stealing your personal information for their own profiteering, to many people such activities seem relatively innocuous—after all, it's all about giving you what you want, and if someone wants to know what kind of cereal I like, or even what dirty pictures I like to look at, fine, go nuts.

But the story deepens a bit when one sees that privacy, while certainly also at stake, is not the key here. This is an extraordinarily ocular culture, and one that rewards the looked-at, so it ought not be surprising that lots of people are ready to be watched. Being looked at, being visible, being known about, is a currency. You can cash it in for money or office, and even if that's not what you're after, the logic of celebrity remains powerful: you aren't anybody until you've been on television. It's the pursuit of publicity, not privacy, that offers the big rewards in this culture. If the fantasy of sailing away from prying eyes is one potent vision, that may only be because the fantasy of being known is its jealous twin.

Indeed, it's the fact that publicity has such payoffs that sends the broadcasting of the "private" into high gear. Publicity culture makes a virtue of being watched, and reality television profits from the desire to witness something real behind self-interested publicity, to see how people look when they do not know they are being seen. The longing captured by *The Truman Show* is a craving for something "real." It's not so much the threats to privacy itself that are bothersome these days but what the private tends to make possible and has come to symbolize: a life you recognize as authentically your own because it is not there for the entertainment of others. The private moment has come to stand for realness, and the awareness of increased surveillance means that fewer and fewer moments qualify. "As private space shrinks," Ellen Goodman has smartly pointed out, "the public's hunger for authenticity grows. As the hunger grows, the deeper we invade private life to find something real, and the shallower it gets." Reality television, moving its cameras into "private," promises exactly the unobserved moments that it makes impossible to deliver.

"Cue the sun," says *The Truman Show's* Christof as he intensifies his search for Truman Burbank. Lately, entertainment media are smitten with this image of their own power, their role as gods manipulating the public and manufacturing reality—the reporter in *Mad City* who "controls" rather than reports a hostage story, the Hollywood producer in *Wag the Dog* who manufactures a made-for-TV war, the producers in *Bulworth* who make and break political careers. And although the manipulative power of media industries is plain and well documented, in many ways media are more like parasites than gods. They feed off social anxieties and broadcast them for profit. The disquieting sense that one is too often watched has more widespread creators than the media gods. Yet once they get in on the game, they set in motion a spiral that is hard to escape. Even if the creators are not as omnipotent as they appear in their own mirrors, that spiral itself is incredibly powerful, in part because the desire to feel one's own life remains, even if buried beneath a pile of *TV Guides,* very powerful. The simultaneous pursuit of publicity and distrust of it, once it enters the realm of television, builds a staircase back to the living room, where we can sit down to watch the watching in the blue-lit privacy of our own homes. As media critic Mark Crispin Miller once put it, "Big Brother is you, watching."

Perhaps in the end it is not really Truman Burbank and Christof who summarize the current state of affairs, but the *Teletubbies.* These four British imports, now trying to recreate their enormous U.K. popularity on America's PBS, are small, goofy alien creatures who bounce around the bright, colorful Teletubbyland ("the place where television is made") in fuzzy head-to-toe pajama-like outfits; their trippy show takes aim at the hitherto-untapped one- to two-year-old market. Po, Laa Laa, Dipsy, and Tinky Winky, who have antennas on their fluffy heads and television screens in their round tummies, live in a beautiful world in which life without television is literally unimaginable. Television lives inside of them. They are TV watchers who are also TV screens. During each show, what looks to be a windmill but turns out to be a TV transmitter begins to emit a signal, and one of the Tubbies' stomach screens starts to glow, until a video of a real-life child (riding a horse or a tricycle or some such thing) begins to play. When the video ends, the Teletubbies call for more. "Again, again," they cry, and we watch them as they turn to watch the mundane clip of life taking place again on one of their own small, glowing bellies.

NAME: ───────────────

DATE: ───────────────

Understanding the Text

1. To what specific contradiction within the American viewing public does Gamson's title, "Look at Me! Leave Me Alone!" refer?

2. How does Gamson account for the popularity of so-called "reality shows" on television? And what is the main effect of our watching these shows?

3. According to Gamson, what is the symbolic import of the show *Teletubbies?*

ADDITIONAL READINGS

Black, Joel. *The Reality Effect: Film Culture and the Graphic Imperative.* New York: Routledge, 2002.

Boorstin, Daniel J. *The Image: A Guide to Pseudo-Events in America.* 1961. New York: Atheneum, 1987.

Braudy, Leo. *The Frenzy of Renown: Fame and Its History.* New York: Oxford UP, 1986.

Bugeja, Michael. *Interpersonal Divide: The Search for Community in a Technological Age.* New York: Oxford UP, 2005.

Coontz, Stephanie. *The Way We Never Were: American Families and the Nostalgia Trap.* New York: BasicBooks, 1992.

Czitrom, Daniel J. *Media and the American Mind: From Morse to McLuhan.* Chapel Hill: U of North Carolina P, 1982.

DeLillo, Don. *White Noise.* New York: Viking, 1985.

Ewen, Stuart. *All Consuming Images: The Politics of Style in Contemporary Culture.* New York: Basic Books, 1988.

Frantz, Douglas and Catherine Collins. *Celebration, U.S.A.: Living in Disney's Brave New Town.* New York: Henry Holt, 1999.

Gabler, Neal. *Life, the Movie: How Entertainment Conquered Reality.* New York: Knopf, 1998.

———. *Walt Disney: The Triumph of the American Imagination.* New York: Knopf, 2006.

Gamson, Joshua. *Claims to Fame: Celebrity in Contemporary America.* Berkeley: U of California P, 1994.

Gitlin, Todd. *Media Unlimited: How the Torrent of Images and Sounds Overwhelms Our Lives.* New York: Metropolitan Books, 2001.

Kunstler, James Howard. *The Geography of Nowhere: The Rise and Decline of America's Man-Made Landscape.* 1993. New York: Touchstone-Simon & Schuster, 1994.

Lazere, Donald, ed. *American Media and Mass Culture: Left Perspectives.* Berkeley: U of California P, 1987.

McKibben, Bill. *The Age of Missing Information.* New York: Random House, 1992.

Miller, Mark Crispin, ed. *Seeing Through Movies.* Pantheon Guide to Popular Culture Series. New York: Pantheon, 1990.

Orvell, Miles. *The Real Thing: Imitation and Authenticity in American Culture, 1880–1940.* Cultural Studies of the United States. Chapel Hill: U of North Carolina P, 1989.

Ross, Andrew. *The Celebration Chronicles: Life, Liberty, and the Pursuit of Property Value in Disney's New Town.* New York: Ballantine, 1999.

Schickel, Richard. *Intimate Strangers: The Culture of Celebrity in America.* 1985. Chicago: Ivan R. Dee, 2000.

Tye, Larry. *The Father of Spin: Edward L. Bernays & The Birth of Public Relations.* New York: Crown, 1998.

How the West Was Spun:
History, Hollywood, and the Narrative of Nationhood

Fighting for the West

Eric Foner and Jon Wiener

"The West as America: Reinterpreting Images of the Frontier, 1820–1920," an exhibit at the Smithsonian Institution's National Museum of American Art, has become the latest target in the assault on "politically correct" thought by longtime conservatives, onetime radicals and academics enamored of campus life before the advent of large numbers of women and minority students. Critics accusing this show of being "P.C." have once again wrapped themselves in the mantle of intellectual liberalism, while accusing their opponents of political indoctrination and thought control (see Alexander Cockburn, "Beat the Devil," May 27 and June 24). But at the Smithsonian, as on most college campuses, abuses inspired by political correctness remain a minor problem. Their significance is dwarfed by the myriad real crises in university and cultural life—among them dwindling public funds, rising corporate influence, the fragmentation of scholarship and widespread illiteracy. "Political correctness" ranks with the swine flu epidemic and comet Kohoutek as molehills transformed into mountains by a gullible media. The Smithsonian controversy suggests that it is the right, not the left, that today poses the real threat to intellectual freedom.

Senator Ted Stevens, the Alaska Republican, made the Smithsonian show a national issue in a Senate Appropriations Committee hearing in May, when he accused the museum of advancing a leftist political agenda and threatened to cut the institution's budget in retaliation. "You're in for a battle," he told Smithsonian officials. Washington Republican Senator Slade Gorton echoed the charge. (Stevens

Eric Foner is a professor of history at Columbia University and widely considered to be the leading authority on Reconstruction, the period following the Civil War. He has published numerous articles in journals and magazines, appeared frequently on television and radio, and contributed to documentaries that have aired on PBS and The History Channel. He has published many seminal books, including *Who Owns History?: Rethinking the Past in a Changing World* (2002), *Slavery and Freedom in Nineteenth-Century America* (1994), and *Reconstruction: America's Unfinished Revolution, 1863–1877* (1988). Jon Wiener is a professor of history at the University of California-Irvine and a contributing editor to *The Nation.* His journalism and scholarly articles have appeared in a wide range of newspapers, magazines, and journals. He is the author of five books, including *Historians in Trouble: Plagiarism, Fraud and Power in the Ivory Tower* (2005), *Gimme Some Truth: The John Lennon FBI Files* (2000), and *Professors, Politics and Pop* (1991).

From "Fighting for the West" by Eric Foner and Jon Wiener. Reprinted with permission from the July 29, 1991 issue of *The Nation.* For subscription information, call 1-800-333-8536. Portions of each week's Nation magazine can be accessed at http://www.thenation.com.

later acknowledged that he had not, in fact, seen the show. What prompted his crusade was a well-publicized remark by former Librarian of Congress Daniel Boorstin in the museum's comment book that the exhibit was "perverse, historically inaccurate, [and] destructive.")

The press quickly entered the fray. *The Washington Post's* Ken Ringle called the show "the most cynical exhibit . . . ever presented under the aegis of your tax dollars and mine." *The New York Times's* senior art critic, Michael Kimmelman, blasted the show's "simplistic" and "forced" analyses. The wildest attack came from political columnist Charles Krauthammer: The exhibit, he wrote, had "a crude half-baked Marxist meanness"; it could have appeared "thirty years ago in Moscow."

Those who actually visit "The West as America" may well be disappointed to discover that the exhibit is decidedly unscandalous. It begins with a seemingly unexceptional premise: that nineteenth-century paintings do not simply record Western "reality." Instead, as a wall label states, they are "products of convention" rooted in the dominant ideologies of their time. Of course, placing the work of artists in historical context is hardly a new idea. What the critics object to is the nature of the historical interpretation presented in tandem with these particular works of art.

In most assaults on "political correctness," the bogyman is "multiculturalism"—the movement to expand subjects like history and literature to include the experiences of previously neglected groups. Critics of "The West as America," however, are after larger game—nothing less than an entire interpretation of the American past. What they want is the kind of relentlessly celebratory account of American development so common in the 1950s. To Krauthammer, the show expresses "contempt for every achievement of Western expansion"; the *Post's* Ringle complained that the show "trashes . . . most of our national history."

Scholars may be excused for finding this somewhat tendentious. As Patricia Nelson Limerick of the University of Colorado at Boulder, a leading historian of the West, puts it, "This show is about as revolutionary as if you had a Southern history exhibit, hung romantic paintings of plantations, and then said slavery was a rough business—not a very wild proposition, and the same kind of proposition this show offers about the West."

Limerick, of course, knows full well that a heroic vision of the West retains a powerful hold on the American imagination. She and others founded the "New Western History," which has transformed our understanding of the region over the past decade or so (see Sarah J. Stage, "Tales of the New West," October 22, 1990). These scholars have hammered the final nail into the coffin of Frederick Jackson Turner's "frontier thesis," which saw westward expansion as a mystical social process in which European culture was stripped away by settlers' encounter with nature. On the frontier emerged the quintessential American, cut free from the European past and devoted to individualism, democracy and equality.

In the New Western History, the West is not a process but a place—a place inhabited by people, not just nature, and fought over by a multi-ethnic cast of characters including

Easterners, Mexicans, Native Americans and blacks. The conquest of the West is a story of success and failure, heroism and betrayal, capitalist triumph and labor exploitation. Colorado miners and Mexican peons are as much a part of the story as pioneers on the Oregon Trail. In other words, the West's development was a complex history, not a simple heroic progress.

Howard Lamar, the Yale historian whose work inspired much of this new history, writes in the exhibition catalogue that the West has always been "a place to project wishes and dreams," and that in so doing, Americans "reveal themselves and their own ideologies." American history contained many Wests, all more or less "invented," all different from the prosaic and intermittently violent reality of white settlement and Native American dispossession. At the Constitutional Convention, Madison argued that the West could save America from Old World class conflict. Half a century later Horace Greeley saw it as a safety valve for oppressed Eastern workers. The doctrine of Manifest Destiny held that the West would fulfill America's divinely ordained role as savior of the world. Economic writers often viewed the West as a passage to India, a route by which America could dominate trade with the Far East. Today, it seems, the New World Order requires a West free of exploitation, racism and other inconvenient realities of American life.

That the West has always existed in the imagination as much as in reality is the theme of the Smithsonian show. *The Washington Post* declared it "curious" that "the art and the arguments of the show's organizers tend to operate at cross-purposes." But that is precisely the show's message. The nineteenth- and early twentieth-century paintings on display celebrated the conquest of the West. The accompanying wall labels challenge viewers not to take the paintings at face value, but to reinterpret them in terms of what historians have come to understand about Western expansion.

The show emphasizes that artists painted the West to conform to the expectations of Easterners, especially wealthy patrons of the arts and railroad companies interested in promoting Western settlement and tourism. Easterners wanted to see a West more honest and clean, more stirring and uplifting, than their own troubled region, suffering in the late nineteenth century from periodic depressions and violent class conflict. The paintings promised settlers a peaceful journey to fertile lands, and the artists paid special attention to "the triumphs of engineering"—railroads, bridges, etc. The wall texts take note of what the paintings left out: abandoned homesteads and mining towns that went bust; social conflict and environmental damage.

Often, artists portrayed the West as if it were entirely uninhabited. When they did depict Native Americans, much of their work tended to be stereotypical. The exhibition section "Inventing the Indian" has turned out to be one of the most controversial. These paintings, the much-maligned wall text declares, "tell more about the feelings and ideas of artists and patrons than about the 'Indians' whose lives they represent." Early in the nineteenth century,

Native Americans were portrayed as noble savages; later, as they were being driven off their land, they were portrayed as violent aggressors (even though they were usually the victims of aggression). Later still, the "doomed Indian" (representing the fantasy that the whole problem might be eliminated by Indians simply dying out) and the acculturated Indian became prominent themes.

The final room, on early-twentieth-century painters, also aroused considerable ire. One guide who has taken groups around the museum reported that while many visitors accept the idea that paintings of Indians are not entirely "accurate," they nevertheless become irate when presented with the idea that the West may not have "really" been the way Frederic Remington painted it.

Nor do they appreciate being confronted by Remington's racism. "Jews— inguns—chinamen—Italians—Huns—" he wrote, were "the rubish of the earth I hate." In the same letter to a friend, he boasted, "I've got some Winchesters and when the massacreing begins . . . I can get my share of 'em and whats more I will." It does not seem entirely far-fetched to speculate, as the wall text does, that Remington's painting *Fight for the Water Hole,* in which some tough-looking Texans defend themselves from Comanche attack, may have been colored by these prejudices. And when the work is placed in the context in which it was painted—America in 1903, thirty years after the event it portrayed—it can be viewed as an allegory in which a native-born white elite is surrounded by menacing and uncivilized immigrants. But Krauthammer ridiculed those interpretations, describing the painting as simply "a classic cowboys vs. Indians gunfight," and *The Washington Post's* Ringle approvingly quoted an assertion that it portrays nothing more or less than "the truth . . . basic reportage."

Critics also objected to the museum's interpretation of *The Captive,* by Irving Crouse, which portrays a helpless young white woman in a flowing white dress, her hands and feet tied, lying unconscious at the feet of an Indian warrior, who quietly stares at her. The wall text suggests that the painting expresses white culture's "fears of miscegenation," which aroused a storm of protest from, among others, *The New York Times* and *Newsweek,* both of which ran reproductions of the painting. The warrior's arrows, on the ground, point at the helpless woman, suggesting a sinister version of Cupid; the catalogue interpreted the arrows as phallic symbols, an idea critics dismissed with contempt.

The painting's sexual imagery is ambiguous, but the critics seem most offended not by the museum's Freudianism (hardly a new idea, even in Stevens's Alaska) but by any effort to interpret a work of art. Krauthammer's argument that Remington painted only "a classic cowboys vs. Indians gunfight" falls into this category. This view reveals the deep strain of anti-intellectualism and provincialism that lies just beneath the surface of the assault on "political correctness."

Some of the show's wall texts are, indeed, didactic—a common failing in museum prose—but the critics are upset by its substance, not just its style. Rather than criticism, however, the exhibition curators deserve praise for the extensive archival work that has enabled them to place these mostly mediocre and forgotten paintings in a historical context. The show includes Henry Farny's 1902 portrait of Ogallala Fire in full warrior regalia. However, as Alex Nemerov's catalogue essay reports, Ogallala Fire was at that time not a warrior on the plains but a janitor in the Cincinnati Art Club. "The hand that erstwhile wielded the tomahawk and scalping knife now handles the broom and dustpan," Farny wrote.

What the catalogue calls "the hopeless separation of Western artists from the era they sought to document" was evident in other cases. A revealing photo of Charles Schreyvogel at work shows him at his easel, in front of a cowboy who crouches as he aims his revolver. They are on the roof of an apartment building in Hoboken, New Jersey, in 1903. Schreyvogel actually went to Colorado to sketch Pike's Peak in 1911; he wrote home to his wife, "I started [sketching] with Pike's Peak in the back ground and it looked fine. I was there at 7:30 A.M. Then the smelters started in and the black smoke just covered the whole valley so that I couldn't see a thing and had to stop." Of course, in his paintings the Western landscape always appears luminous and pristine—a West of the imagination rather than reality.

Although Senators Stevens and Gorton, and many Eastern critics, are outraged by the New Western History, in the West itself the regional political establishment has a different view. Increasingly, it welcomes the new history for its emphasis on the region's diversity of peoples and experiences. The Western Governors' Association invited Limerick and other practitioners of the new history to speak at their conference last summer, and has published a collection of essays on new ways of looking at the region's past, *Beyond the Mythic West*. (The first essay was written by former Secretary of the Interior Stewart Udall.) "Inside the beltway is a special place," Limerick argues, "a place where Western senators dress up as quaint prospectors. But if that exhibit had come to Denver it would get nowhere near the amount of whining it did in D.C."

"The West as America," however, will not travel to Denver. Previously scheduled appearances at the art museums there and in St. Louis have now been canceled. Both museums plead a shortage of funds rather than fear of political controversy, but surely if the exhibit had received the praise it deserved rather than a politically inspired assault, money would have been found to bring the show west.

Despite fears that "The West as America" reflects yet another takeover of a cultural institution by 1960s radicals, Senator Stevens can rest assured that the Smithsonian is no hotbed of political correctness. Most of the exhibitions in its complex of museums are thoroughly conventional. The National Air and Space Museum is nothing more than a celebration of American greatness; it must warm Professor Boorstin's heart. In the Ceremonial Court of the National Museum of American History, the visitor can view ball gowns of the last seven first ladies—with no embarrassing mention of the scandal over Nancy Reagan's requisitioning of hundreds of thousands of dollars' worth of "gifts" from the world's top designers. Nearby is a display of presidential memorabilia: Wilson's golf clubs, Cleveland's trout flies, Harding's riding crop; no Freudian interpretation, no historical context, no mention of Wilson's Red Scare, Cleveland's economic depression or Harding's sexual escapades; just a reliquary.

Indeed, critics of "The West as America" will be delighted to find in the National Museum of American History the show "Westward to Promontory," presenting photos of the building of the transcontinental railroad. Here, the labels are wholly celebratory of "the great enterprise of the nineteenth century." The theme is the triumph of capitalism and the reknitting of the post–Civil War Union, with barely a mention of exploited Chinese laborers or dispossessed Indians, and none at all of the struggle over Reconstruction taking place at the same time.

The Smithsonian, according to one staff member who preferred to remain anonymous, is "the most reactionary place I've ever been. It's anything but liberal." Nonetheless, Stevens's threats have had a chilling effect on an already conservative institution. Curators have changed some of the wall texts for "The West as America" to soften the impact. The changes have not been extensive—five rewritten labels and five new ones out of a total of fifty-five, according to exhibition curator William Truettner. Many of the changes were made in the section "Inventing the Indian." One label no longer states that Indians were considered "racially and culturally inferior." Apparently in response to the complaint that the show has nothing good to say about the paintings, another now credits them with "valuable ethnographic detail."

Truettner insists that the changes were planned before Stevens launched his assault—although they were not executed until the political controversy began. He admits that curators in the future will have to be more "careful" about labels that may offend powerful interests. His observation is reinforced by reports from other Smithsonian employees, speaking off the record, that labels for future shows are being edited to avoid provoking right-wing senators or the White House.

Another example of the chill emanating from Stevens's office can be found at the Hirshhorn Museum, which took the unusual step of posting a warning that visitors "may find disturbing" some of the work in the Awards in the Visual Arts exhibit that opened there in June. The Hirshhorn is part of the Smithsonian, and its curators worried especially about a piece by Adrian Piper depicting a lynching. A museum spokesperson said the warning was posted because of the "climate," which *The Washington Post* took to be a reference to Stevens's threat.

The attack on "The West as America" comes after *The New Republic, Newsweek, Time, New York* magazine and others have blasted away at the campus left, portraying it as "thought police" out to destroy intellectual freedom. Dinesh D'Souza's *Illiberal Education* has reached the best-seller list, arguing as Roger Kimball did in a similar book that "tenured radicals" now control the universities and suppress freedom of speech with tactics that "border on the totalitarian." President Bush himself recently joined the chorus. These laments, however, ring a bit hollow when one reflects that none of these self-proclaimed opponents of censorship have uttered a word of protest against a senator's threat to cut the Smithsonian budget because he dislikes an exhibition's interpretation of American history.

The Smithsonian, it seems certain, will ride out this storm, but the controversy over "The West as America" is a harbinger of more trouble to come. The museum world, like academia, has lately been changing in ways many conservatives find deeply threatening. Long devoted simply to collecting and displaying memorabilia of prominent men and emblems of American greatness, museums are now seeking to present a more complex, diversified and critical portrait of the American past.

The Chicago Historical Society, for example, recently dismantled its Lincoln Gallery, complete with his top hat, ice skate and pieces of wood from his log cabin, and replaced it with an exhibit emphasizing the centrality of slavery and racism in nineteenth-century American history. Richmond's Valentine Museum currently displays a pioneering exhibition on "Jim Crow: Racism and Reaction in the New South." The Museum of the Confederacy in Richmond recently opened a major show on slavery, a far cry from its usual preoccupation with Robert E. Lee, Stonewall Jackson and the Lost Cause. (For reviews of similarly innovative exhibits, see Edward Chappell, "Museums," July 17, 1989, and December 18, 1989.)

"The West as America" is part of this development and represents a significant achievement for the Museum of American Art. We need more shows like this—exhibits that bring forgotten paintings back to life as documents of social and cultural history. Since most of these mediocre genre paintings and banal landscapes long ago lost their status as art, today they are viewed by few people outside the Buffalo Bill Historical Center or the Cowboy Hall of Fame. This exhibition has given us a new way to see them: as images that convey white Americans' obsessive preoccupation with their country's virtue. The Smithsonian, unfortunately, now plans to close this show July 28; it's too bad it can't remain open longer.

All these new exhibits offend some viewers, who go to museums for "old-fashioned" history. But they are appreciated by many others. At "The West as America," the visitors' comment book is filled with perceptive remarks; not everyone wants an exhibit about the West where never is heard a discouraging word. "Where's the paintings the Indians did of the whites?" asks one visitor, a legitimate question. Some comments are sharply critical, but more are rather favorable. "This exhibit," one visitor wrote, "helps me think about the art, the artists, the patrons, the audience, the subjects. Thanks." Is it possible that ordinary people actually appreciate being challenged by new ideas? Senator Stevens, please take note.

Understanding the Text

1. According to Foner and Wiener, what in the Smithsonian exhibit did critics object to? What do Foner and Wiener think of these objections?

2. According to Foner and Wiener, what are the tenets of the "New Western History"?

3. According to historian Howard Lamar, why are our conceptions of the West so important? What do Foner and Wiener claim to be the major "theme" of the exhibit?

Disney's "Politically Correct" Pocahontas

Jacquelyn Kilpatrick

When I walked into the theater to see *Pocahontas,* I had my choice of venue. It was playing on three of six screens, and the line waiting to get in never seemed to diminish. Later, I looked at the film section of the local paper and found that somewhere in the vicinity the movie was starting every fifteen minutes. Now that was a depressing thought.

In an interview with *The New York Times*, Eric Goldberg, the film's codirector (with Mike Gabriel), said, "We've gone from being accused of being too white bread to being accused of racism in *Aladdin* to being accused of being too politically correct in *Pocahontas*. That's progress to me." As much as I wanted to like Disney's production, I must disagree with Goldberg. Instead of progress in depicting Native Americans, this film takes a step backwards—a very dangerous step because it is so carefully glossed as "authentic" and "respectful."

The visual is emotionally more compelling than the written word, to say nothing of being more accessible, and since few people will read about Pocahontas, this film will exist as "fact" in the minds of generations of American children. They will believe in the Romeo and Juliet in the wilds of North America that Disney has presented, which, as Robert Eaglestaff, principal of the American Indian Heritage School in Seattle, has said, is much like "trying to teach about the Holocaust and putting in a nice story about Anne Frank falling in love with a German officer."

It might seem a moot point at best to debate the authenticity or reality of an animated film in

Jacquelyn Kilpatrick is a professor of English at California State University-Channel Islands. She writes on film, drama, and Native American literature.

From *Cineaste,* Vol. 21, No. 4, Fall 1995 by Jacquelyn Kilpatrick. Copyright © 1995 by Cineaste Magazine. Reprinted with permission.

which a tree speaks words of wisdom and the protagonist guides her canoe over a deadly looking waterfall without mussing her hair. If this were a story about a fictional character in a fictional situation, I would agree. I like Mickey Mouse, too. But Pocahontas was a real woman who lived during the pivotal time of first contact with the outside force that would ultimately decimate her people. Although we know of her only from the English reports, and some of the details are a bit hazy, there are some facts that are well supported. For one thing, she was not a voluptuous young woman when she met John Smith but a ten- to twelve-year-old girl, and John Smith was a thirty-something mercenary who more resembled a brick than a blond Adonis.

Smith's report of Pocahontas's brave act in saving his life was nowhere to be found in his initial description of his capture by Powhatan in 1608, surfacing only eight years later in a letter to the queen. There are a couple of possibilities to explain why that might have been. He could have been embarrassed, given the macho community of Jamestown boys, to admit a child had saved his life, or he might have stolen the story, possibly from the account published around the same time about Juan Ortiz and the Utica woman who saved him about eighty years before Smith met Pocahontas.

Assuming she did save his life, it could have been her idea, or it could have been her father's. If Powhatan had his own reasons for wanting Smith to live, he might have instructed her to do as she did to save face. Smith's report said she wanted her father to keep him alive but in captivity so he could make bells and beads for her, which, according to John Gould Fletcher (*John Smith—Also Pocahontas*, 1928), would have provided a cover story to eliminate the censure of the tribe for Powhatan's benevolent act and which would have been in keeping with their traditions.

Assuming Smith stole the story, he could have done so because he turned into a chronicler of his adventures in the New World after it became clear he was not going to be able to return to America to have more of them. He tried repeatedly to return, but even the first settlers in New England were happy to accept his advice but refused his company.

What we do know of Pocahontas is that she met John Smith in 1608, was probably responsible for some trading between the settlers and her people, was kidnapped and raped by the English but later married a tobacco planter named John Rolfe, had a son in 1615 and sailed to England in 1616. She was introduced to Ben Johnson and made such an impression that he wrote her into one of his comedies, *The Staple of News;* she attended a court masque that he wrote and evidently impressed the king and queen as well. She attempted to return home but became ill on the voyage and had to turn back to England, where she died, probably of smallpox, at the age of twenty-two. We have no idea how she or her people felt about any of this, except that some of the contemporary reports said she died "of a broken heart."

That's a pretty interesting story, but not the sort of thing animated Disney films are known for. For one thing, it's much too violent and sad. According to James Pentecost, the film's producer, the changes that were made were due to the fact that Pocahontas's real story was simply too long. He said, "We decided to dramatize what we felt was the *essence* of Pocahontas." Now the logic may be a little tough to follow here, but evidently what that means is that they changed her age, her body, and gave her a motive for her actions that boils down to going gaga over the first white man she sees.

Ignoring for a moment the very non-PC, nonfeminist content of that change, there lies within it a very old stereotype of Native American women. In hundreds of films made during the last century, Indian women have been seen sacrificing themselves and their tribal communities for their white lovers. I'm sure the irony is unintentional in *Pocahontas* as she paddles her canoe along, having just refused to marry the stereotypically stoic and noble Kocoum, singing about the change that is waiting "just around the river bend." The change that waits is another man and another culture in the form of John Smith.

The Disney folks have made much of the fact that Pocahontas is the driving force of this movie, which is, I suppose, to mean it makes some sort of feminist statement. She does sing to John about living naturally in tune with the Earth—also skirting dangerously close to another stereotype, that of the "natural ecologist"—but does she have to do it in an off-the-shoulder miniskirt? And I would love to see a report on the physics of her body. Would she, like Barbie, fall over if really given those dimensions? Glen Keane, the film's supervising animator, researched the paintings of the real Pocahontas but wasn't very impressed, so he made a few "adjustments." Besides her beautiful "more Asian" eyes, he gave her a body with a wasp waist, sexy hips and legs, and breasts that are *truly* impressive. He says, "Some people might see her as sexy, but she's not Jessica Rabbit. I think she looks rather athletic." Uh huh. Mel Gibson (the voice of John Smith) put it more succinctly when he said, "She's a babe." Or, what the heck, maybe she's just drawn that way.

To give the Disney folk their due, they apparently made some effort to be nonoffensive, hiring Native Americans to work on the film and to act as consultants. Unfortunately, there seems to have been some miscommunication of concept. The Disney people were making an animated film about a fictional character. They knew she was fictional because they created her. The Native Americans on the team had other interests. Russell Means, the voice of Powhatan, likes the film, even though they were willing to take his advice about a detail such as the father referring to Pocahontas as Daughter instead of her name, but were unwilling to change important aspects of the image of the Indians as warlike, as established by the return from war at the beginning of the film. He says, "There are scenes where the English settlers admit to historical deceit . . . their animated settlers say they are here to rob, rape, pillage the land and kill Indians. This is the truth that Disney is entrusting with children while the rest of Hollywood won't trust that truth with adults."

As a mixedblood woman, I too am concerned with the truth of the colonization of America, but establishing another stereotype isn't the way to go about it. Even given that

Disney's animated characters are by nature larger than life, the English in the film are extremely one-dimensional in their bumbling greed. As Terry Russio, a screenwriter for Disney, said, "You can judge the sentiments of the country by who you can confidently make fun of. Nowadays the ultimate villain, I suppose, would be a fat, white male terrorist who ran a Fortune 500 company on the side." That fairly well describes the governor in *Pocahontas,* a description which renders the history of first contact literally cartoonish.

Disney also hired Shirley (Little Dove) Custalow-McGowan, a Powhatan who travels through Virginia teaching the history and culture of her people, to work as consultant for the film. When she saw the early rushes, she said, "My heart sorrowed within me . . . Ten-year-old Pocahontas has become twenty-year-old Pocahontas. The movie was no longer historically accurate."

According to the film's producer, James Pentecost, all this talk about historical accuracy is somewhat irrelevant. He believes that "Nobody should go to an animated film hoping to get an accurate depiction of history." Okay, I'll buy that, as long as you're talking about *The Lion King,* but Pocahontas was real, and most people have heard her name even if they know nothing about her reality. Most of the adults who view this film, however, will not have the background to judge whether it is accurate or not, and since the hype has been toward the 'political correctness' of the film, I would think they'd be more apt to trust it than not. And those are the adults. What about the children? As Linda Woolverton, screenwriter for *Beauty and the Beast* and *The Lion King* said, "When you take on a Disney animated feature, you know you're going to be affecting entire generations of human minds." In this case, the effect is one more misconception advertised in the guise of authenticity and respect for Native American values.

As Custalow-McGowan said, "History is history. You're not honoring a nation of people when you change their history."

Understanding the Text

1. Why does Kilpatrick think that Disney's publicity for *Pocahontas* makes the film especially "dangerous"?

2. What "very old stereotype of Native American women" does Kilpatrick especially object to?

3. How does the film represent Pocahontas physically, and what is Kilpatrick's response to this representation?

Prelude to World War II: Racial Unity and the Hollywood Indian

Angela Aleiss

W orld War II laid the foundation for a re-evaluation of the American Indian's screen image. Even before "tolerance," "brotherhood," and "unity" became catchwords in a society engaged within another world conflict, the movie industry had responded to the growing fascism in Europe with more ambiguity in its Indian portrayals. Like Black Americans who would find a place in the racially integrated units of Hollywood's war films (years before actual military desegregation), movie Indians would form a political alliance with their white counterparts.[1] Previous images of menacing warriors who blocked Westward expansion gradually began to fade into one in which Indians stood as allies—rather than as enemies—alongside America's frontier heroes.

Several scholars have noted the transformation of the Indian's screen image throughout the second world war. John A. Price observed that "the decline of Indian stereotyping seems to have begun during World War II when the Germans, Italians, and Japanese replaced the Indian as the major villains," although he argues that both *Geronimo* (1939) and *They Died with Their Boots On* (1941) contain unsympathetic portrayals of their Indian leaders (170).[2] Ted Siminoski concluded in his dissertation, "Sioux Versus Hollywood," that the Sioux's image reversed from a villain to a hero during the war. He explains, however, that the most dramatic shift occurred immediately after World War II when racially liberal attitudes began to influence minority portrayals (60–61). Donald Kaufmann points out that unscrupulous whites often misled otherwise

Angela Aleiss is a lecturer in business communication at California State University, Long Beach. She is the author of *Making the White Man's Indian: Native Americans and Hollywood Movies* (2005).

From *Journal of American Culture,* Vol. 18, No. 2, Summer 1995 by Angela Aleiss. Copyright © 1995 by Journal of American & Comparative Cultures. Reprinted by permission.

friendly Indians in World War II Westerns, but these Native portrayals were merely "caught up in a fad for sympathetic treatment" along with other minorities (499).[3]

While these scholars agree that World War II reshaped the Indian's screen images, several points require further clarification:

1. As studios grew more circumspect about antagonistic Indian/white relations in light of growing European fascism, Americans and their Canadian/British allies would evolve into models of racial diplomacy. Selective Service was enforced by 1940, and scenes of the U.S. Cavalry killing Indians en masse could easily equate American militarism with Gestapo leadership.

2. The pro-interventionist politics of Hollywood studios helped to create a mindset that would reshape the Indian's image at least two years before America's entry into the war. The prevailing anti-fascist mood in the movie industry (best exemplified by the Hollywood Anti-Nazi League, with its roster of studio moguls and liberal screenwriters) peaked in 1936, and studio executives freely trumpeted their anti-Nazi ideology in many pre-forties films.[4] National unity was a powerful weapon against fascism, and Blacks, Indians, and Mexicans soon joined their white counterparts in the movies' effort to "racially integrate" the home front.

3. These "friendly" Indian portrayals were more enduring than a fad. The wartime image of Indians-as-allies would eventually give way to a postwar assimilationist theme: many Westerns further developed the Indian/white brotherhood concept, with *Broken Arrow* (1950) often cited as the most significant example.

Three popular Westerns mark a visible change from the "hostile warrior" stereotype and thus represent the first stage of a trend toward interracial harmony. *Susannah of the Mounties* (1939), *North West Mounted Police* (1940), and *They Died with Their Boots On* (1941) were each produced by major Hollywood studios whose large budgets and aggressive promotion would introduce the films' more complex Indian/white relations to a wider audience.[5] All three films include star performers—Shirley Temple, Gary Cooper, and Errol Flynn—and their established box-office reputations would bolster the pictures' popularity and thus secure these newfound racial themes within the Western genre.[6] Individually, each film exemplifies thematic characteristics that would serve as prototypes for later Indian-theme Westerns; taken together, they reveal an industry struggling to redefine its Indian/white relations in a rapidly changing world. *Susannah* demonstrates, through the perspective of two children, a symbolic interracial brotherhood: its co-mingling of blood between an Indian and a white would not occur again until *Broken Arrow*. *North West Mounted Police* casts Indians as American and Canadian allies against the French—its theme of an interracial allegiance a reverse of *Rose Marie's* (1936) enemy Indians who steal money and hide an American fugitive from the Royal

Canadian Mounted Police. In *They Died with Their Boots On,* the legendary "Indian fighter" of America—George Armstrong Custer—becomes the friend, admirer, and guardian of the Sioux. His role as the Indians' protector—its departure from history notwithstanding—would be a model for other frontier epics like *Buffalo Bill* (1944), in which the hero publicly condemns white exploitation of Indian people.

The Westerns' concept of racial brotherhood was a sharp departure from the previous portrayals of hostile Indian/white relations. During the mid-30s, the 19th-century belief in a Manifest Destiny—the idea of United States' expansion across the North American continent—emerged as a common theme in Hollywood Westerns. The renaissance of the "Western hero" in the mid-30s, writes Andrew Bergman, brought law and government to a strong position in American culture.

> The revival of the cowboys spoke automatically to the benevolence of the federal law, which in turn was vanquishing bad men and releasing the old competitive energies in America. Hollywood constructed a government which it identified with justice and order, and which delivered the nation from external threats to its safety and industry. (169)

The cowboy became the benevolent hero, while the Indian emerged as civilization's alien—and eventually enemy—to progress. Such portrayals often cast Indians in an unambiguously hostile light: King Vidor's *Texas Rangers* (1936), for example, showed that while "savages" rule the plains, Texas is hardly a safe place. Only when the Rangers "put them on the reservation for good" can Texas look forward to real progress. So prevalent was the Indian-as-obstacle theme that a non-Western like Gregory La Cava's *Stage Door* (1937) included Katharine Hepburn's remark: "And if my grandfather hadn't crossed the country in a Conestoga wagon, there would *still* be Indians living in Wichita!"

The French and Indian War was Manifest Destiny displaced into colonial America in George Seitz's *The Last of the Mohicans* (1936), another remake based upon the enduring James Fenimore Cooper novel. The 1920 silent version (directed by Maurice Tourner and Clarence Brown) had blended romantic imagery with a foreboding atmosphere: its enemy Hurons were shadowy figures gliding across moonlit rocks or perched high atop jagged cliffs, and their silhouettes were often framed within cavernous entrances that receded into picturesque backgrounds. Seitz's version instead delivered an unabashed portrayal of bloodthirsty, scalp-hungry (Huron) savages who literally scream into the camera and defy the French and British armistice when they attack Fort William Henry. Magua was "as evil a Huron as ever you pictured him and his misdeeds . . . are even more ghastly than those the original text cited," declared the *New York Times,* noting that the British massacre was especially brutal (September 3, 1936). The more savage the Indians, *Mohicans* seemed to imply, the easier to justify their removal.

America's ability to rid the West of its marauding natives was glorified in Paramount's *Geronimo* (1939). Director Paul Sloan introduces *Geronimo* as "the story of a great enemy," then cautions that the Indian leader (portrayed by "Chief Thundercloud") remains unconquered. President Ulysses S. Grant admits that "our whole handling of the Indian problem has been wrong, unjust," and reiterates Abraham Lincoln's ideology that "the frontiers of the nation must be made safe." The studio's promotional campaign exploited the Apache leader's resistance: Geronimo was "The red terror of the American screen!" and "That most feared Apache that ever ravaged the West," who, obviously, had to be subdued or eliminated in order to open the doors to white settlement.

John Ford's *Stagecoach* (1939) flatly—and unambiguously—declared that white civilization had no room for American Indians. The film's opening titles warn of the Indians' "savage struggle" to oust white settlers and of the name Geronimo that struck terror into the hearts of innocent travelers. *Stagecoach's* references to Indians are consistently ominous: characters remark how Apaches burn every ranch in sight, and one even learns that these Indians strike like rattlesnakes. In a particularly disturbing scene, the charred remains of a house lie smoldering with a woman's body hunched over a burnt chair, her head partly scalped. The final attack upon the stage with the cavalry's fortuitous appearance (similar to *Union Pacific's* 1939 military rescue) suggests that America will be safe only when its hostile natives vanish forever.

The increasing conflict in Europe, however, began to influence Hollywood politics and consequently to reshape minority images even before America's entry into the war. Previous Westerns could boast of conquest, but a national campaign to purge the land of its Indian inhabitants smacked of fascist genocide. At the very least, the Manifest Destiny theme painted a racially intolerant picture of America's frontier heroes. King Vidor's *Northwest Passage* (1940), the story of Rogers' Rangers and their 1759 expedition to destroy the French/Abenaki stronghold in their war against England, shows early signs of ambiguity toward its Indian characters.[7] Rogers (Spencer Tracy) refers to the Indians as "red hellions" who hack and murder whites, steal women, roast officers, and brain babies: "If it were over quick," he explains, "they were lucky." During the village ambush, however, he instructs his men to kill only "every fighting Indian," and when one maniacal Ranger tries to attack two Indian women and a child, another orders him to leave women and young children alone. The deranged man murders a warrior out of sheer delight, infuriating his comrade: "Haven't you had enough?" Rogers tells his men to release the Indian prisoners because "they're not going to do us any good," and he enlists a Mohawk as his scout. Meanwhile, the disturbed Ranger (who has pilfered an Indian head) later plunges to his death—the film's retribution (and the Hay's Office compensation) toward an unfit soldier.[8]

At Twentieth Century-Fox, Darryl Zanuck's pro-interventionist perspective conveyed a theme of racial unity in his World War II Westerns. (As Vice President of Production, Zanuck closely supervised each film script and insisted upon numerous modifications.) Zanuck's sympathy for the French and the British against Nazi Germany developed years before America's entry into the war (he had contributed heavily to William Allen White's Committee to Defend America by Aiding the Allies); his zeal for military preparedness surfaced in *A Yank in the R.A.F.,* a 1941 film that drew much criticism from the media's isolationist factions (Mosley 195, 197).[9] Among his Westerns, a similar theme prevailed: *Hudson's Bay* (1941) favored a British/Canadian alliance against its French counterparts, but Pierre Radisson champions the Indian cause and requests that New France make provisions with the Cree before settling upon Native territory. Zanuck advised during story conferences that a Canadian/Indian alliance dominate the film: thus, Radisson's code of fair dealings with the Indians should be written into Canada's Charter, and the chiefs and white men should show allegiance to the British flag ("Rough Draft" 12). Similarly, the friendly (and comical) Oneida in *Drums Along the Mohawk* (1939) assists the American colonists in the Revolution and reminds whites that he is (in Henry Fonda's words) "as good a Christian as you and me are."

Zanuck's 1939 film, *Susannah of the Mounties,* was an earlier World War II Western whose political tone was noticeably one of racial tolerance. Directed by William A. Seiter and starring Shirley Temple, *Susannah* promotes a pacifist theme that leads to interracial harmony. Susannah is the only survivor of a wagon train massacre; despite the fact that the Indians have killed her grandfather, she befriends a Canadian Blackfoot boy and brings peace between both races. The chief agrees to help locate the Indians who raided the wagon and offers his son "Little Chief" (portrayed by Martin Goodrider, a Blackfeet Indian) as a token of promise to the whites.[10] The Canadian Mounties (who look after Susannah) accept the chief's gesture gratefully, adding, "It will do no harm for your son to learn the ways of the white man." Sue and Little Chief, after a few cultural clashes (he orders her to walk behind him like a squaw) develop a mutual friendship: they later join their fingers in a "blood brother" ceremony—a symbolic gesture that broke the barriers of Manifest Destiny separating Indian and white societies and pointed toward racial unity.

The underlying message is that Canada, England, and the Blackfoot are all united in the national welfare. Canadian expansion occurs through a peaceful resolution—rather than a hostile clash—between both races. When the Indians kidnap Sue's Mountie friend (Randolf Scott) she implores the chief (Maurice Moscovich) for his release: the real culprit is the tribe's warrior (Victor Jory) who has been selling stolen horses to the whites. The Mountie assures the chief that only the Redcoats can speak for England and honor their word; thus, Canada intends to respect Blackfoot territory in the building of the railroad. Zanuck's political sympathies toward the allies helped to shape the film's Indian portrayals: "Don't give impression that the Queen mother will send soldiers to annihilate the Indians—as this may get us in trouble with England" ("Conference . . . 11/12/38" 4–5). The conclusion shows the Mountie, Sue, and two Indians sitting underneath the British flag and sharing the peace pipe—the film's gesture of solidarity during the present European conflict.

Newspapers approvingly took note of *Susannah's* theme. The *New York Evening Journal* noted that Temple "showed the red man and white man how to live together like brothers." The *Star Telegram* argued that the Indians were the movie's real heroes: Little Chief had taught "hostile Susannah how to ride, how to do Indian war dances . . . and at last the meaning of blood brotherhood." Other reviews, however, balked at the film's newfound interracial harmony: "The Indian raids and fights are rather unimpressive," *Variety* alerted exhibitors. Perhaps, the trade journal surmised, audiences might still prefer bloody Indian/white clashes to peace parleys (16).

The Canadian wilderness provided another setting for an American/British alliance with its Indian neighbors in Cecil B. DeMille's *North West Mounted Police* (1940). DeMille began making feature films in 1914 with his production of *The Squaw Man,* based upon Edwin Milton Royle's play about a marriage between an Indian woman and an English man that tragically ends in her suicide. (The miscegenation theme was popular enough, for he remade the same picture twice, in 1918 and 1931). Conversely, in 1917, DeMille directed *The Woman God Forgot,* the story of Montezuma's daughter and her love for and subsequent marriage to a white officer of Cortez's army. Such variety was the spice of DeMille's Indian portrayals, and the producer/director could easily cast them as villains (*The Virginian,* 1914) or as aides (*Girl of the Golden West,* 1915), depending on what the film's story (or even current politics) demanded.

DeMille's later sound Westerns—*The Plainsman* (1936) and *Union Pacific* (1939)—championed the theme of Manifest Destiny with Indians as obstacles to frontier settlement. In *The Plainsman,* production personnel instructed that the audience immediately recognize Indians as "really a menace—burning settlements and massacring whites" (Pine Memo) and the film's promotional campaign boasted of "Heroes of the Dusty Past Slashing an Empire from Savage Hands" ("Advertising Approach").[11] Suggestions for interviews and speeches on *Union Pacific* emphasized the film's timely message of "preserving the unity of this nation," which embraced Irish laborers and Chinese coolies, but not the recalcitrant Indians ("Line on the Golden Spike" 3). "The railroad builders are continually harassed by Indians, who stole supplies, burned houses and killed workmen," the picture's titles warned.

A year later, however, Paramount's *North West Mounted Police* would reevaluate the white relationship to America's natives. The 1885 Métis uprising in Saskatchewan of the French and Indian mixed bloods and their Cree support against the Canadian government (the "Riel Rebellion") was the basis for DeMille's first Technicolor film. DeMille portrayed the French as enemies to Canadian progress and extolled the growth of the British empire; like Zanuck, he "never had any doubt, from the outbreak of World War II, where America must and eventually would take her stand" (Hayne 370).

The film's story of the friendship and mutual respect between Canada and the United States now included its Indian allies (DeMille, "In Chicago" 2–3). The Cree Indians, led by Chief Big Bear (Walter Hampden), initially defy British allegiance and become caught in a power struggle between the Métis and the Canadian government; the Mounties, however, succeed in retaining the chief's loyalty to the British. The American interest is represented by a Texas Ranger (Gary Cooper), who pursues a criminal across the Canadian border where the Mounted Police claim he is also wanted for murder. Americans and Mounties unite to capture the man (Louis Riel, leader of the Métis uprising) and succeed in preventing "a war that might have torn Canada to fragments (DeMille, "In Chicago" 2–3).

DeMille's respect for historical accuracy extended as far as his Anglo-American sympathies would allow. Numerous notations on Indian sign language and dialect accompanied careful research on Cree costumes and equipment; citations included a glossary of Blackfeet words gathered by Henry Schoolcraft and descriptions of Cree camps by Edward Curtis.[12] "History should be honestly and diligently respected," DeMille said in a 1939 interview, but he noted that dramatic license sometimes took precedent over historical truth. "For the sake of dramatic construction, I am justified in making some contradictions or compressions of historical details, so long as I stick to the main facts," he added (Crowther).

DeMille did take liberties in the portrayal of Big Bear by combining his character with Crowfoot, leader of the Blackfoot, who prevented his people from joining the Riel Rebellion (DeMille, Letter 1). (Big Bear actually joined the Métis and was later imprisoned for his part in the rebellion.) In *North West Mounted Police,* Big Bear's composite character supports the British and emerges as a timely metaphor for wartime propaganda: Indians would clearly remain on the side of Canadian and American—rather than French—political interests. When a New York newspaper questioned Big Bear's ability to speak fluent English, DeMille replied with three pages of quoted passages from Crowfoot's eloquent oratory. (The director had explained that both leaders were impressive speakers.) His detailed response carefully positioned Indian chiefs among the ranks of other legendary American heroes: "The Indians of the American continent have produced some great men, and I fear we are all a little apt to confuse these fine philosophers and statesmen with the Indians of the comic strip, whose accepted rhetorical attainment is "ugh!" (DeMille, Letter 3).

The film's villains, then, are the French and Indian Métis. Their leader's daughter is Louvette (Paulette Goddard), whose unsavory habits are intended as a reflection of her mixed-blooded ancestry. Louvette eats on the dirt floor with her hands, prowls barefoot around the campsite, and entices a naive Mountie away from his post when she learns of an attack. Originally named "Lupette" (a parody on the word lupine), Louvette "has the instincts of a wolf, lives by robbing traps, and gets into every possible difficulty" (Rosson Letter).[13] Louvette's connivery is akin to treason: when she seduces the Mountie, she fails to warn Canadian forces of an ambush. This act of treachery immediately casts her as Canada's political enemy, a fitting statement for any pro-British sentiment during the war

The pro-ally sympathies of DeMille and other studio moguls were gradually becoming the rule—rather than the exception—in Hollywood. "The film industry will not shirk from its chance to aid immeasurably in the strengthening of national morale," a *Variety* editorial announced in 1940 (5). Hollywood supported military readiness by providing studio facilities for Army training films and reshaping the movies' content in response to a world fascist threat. Westerns followed with a step toward racial unity: a year before Pearl Harbor, one veteran producer observed that scheming businessmen and crooked bankers began to replace Indians as the frontier's villains (*New York Times*). By 1942, the trend had become noticeable: when MGM resorted to the cowboy-vs.-Indian formula in *Apache Trail,* the results were hackneyed. "The uprising of the Apaches against the whites is something that's long since seen its best picture days," *Variety* complained (MacRae 20).

At Warner Brothers' studio, the concept of racial brotherhood began to influence its Indian/white portrayals at least two years before America's entry into the war. Like his contemporaries at Twentieth Century Fox and Paramount, Jack Warner (Vice President of Production) supported the allies long before the fateful events at Pearl Harbor. In 1940, he sent money to London for the purchase of two fighter planes and produced *London Can Take It,* a documentary that raised thousands of dollars toward British aid. His feature films of the late 30s conveyed the studio's anti-Nazi sentiments; *Confessions of a Nazi Spy* (1939) and Underground (1940) both elicited sharp criticisms from pro-German sympathizers (namely, the German-American Bund) as well as the nation's isolationist groups.[14]

As a member of the Hollywood Anti-Nazi League, Warner joined his colleagues in promoting national unity as democracy's toughest enemy against fascism. The studio's Westerns would echo this same political theme with their symbolic interracial alliance. *Dodge City* (1939) celebrated the building of the West and the settlement of a Kansas town; when a citizen drives a golden spike through the town's railroad terminal, an Indian holds it steady. The community is plagued by villainous cowboys (who were initially reprimanded for killing buffalo on Indian territory); the new threat to law and order is civilization's corruption and greed. Warner's *Santa Fe Trail* (1940) was another variation on the Western theme without the usual cowboy-and-Indian skirmishes and wagon train attacks. The frontier's new villain is the abolitionist leader John Brown (Raymond Massey), whose armed resistance further divides a politically torn Kansas just prior to the Civil War. Brown smuggles rifles in Bible boxes and attacks the people of Harpers Ferry. His "reasons may be good," observes one cavalry officer, "but what he's doing is wrong." Led by George Armstrong Custer and Jeb Stuart, the cavalry finally seizes Brown and orders the rebel hung, a fitting victory against an enemy of the Union and foe of the human race, as one officer puts it.

Santa Fe's pro-Southern sympathy notwithstanding, its friendly Indian character is a barometer of America's changing sentiments during World War II. As Custer eagerly awaits romance, he seeks the advice of an Indian fortune teller. The old woman pokes at the campfire and solemnly predicts that Americans soon will be enemies in battle: a fight has started in the east, a man is lighting a torch, she warns, "but none of us can stop him." The men laugh at her prophecy, but the allusion to a fascist enemy and the urgency for national unity were more than a coincidence. The film skillfully uses Indian mysticism to serve America's political interests.

A year later, Warners' leaning toward Indian/white solidarity grew even more pronounced in *They Died with Their Boots On,* a biography of George Armstrong Custer. "Most Westerns had depicted the Indian as a painted, vicious savage," director Raoul Walsh explained of his 1941 film, in which the real villains are the unscrupulous railroad companies. "In *They Died With Their Boots On,* I tried to show him as an individual who only turned vindictive when his rights as defined by treaty were violated by white men" (qtd. in Walsh 325).

Noting its timely release, Warners seized the opportunity to exemplify American militarism. "In preparing this scenario," screenwriter Aeneas MacKenzie explained in 1941, "all possible consideration was given to the construction of a story which would have the best effect upon public morale in these present days of a national crisis" (Memo).[15] Hence, the studio built an image of an efficient—albeit pompous and bureaucratic—American military. "I need not mention," MacKenzie continued, "that this picture will be released at a moment when thousands of youths are being trained for commissions, and when hundreds of new and traditionless units are being formed" (MacKenzie). Warners' research department noted that during President Grant's era, army officers were appointed as Acting Superintendents for the Indian Service, making "an impressive show of efficiency by enforcing programs for Indian welfare with prompt military action" (Lissauer Memo).[16] In *They Died with Their Boots On,* the United States Army would protect the Indians' best interest.

White paternalism replaced Manifest Destiny as hostile interracial relations became politically unwise for a nation on the throes of fighting genocide in Europe. Warners thus whitewashed Custer's career to create a more racially "sympathetic" hero: the Lieutenant Colonel's massacre of the Cheyenne village in the Battle of Washita was completely ignored, and the events at the Little Bighorn were rearranged so that the loss would not "result from Custer's greed for glory" (Churchill).[17] Further, the hero's feats result from luck rather than foresight: Custer is promoted to (brevet) General by an administrative error, and he claims a victory medal during the Civil War by flouting orders and saving an entire regiment from extermination.

"The Indians need not be presented as lay figures whose sole function in life is to 'mas[s]acre' and be wiped out," advised studio executive Melvin Levy, "but as real people having desires, hopes, loves and hates." Levy thus attempted to convince associate producer Robert Fellows to create a relationship of respect and friendship between Custer and Crazy Horse, as it was "a basis of actuality" (Levy, Memo). Fellows solicited the opinion of his close friend (and history buff) Lee Ryan, who recommended a scene in which Sitting Bull speaks to the chiefs, and Chief Joseph [White Bull] of the Minneconjou Sioux outlines battle strategy. It was "a bit gushy," Ryan explained, to have Custer as the last survivor in a battle not borne out by a conversation with Sioux braves (Memo).[18]

The movie's Custer hero (Errol Flynn) thus emerges as the guardian of Indian welfare: he defends the Sioux's treaty rights and even admires the tactical abilities of the Oglala leader, Crazy Horse (Anthony Quinn).[19] Custer temporarily imprisons Crazy Horse for attacking his wagon train, but he reminds the regiment to treat the Indian leader well. When Crazy Horse escapes, Custer actually praises him as "the only cavalryman I've seen around this fort so far." The narrative titles warn of "a ruthlessly advancing civilization that spelled doom to the red race," and a montage of Indian/cavalry battles follows. Crazy Horse demands a peace pow-wow with Custer: framed equally in low-angle shots, the two face each other mounted on horseback. The Indian leader says that his people will give up everything but the Black Hills, and Custer promises to defend the sacred land against whites. "I listen to my brother," the officer assures him in another wartime gesture toward interracial cooperation.

The Western Railroad Land & Trading Company, however, has other ideas. The railroad's only route is through the Black Hills, and its corrupt owners (including Custer's former West Point classmate) devise a plan to wipe out the Sioux and snatch their territory. Newspapers announce a "Second California gold Rush" in the Black Hills, and Custer warns officials that the Indians will unite in retaliation. "If I were an Indian, I'd fight beside Crazy Horse to the last drop of my blood!" the officer thunders during his court-martial.

Crazy Horse, meanwhile, invites Sitting Bull to a war council, and Indians from several nations convene to plan an attack. The night before, Custer requests that an English soldier escape with a message because he does not want to endanger a foreigner's life. The Briton refuses to leave, and in the spirit of Anglo-American wartime solidarity and racial tolerance, he adds that the Indians are the only real Americans. "You're probably right about that," Custer agrees. The officer ultimately "sacrifices" his regiment at the Battle of Little Bighorn to protect General Alfred Terry and his men; his dying declaration stipulates that the Indians be protected in their right to the existence of their own country—a request that General Philip Sheridan pledges to enforce.[20]

The November 20, 1941, premiere of *They Died with Their Boots On* was just 17 days prior to America's entrance into World War II. The movie's theme of an interracial alliance was not far from wartime rhetoric: as Indians fought in the battlefields, they stood alongside white Americans and gradually melted into society. The Office of Indian Affairs announced that, despite years of discrimination, Native Americans "responded earnestly and enthusiastically" to the challenge of war (Collier, June 1942: 238), and tribes even dropped claims against the United States for "patriotic reasons" (June 1944: 252). The Iroquois Confederacy had issued a declaration of war upon the Axis Powers in 1942 (June 1942: 240), and 18,000 Indians had joined the armed services by 1943 (June 1943: 237). Indians stood beside whites and captured military honors: 75 received the Purple Heart and 16 the Distinguished Flying Cross, while a Second Lieutenant Childers (a Creek) picked up the Congressional Medal of Honor (June 1944: 235–36). Perhaps the most memorable event occurred on Mt. Suribachi in Iwo Jima, where the Pima Indian Ira H. Hayes was one of six men who helped raise the American flag. "The impact of the wartime experience on the Indians was immeasurable," wrote historian Francis Paul Prucha, "for the war suddenly threw thousands of reservation Indians into the midst of white society and greatly accelerated the movement toward assimilation" (1009).

By World War II, the hostile, conniving Indian characters of *The Plainsman* and *Stagecoach* could stand in friendship alongside America's heroes in *Susannah of the Mounties, North West Mounted Police,* and *They Died with Their Boots On.* For a nation preparing to enter yet another world conflict, these Indian/white portrayals offered a powerful message about America's emerging solidarity with its Natives. Three years prior to the formation of the Office of War Information [OWI]—a federal agency that advised the film industry on its promotion of war-related themes—Hollywood had taken a major step toward an Indian/white interracial alliance. "Any form of racial discrimination or religious intolerance, special privileges of any citizen are manifestations of Fascism, and should be exposed as such," the Office lectured Hollywood studios ("Government").[21] The OWI routinely recommended script modifications, advising producers to treat "dark-skinned peoples" as allies to American heroes. "Our sincerity," the agency explained, "is judged by the attitude and treatment we accord those dark-skinned peoples within our own borders" (Rev. of "Road to God's Country" 1).

The OWI's presence war short-lived (Congress slashed its budget in 1943), but the concept of racial brotherhood would continue to permeate Hollywood Westerns. Twentieth Century-Fox's *Buffalo Bill,* released in 1944, signaled the return to frontier epics (following their temporary decline during the war) that would take a close look at racial relations. The film's depiction of William Frederick Cody (Joel McCrea) resembles Warner's Custer: the hero is the Indian's friend and protector, and the villains are the railroad owners. But Cody's relationship with the Indians is more personalized: when his Indian-schoolteacher friend dies in battle, Cody carries her limp body across the field. "They are *all* friends of mind," he confesses to a soldier.

Buffalo Bill was released amidst a growing liberal outlook within the film industry. As American postwar society readjusted to changing social values, political "messages" began cropping up in stories condemning anti-Semitism—*Crossfire* (1947) and *Gentleman's Agreement* (1947)—and those advocating black racial tolerance—*Intruder in the Dust* (1949) and *No Way Out* (1950). Westerns also began examining interracial relations in a more serious light, showing conspicuous tolerance and sympathy toward their Indian characters. *Black Gold* (1947) appeared to promote the racial issue on several fronts: Indian, white, and Chinese. "Use tolerance, Americanism to win heavy publicity," the studio advised. "The picture carries a message that will have a wholesome effect upon the community" ("Use Tolerance"). Similarly, in *The Last Round-Up* (1947), a group of young boys engage in a game of cowboys-and-Indians, and predictably, one of them feigns a scalping. One lad objects because "Indians don't scalp people anymore"—a reminder that traditional beliefs of Indians as bloodthirsty savages should be passé in a more tolerant postwar society.

The movies' themes of a postwar brotherhood pointed to racial assimilation within American society. Although still reluctant to embrace fully this liberal policy (Hollywood would readily promote it by the 1950s), cultural pluralism was growing politically suspect among the industry's conservative ranks. One outspoken adherent to the right-wing faction was the redoubtable Cecil B. DeMille, and his story of Pontiac's rebellion in *Unconquered* (1947) was a fitting analogy to the industry's present communist purge.[22] "America today resists red ideas as it once resisted Red Indians in the pioneer days of *Unconquered*," boasted Paramount's ad campaign ("Suggestions"). Beneath its anti-communist rhetoric, *Unconquered* hinted that a person's "Indianness" was politically risky during a Cold War era.

Equating Indians with communists, however, was the exception and not the rule in postwar Westerns; many instead emerged as allegories of the Cold War mentality in which national unity and conformity stood side by side. Westerns could easily "erase" cultural/racial differences between Indians and whites by assimilating the former into mainstream American society. By 1950, *Broken Arrow* showed that racial tolerance could exist if Indians would agree to compromise. (A peaceful co-existence is achieved only when the Apaches relinquish their warfare and accept the Army's terms.) Several of *Broken Arrow*'s successors—*Battle at Apache Pass* (1950); *Taza, Son of Cochise* (1954); *Apache* (1954); *Chief Crazy Horse* (1955); and *Walk the Proud Land* (1956) advocate Indian/white co-existence as a long-term solution to racial problems.[23] In *White Feather* (1955), a liberal successor to *Broken Arrow,* an interracial marriage between a Cheyenne woman and a white man absorbs Indian culture and produces a mix-blooded offspring who enters the Military Academy at West Point. The transition from a segregated vision of Indian/white relations into one in which assimilation dominated the Westerns' themes had finally been achieved—at least by the movies' standards. Whether the industry openly acknowledged these political implications or not, the Hollywood Indian— once the enemy of the great frontier—was gradually being transformed into a white American.

Notes

[1] Hollywood "racially integrated" military units in many popular war films, including: *Star-Spangled Rhythm* (1942), *Bataan* (1943), *Crash Dive* (1943), *Sahara* (1943), *This Is the Army* (1943). In these films, Black Americans were often performing a service to their country in violation of more traditional "segregated" customs. For a further discussion of this theme, see Thomas Cripps, *Slow Fade to Black: The Negro in American Film, 1900–1942* (New York: Oxford UP, 1977) 249–389. Clayton R. Koppes and Gregory D. Black offer another point of view in "Blacks, Loyalty, and Motion-Picture Propaganda in World War II," *Journal of American History* 73.2 (Sept. 1986).

[2] While I concur with Price's opinion of *Geronimo* as perpetuating another hostile Indian stereotype, *They Died with Their Boots On* portrays the Sioux as allies to Custer, and the railroad owners as the movie's villains. See my discussion in this article.

[3] Michael Hilger disagrees with the aforementioned opinions: he believes instead that the Western heroes' struggle to "conquer and punish the hated Indians parallels the effort of American soldiers to defeat the hated Germans and Japanese" during and after World War II. See *The American Indian in Film* (Metuchen, NJ: Scarecrow, 1986) 54. Hilger's book—an annotated list of Westerns with Indian characters—is a reference guide with no sustained argument.

[4] Many prominent Hollywood executives, writers, and directors were Jewish whose families and relatives in Europe were targets of anti-Semitism long before U.S. entry into the war. Beginning in 1936, the Hollywood Anti-Nazi League openly condemned German fascism and the Japanese invasion of China; so vocal was their opposition that isolationist groups criticized the industry's pro-interventionist (and pro-leftist) politics. For a further discussion of the motion picture community's pre-war sentiments, see Neal Gabler, *An Empire of Their Own: How the Jews Invented Hollywood* (New York: Doubleday, 1988) 311–47.

[5] "Major" studios were the five production companies in Hollywood that owned affiliated dis-tribu-tor and exhibitor chains. They were: Paramount, Metro-Goldwyn-Mayer, Radio-Keith-Orpheum, Twentieth Century-Fox, and Warner Brothers. Major studio films often had greater financing and were more widely marketed than their "minor" counterparts (United Artists, Columbia, and Universal).

[6] Hollywood studios often contracted performers, and their popularity became a key factor in the films' promotion. In 1940, Twentieth Century-Fox studio boasted Shirley Temple as its second popular star; Paramount placed Gary Cooper fourth, and Warner put Errol Flynn third. See *Variety,* 3 Jan. 1940: 29.

[7] The Indian massacre in *Northwest Passage* has prompted many recent scholars to attack the movie as "the single, most ferocious prewar film" ever known. See Raymond Durgnat and Scott Simmon, *King Vidor: American* (Berkeley: U of California P, 1988) 190.

[8] The Hays Office Production Code of 1930–34 insisted upon a moral compensation within motion pictures. Loosely interpreted, this meant that a wrongful death was to be compensated by the death (or arrest) of the perpetrator. Examples abound, but the most contrived is William Wyler's *The Letter* (1940), which added a policeman's arrest of the murderess' murderess in the remote Malaysian jungle. This was a significant departure from the conclusion that W. Somerset Maugham wrote in his original play.

[9] Zanuck espoused the same anti-fascist ideology in several war pictures (all written by him under the pseudonym Melville Crossman); namely, *Secret Agent of Japan* (1942), *To the Shores of Tripoli* (1942), *Tonight We Raid Calais* (1943), and *They Came to Blow Up America* (1943). Zanuck was raised in Nebraska, and his parents were from a Methodist/Episcopal background.

[10] Contrary to critical opinion, Hollywood employed Indians in major roles even prior to World War II. Not only did Chief Thundercloud appear as the Apache leader in *Geronimo* (although his gri-macing character was far from flattering), but films included other Indian performers as well: Redwing (who appeared in DeMille's 1914 *The Squaw Man*) Chief Thunder Bird (who appeared as Sitting Bull in *Annie Oakley,* 1935), Chief John Big Tree (Ford's Indian lead in *Drums Along the Mohawk,* 1939), to name only a few.

[11] All subsequent material from the Brigham Young University Collection will be noted as CBD.

[12] F. Calvin researched and compiled notes for *North West Mounted Police* from the following sources: *Harper's Magazine* (Dec. 1891); *The War Trail of Big Bear* by William Cameron; *History of the*

Northwest Rebellion of 1885 by C. P. Mulvaney; *The Silent Force* by M. Longstreth; *Information Respecting the History, Condition, and Prospects of the Indian Tribes of the United States* by Henry Schoolcraft; and *North American Indians* by Edward S. Curtis (typed Aug.–Oct. 1939, Box 377 Folder 4, CBD).

[13] The letter indicated that DeMille personally had chosen the name Louvette.

[14] In his autobiography, *My First Hundred Years in Hollywood* (New York: Random House, 1964), Jack L. Warner describes—albeit cautiously—his own political sentiments prior to and during World War II. For a detailed discussion of the later 30s films, see Charles Higham, *Warner Brothers* (New York: Scribner, 1975) 139–43. The German-American Bund actually sued Warner for $500,000 in alleged damages from *Confessions of a Nazi Spy.* (The lawsuit was later dropped.)

[15] All production correspondence from *They Died with Their Boots On* was obtained from the Warners' archives at University of Southern California.

[16] Such gestures failed to impress the War Department, which criticized the script's depiction of officers and enlisted men as corrupt or drunk. Executive producer Hal B. Wallis believed that although the military would not assist in production, Warner should incorporate the Army's suggestions so as not to "build up antagonism against possible future cooperation." Colonel E. R. Householder, Letter to William Guthrie (at Warner Brothers), [n.d.], Motion Picture Association of America, and Hal Wallis, Memo to Robert Fellows, 10 June 1941, File 2303.

[17] The studio's liberal interpretation of history prompted MacKenzie to comment that Warner had "an eye more to generosity than to fact."

[18] Although some scholars have incorrectly interpreted Chief Joseph's name (in a studio memo) to mean the Nez Perce leader, a previous citation (File 1018) had referred to *The Battle of the Little Big Horn,* by Chief Joseph White Bull (as told to Stanley Vestal), which describes the latter's role in the battle. Lee Ryan was the captain of Warner's Security Department; how much influence he had on the movie's actual content is questionable. It is worth noting, however, that the film did show Crazy Horse requesting Sitting Bull to join a war council with other Indian leaders.

[19] There has been much disagreement over Anthony Quinn's heritage. According to Quinn's autobiography, *The Original Sin* (A Self-Portrait) (Boston, MA: Little, Brown and Company, 1972) 11, the actor was born in Chihuahua, Mexico in 1915; his father was part Irish and his mother was Mexican with Indian blood.

[20] The movie's depiction of Custer's heroic sacrifice prompted studio head Jack Warner to remark—perhaps, with a twinge of sarcasm: "If Custer died like that, we should applaud him!" Walsh, *Each Man in His Time,* 327.

[21] While it is not within the scope of this article to examine the function of the OWI, it is worth noting that the agency did scrutinize Westerns for domestic and foreign release. Koppes and Black, in "Blacks, Loyalty, and Motion-Picture Propaganda in World War II," *op. cit.* state that every studio (except Paramount) submitted all scripts to the OWI for review, and that by mid-1943, the agency's recommendations were almost always followed (393).

[22] The movie's release in September 1947 was just one month prior to the testimony of Hollywood's 19 "unfriendly" witnesses before the House Un-American Activities Committee in Washington, in which 10 were eventually cited for contempt and sent to prison.

[23] For a further discussion of this trend, see Angela Aleiss, "Hollywood Addresses Postwar Assimilation: Indian/White Attitudes in *Broken Arrow,*" *American Indian Culture and Research Journal* 11.1 (1987): 67–79. John H. Lenihan's *Showdown: Confronting Modern America in the Western Film* (Chicago: U of Illinois P, 1980), devotes an entire chapter to the emerging theme of racial liberalism in Hollywood Westerns (55–89) passim. For better or worse, these fifties Westerns—with their message of tolerance and racial inclusion—echoed the concurrent Federal Termination policy of assimilating Indians into mainstream American society.

Works Cited

"Advertising Approach to *Plainsman.*" C. J. Dunphy staff memo to Zukor, Le Baron, DeMille, Gilliam [n. d.], Box 353, Folder 1, Cecil B. DeMille Collections, Archives and Manuscripts, Harold B. Lee Library, Brigham Young U.

Bergman, Andrew. *We're In the Money: Depression America and Its Films.* New York: New York UP, 1971.

Churchill, Douglas. "A Cowboy's Feud with Hollywood." *New York Times* 19 Oct. 1941.

Collier, John. *Annual Report of the Commissioner of Indian Affairs.* Washington, DC: GPO, June 1942.

———. June 1943.

———. June 1944.

"Conference with Zanuck on Temporary Script of 11/12/38." *Susannah of the Mounties.* Dir. William A. Seiter. With Shirley Temple. 23 Nov. 1938: 4–5, Box FX-PRS-122, Collection 010. Twentieth Century-Fox Film Corp. Produced Scripts, U of California at Los Angeles.

Crowther, Bosley. "DeMille Checks the Facts." *New York Times* 5 July 1939.

DeMille, Cecil B. "In Chicago Tonight." 27 Oct. 1940, Box 387, Folder 6: 2–3, CBD.

———. Letter to Mr. Archer Winsten. (Critic, *New York City Post* [sic]). 28 Nov. 1940: 1, Box 388, Folder 17, CBD.

Geronimo. Dir. Paul Sloan. Paramount, 1939. Paramount Press Sheets from 1 Aug. 1939 to 31 July 1940, Academy of Motion Picture Arts & Sciences, Margaret Herrick Library, Beverly Hills, CA.

"Government Information Manual for the Motion Picture Industry." Summer 1942, Record Group 208, National Archives & Record Administration, Office of War Information, Bureau of Motion Pictures (Hollywood Office), General Records of the Chief, Suitland, Maryland.

Hayne, Donald. Ed. *The Autobiography of Cecil B. DeMille.* New Jersey: Prentice, 1959.

Kaufmann, Donald L. "The Indian as a Media Hand-Me-Down." *The Colorado Quarterly* 23 (Spring 1974): 489–504.

Levy, Melvin. Memo to Robert Fellows, 30 Apr. 1941, File 2303, Warner Brothers Archives, USC.

"Line on the Golden Spike Itself." *Union Pacific* Apr. 1939: 3. Box 374, Folder 7, CBD. Notes for Speeches and Interviews.

Lissauer, Herman [Head, Warner's Research Department]. Memo to Aeneas MacKenzie, 17 June 1941, File 1018, Warner Brothers Archives, USC.

MacKenzie, Aeneas. Memo to Hal Wallis, 13 May 1941, File 2303, Warner Brothers Archives, USC.

MacRae, Henry. "The Perennial Western." Editorial. *Variety* 8 Jan. 1941: 20.

Mosley, Leonard. *Zanuck: The Rise and Fall of Hollywood's Last Tycoon.* Boston: Little, 1984.

"Movies Will Produce Army Training Films: Industry Organizes to Aid Citizen Soldiers." *New York Times* 1 Nov. 1940.

Pine, Bill [Associate Producer]. Memo to DeMille, 18 Feb. 1936. Box 342, Folder 12, CBD.

Price, John A. "The Stereotyping of North American Indians in Motion Pictures." *Ethnohistory* 20.2 (Spring 1973): 153–71.

Prucha, Francis Paul. *The Great Father: The United States Government and the American Indians II.* Lincoln: U of Nebraska P, 1984.

Rev. of *Apache Trail. Variety* 24 June 1942: 8.

Rev. of *Last of the Mohicans. New York Times* 3 Sept. 1936.

Rev. of "Road to God's Country," by Lillian R. Bergquist. 13 Apr. 1943, Record Group 208, OWI.

Rev. of *Susannah of the Mounties. New York Evening Journal* 24 June 1939.

Rev. of *Susannah of the Mounties. New York Star Telegram* 24 June 1939.

Rev. of *Susannah of the Mounties. Variety* 21 June 1939: 16.

Rosson, Gladys. Letter to Baron Valentin Mandelstamm, 29 Jan. 1940, Box 384, Folder 7, CBD.

"Rough Draft of New Line Suggested by Mr. Zanuck." First Draft Continuity of 10/12/37. *Hudson's Bay* 12. Box FX-PRS-809, Collection 010. Dir. Irving Pichel. 20th Century-Fox Film Corp. Produced Scripts, U of California at Los Angeles.

Ryan, Lee. Memo to Robert Fellows, [n.d.], File 2303, Warner Brothers Archives, USC.

Siminoski, Ted. "Sioux Versus Hollywood: The Image of Sioux Indians in American Film." Diss. U of Southern California, 1979.

"Suggestions for Promotion of *Unconquered.*" n.d. Box 430, Folder 7, 6, 10, CBD.

"Use Tolerance, Americanism to Win Heavy Publicity." *Black Gold* Pressbook, New York Public Library at Lincoln Center, Library and Museum of the Performing Arts.

Variety. Editorial. 29 May 1940: 5.

Walsh, Raoul. *Each Man in His Time: The Life Story of a Director.* New York: Farrar, 1974.

Understanding the Text

1. According to Aleiss, what events in Europe prompted Hollywood to change its depiction of Native Americans? What, in particular, did these events make the U.S. government's policy toward Native Americans in the past look like?

2. According to Aleiss, what did Native Americans represent in most Hollywood films before these events? What did they represent during and immediately after?

3. According to Aleiss, how, during the early years of the Cold War, did Cecil B. DeMille in *Unconquered* (1947) choose to depict Native Americans?

What Rough Beast—
New Westerns?

John G. Cawelti

I n *Gunfighter Nation* (1992), the third volume of his monumental study of the myth of the frontier in American culture, Richard Slotkin suggests that the disillusionment resulting from our disastrous involvement in the Vietnam War and our growing uncertainty about the American economy and its future have deeply eroded the ideology of American uniqueness that the traditional western mythicized. Slotkin thinks that the notable decline of the western in the 1970s means that "the western has therefore been relegated to the margins of the 'genre map'" (633) and will never again occupy the central place it once held in the expressive patterns of American culture. Though, according to Slotkin, the western film "reached the peak of its popularity and cultural pre-eminence from 1969 to 1972" (627), its decline has been precipitous since then, and "the failed attempts to revive the western after Vietnam indicate the character and strength of the social and cultural forces that fractured the myth/ideology of the liberal consensus" (628). Just as almost exactly a century ago Frederick Jackson Turner inspired a redefinition of the meaning of American history by his commentary on the end of the frontier, today "it may be time for a post-mortem assessment of the significance of the Frontier *Myth* in American history" (627).

Slotkin goes on to suggest that "the rejection of the western had gone beyond antipathy for a particular ideology to a rejection of the very idea that the Frontier could provide the basis of a national public myth" (632). We have arrived at a "'liminal' moment in our cultural history" when we are "in

John G. Cawelti, a professor of English at the University of Chicago (1957–1980) and at the University of Kentucky (1980–2000), is an eminent scholar of popular culture, especially of genre fiction such as the western and the romance. Among his many books are *Adventure, Mystery and Romance: Formula Stories as Art and Popular Culture* (1976) and *The Six-Gun Mystique* (1971), both of which are classics of contemporary criticism.

ANQ, Vol. 9, No. 3, Summer 1996. Reprinted with permission of the Helen Dwight Reid Educational Foundation. Published by Heldref Publications, 1319 Eighteenth St., NW, Washington, DC 20036-1802. Copyright © 1996.

the process of giving up a myth/ideology that no longer helps us see our way through the modern world" (654). In particular, we need new mythical patterns that express "the fact that our history . . . was shaped from the beginning by the meeting, conversation and mutual adaptation of different cultures." In short, the old epic of the American frontier as locus for white America's conquest of a savage wilderness is in the process of giving way to a new mythical dialectic of multiculturalism that cannot be contained within the patterns of the western.

Slotkin's argument is very persuasive, both in relation to the significance of the frontier myth in American history and in light of the precipitous decline in the creation and popularity of western films and TV programs during the later seventies and throughout most of the eighties. Yet, strangely enough, in the middle of the 1990s, we seem to be in the midst of a remarkable revival of the western. "Today westerns are back, guns blazing" a lead essay in the November 15, 1993, issue of *Time* announced with great éclat (Richard Zoglin, "Return from Boot Hill," 90–95). *Time* traces this upsurge in the production of westerns to the 1989 television mini-series based on Larry McMurtry's *Lonesome Dove,* the popular TV series *Dr. Quinn, Medicine Woman,* and the combined critical and popular acclaim that greeted two recent films, Kevin Costner's *Dances with Wolves* and Clint Eastwood's *Unforgiven.* The popular success of these works paved the way for such productions as three versions of *Geronimo* (PBS, TNT, and Walter Hill), two variations on the Wyatt Earp saga, a new *Maverick,* a plethora of new TV documentary series (Wests "Untold," "Real," and "Native American"), a *Return to Lonesome Dove,* and such gender westerns as *The Ballad of Billie Joe.* Still another Larry McMurtry mini-series based on his *Buffalo Girls* premiered in the spring of 1995.

This flurry of new westerns clearly indicates that the genre is far from dead, but there is some question as to just what this new activity signifies. Is the genre experiencing a revival, that is to say, the continuation of an established tradition after a period of interruption, or can we better characterize what is going on as a rebirth, a much more significant artistic and cultural event that involves not just a revitalization, but a significant transformation of cultural traditions? Although it is clearly premature to attempt a definitive answer to this question, some attempt to see these new western films in the context of other contemporary developments in our understanding of the American West may offer at least some preliminary guesses.

Dances with Wolves seemed to be at once a radical departure and a significant reaffirmation of the major traditions of the western. Most obviously, by making a group of Native Americans the sympathetic protagonists and by showing the U.S. Cavalry as an aggressive and brutal invader, the film reversed the western's mythical polarity between savage Indians and civilizing pioneers. However, as many critics have pointed out, this was not as much of a departure from tradition as it might seem. From the earliest European encounters with non-European cultures, there has always been a certain ambivalence about Native Americans, which manifested itself in divided portrayals of native peoples as diabolical savages on the one hand and noble innocents on the other. As Slotkin points out, this doubleness toward the

Native American was always a significant part of the myth of the West, from James Fenimore Cooper's magnificent Mohicans to what Slotkin calls the "cult of the Indian" in the western film. Was there any significant difference in the way the Native American was portrayed in *Dances with Wolves* than in earlier "cult of the the Indian westerns" such as *Broken Arrow, Soldier Blue,* or *Little Big Man?*

Certainly the film could be criticized for simply revising the old stereotype of the white man's ambiguous encounter with the noble savage. One Native American critic observed that *Dances with Wolves* should really be called *Lawrence of South Dakota.* The movie is clearly connected to earlier westerns and to the long tradition of frontier narrative going back to the seventeenth century by its adaptation of the theme of "captivity," which has always been one of the most potent of western themes. But there are significant departures. The leading female character, Stands-with-a-Fist, is actually a white woman captured as a girl and raised by the Indians. She has even married a warrior, who has recently died, and she sincerely mourns him. Though in traditional terms she has suffered a "fate worse than death," she seems to have thrived on it and has become so completely integrated into the tribe that she has almost forgotten her original language. She becomes the teacher and guide for Lt. Dunbar's willing "captivity" by the tribe. Dunbar himself has "lit out for the territory" after being symbolically killed and reborn in the violent madness of the Civil War. He seeks something better than the "civilized" military culture of madness and destruction. Eventually he relinquishes his former identity and becomes a member of the tribe. When the madness of civilization follows after him, he is forced to leave the tribe. However, he vows to continue his opposition to the destructiveness of white civilization.

There are many similarities between *Dances with Wolves* and *Little Big Man* (1970), which appeared just before the western began its precipitous decline in the early 1970s. Both were strongly influenced by the tragedy of the Vietnam War and portray the invasion of the American West very critically. Both center around a protagonist who becomes integrated into a tribe that is experiencing the destruction of its traditional culture, that of the migratory buffalo hunters of the Great Plains. Finally, both treat Native American cultures—the Sioux in *Dances with Wolves* and the Cheyenne in *Little Big Man*—with some attempt at historical accuracy and complexity as well as great sympathy.

Though *Dances with Wolves* may be overly romantic in its view of Native American cultures, it is still a remarkably effective film and a unique attempt to represent the Native American perspective in a popular cultural form. It does have similarities with *Little Big Man,* but there are some important new elements. Jack Crabb of *Little Big Man* is captured as a child and brought up by the Cheyenne. He has already been acculturated as a Cheyenne when he is taken back by the whites, recaptured again by the Indians, and so on. This is an excellent premise for satirizing cultural differences and inverting conventional perceptions, which *Little Big Man* effectively does. But throughout his story, Jack Crabb remains essentially external to both the cultures he is involved in. To the end, he is, like Huckleberry Finn, always on the outside. Dunbar is not a more complex character, but his role is different. He enables us to participate vicariously in the realization of, and finally the initiation into, a different culture.

This aspect of the narrative is further supported by three other aspects of the film. First, there was the decision to use Native American actors for several of the most important roles. In the traditional western, of course, it was most common to use white actors for the major Indian roles.[1] One of the striking exceptions to this practice, Chief Dan George's delightful portrayal of Old Lodge Skins in *Little Big Man,* was really more caricature than character. On the other hand, Graham Greene's portrayal of Kicking Bird in *Wolves* was a fully rounded and persuasive portrayal of a strong and dignified human being who represented a different set of cultural norms. This effect was reinforced by the use of the Sioux language, which helped give us the sense of encountering the world of another culture. Finally, the film's choice of location was extremely important. Instead of being filmed in the conventional western landscape of desert, mountain, and frontier town, *Wolves* was filmed in South Dakota on the Great Plains, which was, in fact, the real locale of the Sioux culture. This landscape differs enough from the traditional western setting that our sense of the mythical frontier world is subtly displaced, and we do not immediately recognize the familiar mythic West.

Two other recent "Cavalry and Indian" films attempt to acknowledge more fully a Native American perspective. Significantly, both these films center around the most feared and hated of Indian war leaders, the Apache Geronimo. Can anyone forget the famous opening scene of Ford's *Stagecoach,* where the soldiers at an isolated cavalry post suddenly realize that the telegraph wire has been cut, and one of them pronounces in awed tones the dread word "Geronimo!"? In TNT's version, the story is narrated by the aged Geronimo, who has been made into a celebrity by his former enemies, though never really freed from the imprisonment he entered after his surrender. From this standpoint at the end of his life, Geronimo tells a younger Apache warrior, now a West Point Cadet, about his long resistance to the white incursion. The film also contains a few scenes of Apache religious ceremonies and other cultural episodes beyond the stereotypical image of Apaches as fearsome raiders and torturers. Walter Hill's *Geronimo* is an even more complex and powerful film that suggests that the destruction of the Apache culture was not only a historical tragedy but a betrayal as well.

These new representations of the Native American situation in the history of the West are not without unintentional ironies or occasional reversions to the sentimentalizing stereotypes of the noble savage tradition. Still, the films I have been discussing illustrate a new concern for historical complexity and for the acknowledging of different cultural perspectives. In this way, they relate to other important developments in our treatment of the western past.

One of these is particularly evident in the new western history, which rejects the traditional approach to that history as centered around the European settlement of the western frontier. Instead, contemporary historians emphasize the clash of cultures and its lasting implications for the present. Significantly, one of the most widely read of the new histories is Limerick's *The Legacy of Conquest* (1987), which not only rejected the Turnerian emphasis on the uniqueness of America's frontier experience, but insisted on the American West as "an important meeting ground, the point where Indian America, Latin America, Anglo-America, Afro-America, and Asia intersected. . . . The workings of conquest tied these diverse groups into the same story" (27).

Another important contemporary development is the great flowering of Native American fiction and poetry in English. More than anything else, the fascinating novels and poems of writers like N. Scott Momaday, Leslie Silko, James Welch, Gerald Vizenor, and Louise Erdrich have offered a new kind of insight into the cultures and the perspectives on America of a variety of Indian groups. One of the most striking of these works, Leslie Silko's contemporary epic fantasy, *Almanac of the Dead* (1991), startlingly displaces our traditional sense of the West as the victory of American civilization over savagery by representing the present as a time in which the temporary European incursion into the Americas is beginning to show signs of drawing to an end. These Native American fictions should provide a rich literary source for the western films of the future.

A second aspect of recent western films reflects important changes in our understanding of the significance of the West but involves Native Americans only tangentially. This appears in Clint Eastwood's film *Unforgiven* and the television series based on Larry McMurtry's best-selling novel, *Lonesome Dove*. One striking quality shared by both these works is a highly complex and many-sided relationship to the traditional mythology of the West. Both works begin by placing themselves in well-established generic traditions: *Unforgiven* is clearly in the line of gunfighter westerns, most notably perhaps that of *Shane* and its ilk, whereas *Lonesome Dove* relates to cattle-drive westerns such as Howard Hawks's *Red River*. In addition, both films make continual allusions to earlier western films, and this allusive texture is so complex that one is sometimes reminded of modernist novels and poems by writers such as Joyce, Faulkner, Eliot, and Pound, in whose works layers of the mythical past are also continually invoked through allusions. But allusions to western mythology are counterpointed in these films by a constant sense that the characters and action are in continual danger of falling out of the mythical world. In *Unforgiven,* for example, the gunfighter is almost unable to carry out his mission when he nearly dies from a bad case of the flu. In *Lonesome Dove,* accidents, chance encounters, and sudden revelations are continually undercutting and reducing to absurdity the significance of the protagonists' mythical quest. As if to remind us of the falsity of the gunfighter myth, *Unforgiven* provides us with a dime-novel hero accompanied by his writer. English Bob is, in good postmodernist fashion, ambivalently referred to throughout his episode as the "Duke (Duck) of Death" and is literally deconstructed by the sadistic sheriff Little Bill, who reduces him to a pathetic victim. On the other hand, in the film's violent climax, Will Munny actually improves on dime-novel shootouts by escalating the body count when he kills the bar-and-brothel owner, the sheriff, and three deputies.

These works neither affirm nor reject the myth, and that is the way they differ significantly from most previous westerns, which either repeated some version of the myth or claimed to reveal at last the "true" history that lay behind the myth, a "reality" that, more often than not, turned out to be another mythical invention. *Lonesome Dove* and *Unforgiven* manage, it seems to me, to do something still more complex: they show both the power of myth and its dangers, revealing not just the ambiguity of the myths, but the way in which myth and history are engaged in a problematic dialectic. The chaos, randomness, and futility of history call forth the great excitements and simplicities of myth, but once evoked or entered, the mythic world develops an impetus of its own that, imposed on history, can generate a new and more terrifying apocalypse.

In *Lonesome Dove* and *Unforgiven,* the mythic world is associated with the violence and heroism of the protagonists' youths, just as the mythic era of the wild West is associated with an earlier period of America's history. In *Lonesome Dove* Gus and Call have a nostalgic feeling for their earlier lives as Texas Rangers, and they seek to recreate this time of adventure by leaving behind the dull and predictable world of *Lonesome Dove.* William Munny of *Unforgiven* looks back on his violent youth with fear and regret, but he too feels trapped in the present on a wretched hardscrabble farm, trying to raise pigs. The lure of money and adventure draws him once again into a vortex of drunkenness and violence, which leaves a trail of corpses and his best friend dead. It is perhaps the ultimate irony that he is rumored after that to have become a successful merchant in San Francisco.

The ambivalence of these westerns toward the traditional mythic world of the frontier is also related to a more complex treatment of gender issues, for one characteristic of the western was its stereotyping of women by simplification (as in the limitation of women's roles to schoolmarms and dancehall girls) or subordination (by arranging for any important women characters to be converted to the patriarchal code of values). *Lonesome Dove* and *Unforgiven* unfurl a variety of new gender possibilities, from the virtual marriage of Gus McCrae and Woodrow Call to the employer-employee relationship between the victimized prostitutes of *Unforgiven* and the retired gunfighter William Munny. The complexities of gender were even more fascinatingly deployed in another recent western, *The Ballad of Billie Joe,* in which the central character is forced to masquerade as a man to make a decent life for herself in the West. But perhaps in part because this film went even further in its exploratory probing of the absurdity of traditional gender stereotypes as a foundation of the myth of the West, it did not achieve the wide popularity of *Lonesome Dove* and *Unforgiven.*

These changes in the treatment of the West are also reflected in much new fiction and in the revisionist approach to western history. Such cultural phenomena as the extraordinary vitality of Native American and Hispanic writing suggest that the new western is not just part of a momentary revival, but may be one sign of an important cultural renaissance of the sort that another major American region—the South—underwent in the course of the 1920s and 1930s, when a new generation of writers struggled to free themselves from the cultural devastation of another great myth of American history, that of the Lost Cause. In that case, the result was some of the greatest novels and stories ever written about the American dream and its tragic failure. Perhaps today, it is the final decay of the myth of the frontier that makes possible the creativity of the new western literature, film, and history.

Among the themes that express the particular concerns of the new western literature and film are the sense of the loss of a world that seemed to be more fulfilling and more human than the present and the story of the initiation of potentially heroic young men into a world where there is no longer any room for the kind of meaningful action that was once possible.[2] The new western, like many novels of the Southern renaissance, is filled with a deep sense of belatedness and nostalgia for a more unified traditional culture. Larry McMurtry pioneered this genre of western literature with his two early novels of Thalia, Texas, *Horseman, Pass By* (1961) and *The Last Picture Show* (1966). In both these novels, the protagonists not only confront the usual strains of growing up and accepting the knowledge and limitations of adulthood, but also must deal with a very difficult sense of diminishing expectations and of the loss of a bygone time of greater significance and meaning associated with the heyday of the cattle industry and the great cattle drives of the nineteenth century. In *Horseman, Pass By,* the young narrator feels a deep sense of loss: "'Things used to be better around here,' I said. 'I feel like I want something back'" (123). And loss does come to characterize young Lonnie's world, when his beloved grandfather's diseased cattle must be destroyed and the grandfather himself is killed after he is terribly hurt in an accident. *The Last Picture Show* ends with the closing of Thalia's one movie theater and with it, the dream of the old West, which inspired so many of the pictures shown there. Peter Bogdanovich, who directed the excellent movie based on McMurtry's novel, appropriately ended the film with the great scene from Howard Hawks's western *Red River* (1947) in which John Wayne sets off on the first great cattle drive from Texas. In contrast to this heroic moment, the young people of Thalia are left only with the vacuous emptiness of a depressed oil boomtown.

This sense of the end of the heroic West haunts such major works of the new western fiction as Norman Maclean's *A River Runs through It* (1976), in which an old man is haunted by memories of his long-dead father and brother and of the fishing that they shared, and still broods about his inability to save his brother from the violence that destroyed him. In other stories, Maclean evokes a lost world of skill with tools and heroic physical labor and shows how powerful an experience it was to be initiated into such a world. His nonfiction study *Young Men and Fire* (1992) beautifully represents the heroism and tragedy of traditional western work in his reconstruction of the last hours of a fire-fighting crew destroyed by a great fire in Montana in 1949 in the words of an old man who is facing his own encounter with death.

Like the mythical western, these works portray a West that is largely gone, but unlike the once-dominant tales of wild cowtowns and cattle drives, outlaws and marshals, gunfighters and schoolmarms that populated the nation's imagined West, they celebrate the heroism not of gunfighters, but of loggers, miners, forest service workers, and firefighters—those ordinary people who built the West and then saw it transformed into something else.

Thus far, the greatest treatment of the western theme of initiation and belatedness may be found in the transplanted Southerner Cormac McCarthy's novel *All The Pretty Horses* (1992). McCarthy transforms the mythical fantasy world of wild western gunfighters, outlaws, and savage Indians into the last remnant of an age-old world of traditional work in which men are part of the unity of life and find great fulfillment in their actions, because these actions are integral with horses and the rest of nature. Horses, which have been man's primary instrument in the use of nature and the creation of culture for centuries, are, as the novel's title would suggest, the symbol of a traditional unity between man and the world that is being increasingly destroyed by modern technology and industrialism. As McCarthy portrays it, west Texas, once one of the last bastions of traditional pastoralism in America,[3] is already a wasteland of oil derricks and on the verge of the postwar oil boom that will utterly destroy the traditional cattle culture (111).

Like Larry McMurtry's earlier work, *All The Pretty Horses* begins in a depressed west Texas, in the immediate aftermath of World War II. Its protagonist, John Grady Cole, is sixteen years old and very much alone in the world. His father is separated from his mother and is slowly dying from a condition incurred in a prison camp in the war. Cole's grandfather is a rancher, and Cole, loving horses and ranching, would like nothing better than to continue the ranch, but the old man dies, and Cole's mother plans to sell the family ranch and leave the area. To continue the work he loves, Cole crosses the border into Mexico with a young friend, and the two find work on a large hacienda where the traditional work with horses and cattle is still carried on.

However, this momentary recovery of paradise is disrupted when Cole falls desperately in love with the daughter of the great hacienda's proprietor. When she returns his love and the two embark on a passionate affair, her powerful family has Cole wrongfully arrested. After being nearly killed in a Mexican prison, Cole is freed after his lover promises never to see him again. The last section of the novel deals with Cole's revenge on the corrupt Mexican policeman who has betrayed him and stolen his horses. Finally, hardened and matured by his ordeal and deeply saddened by the loss of his love and his encounters with death, Cole returns to Texas.

The Texas he finds is on the verge of the postwar oil boom that will destroy the traditional cattle culture, the same process McMurtry portrayed in his series of Thalia novels and which furnished the background for television's popular western soap opera *Dallas*. Although the traditional culture still exists in the late 1940s on the great haciendas of Mexico, it too is clearly on borrowed time. It is significant that the wealthy hacendado of McCarthy's novel keeps his ranch more as a hobby than a way of life and uses an airplane to fly back and forth between the hacienda and his other life in Mexico City.

John Grady Cole is not only a master of horses but something of a visionary as well, and the story is punctuated by his dreams of horses, which picture an eternal paradise where wild horses symbolize the possibility of man's redemption:

> That night as he lay in his cot he could hear music from the house and as he was drifting to sleep his thoughts were of horses and of the open country and of horses. Horses still wild on the mesa who'd never seen a man afoot and who knew nothing of him or his life yet in whose souls he would come to reside forever. (117–18)

One of the most striking moments in the novel comes in a conversation between Cole, his young friend Rawlins, and an old man who symbolizes the traditional wisdom of the world of natural work. It is this old man who expresses most clearly the full spiritual significance of horses in this traditional vision of the world:

> Finally he said that among men there was no such communion as among horses and the notion that man can be understood at all was probably an illusion. Rawlins asked him in his bad spanish if there was a heaven for horses but he shook his head and said that a horse had no need of heaven. Finally John Grady asked him if it were not true that should all horses vanish from the face of the earth the soul of the horse would not also perish for there would be nothing out of which to replenish it but the old man only said that it was pointless to speak of there being no horses in the world for God would not permit such a thing. (111)

The major thing John Grady Cole must learn in the process of his initiation into mature life is the hardest to accept: that such a world no longer exists for him. The Mexican hacienda is, for him, a Paradise Lost. Even in Mexico, the modern world of politics and revolution, technology and cities, is eroding and destroying the traditions of the countryside, and in the Texas to which he must return, the only vestiges of the traditional world of man and nature are in the few remaining Indian encampments in the midst of the oil fields:

> In tour days' riding he crossed the Pecos at Iraan Texas and rode up out of the river breaks where the pumpjacks in the Yates Field ranged against the skyline rose and dipped like mechanical birds. Like great primitive birds welded up out of iron by hearsay in a land perhaps where such birds once had been. At that time there were still indians camped on the western plains and late in the day he passed in his riding a scattered group of their wickiups propped upon that scoured and trembling waste. They were perhaps a quarter mile to the north, just huts made from poles and brush with a few goathides draped across them. The indians stood

watching him. He could see that none of them spoke among themselves or commented on his riding there nor did they raise a hand in greeting or call out to him. They had no curiosity about him at all. As if they knew all that they needed to know. They stood and watched him pass and watched him vanish upon that landscape solely because he was passing. Solely because he could vanish. (301)

In this profoundly elegiac conclusion McCarthy evokes that mythical western scene of the hero riding off into the sunset, but for John Grady Cole there is no more mythical world to cross over into, there is only "the darkening land, the world to come" (302). In the end, McCarthy's vision of the West is as apocalyptic in its way as Leslie Silko's, though he sees only a darkening wasteland, whereas Silko imagines the ultimate restoration of the land through an ecological catastrophe of modern technological civilization and a return of tribal cultures.

The new western literature, like that of the Southern renaissance before it, is centrally concerned with the failure of white American civilization and with the burden of guilt left by the exploitation of nature and the tragic heritage of racism. The contemporary literary exploration of the history and culture of these regions, once so important as sources of romantic myths of otherness in American culture, has produced compelling reevaluations of the basic myths of American exceptionalism and superiority and powerful critiques of the multiple failures of the American dream.

It's striking, though perhaps not surprising, that these deeply critical literary movements have emerged almost simultaneously with a new surge of political conservatism and fundamentalism in America, also centered in the South and the West and seeking to manipulate the same symbolic and ideological traditions for their own very different purposes. As many commentators have noted, Ronald Reagan tried to reenact the western myth of the shootout between the heroic marshall and the lawless outlaw on the national and international scenes. The new breed of Southern Republicans who have recently become so important in American politics have found that a traditional Southern rhetoric of less government, family values, localism, and even a coded white supremacy disguised as opposition to affirmative action has proved highly effective on the national scene. These reactions are almost always antithetical to those of serious contemporary Southern and Western writers, but though differently focused, they are responses to the same uncertainties that have beset America in the last quarter of the twentieth century: a profound loss of confidence in America's uniqueness, moral superiority, and global omnipotence. In the context of this ongoing spiritual crisis, the South and the West, which once helped define America mythically and symbolically through their otherness, are now being pursued by both intellectual critics and conservative fundamentalists as symbols of the real truth of America.

Notes

[1] One of the most successful of these portrayals was that of the Apache chief Cochise by Jeff Chandler in *Broken Arrow,* a portrayal that Chandler repeated in *The Battle at Apache Pass* and *Taza, Son of Cochise.*

[2] The concern for the loss of a traditional way of life is also reflected in the recent reactions of some westerners against the Federal Government's control of public lands and environmental regulations. These are reported in a recent cover story in *Time* magazine, "Don't Tread On Me: An Inside Look at the West's Growing Rebellion" (October 23, 1995, pp. 52–71). Ironically, if these movements succeed, they will probably accelerate the very transformations they seem to deplore. Similarly, the period of the Southern literary renaissance, the 1920s and 1930s, was also marked by a reactionary resurgence of social movements like the Ku Klux Klan and Protestant fundamentalism, which sought desperately to hold on to the traditional social, racial, and economic patterns of the "Solid South."

[3] West Texas was also the ostensible setting of John Ford's great movie *The Searchers* (1956), a powerful treatment of the clash between pioneers and Indians and of the mythical version of the Indian captivity and the initiation of a young man. Actually, the movie was largely filmed in Ford's favorite locale of Monument Valley. *The Searchers* is considered by many to be the finest of all Western films.

Works Cited

Berger, Thomas. *Little Big Man.* New York: Dial, 1964.

Limerick, Patricia. *The Legacy of Conquest: The Unbroken Past of the American West.* New York: Norton, 1987.

Maclean, Norman. *A River Runs Through It and Other Stories.* Chicago: U of Chicago P, 1976.

———. *Young Men and Fire.* Chicago: U of Chicago P, 1992.

McCarthy, Cormac. *All the Pretty Horses.* New York: Knopf, 1992.

McMurtry, Larry. *Horseman, Pass By.* New York: Harper, 1961.

———. *Lonesome Dove.* New York: Simon and Schuster, 1985.

Understanding the Text

1. Early in his essay, Cawelti wonders whether the "flurry of new westerns" produced in the mid-1990s is the product of a "revival" or a "rebirth" of the genre? What is the difference, in Cawelti's view, and, ultimately, which term does he think is more appropriate? Why do you think so?

2. What, overall, is Cawelti's assessment of *Dances with Wolves?*

3. In his conclusion, Cawelti ties the motifs of "new western literature" to national political trends. What, ultimately, does he say about the relation between the two?

Producing Patriotic Inspiration at Mount Rushmore

Matthew Glass

In an uncharacteristic moment, Mircea Eliade once nodded towards the contentiousness, or better still, the politics, that necessarily shapes the formation of religious landscapes. As an aside in one of his many discussions of sacred space he noted:

> An unknown, foreign, and unoccupied territory (which often means, "unoccupied by our own people") still shares in the fluid and larval modality of chaos. By occupying it and, above all, by settling in it, man symbolically transforms it into a cosmos through a ritual repetition of cosmogony. (31)

Eliade's parenthetical comment provides an important clue for viewing how Americans have gone about investing their lands with sacred significance. "Unoccupied by our own people" suggests that sacred space is a field marked by potential disagreement about the character and contours of the sacred, and that there is a human cost in deciding how to characterize a given place as sacred. It suggests that "our people" will see the landscape differently than "their people." Possession being nine-tenths of the law, it raises the possibility that our people will struggle with their people over the symbolic ownership of place. And if our people are going to see it in a new and different way than their people did, then we are going to have to work diligently, "occupying" and "settling," in order, as Emile Durkheim might have put it, to make ourselves readily visible on the landscape.[1]

This article provides a gloss on Eliade's comments. In particular I want to examine the process

Matthew Glass is a professor of philosophy, religion, and environmental studies and has taught at South Dakota State University, the University of Guelph, and Wilfrid Laurier University. He has published numerous journal articles and a book, *Citizens Against the MX: Public Language in the Nuclear Age* (1993).

Matthew Glass, "Producing Patriotic Inspiration at Mount Rushmore," from *The Journal of the American Academy of Religion*, LXII, No. 2, pages 265–283. Copyright © 1994 by Oxford University Press, used by permission of the Oxford University Press.

of symbolic appropriation that began with the hard work done by the carvers of Mount Rushmore, America's "Shrine of Democracy" and South Dakota's leading tourist attraction, focusing specifically on the production of patriotic inspiration at the memorial. But the efforts of some Americans to view Mount Rushmore as democracy's shrine has given rise to counter-tendencies. As might be concluded from Eliade's suggestion about religion serving to legiti-mate one group taking the land from another, long-running symbolic battles have been fought at Mount Rushmore over its meaning. In conclusion therefore I will juxtapose the production of patriotism with two episodes from the history of symbolic resistance at Mount Rushmore.[2]

I

● ● ● ● ● ● ● ● ● ● ● ● ● ● ●

Since work stopped on the memorial in 1941, the National Park Service (NPS) has sought to excite the curiosity, wonder, and inspiration of the memorial's visitors. Two themes in par-ticular stand out as focal concerns for the interpretive programs run by the NPS: the historical panorama symbolized by the four presidential faces, and the story of the memorial's creation. Together they have enabled many Americans to both commemorate the past and to discover links between the spiritual resources which inspired the lives of their great leaders, and those which are necessary for the conduct of their own lives.

As has become clear through the work on civil religion by Linenthal and Zelinksy, defin-ing the American landscape itself has been central to the formation of nationalism. But unlike battlefield sites, which usually gain an obvious sort of sacred status through the sacrificial spilling of blood, Mount Rushmore has always been subject to some interpretive ambiguity. Just what is it supposed to do? This question surfaced frequently throughout the fourteen years of construction at the memorial, as when Associate Director of the NPS, A.E. Demaray, appearing before the House Appropriations Committee in 1935, said he really did not know what the project portrayed (Fite:167).

Sculptor Gutzon Borglum provided the mountain with its initial interpretation, dramati-cally acknowledging his first view of Rushmore by announcing "American history shall march along that skyline" (R. Smith:33). As a shrine, part of the memorial's aura of sacredness results from condensing the temporal process of American history into a single place. But this itself presents an interpretive problem in an age in which nationalizing forces require the mobiliza-tion of diverse populations and public formation of collective memory. As George Lipsitz has put it, history remains contentious in American life because "what we choose to remember about the past, where we begin and end our retrospective accounts, and who we include and exclude from them—these do a lot to determine how we live and what decisions we make in the present" (34). What should the content of public memory be at Mount Rushmore?

One answer to this appears in the interpretive displays at the Rushmore visitors' center, currently being remodeled to accommodate the memorial's 2.5 million visitors more comfortably. A doorway inside the center leads people into a room furnished with large-screen TV monitors and comfortable family-sized benches from which to view the screens. Visitors entering the room see the memorial itself through twenty-foot high floor-to-ceiling windows. As either prelude or postlude to moving outside they can gather before the monitors to watch a video replaying on demand. Tom Brokaw, NBC news anchor and native South Dakotan, begins his narration:

> It was, critics said, a preposterous idea, an outrage against South Dakota's Black Hills. "What arrogant stone carver could possibly intrude upon God's mountain sculpture?" But as the faces of the great men sprang outright from the mountain, Rushmore simply overwhelmed its critics, and dazzled the world, just as the republican ideals it honors had inspired and dazzled mankind in 1776.

Cameras panning the memorial from the air, recording the play of light and clouds from dawn to sunset, and the brilliant illumination at night all give visitors a chance to extend their temporal view of the memorial beyond the generally brief visits demanded by busy vacation schedules. Interpretive displays of the workers' equipment and photographs of the construction process enable visitors to deepen their experience at Mount Rushmore. Combined with Brokaw's narrative and half-hour talks by rangers, visitors can encounter the testimony of the men who carved Rushmore, anecdotes of their efforts, and an interpretation of its meaning.

Brokaw concludes by saying:

> In both its conception and realization Rushmore is uniquely American, proclaiming bold ideals and big aspirations, celebrating the spirit of our people and the sweep of our civilization, reminding us of the hope a democratic society offers the future. It is a monument no less to the men who working together transformed a lofty dream into a colossal reality, a work of art for the ages.

It is worth noting that Brokaw's narrative seems directly geared towards providing the visitor with a useable, inspirational past, rather than an account of the memorial's development. For instance, the narrative proceeds by regarding the memorial as an accomplished fact, enabling Brokaw to deride the historically out-of-step nay-sayers, those who thought at the time that such a project was a waste and an abomination. In fact there were many, both locally and nationally, who did want to know "what arrogant stone carver could possibly intrude upon God's mountain sculpture?"

Promethean arrogance, denounced in 1925 by South Dakotans basically leery of being saddled with an obligation to provide front money (Fite:55), was a key mythic element in the project, at least for sculptor Gutzon Borglum. Borglum blended a heady mixture of organic evolutionism, Anglo-Saxon nativism, and Whig historiography to lay out the possibilities facing America as a result of his skyline vision. In a piece circulated by the Mount Rushmore National Memorial Commission in 1931 Borglum contrasted the rise and fall of other civilizations with the promethean quality of America's birth.

> Strangely enough, by some humor of nature, out of confusion there grew and developed a small tribe of independent, self-reliant souls, in whose veins flowed the blood of Europe, of Greece, of Rome, of England. . . . They were long enough removed from the trials of their forefathers to think too much of their past, but the hot blood boiled again, and mind and heart got together—and America, a nation, was conceived and born, sired by aeons of upward struggle out of hair and leaves, out of mud and fear, out of slavery in galleys and cells, out of bigotry, out of injustice into fair play. The right of each in his own way to be happy was written by them across the sky, firmly there, where a world could read it. (1931:15)

Borglum's version of the American cosmogony bears little resemblance to pious accounts of providential working. Born into a family that was by turns Mormon, Catholic, and finally given to embracing movements such as new thought and theosophy (Shaff and Shaff), Borglum had little truck with Protestant piety. He tells of America as "conceived and born" out of "hot blood" boiling, "sired" by "upward struggle out of hair and leaves." The American people themselves took on the task of storming heaven, though apparently Borglum saw divine purpose in this. Borglum, carrier of a hefty ego, saw his own production of colossal public sculpture as giving material form to this Promethean spirit, and it is probably not stretching it too far to claim that the carving itself satisfies Eliade's concern for the ritual repetition of cosmogony. He spoke of his "lifting our accomplishments into the heavens and engraving there in the sun our records away from the meddling fingers of ignorance and avarice" (Borglum 1931:16).

As with any divinely-inspired mission, Borglum saw his own, as well as that of the "Anglo-Saxon race," beset with trials and tribulations. In the midst of the project's serious financial difficulties he spoke of the completion of the memorial as a test of spirit.

> If this monument fails to become the first of our great memorials to the Anglo-Saxon in the Western Hemisphere, recording the significance of their civilization in reshaping the philosophy of politics and government throughout the world—if this monument fails to interpret that record, it will be because we ourselves have failed, not only to appreciate our opportunity, but in our abilities to develop what great thought contains. (Borglum 1930:vii)

He maintained the spirits of those involved in the seventeen-year project largely because he remained convinced that American leaders were ripe for apotheosis. In remarks given at the unveiling of the Washington sculpture in 1930, as a gigantic American flag was rolled up to reveal the finished face, Borglum said

> We believe a nation's memorial should, like Washington, Jefferson, Lincoln and Roosevelt, have a serenity, a nobility, a power that reflects the gods who inspired them and the gods that they have become.
>
> Let us place there, carved high, as close to heaven as we can, the words of our leaders, their faces, to show posterity what manner of men they were. Then breathe a prayer that these records will endure until the wind and rain alone shall wear them away. (Borglum 1930:n.p.)

This recognition that American leaders had become gods was certainly not Borglum's alone. Doane Robinson, the South Dakota historian who proposed the idea of carving figures in the Black Hills, put this apotheosis to verse in a Mount Rushmore National Memorial Society brochure published in 1931 to commemorate the sculpting of Jefferson, second figure in the presidential quartet:

> Some sons of God must stand upon the mountain tops,
> And there through all the deathless generations guard
> The continents and guide the gracious stars of fate:
> So God made mountains for thrones such as these.
> Upon this mountain top America enshrines
> Her sturdy sirs; exalts her noblest knight,
> Where children of the earth may lift appraising eye,
> And feel his virtue while his strength invests their souls.
> (Robinson 1931:8)

As has often been noted, apotheosis itself runs deep into American political history. Washington as Moses led the citizenry out of the wilderness and was then translated to the realm of light, as the popular paintings entitled "Apotheosis" by John Barralet (1802) or H. Weishaupt (c.1800) make clear. Lincoln, our own Christ, gave his life to bind up our wounds, as Doane Robinson noticed in a 1941 paean to the two "Greatest Democrats" (Robinson 1941:17). Roosevelt's place at the memorial has always been more of an interpretive problem. Borglum, who supported Roosevelt's Bull Moose Party, saw Roosevelt as the completer of Christopher Columbus's dream, achieved by cutting the Panama Canal (Borglum 1930:vii). And as Columbus's journals indicate, Columbus saw himself as Moses, led on to the terrestrial paradise by the hand of God.

II

From the jaded perspectives of the post-Watergate generation it may be hard to take seriously such ability to turn American politicians into gods. But studies suggest that many Americans do retain this willingness, if not for our contemporaries, then at least for the faces on the mountain (Zelinsky; Schwartz). However, overt political apathy and cynicism in the present does prompt the question of how Mount Rushmore works. If Rushmore remains a potent symbol, exactly how do Americans go about connecting with the power, wisdom or virtue they find there? What makes it possible for visitors to see their visit as "a moment of communion with the very soul of America," as George Bush noted in his dedication in 1991 (Bush:887)? These questions can perhaps only be answered by undertaking an extensive random survey of visitor responses at the memorial. But an initial answer can be gleaned from considering the NPS "strategies" developed to produce the potential for Americans to connect with the sacred qualities carved into the mountain.[3] There are at least three such strategies visible at Mount Rushmore: symbolic limitation, symbolic recentering, and the transference of virtue.

There are at least three such strategies by which NPS staff at MR produce the potential for Americans to connect with the sacred qualities carved into the mountain. The first strategy is actually to qualify or limit the process of symbolic connection. While Gutzon Borglum could easily speak of the memorial being a witness to the achievements of the Anglo-Saxon race, its modern, federal, caretakers cannot.[4] One important National Park Service goal since the heyday of the civil rights movement has been the commitment to present the public with a pluralistic reading of the American experience. The NPS has accomplished this by accepting responsibility for the preservation and interpretation of new historic monuments associated with non-Anglo racial and ethnic groups, and by providing culturally sensitive interpretive programs at all units.[5] At Mount Rushmore it has also included a "toning-down" of the patriotic rhetoric common to the memorial's founders and original promoters.

One might expect that Park Service personnel at Mount Rushmore would acknowledge their role as symbolic custodians and interpreters. But qualitative interviews with staff members at the memorial indicate the extent to which many of them wish to avoid this conclusion.[6] Dan Wenk, park superintendent, doubts that his job has anything to do with protecting, or underscoring, particular symbolic interpretations of Mt. Rushmore. Instead, he sees himself as responsible for budgets, personnel, visitor safety, protection of resources, and mediating between constituencies and adversaries. Wenk does regard Mt. Rushmore as a contemplative place. He is quick to say that the NPS job is to preserve that contemplative quality, though without in any way influencing the direction of contemplation, or affecting the interpretations of visitors.

He notes that these interpretations depend primarily upon individual backgrounds:

Mount Rushmore has a different meaning for every person who visits it. [Take] the veteran from World War II who saw his friends perhaps lose their lives to preserve and maintain our country. Mt. Rushmore affects that person differently than the 16 year old who's never really known conflict, and never really known some of the sacrifices that many of our forefathers, or fathers or brothers have made. And so Mount Rushmore becomes very personal in terms of the history that individuals bring, and that affects them differently as they leave.[7]

For Wenk the personal response to the Memorial means that his duties as protector in no way limit the freedom of perspective held by the visitor. Thus he contends that the Park Service would not consider doing anything to counter derogatory interpretations offered by individuals such as the Lakota holy man John Fire Lame Deer, who saw in the faces merely a legacy of the conquest of his people by the United States.

At the same time, Wenk says that what is most crucial to his job here is to manage affairs in such a way that the visitor can feel a lump in the throat when looking at the mountain. Asked whether he ever gets lumps in his own throat, he responds:

At times. It depends upon the group you're dealing with. If you have a group up here and they're doing a program on the POWs and the MIAs, and you see how that mountain affects them, you can't help but be affected. If you have a group of bikers from the Sturgis rally[8] and you follow them up the trail, and they're rowdy and not paying any attention, and they fall silent, and stand ten minutes and literally don't talk, just look at the mountain, and then when they do talk they talk in hushed tones, you can't help but be affected. When you see the guy walk up that has lost a leg in Vietnam, or is in a wheel chair, you can't help but be affected. When you're here by yourself, and it's a full moon, with no artificial light, you can't help but feel affected.

But he then goes on to say that not everyone is affected.

This recognition of interpretative variety allows the memorial's guardians to serve in some priestly capacities, such as preserving access and order. But at the same time, for Wenk it also distances the NPS from responsibility for the nitty-gritty tasks of symbolic production and control. For Wenk the NPS does not have to produce patriotic spirit or preserve collective memory.

This ambiguity of roles can be illustrated by considering another publication from the Mount Rushmore National Memorial Society. Produced sometime during the early to mid 1960s, the commemorative magazine urges Americans to find strength to endure dark days.

There is a great need in every citizen of the United States to view the great memorials of their historic past, and through them to obtain a more thorough understanding and appreciation of their national heritage.

Today this need is greater than at any other time in our history. Subjected to the unrelenting threats and tensions of an uncertain world, Americans are being drawn in increasing numbers to reestablish contact with the nation's past. From this contact with the past they seek and are able to find the reassurance that through the centuries the United States has weathered every manner of upheaval. From the Revolutionary War, and internal strife during the Civil War, through two world wars and continuing cold war, it lives on today—strong and steadfast. (Mount Rushmore National Memorial Society)

On the one hand the publications of the memorial's support society, staffed by volunteers, can be said to not reflect the official agency line; visitors remain free to purchase commemorative items or not. But on the other hand, as a federal agency, the NPS wields the national power which the memorial legitimates. This becomes awkward when staff members might be personally inclined to support or attack the politically controversial agendas of other agencies. So the official response to brochures urging Americans to find strength to face the Cold War becomes an expression of neutrality, or lack of jurisdiction. Given the awkwardness of symbolic control in a society protecting freedom of religion and expression, NPS employees are justifiably uneasy about serving as the shrine of democracy's priests.

The second strategy for the production of patriotic inspiration operating at Mount Rushmore is perhaps too obvious to mention: one of recentering. Politics has always been a suspicious activity in American eyes. But in the post-Watergate era it is especially dirty business, and the space in which politics is done has become profane space, even polluted. The symbolic trajectories of this particular monument to American nationalism extend along different lines than the great monuments in the national capital. South Dakota carries something of a reputation as "the end of the world," and was even left out of the 1989 Rand MacNally atlas. But this same marginality from the centers of American power might also serve to promote patriotic connections. As one publication from the 1960s put it, Mount Rushmore is "located practically in the center of the North American continent" (Mount Rushmore National Memorial Society). This geographical centering increases the symbolic power of Mount Rushmore. Its location in the continent's heartland suggests its purifying distance from the actual centers of political power. It is far removed from the world of corruption and scandal.

In addition, unlike those memorials in Washington D.C., it appears to be rooted into place, a sculpture that has not been transformed completely from nature to culture. This fact impressed Gutzon Borglum himself, who often told visitors that the faces had always been there. They were not being *carved* into the mountain; they were being brought out. The excess stone was simply being "relieved . . . . from the head" (Fite:80). Mount Rushmore represents the ambiguity facing "nature's nation." Does the monument grow naturally out the ground, or is it a coralling and dominating of the mute earth's forces by inspired human will?

Interpreters and promoters also stress the importance of its rootedness in the earth by linking Mount Rushmore's status as sacred space to the fact that Lakotas and other native, typically more "natural," people themselves saw the Black Hills as sacred. As the *Rapid City Journal* editorialized in 1935 in the wake of appropriations for carving Lincoln:

> Years and years ago, according to old Indian legends, the Black Hills were held sacred by the Indians . . . Its mild climate and the scenic beauty appealed to the hidden religious beliefs of the savages. . . . Now, that the Black Hills have come into the hands of the white men, their value is becoming known more and more. As they served the Indians, so will they serve the folk of modern times. Many persons will find solace and comfort there after the stirring struggles of commerce. (*Rapid City Journal* 5/13/35)

More recently this connection between Lakota and white sacred space was made by the operatic singer White Eagle, whose ancestry is part Lakota and part German. Speaking and singing at the memorial's dedication July 3, 1991, he said that on his mother's Lakota side he had to view the mountain with pain. But then on his father's, German, side he hoped that all Americans might find their unity by connecting with the symbolic power of Mount Rushmore (South Dakota Public Television). His extension of welcome to all carries on the longstanding American tradition of perceiving Indian nobility and hospitality in the exchange of lands. His linking of Indian and white experience, as did the earlier editorial, provides the memorial with a meaningful past—a key problem faced by the American park movement.

The third strategy for producing patriotic inspiration at the mountain depends upon the transfer of virtue, and also stems from the staff's uneasy regard for the mountain's symbolic power. NPS employees interviewed by the author focus their programs more on the memorial's aesthetic qualities than on patriotic significance. Their public talks describe it as primarily a piece of sculpture, and only incidentally a symbol of American nationalism. They highlight the "human" dimension—telling stories of the risks taken, the tools used, and the conditions faced by the men who worked on the mountain for fourteen years.

Kim Weiser, a Black Hills native working at the memorial, spoke about how she handles her interpretive programs. For Weiser the NPS functions to preserve

> our sense of adventure, almost, the American sense of adventure. A lot of people don't get a chance to do it, you know so many people who live in cities never get a chance to put a backpack on and go out in the wilderness for a couple of days. And I think that even though we don't get a chance to do that, that it's something we want to do. You know, as far back as the 1800s when everybody started heading west, that was almost because of a sense of adventure, a restless feeling inside of them. And so I think that we Americans especially, I don't know why I say Americans especially, but it just seems that we do have a real need to get out and do something, and we need to have places to do those things in.[9]

Asked how she sees Mount Rushmore fitting in with this sense of adventure, she says "in maybe a sense that the whole idea of this place is pretty adventurous. You know the idea of climbing a sixty foot face on the mountain, and the idea of having a man hang over that mountain on a bosun's chair, that's pretty adventurous."

This sense of adventure is what she tries to instill in the visitors she meets at Mount Rushmore. She does an entire program on fear, comparing the fears faced by the presidents themselves, the much more vivid fears of those who dangled on cables, burdened with jack-hammers, chisels, and blasting caps, and the fears of her audience.[10] While de-emphasizing her capabilities as an inspirational speaker, she says she tries to "put people who are at the talk in touch with their own fears" so that they might learn to keep their fears from directing their own lives. As she says, "there are things that people can be inspired to go out and do, [to] overcome their fears or create their dreams."

Superintendent Dan Wenk gets at the same inspirational quality when he says that Mount Rushmore is worth government protection because it is a testimony to "man's achievement." As he puts it: "not many people have ever carved a mountain. Borglum I think believed that if the mind's eye could conceive it, man could achieve it."

This focus on the construction as an achievement in and of itself suggests how virtues and other sacred qualities associated with the presidents are transferred to the memorial's visitors. The conquest of fear, the pursuit of adventure, the creation of dreams, these all become available to Americans through their encounters at the memorial. It may be that few Americans aspire any longer to the public actions of a Washington or a Jefferson, but the process of transference at the memorial does not require such lofty aspirations. Rather inspirational focus is much more concrete and tangible, much more connected with everyday life.

In its inception, Mount Rushmore was a means of immortalizing the great deeds that have shaped American society. As Borglum put it the memorial would reflect "the gods who inspired them [the presidents] and the gods that they have become." The carving was to be an embodiment of their spirit. It has become the great deed in its own right however, the accomplishment of ordinary working-class Americans, the "unsung heroes" who did the drilling, jack-hammering and blasting that carved Mount Rushmore, but also built up the substance of twentieth-century America's infrastructure.

Consequently the virtues which Rushmore embodies most tangibly are not political virtues but rather productive, economic virtues. The memorial makes evident, perhaps as does no other artifact within our culture, the American imperative to give the landscape a human visage. The story detailing the memorial's carving provides Americans with a sanctification of the constructive processes by which they have transformed the landscape. The political virtues of the four "nation-builders," to use George Bush's phrase, are made available, incarnated, in the form of the building, constructing, producing done by the memorial's workers. Thus the memorial's material qualities present a model of what Americans have done through their own participation in the industrial economy.

These three strategies, symbolic limitation, transference of virtue, and recentering, may not be the only ones operating at Mount Rushmore. But they do suggest the complexity of a place that despisers of popular culture regard as simply a tourist trap. As attempts to provide an answer to the question of what Mount Rushmore means they remain only partially successful, however. The strategy of symbolic limitation would seem to account for this partial success, chalking it up to a harmonious pluralism at the heart of American civil religion. But recent decades have challenged both the existence and the hope of national consensus or harmonious pluralism.

III

How well will the strategies for producing patriotic inspiration continue to function at Mount Rushmore? This question has a bearing on current developments; the park service recently began groundbreaking for new facilities, and by time of the memorial's dedication on 3 July 1991 the Mount Rushmore National Memorial Society was well along in its $50 million fundraising drive for restoration of the sculpture and expansion of facilities. If the strategies of symbolic appropriation operating at MR are close to the ones presented here there may be some difficulties ahead in the production of patriotic inspiration.

For one, if the memorial does work by conflating political with productive virtues, and if Americans have found their own individual stories written across the skyline, this is likely to be an increasingly difficult interpretive accomplishment in a post-industrial age. Paper-pushers, video terminal operators and motel service staffs, even if inclined to seek patriotic inspiration at Mount Rushmore, may have a harder time than their steel-working, ditch-digging, dragline or chainsaw-operating parents and grandparents. How do the burdens borne by thirtysome-things with overextended credit cards relate to the risks of those who scampered across Washington's nose?

A second difficulty, interpretive conflict, may also stem from our post-industrial setting, which according to Lyotard (65) spawns an increased contentiousness over symbols which elites previously employed to promote social consensus. Certainly there have always been efforts at Mount Rushmore to delegitimate the dominant interpretations, and to offer others in their place. During the years of construction some attacked the choice of figures. In 1935 Congresswoman Caroline O'Day, Eleanor Roosevelt, and others used their influence to place feminist leader Susan B. Anthony's visage on the mountain. Borglum took their complaints seriously enough to try dissuading them with a proposal to include her statue within the mountain's never-completed hall of records (Fite:167, 206).

In recent years, however, the politics of protest have led others to engage in more direct efforts to undercut the strategies of symbolic appropriation at Mount Rushmore. American Indian activists occupied the memorial during the summer of 1971, a time when AIM and the

National Indian Youth Council were turning to re-occupation with some success at Alcatraz, the BIA offices in Washington, D.C., and elsewhere.[11] Charges that AIM members planned to cart dynamite up the mountain or pour red paint down the faces remain somewhat apocryphal. However, having renamed Rushmore "Mount Crazy Horse," it is clear that the Native American activists sought to deflate and defile the sacralized course of American history which they saw marching across Rushmore's sky-line (*Argus Leader* 1971).[12]

John Fire Lame Deer, the Lakota holy man who made the climb up to the top with the young AIM activists, grandmothers and children, expressed the ambiguity found at any sacred place, saying "one man's shrine is another man's cemetery" (93). In order to sever the harmonious connection which the memorial's promoters have cemented between the sacred space of Indians and whites, Lame Deer planted a prayer staff at the top, "in order to make the mountain sacred again." Lame Deer told a curious reporter he was "putting a blanket, or shroud, over the mountain by planting this staff, and the Presidents' faces shall remain dirty until the treaties concerning the Black Hills are fulfilled" (1972:94).

More recently, in October, 1987, Greenpeace and Earth First! activists climbed the memorial in order to drape a banner saying "We the people say no to acid rain" from George Washington's face (*Argus Leader* 1987). The symbolic action failed, those involved having wasted valuable time prior to their apprehension by the NPS in conflict over which to hang first, the hundred-foot banner or a gigantic gas mask (Scarce:166-172). While the action was incomplete, the banner itself indicates a different rationale for protest than was taken up by AIM. "We the people say no to acid rain" is not so much a defilement of the course of history enshrined at the memorial as an effort to drive an interpretive wedge between the democratic values embodied there and the productive capacity which created the mountain. The Greenpeace action, a symbolic revisioning, seemed to entail the strategic assumption that Americans would distinguish between democratic values and the post-war industrial growth which has generated acid rain. But this assumption remains questionable, since it is the productive capacity which seems to have given the memorial its power within American culture.

It was Gutzon Borglum's prayer that the presidential faces would "endure until the wind and rain alone shall wear them away" (Borglum 1930:n.p.). For many of the memorial's interpreters this permanence has implied that the values enshrined there would provoke a consensus of interpretation, extending to far future generations. Gilbert Fite, for instance, concludes his widely-regarded history:

> Regardless of the ultimate destiny of Western civilization, [Borglum's] sculpture would show succeeding generations of men that American society had reached an apex, a highpoint of material greatness. No one could doubt that a civilization which carved a mountain into the heroic likenesses of four men was one of power, audacity and importance. (238)

This brief look at the strategies used to appropriate the mountain as a symbol of American nationalism suggests that such strategies remain fragile, dependent upon social context, subject to political climate. Although the faces themselves will remain, there may be no such permanence of interpretation regarding the mountain's sacred status. The memorial's patriotic interpreters express hope that their sacred vision of America carved in stone will even endure beyond the decline of American institutions. But as Eliade suggests in his parenthetical equation of unoccupied land with "unoccupied by our own people" (31), the next occupiers may well be oblivious to what twentieth-century Americans saw as the sacred qualities of that vision.[13]

Notes

[1] Eliade's comment also serves as a good summation of more recent work done on sacred space by writers such as J.Z. Smith (1978, 1987), David Chidester, David Carrasco, and Edward Linenthal.

[2] For a narrative history of the memorial's development see Fite and R. Smith (1985).

[3] Chidester argues for considering religious action as strategic.

[4] See Shaff and Shaff, particularly chapters 15, 21, and 22, for an account of Borglum's important involvement in the rebirth of the Ku Klux Klan after WWI.

[5] Michael Kammen (444-481) presents the cultural tensions stemming from the federal government's increased role in funding and directing the preservation of collective memory during the late 1920s and the New Deal. Bodnar (169-205) focuses on the park service's role in forming a nationalized sense of public memory. For the impact of racial tensions on interpretive programs during the 1960s and 1970s, see Bodnar (198-200).

[6] Initial interviews were conducted with members of the interpretative staff by the author during the summer of 1990.

[7] Personal interview, Mt. Rushmore National Memorial, 8/24/90.

[8] The Sturgis Rally, or the "Black Hills Motor Classic" is an annual summer event, and the largest gathering of motorcyclists in the world. At its fiftieth celebration, in 1990, it drew over 350,000 people to the Hills.

[9] Personal interview, Mount Rushmore National Memorial, 8/24/90.

[10] See R. Smith (150-71) for a vivid account of the difficult conditions faced by the quarriers and miners who did the carving. The project, as with many public efforts during the Depression, was regarded as good, steady work, attracting men from across the country.

[11] For useful overviews of Native American political and religious resurgence, see Cornell and Hertzberg.

[12] Defilement is a typical maneuver employed to remove the claims of sacredness which a group attaches to a given place. Lame Deer told of a friend, "a Santee Indian who some years ago climbed up here one night a few years ago with a few friends just to pee down on the nose of one of those faces. He called it a 'symbolic gesture.' The way he told me it was quite a feat. They had to form a human

chain just to make it possible for him to do it" (91). For other examples of efforts to both defile and contain the defilement of sacred places see in general Chidester and see Linenthal (68) for a strategy similar to Lame Deer's Santee friend, performed by rock singer Ozzy Ozbourne at the Alamo.

[13] Several people offered comments contributing to this essay. I thank Catherine Albanese, Tom Tweed, Bron Taylor, and Ed Linenthal. Errors, as always, remain my own.

Works Cited

Argus Leader 1971	Sioux Falls, S.D. 6/7.
1987	10/23.
Bodnar, John 1991	*Remaking America: Public Memory, Commemoration, and Patriotism in the Twentieth Century.* Princeton: Princeton University Press.
Borglum, Gutzon 1930	"First Survey and the Development of the Memorial." In *Mount Rushmore National Memorial: A Monument Commemorating the Conception, Preservation and Growth of the Great American Republic.* Mount Rushmore National Memorial Commission. Peter Norbeck Papers, University of South Dakota Archives.
1931	"Colossal Sculpture: Its Value to Civilization." In *Mount Rushmore National Memorial, Jefferson Number.* Mount Rushmore National Memorial Society. Norbeck Papers.
Bush, George 1991	"Remarks on the Fiftieth Anniversary of the Mount Rushmore National Memorial in the Black Hills of South Dakota, 7/3/91." *Weekly Compilation of Presidential Documents: Administration of George Bush.* Vol. 27. Washington, DC: GPO.
Carrasco, David 1987	"Myth, Cosmic Terror, and the Templo Mayor." In *The Great Temple of Tenotchtitlan,* 124-162. Ed. by Johanna Brody, David Carrasco, and Eduardo Matos Moctezuma. Berkeley: University of California Press.
Chidester, David 1988	*Salvation by Suicide: An Interpretation of Jim Jones, the People Temple, and Jonestown.* Bloomington: University of Indiana Press.
Cornell, Stephen 1988	*The Return of the Native: American Indian Political Resurgence.* New York: Oxford University Press.
Eliade, Mircea 1959	*The Sacred and the Profane: The Nature of Religion.* New York: Harper and Row.
Fite, Gilbert C. 1952	*Mount Rushmore.* Norman: University of Oklahoma Press.

Hertzberg, Hazel W.
1971
The Search for an American Indian Identity. Syracuse: Syracuse University Press.

Kammen, Michael
1991
The Mystic Chords of Memory: The Transformation of Tradition in American Culture. New York: Alfred A. Knopf.

Lame Deer, John Fire, and Richard Erodes
1972
Lame Deer, Seeker of Visions: The Life of a Sioux Medicine Man. New York: Simon and Schuster.

Linenthal, Edward
1991
Sacred Ground: Americans and Their Battlefields. Urbana: University of Illinois Press.

Lipsitz, George
1990
"Precious and Communicable: History in an Age of Popular Culture." In *Time Passages: Collective Memory and American Popular Culture,* 21-39. Minneapolis: University of Minnesota Press.

Lyotard, Jean-Francois
1984
The Postmodern Condition: A Report on Knowledge. Minneapolis: University of Minnesota Press.

Mount Rushmore National Memorial Society
n.d.
Mount Rushmore National Memorial: The Shrine of Democracy. Norbeck Papers.

Rapid City Journal
1935
Rapid City, S.D.

Robinson, Doane
1931
"The History of the Memorial." In *Mount Rushmore National Memorial: Jefferson Number.* Mount Rushmore National Memorial Society. Norbeck Papers.

1941
"The Greatest Democrats." In *Mount Rushmore National Memorial: Shrine of Democracy.* Mount Rushmore National Memorial Commission. Norbeck Papers.

Scarce, Rik
1990
Eco-warriors: Understanding the Radical Environmental Movement. Chicago: Noble.

Schwartz, Barry
1987
George Washington: The Making of an American Symbol. Athens, GA: University of Georgia Press.

Shaff, Howard, and Audrey Karl
1985
Six Wars at a Time: The Life and Times of Gutzon Borglum, Sculptor of Mount Rushmore. Sioux Falls: Center for Western Studies.

Smith, Jonathan Z.
1978
Map Is not Territory. The Hague: Leyden and Brill.

1987
To Take a Place: Toward Theory in Ritual. Chicago: University of Chicago Press.

Smith, Rex Allen
1985
The Carving of Mount Rushmore. New York: Abbeville.

South Dakota
Public Television
1991
"Mount Rushmore's Golden Anniversary."

Zelinsky, Wilbur
1988
Nation into State: The Shifting Symbolic Foundations of American Nationalism. Chapel Hill: University of North Carolina Press.

Understanding the Text

1. Glass refers to the various competing interpretations of Mt. Rushmore. Briefly describe those of Gutzon Borglum and John Fire Lame Deer.

2. According to Glass, how do the National Park Service employees at Mt. Rushmore view their role at the site? Does Glass fully agree with their view? Why or why not?

3. According to Glass, which virtues are most evident at Mt. Rushmore?

The Rhetoric of Imperialism in the Lewis and Clark Journals: The Trope of Surveillance[1]

Joan K. W. Dolence

Joan W. K. Dolence earned her M.A. in English at South Dakota State University and has taught English there and at the University of Wisconsin at Green Bay. She also has worked as a writer and editor for a variety of publications and institutions.

In *The Rhetoric of Empire,* David Spurr's discussion of the trope of surveillance found in journalism, travel writing, and imperial administration focuses on three objects Western travel writers have set their eyes and pens upon: landscapes, interiors, and bodies. To report on any of the three, the traveler must survey them first by assuming a position of detachment from which to observe and judge the scene. Spurr suggests that this "commanding view" offers "aesthetic pleasure on one hand, information and authority on the other." The explorer delights in both the data gathered and the visual control he or she wields over the subject, object, or vista. "At the same time the commanding view is an originating gesture of colonization itself, making possible the exploration and mapping of territory which serves as the preliminary to a colonial order" (15-16).

To illustrate the trope of surveillance as writers use it to describe non-Western landscapes, Spurr turns to Mary Louise Pratt's definition of the "monarch-of-all-I-survey" scene included in much mid-nineteenth century travel and adventure writing. Pratt explains that in writing the "monarch-of-all-I-survey" scene, the explorer/writer records the landscape by employing different types of descriptions which, combined, create measurable meaning and value for future readers of the explorer's account. The writer first draws the scene in painterly terms—the lens fills with lush images conveyed in writing through excessive use of adjectives to modify the objects viewed. The view brings such delight to the writer and to the reader that

Two chapters from Master's Thesis by Joan K. W. Dolence. Reprinted by permission of the author.

the voyage is rendered worthwhile simply for the pleasure of seeing or reading about the scene. The writer also commands the view—the images the writer conveys through words and how the writer orders the landscape constitute the extent of the scene's meaning. As far as the reader knows, the writer's account represents all that exists in the landscape (Pratt 204-05).

In mapping the use of this trope, Pratt quotes from British explorer Richard Burton's description of his discovery of Lake Tanganyika in *The Lake Regions of Central Africa: A Picture of Exploration* (1860). Burton writes, "Nothing in sooth could be more picturesque than this first view of the Tanganyika Lake, as it lay in the lap of the mountains, basking in the gorgeous tropical sunshine." He describes "glistening yellow sand," and "waters . . . of the lightest and softest blue," as well as "steel-coloured mountains, here flecked and capped with pearly mist, there standing sharply pencilled against the azure air" (qtd. in Pratt 201-02). Burton's effusive descriptive style never betrays his physical condition as he takes in the view: too ill to walk, he was carried to the site by the native guides in his employ. Thus, Pratt writes, "discovery, in this context consisted of a gesture of converting local knowledges (discourses) into European national and continental knowledges associated with European forms and relations of power" (202). Although the guides do the work, Burton, in writing about his "discovery," receives the credit for it.

Despite Burton's insistence that "Nothing . . . could be more picturesque than [his] first view" of the lake, he does not hesitate to suggest improvements:

> Villages, cultivated lands, the frequent canoes of the fishermen upon the shore, give a something of variety, of movement, of life to the landscape, which, like all the fairest prospects in these regions, wants but a little of the neatness and finish of art—mosques and kiosks, palaces and villas, gardens and orchards—contrasting with the profuse lavishness and magnificence of nature . . . . (qtd. in Pratt 202)

Although Burton views the landscape as beautiful and potentially exploitable (farmers, fishermen, and villagers bustle below), he proposes changes that would add order and a touch of "art" to what he considers wilderness.

Spurr further illustrates Pratt's "monarch-of-all-I-survey" scene through a description of landscape included in journalist and explorer Henry Morton Stanley's 1871 writings about the interior of Africa, *Despatches to the New York Herald* (reprinted in 1970). Stanley adopts much the same expansive yet authoritative style as Burton, writing, "if you look to the west, you will see Unyamwezi recede into the far blue, mysterious distance in a succession of blue waves of noble forest, rising and subsiding like the blue waves of an ocean . . ." (qtd. in Spurr 17). From above, "Stanley's eye . . . ranges freely over the scene, providing general outline and points of focus, bringing about spatial order from a fixed point of view" (Spurr 17). Like

Burton, he adds to this foreign scene sights more familiar to the Western imagination: "Hills of syenite are seen dotting the vast prospect, like islands in the sea, presenting in their external appearance, to an imaginative eye, rude imitations of castellated fortresses and embattled towers" (qtd. in Spurr 17). While Burton's "mosques and kiosks, palaces and villas, gardens and orchards" bring to mind cultured order, Stanley's "castellated fortresses and embattled towers" endow the scene with "a strategic value . . . showing that it could be held, safeguarded, protected" (Spurr 18). By adding these familiar images to the scenes, both Burton and Stanley infuse their descriptions with significant meaning to the Western reader.

Although Lewis and Clark wrote their journals more than a half century before those of the adventurers Pratt cites and almost seventy years before Stanley described Unyamwezi, the "rhetoric of presence" (Pratt 205) apparent in the "monarch-of-all-I-survey" scene is evident in their field notes written during the summer and fall of 1804. In this passage dated July 4, 1804, Clark looks out over the landscape and describes the following scene:

> We camped in the plain ² one of the most butifull Plains, I ever Saw, Open & butifully diversified with hills and vallies all presenting themselves to the river . . . a handsom Creek meandering thro at this place . . . . the Plains of this countrey are covered with Leek Green Grass, well calculated for the sweetest and most nourishing hay—interspersed with cops [copses]³ of trees, Spreding their lofty branchs over Pools Springs or Brooks of fine water. Groops of Shrubs covered with the most delicious froot is to be seen in every direction, and nature appears to have exerted herself to butify the Senery by the variety of flours Delicately and highly flavered raised above the Grass, which Strikes and profumes the Sensation, and amuses the mind throws it into Conjectering the cause of So magnificent a Senery . . . in a Country thus Situated far removed from the Sivilised world to be enjoyed by nothing but the Buffalo Elk Deer & Bear in which it abounds & . . . Savage Indians. (Moulton 2: 346-47)

In this scene, Clark personifies nature as having put forth extra effort in order to "profume the Sensation, and amuse the mind." In wondering why this splendid scene is wasted on the beasts and the "Savage Indians," he communicates his good fortune at having happened upon the view and arouses the reader's desire to participate in the splendor. Clark, therefore, accomplishes the first mode of description in Pratt's "monarch-of-all-I-survey" scene—he offers an aesthetic representation of the landscape and suggests that experiencing such a scene is well worth the trip.

In describing this experience, Clark spares no modifiers. He crowds the landscape with lofty trees, handsome waters, delicious fruits, and delicate flowers; this overabundant land cries to the "sivilized" world to experience it. Also reflected in Clark's reading of the landscape are the values the explorer brings to his enterprise. He laments that "nothing but" the wildlife and the "Savage Indians" can experience such a scene every day. What Clark feels privileged to see and enjoy, this statement suggests, cannot be seen or enjoyed in the same way by the natives of the region. Ironically, Pratt points out that aside from the effort expended to reach a natural wonder, the act of "discovering" really consists of a rather passive experience—seeing. Only in writing down observations and publishing them back home do explorers truly "discover."[4] And the thing discovered consists, in most cases, of something the natives have known for years, something they had "discovered" long ago (Pratt 202), as with Burton's "discovery" of Lake Tanganyika. In the "monarch-of-all-I-survey" scene, then, "the esthetic qualities of the landscape constitute the social and material value of the discovery to the explorers' home culture, at the same time as its esthetic deficiencies suggest a need for social and material intervention by the home culture" (Pratt 205). This example from Clark's notes reveals both the beauty of the Missouri River plains and the need for someone to appreciate that beauty—specifically, civilized, white Americans.

In his "Instructions to Captain Lewis" (1803), Thomas Jefferson directed Lewis and Clark to employ the commanding view in order to survey the West with the goal of discovering "for the purposes of commerce" a direct water route to the Pacific:

> Beginning at the mouth of the Missouri, you will take observations of latitude and longitude at all the remarkable points on the river, & especially at mouths of rivers, at rapids, at islands & other places & objects distinguished by such natural marks & characters of durable kind, as that they may with certainty be recognized hereafter . . . . Other objects worthy of notice will be the soil & face of the country, its growth & vegetable productions . . . . the animals of the country . . . . The remains & accounts of any which may be deemed rare or extinct; the mineral productions of every kind . . . . climate as characterized by the thermometer . . . . the dates at which particular plants put forth and lose their flowers, or leaf, times of appearance of particular birds, reptiles or insects . . . . the character and extent of the country watered by [the Missouri's] branches, and especially on it's southern side. (Jefferson 1127-29)

Jefferson instructed the captains to survey (using compass, sextant, etc.) the entire route and note every thing and everyone they saw (1127). In mapping the West, Lewis and Clark followed Jefferson's orders. They also followed geographical precedent by employing the trope of surveillance in their expedition journals. John Logan Allen, a geographer and the author of *Passage Through the Garden: Lewis and Clark and the Image of the American Northwest* (1975), contends that most adventurers enter into their journeys with the ideological aims of "those who seek to have blank spaces on the map filled" in mind. Explorers, therefore, cannot "be separated from the greater historical realities of their time and place" (xiii). The greater historical reality of the early nineteenth century included fierce competition between Britain, France, Spain, Russia, and the United States for control of the lucrative fur trade in the American West (Allen 40-41, 64), and the equally competitive rush to discover an easy water route across the continent in order to facilitate trade with the Orient.

With these pressures in mind, we should not be surprised to find the trope of surveillance in Lewis and Clark's journals of 1804. During this period, although the expedition covered previously mapped territory, most members of the group experienced the region for the first time. Lewis spent the summer and fall identifying and describing the flora and fauna of the region, taking celestial readings, and fixing the expedition's longitude and latitude as the group proceeded up the river. In addition to assisting Lewis with these tasks, Clark wrote daily entries in the expedition journals describing the group's progress and activities; he also began work on a map of the Missouri River, its tributaries, and the adjacent lands. When the expedition halted on July 23, 1804, to refresh the men and dry some of the provisions, Clark reported: "commenced Coppying my map of the river to Send to the Presdt. of U S." (Moulton 2: 415). Surveying was a requirement of the expedition and both Lewis and Clark spent time walking along the shore, later transferring what they saw into written and pictorial descriptions of the landscape.

In his discussion of surveillance, Spurr recognizes that seeing and naming that which exists around you is less than an innocent act. "It is, on the contrary, a mode of thinking and writing wherein the world is radically transformed into an object of possession . . . . The writer's eye is always in some sense colonizing the landscape, mastering and portioning, fixing zones and poles . . ." (27). Lewis and Clark undertook this very task as they moved north and west against the current of the Missouri River. In many journal entries they succeed in colonizing the landscape, reconceptualizing unfamiliar territory into organized, familiar, pastoral scenes. On June 19, 1804, Clark noted that "the Lands on the North Side of the river is rich and Sufficiently high to afford Settlements" (Moulton 2: 309), and on July 2, he reported that "The french formerly had a Fort at this place, to protect the trade of this nation, the Situation appears to be a verry eligable one for a Town, the valley rich & extensive, with a Small Brook Meanding [meandering] through it and one part of the bank affording yet a good Landing for Boats" (2: 341). Several days later, on July 7, 1804, Clark remarked that the expedition "passed a butifull Prarie on the right Side which extends back, those Praries has much the appearance from the river of farms, Divided by narrow Strips of woods" (2: 355); and previously, on June 16, he had taken note of "a Kind of Grass resembling Timothey which appeared well calculated for Hay" (2: 304). In organizing the landscape this way, Lewis and Clark succeed in producing a perceptual map of the area, a map filled with towns, farms, and fields suitable for cultivation.

Lewis and Clark's journals of this period also reflect their tendency to survey the area with a view toward establishing commercial and military structures. On June 28, 1804, Clark wrote that "the high lands Coms to the river Kanses on the upper Side at about a mile, full in view, and a butifull place for a fort" (Moulton 2: 327). Similarly, on July 4, 1804, Clark noted that they encamped in an area once occupied by a large group of Kansas Indians. He wrote,

"I observed Spring braking out of the bank, a good Situation for a fort on a hill at the upper part" (2: 348). Four days earlier, in describing the Little Shoal River in present-day Platte County, Missouri, Clark envisioned the area's potential for commercial success. He reported that "this river is about 70 yds. Wide and has Several rapids & falls, well Calculated for mills" (2: 333). After a peaceful council with the Oto and Missouri Indians, in a long journal entry dated August 3, 1804, Clark considered the possibilities of white settlements of many types in the area:

> The Situation of this place which we Call *Council Bluff* which is handsom ellevated a Spot well Calculated for a Tradeing establishment, the Bank high & leavel on top well Calculated for a fort to Command the Countery and river the low bottom above high water & well Situated under the Command of the Hill for Houses to trade with the Natives a butifull Plain both above and below . . . . those Bluffs afford good Clay for Brick . . . . the Situation I am informed is, within 1 Days march of the Ottoes, 1½ of the Panieas, 2 of the Mahars, & 2½ of the Loups Villages, also Convenient to the roveing Bands of Soux, Those people are now at war with each other, an establishment here would bring about peace and be the means of Keeping of it. (Clark's emphasis, Moulton 2: 440)

Jefferson initially planned to designate the lands west of the Mississippi River an extensive reservation for eastern tribes. After serving as both employees (trappers) and consumers in the American fur trade, they would settle into farming communities and "become civilized, so that they could be incorporated into the body politic" (Ambrose 57). According to Ambrose, Jefferson envisioned only the eventual settlement of white farmers into the area (57). He took it for granted that whites already living west of the Mississippi River would gladly move east, and that American Indians both east and west of the Mississippi would not resist this imposition of "order" upon their land and way of life. Regardless, it was Jefferson's vision of an agrarian West filled with trading houses and policed by the military that Lewis and Clark had in mind as they surveyed and mapped this section of the Missouri River and its adjacent lands.

The trope of surveillance and the "monarch-of-all-I-survey" scene reveal the explorer's joy at "discovering" the view described; they also reveal the explorer's suggestions for its improvement. In either case, writers of these accounts assert their authority over the landscape. As Spurr suggests, "The writer literally sees the landscape of the non-Western world in terms either of the promise for westernized development or of the disappointment of that promise" (19). The journalist/explorer assumes the power to pass judgment over the landscape, to view it primarily in terms of its usefulness to the culture he represents.

Spurr writes that "the gaze of the Western writer penetrates the interiors of human habitation, and it explores the bodies and faces of people with the same freedom it brings to the survey of a landscape" (19). While their gazes penetrate native buildings and faces with great freedom, explorers who survey territory in order to possess it, find it more convenient in their writings to ignore native habitations and native bodies or to acknowledge them as deserted or depraved. If the landscape contains few dwellings, and if those dwellings sit abandoned by their inhabitants because of a nomadic lifestyle or a dramatic decline in population, the explorer can render the land open and ready for use. Pratt writes:

> The European improving eye produces subsistence habitats as "empty" landscapes, meaningful only in terms of their potential for producing a marketable surplus. From the vantage point of their inhabitants, of course, these same spaces are lived as intensely humanized, saturated with local history and meaning, where plants, creatures, and geographical formations have names, uses, symbolic functions, histories, places in indigenous knowledge formations. (61)

Two entries from August 14, 1804, reveal the tendency of Lewis and Clark to produce the landscape as empty and to ignore the importance native inhabitants placed on the spaces they occupied. In these entries, Clark discusses the plight of the much-reduced Mahar (Omaha) Indians, whom the expedition hoped to meet. After sending a party out to talk with the Mahars in their nearby village and finding no one around, Clark wrote, "The Situation of this Village, now in ruins Siround by . . . [innumerable] hosts of graves[s] the ravages of the Small Pox (4 years ago) they follow the Buf: and tend no Corn" (Moulton 2: 478). In the second passage for that day, Clark continues his description of the Mahars and their town:

> Those people haveing no houses no Corn or any thing more than the graves of their ancestors to attach them to the old Village, Continue in pursuite of the Buffalow longer than others who had greater attachments to their native Village—the ravages of the Small Pox (which Swept off 400 men & women & Children . . .) has reduced this nation not exceeding 300 men and left them to the insults of their weaker neighbours which before was glad to be on friendly turms with them— I am told whin this fatal malady was among them they Carried ther franzey to verry extroadinary length, not only of burning their Village, but they put their wives & Children to *D[e]ath* with a view of their all going together to Some better Countrey— They burry their Dead on the tops of hills and rais mounds on the top of them,— The cause or way those people took the Small Pox is uncertain, the most Probable from Some other Nation by means of a warparty. (Clark's emphasis, Moulton 2: 479)

Clark's reading of the landscape focuses on the lack of importance the Mahars place on their land based on the absence of crops and the preponderance of graves. The Mahars' semi-nomadic lifestyle, the idea that having lost so many of their people to disease they now "follow the Buf: and tend no Corn," suggests to Clark that they have few ties to their old village— graves alone not serving, in Clark's mind, as ties as strong as houses or corn. The Mahars' stereotypically "savage" response to the devastation of disease—the killing of their own women and children—suggests as well that they lack the self-control and reason to determine their own fate; as Clark points out, even their former, weaker friends now seek to control them. He depicts the Mahars as a group to be dominated. In the August 3, 1804, entry above, Clark envisions Council Bluff as the perfect spot from which to control the military and economic affairs of the Indians. The Mahars' burning or abandonment (even seasonal abandonment) of their villages, as Clark tells it, lends support to the captains' view that this territory lay open and in need of American intervention.

On August 11, just three days before Clark witnessed the remains of the Omaha village described above, the expedition came across the mound grave of the Omaha chief, Blackbird, and, in a gesture of respect marked nonetheless by proprietary undertones, they raised a white flag bound in red, white, and blue atop the mound. Blackbird, "a notorious character along the Missouri, noted for his friendship with white traders and his strong rule over his own people" (Moulton 2: 470), had died of smallpox four years earlier. Clark's remark in the August 14 entry that the Omaha had probably contracted smallpox from other war parties reveals his assumption that regardless of the Omahas' well-known and frequent trade with whites (according to Gary Moulton, "Legend has it that [Blackbird] was buried seated on the back of his horse, on the hilltop where he used to watch for the coming of his friends the traders" [2: 470]), the Omahas contracted smallpox from warring Indians, not the white traders who introduced the disease. By the time the expedition passed the Omaha village, smallpox had so reduced the tribe that "Thereafter they did not appear as an obstacle to white expansion" (Moulton 2: 482). Lewis and Clark expected to meet the powerful Omaha nation headed by powerful men, but their view of the empty, burnt-out village offered more support to their impression of the area as one available for American settlement.

In discussing nineteenth-century European travelers to South America, Pratt observes that the men who traveled in search of commercial opportunities spent much time surveying landscapes (potential resources) and people (a potential work force), but little time surveying interiors. In accounts written by these men who sought to "collect and possess everything," she writes, "one is hard pressed indeed to find even an interior description of a house" (159). This holds true of Lewis and Clark's journals from the summer and fall of 1804. Several possible reasons for this exist: members of the expedition spent most of their time outside, in their boats or walking and camping along the shore; in addition, relatively few intact dwellings existed along the way to describe, particularly in proportion to landscapes. However, of the possible interiors—the houses of St. Charles and La Charette (two of the westernmost white settlements on the Missouri River), the villages of the Yankton and Teton Sioux, or the permanent dwellings of the Arikara and Hidatsa villages—they described very few. For example, although Lewis and Clark dined in the home of a St. Charles family (that of François Duquette, originally from Canada [Moulton 1: 234]), Clark limited his May 16, 1804, description to the following: "This village Contns. About 100 houses, the most of them Small and indefferent and about 450 inhabitants Cheifly French, those people appear pore, polite & harmonious."

About Duquette's household specifically, Clark merely wrote, "he has a Charming wife an eligent Situation on the hill Serounded by orchards & a excellent gardain" (Moulton 2: 233).

Unlike Clark, Lewis included a lengthy description of St. Charles in his notes, although, like Clark, he too failed to describe a single interior. Lewis's description, however, proves interesting both for its rarity (Clark wrote most of the surviving journal entries covering the summer and fall of 1804) and for its insight into Lewis's prejudices even in regard to the white inhabitants the expedition met. On May 20, 1804, Lewis wrote:

> The Vilage contains a Chappel, one hundred dwelling houses, and about 450 inhabitants; their houses are generally small and but illy constructed; a great majority of the inhabitants are miserably pour, illiterate and when at home excessively lazy, tho' they are polite hospitable and by no means deficient in point of natural genious, they live in a perfect state of harmony among each other; and plase as implicit confidence in doctrines of their speritual pastor, the Roman Catholic priest, as they yeald passive obedience to the will of their temporal master the commandant [JW: Charles Tayon, the Spanish authority in the town]. a small garden of vegetables is the usual extent of their cultivation, and this is commonly imposed on the old men and boys; the men in the vigor of life consider the cultivation of the earth a degrading occupation, and in order to gain the necessary subsistence for themselves and families, either undertake hunting voyages on their own account, or engage themselves as hirelings to such persons as possess sufficient capital to extend their traffic to the natives of the interior parts of the country; on these voyages in either case, they are frequently absent from their families or homes the term of six twelve or eighteen months and alwas subjected to severe and incessant labour, exposed to the ferocity of the lawless savages, the vicissitudes of weather and climate, and dependent on chance or accident alone for food, raiment or relief in the event of malady. These people are principally the decendants of the Canadian French, and it is not an inconsiderable proportion of them that can boast a small dash of the pure blood of the aborigenees of America. (Moulton 2: 241-42).

Perhaps in preparation for the ethnographic notes he would take along the journey, Lewis here focuses on the character of the town and its people, not the physical nature of the dwellings. About the people he comments that "when at home" the men appear "excessively lazy," and then enumerates the hardships and the "severe and incessant labour" they endure while out hunting on their own or trading with the Indians. Lewis's interpretation of the townspeople's excessive laziness, docility, and gullibility translates into a need for intervention from efficient, agrarian Americans. Pratt finds a similar tendency among the "capitalist vanguard" in South America—Europeans who went to South America in the nineteenth century as advance-men for their companies in order to scout out territory appropriate for exploitation. Writing about this group, she asserts that "Ideologically, the vanguard's task is to reinvent America as backward and neglected, to encode its non-capitalist landscapes and societies as manifestly in need of the rationalized exploitation the Europeans bring" (152). The mixed-blooded inhabitants of St. Charles, like the Mahar Indians, seem to prize superstition (in the form of the Catholic Church) and senseless labor in the wilderness over sedentary agriculture—the American ideal in Jefferson's eyes. As with the Mahars, the United States could easily contain the residents of St. Charles and transfer their lands to more useful purposes—trading, farming, and fort-building.

In his description of St. Charles, Lewis focuses attention on the character of the mixed-blooded people. Spurr makes several points about the surveillance of non-Western bodies (whether native or of mixed-blood) by journalists, travel writers, and imperial administrators. He points out that "primitives" are known for their bodies. Clark's remark that "nothing but the Buffalo Elk Deer & Bear . . . & . . . Savage Indians" (Moulton 2: 346-47) have the good fortune of enjoying the beautiful plains of the "uncivilized" lower Missouri, categorizes the "Savage Indians" with the beasts Jefferson sent the expedition to collect and describe. Further, the observer tends to either inspect the non-Western body closely, moving from part to part, detail to detail (as one would describe a landscape), or to view the body hastily and then dismiss it in favor of the surrounding landscape (Spurr 22-23). The writer's close inspection of the non-Western body renders that body a possession—something to be objectified or aestheticized—while hasty dismissal of the non-Western body in favor of the landscape shows the importance in the Western mind of the latter over the former.

Most of Lewis and Clark's remarks about bodies focus on either the absence of bodies—Indians dead from disease and war or absent on the hunt; the composition of bodies—what people look like and how they dress (along with some judgment about the quality of their bodies); and, counter to Spurr's generalized rhetors of imperialism, the captains' very real concern about bodies watching them—their realization of the possible resistance their journey into the contact zone will provoke. In the fall of 1804, Clark makes frequent mention of Indians lining the banks to observe them, particularly after several dangerous encounters with the Teton Sioux in which both the Sioux and members of the expedition drew their weapons and prepared to fight.

Early in the summer of 1804, however, Lewis and Clark focused more often on the absence of people on the plains because of disease, war, or summer hunting, as with the Mahars above. Descriptions of human absence accompany descriptions of the beauty of the plains, allowing for the possibility of Western enjoyment of the area without the interference of native "intruders." One entry by Clark representative of this mode of description appears in his writings for June 13, 1804. As the expedition passed through present north-central Missouri, Clark described the plight of the Missouri Indians who had lived along the river in Missouri as late as 1798. After passing two creeks, he wrote:

> between those Creeks . . . is a butifull Prarie, in which the antient Missourie Indians had a Village, at this place 300 of them were killed by the Saukees, a fair Day . . . . this nation once the Most Noumerous is now almost extinct, about 30 of them, living with Otteaus on the R. Platt, the remainder all distroyed . . . . a Butifull open Prarie Coms to the river below its mouth, we landed and walked to the hills which is abt. ½ a mile. The Lower prarie over flows. The hunters Killd. a Bare and Dere, this is a butifull place the Prarie rich & extinsive . . . . (Moulton 2: 295-96)

Clark juxtaposes the Missouri's exit from the land with a discussion of the area's beauty, absentmindedly dismissing the Sauks' killing of 300 Missouris with the day's weather report: "a fair day." In "The Problem of the Discoverer's Authority in Lewis and Clark's *History*" (1991), literary critic Bruce Greenfield asserts that Lewis and Clark's "descriptions of Indian cultures show a strong tendency to coalesce around theories in which their decline was inevitable, and the whole process appeared as a natural rather than a political phenomenon" (18). The movement of the Missouris up the river to live with the Otos, who are themselves "declineing," in Clark's words, leaves this beautiful plain uninhabited and therefore available for American enjoyment.

When Indian peoples present themselves to Lewis and Clark, the captains either dismiss them with only a mention or they include a full description of the bodies. Of the important Teton Sioux, for instance, Clark wrote the following lengthy description:

> Those people are Spritely Small legs ille looking Set men perticularly, they grease & Black themselves when they dress, make use of Hawks feathers about their heads, cover with a Roab each a polecat Skin to hold their Smokeables, fond of Dress. Badly armed. Ther women appear verry well, fin[e] Teeth, High Cheek [bones] Dress in Skin Peticoats . . . . they doe all the Laborious work, and I may say are perfect Slaves to their husbands . . . as all Squars of nations much at war, or where the womin are more noumerous than the men. (Moulton 3: 115-17)

Clark moves from part to part, focusing on the clothing the Teton men and women wear and the fact that they are "badly armed." The conclusion he draws about the flashy but poorly armed men and the status of women in "nations much at war" registers what Pratt calls the "normalizing, generalizing voice of the ethnographic manners-and-customs portrait." The writer of such a description:

> is distinct from, but complementary to, the landscape narrator. Both are authorized by the global project of natural history: one produces land as landscape and territory, scanning for prospects; the other produces the indigenous inhabitants as bodyscapes, scanned also for prospects. Together they dismantle the socioecological web that preceded them and install a

Eurocolonial discursive order whose territorial and visual forms of authority are those of the modern state. Abstracted away from the landscape that is under contention, indigenous people are abstracted away from the history that is being made—a history into which Europeans intend to reinsert them as an exploited labor pool. (64-65)

In the case of Lewis and Clark, Jefferson hoped to use the Indians not only as an exploited labor pool (to gather furs, act as guides, and, eventually, farm the land), but as an exploited customer base for American products in American trading posts. And while the women show diligence and allegiance—acting as "perfect Slaves" to the men, the Teton men, who repeatedly challenge Lewis and Clark with demands for gifts and rides on the keelboat, and with the might of their warriors, must, according to Lewis and Clark, be controlled in order for the United States to run a successful trade operation in the West. In a letter dated July 20, 1806, written to North West Company trader Hugh Heney, Lewis and Clark argue that "until some effectual measure be taken to render them pacific," the Sioux would continue to threaten traders on the upper Missouri River (Ronda 41). Lewis and Clark surveyed the Teton Sioux with trade considerations in mind, and they reflect these considerations in their descriptions of Sioux bodies.

After challenges to their authority by Teton Sioux chiefs and warriors, Lewis and Clark modified their interactions with the Indians they met. Clark's entries of September and October, 1804, reflect these changes. No longer eager to hold prolonged meetings with groups of (mainly) Sioux, and anxious to reach the Mandan villages before the onset of winter, they hurried past groups of Indians intent on getting the expedition's attention. And while they had been cautious of possible attack all through the summer and fall, the large number of Indian "spectators" along the Missouri River banks seems to have magnified the captains' worries—in the late fall of 1804, the surveyors, Lewis and Clark, become intensely aware of being surveyed.

On September 29, 1804, just two days after leaving the Teton Sioux, Lewis and Clark set off from their camp located between present-day Sully and Stanley counties, South Dakota. According to Clark, the group:

> had not proceeded on far before we discovered an Indn. Running after us, he . . . requested to come on bord and go up to the *recorees* [JW: Arikaras] we refused to take any of that band on board . . . . Soon after I discovered on the hills at a great distance great numbers of Indians which appeared to be making to the river above us, we proceeded on under a Double reafed Sail. (Clark's emphasis, Moulton 3: 129)

In the same entry, Clark reported seeing two more Indians who "looked at us . . . about ½ an hour & went over the hills." He closed the entry by noting, "a verrey Cold evening, all on ou[r] guard" (3: 130). Several days later, on October 2, 1804, the expedition again passed a group of Indians on the banks of the Missouri and Clark wrote, "one Came to the river & fired off his gun and asked us to come he wish us to go to his Camp near at hand we refused, passed a large Island . . . here we expected the Tetons would attempt to Stop us, and prepared for action" (Moulton 3: 138). Incidents such as these occurred frequently during the weeks following the expedition's departure from the Teton Sioux—Indians attempted to get the expedition's attention and the expedition largely ignored them or gave them bits of tobacco or a bite to eat and then moved on. These entries show the haste with which Lewis and Clark pushed up the river toward the Arikara, Mandan, and Hidatsa villages, and the suspicions they harbored against the Tetons. Writing about this segment of the journey, Ronda suggests that Lewis and Clark's awareness that "they would soon be with the Arikaras did not allay the ever present dread of Teton ambush" (43). Although the captains found their fears unfulfilled, they nonetheless maintained a heightened sense of their vulnerable position on the river with unknown numbers of Indians just beyond the banks. Aware of others watching them, they did not pause to do the same.

The feeling of threat did not diminish as Lewis and Clark came upon the first populated Arikara village on an island near present-day Mobridge, South Dakota. On October 9, 1804, Clark noted that, "Great numbers of those People came on the Island to See us pass . . . . all things arranged both for Peace or War" (Moulton 3: 152). Clark's awareness of native surveillance continued as the captains waited for the weather to improve so they could meet with the Arikara chiefs. On October 10, 1804, Clark wrote, "many Came to view us all day, much asstonished at my black Servent, who did not lose the oppertunity of his powers . . . .This nation never Saw a black man before" (3: 155). Even among the Arikara, members of the expedition felt themselves watched by the Indians they had come to observe.

After a successful meeting with the Arikara and upon the expedition's departure from them, Clark set down his description of the group. He wrote:

> The Ricaras Are about 500 men . . . able to bear arms, and the remains of ten different tribes of Panias reduced by the Small Pox & war[s] with the Sioux, they are tall Stout men corsily featured, their womin Small & industerous raise great quantities of corn beans &c also Tobacco for the men to Smoke, they collect all the wood and doe the Drudgery common amongst Savages . . . .They are Dirty, Kind, pore, & extravegent; possessing natural pride, no begers, rcive what is given them with pleasure . . . . (Moulton 3: 161-62)

Clark implicitly compares the Arikaras, who gratefully receive what the captains give them, with the Teton Sioux, who seemed always to ask for something more. He does, however, come to a similar conclusion about the Arikara women as he had about the Teton Sioux—they act as slaves to the men. These "Dirty, Kind, pore, and extravegent" people posed less of a threat to the captains than did the aggressive Sioux, and Clark takes the time to describe them carefully (he had described the Sioux carefully as well, but had then quickly moved on, ignoring the many individual Sioux who came to the River to see the expedition). In describing the Arikaras, Clark again employs his ethnographic "manner- and-customs" description, just as he had employed the "monarch-of-all-I-survey" scene in his descriptions of land. In both cases, he assumes the authority to survey and judge—to measure what is good and useful about the people and to decide what should be changed in order to adapt them to the American agrarian ideal.

As they approached the Mandan villages in present-day North Dakota, then, Lewis and Clark surveyed landscapes and bodyscapes and infused them with meaning for future readers of their accounts—placing a farm here and a fort or mill there, judging one tribe dirty and poor and another handsome and dangerous. They did not show much interest in interiors, preferring instead to point out the considerable seasonal and permanent abandonment of once-populated landscapes and the beauty and richness of the land. Increased awareness of the natives' eyes watching them during this period changed (at least temporarily) the captains' way of interacting with the natives they saw, causing them to practice stricter caution and greater haste when confronted by Indians—particularly the Teton Sioux. While writers often depict the expedition's encounters with the Teton Sioux as situations during which the expedition dominated the Indians, the captains' awareness (revealed in their journal entries) of both native presence and native power to threaten the expedition's success and the lives of its members offers a more realistic image of relations in this contact zone.

CONCLUSION

I have argued that in writing their journals, Lewis and Clark employed imperialist rhetoric. Of course, they were not the first to do so. They followed a long line of explorers, diplomats, scientists, and colonial administrators who also depicted "foreign" lands and peoples as both objects of desire and objects in need of improvement—in either case, commodities to be exploited and controlled. In the United States, Lewis and Clark have likewise been followed by many more explorers, diplomats, missionaries, Indian agents, and private citizens who considered Indian peoples less than equal and Indian lands free for the taking. With exceptions, this tradition continues today, particularly in areas of the country where Indian tribes control resources white people desire—among them, mineral-rich regions, prime hunting, fishing, and recreation lands and waters, and economically-successful enterprises such as casinos. Lewis and Clark helped to promote and perpetuate this attitude by depicting the trans-Missouri River West "as an object of desire—a virgin wilderness" (Goetzmann 4)—an area to be surveyed, aestheticized, and appropriated.

In South Dakota, philosophical differences about ownership and use of land and about recognition of Indian heritage continue to divide some Indians and whites. In his 1995 article,

"Views from the Mount," *Minneapolis Star Tribune* staff writer Robert Franklin reports on the many controversies surrounding the Black Hills and Mount Rushmore National Memorial in western South Dakota. Indians of South Dakota consider the Black Hills sacred land, and South Dakota tribes, according to Franklin, "have refused a congressional payment (amounting to more than $350 million, with interest) to compensate them for the seizure of the Black Hills in the 1870s. They want the return of 1.3 million acres of federal land" (24A). Thomas Jefferson's policy of encouraging "good and influential" Indians to become indebted to government trading houses in order to force them to pay their debts by ceding land, a policy he explained to William Henry Harrison in 1803 (qtd. in Ford 1118), coincides with the existing practice of attempting to negotiate for lands worth more to the Indians—in both spiritual and financial terms than the government recognizes.

Mount Rushmore National Memorial poses a slightly different but interrelated set of problems for American Indians, according to Charlotte Black Elk, the 1995 secretary of the Black Hills Steering Committee. An 1868 treaty between the United States and the Lakota (Teton Sioux) Nation recognized the Black Hills and other areas of Wyoming and the Dakotas as Lakota territory (Matthiessen xx). However, with the discovery of gold in the Black Hills, the government abandoned the treaty and seized the lands. The steering committee represents South Dakota tribal members striving to gain back these lands. Black Elk points out that "the four gentlemen on Mount Rushmore capsulize the whole 200 years of dishonor by the United States government," and further asserts that the Louisiana Purchase, orchestrated by Jefferson (one of the four presidents whose likeness appears on Mount Rushmore), helped to establish the attitude among whites that "it's ours without having any responsibility for another culture" (qtd. in Franklin 24A). This controversy has led to disagreements over who should administer the monument site. When the Federal Government threatened cutbacks to national parks in the mid-1990s, South Dakota Governor William Janklow proposed that the state administer Mount Rushmore. However, Black Elk contends that the tribes should be given the chance to operate the site in order to "tell a more correct story" (qtd. in Franklin 24A). While to some Americans, Mount Rushmore symbolizes freedom and democracy, to many American Indians, the rock carvings of the four American presidents—Washington, Jefferson, Lincoln, and Theodore Roosevelt—serve as a reminder of lands and rights taken away.

Closer to my home in eastern South Dakota, I hear echoes of imperialist rhetoric each evening when I turn on the local news. "Here's what's happening in the Sioux Empire today," local newscasters announce as they begin their discussion of the day's events—stories dominated by news of white South Dakotans. The local mall, the quintessential representation of white capitalist values, also bears the name "The Empire"—another irony in an area once traversed by Lewis and Clark, who added momentum to the demise of the Sioux "empire" and helped to establish American cultural and trade hegemony in the region. Black Elk asserts that "Western culture worships people and things, and that's not our culture" (qtd. in Franklin

24A), however, Joe Eagle Elk, a healer on the Rosebud Reservation, explains that Indian children "want a lot of things that they see on TV, but there are no jobs for them anywhere, nothing for them to do, and meanwhile everything is so expensive" (qtd. in Matthiessen xxxv). "The Empire" continues to prove both culturally and economically costly to American Indians.

Analyzing the rhetoric of important historical documents such as the Lewis and Clark journals sheds light on the source of current negative or dismissive attitudes toward American Indians and helps to explain the continuing challenges tribes face, after hundreds of years of representation by both ill- and well-meaning whites. Awareness of the rhetoric of imperialism, a rhetoric that has shaped American attitudes about rights to land and resources and about peoples existing apart from the politically dominant culture, will perhaps lead to more respectful treatment of American lands and all American people.

Notes

[1] I use the terms American Indian, Indian, and native or native peoples interchangeably. In *The Indian Affair,* attorney, theologian, writer, and American Indian activist Vine Deloria points out that confusion has always surrounded the words used to refer to American Indians. Anthropologists use the term "Amerindians," and some younger Indians prefer the term "Native Americans." However, he writes that "In all probability no name other than 'Indians' will ever satisfy most of the people known popularly as 'Indians'" (6). I employ the term American Indian in order to distinguish this native group from other native or (East) Indian groups discussed by theorists such as Pratt, Spurr, and Said. In discussing material from Lewis and Clark's journals, I generally use the term Indian or native, terms both captains used in writing about American Indians. I do so in order to make my terminology consistent with Jefferson's, Lewis's, and Clark's.

[2] Clark often substituted several spaces for a comma or a period in his entries.

[3] In quoting from Gary Moulton's edition of the Lewis and Clark journals, I have retained his bracketed additions to their material. I have indicated my own bracketed additions to material from the journals by placing my initials, JW, before the added material. During the summer and fall of 1804, Clark wrote at least two largely repetitious entries for each day; in some cases I have included in brackets information from other entries for that day, and although the wording is Clark's, I have indicated my reordering of the material by placing my initials in the bracket containing the addition. Where my initials do not appear, the additions are Moulton's or a previous editor's.

[4] In the case of Lewis and Clark, Pratt's point about "discovery" proves particularly ironic since the captains failed to publish an account of their journey until 1814, eight years after the return of the expedition, while a full account did not appear until 1904. The 1814 publication lacked most of Lewis's natural history notes. "As a result," Stephen Ambrose notes, "Lewis and Clark got no credit for most of their discoveries" (480).

Works Cited

Allen, John Logan. *Passage Through the Garden: Lewis and Clark and the Image of the American Northwest.* Urbana: U of Illinois P, 1975.

Ambrose, Stephen. *Undaunted Courage: Meriwether Lewis, Thomas Jefferson, and the Opening of the American West.* New York: Touchstone, 1997.

Deloria, Vine, Jr. *The Indian Affair.* New York: Friendship Press, 1974.

Ford, Paul Leicester, ed. *The Writings of Thomas Jefferson: Vol. VIII. 1801–1806.* By Thomas Jefferson. 10 vols. New York York and London: G. P. Putnam's Sons, 1892–1899.

Franklin, Robert. "Views from the Mount: Mount Rushmore National Memorial. S.D." *Minneapolis Star Tribune* 8 Oct. 1995, metro ed.: 24A.

Goetzmann, William H. *Exploration and Empire: The Explorer and the Scientist in the Winning of the American West.* New York: Knopf, 1966.

Greenfield, Bruce. "The Problem of the Discoverer's Authority in Lewis and Clark's *History.*" *Macropolitics of Nineteenth-Century Literature: Nationalism, Exoticism, Imperialism.* Ed. Jonathan Arac and Harriet Ritvo. Philadelphia: U of Pennsylvania P, 1991. 12–36.

Jefferson, Thomas. "Expedition to the Pacific: Instructions to Captain Lewis." *Thomas Jefferson: Writings.* Ed. Merrill D. Peterson. New York: Library of America, 1984.

Matthiessen, Peter. *In the Spirit of Crazy Horse.* New York: Penguin, 1992.

Moulton, Gary E. ed. *Atlas of the Lewis and Clark Expedition.* Lincoln: U of Nebraska P, 1983.

———. *The Journals of the Lewis and Clark Expedition: Vol. 2. August 30, 1803–August 24, 1804.* By Meriwether Lewis and William Clark. 11 vols. Lincoln: U of Nebraska P, 1983–1997.

———. *The Journals of the Lewis and Clark Expedition: Vol. 3. August 25, 1804–April 6, 1805.* By Meriwether Lewis and William Clark. 11 vols. Lincoln: U of Nebraska P, 1983–1997.

Pratt, Mary Louise. *Imperial Eyes: Travel Writing and Transculturation.* London and New York: Routledge, 1994.

Ronda, James P. *Lewis and Clark among the Indians.* Lincoln: U of Nebraska P, 1984.

Said, Edward. *Culture and Imperialism.* New York: Knopf, 1993.

Spurr, David. *The Rhetoric of Empire: Colonial Discourse in Journalism, Travel Writing, and Imperial Administration.* Durham and London: Duke UP, 1996.

Understanding the Text

1. Briefly define the trope of surveillance and explain how it functions in the writing of those who describe cultures foreign to their own.

2. According to Dolence, how does the trope of surveillance influence Lewis and Clark's attempts to represent Native peoples and their land?

3. How does Dolence interpret the name of the major shopping mall in Sioux Falls, South Dakota—The Empire?

Opening the Black Hills

Custer's Report.[1]

Headquarters Black Hills Expedition,
Eight and one-half miles southeast of
Harney's Peak, Aug. 2.[2]
(Via. Fort Laramie, Wyo., 8, 1874.)[3]

George Armstrong Custer

Assistant Adjutant-General.,

Department of Dakota, St. Paul., Minn.:

My last dispatch was dated July 15, and sent from Prospect Valley, Dakota, longitude 103 degrees and 46 minutes, latitude 45 degrees and 29 minutes. Two of my Indian scouts left as bearers of the dispatch as soon as their departure could be concealed by the darkness. After leaving that point this expedition moved in a southwesterly direction until it reached the valley of the Little Missouri River, up which we moved 21 miles. Finding this valley almost destitute of grazing along our line of march, I ordered the water kegs to be filled and a supply of wood placed in the wagons, and left the valley in search of a better campground. During our passage up the valley of the Little Missouri we had entered and were about to leave the territory of Montana. Our course was nearly due south. After further march of about nine miles, we arrived before sundown at a point capable of furnishing us good grazing and water for our animals, having marched over thirty miles since breaking camp in the morning. From this point to the valley of the Belle Fourche we found the country generally barren and uninviting, save in a few isolated places. We reached the Belle Fourche on the

George Armstrong Custer (1839-1876) was an Army cavalry commander in the Civil War and in the federal government's sustained campaigns against the Native peoples of the plains. Known in his own day for both his bravery and ostentatious behavior, Custer is now best remembered for his defeat at the hands of the Sioux tribes, led by Sitting Bull and Crazy Horse, at the Battle of the Little Bighorn. After his death, his wife, Elizabeth, wrote three books about her husband's career and thus helped to promote him as a military hero and cultural icon. Custer himself wrote a book about his military exploits, entitled *My Life on the Plains* (1874).

From South Dakota Historical Collection, 1914.

evening of the 18th of July, encamping where good grass, wood, and water were abundant, and at a point a short distance above that marked fifteen (15) on Reynold's map, just west of the line separating Dakota from Wyoming. The following day was spent in camp.

On the 20th we crossed the Belle Fourche and began, as it were, skirmishing with the Black Hills. We began by feeling our way carefully along the outlaying ranges of hills, seeking a weak point through which we might take our way to the interior. We continued from the time we ascended from the valley of the Belle Fourche to move through a very superior country, covered with the best of grazing and an abundance of timber, principally pine, poplar, and several varieties of oak. As we advanced, the country skirting the Black Hills to the southward became each day more beautiful. On the evening of the 22nd, we halted and encamped east of and within four miles of the Cave of Inyan Kara.[4] Desiring to aside (ascend?) that peak the following day, it being the highest on the western range of the Black Hills, I did not move camp the following day, but, taking a small party with me, proceeded to the highest point of this prominent landmark, whose height is given as 6,600 feet.[5] The day was not favorable for obtaining distant views, but I decided on the following morning to move due east and attempt the passage of the hills. We experienced considerable delay from fallen timber which lay in our pathway. With this exception, and a very little digging rendered necessary in descending into a valley, the pioneers prepared the way for the train, and we reached camp by 2 o'clock, having marched eleven miles. We here found grass, water, and wood of the best quality, and in great abundance. On the following day we resumed our march up this valley, which I had explored the preceding evening, and which led us by an easy ascent almost southeast.

After marching nearly 12 miles, we encamped at an early hour in the same valley. This valley, in one respect, presented the most wonderful as well as beautiful aspect. Its equal I have never seen: and such, too, was the testimony of all who beheld it. In no private or public park have I ever seen such a profuse display of flowers. Every step of our march that day was amid flowers of the most exquisite colors and perfume. So luxuriant in growth were they that men plucked them without dismounting from the saddle. Some belonged to new or unclassified species. It was a strange sight to glance back at the advancing columns of cavalry and behold the men with beautiful bouquets of flowers in their hands, while the headgear of the horses was decorated with wreaths of flowers fit to crown a queen of May. Deeming it a most fitting appellation, I named this Floral Valley. General Forsyth, at one of our halting places, plucked 17 beautiful flowers belonging to different varieties, and within a space of twenty feet square. The same evening, while seated at the mess table, one of the officers called attention to the carpet of flowers strewn under our feet, and it was suggested that it be determined how many different flowers could be plucked without leaving our seat at dinner table. Seven beautiful varieties were thus gathered. Prof. Donaldson, the botanist of the expedition, estimated the number of flowers in bloom in Floral Valley at 50, while an equal number of varieties had bloomed, or were yet to bloom. The number of trees, shrubs and grasses was estimated at 25, making the total flora of the valley embrace 125 species. Through this beautiful valley meanders a stream of crystal water so cold as to render ice undesirable even at noon day. The temperature of two of the many springs found flowing into it was taken, and ascertained to be 44 and 44 1-2 degrees respectively. The next morning, although loath to leave so enchanting a locality, we continued to ascend this valley, until gradually, almost imperceptibly, we discovered that we were on the crest of the western ridge of the Black Hills, and instead of being among barren peaks, as might be supposed, we found ourselves wending our way through a little park, whose natural beauty may well bear comparison with the lovliest portions of Central Park. Favored as we had been in having Floral Valley for our roadway to the crest of the Black Hills, we were scarcely less fortunate in the valley which seemed to rise to meet us in the interior slope. The rippling stream of clear, cold water, the counterpart of that we had ascended the day before, flowed at our feet and pointed out the way before us, while along its banks grew beautiful flowers, surpassed but little in beauty and profusion by their sisters who had greeted us the day before. After advancing down this valley about fourteen miles, our course being almost southeast, we encamped in the midst of grazing whose only fault, if any, was the great luxuriance. Having preceded the main column, as usual, with an escort of two companies of cavalry (E and C) and Lieutenant Wallace's detachment of scouts, I came upon an Indian camp fire still burning, and which, with other indications, showed that a small party of Indians had encamped there the previous night, and had evidently left that morning in ignorance of our close proximity. Believing they would not move far, and that a collision might take place at any time unless a friendly understanding was arrived at, I sent my head scout, "Bloody Knife," and twenty of his braves to advance a few miles and reconnoiter the valley. This party had been gone but a few minutes when two of Bloody Knife's young men came galloping back and informed me that they had discovered five Indian lodges a few miles down the valley, and that Bloody Knife, as directed, had concealed his party in a wooded ravine where they awaited further orders. Taking a company with me, which was afterwards reinforced by the remainder of the scouts, and Colonel Hart's company, I proceeded to the ravine where Bloody Knife and his party lay concealed, and from the crest beyond obtained a full view of the five Indian lodges, about which a considerable number of ponies were grazing. I was enabled to place my command still nearer to the lodges undiscovered. I then dispatched a guard, the interpreter, with a flag of truce, accompanied by two of our Sioux scouts, to acquaint the occupants of the lodge that we were friendly disposed and desired to communicate with them. To prevent either treachery or flight on their part, I galloped the remaining portion of my advance and surrounded the lodges. This was accomplished almost before they were aware of our presence. I then entered the little village and shook hands with the occupants, assuring them, through the interpreter, that they had no cause to fear, as we were not there to molest them. I invited them to visit our camp and promised presents of flour, sugar, and coffee to all who would accept. This invitation was accepted. At the same time, I entered into an agreement with the leading men they should encamp with us a few days and give us such information concerning the country as we might desire, in return for which service I was to reward them with rations. With this understanding, I left them. The entire party numbered twenty-seven. Later in the afternoon, four of the men, including the chief, "One Stab," visited our camp and desired the promised rations, saying their entire party would move up and join us the following morning, as agreed upon. I ordered presents of sugar, coffee, and bacon to be given them, and to relieve them of their pretended anxiety for the safety of their village during the night, I ordered a party of 15 of my command to return with them and protect them during the night. But from their great disinclination to wait a few minutes, till the party could saddle up, and from the fact that two of the four had already slipped away, I was of the opinion that they were not acting in good faith. In this I was confirmed, when the two remaining ones set off at a gallop in the direction of their village. I sent a party of our scouts to overtake them and request them to return. Not complying with this request, I sent a second party with orders to repeat the request, and if not complied with, to take hold of the bridles of their ponies and lead them back, but to offer no violence. When overtaken by our scouts, one of the two Indians seized the musket of one of the scouts and endeavored to wrest it from him. Failing in this he released his hold, after the scout became dismounted in the struggle, and set off as fast as his pony would carry him, but not before the musket of the scout was discharged. From blood discovered afterward, it was very evident that either the Indian or his pony was wounded. I hope that neither was seriously hurt, although the Indians have their own bad faith as the sole ground for the collision. "One Stab," the chief, was brought back to camp. The scouts galloped down the valley to the site of the village, when it was discovered that the entire party had packed up their lodges and fled, and the visit of the four Indians to our camp was not only to obtain their rations promised them in return for future services, but to cover the flight of the lodges. I have effected arrangements by which the chief One Stab will be with us as guide three days longer, when he will take his departure and rejoin his band. He claims to belong to both Red Cloud's and Spotted Tail's agencies, but has been to neither for a long time. He has recently returned from the hostile camp on Powder River, and represents that the Indians lost 10 killed in their fights with the Bozeman exploring party. The creek which led us down into the interior of the Black Hills is bordered by high bluffs, on the crests of which are located prominent walls of solid rock, presenting here and there the appearance of castles constructed of masonry. From their marked resemblance, I named this stream Castle Creek. The direction of Castle Creek having commenced to lead us more to the northeast than we were prepared to go, and the valley having become narrow and broken, I left this water course and ascended the valley of a small tributary, which again gave us a southeasterly course. After a march of fourteen miles, encamped on a small creek furnishing us an abundance of water and grass. The direction of this creek was nearly east. On the 30th, moved in the continuation of our previous course, and through a fine open country covered with excellent grazing. After a march of over ten miles, we encamped early in the day about five miles from the western base of Harney's Peak—finding water and grass and wood abundant, with springs of clear cold water running through camp. On the following day the command remained in camp, except the exploring parties sent out in all directions. With a small party I proceeded to Harney's Peak, and after great difficulty made the ascent to its crest. We found this to be the highest point in the Black Hills. From the highest point we obtained a view of Bear Butte, in the north part of plains to the east, far beyond the Cheyenne River. Our party did not reach camp till near 1 o'clock that night, but we were amply repaid for our labor by the magnificence of the views obtained. While on the highest point, we drank the health of the veteran out of compliment to whom the peak was named. On the 1st of August we moved camp a few miles, simply to obtain fresh grass, still keeping near the base of the hills to the east of us. This a. m. I dispatched two companies, under Colonel Hart, in a southeasterly direction, to extend our exploration with the South Fork of the Cheyenne River. Tomorrow morning at 5 o'clock I will set out with five companies of cavalry and endeavor to reach the same stream in a southwesterly direction from Harney's Peak. Reynolds, the scout who is to carry this dispatch to Fort Laramie, will go with us as far as we go in that direction, when he sets out alone to reach his destination, traveling mainly by night. The country through which we have passed since leaving the Belle Fourche River has been generally open and extremely fertile. The main portion of that passed over since entering the unexplored portion of the Black Hills consists of beautiful parks and valleys, through which flows a stream of clear, cold water, perfectly free from alkali, while bounding these parks or valley is invariably found unlimited supplies of timber, much of it capable of being made into good lumber. In no portion of the United States, not excepting the famous blue grass region of Kentucky, have I ever seen grazing superior to that found growing wild in this hitherto unknown region. I know of no portion of our country where nature has done so much to prepare homes for husbandmen, and left so little for the latter to do, as here. The open and timbered spaces are so divided that a partly prepared farm of almost any dimensions, of an acre and upward, can be found here. Not only is the land cleared and timbered, both for fuel and building, conveniently located, with streams of pure water flowing through its length and breadth, but nature oft times seems to have gone further and placed beautiful shrubbery and evergreens in the most desirable locations for building sites, while on Harney's Peak I could contrast the bright green verdure of these lovely parks with the sunburned and dried yellow herbage to be seen on the outer plains. Everything indicates an abundance of moisture with in the space inclosed by the Black Hills. The soil is that of a rich garden, and composed of a dark mold of exceedingly fine grain. We have found the country in many places covered with wild raspberries, both black and red varieties. Yesterday and today I have feasted on the latter. It is no unusual sight to see hundreds of soldiers gathering wild raspberries. Nowhere in the States have I tasted cultivated raspberries of equal flavor to those found growing wild here, nor have I ever seen them as large or in as great profusion as I have seen hundreds of acres of them here. Wild strawberries, wild currants, gooseberries, two varieties of pure berries, and wild cherries are also found in great profusion and of exceedingly pure quality. Cattle could winter in these valleys without other food or shelter than that to be obtained from running at large. As there are scientists accompanying the expedition who are examining into the mineral resources of this region, the result of whose researches will accompany my detailed report, I omit all present reference to that portion of our explorations until the return of the expedition, except to state, what will appear in any event in the public prints, that gold has been found at several places, and it is the belief of those who are giving their attention to this subject that it will be found in paying quantities. I have upon my table 40 or 50 small particles of pure gold, in size averaging that of a small pin head, and most of it obtained today from one panful of earth. As we have never remained longer at our camp than one day, it will be readily understood that there is no opportunity to make a satisfactory examination in regard to deposits of valuable minerals. Veins of lead and strong indications of the existence of silver have been found. Until further examination is made regarding the richness of the gold, no opinion should he formed.

Veins of what the geologists term gold-bearing quartz crop out on almost every hillside. All existing geological or geographical maps of this region have been found incorrect. This will not seem surprising when it is remembered that both have been compiled by guess-work and without entering the country attempted to be represented. The health of the command continues excellent. I will begin my northward march in four days from this date. I do not expect to arrive at Fort Lincoln until the 31st of August.

G. A. Custer

● ● ● ● ● ● ● ● ● ● ● ● ● ● ●

Bear Battle,[6] Dak., August 15, (via Bismarck.)
Headquarters Black Hills Expedition.
Bear Battle, Dak., August 15, (via Bismarck.)

My last dispatch was written on the 2nd and 3rd instant, and sent from the south fork of the Cheyenne, from a point on the latter nearest to Fort Laramie. On the morning of the 4th instant I began my return march to our main camp, near Harney's Peak, arriving there by a different route on the 6th. On the morning of the 7th the expedition began its march northward, Bear Butte being our next objective point. We advanced without serious obstacle until ten or twelve miles of Bear Butte, when we found our further progress barred by a high range of impassable hills. We attempted to effect a passage through some one of the many valleys whose water courses ran directly through the hills in the desired direction, but in every instance we were led into deep broken canyons, impassable even to horsemen.

Through one of these I made my way on foot, and from a high point near its mouth obtained a view of the plains outside. Retracing my steps I placed the command in camp in a fine valley, in which it had halted, and devoted the remainder of the day to a further search for a practicable route through the hills. The result decided me to follow down a water course, which led us first toward the south, and afterwards toward the east. This stream proved to be Elk Creek, the valley of which, as well as the stream itself, proved to be at least equal in beauty and extent to any passed through during our march. We camped twice on this stream, and as far as we proceeded down its course we had a most excellent road; but finding that, like nearly all other streams leaving the hills, its course would take us into a canon which could be barely made practicable for our wagons, I searched for and discovered a narrower gap in the rocky wall which forms the northern boundary of the valley, and which was conveniently large to allow our wagons to pass through. A march of an hour up a gradual ascent, and through a pine forest, brought us to a beautiful park, containing thousands of acres, and from which we obtained a fine view, in the distance, of our old acquaintance—the plains. Here we pitched our tents for the last time in the Black Hills; nearly every one being loathe to leave a region which had been found so delightful in almost every respect. Behind us the grass and foliage were clothed in green of the freshness of May. In front of us, as we cast our eyes over the plains below, we saw nothing but a comparatively parched, dried surface, the sunburnt pasture of which offered a most uninviting prospect both to horse and rider, when remembering the rich abundance we were leaving behind us. A march of 26 miles, gradually bearing northward, brought us to the base of Bear Butte, at which point I concluded to remain one day before beginning our return march. I propose to return by a different, although, perhaps, not shorter, route than that adopted in coming to the Black Hills. I am induced to make this change in order to embrace a larger extent of unexplored country within the limits of our explorations, and particularly to enable us to locate as much as possible of that portion of the Little Missouri of which nothing is now known. I expect the expedition to reach Fort Lincoln on the 31st of August. The health of the command has been, and is, most excellent. This expedition entered the Black Hills from the west side, penetrated through the eastern and most southern ranges, explored the major portions of the interior, and passed out the most eastern ranges which form the boundary of the Black Hills. From the fact that in all our principal marches through the Black Hills we have taken, without serious obstacle, a heavily laden train of over 100 wagons, it may be inferred that the Black Hills do not constitute the impenetrable region heretofore represented.

In entering the Black Hills from any direction, the most serious, if not the only, obstacles were encountered at once, near the outer base. This probably accounts for the mystery which has so long existed regarding the character of the interior. Exploring parties have contented themselves with marching around the exterior base, and, from the forbidding aspect of the hills as viewed at a distance, inferred that an advance toward the interior would only encounter increased obstacles. In regard to the character of the country inclosed by the Black Hills, I can only repeat what I have stated in previous dispatches.

No portion of the United States can boast of a richer or better pasturage, purer water, the natural temperature of which in midsummer, as it flows from the earth, is but 12 degrees above the freezing point, and of greater advantages generally to the farmer or stock raiser than are to be found in the Black Hills. Building stone of the best quality is to be found in inexhaustable quantities. Wood for fuel and lumber sufficient for all time to come. Rains are frequent, with no evidence in the country of either drought or freshets. The season, perhaps, is too short and the nights too cool for corn, but I believe all other grain could he produced here in wonderful abundance. Wheat would particularly yield largely. There is no doubt as to the existence of various minerals throughout the hills, as this subject has received special attention of experts who accompany the expedition, and will be reported upon in detail. I will only mention the fact that iron and plumbago have been found, and beds of gypsum of apparently inexhaustible extent.

I referred in a former dispatch to the discovery of gold. Subsequent examinations at numerous points confirm and strengthen the fact of the existence of gold in the Black Hills. On some of the water courses almost every panful of earth produced gold in small, yet paying quantities. Our brief halts and rapid marching prevented anything but a very hasty examination of the country in this respect; but in one place, and the only one within my knowledge where so great a depth was reached, a hole was dug 8 feet in depth. The miners report that they found gold among the roots of the grass, and, from that point to the lowest point reached, gold was found in paying quantities. It has not required an expert to find gold in the Black Hills, as men without former experience in mining have discovered it at an expense of but little time or labor. As an evidence of the rich pasturage to be found in this region, I can state the fact that my beef herd, after marching upward of 600 miles, is in better condition than when I started, being now as fat as is consistent with marching condition. The same may be said of the mules of the wagon train. The horses of the command are in good working condition. I have never seen as many deer as in the Black Hills. Elk and bear have also been killed. We have had no collision with hostile Indians.

G. A. Custer,

Brevet Major-General, Commanding Expedition.

To Assistant Adjutant-General,

    Department of Dakota, St. Paul.

Notes

[1] This report was published as Executive Document 32, 43rd Congress Second session. For editorial notes consult Donaldson's report ante.

[2] Written from the camp on French Creek a short distance below Custer City.

[3] This report was carried by Charley Reynolds the scout to Fort Laramie when it was sent by wire to Saint Paul. Reynolds was killed in the battle of the Little Bighorn, June 25, 1876.

[4] Cave is evidently a misciphering of the dispatch. There is no cave of consequence at Inyan Kara. From the context it may have been "peak" Inyan Kara.

[5] According to modern measurements the peak is 6,313 feet high.

[6] This is certainly intended for Bear Butte.

Understanding the Text

1. In his descriptions of the Black Hills, what does Custer seem most interested in? What might this interest suggest, in part, about the purpose of the expedition?

2. How does Custer interpret the encounter with Indians? In your view, is this interpretation entirely fair? Why or why not?

3. The editor of Custer's reports has assigned to them the title, "Opening the Black Hills." In your view, what does this title—especially the word "opening"—signify?

The Custer Black Hills Expedition

Annie D. Tallent

On July 2d, 1874, an expedition under the command of Gen. Geo. A. Custer, left Fort Abraham Lincoln with ten companies of cavalry, two of infantry, a detachment of white and Indian scouts, interpreters, miners, teamsters, etc., in all about 1,000 men, under orders from the Governmental Department, to make a reconnoissance of the country from that point to Bear Butte on the north of the Hills, and explorations of the country adjacent thereto, on the southwest, south, and southeast, and into the interior eastward for the purpose presumably of learning something of the topography and geological formation of the Hills, and also of their general character and possible resources. The prime object of the expedition, however, would appear to be to ascertain their exact geographical position, relative to the military posts, Lincoln and Laramie, with a view to the establishment of other posts within or near the Black Hills, in case future complications with the Sioux rendered it necessary.

The following extract from the report of William Ludlow, chief of engineers, Department of Dakota, accompanying the expedition, will make clear its real object: —

"In case of any future complication with the Sioux, or the needs of bordering civilization should make it necessary to establish military posts on this reservation, indications all point to the Black Hills as the most suitable point, both on account of their geographical position, and on the abundance of wood, water, and grass to be found there. To explain the value of its position, it should be stated that the trails from the camp of the hostile Sioux

Annie D. Tallent is reported to have been the first white woman to travel through the Black Hills, which she did in 1874. In 1899, she published *The Black Hills; or the Last Hunting Ground of the Dakotahs,* a book that describes the efforts of whites to wrest control of the Hills from the Sioux Indians and that also reflects the racial and cultural prejudices of the times.

From *The Black Hills* by Annie D. Tallent, Nixon-Jones Printing Company, 1899.

on the Yellowstone to the agencies near the Missouri, where live the reservation Indians, and where the issues of annuities are made, lead by a southeasterly course through the Hills, the abundance of game, and ample security of which make them a ready refuge in time of war, and a noble hunting ground in time of peace. It was therefore desirable to gain positive information regarding them, and to connect them as well, by reconnoissance with the posts of Lincoln and Laramie. To accomplish these results was the object of this expedition."

In this connection the opinion is ventured that there might have been another object underlying the action of the government, and one of more vital interest to the people of the country, who were looking with covetous eyes towards this rich domain, namely, their ultimate redemption from the hands of the Indians, and their consequent opening to white settlement, in case the vague rumors that had reached the world, of their fabulous richness, should be borne out by the facts.

Be that as it may, a hasty exploration was made—all that was possible in the limited time fixed for the work (sixty days time), sufficiently extensive, however, to answer the purpose for which the expedition was organized, and to gain a partial knowledge of the formation of the Hills, and their general topographical features.

The expedition entered the Hills on the west, at a point near Inyan-Kara, penetrated southeastward as far as Harney's Peak, thence southward across the southern limits of the Hills to the south fork of the Cheyenne river.

From this point, Charlie Reynolds, Custer's chief of scouts, was sent alone across the Indian infested country with dispatches to Fort Laramie, and it is alleged that the famous scout suffered exposure and privations on the journey, from the effects of which he never fully recovered.

Returning to Harney's Peak the expedition spent a few days prospecting in the region of the Peak, then took up their march along the Box Elder, and finally after some difficulty found its way out of the Hills at a point nearly opposite Bear Butte, which embraced all the territory explored.

But very little prospecting was done, and that principally on the heads of the streams draining the area around Harney's Peak, where only five days were spent, the longest time at any one point, in proof of which I will quote from General Custer's Report to the War Department, in detailing the work of the expedition, the following: —

"It will be understood that within the limits of the Black Hills we were almost constantly marching, never halting at any one point for a longer time than one day—except one, and that was near Harney's Peak, where we remained five days; most of the command, however, being employed in operations during the halt. From this it will be seen that no satisfactory or conclusive examination of the country could be made regarding its mineral deposits; enough, however, was determined to establish the fact that gold is distributed throughout an extensive area within the Black Hills. No discoveries, as far as I am aware, were made of gold deposits in quartz, although there is every reason to believe that a more thorough and extended search would have discovered it. Seeking for gold was not one of the objects of the expedition; consequently, we were but illy-prepared to institute or successfully prosecute a search for it, even after we became aware of its existence in the country."

It will be seen from the above that, although prospects of gold were found in the gulches of the streams flowing from the region of Harney's Peak, no deposits of gold in quartz were discovered. The fact was revealed to the pioneers of 1874 in their search for gold, very shortly after, that the prospecting done by the Custer expedition was a mere bagatelle; besides, there was such a wide discrepancy of statement in the reports of the experts accompanying the expedition, in regard to even the existence of gold in the Black Hills, that the public mind was thrown into a greater degree of uncertainty than before, for, while General Custer and the mining experts of the expedition claimed to have found gold, Prof. Winchell, geologist, was equally positive in his claim that he did not see a single one of the shining particles. The sequel has demonstrated, however, that the Professor probably did not see the gold because he wouldn't. There is an old adage which says: "There are none so blind as those who won't see."

Be that as it may, it was left to the pioneers of 1874 to relieve the public mind from the uncertainty into which it was thrown by these conflicting reports, and to prove to them beyond any doubt the existence of the precious metal in which the people of the country were, at the time, more deeply interested than in any other question. In this state of uncertainty they awaited, with no little anxiety, a report from the pioneers who were already on their perilous way before the final reports of the Custer expedition were made public.

Understanding the Text

1. According to Tallent, what was the true purpose of the Custer expedition?

2. Briefly describe Tallent's tone as it pertains to her discussion of the Sioux. Which phrases seem especially revealing?

3. According to Tallent, was the search for gold a major object of the Custer expedition?

ADDITIONAL READINGS

Ambrose, Stephen E. *Undaunted Courage: Meriwether Lewis, Thomas Jefferson, and the Opening of the American West.* 1996. New York: Touchstone-Simon & Schuster, 1997.

Bellesiles, Michael. A. *Arming America: The Origins of a National Gun Culture.* New York: Knopf, 2000.

Berkhofer, Robert. *The White Man's Indian: The History of an Idea from Columbus to the Present.* New York: Knopf, 1978.

Brown, Dee. *Bury My Heart at Wounded Knee: An Indian History of the American West.* New York: Holt, Rinehart, and Winston, 1970.

Cawelti, John G. *The Six-Gun Mystique Sequel.* Bowling Green, OH: Bowling Green State University Popular Press, 1999.

Chidester, David and Edward T. Linenthal, eds. *American Sacred Space.* Religion in North America. Bloomington: Indiana UP, 1995.

Deloria, Vine, Jr., ed. *American Indian Policy in the Twentieth Century.* Norman: U of Oklahoma P, 1985.

———. *Behind the Trail of Broken Treaties: An American Declaration of Independence.* New York: Delacourt, 1974.

———. *Custer Died for Your Sins: An Indian Manifesto.* New York: Avon, 1969.

DeVoto, Bernard. *The Journals of Lewis and Clark.* 1953. Boston: Mariner-Houghton Mifflin, 1981.

Fire, John (Lame Deer) and Richard Erdoes. *Lame Deer, Seeker of Visions: The Life of a Sioux Medicine Man.* New York: Simon and Schuster, 1972.

Hutton, Paul Andrew, ed. *The Custer Reader.* Lincoln: U of Nebraska P, 1992.

Larner, Jesse. *Mount Rushmore: An Icon Reconsidered.* New York: Thunder's Mouth Press-Nation Books, 2002.

Leckie, Shirley. A. *Elizabeth Bacon Custer and the Making of Myth.* Norman: U of Oklahoma P, 1993.

Limerick, Patricia Nelson. *The Legacy of Conquest: The Unbroken Past of the American West.* New York: Norton, 1987.

Matthiessen, Peter. *In the Spirit of Crazy Horse.* 1983. New York: Viking, 1991.

McMurtry, Larry. *The Colonel and Little Missie: Buffalo Bill, Annie Oakley, and the Beginnings of Superstardom in America.* New York: Simon & Schuster, 2005.

Moses, L.G. *Wild West Shows and the Images of American Indians, 1883–1933.* Albuquerque: U of New Mexico P, 1996.

Rorabaugh, W.J. *The Alcoholic Republic: An American Tradition.* New York: Oxford UP, 1979.

Ronda, James P. *Lewis and Clark among the Indians.* Lincoln: U of Nebraska P, 1984.

Slotkin, Richard. *The Fatal Environment: The Myth of the Frontier in the Age of Industrialization, 1800–1890.* New York: Atheneum, 1985.

———. *Gunfighter Nation: The Myth of the Frontier in Twentieth-Century America.* New York: Atheneum, 1992.

———. *Regeneration Through Violence: The Mythology of the American Frontier, 1600–1860.* Middletown, CT: Wesleyan UP, 1973.

Smith, Henry Nash. *Virgin Land: The American West as Symbol and Myth.* Cambridge: Harvard UP, 1950.

Spurr, David. *The Rhetoric of Empire: Colonial Discourse in Journalism, Travel Writing, and Imperial Administration.* Post-Contemporary Interventions. Durham: Duke UP, 1993.

Tallent, Annie D. *The Black Hills; or, The Last Hunting Ground of the Dakotahs.* St Louis: Nixon-Jones, 1899.

Taylor, Alan. *American Colonies. The Penguin History of the United States.* New York: Viking, 2001.

Tompkins, Jane. *West of Everything: The Inner Life of Westerns.* New York: Oxford UP, 1992.

Turner, Frederick Jackson. *The Significance of the Frontier in American History.* New York: Holt, 1947.

Wallis, Michael. *The Real Wild West: The 101 Ranch and the Creation of the American West.* New York: St. Martin's, 1999.

Ward, Geoffrey C. *The West: An Illustrated History.* Boston: Little Brown, 1996.

Wert, Jeffrey D. *The Controversial Life of George Armstrong Custer.* New York: Simon & Schuster, 1996.

Wills, Garry. *John Wayne's America: The Politics of Celebrity.* New York: Simon and Schuster, 1997.